STRATEGIC MARKETING PROBLEMS

STRATEGIC MARKETING PROBLEMS

Cases and Comments

SEVENTH EDITION

Roger A. Kerin
Southern Methodist University

Robert A. Peterson
University of Texas

PRENTICE HALL, Englewood Cliffs, New Jersey 07632

Library of Congress Cataloging-in-Publication Data

Kerin, Roger A.
   Strategic marketing problems : cases and comments / Roger A.
Kerin, Robert A. Peterson. -- 7th ed.
     p. cm.
   Includes bibliographical references and index.
   ISBN 0-205-161707-7 (case)
    1. Marketing--Decision making--Case studies. 2. Marketing-
-Management--Case studies. I. Peterson, Robert A. II. Title.
HF5415.135.K47 1995
658.8'02--dc20   94-12524
                                                  CIP

Acquisitions Editor: David Borkowsky
Managing Editor: Fran Russello
Production Editor: Cathleen Profitko
Cover Designer: Tom Nery
Copy Editor: Brenda Melissaratos
Proofreader: Amy Hinton
Buyer: Marie McNamara
Assistant Editor: Melissa Steffens
Production Assistant: Renee Pelletier
Editorial Assistant: Aviva Rosenberg

© 1995, 1993, 1990, 1987, 1984, 1981, 1978 by Prentice Hall, Inc.
A Simon & Schuster Company
Englewood Cliffs, New Jersey 07632

Printed in the United States of America

10 9 8 7 6 5 4 3 2 1

ISBN 0-205-161707-7

Prentice-Hall International (UK) Limited, *London*
Prentice-Hall of Australia Pty. Limited, *Sydney*
Prentice-Hall Canada Inc., *Toronto*
Prentice-Hall Hispanoamericana, S.A., *Mexico*
Prentice-Hall of India Private Limited, *New Delhi*
Prentice-Hall of Japan, Inc., *Tokyo*
Simon & Schuster Asia Pte. Ltd., *Singapore*
Editora Prentice-Hall do Brasil, Ltda., *Rio de Janeiro*

To Our Families

Contents

Preface   *xi*

CHAPTER 1
Foundations of Strategic Marketing Management   **1**

CHAPTER 2
Financial Aspects of Marketing Management   **16**

CHAPTER 3
Marketing Decision Making and Case Analysis   **31**

CHAPTER 4
Opportunity Analysis and Market Targeting   **41**

   Importatores Quetzal   49
   Roger A. Kerin and Robert A. Peterson

   Jones•Blair Company   52
   Roger A. Kerin

   Frito-Lay's® Dips   62
   Roger A. Kerin and Jeanne Bertels

   Curtis Automotive Hoist   74
   Gordon H. L. McDougell

   The Upjohn Company: Rogaine Topical Solution   84
   Roger A. Kerin

   Nestlé Italy   96
   John A. Quelch and Michele Costabile

CHAPTER 5
Marketing Research   **111**

   South Delaware Coors, Inc.   119
   James E. Nelson and Eric J. Karson

   Ms-Tique Corporation   130
   Roger A. Kerin

   MacTec Control AB   137
   James E. Nelson

   Bateson Battery Chargers   145
   James E. Nelson

CHAPTER 6
Product and Service Strategy and Management   **156**

   Frito-Lay, Inc.: SunChips™ Multigrain Snacks   167
   Roger A. Kerin and Kenneth R. Lukaska

   Price Waterhouse   186
   Roger A. Kerin, Angela Bullard and Lawrence Cervetti

   Manor Memorial Hospital   199
   Roger A. Kerin

   Swisher Mower and Machine Company   121
   Roger A. Kerin and Wayne Swisher

   American Airlines, Inc: Proposal for a Three-Class Transcon System   224
   A. Dhebar

   Procter & Gamble, Inc.: Scope   243
   Gordon H. G. McDougall and Franklin Ramsoomair

Logitech
Adrian B. Ryans and Brock Smith   256

CHAPTER 7

Marketing Communications Strategy and Management   **271**

Morgantown Furniture Inc. (A)   282
Roger A. Kerin

Morgantown Furniture Inc. (B)   293
Roger A. Kerin

Cadbury Beverages, Inc.: CRUSH® Brand   296
Roger A. Kerin

Godiva Europe   312
Jean-Jaques Lambin

Honeywell, Inc.: Spectronics Division   331
Roger A. Kerin and Angela Schuetze

Club Med España   345
Dominique Turpin and Alex Bloom

CHAPTER 8

Marketing Channel Strategy and Management   **362**

Zoëcon Corporation: Insect Growth Regulators   372
Roger A. Kerin and Larry Smith

Hendison Electronics Corporation   383
Roger A. Kerin

Goodyear Tire and Rubber Company   390
Roger A. Kerin

Konark Television India   403
James E. Nelson and Piyush K. Sinha

Carrington Carpet Mills, Inc.   416
Roger A. Kerin

CHAPTER 9

Pricing Strategy and Management   **421**

Burroughs Wellcome Company: Retrovir   430
Roger A. Kerin

Augustine Medical, Inc.: The Bair Hugger™ Patient Warming System   443
Roger A. Kerin, Michael Gilbertson, and William Rudelius

U. S. SemiCon Corporation: Facsimile Technology Program   454
Roger A. Kerin

Proctor & Gamble, Inc.: Downy Enviro-Pak   468
Adrian B. Ryans, Janet Lahey and Chris Lane

Warner-Lambert Ireland: Niconil   476
John A. Quelch and Susan P. Smith

WilTel, Inc.   492
Robert A. Peterson and William R. Wilson

CHAPTER 10

Marketing Strategy Reformulation: The Control Process   **506**

Tostitos® Brand Tortilla Chips   516
Roger A. Kerin and Jane Lovett

Marshall Museum of Art   528
Roger A. Kerin

Hanover-Bates Chemical Corporation   539
Robert E. Witt

Dell Computer Corporation: Reformulation Strategy   546
Robert A. Peterson

CHAPTER 11

Comprehensive Marketing Programs   **563**

Tyler Pet Foods, Inc.   568
Roger A. Kerin

Chun King Corporation   579
Robert A. Peterson and Nick Mihnovets

The Circle K Corporation   590
Roger A. Kerin

Volvo Trucks Europe   602
Jean-Jacques Lambin and Tammy Bunn Hiller

Colgate-Palmolive Canada: Arctic Power Detergent   617

Gordon H. G. McDougall and Douglas Snetzinger

Swatch 637
Heĺen C. Kimball and Christian Pinson

Żantac (A) 671
Reinhard Angelmar and Christian Pinson

APPENDIX
Preparing a Written Case Analysis **709**

**Republic National Bank of Dallas—
NOW Accounts** 709

Roger A. Kerin

**Student Analysis: Republic National Bank
of Dallas—NOW Accounts** 719

**Selected Glossary of Marketing
Terms and Concepts** 727

Subject, Brand, and Company Index 731

Preface

Decision making in marketing is first and foremost a skill. Like most skills, it possesses tools and terminology. Like all skills, it is best learned through practice. This book is dedicated to the development of decision-making skills in marketing. Textual material introduces concepts and tools useful in structuring and solving marketing problems. Case studies describing actual marketing problems provide an opportunity for those concepts and tools to be employed in practice. In every case study, the decision maker must develop a strategy consistent with the underlying factors existing in the situation presented and must consider the implications of that strategy for the organization and its environment.

The seventh edition of *Strategic Marketing Problems: Cases and Comments* seeks a balance between marketing management content and process. The book consists of eleven chapters and forty-five cases.

Chapter 1, "Foundations of Strategic Marketing Management," provides an overview of the strategic marketing management process. The principal emphasis is on defining an organization's business and purpose, identifying opportunities, formulating strategies, budgeting, controlling the marketing effort, and developing contingency plans.

Chapter 2, "Financial Aspects of Marketing Management," reviews basic concepts of managerial accounting and managerial finance that are useful in marketing management. Primary emphasis is placed on such concepts as cost structure, relevant versus sunk costs, margins, contribution analysis, liquidity, operating leverage, and preparing *pro forma* income statements.

Chapter 3, "Marketing Decision Making and Case Analysis," introduces a systematic process for decision making and provides an overview of various aspects of case analysis. A sample case and written student analysis are presented in the appendix at the end of the book. The student analysis illustrates the nature and scope of a written case presentation, including the qualitative and quantitative analyses essential to a good presentation.

Chapter 4, "Opportunity Analysis and Market Targeting," focuses on the identification and evaluation of marketing opportunities. Market segmentation, market targeting, and market potential and profitability issues are considered in some depth.

Chapter 5, "Marketing Research," deals with the effective management of marketing information. Decisions involved in assessing the value of marketing information and managing the information acquisition process are highlighted.

Chapter 6, "Product and Service Strategy and Management" focuses on the management of the organization's offering. New-offering development, life cycle management, product or service positioning, branding, and product-service mix decisions are emphasized.

Chapter 7, "Marketing Communications Strategy and Management," raises issues in the design, execution, and evaluation of the communications mix. Decisions concerned with communications objectives, strategy, budgeting, programming, and effectiveness, as well as sales management are addressed.

Chapter 8, "Marketing Channel Strategy and Management," introduces a variety of considerations affecting channel selection and modification as well as trade relations. Specific decision areas covered include direct versus indirect distribution, dual distribution, cost-benefit analysis of channel choice and management and marketing channel conflict and coordination.

Chapter 9, "Pricing Strategy and Management," highlights concepts and applications in price determination and modification. Emphasis is placed on evaluating demand, cost, and competitive influences when selecting or modifying pricing strategies for products and services.

Chapter 10, "Marketing Strategy Reformulation: The Control Process," focuses on the appraisal of marketing actions for the purpose of developing reformulation and recovery strategies. Considerations and techniques applicable to strategic and operations control are introduced.

Chapter 11, "Comprehensive Marketing Programs," raises issues in developing integrated marketing strategies. Attention is directed to marketing strategy decisions for new and existing products and services.

The case selection in this book reflects a broad overview of contemporary marketing problems and applications. Seventy percent of the cases are dated in the 1990s. Of the forty-five cases included, thirty deal with consumer products and services, and fifteen have a business-to-business marketing orientation. Fourteen cases introduce marketing issues in the international arena. Marketing of services is addressed in seven cases, and four cases raise issues related to ethics and social responsibility in marketing. Sixty percent of the cases are new, revised, or updated for this edition, and many have spreadsheet applications embedded in the case analysis. All text and case material has been classroom-tested.

Computer-assisted programs and a student manual are available for use with seventeen of the cases in the book. The manual contains all the materials necessary to use spreadsheets. It includes a sample case demonstration, instructions for use with specific cases, and input and output forms. If this material is not available from your instructor or bookstore, please write to the publisher.

The efforts of many people are reflected here. First, we thank those institutions and individuals who have kindly granted us permission to include their cases in this edition. The cases contribute significantly to the overall quality of the book, and each individual is prominently acknowledged in the Contents and at the bottom of the page on which the case begins. We specifically wish to thank the Harvard Business School, The University of Western Ontario, INSEAD, and IMD for granting permission to reproduce cases authored by their faculty. Second, we wish to thank our numerous collaborators, whose efforts made the difference between good cases and excellent cases. Third, we thank the adopters of the previous six editions of the book for their many comments and recommendations for improvements. Their insights and attention to detail are, we hope, reflected here. Finally, we wish to thank the numerous reviewers of this and previous editions for their conscientious reviews of our material. Naturally, we bear full responsibility for any errors of omission and commission in the final product.

R. A. K
R. A. P

STRATEGIC MARKETING PROBLEMS

CHAPTER 1

Foundations of Strategic Marketing Management

 The primary purpose of marketing is to create long-term and mutually beneficial exchange relationships between an organization and the publics (individuals and organizations) with which it interacts. Though this fundamental purpose of marketing is timeless, the manner in which organizations undertake it continues to evolve. No longer do marketing managers function solely to direct day-to-day operations; they must make strategic decisions as well. This elevation of marketing perspectives and practitioners to a strategic position in organizations has resulted in expanded responsibilities for marketing managers. Increasingly, they find themselves involved in charting the direction of the organization and contributing to decisions that will create and sustain a competitive advantage and affect long-term organizational performance. The transition of the marketing manager from being only an implementer to being a maker of organization strategy as well has prompted the emergence of strategic marketing management as a course of study and practice.

Strategic marketing management consists of six complex and interrelated analytical processes:[1]

1. Defining the organization's business
2. Specifying the purpose of the organization
3. Identifying organizational opportunities
4. Formulating product-market strategies
5. Budgeting financial, production, and human resources
6. Developing reformulation and recovery strategies

The remainder of this chapter discusses each of these processes and their relationships to one another.

DEFINING THE ORGANIZATION'S BUSINESS

Business definition is the first step in the application of strategic marketing management. An organization should define its business in terms of the type of customers it wishes to serve, the particular needs of these customers, and the means or technology by which the organization will serve these needs.[2] The definition of an organization's business, in turn, specifies the market niche(s) that the organization seeks to occupy and how it will compete. Ultimately, the business definition affects the growth prospects for the organization itself by establishing guidelines for pursuing and evaluating organizational opportunities in the context of identified environmental opportunities, threats, and organizational capabilities.

The following three examples illustrate the concept of business definition in practice. First consider the hand-held calculator industry, in which Hewlett-Packard and Texas Instruments seemingly competed with each other in the early 1980s. Although both firms excelled in marketing and technical expertise, each carved out a different market niche based on different business definitions. Hewlett-Packard's products were designed primarily for the technical user (customer type) who required highly sophisticated scientific and business calculations (customer needs). Hewlett-Packard's heavy development expenditures on basic research (means) made the products possible. On the other hand, Texas Instruments' products were designed for the household consumer (customer type) who required less sophisticated calculator capabilities (customer needs). Texas Instruments' efficient production capabilities (means) made its products possible.

A second example could be found in the overnight-courier industry, in the differences between Federal Express and Purolator in the late 1980s.[3] Although both firms competed for the same customer group—businesses that wanted next-morning delivery of letters and packages—each used very different means for satisfying different customer needs. Federal Express satisfied a customer's desire to ship items over distances of more than 350 miles (customer needs) and relied on a fleet of airplanes (means) for this purpose. By comparison, Purolator satisfied a customer's desire to ship items less than 350 miles (customer needs) and relied on a fleet of trucks (means). The differences in business definition were reflected in the companies' respective competitive positions. Purolator captured over 75 percent of the next-morning, short-haul (under 350 miles) courier volume, whereas Federal Express captured about 10 percent. Federal Express, however, captured over 53 percent of the next-morning, long-haul (over 350 miles) courier volume, whereas Purolator captured only about 7 percent.

Environmental and market forces sometimes require an organization to alter an aspect of its business definition. However, major changes in two or three dimensions are often difficult for organizations and frequently produce unfavorable results. Sears, Roebuck and Company is a case in point.[4] The retailing giant found itself in a retailing environment where discounters and specialty outlets were attracting its traditional middle-class customers. The company tinkered with its marketing strategy throughout the 1980s and early 1990s. It promoted itself variously as an upscale, fashion-oriented department store for more affluent customers and as a discounter with budget shops featuring store or private-label brands and discounted prices. Sears then attempted to portray itself as a store with "everyday low pricing" and as a collection of "power formats" focusing on popular brands of merchandise. Recently,

Sears's top management acknowledged that, "We need to much more clearly identify our target customers and needs," which meant that Sears would focus its marketing strategy on "the middle 60 percent of the population that recognizes value." Having defined the company's customer group and need(s) to be satisfied, the Sears merchandising formula (means) had to be modified, thus demonstrating the tight linkage among all three aspects of business definition.

SPECIFYING THE PURPOSE OF THE ORGANIZATION

The purpose of an organization is derived from its business definition. Purpose specifies the aspirations of the organization and what it wishes to achieve, with full recognition given to environmental opportunities, threats, and organizational capabilities.

From a strategic marketing management perspective, aspirations are objectives and desired achievements are goals. Objectives and goals represent statements of expectations or intentions, and they often incorporate the organization's business definition. For example, consider the marketing objectives outlined in the Hendison Electronics Corporation case in Chapter 8 of this text. Hendison Electronics aspires

> . . . to serve the discriminating purchasers of home entertainment products who approach their purchase in a deliberate manner with heavy consideration of long-term benefits. We will emphasize home entertainment products with superior performance, style, reliability, and value that require representative display, professional selling, trained service, and brand acceptance—retailed through reputable electronic specialists to those consumers whom the company can most effectively service.

Hendison Electronics intends to achieve, in every market served, a market position of at least $6.50 sales per capita in the current year.

In practice, business definition provides direction in setting goals and objectives. Capabilities of the organization and environmental opportunities and threats determine the likelihood of attainment. Goals and objectives divide into three major categories: production, finance, and marketing. Production expectations relate to the use of manufacturing and service capacity and to product and service quality. Financial goals and objectives relate to return on investment, return on sales, profit, cash flow, and shareholder wealth. Marketing goals and objectives relate to market share, marketing productivity, sales volume, profit, and customer satisfaction and value. When production, finance, and marketing goals and objectives are combined, they represent a composite picture of organizational purpose. Accordingly, they must complement one another.

Finally, goal and objective setting should be problem-centered and future-oriented. Because goals and objectives represent statements of where the organization should be, they implicitly arise from an understanding of the current situation. Therefore, managers need an appraisal of operations, or a *situation analysis*, to determine reasons for the gap between what was or is expected and what has happened or will happen. If performance has met expectations, the question arises as to future directions. If performance has not met expectations, managers must diagnose the reasons for this difference and enact a program for remedying the situation. Chapter 3 provides an expanded discussion on performing a situation analysis.

IDENTIFYING ORGANIZATIONAL OPPORTUNITIES

Organizational opportunities and strategic direction result from matching environmental opportunities with organizational capabilities, acceptable levels of risks, and resource commitments. Three questions capture the essence of the decision-making process at this stage:

- What might we do?
- What do we do best?
- What must we do?

Each of these questions highlights major concepts in strategic marketing management. The *what might we do* question introduces the concept of environmental opportunity. Unmet needs, unsatisfied buyer groups, and new means for delivering value to prospective buyers—each represents a type of *environmental opportunity*.

The *what do we do best* question introduces the concept of organizational capability, or distinctive competency. *Distinctive competency* describes an organization's principal strengths or qualities, its skills in areas such as technological innovation, marketing prescience and prowess, manufacturing or service delivery, and managerial talent.[5] In order for any of an organization's qualities to be considered truly distinctive and a source of competitive advantage, two criteria must be satisfied. First, the quality must be imperfectly imitable by competitors. That is, competitors cannot replicate a quality (such as the delivery competency of Domino's Pizza) easily or without a sizable investment. Second, the quality should make a significant contribution to the benefits perceived by customers and, by doing so, provide superior value to them. For example, technological innovation that is wanted and provides value to customers is a distinctive competency. Consider the Safety Razor Division of the Gillette Company. Its distinctive competency lies in three areas: (1) shaving technology and development, (2) high-volume manufacturing of precision metal and plastic products, and (3) marketing of mass-distributed package goods.[6] This distinctive competency was responsible for the Sensor razor blade, which revolutionized the shaving industry in the early 1990s.

Finally, the *what must we do* question introduces the concept of success requirements in an industry or market. *Success requirements* are basic tasks that must be performed in a market or industry to compete successfully. These requirements are subtle in nature and often overlooked. For example, distribution and inventory control are critical in the cosmetics industry. Firms competing in the personal computer industry recognize that the requirements for success include low-cost production capabilities, access to retail distribution channels, and strengths in software development.[7]

The linkage among environmental opportunity, distinctive competency, and success requirements will determine whether an organizational opportunity exists. A clearly defined statement of success requirements serves as a device for matching environmental opportunity with an organization's distinctive competency. If *what must be done* is inconsistent with *what can be done* to pursue an environmental opportunity, an organizational opportunity will fail to materialize. Too often organizations ignore this linkage and embark on ventures that are doomed from the start. Exxon Corporation learned this lesson painfully after investing $500 million in the office-products market over a ten-year period. After the company abandoned this venture, a former Exxon executive summed up what had been learned: "Don't get involved where you don't have the skills. It's hard enough to make money at what you're good at."[8] By clearly establishing the linkages necessary for success before taking any action, an organization can minimize the risk. A Hanes Corporation executive illustrates this point in specifying his organization's new-venture criteria:

> . . . products that can be sold through food and drugstore outlets, are purchased by women, . . . can be easily and distinctly packaged, and comprise at least a $500 million retail market not already dominated by one or two major producers.[9]

When one considers Hanes's past successes, it is apparent that whatever Hanes decides to do in the future will be consistent with what Hanes can do best, as illustrated by past achievements in markets whose success requirements are similar. An expanded discussion of these points is found in Chapter 4.

In actuality, organizational opportunities emerge from existing markets or from newly identified markets. Opportunities also arise for existing, improved, or new products and services. Matching products and markets to form product-market strategies is the subject of the next set of decision processes.

FORMULATING PRODUCT-MARKET STRATEGIES

Product-market strategies consist of plans for matching existing or potential offerings of the organization with the needs of markets, informing markets that the offering exists, having the offering available at the right time and place to facilitate exchange, and assigning a price to the offering. In practice, a product-market strategy involves selecting specific markets and profitably reaching them through a program called a *marketing mix*.

Exhibit 1.1 classifies product-market strategies according to the match between offerings and markets. The operational implications and requirements of each strategy are briefly described in the following subsections.[10]

EXHIBIT 1.1

Product-Market Strategies

		Markets	
		Existing	*New*
Offerings	*Existing*	Market penetration	Market development
	New	New offering development	Diversification

Source: This classification is adapted from H. Igor Ansoff, *Corporate Strategy* (New York: McGraw-Hill, 1964), Chapter 6. An extended version of this classification is presented in G. Day, "A Strategic Perspective on Product Planning," *Journal of Contemporary Business* (Spring 1975): 1–34.

Market-Penetration Strategy

A market-penetration strategy dictates that an organization seek to gain greater dominance in a market in which it already has an offering. This strategy involves attempts to increase present buyers' usage or consumption rate of the offering, attract buyers of competing offerings, or stimulate product trial among potential customers. The mix of marketing activities might include lower prices for the offerings, expanded distribution to provide wider coverage of an existing market, and heavier promotional efforts extolling the "unique" advantages of an organization's offering over competing offerings. Anheuser-Busch uses all of these activities in attempting to achieve its announced goal of capturing 50 percent of the U.S. beer market in the 1990s.[11]

Several organizations have attempted to gain dominance by promoting more frequent and varied usage of their offering. For example, the Florida Orange Growers Association advocates drinking orange juice throughout the day rather than for breakfast only. Airlines stimulate usage through a variety of reduced-fare programs and various family-travel packages, designed to reach the primary traveler's spouse and children.

Marketing managers should consider a number of factors before adopting a penetration strategy. First, they must examine market growth. A penetration strategy is usually more effective in a growth market. Attempts to increase market share when volume is stable often result in aggressive retaliatory actions by competitors. Second, they must consider competitive reaction. Procter and Gamble implemented a penetration strategy for its Folger's coffee in selected East Coast cities, only to run head-on into an equally aggressive reaction from General Foods' Maxwell House Division. According to one observer of the competitive situation:

> When Folger's mailed millions of coupons offering consumers 45 cents off on a one-pound can of coffee, General Foods countered with newspaper coupons of its own. When Folger's gave retailers 15 percent discounts from the list price..., General Foods met them head-on. [General Foods] let Folger's lead off with a TV blitz.... Then [General Foods] saturated the airwaves.[12]

The result of this struggle was no change in market share for either firm. Third, marketing managers must consider the capacity of the market to increase usage or consumption rates *and* the availability of new buyers. Both are particularly relevant when viewed from the perspective of the *costs of conversion* involved in gaining buyers from competitors, stimulating usage, and attracting new users.

Market-Development Strategy

A market-development strategy dictates that an organization introduce its existing offerings to markets other than those it is currently serving. Examples include introducing existing products to different geographical areas (including international expansion) or different buying publics. For example, Adolph Coors and Company engaged in a market-development strategy when it entered states east of the Mississippi River. O. M. Scott and Sons Company employed this strategy when it moved from the home lawn-improvement market to large users of lawn-care products, such as golf courses and home construction contractors.

The mix of marketing activities used must often be varied to reach different markets with differing buying patterns and requirements. Reaching new markets often requires modification of the basic offering, different distribution outlets, or a change in sales effort and advertising.

Apple Computer is a case in point. Apple originally focused on the home and education markets. In the mid-1980s, however, the company set as its target the business and technical markets. In the late 1980s, 50 new products were introduced and software developers were recruited to create basic programs for graphics, spreadsheet applications, and desktop publishing. A heavier emphasis was placed on advertising, a company sales force was put into place, and the dealer network was modified. As a result, Apple tripled its share of the business and technical market.[13]

Like the penetration strategy, market development involves a careful consideration of competitive strengths and weaknesses and retaliation potential. Moreover, because the firm seeks new buyers, it must understand their number, motivation, and buying patterns in order to develop marketing activities successfully. Finally, the firm must consider its strengths, in terms of adaptability to new markets, in order to evaluate the potential success of the venture.

Market development in the international arena has grown in importance and usually takes one of four forms: (1) exporting, (2) licensing, (3) joint venture, or (4) direct investment.[14] Each option has advantages and disadvantages. *Exporting* involves marketing the same offering in another country either directly (through sales offices) or through intermediaries in a foreign country. Since this approach typically requires minimal capital investment and is easy to initiate, it is a popular option for developing foreign markets. Procter and Gamble, for instance, exports its deodorants, soaps, fragrances, shampoos, and other health and beauty products to the newly emerging democracies in Eastern Europe and the former Soviet Union. *Licensing* is a contractual arrangement whereby one firm (licensee) is given the rights to patents, trademarks, know-how, and other intangible assets by their owner (licensor) in return for a royalty (usually 5 percent of gross sales) or a fee. For example, Cadbury Schweppes PLC, a London-based multinational firm has licensed Hershey Foods to sell its candies in the United States for a fee of $300 million. Licensing provides a low-risk, quick, and capital-free entry into a foreign market. However, the licensor usually has no control over production and marketing by the licensee. A *joint venture*, often called a strategic alliance, involves investment by both a foreign firm and a local company to create a new entity in the host country. The two companies share ownership, control, and profits of the entity. Joint ventures are popular because one company may not have the necessary financial, technical, or managerial resources to enter a market alone. This approach also often ensures against trade barriers being imposed on the foreign firm by the government of the host company. Japanese companies frequently engage in joint ventures with American and European firms to gain access to foreign markets. A problem frequently arising from joint ventures is that the partners do not always agree on how the new entity should be run. *Direct investment* in a manufacturing and/or assembly facility in a foreign market is the most risky option and requires the greatest commitment. However, it brings the firm closer to its customers and may be the most profitable approach toward developing foreign markets. For these reasons, direct investment must be evaluated closely in terms of benefits and costs. Direct investment often follows one of the three other approaches to foreign-market entry. For example, PepsiCo first exported Pepsi-Cola to the then Soviet Union in 1972. By 1994, PepsiCo operated over 30 bottling plants there.

Product-Development Strategy

A product-development strategy dictates that the organization create new offerings for existing markets. The approach taken may be to develop totally new offerings *(product innovation)*, to enhance the value to customers of existing offerings *(product augmentation)*, or to broaden the existing line of offerings by adding different sizes, forms, flavors, and so forth *(product line extension)*. Rollerblades are an example of product innovation, as is the introduction of the "Cash Management Account" by Merrill Lynch in the financial services industry. Product augmentation can be achieved in numerous ways. One is to bundle complimentary items or services with an existing offering. For example, programming services, application aids, and training programs for buyers enhance the value of personal computers. Another way is to improve the functional performance of the offering. Producers of facsimile machines have done this by improving print quality. Many types of product line extensions are possible. Personal-care companies market deodorants in powder, spray, and liquid forms; Quaker Oats produces several flavors of Gatorade; and Frito-Lay offers its Lay's potato chips in a number of sizes.

Companies successful at developing and commercializing new offerings lead their industries in sales growth and profitability. The likelihood of success is increased if the development effort results in offerings that satisfy a clearly understood buyer need. In the toy industry, for instance, these needs translate into products with three qualities: (1) lasting play value, (2) the ability to be shared with other children, and (3) the ability to stimulate a child's imagination.[15] Successful commercialization occurs when the offering can be communicated and delivered to a well-defined buyer group at a price it is willing and able to pay.

Important considerations in planning a product-development strategy concern the market size and volume necessary for the effort to be profitable, the magnitude and timing of competitive response, the impact of the new product on existing offerings, and the capacity (in terms of human and financial investment and technology) of the organization to deliver the offering to the market(s). The failure of DuPont's attempt to introduce Corfam (a synthetic leather) has been attributed to the magnitude of competitive response generated by Leather Industries of America (a trade association) and to the fact that the company could not develop competitive prices for the product because of an inability to lower production costs.

The potential for *cannibalism* must be considered with a product-development strategy.[16] Cannibalism occurs when sales of a new product or service come at the expense of sales of existing products already marketed by the firm. For example, it is estimated that two-thirds of Gillette's Sensor razor volume came from the company's other razors and shaving systems. Cannibalism of this degree is likely to occur in many product-development programs. The issue faced by the manager is whether it detracts from the overall profitability of the organization's total mix of offerings.

Diversification

Diversification involves the development or acquisition of offerings new to the organization and the introduction of those offerings to publics not previously served by the organization. Many firms have adopted this strategy in recent years to take advantage of growth opportunities. Yet diversification is often a high-risk strategy because both the offering and the public or market served are new to the organization.

Consider the following examples of diversification.[17] General Foods announced a $39 million write-off after its entry into the business of fast-food chains failed. Rohr Industries, a subcontractor in the aerospace industry, reported a $59.9 million write-off on a mass-transit diversification. Singer's effort to develop a business-machines venture over a ten-year period was abandoned while still unprofitable. Gerber Products Company, which holds 70 percent of the U.S. baby-food market, has been mostly unsuccessful in diversifying into child-care centers, toys, furniture, and adult food and beverages. Coca-Cola's many attempts at diversification—acquiring wine companies, a movie studio, and a pasta manufacturer, and producing television game shows—have also proven to be largely unsuccessful. These examples highlight the importance of understanding the link between market success requirements and an organization's distinctive competency. In each of these cases, a bridge was not made between these two concepts and thus an opportunity was not realized.

Still, diversifications can be successful. Successful diversifications typically result from an organization's attempt to apply its distinctive competency in reaching new markets with new offerings. By relying on its marketing expertise and extensive distribution system, Borden has had success with offerings ranging from milk to glue, and Procter and Gamble with offerings ranging from cake mixes to disposable diapers.

Strategy Selection

A recurrent issue in strategic marketing management is determining the consistency of product-market strategies with the organization's mission and capacity, market capacity and behavior, environmental forces, and competitive activities. Proper analysis of these factors depends on the availability and evaluation of relevant information. Information on markets should include data on size, buying behavior, and requirements. Information on environmental forces such as social, legal, political, and economic changes is necessary to determine the future viability of the organization's offerings and the markets served. In recent years, for example, organizations have had to alter or adapt their product-market strategies because of political actions (deregulation), social changes (increase in the number of employed women), economic fluctuations (income shifts and the decline in disposable personal income), attitudes (value consciousness) and population shifts (city to suburb and northern to southern United States)—to name just a few of the environmental changes. Competitive activities must be monitored to ascertain their existing or possible strategies and performance in satisfying buyer needs. Considerations in the acquisition and management of information are discussed in Chapter 5.

In practice, the strategy selection decision is based on an analysis of the costs and benefits of alternative strategies and their probabilities of success. For example, a manager may compare the costs and benefits involved in further penetrating an existing market to those associated with introducing the existing product to a new market. It is important to make a careful analysis of competitive structure; market growth, decline, or shifts; and *opportunity costs* (potential benefits *not* obtained). The product or service itself may dictate a strategy change. If the product has been purchased by all of the buyers it is going to attract in an existing market, opportunities for growth beyond replacement purchases are reduced. This situation would indicate a need to search out new buyers (markets) or to develop new products or services for present markets.

The probabilities of success of the various strategies must then be considered. A. T. Kearney, a management consulting firm, has provided rough probability esti-

E X H I B I T   1.2

Decision-Tree Format

Action	Response	Outcome

A_1 — R_1 ——————→ O_1

A_1 — R_2 ——————→ O_2

A_1 — R_1 ——————→ O_1

A_1 — R_2 ——————→ O_2

mates of success for each of the four basic strategies.[18] The probability of a successful diversification is 1 in 20. The probability of successfully introducing an existing product into a new market (market-development strategy) is 1 in 4. There is a 50-50 chance of success for a new product being introduced into an existing market (product-development strategy). Finally, minor modification of an offering directed toward its existing market (market-penetration strategy) has the highest probability of success.

A useful technique for gauging potential outcomes of alternative marketing strategies is to array possible actions, the responses to these actions, and the outcomes in the form of a *decision tree*, so named because of the branching out of responses from action taken. This implies that for any action taken, certain responses can be anticipated, each with its own specific outcomes. Exhibit 1.2 shows a decision tree.

As an example, consider a situation in which a marketing manager must decide between a market-penetration strategy and a market-development strategy. Suppose the manager recognizes that competitors may react aggressively or passively to either strategy. This situation can be displayed vividly using the decision-tree scheme, as shown in Exhibit 1.3. This representation allows the manager to consider actions, responses, and outcomes simultaneously. The decision tree shows that the highest profits will result *if* a market-development strategy is enacted *and* competitors react passively. The manager must resolve the question of competitive reaction because an aggressive response will plunge the profit to $1 million, which is less than either outcome under the market-penetration strategy. The manager must rely on informed judgment to assess subjectively the likelihood of competitive response. Chapter 3 presents a more detailed description of decision analysis.

The Marketing Mix

Matching offerings and markets requires recognition of the other marketing activities available to the marketing manager. Combined with the offering, these activities form the marketing mix.

A marketing mix typically encompasses activities controllable by the organization. These include the kind of product, service, or idea offered (product strategy), how it will be communicated to buyers (promotion strategy), the method for dis-

EXHIBIT 1.3

Sample Decision Tree

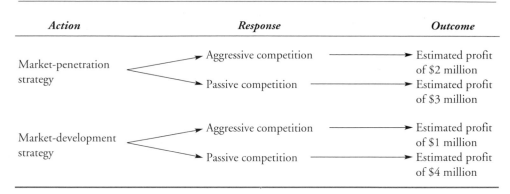

Action	Response	Outcome
Market-penetration strategy	Aggressive competition	Estimated profit of $2 million
	Passive competition	Estimated profit of $3 million
Market-development strategy	Aggressive competition	Estimated profit of $1 million
	Passive competition	Estimated profit of $4 million

tributing the offering to buyers (channel strategy), and the amount buyers will pay for the offering (price strategy). Each of these individual strategies is described later in this book. Here it is sufficient to note that each element of the marketing mix plays a role in stimulating a market's willingness and ability to buy. For example, promotion—personal selling, advertising, sales promotion, and public relations—informs and assures buyers that the offering will meet their needs. Marketing channels satisfy buyers' shopping patterns and purchase requirements in terms of point-of-purchase information and offering availability. Price represents the value or benefits provided by the offering.

The appropriate marketing mix for a product or service depends on the success requirements of the markets at which it is directed. The "rightness" of a product, promotion, channel, or price strategy can be interpreted only in the context of markets served. Recognition of this fact has prompted the use of *regional marketing*, whereby different marketing mixes are employed to accommodate unique consumer preferences and competitive conditions in different geographical areas. For instance, Frito-Lay's Tostitos® brand of tortilla chips is marketed as a specialty product sold mostly through delicatessens in some northeastern states. The brand's promotion and price policies are not aggressive in these states because of fragmented competition. Tortilla chips in southwestern states are a commodity-type product sold by many competitors through supermarkets. The Tostitos® brand is therefore supported in that geographical area by more aggressive price and promotion programs. Firms that market products and services worldwide often "glocalize" their marketing mixes. That is, global decisions are made in such areas as product development, but decisions related to advertising, pricing, and distribution are arrived at by local (country-specific) marketing managers. A prime example of glocalization is found in the marketing of Swatch watches.[19] In developed countries, Swatch watches are marketed as a fashion item; in less developed countries, the marketing mix emphasizes simple design, affordable cost, and functional qualities.

In addition to being consistent with the needs of markets served, a marketing mix must be consistent with the organization's capacity, and the individual activities must complement one another. Several questions offer direction in evaluating an organization's marketing mix. First, is the marketing mix *internally consistent?* Do the individual activities complement one another to form a whole, as opposed to fragmented pieces? Does the mix fit the organization, the market, and the environment into which it will be introduced? Second, are buyers more *sensitive* to some marketing mix activities than to others? For example, are they more likely to respond favorably to a decrease in price or an increase in advertising? Third, what are the *costs* of performing marketing mix activities? Do the costs exceed the benefits in terms of buyer response? Can the organization afford the marketing mix expenditures? Finally, is the marketing mix properly *timed?* For example, is promotion scheduled to coincide with product availability? Is the entire marketing mix timely with respect to the nature of the markets and environmental forces?

The implementation of a marketing strategy is as much an art as a science. Implementation requires an integration of markets, environmental forces, organizational capacity, and marketing mix activities. These topics are raised again in Chapter 11.

An example of an implementation with less than successful results is that of A&P's WEO (Where Economy Originates) program. Prior to implementing the program, A&P had watched its sales volume plateau with shrinking profits, while other supermarket chains continued to increase sales volume and profits. When the WEO program was initiated, it emphasized discount pricing (price strategy) with heavy promotional expenditures (promotion strategy). The program increased sales volume by $800 million but produced a profit loss of over $50 million. In the words of one industry observer at the time:

> Its competitors are convinced that A&P's assault with WEO was doomed from the start. Too many of its stores are relics of a bygone era. Many are in poor locations [distributional strategy]. . . . They are just not big enough to support the tremendous volume that is necessary to make a discounting operation profitable [capacity] . . . stores lack shelf space for stocking general merchandise items, such as housewares and children's clothing [product strategy].[20]

The product-market strategy employed by A&P could be classified as a market-penetration strategy. Its implementation, however, could be questioned in terms of internal consistency, costs of the marketing mix activities, and fit with organizational capacity. Moreover, the retail grocery industry was plagued at the time by rising food costs, an environmental force that had a destructive effect on strategy success.

BUDGETING FINANCIAL, PRODUCTION, AND HUMAN RESOURCES

The culmination of all strategic decisions is reflected in the *master budget* for the organization. A well-prepared budget quantitatively expresses marketing strategy and also integrates the goals of all functional areas of the organization.

The sales forecast is the foundation of the master budget. Financial, production, and human resource allocations, depicted in dollar terms, illustrate how the sales goals will be achieved. The end result is the profit or loss projection.

A complete description of the budgetary process is beyond the scope of this section. However, Chapter 2, Financial Aspects of Marketing Management, provides an overview of cost concepts and behavior. It also describes useful analytical tools for dealing with the financial dimensions of marketing management, including the preparation of *pro forma* income statements.

DEVELOPING REFORMULATION AND RECOVERY STRATEGIES

Reformulation and recovery strategies form the cornerstone of adaptive behavior in organizations. Strategies are rarely timeless. Changing markets and competitive behavior require periodic, if not sudden, adjustments in strategy.

Marketing audit and control procedures are fundamental to the development of reformulation and recovery strategies. The marketing audit has been defined as follows:

> A marketing audit is a comprehensive, systematic, independent, and periodic examination of a company's—or business unit's—marketing environment, objectives, strategies, and activities with a view of determining problem areas and opportunities and recommending a plan of action to improve the company's marketing performance.[21]

The audit process directs the manager's attention to both the strategic fit of the organization with its environment and the operational aspects of the marketing program. Strategic aspects of the marketing audit address the synoptic question "Are we doing the right things?" Operational aspects address an equally synoptic question "Are we doing things right?"

The distinction between strategic and operational perspectives, as well as the implementation of each, is examined in Chapter 10. Suffice it to say here that marketing audit and control procedures underlie the process of defining the organization's business and purpose, identifying opportunities and strategic direction, and formulating product-market strategies and marketing mix activities.

The intellectual process of developing reformulation and recovery strategies during the planning process serves two important purposes. First, it forces the manager to consider the "what if" questions. For example, "What if an unexpected environmental threat arises that renders a strategy obsolete?" or "What if competitive and market response to a strategy is inconsistent with what was originally expected?" Such questions focus the manager's attention on the sensitivity of results to assumptions made in the strategy development process. Second, preplanning of reformulation and recovery strategies, or *contingency plans*, leads to a faster reaction time in implementing remedial action. Marshaling and reorienting resources is a time-consuming process itself without additional time lost in planning.

ETHICS AND SOCIAL RESPONSIBILITY

Matters of ethics and social responsibility permeate every aspect of the strategic marketing management process. Indeed, most marketing decisions involve some degree of moral judgment and reflect an organization's orientation toward the publics with which it interacts.[22] Enlightened marketing executives no longer subscribe to the view that if an action is legal, then it is also ethical and socially responsible. These executives are sensitive to the fact that the marketplace is populated by individuals and groups with diverse value systems. Moreover, they recognize that their actions will be judged publicly by others with different values and interests.

Enlightened ethical and socially responsible decisions arise from the ability of marketers to discern the precise issues involved and their willingness to take action even when the outcome may negatively affect their standing in an organization or the company's financial interests. Although the moral foundations on which marketing decisions are made will vary among individuals and organizations, failure to recognize issues and take appropriate action is the least ethical and most socially irresponsible approach.

A positive approach to ethical and socially responsible behavior is evident in Anheuser-Busch's "Know When to Say When" campaign, which advocates responsible drinking of alcoholic beverages.[23] The company spends as much for advertising on this campaign as it does for its flagship brands (Michelob, Busch, and Natural Light), or about $30 million annually. Anheuser-Busch executives acknowledge the potential for alcohol abuse and are willing to forgo business generated by misuse of the company's products. These executives have discerned the issues and have recognized an ethical obligation to present and potential customers. They have also recognized the company's social responsibility to the general public by encouraging safe driving and responsible drinking habits.

NOTES

1. This sequence of analytical processes was influenced by the work of D. Abell and J. Hammond, *Strategic Market Planning: Problems and Analytical Approaches* (Englewood Cliffs, NJ: Prentice Hall, 1979): 9.

2. D. Abell, *Defining the Business* (Englewood Cliffs, NJ: Prentice Hall, 1980).

3. "Federal Express Corporation," in J. B. Quinn, H. Mintzberg, and R. James, *Strategy Process: Concepts, Contexts, and Cases* (Englewood Cliffs, NJ: Prentice Hall, 1991).

4. Susan Caminiti, "Sears' Need: More Speed," *Fortune* (July 15, 1991): 88–90; "American Retailing: Back to the Future," *The Economist* (October 9, 1993): 74–75.

5. For a thorough discussion of distinctive competency, see C. K. Prahalad and Gary Hamel, "The Core Competence of the Corporation," *Harvard Business Review* (May–June 1990): 79–91; Gary Hamel and C. K. Prahalad, "Corporate Imagination and Expeditionary Marketing," *Harvard Business Review* (July–August 1991): 81–92.

6. "Gillette Safety Razor Division: The Blank Cassette Project," HBS #9-574-058.

7. "The Power Surge in Home PCs," *Business Week* (August 26, 1991): 65–66.

8. "Exxon's Flop in Field of Office Gear Shows Diversification Perils," *Wall Street Journal* (September 3, 1985): 1ff.

9. "Hanes Expands L'eggs to the Entire Family," *Business Week* (June 14, 1975): 57ff.

10. For an extended discussion on product-market strategies, see Roger A. Kerin, Vijay Mahajan, and P. Rajan Varadarajan, *Contemporary Perspectives on Strategic Market Planning* (Boston: Allyn and Bacon, 1990), Chapter 6.

11. Patricia Sellers, "Busch Fights to Have It All," *Fortune* (January 15, 1990): 81ff.

12. H. Menzies, "Why Folger's Is Getting Creamed Back East," *Fortune* (July 17, 1978): 69.

13. B. O'Rielly, "Growing Apple Anew for the Business Market," *Fortune* (January 4, 1988): 36–37; and L. Strazewski, "Apple Uses New Marketing Strategy to Take a Slice of Competition's Pie," *Marketing News* (September 12, 1988): 7–8.

14. This discussion is based on Subhash C. Jain, *International Marketing Management*, 3rd ed. (Boston: PWS-Kent, 1990): 35–40.

15. "Hasbro, Inc.," in Eric Berkowitz, Roger Kerin, Steven Hartley, and William Rudelius, *Marketing*, 3rd ed. (Homewood, IL: Richard D. Irwin, 1992): 683–685.

16. For an extended treatment of this topic and additional examples, see Roger Kerin and Dwight Riskey, "Product Cannibalism," in Sidney Levy, ed., *Marketing Manager's Handbook* (Chicago: Dartnell Company, 1994).

17. The examples are from "Some Things Don't Go Better with Coke," *Forbes* (March 21, 1988): 34–35; and "Gerber Goes Global with 'Superbrand' Concept," *Marketing News* (September 16, 1991): 21.

18. These estimates were reported in "The Breakdown of U.S. Innovation," *Business Week* (February 16, 1976): 56ff.

19. *Management Briefing: Marketing* (New York: Conference Board, January 1990): 5.

20. E. Tracy, "How A&P Got Creamed," *Fortune* (January 1973): 104. Items in brackets added for illustrative purposes.

21. Philip Kotler, *Marketing Management*, 8th ed. (Englewood Cliffs, NJ: Prentice Hall, 1994): 758.

22. For an extensive discussion of ethics in marketing, see Gene Lazniak and Patrick E. Murphy, *Ethical Marketing Decisions: The Higher Road* (Boston: Allyn and Bacon, 1993).

23. This example is based on "Anheuser Boosting Public Service Ads," *Wall Street Journal* (June 28, 1989): 86; and "Selling Sobriety," *Dallas Times Herald* (March 19, 1990): A9.

CHAPTER 2

Financial Aspects of Marketing Management

 Marketing managers are accountable for the impact of their actions on profits. Therefore, they need a working knowledge of basic accounting and finance. This chapter provides an overview of several concepts from managerial accounting and managerial finance that are useful in marketing management: (1) variable and fixed costs, (2) relevant and sunk costs, (3) margins, (4) contribution analysis, (5) liquidity, and (6) operating leverage. In addition, considerations for preparing *pro forma* income statements are described.

VARIABLE AND FIXED COSTS

An organization's costs divide into two broad categories: variable costs and fixed costs.

Variable Costs

Variable costs are expenses that are uniform per unit of output within a relevant time period (usually defined as a budget year); yet total variable costs fluctuate in direct proportion to the output volume of units produced. In other words, as volume increases, total variable costs increase.

Variable costs are divided into two categories, one of which is *cost of goods sold.* For a manufacturer or a provider of a service, cost of goods sold covers materials, labor, and factory overhead applied directly to production. For a reseller (wholesaler or retailer), cost of goods sold consists primarily of the costs of merchandise. The second category of variable costs consists of expenses that are not directly tied to production but that nevertheless vary directly with volume. Examples include sales commissions, discounts, and delivery expenses.

Fixed Costs

Fixed costs are expenses that do not fluctuate with output volume within a relevant time period (the budget year) but become progressively smaller per unit of output as volume increases. The decrease in per-unit fixed cost results from the increase in the number of output units over which fixed costs are allocated. Note, however, that no matter how large volume becomes, the absolute size of fixed costs remains unchanged.

Fixed costs divide into two categories: programmed costs and committed costs. *Programmed costs* result from attempts to generate sales volume. *Marketing expenditures are generally classified as programmed costs.* Examples include advertising, sales promotion, and sales salaries. *Committed costs* are those required to maintain the organization. They are usually nonmarketing expenditures such as rent and administrative and clerical salaries.

It is important to understand the concept of fixed cost. Remember that total fixed costs do not change during a budget year, regardless of changes in volume. Once fixed expenditures for a marketing program have been made, they remain the same whether or not the program causes unit volume to change.

Despite the clear-cut classification of costs into variable and fixed categories suggested here, cost classification is not always apparent in actual practice. Many times costs have a fixed and a variable component. For example, selling expenses often have a fixed component (such as salary) and a variable component (such as commissions or bonus) that are not always evident at first glance.

RELEVANT AND SUNK COSTS

Relevant Costs

Relevant costs are expenditures that (1) are expected to occur in the future as a result of some marketing action and (2) differ among marketing alternatives being considered. In short, relevant costs are future expenditures unique to the decision alternatives under consideration.

The concept of relevant cost can best be illustrated by an example. Suppose a manager considers adding a new product to the product mix. Relevant costs include potential expenditures for manufacturing and marketing the product, plus salary costs arising from the time sales personnel give to the new products at the expense of other products. If this additional product does not affect the salary costs of sales personnel, salaries are not a relevant cost.

As a general rule, opportunity costs are also a relevant cost. Opportunity costs are the forgone benefits from an alternative not chosen.

Sunk Costs

Sunk costs are the direct opposite of relevant costs. Sunk costs are past expenditures for a given activity and are typically irrelevant in whole or in part to future decisions. In a marketing context, sunk costs include past research and development expenditures (including test marketing) and last year's advertising expense. These expenditures, although real, will neither recur in the future nor influence future expenditures.

When marketing managers attempt to incorporate sunk costs into future decisions affecting new expenditures, they often fall prey to the *sunk cost fallacy*—that is, they attempt to recoup spent dollars by spending still more dollars in the future.

MARGINS

Another useful concept for marketing managers is that of *margin,* which refers to the difference between the selling price and the "cost" of a product or service. Margins are expressed on a total volume basis or on an individual unit basis, in dollar terms or as percentages. The three described here are gross, trade, and net profit margins.

Gross Margin

Gross margin, or gross profit, is the difference between total sales revenue and total cost of goods sold, or, on a per-unit basis, the difference between unit selling price and unit cost of goods sold. Gross margin may be expressed in dollar terms or as a percentage.

Total Gross Margin	Dollar Amount	Percentage
Net sales	$100	100%
Cost of goods sold	−40	−40
Gross profit margin	$ 60	60%
Unit Gross Margin		
Unit sales price	$1.00	100%
Unit cost of goods sold	−0.40	−40
Unit gross profit margin	$0.60	60%

Gross margin analysis is a useful tool because it implicitly includes unit selling prices of products or services, unit costs, and unit volume. A decrease in gross margin is of immediate concern to a marketing manager, because such a change has a direct impact on profits, providing that other expenditures remain unchanged. Changes in total gross margin should be examined in depth to determine whether the change was brought about by fluctuations in unit volume, changes in unit price or unit cost of goods sold, or a modification in the sales mix of the firm's products or services.

Trade Margin

Trade margin is the difference between unit sales price and unit cost at each level of a marketing channel (for example, manufacturer → wholesaler → retailer). A trade margin is frequently referred to as a *markup* or *mark-on* by channel members, and it is often expressed as a percentage.

Trade margins are occasionally confusing, since the margin percentage can be computed on the basis of cost or selling price. Consider the following example. Suppose a retailer purchases an item for $10 and sells it at a price of $20—that is, a $10 margin. What is the retailer's margin percentage?

Retailer margin as a percentage of cost is

$$\frac{\$10}{\$10} \times 100 = 100 \text{ percent}$$

Retailer margin as a percentage of selling price is

$$\frac{\$10}{\$20} \times 100 = 50 \text{ percent}$$

Differences in margin percentages show the importance of knowing the base (cost or selling price) on which the margin percentage is determined. *Trade margin percentages are usually determined on the basis of selling price*, but practices do vary among firms and industries.

Trade margins affect the pricing of individual items in two ways. First, suppose a wholesaler purchases an item for $2.00 and seeks to achieve a 30 percent margin on this item based on selling price. What would be the selling price?

$2.00 = 70 percent of selling price

or

Selling price = $2.00/0.70 = $2.86

Second, suppose a manufacturer suggests a retail list price of $6.00 on an item for ultimate sales to the consumer. The item will be sold through retailers whose policy is to obtain a 40 percent margin based on selling price. For what price must the manufacturer sell the item to the retailer?

$$\frac{x}{\$6.00} = 40 \text{ percent of selling price}$$

where x is the retailer margin. Solving for x indicates that the retailer must obtain $2.40 for this item. Therefore, the manufacturer must set the price to the retailer at $3.60 ($6.00 − $2.40).

The manufacturer's problem of suggesting a price for ultimate resale to the customer becomes more complex as the number of intermediaries between the manufacturer and the final consumer increases. This complexity can be illustrated by expanding the above example to include a wholesaler between the manufacturer and retailer. The retailer receives a 40 percent margin on the sales price. If the retailer must receive $2.40 per unit, the wholesaler must sell the item for $3.60 per unit. In order for the wholesaler to receive a 20 percent margin, for what price must the manufacturer sell the unit to the wholesaler?

$$\frac{x}{\$3.60} = 20 \text{ percent wholesaler margin on selling price}$$

where x is the wholesaler margin. Solving for x shows that the wholesaler's margin is $0.72 for this item. Therefore, the manufacturer must set the price to the wholesaler at $2.88.

This example shows that a manager must work backward from the ultimate price to the consumer through the marketing channel to arrive at a product's selling price. Assuming that the manufacturer's cost of goods sold is $2.00, we can calculate the following margins, which incidentally show the manufacturer's gross margin of 30.6 percent.

	Unit Cost of Goods Sold	*Unit Selling Price*	*Gross Margin as a Percentage of Selling Price*
Manufacturer	$2.00	$2.88	30.6%
Wholesaler	2.88	3.60	20.0
Retailer	3.60	6.00	40.0
Consumer	6.00		

Net Profit Margin (before Taxes)

The last margin to be considered is the net profit margin before taxes. This margin is expressed as a dollar figure or a percentage. *Net profit margin* is the remainder after cost of goods sold, other variable costs, and fixed costs have been subtracted from sales revenue. The place of net profit margin in an organization's income statement is illustrated by the following:

	Dollar Amount	Percentage
Net sales	$100,000	100%
Cost of goods sold	−30,000	−30
Gross profit margin	$ 70,000	70%
Selling expenses	−20,000	−20
Fixed expenses	−40,000	−40
Net profit margin	$ 10,000	10%

Net profit margin dollars represent a major source of funding for the organization. As will be shown later, net profit influences the working-capital position of the organization; hence the dollar amount ultimately affects the organization's ability to pay its cost of goods sold plus its selling and administrative expenses. Furthermore, net profit also affects the organization's cash flow position.

CONTRIBUTION ANALYSIS

Contribution analysis is an important concept in marketing management. *Contribution* is the difference between total sales revenue and total variable costs, or, on a per-unit basis, the difference between unit selling price and unit variable cost. Contribution analysis is particularly useful in assessing relationships among costs, prices, and volumes of products and services.

Break-Even Analysis

Break-even analysis is one of the simplest applications of contribution analysis.[1] *Break-even analysis* identifies the unit or dollar sales volume at which an organization neither makes a profit nor incurs a loss. Stated in equation form:

Total revenue = total variable costs + total fixed costs

Since break-even analysis identifies the level of sales volume at which total costs (fixed and variable) and total revenue are equal, it is a valuable tool for evaluating an organization's profit goals and assessing the riskiness of actions.

Break-even analysis requires three pieces of information: (1) an estimate of unit variable costs, (2) an estimate of the total dollar fixed costs to produce and market the product or service unit (note that only relevant costs apply), and (3) the selling price for each product or service unit.

The formula for determining the number of units required to break even is as follows:

$$\text{Unit break-even volume} = \frac{\text{total dollar fixed costs}}{\text{unit selling price} - \text{unit variable costs}}$$

The denominator in this formula (unit selling price minus unit variable costs) is called *contribution per unit.* Contribution per unit is the dollar amount that each unit sold "contributes" to the payment of fixed costs.

Consider the following example. A manufacturer plans to sell a product for $5.00. The unit variable costs are $2.00, and total fixed costs assigned to the product are $30,000. How many units must be sold to break even?

$$
\begin{aligned}
\text{Fixed costs} &= \$30,000 \\
\text{Contribution per unit} &= \text{unit selling price} - \text{unit variable cost} \\
&= \$5 - \$2 = \$3 \\
\text{Unit break-even volume} &= \$30,000/\$3 = 10,000 \text{ units}
\end{aligned}
$$

This example shows that for every unit sold at $5.00, $2.00 is used to pay variable costs. The balance of $3.00 "contributes" to fixed costs.

A related question is what the manufacturer's dollar sales volume must be to break even. The manager need only multiply unit break-even volume by the unit selling price to determine the dollar break-even volume: 10,000 units × $5 = $50,000.

A manager can calculate a dollar break-even point directly without first computing unit break-even volume. First the *contribution margin* must be determined from the formula:

$$
\text{Contribution margin} = \frac{\text{unit selling price} - \text{unit variable costs}}{\text{unit selling price}}
$$

Using the figures from our example, we find that the contribution margin is 60 percent:

$$
\text{Contribution margin} = \frac{\$5 - \$2}{\$5} = 60 \text{ percent}
$$

Then the dollar break-even point is computed as follows:

$$
\text{Dollar volume} = \frac{\text{total fixed costs}}{\text{contribution margin}} = \frac{\$30,000}{0.60} = \$50,000
$$

Sensitivity Analysis

Contribution analysis can be applied in a number of different ways, depending on the manager's needs. The following illustrations show how the break-even points in our example can be varied by changing selling price, variable costs, and fixed costs.

1. What would break-even volume be if fixed costs were increased to $40,000 while the selling price and variable costs remained unchanged?

$$
\begin{aligned}
\text{Fixed costs} &= \$40,000 \\
\text{Contribution per unit} &= \$3 \\
\text{Unit break-even volume} &= \$40,000/\$3 = 13,333 \text{ units} \\
\text{Dollar break-even volume} &= \$40,000/0.60 = \$66,667
\end{aligned}
$$

Note that the difference between the dollar break-even volume calculated from the contribution margin and the result of simply multiplying unit selling price by unit break-even volume (13,333 × $5 = $66,665) is due to rounding.

2. What would break-even volume be if selling price were dropped from $5.00 to $4.00 while fixed and variable costs remained unchanged?

$$\text{Fixed costs} = \$30,000$$
$$\text{Contribution per unit} = \$2$$
$$\text{Unit break-even volume} = \$30,000/\$2 = 15,000 \text{ units}$$
$$\text{Dollar break-even volume} = \$30,000/0.50 = \$60,000$$

3. Finally, what would break-even volume be if unit variable cost per unit were reduced to $1.50, selling price remained at $5.00, and fixed costs were $30,000?

$$\text{Fixed costs} = \$30,000$$
$$\text{Contribution per unit} = \$3.50$$
$$\text{Unit break-even volume} = \$30,000/\$3.50 = 8,571 \text{ units}$$
$$\text{Dollar break-even volume} = \$30,000/0.70 = \$42,857$$

Contribution Analysis and Profit Impact

No manager is content to operate at the break-even point in unit or dollar sales volume. Profits are necessary for the continued operation of an organization. A modified break-even analysis is used to incorporate a profit goal.

In simple break-even analysis, contribution per unit is the dollar amount available to pay fixed costs. To modify the break-even formula to incorporate the dollar profit goal, we need only regard the profit goal as an additional fixed cost, as follows:

$$\frac{\text{Unit volume to}}{\text{achieve profit goal}} = \frac{\text{total dollar fixed costs} + \text{dollar profit goal}}{\text{contribution per unit}}$$

Suppose a firm has fixed costs of $200,000 budgeted for a product or service, the unit selling price is $25.00, and the unit variable costs are $10.00. How many units must be sold to achieve a profit goal of $20,000?

$$\text{Fixed costs} + \text{profit goal} = \$200,000 + \$20,000 = \$220,000$$
$$\text{Contribution per unit} = \$25 - \$10 = \$15$$
$$\text{Unit volume to achieve profit goal} = \$220,000/\$15$$
$$= 14,667 \text{ units}$$

Many firms specify their profit goal as a percentage of sales rather than as a dollar amount ("Our profit goal is a 20 percent profit on sales"). This objective can be incorporated into the break-even formula by including the profit goal in the contribution-per-unit calculation. If the goal is to achieve a 20 percent profit on sales, each dollar of sales must "contribute" $0.20 to profit. In our example, each unit sold for $25.00 must contribute $5.00 to profit. The break-even formula incorporating a percent profit on sales goal is as follows:

$$\frac{\text{Unit volume to}}{\text{achieve profit goal}} = \frac{\text{total dollar fixed costs}}{\text{unit selling price} - \text{unit variable costs}}$$

The unit volume break-even point to achieve a 20 percent profit goal is 20,000 units:

$$\text{Fixed costs} = \$200,000$$
$$\text{Contribution per unit} = \$25 - \$10 - \$5 = \$10$$
$$\text{Unit volume to achieve profit goal} = \$200,000/\$10$$
$$= 20,000 \text{ units}$$

Contribution Analysis and Market Size

An important consideration in contribution analysis is the relationship of break-even unit or dollar volume to market size. Consider the situation in which a manager has conducted a break-even analysis and found the unit volume break-even point to be 50,000 units. This number has meaning only when compared with the potential size of the market segment sought. If the market potential is 100,000 units, the manager's product or service must capture 50 percent of the market sought to break even. An important question to be resolved is whether such a percentage can be achieved. A manager can assess the feasibility of a venture by comparing the break-even volume with market size and market-capture percentage.

Contribution Analysis and Performance Measurement

A second application of contribution analysis lies in performance measurement. For example, a marketing manager may wish to examine the performance of products. Consider an organization with two products, X and Y. A description of each product's financial performance follows:

	Product X (10,000 volume)	Product Y (20,000 volume)	Total (30,000 volume)
Unit price	$ 10	$ 3	
Sales revenue	100,000	60,000	$160,000
Unit variable costs	4	1.50	
Total variable costs	40,000	30,000	70,000
Unit contribution	6	1.50	
Total contribution	60,000	30,000	90,000
Fixed costs	45,000	10,000	55,000
Net profit	$ 15,000	$20,000	$35,000

The net profit figure shows that Product Y is more profitable than Product X. Product X is four times more profitable than Product Y on a unit-contribution basis, however, and generates twice the contribution dollars to overhead. The difference in profitability comes from the allocation of fixed costs to the products. In measuring performance, it is important to consider which products contribute most heavily to the organization's total fixed costs ($55,000 in this example) and then to total profit.

Should a manager look only at net profit, a decision might be made to drop Product X. Product Y would then have to cover total fixed costs, however. If the fixed costs remain at $55,000 and only Product Y is sold, this organization will experience a *net loss* of $25,000, assuming no change in Product Y volume.

Assessment of Cannibalization

A third application of contribution analysis is in the assessment of cannibalization effects. Cannibalization is the process by which one product or service sold by a firm gains a portion of its revenue by diverting sales from another product or service also sold by the firm. For example, sales of Brand X's new gel toothpaste may be at the expense of sales of Brand X's existing opaque white toothpaste. The problem facing a marketing manager is to assess the financial effect of cannibalization.

Consider the following data:

	Existing Opaque White Toothpaste	*New Gel Toothpaste*
Unit selling price	$1.00	$1.10
Unit variable costs	−0.20	−0.40
Unit contribution	$0.80	$0.70

The gel toothpaste can be sold at a slightly higher price, given its formulation and taste, but the variable costs are also higher. Hence the gel toothpaste has a lower contribution per unit. Therefore, for every unit of the gel toothpaste sold instead of a unit of the opaque white toothpaste, the firm "loses" $0.10. Suppose further that the company expects to sell 1 million units of the new gel toothpaste in the first year after introduction and that, of that amount, 500,000 units will be diverted from the opaque white toothpaste, of which the company had expected to sell 1 million units. The task of the marketing manager is to determine how the introduction of the new gel toothpaste will affect Brand X's total contribution dollars.

One approach to assessing the financial impact of cannibalization is shown below:

1. Brand X expects to lose $0.10 for each unit diverted from the opaque white toothpaste to the gel toothpaste.
2. Given that 500,000 units will be cannibalized from the opaque white toothpaste, the total contribution *lost* is $50,000 ($0.10 × 500,000 units).
3. However, the new gel toothpaste will sell an additional 500,000 units at a contribution per unit of $0.70, which means that $350,000 ($0.70 × 500,000 units) in additional contribution will be generated.
4. Therefore, the net financial effect is a positive increase in contribution dollars of $300,000 ($350,000 − $50,000).

Another approach to assessing the cannibalization effect is as follows:

1. The opaque white toothpaste alone had been expected to sell 1 million units with a unit contribution of $0.80. Therefore, contribution dollars without the gel would equal $800,000 ($0.80 × 1,000,000 units).
2. The gel toothpaste is expected to sell 1 million units with a unit contribution of $0.70.
3. Given the cannibalism rate of 50 percent (that is, one-half of the gel's volume is diverted from the opaque white toothpaste), the combined contribution can be calculated as follows:

Product	Unit Volume	Unit Contribution	Contribution Dollars
Opaque white toothpaste	500,000	$0.80	$400,000
Gel toothpaste:			
Cannibalized volume	500,000	0.70	350,000
Incremental volume	500,000	0.70	350,000
Total	1,500,000		$1,100,000
Less original forecast volume for opaque white toothpaste	1,000,000	0.80	800,000
Total	+500,000		+$300,000

Both approaches arrive at the same conclusion: Brand X will benefit by $300,000 from the introduction of the gel toothpaste. The manager should use whichever approach he or she is more comfortable with in an analytic sense.

It should be emphasized, however, that the incremental fixed costs associated with advertising and sales promotion or any additions or changes in manufacturing capacity must be considered to complete the analysis. If the fixed costs approximate or exceed $300,000, the new product should be viewed in a very different light.

LIQUIDITY

Liquidity refers to an organization's ability to meet short-term (usually within a budget year) financial obligations. A key measure of an organization's liquidity position is its working capital. *Working capital* is the dollar value of an organization's *current assets* (such as cash, accounts receivable, prepaid expenses, inventory) *minus* the dollar value of *current liabilities* (such as short-term accounts payable for goods and services, income taxes).

A manager should be aware of the impact of marketing actions on working capital. Marketing expenditures precede sales volume; therefore, cash outlays for marketing efforts reduce current assets. If marketing expenditures cannot be met out of cash, accounts payable are incurred. In either case, working capital is reduced. In a positive vein, a marketing manager's creation of sales volume, with corresponding increases in net profit, contributes to working capital. Since the timing of marketing expenditures and sales volume is often lagged, a marketing manager must be wary of marketing efforts that unnecessarily deplete working capital and must assess the likelihood of potential sales, given a specified expenditure level.

OPERATING LEVERAGE

A financial concept closely akin to break-even analysis is operating leverage. *Operating leverage* refers to the extent to which fixed costs and variable costs are used in the production and marketing of products and services. Firms that have high total fixed costs relative to total variable costs are defined as having high operating leverage. Examples of firms with high operating leverage include airlines and heavy-equipment manufacturers. Firms with low total fixed costs relative to total variable costs are defined as having low operating leverage. Firms typically having low operating leverage include residential contractors and wholesale distributors.

The higher a firm's operating leverage, the faster its total profits will increase once sales exceed break-even volume. By the same token, however, those firms with high operating leverage will incur losses at a faster rate once sales volume falls below the break-even point.

Exhibit 2.1 illustrates the effect of operating leverage on profit. The base case shows two firms that have identical break-even sales volumes. The cost structures of the two firms differ, however, with one having high fixed and low variable costs and the other having low fixed and high variable costs. Note that when sales volume is increased 10 percent, the firm with high fixed and low variable costs achieves a much higher profit than the firm with low fixed and high variable costs. When sales volume declines, however, just the opposite is true. That is, the firm with high fixed and low variable costs

EXHIBIT   2.1

Effect of Operating Leverage on Profit

	Base Case		10% Increase in Sales		10% Decrease in Sales	
	High-Fixed-Costs Firm	High-Variable-Costs Firm	High-Fixed-Costs Firm	High-Variable-Costs Firm	High-Fixed-Costs Firm	High-Variable-Costs Firm
Sales	$100,000	$100,000	$110,000	$110,000	$90,000	$90,000
Variable costs	20,000	80,000	22,000	88,000	18,000	72,000
Fixed costs	80,000	20,000	80,000	20,000	80,000	20,000
Profit	$ 0	$ 0	$ 8,000	$ 2,000	($8,000)	($2,000)

incurs losses at a faster rate than the firm with high variable and low fixed costs once sales fall below the break-even point.

The message of operating leverage should be clear from this example. Firms with high operating leverage benefit more from sales gains than do firms with low operating leverage. At the same time, firms with high operating leverage are more sensitive to sales-volume declines, since losses will be incurred at a faster rate. Knowledge of a firm's cost structure will therefore prove valuable in assessing the gains and losses from changes in sales volume brought about by marketing efforts.

PREPARING A PRO FORMA INCOME STATEMENT

Since marketing managers are accountable for the profit impact of their actions, they must translate their strategies and tactics into *pro forma*, or projected, income statements. A *pro forma* income statement displays projected revenues, budgeted expenses, and estimated net profit for an organization, product, or service during a specific planning period, usually a year. *Pro forma* income statements include a sales forecast and a listing of variable and fixed costs that can be programmed or committed.

Pro forma income statements can be prepared in different ways and reflect varying levels of specificity. Exhibit 2.2 shows a typical layout for a *pro forma* income statement consisting of six major categories or line items:

1. *Sales*—forecasted unit volume times unit selling price.
2. *Cost of goods sold*—costs incurred in buying or producing products and services. Generally speaking, these costs are constant per unit within certain volume ranges and vary with total unit volume.
3. *Gross margin* (sometimes called gross profit)—represents the remainder after cost of goods sold has been subtracted from sales.
4. *Marketing expenses*—generally, programmed expenses budgeted to produce sales. Advertising expenses are typically fixed. Sales expenses can be fixed, such as a salesperson's salary, or variable, such as sales commissions. Freight or delivery expenses are typically constant per unit and vary with total unit volume.
5. *General and administrative expenses*—generally, committed fixed costs for the planning period, which cannot be avoided if the organization is to operate. These costs are frequently called overhead.

EXHIBIT   2.2

**Pro Forma Income Statement for the 12-Month Period
Ended December 31, 19__**

Sales		$1,000,000
Cost of goods sold		500,000
Gross margin		$ 500,000
Marketing expenses		
Sales expenses	$170,000	
Advertising expenses	90,000	
Freight or delivery expenses	40,000	300,000
General and administrative expenses		
Administrative salaries	$120,000	
Depreciation on buildings and equipment	20,000	
Interest expense	5,000	
Property taxes and insurance	5,000	
Other administrative expenses	5,000	155,000
Net profit before (income) tax		$ 45,000

6. *Net income before (income) taxes* (often called net profit before taxes)—the remainder after all costs have been subtracted from sales.

A *pro forma* income statement reflects a marketing manager's expectations (sales) given certain inputs (costs). This means that a manager must think specifically about customer response to strategies and tactics and focus attention on the organization's financial objectives of profitability and growth when preparing a *pro forma* income statement.

SUMMARY

This chapter provides an overview of basic accounting and financial concepts. A word of caution is necessary, however. Financial analysis of marketing actions is a necessary but insufficient criterion for justifying marketing programs. A careful analysis of other variables impinging on the decision at hand is required. Thus, judgment enters the picture. "Numbers" serve only to complement general marketing analysis skills and are not an end in themselves. In this regard, it is wise to consider some words of Albert Einstein: "Not everything that counts can be counted, and not everything that can be counted counts."[2]

NOTES

1. For a straightforwad tutorial on break-even analysis, see "Break-Even Analysis," *Small Business Report* (August 1986): 22–24.

2. "Informed Source," *Dallas Times Herald* (February 11, 1991): A2.

EXERCISES

1. Executives of Studio Recordings, Inc., produced the latest compact disc by the Starshine Sisters Band, entitled *Sunshine/Moonshine*. The following cost information pertains to the new CD:

CD package and disc (direct material and labor)	$1.25/CD
Songwriters' royalties	$0.35/CD
Recording artists' royalties	$1.00/CD
Advertising and promotion	$275,000
Studio Recordings, Inc., overhead	$250,000
Selling price to CD distributor	$9.00

Calculate the following:
  a. Contribution per CD unit
  b. Break-even volume in CD units and dollars
  c. Net profit if 1 million CDs are sold
  d. Necessary CD unit volume to achieve a $200,000 profit

2. The group product manager for ointments at American Therapeutic Corporation was reviewing price and promotion alternatives for two products: Rash-Away and Red-Away. Both products were designed to reduce skin irritation, but Red-Away was primarily a cosmetic treatment whereas Rash-Away also included a compound that eliminated the rash.

The price and promotion alternatives recommended for the two products by their respective brand managers included the possibility of using additional promotion or a price reduction to stimulate sales volume. A volume, price, and cost summary for the two products follows:

	Rash-Away	*Red-Away*
Unit price	$2.00	$1.00
Unit variable costs	1.40	0.25
Unit contribution	$0.60	$0.75
Unit volume	1,000,000 units	1,500,000 units

Both brand managers included a recommendation to either reduce price by 10 percent or invest an incremental $150,000 in advertising.
  a. What absolute increase in unit sales and dollar sales will be necessary to recoup the incremental increase in advertising expenditures for Rash-Away? For Red-Away?
  b. How many additional sales dollars must be produced to cover each $1.00 of incremental advertising for Rash-Away? For Red-Away?
  c. What increase in absolute unit sales and dollar sales will be necessary to maintain the level of total contribution dollars if the price of each product is reduced by 10 percent?

3. After spending $300,000 for research and development, chemists at Diversified Citrus Industries have developed a new breakfast drink. The drink, called Zap, will provide the consumer with twice the amount of Vitamin C currently available in breakfast drinks. Zap will be packaged in an eight-ounce can and will be introduced to the breakfast drink market, which is estimated to be equivalent to 21 million eight-ounce cans nationally.

One major management concern is the lack of funds available for advertising. Accordingly, management has decided to use newspapers (rather than television) to promote the product in the introductory year in major metropolitan areas that account for 65 percent of U.S. breakfast drink volume. Newspaper advertising will carry a coupon that will entitle the consumer to receive $0.20 off the price of the first can purchased. The retailer will receive the regular margin and be reimbursed by Diversified Citrus Industries. Past experience indicates that for every five cans sold during the introductory year, one coupon will be returned. The cost of the newspaper advertising campaign (excluding coupon returns) will be $250,000. Other fixed overhead costs are expected to be $90,000 per year.

Management has decided that the suggested retail price to the consumer for the eight-ounce can will be $0.50. The only unit variable costs for the product are $0.18 for materials and $0.06 for labor. The company intends to give retailers a margin of 20 percent off the suggested retail price and a wholesalers' margin of 10 percent of the retailers' cost of the item.

    a. At what price will Diversified Citrus Industries be selling its product to wholesalers?

    b. What is the contribution per unit for Zap?

    c. What is the break-even unit volume in the first year?

    d. What is the first-year break-even share of market?

    4. Max Leonard, Vice President of Marketing for Dysk Computer, Inc., must decide whether to introduce a mid-priced version of the firm's DC6900 minicomputer product line—the DC6900-X minicomputer. The DC6900-X would sell for $3,900, with unit variable costs of $1,800. Projections made by an independent marketing research firm indicate that the DC6900-X would achieve a sales volume of 500,000 units next year, in its first year of commercialization. One-half of the first year's volume would come from competitors' minicomputers and market growth. However, a consumer research study indicates that 30 percent of the DC6900-X sales volume would come from the higher-priced DC6900-Omega minicomputer, which sells for $5,900 (with unit variable costs of $2,200). Another 20 percent of the DC6900-X sales volume would come from the economy-priced DC6900-Alpha minicomputer, priced at $2,500 (with unit variable costs of $1,200). The DC6900-Omega unit volume is expected to be 400,000 units next year, and the DC6900-Alpha is expected to achieve a 600,000-unit sales level. The fixed costs of launching the DC6900-X have been forecast to be $2 million during the first year of commercialization. Should Mr. Leonard add the DC6900-X model to the line of minicomputers?

    5. (To be discussed after reading Chapter 3 and 5.) A marketing manager for the Dental Products Division of a large firm is considering whether to introduce Product A, a toothpaste with stain remover compounds, or Product B, a toothpaste with added decay-prevention compounds. The manager's assistant prepared the following table, which includes the profit expectations for each of three possible market shares developed from marketing research:

	Market Share		
	20%	*10%*	*5%*
Introduce Product A	$20 million	$10 million	−$8 million
Introduce Product B	$15 million	$9 million	−$3 million

The estimated profit/loss identified for the 5 percent market-share estimate prompted the manager to review ten case studies of previous product introductions. The review indicated that three new products achieved a 20 percent market share, five new products achieved a 10 percent market share, and two new products recorded a 5 percent market share.

a. What is the expected monetary value for Product A? For Product B? Given the data provided, should the marketing manager introduce Product A or Product B?

b. Concern over whether either product would achieve the market-share projections has prompted consideration of a test market. What is the maximum amount of money that the manager should budget for a test market?

6. The annual planning process at Century Office Systems, Inc., had been arduous but produced a number of important marketing initiatives for the next year. Most notably, company executives had decided to restructure its product-marketing team into two separate groups: (1) Corporate Office Systems and (2) Home Office Systems. Angela Blake was assigned responsibility for the Home Office Systems group, which would market the company's word-processing hardware and software for home and office-at-home use by individuals. Her marketing plan, which included a sales forecast for next year of $25 million, was the result of a detailed market analysis and negotiations with individuals both inside and outside the company. Discussions with the sales director indicated that 40 percent of the company sales force would be dedicated to selling products of the Home Office Systems group. Sales representatives would receive a 15 percent commission on sales of home office systems. Under the new organizational structure, the Home Office Systems group would be charged with 40 percent of the budgeted sales force expenditure. The sales director's budget for salaries and fringe benefits of the sales force and noncommission selling costs for both the Corporate and Home Office Systems groups was $7.5 million.

The advertising and promotion budget contained three elements: trade magazine advertising, cooperative newspaper advertising with Century Office Systems, Inc., dealers, and sales promotion materials including product brochures, technical manuals, catalogs, and point-of-purchase displays. Trade magazine ads and sales promotion materials were to be developed by the company's advertising and public relations agency. Production and media placement costs were budgeted at $300,000. Cooperative advertising copy for both newspaper and radio use had budgeted production costs of $100,000. Century Office Systems, Inc.'s, cooperative advertising allowance policy stated that the company would allocate 5 percent of company sales to dealers to promote its office systems. Dealers always used their complete cooperative advertising allowances.

Meetings with manufacturing and operations personnel indicated that the direct costs of material and labor and direct factory overhead to produce the Home Office System product line represented 50 percent of sales. The accounting department would assign $600,000 in indirect manufacturing overhead (for example, depreciation, maintenance) to the product line and $300,000 for administrative overhead (clerical, telephone, office space, and so forth). Freight for the product line would average 8 percent of sales.

Blake's staff consisted of two product managers and a marketing assistant. Salaries and fringe benefits for Ms. Blake and her staff were $250,000 per year.

a. Prepare a *pro forma* income statement for the Home Office Systems group given the information provided.

b. Prepare a *pro forma* income statement for the Home Office Systems group given annual sales of only $20 million.

c. At what level of dollar sales will the Home Office Systems group break even?

CHAPTER 3

Marketing Decision Making and Case Analysis

 Skill in decision making is a prerequisite to being an effective marketing manager. Indeed, Nobel laureate Herbert Simon viewed managing and decision making as being one and the same.[1] Another management theorist, Peter Drucker, has said that the burden of decision making can be lessened and better decisions can result if a manager recognizes that "decision making is a rational and systematic process and that its organization is a definite sequence of steps, each of them in turn rational and systematic."[2]

One objective of this chapter is to introduce a systematic process for decision making; another is to introduce basic considerations in case analysis. Just as decision making and managing can be viewed as being identical in scope, so the decision-making process and case analysis go hand in hand.

DECISION MAKING

Although no simple formula exists that can assure a correct solution to all problems at all times, use of a systematic decision-making process can increase the likelihood of arriving at better solutions.[3] The decision-making process described here is called DECIDE:[4]

Define the problem.

Enumerate the decision factors.

Consider relevant information.

Identify the best alternative.

Develop a plan for implementing the chosen alternative.

Evaluate the decision and the decision process.

A definition and a discussion of the implications of each step follow.

Define the Problem

The philosopher John Dewey observed that "a problem well defined is half solved." What this statement means in a marketing setting is that a well-defined problem outlines the framework within which a solution can be derived. This framework includes the *objectives* of the decision maker, a recognition of *constraints*, and a clearly articulated *success measure*, or goal, for assessing progress toward solving the problem.

Consider the situation faced by El Nacho Foods, a marketer of Mexican foods. The company had positioned its line of Mexican foods as a high-quality brand and used advertising effectively to convey that message. Shortly after the company's introduction of frozen dinners, two of its competitors began cutting the price of their frozen dinner entrees. The firm lost market share and sales as a result of these price reductions; this loss led to reductions in the contribution dollars available for advertising and sales promotion. How might the problem be defined in this situation? One definition of the problem leads to the question "Should we reduce our price?" A much better definition of the problem leads one to ask: "How can we maintain our quality brand image (objective) and regain our lost market share (success measure), given limited funds for advertising and sales promotion (constraint)?"

The first problem definition asks for a response to an immediate issue facing the company. It does not articulate the broader and more important considerations of competitive positioning. Hence the problem statement fails to capture the significance of the issue raised. The second definition provides a broader perspective on the immediate issue posed and allows the manager greater latitude in seeking solutions.

In a case study, the analyst is frequently given alternative courses of action to consider. The narrow approach to case analysis is simply to compare these different options. Such an approach often leads to the selection of alternative A or alternative B without regard for the significance of the choice in the broader context of the situation facing the company or the decision maker.

Enumerate the Decision Factors

Two sets of decision factors must be enumerated in the decision-making process: (1) *alternative courses of action* and (2) *uncertainties* in the competitive environment. Alternative courses of action are controllable decision factors because the decision maker has complete command of them. Alternatives are typically product-market strategies or changes in the various elements of the organization's marketing mix (described in Chapter 1). Uncertainties, on the other hand, are uncontrollable factors that the manager cannot influence. In a marketing context, they often include actions of competitors, market size, and buyer response to marketing action. Assumptions often have to be made concerning these factors. These assumptions need to be spelled out, particularly if they will influence the evaluation of alternative courses of action.

A recent experience of Cluett Peabody and Company, the maker of Arrow shirts, illustrates how the combination of an action and uncertainties can spell disaster. Arrow departed from its normal practice of selling classic men's shirts to offer a new line featuring bolder colors, busier patterns, and higher prices (action). The firm soon realized that men's tastes had changed to more conservative styles (environmental uncertainties). The result? The company posted a $4.5 million loss. According to the company president, "We tried to be exciting, and we really didn't look at the market."[5]

Case analysis provides an opportunity to relate alternatives to uncertainties, and these factors *must* be related if decision making is to be effective. No expected outcome, financial or otherwise, of a chosen course of action can realistically be considered apart from the environment into which it is introduced.

Consider Relevant Information

The third step in the decision-making process is the consideration of relevant information. *Relevant information*, like the relevant costs discussed in Chapter 2, consists of information that relates to the alternatives identified by the manager as being likely to affect future events. More specifically, relevant information might include characteristics of the industry or competitive environment, characteristics of the organization (such as competitive strengths and position), and characteristics of the alternatives themselves.

Identifying relevant information is difficult both for the practicing manager and for the case analyst. There is frequently an overabundance of facts, figures, and viewpoints available in any decision setting. Determining what matters and what does not is a skill that is best gained through experience. Analyzing many and varied cases is one way to develop this skill.

Two notes of caution are necessary. First, the case analyst must resist the temptation to consider *everything* in a case as "fact." Many cases, including actual marketing situations, contain conflicting data. Part of the task in any case analysis is to exercise judgment in assessing the validity of the data presented. Second, in many instances relevant information must be created. An example of creating relevant information is the blending together of several pieces of data, as in the calculation of a simple break-even point.

It should be clear at this point that even though the consideration of relevant information is the third step in the decision-making process, relevant information will also affect the two previous steps. As the manager or case analyst becomes more deeply involved in considering and evaluating information, the problem definition may be modified or the decision factors may change.

Upon the conclusion of the first three steps, the manager or case analyst has completed a *situation analysis*. The situation analysis should produce an answer to the synoptic question "Where are we now?" (Specific questions relating to situation analysis are found in Exhibit 3.3 later in this chapter.)

Identify the Best Alternative

Identifying the best alternative is the fourth step in the decision-making process. The selection of a course of action is not simply a matter of choosing Alternative A over other alternatives but, rather, of evaluating identified alternatives and the uncertainties apparent in the problem setting.

A framework for identifying the best alternative is *decision analysis*, which was introduced in Chapter 1. In its simplest form, decision analysis matches each alternative identified by the manager with the uncertainties existing in the environment and assigns a quantitative value to the outcome associated with each match. Managers implicitly use a decision tree and a payoff table to describe the relationship among alternatives, uncertainties, and potential outcomes. The use of decision analysis and the application of decision trees and payoff tables can be illustrated by referring back to the situation faced by El Nacho Foods.

Suppose that at the conclusion of Step 2 in the DECIDE process (that is, enumerating decision factors), El Nacho executives identified two alternatives: (1) reduce the price on frozen dinners or (2) maintain the price. They also recognized two uncertainties: (1) competitors could maintain the lower price or (2) competitors could reduce the price further. Suppose further that at the conclusion of Step 3 in the DECIDE process (considering relevant information), El Nacho executives examined the changes in market share and sales volume that would be brought about by the pricing actions. They also calculated the contribution per unit of frozen dinners for each alternative for each competitor response. They performed a contribution analysis because the problem was defined in terms of contribution to advertising and sales promotion in Step 1 of the DECIDE process (defining the problem).

Given two alternatives, two competitive responses, and a calculated contribution per unit for each combination, they identified four unique financial outcomes. These outcomes are displayed in the decision tree shown in Exhibit 3.1.

It is apparent from the decision tree that the largest contribution will be generated if El Nacho maintains its price on frozen dinners *and* competitors maintain their lower price. If El Nacho maintains its price and competitors reduce their price further, however, the lowest contribution among the four outcomes identified will be generated. The choice of an alternative obviously depends on the likelihood of occurrence of uncertainties in the environment.

A *payoff table* is a useful tool for displaying the alternatives, uncertainties, and outcomes facing a firm. In addition, a payoff table includes another dimension—management's subjective determination of the probability of the occurrence of an uncertainty. Suppose, for example, that El Nacho management believes that competitors are also operating with slim contribution margins and hence are most likely to maintain the lower price regardless of El Nacho's action. They believe that there is a 10 percent chance that competitors will reduce the price of frozen dinners even further.[6] Since only two uncertainties have been identified, the subjective probability of competitors' maintaining their price is 90 percent (note that the probabilities assigned to the uncertainties must total 1.0, or 100 percent). Given these probabilities, the payoff table for El Nacho Foods is as shown in Exhibit 3.2.

The payoff table allows the manager or case analyst to compute the "expected value" of each alternative. The expected value is calculated by multiplying the outcome for each uncertainty by its probability of occurrence and then totaling across

EXHIBIT   3.1

Decision Tree for El Nacho Foods

Company Action	Competitive Response	Financial Outcome
Reduce price	Maintain price	$150,000
	Reduce price further	$110,000
Maintain price	Maintain price	$175,000
	Reduce price further	$90,000

EXHIBIT 3.2

Payoff Table for El Nacho Foods

		Uncertainties	
		Competitors maintain price (probability = 0.9)	Competitors reduce price (probability = 0.1)
Alternatives	Reduce price	$150,000	$110,000
	Maintain price	$175,000	$90,000

the uncertainties for each alternative. The expected value of an alternative can be viewed as the value that would be obtained if the manager were to choose the same alternative many times under the same conditions.

The expected value of the price-reduction alternative equals the probability that competitors will maintain prices, multiplied by the financial contribution if competitors maintain prices, plus the probability that competitors will further reduce prices, multiplied by the financial contribution if competitors further reduce prices. The calculation is

$$(0.9)(\$150,000) + (0.1)(\$110,000) = \$135,000 + \$11,000 = \$146,000$$

The expected value of maintaining the price is

$$(0.9)(\$175,000) + (0.1)(\$90,000) = \$157,500 + \$9,000 = \$166,500$$

The higher average contribution of $166,500 for maintaining the price indicates that El Nacho's management should maintain the price. The contribution is higher because competitors are expected to maintain their prices nine times out of ten. Under the same conditions (same outcomes, same probability estimates), El Nacho would achieve an average contribution of $146,000 if the price-reduction alternative were chosen. A rational management would therefore select the price-maintenance alternative.

Familiarity with decision analysis is important for four reasons. First, decision analysis is a fundamental tool for considering "what if" situations. By organizing alternatives, uncertainties, and outcomes in this manner, a manager or case analyst becomes sensitive to the dynamic processes present in a competitive environment. Second, decision analysis forces the case analyst to quantify outcomes associated with specific actions. Third, decision analysis is useful in a variety of settings. For example, Ford Motor Company used decision analysis in deciding whether to produce its own tires; Pillsbury used it in determining whether to switch from a box to a bag for a certain grocery product.[7] Fourth, an extension of decision analysis can be used in determining the value of "perfect" information; this topic is discussed in Chapter 5.

Develop a Plan for Implementing the Chosen Alternative

The selection of a course of action must be followed by development of a plan for its implementation. Simply deciding what to do will not make it happen. The execution phase is critical, and planning for it forces the case analyst to consider resource allocation and timing questions. For example, if a new product launch is recommended, it is important to consider how managerial, financial, and manufacturing resources will be allocated to this course of action. If a price reduction is recommended, it will be important to monitor whether the reduced prices are reaching the final consumer and not being absorbed by resellers in the marketing channel. Timing is crucial, since a marketing plan takes time to develop and implement.

As a final note, it is important to recognize that strategy formulation and implementation are not necessarily separate sequential processes. Rather, an interactive give-and-take occurs between formulation and implementation until the case analyst realizes that "what might be done can be done," given organizational strengths and market requirements. Another reading of the discussion on the marketing mix in Chapter 1 will highlight these points.

Evaluate the Decision and the Decision Process

The last step in the decision-making process is evaluating the decision made and the decision process itself. With respect to the decision itself, two questions should be asked. First, *Was a decision made?* This seemingly odd question addresses a common shortcoming of case analyses, whereby a case analyst does not make a decision but, rather, "talks about" the situation facing the organization.

The second question is, *Was the decision appropriate, given the situation identified in the case setting?* This question speaks to the issue of insufficient information on the one hand and the failure to consider and interpret information on the other. In many marketing cases, and indeed in some actual business situations, some of the information needed to make a decision is simply not available. When information is incomplete, assumptions must be made. A case analyst is often expected to make assumptions to fill in gaps, but such assumptions should be logically developed and articulated. Merely making assumptions to make the "solution" fit a preconceived notion of the correct answer is a death knell in case analysis and business practice.

The case analyst should constantly monitor how he or she applies the decision-making process. The mere fact that one's decision was right is not sufficient reason to think that the decision process was appropriate. For example, we have all found ourselves lost while trying to locate a home or business from an address. Eventually we somehow find it, but are again at a loss when later asked to direct someone else to the same address. Analogously, the case analyst may arrive at the "correct" solution but be unable to outline (map) the process involved.

After completing a class discussion of a case, a written case assignment, or a group presentation, the case analyst should critically examine his or her performance by answering the following questions:

1. Did I define the problem adequately?

2. Did I identify all pertinent alternatives and uncertainties? Were my assumptions realistic?

3. Did I consider all information relevant to the case?

4. Did I recommend the appropriate course of action? If so, was my logic consistent with the recommendation? If not, were my assumptions different from the assumptions made by others? Did I overlook an important piece of information?

5. Did I consider how my recommendation could be implemented?

Honest answers to these questions will improve the chances of making better decisions in the future.

CASE ANALYSIS

How do I prepare a case? This question is voiced by virtually every student exposed to the case method for the first time. One of the most difficult tasks in preparing a case for presentation—or, more generally, resolving an actual marketing problem—is structuring your thinking process to address relevant forces confronting the organization in question. The previous discussion of the decision-making process should be of help in this regard. The remainder of this chapter provides some useful hints to assist you in preparing a marketing case.

Approaching the Case

On your first reading of a marketing case, you should concentrate on becoming acquainted with the situation in which the organization finds itself. This first reading should provide some insights into the problem requiring resolution, as well as background information on the environment and organization.

Then read the case again, paying particular attention to key facts and assumptions. At this point, you should determine the relevance and reliability of the quantitative data provided in the context of what you see as the issues or problems facing the organization. Valuable insights often arise from analyzing two or more bits of quantitative information concurrently. It is essential that extensive note taking occurs during the second reading. Working by writing is very important; simply highlighting statements or numbers in the case is not sufficient. Behavioral scientists estimate that the human mind can focus on only eight facts at a time and that our mental ability to link these facts in a meaningful way is limited without assistance.[8] Experienced analysts and managers always work out ideas on paper—whether they are working alone or in a group.

There are three pitfalls you should avoid during the second reading. First, *do not rush to a conclusion*. If you do so, information is likely to be overlooked or possibly distorted to fit a preconceived notion of the answer. Second, *do not "work the numbers"* until you understand their meaning and derivation. Third, *do not confuse supposition with fact*. Many statements are made in a case, such as "Our firm subscribes to the marketing concept." Is this a fact, based on an appraisal of the firm's actions and performance, or a supposition?

Formulating the Analysis

The previous remarks should provide some direction in approaching a marketing case. The marketing case analysis worksheet shown in Exhibit 3.3 provides a framework for organizing information. Four analytical categories are shown, with illustrative questions pertaining to each. You will find it useful to consider each analytical category when preparing a case.

Nature of the Industry, Market, and Buying Behavior   The first analytical category focuses on the organization's environment—the context in which the organization operates. Specific topics of interest include (1) an assessment of the structure,

EXHIBIT   3.3

Marketing Case Analysis Worksheet

Specific Points of Interest

Nature of the industry, market, and buyer behavior	1. What is the nature of industry structure, conduct, and performance?
	2. Who are the competitors, and what are their strengths and weaknesses?
	3. How do consumers buy in this industry or market?
	4. Can the market be segmented? How? Can the segments be quantified?
	5. What are the requirements for success in this industry?
The organization	1. What are the organization's mission, objectives, and distinctive competency?
	2. What is its offering to the market? How can its past and present performance be characterized? What is its potential?
	3. What is the situation in which the manager or organization finds itself?
	4. What factors have contributed to the present situation?
A plan of action	1. What actions are available to the organization?
	2. What are the costs and benefits of each action in both qualitative and quantitative terms?
	3. Is there a disparity between what the organization wants to do, should do, can do, and must do?
Potential outcomes	1. What will be the buyer, trade, and competitive response to each course of action?
	2. How will each course of action satisfy buyer, trade, and organization requirements?
	3. What is the potential profitability of each course of action?
	4. Will the action enhance or reduce the organization's ability to compete in the future?

conduct, and performance of the industry and competition and (2) an understanding of who the buyers are and why, where, when, how, what, and how much they buy.

The Organization It is important to develop an understanding of the organization's financial, human, and material resources, its strengths and weaknesses, and the reasons for its success or failure. Of particular importance is an understanding of what the organization wishes to do. The "fit" between the organization and its environment represents the first major link drawn in case analysis. This link is the essence of the situation analysis, since it is an interpretation of where the organization currently stands.

A Plan of Action You should be prepared to identify possible courses of action on the basis of the situation analysis. More often than not, several alternatives are possible, and each should be fully articulated. Each course of action typically has associated costs and revenues. These should be carefully calculated on the basis of realistic estimates of the magnitude of effort expected in their pursuit.

Potential Outcomes Finally, the potential outcomes of all courses of action identified should be evaluated. On the basis of the appraisal of outcomes, one course of action or strategy should be recommended. The evaluation, however, must indicate not only why the recommendation was preferred, but also why other actions were dismissed.

Though it is always useful to consider each of the analytical categories just described, the method in which they are arranged may vary. There is no one way to analyze a case, just as there is no single correct way to attack a marketing problem. Just be sure to cover the bases.

Communicating the Analysis

Three means exist for communicating case analyses: (1) class discussion, (2) group presentation, and (3) written report.

Class Discussion Discussing case studies in the classroom setting can be an exciting experience, provided that each student actively prepares for and participates in the discussion. Preparation involves more than simply reading the case prior to the scheduled class period—the case should be carefully analyzed, using the four analytical categories described earlier. Four to five hours of preparation are usually required for each assigned case. The notes developed during the preparation should be brought to class.

Similarly, participation involves more than talking. Other students should be carefully watched and listened to during a class discussion. Attentiveness to the views of others is necessary in order to build on previous comments and analyses. Most class discussions follow a similar format. Class analysis begins with a discussion of the organization and its environment. This discussion is followed first by a discussion of the alternative courses of action and then by a consideration of possible implementation strategies. Knowing where the class is in the discussion is important both for organizing the multitude of ideas and analyses presented and for preparing remarks for the subsequent steps in the class discussion.

Immediately after the class discussion, you should prepare a short summary of the analysis developed in class. This summary, which should include the specific facts, ideas, analyses, and generalizations developed, will be useful in comparing and contrasting case situations.

Group Presentation Group presentation of a case requires a slightly different set of skills. Usually a group of three to five students conducts a rigorous analysis of a case and presents it to classmates. Role-playing may be featured: class members may serve as an executive committee witnessing the presentation of a task force or project team.

If the instructor asks you to form your own groups, do not form groups solely on the basis of friendship. Rather, try to develop a balanced team where various skills complement one another (financial skills, oral presentation skills, and so on). Seek out individuals who are committed and dependable. Finally, organize the efforts of the group around individual interests and skills.

A polished presentation is very important. Thus, the group should rehearse its presentation, with group members seriously critiquing one another's performance. At the very least, the group should prepare an outline of the presentation (including important exhibits) and distribute it to the class. It is a good idea to use transparencies to highlight important points and unique analyses, but *don't* read transparencies to your audience. For further information, consult a text on oral presentations or guidelines for effective speaking.

Written Report What you need to do to generate a written analysis of a case assignment is similar to what you should do to prepare for class discussion. The only difference is in the submission of the analysis; a written report should be carefully organized, legible (preferably typed), and grammatically correct.

There is no one correct approach to organizing a written case analysis. However, it is usually wise to think about the report as having three major sections: (1) identification of the strategic issues and problems, (2) analysis and evaluation, and (3) recommendations.[9] The first section should contain a focused paragraph that defines the problem and specifies the constraints and options available to the organization. Material in the second section should provide a carefully developed assessment of the industry, market and buyer behavior, the organization, and the alternative courses of action. *Analysis and evaluation should represent the bulk of the written report.* This section should not contain a restatement of case information; it should contain an assessment of the facts, quantitative data, and management views. The last section should consist of a set of recommendations. These recommendations should be documented with references to the previous section and should be operational given the case situation. By all means, commit to a decision!

A case and a written student analysis of it are presented in the appendix at the end of the book. It is recommended that you carefully analyze the case before reading the student analysis.

NOTES

1. Herbert A. Simon, *The New Science of Management Decision* (New York: Harper & Row, 1960).

2. Peter Drucker, "How to Make a Business Decision," *Nation's Business* (April 1956): 38–39.

3. There are a variety of systematic approaches to the decision-making process. For a review, see Ernest R. Archer, "How to Make a Business Decision: An Analysis of Theory and Practice," *Management Review* (February 1980): 54–61; Beverly Geber, "Decisions, Decisions," *Training* (April 1988): 52–62; and James R. Evans, *Creative Thinking in the Decision and Management Sciences* Cincinnatti, OH: South-Western Publishing, 1991).

4. DECIDE acronym copyright © by William Rudelius. It is used here with permission.

5. "Cluett Peabody & Co. Loses Shirt Trying to Jazz Up the Arrow Man," *Wall Street Journal* (July 28, 1988): 24.

6. An issue that frequently arises in developing these subjective probabilities is how to select them. One source is past experience, in the form of statistics such as A. T. Kearney's probabilities of success for alternative strategies, presented in Chapter 1. Alternatively, case information can be used to develop probability estimates. At the very least, when two possible uncertainties exist, a subjective probability of .5 can be assigned to each. This means that the two uncertainties have an equal chance of occurring. These probabilities can then be revised up or down, depending on case information.

7. These examples and others are found in Jacob W. Ulvila and Rex V. Brown, "Decision Analysis Comes of Age," *Harvard Business Review* (September–October 1982): 130–141.

8. Amitai Etzioni, "Humble Decision Making," *Harvard Business Review* (July–August 1989): 122–126.

9. For an expanded discussion on these headings, see A. J. Strickland III and Arthur A. Thompson, Jr., *Cases in Strategic Management*, 7th ed. (Homewood, IL: R. D. Irwin, 1993): 280–290.

CHAPTER 4

Opportunity Analysis and Market Targeting

 The development and implementation of marketing strategy are complicated and challenging tasks. At its pinnacle, marketing strategy involves the selection of markets and the development of programs to reach these markets. This process is carried out in a manner that simultaneously benefits both the markets selected (satisfying the needs or wants of buyers) and the organization (typically in dollar-profit terms).

Within this framework, a necessary first task is opportunity analysis and market targeting. This chapter describes analytical concepts and tools that marketing managers find useful in performing opportunity analyses and selecting market targets.

OPPORTUNITY ANALYSIS

Opportunity analysis consists of three interrelated processes:

- Opportunity identification
- Opportunity-organization matching
- Opportunity evaluation

Opportunities arise from identifying new types or classes of buyers, uncovering unsatisfied needs of buyers, or creating new ways or means for satisfying buyer needs. In short, opportunity analysis focuses on finding a market niche for the organization.

The case of Reebok International, Ltd., highlights the value of careful *opportunity identification*. In 1981, Reebok was known primarily for its custom running shoes. Consumer interest in running had plateaued, however, and new opportunities had to be identified for the company to grow. Careful investigation revealed that there existed numerous opportunities for product development based on buyer types and needs. In quick succession, Reebok introduced an aerobic dance shoe in 1982, a tennis shoe in 1984, a basketball shoe and a children's shoe in 1984, a walking shoe in 1986, an all-purpose shoe in 1988, step-trainers in 1991, and hiking shoes in 1994. Reebok had identified buyer needs based on athletic activities (tennis, basketball, walking) and buyer types (men, women, and children). By doing so, Reebok increased sales from $1 million to more than $3 billion in 13 years.[1]

Opportunity-organization matching determines whether an identified market niche is consistent with the definition of the organization's business, purpose, and distinctive competency. This determination usually requires an assessment of the organization's purpose, strengths, and weaknesses and an identification of the requirements for operating profitably in the market niche. The lack of a match between opportunity and organization may account for the fact that the Gillette Company never took advantage of the market opportunity for feminine hygiene sprays, even though it had the aerosol technology and marketing experience in introducing feminine products. The product simply was inconsistent with Gillette's business definition. (This situation allegedly occurred because Gillette executives could not bring themselves to mention certain parts of the female anatomy in their business conversations.)[2] Similarly, no steam locomotive manufacturers entered the field of diesel locomotives, and most manufacturers of safety razor blades do not produce electric shavers. The main cause of such actions is usually unwillingness to modify organizational strategy.

Opportunity evaluation typically has two distinct phases—one qualitative and one quantitative. The qualitative phase focuses on matching the attractiveness of an opportunity with the potential for uncovering a market niche. Attractiveness is dependent on (1) competitive activity; (2) buyer requirements; (3) market demand and supplier sources; (4) social, political, economic, and technological forces; and (5) organizational capabilities.[3] Each of these factors in turn must be tied to its impact on the types of buyers sought, the needs of buyers, and the means for satisfying these needs. Exhibit 4.1 is an opportunity evaluation matrix containing illustrative questions useful in the qualitative analysis of a market opportunity. The quantitative phase yields estimates of market potential, estimates of organization sales potential, and sales forecasts. It also produces budgets for financial, human, marketing, and production resources, which are necessary to assess the profitability of a market opportunity.

Opportunity identification, matching, and evaluation are challenging assignments, since subjective factors play a large role and managerial insight and foresight are necessary. These processes are even more difficult in the global arena, where social and political forces and uncertainties related to organizational capabilities in unfamiliar economic environments assume a significant role.

WHAT IS A MARKET?

The fact that an opportunity has been identified does not necessarily imply that a market exists for the organization. Although definitions vary, a *market* may be considered to be the prospective buyers (individuals or organizations) willing and able to purchase the existing or potential offering (product or service) of an organization.

This definition of a market has several managerial implications. First, the definition focuses on buyers, not on products or services. People and organizations whose idiosyncrasies dictate whether and how products and services will be acquired, consumed, or used make up markets. Second, by highlighting the buyer's willingness and ability to purchase a product or service, this definition introduces the concept of *effective de-*

EXHIBIT 4.1

Opportunity Evaluation Matrix: Attractiveness Criteria

Market Niche Criteria	Competitive Activity	Buyer Requirements	Demand/ Supply	Political, Technological, and Socioeconomic Forces	Organizational Capabilities
Buyer type	How many and which firms are competing for this user group?	What affects the willingness and ability to buy?	Do different buyer types have different levels of effective demand? How important are adequate sources of supply?	How sensitive are different buyers to these forces?	Can we gain access to buyers through marketing-mix variables? Can we supply these buyers?
Buyer needs	Which firms are satisfying which buyer needs?	Are there needs that are not being satisfied? What are they?	Are buyer needs likely to be long term? Do we have or can we acquire resources to satisfy buyer needs?	How sensitive are buyer needs to these forces?	Which needs can our organization satisfy?
Means for satisfying buyer needs	What are the strategies being employed to satisfy buyer needs?	Is the technology for satisfying needs changing?	To what extent are the means for satisfying buyer needs affected by supply sources? Is the demand for the means for satisfying buyer needs changing?	How sensitive are the means for satisfying buyer needs to these forces?	Do we have the financial, human, technological, and marketing expertise to satisfy buyer needs?

mand. Even if buyers are willing to purchase a product or service, exchange cannot occur unless they are able to do so. Likewise, if buyers are able to purchase a product or service but are unwilling to do so, exchange will not occur. These relationships are important to grasp because a marketing strategist must ascertain the extent of effective demand for an offering in order to determine whether a market exists. To a large degree, the extent of effective demand will depend on the marketing-mix activities of the organization. Third, use of the term *offering*, rather than *product* or *service*, expands the definition of what organizations provide for buyers. Products and services are not purchased for the sake of purchase; they are purchased for the values or benefits that buyers expect to derive from them. It is for this reason that the late Charles Revson of Revlon Cosmetics continually reiterated that his company did not sell cosmetics but, rather, hope. This expanded definition of an offering requires strategists to consider benefits provided by a product or service apart from its tangible nature.

Frequently one hears or reads about the automobile market, the soft-drink market, or the health-care market. These terms can be misleading because each refers to a composite of multiple minimarkets. Viewing a market as composed of mini-

EXHIBIT   4.2

Market Structure for Coffee

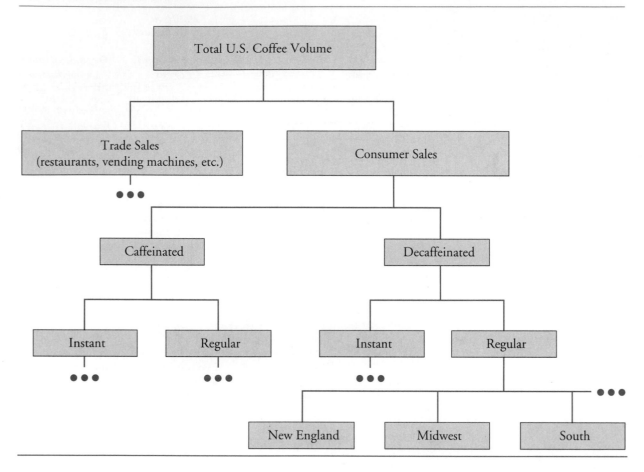

markets allows a marketer to better gauge opportunities. Consider, for example, the "coffee market." Exhibit 4.2 shows how the coffee market might be broken down into multiple markets by a marketing manager for Maxwell House or Folger's. With this breakdown, the manager can more effectively identify who is competing in the caffeinated versus the decaffeinated markets and how they are competing, monitor changes in sales volume for instant decaffeinated coffee, and appreciate differences between buyer taste preferences and competition in the South and in New England. (For these reasons, among others, regional marketing has become popular.)[4]

Finally, how a market is defined has a crucial effect on the concept of market share. *Market share* can be defined as the sales of a firm, product, or brand divided by the sales of the "market." Obviously, market definition is critical in calculating this percentage. For example, consider the market share of Brand X, an instant, decaffeinated coffee brand with annual sales of $1 billion. Depending on the definition of the market, the brand's share will range from 12.5 percent to 50 percent, as shown in the following table.

Market Definition	*Dollar Sales*	*Brand X Sales*	*Market Share*
U.S. coffee market	$8 billion	$1 billion	12.5%
U.S. decaffeinated coffee market	$4 billion	$1 billion	25.0%
U.S. instant decaffeinated coffee market	$2 billion	$1 billion	50.0%

MARKET SEGMENTATION

A useful technique for structuring markets is *market segmentation*—the breaking down or building up of potential buyers into groups. These groups are typically termed *market segments*. Each segment is thought of as possessing some sort of homogeneous characteristic relating to its purchasing or consumption behavior, which is ultimately reflected in its responsiveness to marketing programs. Market segmentation grew out of the recognition that, in general, an organization cannot be all things to all people.

Although Henry Ford is reputed to have said that buyers of his automobiles could have any color they desired as long as it was black, most marketers agree that such an undifferentiated marketing strategy is no longer appropriate. For a variety of reasons, the idea that an organization can effectively apply one marketing strategy to all possible buyers is no longer viable.

At the other extreme, unless the organization is highly specialized and sells only to, say, one buyer, it is not feasible to treat each potential buyer as unique. Thus, as Ben Enis has so aptly written, market segmentation "is a compromise between the ineffectiveness of treating all customers alike and the inefficiency of treating each one differently."[5]

Segmentation offers two principal benefits with regard to the development of marketing strategy. First, needs, wants, and behaviors of specific groups of buyers can be more precisely determined. More specifically, the following six fundamental questions can be answered for each market segment:

1. Who are they?
2. What do they want to buy?
3. How do they want to buy?
4. When do they want to buy?
5. Where do they want to buy?
6. Why do they want to buy?

Second, resources can be more effectively allocated to marketing-mix activities designed to satisfy the needs, wants, and behaviors of buyer segments. For example, Procter and Gamble markets its Crest toothpaste with different advertising and promotion campaigns directed at six different market segments, including children, Hispanics, and senior citizens.

These advantages, though, are not without their costs. There are research costs associated with identifying appropriate market segments. And designing more than one marketing strategy is likely to increase expenses for such items as offering design, salesperson training, and channel selection.

A variety of measures are useful for segmenting markets. A brief listing includes the following:

- Socioeconomic characteristics, such as sex, age, occupation, income, family life cycle, education, or geographic location

- Buying and usage characteristics, such as end use versus intermediate use, buying for another versus buying for self, size of purchase, or volume of consumption
- Benefits sought from products or services, such as status, economy, taste, or convenience of use

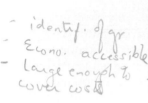

In selecting the measures to use for segmenting a particular market, the manager must depend on his or her knowledge of their relative contributions to buyer behavior and effective demand. Whichever measures are selected must satisfy a number of important requirements. First, the measures should assist in the identification of distinct groups of prospective buyers. Second, the groups identified should be economically accessible to a product or service organization through existing or possible marketing programs. Finally, the groups should be large enough in terms of sales volume potential to support the costs of the organization serving them.

OFFERING-MARKET MATRIX

A useful procedure for investigating markets is to construct an *offering-market matrix*. Such a matrix relates offerings to selected groups of buyers. Exhibit 4.3 shows an illustrative matrix for hand-held calculators. Four possible user groups (or market segments) are business, scientific, home, and school. Displaying offerings and user groups in this manner facilitates identification of gaps in the calculator market. In other words, it makes it easier to identify which user groups are not being satisfied. Furthermore, competitors and their product offerings can be assigned to specific *cells* in the matrix. Knowing where competitors are active provides a basis for

EXHIBIT 4.3

Offering-Market Matrix for Hand-Held Calculators

Computational Characteristics	Market Segments (User Groups)			
	Business	Scientific	Home	School
Simple (arithmetic operations only)				
Moderate (arithmetic operations, squares, and square roots)				
Complex (all of the above plus trigonometric functions)				
Very complex (all of the above plus programmable features)				

determining whether a market opportunity exists. Identification of gaps in the market and knowledge of competitive activities in specific offering-market cells should assist the marketing manager in gauging the effective demand for an organization's offering and the likelihood of developing a profitable marketing program. Regardless of whether the organization is investigating a potential or an existing market, development of an offering-market matrix is often a prerequisite for market targeting.

MARKET TARGETING

After a market has been segmented, it is necessary to select the segment(s) on which marketing efforts will be focused. *Market targeting* (or target marketing) is merely the specification of the segment(s) the organization wishes to pursue. Once the manager has selected the target market(s), the organization must decide which marketing strategies to employ.

For example, recognizing that Wal-Mart and Home Depot were targeting the home-improvement "do-it-yourselfer" segment for home repairs and remodeling, Payless Cashways targeted the professional remodeler segment. Once decided, the company modified its merchandise assortment, changed its credit and delivery policies, and added a sales force to call on contractors. The result? Sales to professionals grew to 45 percent of Payless's revenues, up from 25 percent of sales in previous years. Profits also improved.[6]

Two frequently used approaches are *differentiated marketing* and *concentrated marketing*. In a differentiated marketing approach, the organization simultaneously pursues several different market segments, usually with a unique marketing strategy for each. An example of this type of marketing is the strategy of Coca-Cola, which simultaneously markets a variety of soft drinks—Coca-Cola Classic, Diet Coke, and Sprite, to name a few—to various market segments. In a concentrated marketing approach, the organization focuses on a single market segment. An extreme case would be where an organization marketed a single product offering to a single market segment. More commonly, an organization will offer a product line to a single segment. For many years Gerber proclaimed that "babies are our only business." Today, Gerber further segments the "baby" segment into infants (one year old or less) and toddlers (12 to 30 months) and provides specially prepared foods for each subsegment.[7]

DETERMINING MARKET POTENTIAL AND PROFITABILITY

Before an organization can employ target marketing, it is necessary to evaluate how much various possible market segments are worth. This is done first by determining the market potential of a segment and then estimating its sales potential—the sales a particular organization might expect to obtain from the segment. From the sales estimate it is possible to compute the potential profitability of the segment.

Market-potential analysis provides a quantitative assessment of the unit or dollar sales volume in a specific, defined market segment. Estimating market potential for an offering is a difficult task even for the seasoned marketing executive. Markets and offerings can be defined in numerous ways that can lead to very different quantitative estimates of potential. Estimates can be based on trend analysis when generally accepted definitions of markets and offerings exist. For innovative offerings and new markets, the marketing analyst must often rely almost entirely on judgment and creativity. Estimating the market potential for high-definition television when the technology is still evolving and prospective market segments are uncertain is a case in point. Even in such instances, however, a marketing analyst should be prepared to describe the approach used and assumptions made in arriving at quantitative estimates. Once determined, the quantitative assessment serves as the basis for estimating what the sales potential might be within a market segment. Sales potential is due, to a large extent, to the organization's marketing program.

A profitability analysis can then be conducted on the basis of market-sales potential, by deducting the likely costs of marketing programs from the estimated sales revenues. Market segments that provide the greatest profit contribution represent viable market targets for the organization.

NOTES

1. Reebok's experience is detailed in "Sneakers That Don't Specialize," *Business Week* (June 6, 1988): 146; "Reebok's Recent Blisters Seem to Be Healing," *Business Week* (August 3, 1987): 62; "Where Nike and Reebok Have Plenty of Running Room," *Business Week* (March 11, 1991): 56–60; and "Can Reebok Regain Its Balance?" *Business Week* (December 20, 1993): 108–109.

2. W. Corley, "Gillette Co. Strategies as Its Rivals Slice at Fat Profit Margins," *Wall Street Journal* (February 2, 1972): 1ff.

3. D. Abell and J. Hammond, *Strategic Market Planning: Problems and Analytical Approaches* (Englewood Cliffs, NJ: Prentice Hall, 1979), Chapter 2.

4. For an extensive discussion of regional marketing, see S. McKenna, *The Complete Guide to Regional Marketing* (Homewood, IL: R. D. Irwin, 1992).

5. Ben M. Enis, *Marketing Principles: The Management Process*, 2nd ed. (Pacific Palisades, CA: Goodyear, 1977): 241.

6. C. Palmeri, "Remodeling Your Business," *Forbes* (August 16, 1993): 43.

7. "Baby Food Is Growing Up," *American Demographics* (May 1993): 20–22.

Importadores Quetzal

Importadores Quetzal (Quetzal Importers, in English) is an importer and distributor of a wide variety of South American and African artifacts. It is also a major source of southwestern Indian—especially Hopi and Navajo—authentic jewelry and pottery. Although the firm's headquarters is located in Phoenix, Arizona, there are currently branch offices in Los Angeles, Miami, and Boston.

Quetzal (named after the national bird of Guatemala) originated as a trading post operation near Tucson, Arizona, in the early 1900s. Through a series of judicious decisions, the firm established itself as one of the more reputable dealers in authentic southwestern jewelry and pottery. Over the years, Quetzal gradually expanded its product line to include pre-Columbian artifacts from Peru and Venezuela (see Exhibit 1) and tribal and burial artifacts from Africa. Through its careful verification of the authenticity of these South American and African artifacts, Quetzal developed a national reputation as one of the most respected importers of these types of artifacts.

In the late 1980s Quetzal further expanded its product line to include items that were replicas of authentic artifacts. For example, African fertility gods and masks were made by craftspeople who took great pains to produce these items so that only the truly knowledgeable buyer—a collector—would know that they were replicas. Quetzal now has native craftspeople in Central America, South America, Africa, and the southwestern United States who provide these items. Replicas account for only a small portion of total Quetzal sales; the company agreed to enter this business only at the prodding of the firm's clients, who desired an expanded line. The replicas have found most favor among gift buyers and individuals looking for novelty items.

Quetzal's gross sales are about $12 million and have increased at a constant rate of 20 percent per year over the last decade, despite a recession and little price inflation. Myron Rangard, the firm's national sales manager, attributed the sales increase to the popularity of Quetzal's product line and to the expanded distribution of South American and African artifacts:

> For some reason, our South American and African artifacts have been gaining greater acceptance. Two of our department store customers featured examples of our African line in their Christmas catalogs last year. I personally think consumer tastes are changing from the modern and abstract to the more concrete, like our products.

Quetzal distributes its products exclusively through specialty shops (including interior decorators), firm-sponsored showings, and a few exclusive department stores. Often the company is the sole supplier to its clients. Rangard recently expressed the reasons for this highly limited distribution:

This case was prepared by Professors Roger A. Kerin, of the Edwin L. Cox School of Business, Southern Methodist University, and Robert A. Peterson, of the University of Texas, as a basis for class discussion and is not designed to illustrate effective or ineffective handling of an administrative situation. Names have been disguised. Copyright © by Roger A. Kerin and Robert A. Peterson. No part of this case may be reproduced without the written permission of the copyright holder.

EXHIBIT   1

Pre-Columbian Water Vessel from Peru

Our limited distribution has been dictated to us because of the nature of our product line. As acceptance grew, we expanded our distribution to specialty shops and some exclusive department stores. Previously, we had to push our products through our own showings. Furthermore, we just didn't have the product. These South American artifacts aren't always easy to get and the political situation in Africa is limiting our supply. Our perennial supply problem has become even more critical in recent years for several reasons. Not only must we search harder for new products, but the competition for authentic artifacts has increased tenfold. On top of this, we must now contend with governments' not allowing exportation of certain artifacts because of their "national significance."

The problem of supply has forced Quetzal to add three new buyers in the last two years. Whereas Quetzal identified 5 major competitors a decade ago, there are 11 today. "Our bargaining position has eroded," noted David Olsen, Director of Procurement. "We have watched our gross margin slip in recent years due to aggressive competitive bidding by others."

"And competition at the retail level has increased also," injected Rangard. "Not only are some of our specialty and exclusive department store customers sending out their own buyers to deal directly with some of our Hopi and Navajo suppliers, but we are often faced with amateurs or fly-by-night competitors. These people move into a city and dump a bunch of inauthentic junk on the public at exorbitant prices. Such antics give the industry a bad name."

In recent years several mass-merchandise department store chains and a number of upper-scale discount operations have begun to sell merchandise similar to that offered by Quetzal. Even though product quality was often mixed and most items were replicas, occasionally an authentic group of items was found in these stores, according to company sales representatives. Subsequent inquiries by both Rangard and Olsen revealed that other competing distributors had signed purchase contracts with these outlets. Moreover, the items were typically being sold at retail prices below those charged by Quetzal's dealers.

Late one spring morning, Rangard was contacted by a mass-merchandise department store chain concerning the possibility of carrying a complete line of Quetzal products and particularly a full assortment of authentic items. The chain was currently selling a competitor's items but wished to add a more exclusive product line. A tentative contract submitted by the chain stated that it would buy at 10 percent below Quetzal's existing prices, and that its initial purchase would be for no less than $250,000. Depending on consumer acceptance, purchases were estimated to be at least $1 million annually. An important clause in the contract dealt with the supply of replicas. Inspection of this clause revealed that Quetzal would have to triple its replica production to satisfy the contractual obligation. Soon after Quetzal executives began discussing the contract, the president mentioned that accepting the contract could have a dramatic effect on how Quetzal defined its business.

Jones•Blair Company

Alexander Barrett, President of Jones•Blair Company, slumped back in his chair as his senior management executives filed out of the conference room. "Another meeting and still no resolution," he thought. The major point of disagreement among the executives was where and how to deploy corporate marketing efforts among the various trade paint markets served by the company. He asked his secretary to schedule another meeting for next week.

THE PAINT INDUSTRY

The market for paint coatings can be divided into *trade sales* and *industrial sales*. Trade sales include sales of products known as *shelf goods* primarily for households, contractors, and professional painters. Industrial sales include sales of numerous products for original application by manufacturers. Principal industrial customers are manufacturers of furniture, appliances, transportation equipment (autos, ships, trucks), construction components, and farm implements. Most coatings sold to industrial customers are special formulations designed to meet specific needs and application methods. Total sales of paint coatings in the United States are divided equally between trade and industrial sales.

Market Outlook for Trade Paint Sales

Industry sources estimated U.S. trade sales of paint and allied products (brushes, paint thinners, etc.) to be $5.1 billion in 1984, with projected sales of $6 billion in 1987. The average annual growth rate in dollar sales during the 1980s was considerably below the growth rate observed in the 1960s and 1970s. Some observers expected the rate of increase in paint volume to slow down further in the late 1980s, for a variety of reasons. First, there would be increased use of materials such as aluminum, plastics, and other nonwood products that require little or no painting. Second, producers of coatings had developed more durable products, and industrial paint users had developed more efficient application techniques. Third, improvements in paint quality had reduced the amount of paint necessary per application and the frequency of repainting. Counteracting these factors, industry observers foresaw increasing demand for miscellaneous products such as paint-brushes, rollers, and other paint sundries.

Paint manufacturers in general had had to contend with a cost-price squeeze in the early 1980s, and there was no end in sight. Cost of raw materials and increased competition were expected to remain major threats to industry profitability.

This case was prepared by Professor Roger A. Kerin, of the Edwin L. Cox School of Business, Southern Methodist University, as a basis for class discussion and is not designed to illustrate effective or ineffective handling of an administrative situation. Certain names and all market and sales data have been disguised and are not useful for research purposes. Copyright © by Roger A. Kerin. No part of this case may be reproduced without the written permission of the copyright holder.

Competition

There were an estimated 1,200 paint manufacturers in the United States in 1985, compared with 1,600 manufacturers in 1968. The increased concentration of paint manufacturing was due to business failures and acquisition of regional manufacturers by national firms. Still, because of a readily available technology and differences in paint formulations associated with regional climate needs, a large number of regional manufacturers have competed effectively against national manufacturers.

Major producers of paint for trade sales are Sherwin-Williams, Glidden, PPG Industries, and Benjamin Moore. These producers capture upward of 30 percent of the total U.S. trade sales market. Glidden, which was acquired by Imperial Chemicals Industries of Great Britain through the purchase of its parent company, SCM Corporation, in early 1986, is considered to be the leader in the do-it-yourself segment of the trade sales market. Sherwin-Williams is second in market share.

About 50 percent of trade paint sales is private brands. Montgomery Ward, Kmart, and Sears are major suppliers. Sears has expressed a commitment to holding its share of the paint business, if not increasing it.

Paint stores and hardware stores selling paint have been able to compete in the paint business despite the presence of private brands, mass merchandisers, and home improvement centers (such as Home Depot). Industry sources estimate that paint stores are the recipient of about 36 percent of exterior and interior paint sales; hardware stores and lumber yards receive 14 percent. These figures have remained unchanged over the past decade. Furthermore, paint and hardware stores and lumber yards in nonmetropolitan areas have outdistanced mass merchandisers and home improvement centers as a source of paint. This is largely attributable to a lack of home improvement centers and mass-merchandise distribution in these areas and to paint-store customer relations and service. However, Wal-Mart has been an effective competitor in some rural markets.

Trade Sales Purchase Patterns

Approximately 45 percent of trade sales are accounted for by households. Contractors and professional painters account for another 35 percent. The remainder are accounted for by government purchases, exports, and miscellaneous commercial applications.

Approximately one in four households purchases interior house paint in any given year. About 15 percent of U.S. households purchase exterior house paint. Industry observers believe that a majority of the paint purchased by the general public is applied by the purchaser. The popularity of do-it-yourself painting has necessitated an expanded product line of paint and sundry items carried by retail outlets, which partially accounts for the development of manufacturer-owned and -operated retail outlets such as Sherwin-Williams.

Contractors are typically involved in large-scale painting jobs such as new home and building construction. Professional painters, by comparison, typically paint the exterior and interior of individual homes or serve in a maintenance capacity for property management firms.

"Paint has become a commodity," commented Barrett. "Household purchasers view paint as paint—a covering—and try to get the best price. But there are a significant number of people who desire service as well in the form of information about application, surface preparation, and durability," he added. He conceded that "once paint is on the wall, you can't tell the difference between premium-priced and competitively priced paint.

"There is a difference between contractors and professional painters, however," he continued. "Pot and brush guys [professional painters] do seek out quality products, since their reputation is on the line and maintenance firms don't want to have to paint an office each time a mark appears on a wall. They want paint that is durable, washable, and will cover in a single coat. Contractors want whitewash in many instances and strive for the lowest price, particularly on big jobs."

JONES•BLAIR SERVICE AREA

Jones•Blair markets its products in over 50 counties in Texas, Oklahoma, New Mexico, and Louisiana. Dallas-Fort Worth (DFW), with a population of 3 million, is the major urban center in the company's service area. DFW, the business and financial center for the Jones•Blair service area, is a city that benefited from migration in the early 1980s because of its prosperous economy. A similar pattern of growth occurred in the entire 50-county service area. According to the U.S. census, the population growth rate for the entire area has exceeded the DFW growth rate. The total population in the 50-county service area is 6 million.

Competition at both retail and manufacturing levels has accelerated in recent years. Sears and Kmart have multiple outlets in DFW, as do Sherwin-Williams and Home Depot. Competition for retail selling space in paint stores, lumberyards, and hardware stores has also increased. "Our research indicates that 1,000 of these outlets now operate in the 50-county service area, and DFW houses 300 of them," noted Barrett. "When you consider that the typical lumberyard or hardware store gets 10 percent of its volume ($30,000) from paint and the typical paint store has annual sales of $125,000 with three brands, you can see that getting and keeping widespread distribution is a key success factor in this industry. Over 1,200 outlets were in operation in the area in 1975; about 600 were situated in DFW or its suburbs at the time."

Competition at the manufacturing level has increased as well. The major change in competitive behavior has occurred among paint companies that sell to contractors serving the housing industry. The companies have aggressively priced their products to capture a higher percentage of the home construction market. "These companies have not pursued the 300 or so professional painting firms in DFW and the 100 painters in rural areas or the household market as yet," said Barrett. "They have not been able to gain access to retail outlets, but they may buy their way in through free goods, promotional allowances, or whatever means are available to them.

"We believe that mass merchandisers control 50 percent of the household paint market in the DFW metropolitan area. Price seems to be the attraction, but we can't quarrel with their quality," noted Barrett.

The estimated dollar volume of trade paint and allied products sold in Jones•Blair's service area in 1986 was $55 million (excluding contractor sales). DFW was estimated to account for 60 percent of this figure, with the remaining volume being sold in rural areas. Do-it-yourself household buyers were believed to account for 70 percent of non-contractor-related volume in DFW and 90 percent of volume in rural areas. A five-year summary of trade paint and allied product sales in the Jones•Blair service area is shown in Exhibit 1.

EXHIBIT   1

Trade Paint and Allied Product Sales Volume (Millions of Dollars)

Year	Total Dollar Sales	DFW Area Sales	Rural Sales
1982	$43.2	$33.2	$10.0
1983	46.2	33.7	12.5
1984	49.4	33.8	15.6
1985	52.4	33.9	18.5
1986	55.0	33.0	22.0

JONES•BLAIR COMPANY

Jones•Blair Company is a privately held corporation that is involved in trade paint sales under the Jones•Blair brand name. In addition to producing a full line of paints, the company sells paint sundries (brushes, rollers, thinners, etc.) under the Jones•Blair name, even though these items are not manufactured by the company. The company also operates a very large industrial-coatings division, which sells its products nationwide.

Company trade paint and allied products sales volume in 1986 was $4.67 million, and net profit before taxes was $450,000. Dollar sales had increased at an average annual rate of 10 percent per year over the past decade. Paint gallonage, however, had remained stable over the past five years (see Exhibit 2). "We have been very aggressive in raising our prices to cover increased material and labor costs, but I'm afraid we've crossed the threshold." Barrett said. "We are now the highest-priced paint in the markets we serve." In 1986, cost of goods sold, including freight expenses, was 60 percent of net sales.

Distribution

The company distributes its products through 200 independent paint stores, lumberyards, and hardware outlets. Forty percent of its outlets are located in DFW. The remaining outlets are situated in rural areas in the 50-county service area. Jones•Blair

EXHIBIT   2

Jones•Blair Company Trade Sales and Volume Performance

Year	Total Gallons	Total Dollar Sales Sold(Millions)[a]
1982	594,290	$3.19
1983	594,300	3.51
1984	594,390	3.86
1985	594,400	4.25
1986	594,412	4.67

[a]Includes sales of allied products, such as brushes and rollers.

sales are distributed evenly between DFW and rural accounts. Exhibit 3 shows the account and sales volume distribution by size of dollar purchase per year.

Retail outlets in rural areas with paint and sundry purchases exceeding $15,000 annually carry only the Jones•Blair product line. However, except for 14 outlets in DFW (those with purchases greater than $30,000 annually), which carry the Jones•Blair line exclusively, DFW stores carry two or three lines, with Jones•Blair's line being premium priced. "Our experience to date shows that in our DFW outlets, the effect of multiple lines has been to cause a decline in gallonage volume. The rural outlets, by comparison, have grown in gallonage volume. When you combine the two, you have flat gallonage volume," remarked Barrett.

Promotional Efforts for Trade Sales

Jones•Blair employs eight sales representatives, who are responsible for monitoring inventories of Jones•Blair paint and sundry items in each retail outlet, as well as for order taking, assisting in store display, and coordinating cooperative advertising programs. A recent survey of Jones•Blair paint outlets indicated that the sales representatives were well liked, helpful, and knowledgeable about paint. Commenting on the survey findings, Barrett said, "Our reps are on a first-name basis with their customers. It is not uncommon for our reps to discuss business and family over coffee during a sales call, and some of our people even 'mind the store' when the proprietor has to run an errand or two." Sales representatives are paid a salary and a 1 percent commission on sales.

The company spends approximately 3 percent of net sales on advertising and sales promotion efforts. Approximately 55 percent of advertising and sales promotion dollars are allocated to cooperative advertising programs with retail accounts. The cooperative program, whereby Jones•Blair pays a portion of an account's media costs based on the amount purchased from Jones•Blair, applies to newspaper advertising and seasonal catalogs distributed door to door in a retailer's immediate trade area. The remainder of the advertising and sales promotion budget is spent on in-store displays, on corporate brand advertising on outdoor signs and in regional magazines, on premiums, and on advertising production costs. Exhibits 4 and 5 show Jones•Blair print advertisements.

EXHIBIT 3

Account and Sales Volume Distribution by Dollar Purchase per Year

	Accounts			*Sales Volume*		
Dollar Purchase/Year	*Urban*	*Rural*	*Total*	*Urban*	*Rural*	*Total*
$30,000+	7%	10%	17%	28%	28%	56%
$15,000–$30,000	14	20	34	13	13	26
Less than $15,000	19	30	49	9	9	18
Total	40%	60%	100%	50%	50%	100%

EXHIBIT 4

Jones•Blair Print Advertisement

DON'T GO BANANAS MATCHING COLORS!

Get the color you want with Jones·Blair Paint

SATIN-X LATEX WALL PAINT
This premium paint is customer proven for interior walls. Not only can you choose ready-mixed or 1,000 custom-mixed colors, the beautiful, one-coat matte finish is tough enough to wash with soap and water. Satin-X dries quick, cleans up easy and lasts longer.

VALUE PRICED $**00**⁰⁰

Choose from 1000 colors or bring your sample to match

Jones·Blair 𝑱𝑩™

SEE YOUR JONES·BLAIR DEALER FOR THE RIGHT PAINT AND BEST ADVICE!

DEALER NAME

Your Home Is Worth Jones·Blair Paint

EXHIBIT 5

Jones•Blair Print Advertisement

PLANNING MEETING

Senior management executives of Jones•Blair Company assembled again to consider the question of where and how to deploy corporate marketing efforts among the various trade paint markets served by the company. Barrett opened the meeting with a statement that it was absolutely necessary to resolve this question at the meeting in order for the tactical plan to be developed.

Vice President of Advertising: Alex, I still believe that we must direct our efforts toward bolstering our presence in the DFW market. I just received the results of our DFW consumer advertising awareness study. As you can see (Exhibit 6), awareness is related to paint purchase behavior. Furthermore, industry research on paint purchase behavior indicates that a majority of consumers decide ahead of time what brand they will buy before shopping for paint and do think about paint they have seen advertised when choosing a brand. It seems to me that we need an awareness level of at least 30 percent to materially affect our market share.

Preliminary talks with our ad agency indicate that an increase of $150,000 in corporate brand advertising beyond what we are now spending, with an emphasis on television, will be necessary to achieve this awareness level. Furthermore, this television coverage will reach rural consumers as well.

Vice President of Operations: I don't agree. Advertising is not the way to go, and reference to the DFW area alone is too narrow a focus. We have to be com-

E X H I B I T   6

Percentage of DFW Population Who Were Aware of Paint Brands and Purchased Paint in the Past 12 Months

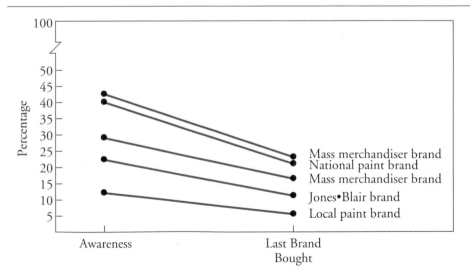

Awareness Question: "What brands come to mind when you think of paint?"

Last Brand Bought: "What paint brand did you purchase the last time you bought paint?"

Note: Sample size was $N = 400$. Percentages are subject to a 5 percent sampling error.

petitive in the household paint market, period. Our shopper research program indicated that dealers will quickly back off from our brand when the customer appears price-sensitive. We must cut our price by 20 percent on all paint products to achieve parity with national paint brands. Look here. In today's newspaper, we advertise a price-off special on our exterior paint, and our price is still noticeably higher than a mass merchandiser's everyday price. With both ads on the same page, a customer would have to be an idiot to patronize one of our dealers.

Vice President of Sales: Forget the DFW market. We ought to be putting our effort into the rural market, where half of our sales and most of our distributors exist right now. I hate to admit it, but our sales representatives are actually on a milk run. We have only added five new accounts in the last five years; our account penetration in rural areas is only 17 percent. I'm partially at fault, but I'm ready to act. We should add one additional sales representative whose sole responsibility is to develop new retail account leads and presentations or call on professional painters. I've figured the direct cost to keep one rep in the field at $50,000 per year.

Vice President of Finance: Everyone is proposing a change in our orientation. Let me be the devil's advocate and favor pursuing our current approach. We now sell to both the home owner and the professional painter in DFW and rural markets through our dealers. We have been and will continue to be profitable by judiciously guarding our margins and controlling costs. Our contribution margin is 35 percent. Everyone suggests that increasing our costs will somehow result in greater sales volume. Let me remind you, Alex, we have said that it is our policy to recoup noncapital improvement expenditures within a one-year time horizon. If we increase our advertising by an incremental amount of $150,000, then we had better see the incremental sales volume as well. The same goes for additional sales representatives and, I might add, the across-the-board cut in prices.

Mr. Barrett: We keep going over the same ground. All of you have valid arguments, but we must prioritize. Let's quit pushing our pet projects and think about what's best for all of us.

Increased advertising seems reasonable, since national paint firms and mass merchandisers outspend us tenfold. You are right in saying people have to be aware of us before they will buy, or even consider, Jones•Blair. But I am not sure what advertising will do for us given that about 75 percent of the audience is not buying paint. Your reference to DFW as being our major market has been questioned by others. Can't we take that $150,000 of incremental advertising and apply it toward newspapers and catalogs in rural areas?

The price cut is a more drastic action. We might have to do it just to keep our volume. It would appear from our sales representatives' forecast that the demand for paint in our area will not increase next year despite the population growth. Any increases will have to come out of a competitor's hide. Moreover, since our costs are unlikely to decline, we must recoup gross profit dollars from an increase in volume. Is this possible?

The idea of hiring additional representatives has merit, but what do we do with them? Do they focus on the retail account side or on the professional painter? Our survey of retail outlets indicted that 70 percent of sales through our DFW outlets went to the professional painter, while 70 percent of sales through our rural outlets went to households. These figures are identical to the 1980 survey of retail outlets. Our contractor sales in DFW and rural areas are minimal. We would need a 40 percent price cut to attract contractors, not to mention the increased costs, expertise, and headaches of competitive bidding for large jobs.

Now that I've had my say, let's think about your proposals again.

Frito-Lay's® Dips

In late 1986, Ben Ball, Marketing Director, and Ann Mirabito, Product Manager, had just completed the planning review for the line of dips sold by Frito-Lay, Inc. Frito-Lay's® Dips were a highly profitable product line and had shown phenomenal sales growth in the past five years. Sales in 1985 were $87 million, compared with $30 million in 1981.

A major issue raised at the planning meeting was where and how Frito-Lay's® Dips could be developed further. Two different viewpoints were expressed. One view was that the dip line should be more aggressively promoted in its present market segment. This segment was broadly defined as the "chip dip" category. The other view was that Frito-Lay should also actively pursue the "vegetable dip" category. The company had recently introduced a shelf-stable, sour cream–based French onion dip nationally, and 1986 sales were forecasted to be $10 million. The new dip was the first sour cream–based dip introduced by Frito-Lay. Some executives felt that this dip could provide a bridge to the vegetable dip category, which could be further developed.

Frito-Lay executives had yet to decide how much emphasis to place on each category in 1987. Furthermore, expense budgets would need special consideration. More aggressive marketing would require higher marketing investment or at least a reallocation of funds, while at the same time the gross margin and profit contribution of dips would have to be preserved.

DIP CATEGORY

Dips are typically used as an appetizer, snack, or accompaniment to a meal. Dip popularity has risen in recent years as a result of the convenience of use, multiple uses, and "grazing" trends in the United States. Dips can be served along with chips, crackers, or raw vegetables.

The market for dips is highly fragmented and difficult to measure; however, upward of 80 percent of dip sales are accounted for by supermarkets. According to industry estimates, total dip retail dollar sales volume through supermarkets was $620 million in 1985. Two-thirds of this dollar volume was captured by prepared dips; the remaining one-third was accounted for by dip mixes for at-home preparation. About 55 percent of the prepared dips sold in supermarkets required refrigeration. The major competitors in this segment were Kraft, Borden, a large number of regional dairies, and numerous store brands. Refrigerated dip retail prices were typically in the range from $0.07 to $0.15 per ounce. About 45 percent of prepared dips were "shelf sta-

This case was prepared by Jeanne Bertels, graduate student, under the supervision of Professor Roger A. Kerin, of the Edwin L. Cox School of Business, Southern Methodist University, as a basis for class discussion and is not designed to illustrate effective or ineffective handling of an administrative situation. The cooperation of Frito-Lay, Inc., is gratefully acknowledged. Selected financial and market data have been disguised or approximated and are not useful for research purposes. Copyright © by Roger A. Kerin. No part of this case may be reproduced without the written permission of the copyright holder.

ble" (that is, they were packaged in metal cans and required no refrigeration). These dips could be displayed virtually anywhere in a supermarket, though they were typically located near snack foods. Frito-Lay was the major competitor in shelf-stable dips, followed by regional chip manufacturers. Shelf-stable dip retail prices were in the range from $0.13 to $0.20 per ounce. By comparison, prices of dip mix were typically $0.09 per ounce (including the cost of a sour cream mixer or base).

Exhibit 1 shows a breakdown of the $620 million sales of dips in supermarkets by product type. Industry research indicates that dip dollar sales are growing at 10 percent per year, but this growth has come about because of price (inflationary) increases. No real growth is evident. Virtually all of the growth in 1984 and 1985 was accounted for by cheese-based dips, which captured market share from other dip flavors.

Flavor Popularity and Usage

Sour cream–based dips are the most popular flavor. Sour cream–based prepared dips and dip mixes account for about 50 percent of total dip sales. Cheese-based dips are the second most popular segment and account for about 25 percent of total dip sales. Bean and picante dips account for about 10 percent of total dip sales, and cream cheese–based dips account for the remaining 15 percent.

Dips are most frequently used with salty snacks, such as potato chips and corn chips. Whereas about 67 percent of total dip sales are linked to salty snack usage, virtually all bean and picante dips are consumed with salty snacks. One-fourth of cream cheese–based dip volume and 85 percent of cheese-based volume are linked with chip usage. Shelf-stable dips and many dip mixes are located adjacent to salty snack foods in supermarkets. Dry soup mixes are typically shelved with canned soups. Approximately 33 percent of all dip sales ($207 million) are linked to vegetable usage, and most of this volume is sold through supermarkets. Vegetable dips are located throughout supermarkets, in produce, soup mix, salad dressing, and snack sections, since they are viewed as a complementary as opposed to a primary product. Two brands—Libby's Dip Mixes and Bennett's Toppings/Dips—are located in the produce section, but each is sold only on a regional basis. Numerous local brands are also shelved in the produce section.

The popularity of Mexican food, including nachos, has fueled the growth of cheese-based dips in particular. New product introductions and accompanying market expenditures have also stimulated trial and acceptance of Mexican-style dips. For instance, Kraft, a major competitor in cheese dips, added Mexican flavors to both new and existing product lines in 1984. New products included Kraft Nacho Cheese Dip and Kraft Premium Jalapeno Cheese Dip. Kraft also added a Mexican zest to two of its popular products: Velveeta Mexican process cheese spread features jalapeno peppers, and Kraft Cheese Whiz is offered in variations of hot salsa and mild salsa. Kraft competes primarily in the refrigerated segment of the dip market. In late 1985, however, Kraft entered the shelf-stable market with Kraft Nacho Dip and Kraft Hot Nacho Dip.

Dip Substitutes

Even though the market for dips is large; it is estimated that about 20 percent of all dip volume consumed by households in the United States is homemade. In addition, many consumers use refrigerated salad dressings for dips, especially for vegetables. It is estimated that 35 percent of refrigerated salad dressing volume is used for dips. These re-

EXHIBIT 1

Estimated 1985 Supermarket Dip Sales at Retail Prices

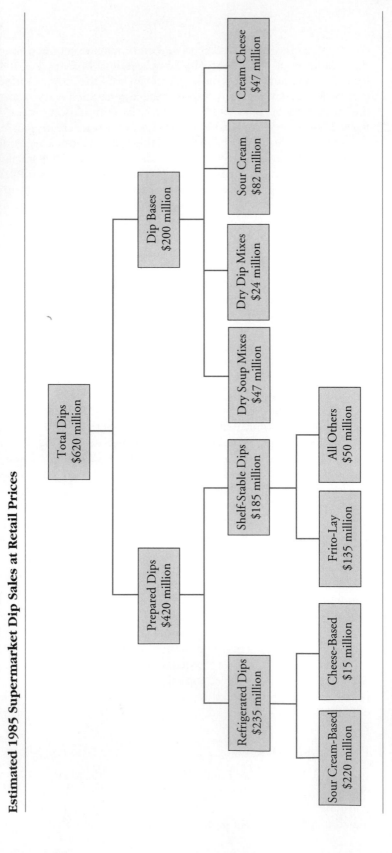

Source: Frito-Lay, Inc., company records.

frigerated salad dressings are typically located in the produce section of supermarkets and include such brands as Marie's, Bob's Big Boy, Marzetti's, and Walden Farms, as well as a few local brands in different areas of the country. Market research indicates that refrigerated salad dressings sold in the produce section of supermarkets account for $67 million in retail sales annually. Retail sales of refrigerated salad dressings have been growing at a compound annual rate of 18 percent since 1978.

Competitive Activity

Competitive activity in the dip market accelerated in 1984 and 1985. During these two years, numerous new products were introduced, and advertising expenditures increased. Industry sources estimated that dip competitors combined (excluding Frito-Lay) spent $58 million for consumer advertising alone in 1985. This figure was 25 percent higher than in 1984.

Equally noteworthy is the fact that large, well-financed companies began to aggressively pursue the dip market. For example, Campbell Soup introduced a nacho soup/dip and a line of vegetable dip mixes in 1985, and Lipton expanded its line of vegetable dip mixes and upgraded its packaging in 1985. According to Ann Mirabito, "These companies, coupled with Borden, Kraft, and regional chip manufacturers, have dramatically altered the competitive environment for chip dips in the past two years."

FRITO-LAY, INC.

Frito-Lay, Inc., is a division of PepsiCo, Inc., a New York-based diversified consumer goods and services firm. Other PepsiCo, Inc. divisions include Pizza Hut, Taco Bell, Pepsi Cola Bottling Group, Kentucky Fried Chicken, and PepsiCo Foods International. PepsiCo, Inc., recorded net sales of over $8 billion in 1985.

Frito-Lay is a nationally recognized leader in the manufacture and marketing of salty snack foods. The company's major salty snack products and brands include potato chips (Lay's®, O'Grady's®, Ruffles®, Delta Gold®), corn chips (Fritos®), tortilla chips (Doritos®, Tostitos®), cheese puffs (Cheetos®), and pretzels (Rold Gold®). Other well-known products include Baken-Ets® brand fried pork skins, Munchos® brand potato chips, and Funyuns® brand onion-flavored snacks. In addition, the company markets a line of nuts, peanut butter crackers, processed beef sticks, Grandma's® brand cookies and snack bars, and assorted other snacks. Frito-Lay's net sales in 1985 approached $3 billion.

Given the nature of its products, Frito-Lay competes primarily with what is termed the salty snack food segment of the snack food market. In 1985, Frito-Lay captured about 33 percent of the salty snack food tonnage sold in the United States.

The Dip Business

The first two dips introduced by Frito-Lay were Frito-Lay's® Jalapeno Bean Dip and Enchilada Bean Dip. These dips, marketed in the 1950s, were viewed as a logical complement to the company's Fritos® corn chips. A Picante Sauce Dip was introduced in 1978 to complement the newly introduced Tostitos® tortilla chips. These three dips were the only Frito-Lay dips sold until 1983.

Dip popularity accelerated extension of the dip product line in 1983. In late 1983 and early 1984, Frito-Lay introduced a number of cheese-based dips, including Mild Cheddar, Cheddar and Herb, Cheddar and Jalapeno, and Cheddar and Bacon, all of which were packaged in nine-ounce cans like the Mexican-style dips. According to Ben Ball, "Cheese dips were an extension of Frito-Lay's tortilla chip business and were a response to the Mexican food phenomenon sweeping the country." These new dips were shelf stable and were sold under the Frito-Lay's® brand name. Ball commented, "There was some discussion about whether or not we should use the Frito-Lay's® brand name with the cheese dips. However, we chose to stay with the Frito-Lay's® name to trade off the company's equity in salty snacks and capitalize on the company's strengths in marketing and distribution." The cheese dips, like their predecessors, were displayed in the salty snack section of supermarkets.

In 1986, Frito-Lay introduced its first sour cream–based, shelf-stable dip. This dip carried the Frito-Lay's® brand name and was displayed in the salty snack section of supermarkets. Its French onion flavor was viewed as an ideal accent for the company's potato chips. Industry data indicated that about 50 percent of salty snack volume sold in the United States was accounted for by potato chips. In addition, this onion dip was also deemed suitable as a vegetable dip.

Frito-Lay's dip sales for the period 1981–1985 are shown in Exhibit 2. Jalapeno Bean Dip and Picante Sauce Dip showed consistent, although slow, growth in these years. Enchilada Bean Dip was dropped from the Mexican dip line in mid-1985 as a result of falling sales. Sales trends indicated that Mexican dips would show a 4 percent increase in sales in 1986. Cheese dips, by comparison, represented a huge success and outsold Mexican dips in their introductory year. Nevertheless, total dollar sales of dips declined in 1985, and 1986 sales of cheese dips would be unchanged from the previous year. Ann Mirabito attributed the decline to three factors. First, the novelty of shelf-stable cheese dips had passed. Mirabito commented, "We had good initial penetration for the products; however, with the passage of time, we settled down to a core group of customers." Second, she believed that increased competitive activity had played a part in slowing Frito-Lay's dip volume growth. Third, discontinuance of Enchilada Bean Dip had had an unexpected effect. It had been expected that consumers would switch to Frito-Lay's other Mexican dips. "They didn't, and we lost customers," Mirabito noted. Nevertheless, dips were a highly profitable product line. Exhibit 3 shows the 1985 income statement for the dip product line.

EXHIBIT   2

Dollar Sales of Frito-Lay's® Dips (In millions of Dollars)

Year	Mexican Dips	Cheese Dips	Sour Cream Dip	Total Dips
1986 (forecast)	$41	$48	$10	$99
1985	39	48	—	87
1984	40	55	—	95
1983	38	5	—	43
1982	35	—	—	35
1981	30	—	—	30

EXHIBIT 3

Income Statement for Frito-Lay's® Dips, 1985 (In Thousand of Dollars)

	Mexican Dip	Cheese Dip	Total Dip
Net sales	$39,040	$48,296	$87,336
Gross margin	19,146	21,876	41,022
Marketing expense:			
Selling	8,798	11,044	19,842
Freight	1,464	1,825	3,289
Consumer advertising	60	87	147
Consumer and trade promotion	851	1,352	2,203
Total marketing expense	11,173	14,308	25,481
General and administrative overhead	2,781	3,791	6,572
Profit contribution	$ 5,192	$ 3,777	$ 8,969

Note: Selling and freight expenses are variable costs, consumer advertising and consumer and trade promotion are fixed costs budgeted annually, and general and administrative overhead expenses are fixed costs.

Dip Distribution and Sales Effort

Frito-Lay distributes its products through 350,000 outlets nationwide. In 1985, 34,000 outlets were supermarkets, 47,000 were convenience stores, and 20,000 were nonfood outlets. The remainder of Frito-Lay's 350,000 outlets were small grocery stores, liquor stores, service stations, and a variety of institutional customers. The great majority of Frito-Lay's® Dips, however, are sold through supermarkets.

Frito-Lay's distribution system is organized around four geographical zones that cover the entire United States. Each zone contains distribution centers that inventory products for the Frito-Lay sales force, which is composed of over 10,000 individuals who make 400,000 sales and delivery calls during an average workday. Each Frito-Lay salesperson follows a specific, assigned route and is responsible for selling company products to present and potential customers on his or her route.

Frito-Lay uses a "front-door store delivery system," in which one person performs the sales and delivery functions. During a visit to a store, the driver/salesperson takes orders, unloads the product, stocks and arranges the shelves, and handles in-store merchandising. This sales and delivery system is particularly suited to the 270,000 nonchain outlets serviced by Frito-Lay. Experience has indicated, however, that sales calls on chain-store accounts, which include most supermarkets, virtually always require participation by a Frito-Lay Region or Division Manager. Such participation is necessary because chain-store snack buyers purchase for all outlets in the chain and approve in-store merchandising plans as well. Furthermore, the sales task and account servicing are more time-consuming and complex, although no less important, than those required for individual outlets (for example, "mom-and-pop" grocery stores and liquor stores).

Dip Marketing

Prior to 1983, the Frito-Lay's® Dips line was viewed as a nonpromoted profit producer. With the introduction of cheese dips in 1983, Frito-Lay began promoting dips, but virtually all marketing and promotion was directed toward retail-store snack food buyers in the form of trade-oriented promotions. In 1985, the emphasis shifted to consumer promotions such as product sampling and couponing to generate trial of the new products, and television and radio advertising was used for the first time since the 1950s. Frito-Lay's new product effort, coupled with increased competitive activity, resulted in further planned increases in consumer advertising and promotion in 1986. Exhibit 4 summarizes the advertising and merchandising expenditures for dips for the period 1983–1986. Exhibit 5 illustrates a typical consumer promotion, and Exhibit 6 shows a typical trade promotion. A Frito-Lay's® Dip television commercial is shown in Exhibit 7.

Ann Mirabito provided the following rationale for the change in promotion emphasis:

> The phenomenal success of Frito-Lay's® Dips was due to two factors. First, we had the right products—cheese dips were novel, and our flavors were innovative. Second, we had the right merchandising location next to salty snacks. Prior to 1985, all of our advertising and merchandising spending was trade-oriented because our goal was to gain distribution in supermarkets and shelf space rapidly. Our consumer household penetration increased from 12 percent in 1983 to 20 percent in 1984, driven largely by placing cheese dips near salty snacks. In 1985, penetration flattened, indicating a need for consumer-pull marketing.

For the most part, dips were promoted jointly with Frito-Lay salty snacks, particularly Doritos® tortilla chips. According to Ben Ball, this approach was adopted because "dips are a complementary product." He added, "Growth occurred when our dips were displayed in conjunction with a natural carrier. That's how we built the chip dip business. This association was conveyed in our promotion and in our shelf placement with salty snacks."

FUTURE GROWTH OPPORTUNITIES

Two opportunities for the Frito-Lay's® Dips product line were raised at the planning review meeting. Frito-Lay could continue to develop the chip dip market, where it already had a strong foothold, or it could pursue the vegetable dip market as well, using the new sour cream–based dip as a spearhead. The decision would have sig-

EXHIBIT   4

Frito-Lay's® Dips Advertising and Merchandising Expenditures, 1983–1986

Year	Consumer Advertising[a]	Consumer Promotion[b]	Trade Promotion[c]	Total
1986	$1,170,000	$3,389,220	$169,290	$4,728,510
1985	147,045	1,459,050	744,101	2,350,196
1984	None	535,266	312,180	847,446
1983	None	22,322	425,478	447,800

[a]Television and radio advertising.
[b]Product sampling, cents-off coupons, etc.
[c]Trade discounts, advertising to store buyers, etc.

EXHIBIT 5

Frito-Lay's® Dips Consumer Promotion

nificant resource allocation consequences, since it was unlikely that funds for dip advertising and merchandising would be increased in 1987 beyond the $4.73 million budgeted for 1986.

Chip Dip Opportunity

One view expressed at the planning meeting was that Frito-Lay should capitalize on its foothold in the chip dip market and attempt to expand the market and build market share. Several arguments were made for this strategy. First, research indicated that only 20 percent of chips were currently eaten with dips; furthermore, only 45 percent of all U.S. households used dips in 1985, whereas 97 percent used salty snacks. "This indicated a major opportunity to build penetration through more aggressive advertising," according to a Frito-Lay executive. Second, research indicated that in 1985 the average number of times shelf-stable dips were purchased by households was four. It was felt that this frequency could be increased through frequency-building promotions such as on-pack coupon offers to encourage repeat sales. In 1985, the purchase frequency of all Frito-Lay's® Dips was 3.6 times per year. A third argument in favor of focusing attention on the chip dip market was the increased competitive

EXHIBIT 6

Frito-Lay's® Dips Trade Promotions

activity: 40 new Mexican-style cheese dips had been introduced since 1983. Although many were regional products, each vied for shelf space in or near the salty snack section of supermarkets. At the same time, it was believed that Kraft would be introducing additional products that would compete in the chip dip market. A fourth argument was that historically Frito-Lay had not promoted dips aggressively. It was

EXHIBIT 7

Frito-Lay's® Dips Television Commercial

TRACY-LOCKE
CLIENT: Frito-Lay, Inc.
PRODUCT: Frito Lay's® Dips

TITLE: "Magnetism"
LENGTH: 15 Seconds
COMM'L. NO.: PECD 6193
FIRST AIR DATE: 2/21/86

SFX: LABORATORY SOUNDS
SCIENCE EDITOR: Do you forget Frito-Lay's®
Dip?

Use the theory of magnetism,

so when you pick up the chips you automatically
. . .

SFX: METALLIC CLINK
SCIENCE EDITOR: pick up the Dip.

ANNCR (VO) AND SCIENCE EDITOR EATING:
The best way to remember Frito-Lay's® Dip is to
taste [CRUNCH! Mmmmm!] what it does to our
chips.

SCIENCE EDITOR: What an attractive concept!

believed that the typical ratio of advertising and merchandising spending to sales (A/S ratio) for prepared dips was 10 percent.[1] Refrigerated salad dressings had an A/S ratio of 3 percent, and salad dressing dry mixes had an A/S ratio of 13.6 percent. In 1985, Frito-Lay's A/S ratio for its dip product line was 2.7 percent. Therefore, the 1986 advertising and merchandising budget had been more than double 1985 expenditures. (A breakdown of these expenses is shown in Exhibit 8). A fifth argument was that Frito-Lay could spin off other products from its sour cream–based dip.

Other executives argued that the opportunity in the chip dip category was less promising. They based their argument on three points. First, competitive activity was such that Frito-Lay could only hope to hold, not improve, its position in the chip dip category. The effort and expense necessary to increase penetration and/or increase purchase frequency in the congested chip dip category could be better spent on attacking vegetable dips, where the competition (such as Marie's) was less formidable and more fragmented. Second, Frito-Lay's recent sales growth in dips was due to new products (for example, cheese-based dips), and it was not clear that further product line extensions could produce continued growth. There was also significant potential for cannibalization of existing cheese dips if the line was expanded further. Third, the new sour cream dip represented a break with Mexican-style dips and cheese dips and was probably more suitable for vegetable dipping. To promote and distribute this new dip solely as a chip dip rather than as a vegetable dip could mean a missed opportunity.

Vegetable Dip Opportunity

Executives who voiced concern about focusing on the chip dip category also raised several points in favor of the vegetable dip opportunity. First, they noted that 33 percent of dip sales were linked to vegetables. Moreover, industry research indicated that only one-fourth of the dollar volume associated with vegetable dipping was accounted for by refrigerated salad dressings, such as Marie's. The remainder was accounted for by dip mixes and refrigerated dips, and no major competitors had a strong competitive position in the market. Second, research indicated that sour

EXHIBIT 8

Planned Frito-Lay's® Dips Advertising and Merchandising Expenditures by Product Line, 1986

Product Line	Consumer Advertising	Consumer Promotion	Trade Promotion	Total
Mexican and cheese dips[a]	$1,170,000	$2,740,320	$ 56,790	$3,967,110
Sour cream dip	0	648,900	112,500	761,400
Total	$1,170,000	$3,389,220	$169,290	$4,728,510

[a]Total advertising and merchandising expenditures for Mexican and cheese dips were roughly proportional to 1985 sales of the two product lines.

---

[1]The A/S ratio is calculated by dividing total expenditures for consumer advertising and promotion and trade promotion by total sales for a given year.

cream–based dips were more popular than cheese dips for vegetable dipping. Third, trend data indicated that consumers were becoming concerned about the nutritional value and salt content of prepared foods.[2] It was felt that this trend could affect preferences for vegetables and salty snacks and, as a result, dips. Fourth, the Frito-Lay's® Dips line now had a sour cream–based dip that had not yet been promoted and merchandised for vegetable dipping. Fifth, no major competitor had introduced a shelf-stable dip for vegetables. Frito-Lay had pioneered the shelf-stable business for chip dips, and some executives felt that a similar opportunity existed for vegetable dips. Finally, a cost analysis indicated that the gross margins would be largely unaffected. The gross margin on Frito-Lay's sour cream dip was 45 percent.

Other executives expressed the view that pursuing the vegetable dip segment would not be easy, however. These executives cited research indicating that supermarket executives preferred that dips suitable for vegetable dipping be handled by their produce warehouse. This meant that Frito-Lay's front-door delivery system would not be favored. Distribution through the produce warehouse would also involve dealing with supermarket produce buyers and managers. Frito-Lay had never dealt with these individuals in the past, and some company executives believed that a totally new sales approach would be necessary. Even though a complete cost analysis had not been conducted, it was estimated that selling expenses could increase to 25 percent of sales. Current sales expense was 22.7 percent. Freight expense would not be affected. As of 1986, the sour cream dip was not allocated any general and administrative overhead. Furthermore, Frito-Lay driver/salespeople were unfamiliar with merchandising practices in the produce section of supermarkets. This same research indicated that any new vegetable dip should be shelved next to refrigerated salad dressing or near produce.

A second concern was that Frito-Lay's® Dips would lose some economies in advertising and merchandizing. Frito-Lay's® Dips had been promoted jointly with the company's chips in the past and thus traded on the "halo effect" of Frito-Lay salty snacks. Mirabito acknowledged that vegetable dips would have to "go it alone" because Frito-Lay's halo effect might not translate to vegetable dips.

A third concern expressed at the meeting was that any foray into vegetable dips would require more than a single item. In addition to the French onion flavor, other flavors (such as ranch style) would be necessary. Such line extensions would require added research and development expenses and promotional support, as had been the case with the successful introduction of cheese dips.

The planning meeting adjourned without resolution of the issue. Ben Ball asked Ann Mirabito to give the "chip dip versus vegetable dip" question further consideration. She was to prepare a recommendation for another meeting to be scheduled within 30 days.

---

[2]Bob Messenger, "Consumers See the Light . . . and the Lean, with a Touch of Pizzazz," *Prepared Foods* (November 1985): 46–49.

Curtis Automotive Hoist

In September 1990, Mark Curtis, President of Curtis Automotive Hoist (CAH), had just finished reading a feasibility report on entering the European market in 1991. CAH manufactures surface automotive hoists, a product used by garages, service stations, and other repair shops to lift cars for servicing (Exhibit 1). The report, prepared by CAH's Marketing Manager, Pierre Gagnon, outlined the opportunities in the European Economic Community and the entry options available.

Curtis was not sure if CAH was ready for this move. Although the company had been successful in expanding sales into the U.S. market, Curtis wondered if this success could be repeated in Europe. He thought that, with more effort, sales could be increased in the United States. On the other hand, there were some positive aspects to the European idea. He began reviewing the information in preparation for a meeting the following day with Gagnon.

CURTIS LIFT

Curtis, a design engineer, had worked for eight years for the Canadian subsidiary of a U.S. automotive hoist manufacturer. During those years, he had spent considerable time designing an above-ground (or surface) automotive hoist. Although Curtis was very enthusiastic about the unique aspects of the hoist, including a scissor lift and wheel alignment pads, senior management expressed no interest in the idea. In 1980, Curtis left the company to start his own business with the express purpose of designing and manufacturing the hoist. He left with the good wishes of his previous employer, who had no objections to his plans to start a new business.

Over the next three years, Curtis obtained financing from a venture capital firm, opened a plant in Lachine, Quebec, and began manufacturing and marketing the hoist, called the Curtis Lift (Exhibit 1).

From the beginning, Curtis took considerable pride in the development and marketing of the Curtis Lift. The original design included a scissor lift and a safety locking mechanism that allows the hoist to be raised to any level and locked in place. In addition, the scissor lift offers easy access for the mechanic to work on the raised vehicle. Because the hoist is fully hydraulic and has no chains or pulleys, it requires little maintenance. Another key feature is the alignment turn plates that are an integral part of the lift. The turn plates enable mechanics to accurately and easily perform wheel alignment jobs. Because it is a surface lift, the Curtis Lift can be installed in a garage in less than a day.

Curtis continually made improvements to the product, including adding more safety features. In fact, the Curtis Lift is considered a leader in automotive lift safety.

This case was prepared by Professor Gordon H. G. McDougall, of the School of Business and Economics, Wilfrid Laurier University. Used with permission.

EXHIBIT 1

Examples of Automotive Hoists

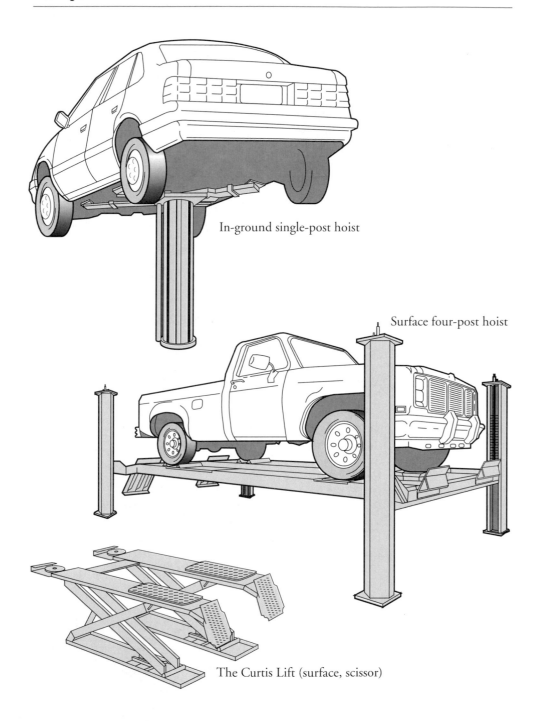

In-ground single-post hoist

Surface four-post hoist

The Curtis Lift (surface, scissor)

Safety is an important factor in the automotive hoist market. Although hoists seldom malfunction, when one does, it often results in a serious accident.

The Curtis Lift developed a reputation in the industry as the "Cadillac" of hoists; the unit is judged by many as superior to competitive offerings because of its design, the quality of the workmanship, the safety features, the ease of installation, and the five-year warranty. Curtis holds four patents on the Curtis Lift, including the lifting mechanism on the scissor design and a safety locking mechanism. A number of versions of the product were designed that make the Curtis Lift suitable (depending on the model) for a variety of tasks, including rustproofing, muffler repairs, and general mechanical repairs.

In 1981, CAH sold 23 hoists and had sales of $172,500. During the early years, the majority of sales were to independent service stations and garages specializing in wheel alignment in the Quebec and Ontario market. Most of the units were sold by Pierre Gagnon, who was hired in 1982 to handle the marketing side of the operation. In 1984, Gagnon began using distributors to sell the hoist to a wider geographic market in Canada. In 1986, he signed an agreement with a large automotive wholesaler to represent CAH in the U.S. market. In 1989, the company sold 1,054 hoists and had sales of $9,708,000 (Exhibit 2). About 60 percent of those sales were to the United States with the remaining 40 percent to the Canadian market.

INDUSTRY

Approximately 49,000 hoists are sold each year in North America. Typically hoists are purchased by automotive outlets that service or repair cars including new car dealers, used car dealers, specialty shops (for example, muffler, transmission, or wheel alignment shops), chains (for example, Firestone, Goodyear, Canadian Tire), and independent garages. It is estimated that new car dealers purchase 30 percent of all units sold in a given year. In general, the specialty shops focus on one type of repair, such as mufflers or rustproofing, while "nonspecialty" outlets handle a variety of repairs. Although there is some crossover, in general, CAH competes for the business of the specialty shop segment, particularly those shops that deal with wheel alignment. This segment includes chains such as Firestone and Canadian Tire as well as new car deal-

EXHIBIT 2

Selected Financial Statistics for Curtis Automotive Hoist, 1987–1989

	1989	1988	1987
Sales	$9,708,000	$7,454,000	$6,218,000
Cost of sales	6,990,000	5,541,000	4,540,000
Contribution	2,718,000	1,913,000	1,678,000
Marketing expenses[a]	530,000	510,000	507,000
Administrative expenses	840,000	820,000	810,000
Earnings before tax	$1,348,000	$583,000	$361,000
Units sold	1,054	847	723

Source: Company records.

[a]Marketing expenses in 1989 included advertising ($70,000), four salespeople ($240,000), and marketing manager and three sales support staff ($220,000).

ers (for example, Ford) that devote a certain percentage of their lifts to the wheel alignment business and independent garages that specialize in wheel alignment.

The purpose of a hoist is to lift an automobile into a position where a mechanic or service person can easily work on the car. Because different repairs require different positions, a wide variety of hoists has been developed to meet specific needs. For example, a muffler repair shop requires a hoist that allows the mechanic to gain easy access to the underside of the car. Similarly, a wheel alignment job requires a hoist that offers a level platform where the wheels can be adjusted as well as providing easy access for the mechanic. Pierre Gagnon has estimated that 85 percent of CAH's sales are to the wheel alignment market comprising service centers such as Firestone, Goodyear, and Canadian Tire and independent garages that specialize in wheel alignment. About 15 percent of sales are made to customers who use the hoist for general mechanical repairs.

Firms purchasing hoists are part of an industry called the automotive aftermarket. This industry is involved in supplying parts and service for new and used cars and was worth over $54 billion at retail in 1989, while servicing the approximately 11 million cars on the road in Canada. The industry is large and diverse; in 1989, there were over 4,000 new car dealers in Canada, over 400 Canadian Tire stores, over 100 stores in each of the Firestone and Goodyear chains, and over 200 stores in the Rust Check chain.

The purchase of an automotive hoist is often an important decision for the service station owner or dealer. Because the price of hoists ranges from $3,000 to $15,000, it is a capital expense for most businesses.

For the owner/operator of a new service center or car dealership, the decision involves determining what type of hoist is required, then what brand will best suit the company. Most new service centers or car dealerships have multiple bays for servicing cars. In these cases, the decision will involve what types of hoists are required (for example, in-ground, surface). Often more than one type of hoist is purchased, depending on the needs of the service center/dealership.

Experienced garage owners seeking a replacement hoist (the typical hoist has a useful life of 10 to 13 years) will usually determine what products are available and then make a decision. If the garage owners are also mechanics, they will probably be aware of two or three types of hoists but will not be very knowledgeable about the brands or products currently available. Garage owners or dealers who are not mechanics probably know very little about hoists. The owners of car or service dealerships often buy the product that is recommended and/or approved by the parent company.

COMPETITION

Sixteen companies compete in the automotive lift market in North America: 4 Canadian and 12 U.S. firms. Hoists are subject to import duties. Duties on hoists entering the U.S. market from Canada were 2.4 percent of the selling price; from the United States entering Canada the import duty was 7.9 percent. The Free Trade Agreement signed in 1989 specified that the duties between the two countries would be phased out over a ten-year period. For Curtis, the import duties had never played a part in any decisions: the fluctuating exchange rates between the two countries had a far greater impact on selling prices.

A wide variety of hoists are manufactured in the industry. The two basic types of hoists are in-ground and surface. As the names imply, in-ground hoists require that a pit be dug "in-ground" where the piston that raises the hoist is installed. In-ground hoists are either single post or multiple post, are permanent, and obviously cannot be moved. In-ground lifts constituted approximately 21 percent of total lift sales in 1989 (Exhibit 3). Surface lifts are installed on a flat surface, usually concrete. Surface lifts come in two basic types: post lift hoists and scissor hoists. Surface lifts, compared to in-ground lifts, are easier to install and can be moved, if necessary. Surface lifts constituted 79 percent of total lift sales in 1989. Within each type of hoist (for example, post lift surface hoists), there are numerous variations in terms of size, shape, and lifting capacity.

The industry is dominated by two large U.S. firms, AHV Lifts and Berne Manufacturing, which together hold approximately 60 percent of the market. AHV Lifts, the largest firm with approximately 40 percent of the market and annual sales of about $60 million, offers a complete line of hoists (that is, in-ground and surface) but focuses primarily on the in-ground market and the two-post surface market. AHV Lifts is the only company that has its own direct sales force; all other companies use (1) only wholesalers or (2) a combination of wholesalers and company sales force. AHV Lifts offers standard hoists with few extra features and competes primarily on price. Berne Manufacturing, with a market share of approximately 20 percent, also competes in the in-ground and two-post surface markets. It uses a combination of wholesalers and company salespeople and, like AHV Lifts, competes primarily on price.

Most of the remaining firms in the industry are companies that operate in a regional market (for example, California or British Columbia) and/or offer a limited product line (for example, four-post surface hoist).

Curtis has two competitors that manufacture scissor lifts. AHV Lifts markets a scissor hoist that has a different lifting mechanism and does not include the safety locking features of the Curtis Lift. On average, the AHV scissor lift sells for about 20 percent less than the Curtis Lift. The second competitor, Mete Lift, is a small regional company with sales in California and Oregon. It has a design that is very similar to

EXHIBIT 3

North American Unit Sales of Automotive Lifts, by Type, 1987–1989

	1987	1988	1989
In-ground			
Single post	5,885	5,772	5,518
Multiple post	4,812	6,625	5,075
Surface			
Two post	27,019	28,757	28,923
Four post	3,862	3,162	3,745
Scissor	2,170	2,258	2,316
Other	4,486	3,613	3,695
Total	48,234	50,187	49,272

Source: Company records.

the Curtis Lift but lacks some of its safety features. The Mete Lift, regarded as a well-manufactured product, sells for about 5 percent less than the Curtis Lift.

MARKETING STRATEGY

As of early 1990, CAH had developed a reputation for a quality product backed by good service in the hoist lift market, primarily in the wheel alignment segment.

The distribution system employed by CAH in the 1980s reflected the need to engage in extensive personal selling. Three types of distributors were used: a company sales force, Canadian distributors, and a U.S. automotive wholesaler. The company sales force consisted of four salespeople and Pierre Gagnon. Their main task was to service large "direct" accounts. The initial step was to get the Curtis Lift approved by large chains and manufacturers and then, having received the approval, to sell to individual dealers or operators. For example, if General Motors approved the hoist, then CAH could sell it to individual General Motors dealers. CAH sold directly to the individual dealers of a number of large accounts including General Motors, Ford, Chrysler, Petro-Canada, Firestone, and Goodyear. CAH had been successful in obtaining manufacturer approval from the big three automobile manufacturers in both Canada and the United States. In addition, CAH had received approval from service companies such as Canadian Tire and Goodyear. To date, CAH had not been rejected by any major account but, in some cases, the approval process had taken over four years.

In total, the company sales force generated about 25 percent of the unit sales each year. Sales to the large "direct" accounts in the United States went through CAH's U.S. wholesaler.

The Canadian distributors sold, installed, and serviced units across Canada. These distributors handled the Curtis Lift and carried a line of noncompetitive automotive equipment products (for example, engine diagnostic equipment, wheel balancing equipment) and noncompetitive lifts. These distributors focused on the smaller chains and the independent service stations and garages.

The U.S. wholesaler sold a complete product line to service stations as well as manufacturing some equipment. The Curtis Lift was one of five different types of lifts that the wholesaler sold. Although the wholesaler provided CAH with extensive distribution in the United States, the Curtis Lift was a minor product within the wholesaler's total line. Although Gagnon did not have any actual figures, he thought that the Curtis Lift probably accounted for less than 20 percent of the total lift sales of the U.S. wholesaler.

Both Curtis and Gagnon felt that the U.S. market had unrealized potential. With a population of 248 million people and over 140 million registered vehicles, the U.S. market was over ten times the size of the Canadian market (population of 26 million, and approximately 11 million vehicles). Gagnon noted that the six New England states (population over 13 million), the three largest mid-Atlantic states (population over 38 million), and the three largest mideastern states (population over 32 million) were all within a day's drive of the factory in Lachine. Curtis and Gagnon had considered setting up a sales office in New York to service these states, but they were concerned that the U.S. wholesaler would not be willing to relinquish any of its territory. They had also considered working more closely with the wholesaler to encourage it to "push" the Curtis Lift. It appeared that the wholesaler's major objective was to sell a hoist, not necessarily the Curtis Lift.

CAH distributed a catalogue-type package with products, uses, prices, and other required information for both distributors and users. In addition, CAH advertised in trade publications (for example, *Service Station & Garage Management*), and Gagnon traveled to trade shows in Canada and the United States to promote the Curtis Lift.

In 1989, Curtis Lifts sold for an average retail price of $10,990, and CAH received, on average, $9,210 for each unit sold. This average reflected the mix of sales through the three distribution channels: (1) direct (where CAH received 100 percent of the selling price), (2) Canadian distributors (where CAH received 80 percent of the selling price), and (3) the U.S. wholesaler (where CAH received 78 percent of the selling price).

Both Curtis and Gagnon felt that the company's success to date was based on a strategy of offering a superior product that was primarily targeted to the needs of specific customers. The strategy stressed continual product improvements, quality workmanship, and service. Personal selling was a key aspect of the strategy; salespeople could show customers the benefits of the Curtis Lift over competing products.

THE EUROPEAN MARKET

Against this background, Mark Curtis was thinking of ways to continue the rapid growth of the company. One possibility that kept coming up was the promise and potential of the European market. The fact that Europe would become a single market in 1992 suggested that it was an opportunity that should at least be explored. With this in mind, Curtis asked Gagnon to prepare a report on the possibility of CAH entering the European market. The highlights of Gagnon's report follow.

History of the European Community

The European Community (EC) stemmed from the 1953 Treaty of Rome, whereby five countries decided it would be in their best interest to form an internal market. These countries were France, Spain, Italy, West Germany, and Luxembourg. By 1990, the EC consisted of 12 countries (the additional 7 were Belgium, Denmark, Greece, Ireland, the Netherlands, Portugal, and the United Kingdom) with a population of over 325 million people.[1] In 1992, virtually all barriers (physical, technical, and fiscal) were scheduled to be removed for companies located within the EC. This would allow the free movement of goods, persons, services, and capital.

In the five years prior to 1991, many North American and Japanese firms established themselves in the EC. The reasoning for this was twofold. First, these companies regarded the community as an opportunity to increase global market share and profits. The market was attractive because of its sheer size and lack of internal barriers. Second, in 1992, companies that were established within the community were subject to protection from external competition via EC protectionism tariffs, local contender, and reciprocity requirements. EC protectionism tariffs were only

---

[1] At the end of 1990, West Germany and East Germany were reunified. East Germany had a population of approximately 17 million people.

temporary and would be removed at a later date. It would be possible for companies to export to or get established in the community after 1992, but there was some risk attached.

Market Potential

The key indicator of the potential market for the Curtis Lift hoist was the number of passenger cars and commercial vehicles in use in a particular country. Four countries in Europe had more than 20 million vehicles in use, with West Germany having the largest domestic fleet of 34 million vehicles followed in order by France, Italy, and the United Kingdom (Exhibit 4). The number of vehicles was an important indicator because the more vehicles in use meant a greater number of service and repair facilities that needed vehicle hoists and potentially the Curtis Lift.

An indicator of the future vehicle repair and service market was the number of new vehicle registrations. The registration of new vehicles was important, since this maintained the number of vehicles in use by replacing cars that had been retired. Again, West Germany had the most new cars registered in 1988 and was followed in order by France, the United Kingdom, and Italy.

Based primarily on the fact that a large domestic market was important for initial growth, the selection of a European country should be limited to the "Big Four" industrialized nations: West Germany, France, the United Kingdom, and Italy. In an international survey, companies from North America and Europe ranked European countries on a scale of 1 to 100 on market potential and investment site potential. The results showed that West Germany was favored for both market potential and investment site opportunities; France, the United Kingdom, and Spain placed second, third, and fourth, respectively. Italy did not place in the top four in either market or investment site potential. However, Italy had a large number of vehicles in use, had the second largest population in Europe, and was an acknowledged leader in car technology and production.

Little information was available on the competition within Europe. There was, as yet, no dominant manufacturer as was the case in North America. There was one firm in Germany that manufactured a scissor-type lift. The firm sold most of its units within the German market. The only other available information was that 22 firms in Italy manufactured vehicle lifts.

EXHIBIT 4

Number of Vehicles, 1988, and Population, 1989

	Vehicles in Use (thousands)		New Vehicle Registrations (thousands)	Population (thousands)
Country	*Passenger*	*Commercial*		
West Germany	29,970	4,223	2,960	60,900
France	28,304	1,814	2,635	56,000
Italy	22,500	1,897	2,308	57,400
United Kingdom	20,605	2,915	2,531	57,500
Spain	9,750	1,750	1,172	39,400

Investment Options

Gagnon felt that CAH had three options for expansion into the European market: licensing, joint venture, or direct investment. The licensing option was a real possibility, since a French firm had expressed an interest in manufacturing the Curtis Lift.

In June 1990, Gagnon had attended a trade show in Detroit to promote the Curtis Lift. At the show, he met Phillipe Beaupre, the marketing manager for Bar Maisse, a French manufacturer of wheel alignment equipment. The firm, located in Chelles, France, sold a range of wheel alignment equipment throughout Europe. The best-selling product was an electronic modular aligner that enabled a mechanic to utilize a sophisticated computer system to align the wheels of a car. Beaupre was seeking a North American distributor for the modular aligner and other products manufactured by Bar Maisse.

At the show, Gagnon and Beaupre had a casual conversation in which each explained what their respective companies manufactured; they exchanged company brochures and business cards, and both went on to other exhibits. The next day, Beaupre sought out Gagnon and asked if he might be interested in having Bar Maisse manufacture and market the Curtis Lift in Europe. Beaupre thought that the lift would complement Bar Maisse's product line and the licensing would be of mutual benefit to both parties. They agreed to pursue the idea. Upon his return to Lachine, Gagnon told Curtis about these discussions, and they agreed to explore this possibility.

Gagnon called a number of colleagues in the industry and asked them what they knew about Bar Maisse. About half had not heard of the company, but those who had commented favorably on the quality of its products. One colleague, with European experience, knew the company well and said that Bar Maisse's management had integrity and the firm would make a good partner. In July, Gagnon sent a letter to Beaupre stating that CAH was interested in further discussions and enclosed various company brochures including price lists and technical information on the Curtis Lift. In late August, Beaupre responded stating that Bar Maisse would like to enter a three-year licensing agreement with CAH to manufacture the Curtis Lift in Europe. In exchange for the manufacturing rights, Bar Maisse was prepared to pay a royalty rate of 5 percent of gross sales. Gagnon had not yet responded to this proposal.

The second possibility was a joint venture. Gagnon had wondered if it might not be better for CAH to offer a counterproposal to Bar Maisse for a joint venture. He had not worked out any details but felt that CAH would learn more about the European market and probably make more money if it were an active partner in Europe. Gagnon's idea was a 50-50 arrangement whereby the two parties shared the investment and the profits. He envisioned a situation in which Bar Maisse would manufacture the Curtis Lift in its plant with technical assistance from CAH. Gagnon also thought that CAH could get involved in the marketing of the lift through the Bar Maisse distribution system. Further, he thought that the Curtis Lift, with proper marketing, could gain a reasonable share of the European market. If that happened, Gagnon felt that CAH was likely to make greater returns with a joint venture.

The third option was direct investment; that is, CAH would establish a manufacturing facility and set up a management group to market the lift. Gagnon had contacted a business acquaintance who had recently been involved in manufacturing fabricated steel sheds in Germany. On the basis of discussions with his acquaintance,

Gagnon estimated the costs involved in setting up a plant in Europe at: (1) $250,000 for capital equipment (welding machines, cranes, and other equipment), (2) $200,000 in incremental costs to set the plant up, and (3) carrying costs to cover $1 million in inventory and accounts receivable. Although the actual costs of renting a building for the factory would depend on the site location, he estimated that annual building rent including heat, light, and insurance would be about $80,000. Gagnon recognized that these estimates were guidelines, but he felt that the estimates were probably within 20 percent of actual costs.

THE DECISION

As Mark Curtis considered the contents of the report, a number of thoughts crossed his mind. He began making notes concerning the European possibility and the future of the company.

- If CAH decided to enter Europe, Pierre Gagnon would be the obvious choice to head up the direct investment option or the joint venture option. Curtis felt that Gagnon had been instrumental in the success of the company to date.
- Although CAH had the financial resources to go ahead with the direct investment option, the joint venture would spread the risk (and the returns) over the two companies.
- CAH had built its reputation on designing and manufacturing a quality product. Regardless of the option chosen, Curtis wanted the firm's reputation to be maintained.
- Either the licensing agreement or the joint venture appeared to build on the two companies' strengths; Bar Maisse had knowledge of the market and CAH had the product. What troubled Curtis was whether this apparent synergy would work or Bar Maisse would seek to control the operation.
- It was difficult to estimate sales under any of the options. With the first two (licensing and joint venture), they would depend on the effort and expertise of Bar Maisse; with the third option, they would depend on Gagnon.
- CAH's sales in the U.S. market could be increased if the U.S. wholesaler would "push" the Curtis Lift. Alternatively, the establishment of a sales office in New York to cover the eastern states could also increase sales.

As Curtis reflected on the situation, he knew he should probably get additional information—but it wasn't obvious exactly what information would help him make a yes or no decision. He knew one thing for sure—he was going to keep his company on a "fast growth" track, and at tomorrow's meeting he and Gagnon would decide how to do it.

The Upjohn Company
Rogaine Topical Solution

In early 1992, the Upjohn Company began marketing Rogaine Topical Solution to women supported by an advertising, promotion, and sales budget of $20 million. Marketing to women "opens up a great opportunity for continued growth of Rogaine in 1992" noted Keith Barton, Vice President of the Upjohn Dermatology Division.[1]

Rogaine, the only drug approved by the U.S. Federal Drug Administration (FDA) to restore hair growth, is a 2 percent solution of minoxidil applied to the head to treat men with male pattern baldness and women with hereditary hair loss. First marketed to men in the United States with FDA approval in 1988, this prescription drug has been used by over 2 million men worldwide under the Rogaine and Regaine (outside the United States) brand names.[2] FDA approval for Rogaine use by women in the United States was granted in August 1991.

Even though worldwide sales of Rogaine (Regaine) approached $150 million in 1991 and cumulative sales of the product exceeded $500 million since its commercialization, several issues were apparent. First, Rogaine had not achieved its sales potential according to pharmaceutical industry observers. For example, Wall Street financial analysts believed Rogaine's ability to reverse some forms of baldness in men would rapidly produce $400 to $500 million in annual sales.[3] Marketing analysts also expressed doubts about the marketing program behind Rogaine. According to one analyst:

> Upjohn Co.'s Rogaine has failed to develop into the "miracle" hair-restorer everyone anticipated. Instead, the prescription drug has fizzled, failing to arouse much interest from the millions of men originally expected to rush to buy the first proven baldness treatment.[4]

Responding to comments such as this, a company spokesperson noted: "There were no textbooks to go to. We've had to write the book as we've gone along."[5] A

---

[1]Stuart Elliott, "Upjohn Turns to Women to Increase Rogaine Sales," *Advertising Age* (January 2, 1992): 4; "Rogaine for Women Gets $20MM in Support," *Advertising Age* (January 6, 1992): 1, 8.

[2]William G. Flanagan and David Stix, "The Bald Truth," *Forbes* (July 22, 1991): 309–310.

[3]"For Rogaine, No Miracle Cure—Yet," *Business Week* (June 4, 1990): 100. The Upjohn Company has neither confirmed nor denied these sales projections.

[4]Laurie Freeman, "Can Rogaine Make Gains via Ads?" *Advertising Age* (September 11, 1989): 12.

[5]Stuart Elliott, "Upjohn Turns to Women to Increase Rogaine Sales," *Advertising Age* (January 2, 1992): 4.

This case was prepared by Professor Roger A. Kerin, of the Edwin L. Cox School of Business, Southern Methodist University, as a basis for class discussion and is not designed to illustrate effective or ineffective handling of an administrative situation. This case is based on published sources, including the Upjohn Company Annual Reports and 10-K reports, and interviews with individuals knowledgeable about the industry. Quotes, statistics, and published operating information are footnoted for reference purposes. Copyright © by Roger A. Kerin. No part of this case may be reproduced without the written permission of the copyright holder.

second issue concerned the U.S. patent for Rogaine. The patent was due to expire in 1996. While the ultimate sales and profit impact of this factor was yet to be determined, sales of Regaine, the foreign equivalent of Rogaine, had recently plateaued in the face of competition from generic brands and substitute products entering foreign markets.[6] Moreover, pharmaceutical industry analysts estimate that it was common for patented drugs to lose up to 60 percent of their volume within six months after their patent expired.[7] A third issue concerned the dollar sales growth of Rogaine in the United States (see Exhibit 1). Even though Rogaine continued to post dollar sales gains, the growth rate had slowed, according to industry analysts' estimates, even with average price increases in the range of 3 to 4 percent per year.[8]

FDA approval to market Rogaine to women in the United States was expected to broaden the target market for the product by making its potential use more widespread. An estimated 20 million women in the United States are experiencing hair loss. Survey research indicates that 38.6 percent of women say they would seek treatment if they were losing their hair compared with 30.4 percent of men who say they

EXHIBIT 1

Rogaine and Regaine Dollar Sales, 1989–1991 (Sales Reported Using Manufacturer Prices)

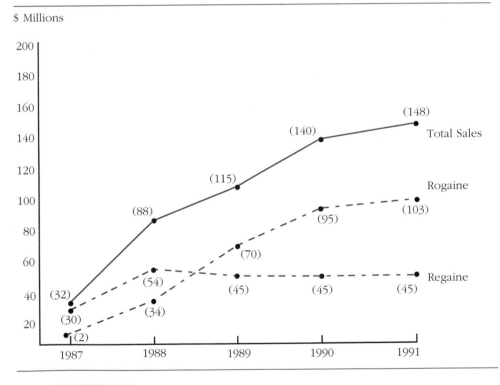

$ Millions

6 *The Upjohn Company Annual Report: 1991*, p. 20.

7 Patricia Winters, "Prescription Drug Ads Up," *Advertising Age* (January 18, 1993): 10, 50.

8 Sales figures and price information were obtained from estimates made by Bear, Stearns & Company and Prudential-Bache industry analysts and data reported in "For Rogaine, No Miracle Cure—Yet," *Business Week* (June 4, 1990): 100; "Blondes, Brunettes, Redheads, and Rogaine," *American Druggist* (June 1992): 39–40.

would seek treatment. However, this research also reported that 13.3 percent of surveyed women who were actually experiencing hair loss actually sought treatment, while 9.9 percent of men experiencing hair loss actually sought treatment.[9] Converting these potential users into actual users has been a continuing challenge for the Upjohn Company and raises a variety of important questions. For example, what is a realistic sales potential for Rogaine use by men and women in the United States through 1995? What, for instance, may be potential sources of consumer resistance to the product, and how might they be overcome for Rogaine to achieve its sales potential? How might the Rogaine marketing strategy be modified in the United States so that the product achieves its sales potential and does so profitably?

TREATMENTS FOR BALDING

There are about 300,000 hairs on the scalp of a person considered to have a "full" head of hair.[10] The exact number of hairs on a person's head depends on the number of hair follicles, which is established before birth. On average, a person will shed 100 to 150 hairs per day from the scalp, and a new hair begins to emerge from the follicle. However, many people experience permanent hair loss on the scalp. Called *androgenetic alopecia*, both men and women can have this condition. With male pattern baldness, the most common form of *alopecia*, normal hair is lost initially from the temples and crown, where it is replaced by fine, downy hair. The affected area gradually becomes wider as the line of normal hair recedes. This process of hair loss is inherited and the typical progression in men is shown in Exhibit 2. Women also experience hair loss, a condition referred to as diffuse hair loss. This condition is manifested by thinning hair all over the head, rather

EXHIBIT 2

Typical Progression of Male Pattern Baldness

[9]Laurie Freeman, "Upjohn Takes a Shine to Balding Women," *Advertising Age* (February 27, 1989): S1. These statistics are based on a Gallup Organization survey of 1,000 adults in the United States.

[10]This material is based on Charles B. Clayman, ed., *The American Medical Association Encyclopedia of Medicine* (New York: Random House, 1989), 88, 504; William G. Flanagan and David Stix, "The Bald Truth," *Forbes* (July 22, 1991): 309–310; "Baldness: Is There Hope?" *Consumer Reports* (September 1988): 533–547.

than the progression typical of male pattern baldness, although young women and women who have passed menopause occasionally exhibit this progression.

People with hair loss who seek remedies have numerous options to treat this condition. The most popular treatments involve prescription and nonprescription hair shampoos, lotions, and conditioners. These hair-thickening products are often used to treat thinning hair. It is estimated that there are 30 million balding men in the United States and they spend upward of $300 million annually on these kinds of products. Exhibit 3 shows the amount of money men and women are willing to spend per year for the treatment of balding. Hairpieces or wigs, hair transplants, and prescription drugs, such as Rogaine, can be used when hair loss is prominent.

Hairpieces or Wigs

Hairpieces (or toupees) and wigs are worn by over 2 million Americans. About $350 million is spent annually for these products, including periodic cleaning and styling. Hairpieces and wigs can be made from real human hair or from synthetic material, usually nylon. Hairpieces made from human hair usually last no more than one year. Synthetic hair will last up to two years. The cost of a small filler hairpiece for a balding man's crown and made from human hair can be purchased for as little as $325; a full women's wig can cost $2,000 or more. A typical man's hairpiece made of human hair costs from $1,000 to $3,500. Synthetic hairpieces for men cost between $1,800 and $2,500. Hairpieces require maintenance every two to four weeks with the average cost for cleaning and styling being $40. Spirit gum or a double-faced tape is used to hold the hairpiece or wig on the scalp.

Hair Transplants

A hair transplant consists of a surgical cosmetic operation in which hairy sections of the scalp are removed and transplanted to hairless areas. One or a combination of the following procedures may be used. "Punch grafting" is the most common procedure. With this procedure, a punch is used to remove small areas of bald scalp (about one-quarter

EXHIBIT 3

Amount that Adults in the United States are Willing to Spend for the Treatment of Balding

Amount	Men	Women
$1,000–$10,000	11.3%	11.1%
600–1,000	7.1	5.3
300–599	13.5	9.7
100–299	14.2	13.5
99 or less	27.0	28.5
Don't Know	26.9	31.9
	100.%	100.0%

Source: Gallup Organization Survey of 1,000 U.S. adults commissioned by *Advertising Age.* Reported in Laurie Freeman, "Upjohn Takes a Shine to Balding Women," *Advertising Age* (February 27, 1989): S1. Reproduced with the permission of *Advertising Age.*

inch across), which are replaced with areas of hairy scalp. The grafts are taped into position until the natural healing process takes effect. "Strip grafting" is a procedure whereby strips of bald skin are removed from the scalp and replaced with strips of hairy scalp that are stitched into position. "Flap grafting" is similar to strip grafting, except that flaps of hairy skin are lifted from the scalp, swiveled, and stitched to replace areas of bald skin. This procedure is typically used to form a new hairline. "Male pattern baldness reduction" consists of cutting out areas of bald scalp and then stretching surrounding areas of hairy scalp to replace the bald area. Hair transplants, no matter how successful, do not last indefinitely. As time passes, transplanted areas become bald.

Approximately $250 million is spent each year for hair transplants in the United States. Hair transplant procedures of the grafting variety cost patients $10,000 to $15,000. Male pattern baldness reduction often costs $1,500 to $2,000. These procedures are usually not covered by medical insurance.

Prescription Drugs

Although many topical ointments and elixirs are promoted, only one product has been approved by the FDA as a drug to restore hair growth for men and women. Rogaine Topical Solution, produced by the Upjohn Company, received FDA approval for use by men in the United States in August 1988 and for women in August 1991. Rogaine is a 2 percent solution of minoxidil that is applied twice daily to areas of the scalp that have thinning hair or no hair. Based on clinical tests conducted by the Upjohn Company, investigators concluded that 39 percent of patients achieved moderate to dense hair growth after one year—a claim approved by the FDA. Hair growth appeared to be more pronounced for patients under 30 years of age and those in the early stages of the male pattern baldness progression. An estimated 35 percent of men under age 30 experience hair loss. The properties of minoxidil and its use as a topical ointment for hair growth are such that if not applied twice daily, hair loss results. In other words, minoxidil is a lifetime treatment if its effects on hair growth and retention are to be permanent.

Treatment with Rogaine requires a physician's prescription. A one-month supply of the product typically costs a patient $50 to $60 and up to $125 if the product is used in high concentrations, or if mixed with other drugs such as Retin-A. In addition, periodic physician office fees can raise the annual patient cost for treatment. Rogaine is not typically covered by medical insurance.

THE UPJOHN COMPANY

The Upjohn Company, with corporate headquarters in Kalamazoo, Michigan, is a Fortune 500 company and is one of the largest drug manufacturing firms in the United States based on annual sales. In addition, the company ranks highly in the *Fortune* magazine poll of "most admired" corporations in the United States. In 1991, the company recorded net sales of $3.4 billion and net earnings of $537.4 million (see Exhibit 4 for summary revenue and expense information). Approximately 37 percent of company sales come from operations outside the United States.

The company operates in two business segments: (1) human health care and (2) agricultural business. Human health care accounted for 80.5 percent of sales and 92 percent of company operating profit in 1991.

EXHIBIT 4

The Upjohn Company Net Sales and Disposition of Net Sales Dollar, 1988–1991 (Year End, December 31)

	1988	*1989*	*1990*	*1991*
NET SALES (in millions)	$2,524.1	$2,724.8	$3,020.9	$3,401.8
DISPOSITION OF NET SALES DOLLAR:				
Cost of products sold	31¢	30¢	27¢	26¢
Marketing and administration	37¢	38¢	38¢	39¢
Research and development	14¢	14¢	14¢	14¢
Restructuring, nonrecurring and discontinued operations	—	7¢	—	—
Income taxes	5¢	5¢	6¢	5¢
Net earnings	13¢	6¢	15¢	16¢
	$1.00	$1.00	$1.00	$1.00

Source: The Upjohn Company Annual Report: 1988–1991.

Human Health Care Business

The Upjohn Company engages primarily in the research, development, production, and marketing of prescription pharmaceuticals, including central nervous system agents, nonsteroidal anti-inflammatory and analgesic agents, antibiotics, steroids, oral antidiabetes agents, and a hair growth product—Rogaine Topical Solution.[11] The company produces two major drugs for central nervous system disorders. Xanox tablets are used for symptomatic relief of anxiety with and without depressive symptoms and for the treatment of panic disorder. Halcion tablets are a hypnotic agent for the treatment of insomnia. The company's two major nonsteroidal anti-inflammatory and analgesic agents are Ansaid tablets and Motrin tablets. Ansaid tablets are used for the treatment of osteoarthritis and rheumatoid arthritis. Motrin tablets are used in the treatment of rheumatoid arthritis and osteoarthritis and as a general analgesic for mild to moderate pain, including dysmennorrhea. Micronase tablets are the company's major oral antidiabetes agent. In March 1992, the company received FDA approval to market Glynase PresTab tablets for the treatment of non-insulin-dependent diabetes. The company's broad line of antibiotic products includes Cleocin Phosphate Sterile Solution for the treatment of certain life-threatening anaerobic infections and Lincocin, which is used to treat serious infections caused by many strains of gram-positive bacteria. The company also markets several steroid hormones for a variety of uses, including the treatment of allergic reactions, inflammation, asthma, and certain hormone deficiencies.

The Upjohn Company also manufactures and distributes many other familiar products that do not require a prescription, including Motrin IB Tablets and Caplets, used as an analgesic; Kaopectate products, for diarrhea; Cortaid products, which are anti-inflammatory topical products containing hydrocortisone; the family of Unicap vitamin products; Dramamine products, which are anti–motion sickness medicines acquired from the Procter and Gamble Company; and Mycitracin, an antibiotic ointment for treatment of minor skin infections and burns. The company also holds a

---

[11]This material is based on *The Upjohn Company Annual Report: 1991* and 10-K Report.

license from Hoechst-Roussel Pharmaceuticals Inc. for exclusive U.S. rights to the nonprescription laxative products Doxidan and Surfak.

Competition in the human health-care business is intense. There are at least 50 competitors in the United States that market prescription and nonprescription pharmaceutical products. Companies compete on the basis of product development and their effectiveness in introducing new or improved products for the treatment and prevention of disease. Other competitive features include product quality, pricing to and through marketing channels, and the dissemination of technical information and medical support and advice to health care professionals.

The Upjohn Company pharmaceutical sales force of 3,800 technically trained representatives calls on physicians, pharmacists, hospital personnel, health maintenance organizations (HMOs) and other managed health-care organizations, and wholesale drug outlets. Most sales of pharmaceutical products are made directly to pharmacies, hospitals, chain warehouses, wholesalers, and other distributors, but the company also sells to physicians and governments. Product advertising is directed mostly toward health-care professionals for prescription drugs, while nonprescription drugs, such as Motrin IB, are advertised directly to consumers using broadcast and print media. This practice is necessary because of long-standing FDA regulations that require virtually all prescription drug advertising to list all product use side effects and contraindications. Complete disclosure of such information for the great majority of prescription drugs would be cost-prohibitive for television advertising and print advertisements directed at consumers due to time and space requirements and technical language.

Development of Rogaine Topical Solution[12]

The development of Rogaine can be traced to the mid-1960s when researchers at the Upjohn Company observed that a drug, originally thought to be a possible antacid agent, lowered the blood pressure in laboratory animals. Subsequent research produced a drug, given the generic name minoxidil, which proved to be a potent agent for lowering high blood pressure in humans. Assigned the trade name Loniten, the drug was given FDA approval for marketing in 1979.

Clinical research on minoxidil as an antihypertensive drug led to an unexpected discovery in 1971 when investigators noticed unusual hair growth in some patients who were taking minoxidil orally. Then, in 1973, a patient taking minoxidil for hypertension began to grow hair on a previously bald spot on his head. Additional clinical trials of minoxidil and related studies were conducted between 1977 and 1982 with more than 4,000 patients. The primary clinical study at 27 different testing sites tracked 2,326 patients who were nearly all men in good health, aged 18 to 49 and diagnosed as exhibiting male pattern baldness. This study concluded that a 2 percent minoxidil solution applied twice daily to the head offered the best safety and effectiveness profile for this group. The safety and effectiveness of this solution for people under age 18 were not tested (Rogaine is not recommended for persons under 18 years of age). Some side effects of the drug included itching, skin irritation, and a possible rise in heartbeat. In terms of effectiveness, 48 percent of the patients felt they had achieved moderate to dense hair growth after one year of use.

---

[12]This description is based on *The Upjohn Company Annual Report: 1988*, pp. 10–11; Steven W. Quickel, "Bald Spot," *Business Month* (November 1989); 36–43; "Baldness: Is There Hope?" *Consumer Reports* (September 1988); 533–547.

Investigators felt that 39 percent of the patients achieved moderate to dense hair growth. These data were submitted to the FDA in 1985. The FDA approved the 39 percent moderate to dense hair growth claim. In 1986, the Upjohn Company began selling the 2 percent minoxidil solution outside the United States under the trade name Regaine. However, more stringent and time-consuming review procedures by the FDA slowed the approval process in the United States.

Continued study on minoxidil led company researchers to draw two basic conclusions:

> First, it was clear after four months that topical minoxidil could grow hair on some scalps. Second, efficacy seemed to be related in many cases to the age of the patient, the extent of his baldness and how long he had been bald. Younger men who were not as far into the balding process seemed to respond better to the drug. There are exceptions to this finding, however, and the correlation of age to efficacy has not been scientifically established.[13]

In 1987, the company established the Hairgrowth Research Unit to determine the mechanism of action of minoxidil, develop new and better minoxidil analogs, and investigate other agents that affect hair growth or loss. At the time, researchers could only theorize why minoxidil stimulated hair growth in some patients. According to the company's director of dermatology:

> The most plausible theory is that minoxidil somehow stimulates the matrix cell of the hair follicle to regrow when it is destined to turn off. It's an overcoming of the genetic propensity to shut down. But we don't know how minoxidil modifies the metabolic activity of that cell.[14]

In the same year, the Upjohn Company signed an agreement with the Procter and Gamble Company to "develop improved formulations and delivery systems for topical minoxidil and to engage in research and development of hair growth products."

Two noteworthy developments occurred in 1988. First, an eight-month clinical study on Rogaine use for female hair loss was completed. Clinical studies conducted by physicians in 11 U.S. medical centers involving 256 women with hair loss were reported. Based on patient evaluations of regrowth after eight months, 19 percent of the women using Rogaine had at least moderate regrowth compared with 7 percent of women using a placebo (no active ingredient). No regrowth was reported by 41 percent of the women using Rogaine and 60 percent of the women using a placebo.[15] Clinical reports submitted to the FDA ultimately led to agency approval to market the minoxidil solution to women in August 1991. Pregnant women and nursing mothers were advised not to use Rogaine, however. In August 1988, the FDA granted approval to market the solution to men in the United States. However, the Regaine name was replaced with the Rogaine name because an FDA official believed the Regaine name suggested that the minoxidil solution would result in complete hair growth. During this time, minoxidil had received considerable publicity in the consumer and marketing media and in the financial community as a miracle cure for baldness.[16]

---

[13] *The Upjohn Company Annual Report: 1988*, p. 11.

[14] "Baldness: Is There Hope?" *Consumer Reports* (September 1988): 544.

[15] Based on information reported in Rogaine print advertisement for women.

[16] "The Hottest Products: Baldness Treatment," *Adweek* (November 7, 1988): 6.

MARKETING PROGRAM FOR ROGAINE TOPICAL SOLUTION

Marketing plans for Rogaine in the United States were developed concurrently with the FDA approval process. The announced marketing objective for Rogaine was "to maximize sales of Rogaine in the new U.S. market."[17] Since Rogaine had FDA approval as a prescription drug, Upjohn's initial attention was placed on educating its sales force who called on physicians, dermatologists, and other health-care professionals. Rogaine was introduced to the medical community by its sales force and through advertisements in medical journals and periodicals. An Upjohn Company spokesperson said, "We couldn't begin marketing Rogaine to consumers until we felt the awareness level was adequate in the medical community."[18]

Consumer Advertising Program

Consumer advertising for Rogaine, targeted at 25- to 49-year-old males, began in November 1988 (see Exhibit 5 for an age and income summary for U.S. males and females). This start date, two months earlier than planned, was prompted by slow prescription sales. The television campaign began on November 23, 1988, during ABC's "War and Remembrance" miniseries. The print campaign featured advertisements in popular consumer magazines and newsstand business publications.

Television and print advertising message emphasized a soft-sell that urged consumers to "see your doctor . . . if you're concerned about hair loss." These advertisements contained no mention of Rogaine, since federal regulations at the time prohibited the use of brand names in prescription-drug advertising to consumers. However, the Upjohn Company name appeared in the advertisements. With a sales rate of $4 million per month for the first quarter of 1989, a decision was made to revamp the advertising campaign. The new campaign featured a bald man standing before his bathroom mirror. Like the earlier message, viewers were again urged to see their doctor. Sales improved, reaching $70 million for 1989. A third advertising campaign was developed and launched in February 1990 with print advertisements featuring the Rogaine name for the first time with FDA approval. Advertisement copy emphasized that Rogaine was the only FDA-approved product for hair growth with the headline: "The good news is there's only one product that's proven to grow hair . . . Rogaine." Companion television advertising, however, did not mention Rogaine. Rogaine sales in 1990 totaled $95 million. This campaign continued in 1991; however, the Rogaine name now appeared in television advertisements with FDA approval. Year-end Rogaine sales totaled $103 million in 1991. Industry sources

---

[17] *The Upjohn Company Annual Report: 1988*, p. 11. The following material is based on Stuart Elliott, "Upjohn Turns to Women to Increase Rogaine Sales," *Advertising Age* (January 2, 1992): 4; "Rogaine for Women Gets $20M in Support," *Advertising Age* (January 6, 1992): 1; "New Hope for the Hair-Impaired," *Business Week* (August 17, 1992): 105; "For Rogaine, No Miracle Cure—Yet," *Business Week* (June 4, 1990): 100; "Britain Approves Upjohn Hair Drug," *The New York Times* (April 6, 1990): 4; Laurie Freeman, "Can Rogaine Make Gains via Ads," *Advertising Age* (September 11, 1989): 12; Stephen W. Quickel, "Bald Spot," *Business Month* (November 1989): 36–37ff; Laurie Freeman, "Upjohn Takes a Shine to Balding Women," *Advertising Age* (February 27, 1989): S1; Patricia Winters and Laurie Freeman, "Nicorette, Rogaine Seek TV OK," *Advertising Age* (November 27, 1989): 31; "Minoxidil," *Vogue* (September 1989): 56; "Hair Today: Rogaine's Growing Pains," *New York* (October 30, 1990): 20; "Blondes, Brunettes, Redheads, and Rogaine," *American Druggist* (June 1992): 39–40.

[18] Steven W. Quickel, "Bald Spot," *Business Month* (November 1989): 40.

EXHIBIT 5

Age and Income of Persons in the United States, 1990

Age Category	Persons (millions)	Percent distribution by income level							
		Less than $2,500	$2,500–$4,999	$5,000–$9,999	$10,000–$14,999	$15,000–$24,999	$25,000–$49,999	$50,000–$74,999	$75,000 or more
Males									
15–24	17.4	28.1	15.1	22.0	14.9	14.8	4.9	.3	—
25–34	21.3	3.1	3.7	10.0	13.8	28.6	34.4	4.7	1.7
35–44	19.0	2.6	2.8	6.5	8.3	20.1	41.8	11.8	6.0
45–54	12.4	3.0	2.4	6.3	8.5	18.4	39.3	13.9	8.1
55–64	10.2	3.1	4.1	10.8	11.2	21.1	33.1	10.1	6.4
65 and over	12.5	1.9	5.8	24.7	20.9	24.2	16.0	3.9	2.6
Total Males	92.8								
Females									
15–24	17.5	31.0	19.7	22.8	13.1	10.5	2.7	.1	—
25–34	21.6	15.7	8.8	16.5	15.3	25.0	17.2	1.2	.4
35–44	19.6	14.9	7.6	14.8	13.8	23.0	22.2	2.7	1.0
45–54	13.3	14.7	7.9	15.3	14.2	21.7	22.2	3.0	1.0
55–64	11.2	17.0	14.8	20.4	14.5	17.0	13.0	2.5	.8
65 and over	17.5	5.0	19.4	37.0	16.7	13.8	6.8	.9	.5
Total Females	100.7								

Source: U.S. Bureau of the Census, *Current Population Reports.*

estimated that the amount spent on consumer measured media advertising for Rogaine
was $4,914,500 in 1989, $9,347,500 in 1990, and $3,443,000 in 1991.[19]

Price-Sales Promotion Program

A one-year supply of Rogaine could cost a user between $600 and $720 depending
on pharmacist margins.[20] The total out-of-pocket cost to patients, including periodic
physician office fees, could be as high as $800 to $900 per year, since patients were
advised to visit their physicians twice per year after the initial consultation.

A variety of price incentives and sales promotion activities were also implemented to stimulate physician visits. For instance, the Upjohn Company offered rebates to people who received a Rogaine prescription from their physician. The patient
would either get a certificate worth $10 toward the purchase of the first bottle of
Rogaine, or $20 for sending in the box tops for the first four bottles used. Selected
barbershops and salons were also provided information packets to be given to customers worried about hair loss, including 150,000 copies of informational videos.
Consumer advertising also included an 800 number to call to receive information
about the product. By 1991, some 1 million calls had been made to the Upjohn
Company. It is estimated that the Upjohn Company has spent between $40 and $50
million annually to market Rogaine since its introduction. This cost included professional and consumer advertising, the price-sales promotion program, and selling
expenses.

In September 1991, the price-sales promotion program for Rogaine was the subject of a day-long congressional hearing in Washington, D.C.[21] Several members of
Congress expressed criticism of the practice of using consumer rebates and cash incentives to market a prescription drug. An FDA official said, "We are concerned
about this kind of tactic." Commenting on prescription drug consumer advertising
in general, FDA Commissioner Dr. David Kessler commented, "We believe the public, in general, is not well-served by ads for prescription drugs." An FDA spokesperson later said the agency "will let [the current Rogaine campaign] continue as it is,
though we are not going to tip our hand as to what might happen in the future."

Even though the FDA and some physicians did not favor prescription-drug advertising, consumer response to prescription-drug advertising has been generally favorable.[22] A 1989 survey of 2,000 adult consumers in the United States reported that
40 percent said they had talked to a physician because of an advertisement they had
seen, 72 percent of consumers in the survey said the advertising was an educational
tool, and 71 percent thought prescription-drug advertising was worthwhile.

---

[19]*Measured media* refers to newspapers, consumer magazines and Sunday magazines, outdoor
billboards, network, spot, syndicated and cable television, and network and spot radio. *Unmeasured
media* include direct mail, co-op advertising, couponing, catalogs, and business publications and is not
included in the measured media figures.

[20]Although pharmacy margins varied, pharmacists typically obtained a gross profit margin of 10
percent based on the selling price to the consumer, based on "Blondes, Brunettes, Redheads, and
Rogaine," *American Druggist* (June 1992): 40.

[21]Steven W. Colford and Pat Sloan, "Feds Take Aim at Rogaine Ads," *Advertising Age* (September
16, 1991): 47.

[22]"Upswing Seen in R_x Drug Ads Aimed Directly at Consumer, *American Medical News* (June 1,
1990): 13, 15.

Product and Market Development

The Upjohn Company has continued its product and market development efforts on Rogaine since its introduction in 1988. For example, a different concentration of minoxidil has been examined that would require only one application per day rather than two. This development would improve the product's convenience of use because, as one former company executive conceded, "It's hard to use something twice a day, come hell or high water."[23] Also, an easier-to-use gel is being introduced to Europe. In early 1989, the Upjohn Company introduced Progaine Shampoo, a hair-thickener shampoo product, for use by men and women. This product does not promote hair growth, but serves as a treatment for thinning hair. It is believed the shampoo will benefit form the sound-alike name and be considered a companion to Rogaine. In April 1990, the company received approval to market Rogaine in Great Britain, which opened another market for the product in 1991. By 1991, Rogaine (Regaine) was sold in over 50 countries.

Rogaine for Women[24]

FDA approval for Rogaine use by women was granted in August 1991, and the advertising and promotion program directed at women would begin in February 1992. The female-market entry plan mirrored the marketing program for males, including the same price and reference to the Rogaine name in advertisements. Extensive use of consumer print advertising was scheduled to appear in *Cosmopolitan*, *People*, *US*, *Vogue*, and *Woman's Day*, as well as other magazines. The advertising copy for Rogaine advertising directed toward women would differ from that used for men, however, because the topic of hair loss is discussed among men, but less often among women. According to an Upjohn Company official, women who suffer from hair loss "feel very much alone because no one talks about it."[25] This view would materialize in the message conveyed in Rogaine print advertisements for women. For example, a woman in a Rogaine print advertisement says: "Finally I can do a lot more about my hair loss than just sit back and take it." The advertisement concludes by saying: "Take the control you've always wanted, and do it now." Television commercials were also scheduled to appear in major U.S. metropolitan markets during daytime, early evening, and weekend programs on local stations and cable networks. In the television commercials, a woman portraying a news reporter says: "On this job, you cannot do a story until you get the facts. So when I heard about Rogaine with minoxidil, I wanted to get all the facts for myself."

The price-sales promotion program would include a $10 incentive to visit a physician or dermatologist and an 800 number to call to receive an informational brochure about the product. Brochures will be made available at drugstores and doctors' offices. An extensive professional effort evident in journal advertising, direct mail, and sales-staff support would launch the product, including new print and video materials for pharmacists. The total marketing budget for the female market was reported to be $20 million.

---

[23]"For Rogaine, No Miracle Cure—Yet," *Business Week* (June 4, 1990): 100.

[24]This discussion is based on "Blondes, Brunettes, Redheads, and Rogaine," *American Druggist* (June 1992): 39–40; Steven W. Colford and Pat Sloan, "Feds Take Aim at Rogaine Ads," *Advertising Age* (September 16, 1991): 47; Stuart Elliott, "Upjohn Turns to Women to Increase Rogaine Sales," *Advertising Age* (January 2, 1992): 4.

[25]Stuart Elliott, "Upjohn Turns to Women to Increase Rogaine Sales," *Advertising Age* (January 2, 1992): 4.

Nestlé Italy

Giorgio Baruffa, Product Manager for Nescafé instant coffee at Nestlé Italy, was considering options for the future marketing strategy of the brand. Nescafé had been marketed in Italy for 30 years but held less than a 1 percent share of the Italian coffee market. In a recent single city test, Nescafé had experimented with a 14 percent price decrease with the objective of increasing market share. The price reduction increased short–term sales volume by 25 percent, but did not have a sustained impact on market share and weakened user and nonuser perceptions of Nescafé's quality and reliability.

Mr. Bechi, Marketing Director of Nestlé Italy, and Mr. Baruffa called a meeting in March 1989 to discuss Nescafé's strategic options. The group—which included Mr. Mazzei, the Chief Financial Officer, Mr. Giuliani, head of strategic planning, and Mr. Baruffa's brand assistant—had to decide whether Nescafé should aim to penetrate further its current target market or seek out one or more new target groups.

COMPANY BACKGROUND

Nestlé was founded in Switzerland in 1866 to process dairy products. Nestlé became well known as a manufacturer of infant feeding formulas, developing successful products such as Nestlé Powdered Milk and Condensed Milk. The company grew through new product introductions and acquisitions of other companies, both inside and outside the food industry. By 1988, Nestlé S.A. generated revenues of $20 billion. It had 160,000 employees working in 200 plants worldwide. Decision-making responsibility was decentralized to ensure that the operating unit in each country responded to local market conditions. Nestlé competed worldwide in a variety of product groups including:

- Chocolate, with the Gala and Frigor brands
- Instant coffee, with the Taster's Choice and Nescafé brands
- Instant beverages, with the Nesquick (or Quik) and Orzoro brands
- Soups and bouillon cubes, with the Maggi brand
- Preserves and fruit juices
- Pharmaceuticals and cosmetics, with the L'Oreal line

Nestlé was the world's largest buyer of raw coffee beans and a major producer of instant coffee. In the 1930s, when raw coffee supply exceeded demand, Nestlé re-

Professor John A. Quelch prepared this case in association with Michele Costabile, SDA Bocconi, Italy, as the basis for class discussion rather than to illustrate either effective or ineffective handling of an administrative situation. Copyright © 1992 by the President and Fellows of Harvard College. No part of this publication may be reproduced, stored in a retrieval system, used in a spreadsheet, or transmitted in any form or by any means—electronic, mechanical, photocopying, recording, or otherwise—without the permission of Harvard Business School. Used with permission.

searchers perfected a dehydration process to preserve coffee in a concentrated and soluble form while maintaining its flavor and aroma. The Nescafé brand of instant coffee was launched in 1938 just before World War II. It was adopted by the armed forces due to its convenience and ease of use. Instant coffee quickly gained worldwide acceptance. By 1988, the world drank more than 170 million cups of Nescafé a day. In 1988, Nestlé's advertising budget to promote Nescafé worldwide was $312 million.

Nestlé Italy, a Milan-based company, sold over 80 products in 10 categories and generated about $1 billion in sales in 1988. Nestlé Italy was the share leader in milk modifiers (with Nesquick) and instant coffee. In Italy, Nescafé was offered in three blends: Nescafé Classic, Nescafé Gran Aroma (a stronger, premium quality coffee), and Nescafé Relax (a decaffeinated coffee). Nescafé contributed 3 percent of Nestlé Italy revenues and 7 percent of net profits in 1988. Nescafé accounted for 5 percent of Nestlé Italy's total advertising expenditures and 2 percent of total consumer and trade promotion expenditures.

COFFEE CONSUMPTION IN ITALY

The Arabs discovered the process of roasting coffee beans at the end of the fourteenth century. Since then, coffee had been consumed both in the home and in public as a social beverage. From the eighteenth century, coffeehouses in Europe were patronized by intellectuals who used the stimulus of the aromatic beverage to sustain their poetic or political dissertation. In Italy, coffeehouses were once called "schools of knowledge."

The range of blends, degree of roasting, methods of preparation, and reasons for coffee consumption varied widely across countries. Different consumer segments viewed coffee as a stimulant, as a thirst quencher, or, when mixed with a small amount of water, as an elixir.

In 1988, the highest per capita coffee consumption was in Scandinavia at 12 kg., followed by the Netherlands (9), Germany (7), France (6), United States (4.6), Italy (4.3), United Kingdom (2), Greece (2), and Spain (2). The Italian instant coffee market was comparatively underdeveloped. In Italy, instant coffee accounted for 1 percent of total coffee consumption in 1988 versus 8 percent in the Netherlands, 10 percent in Germany, 30 percent in France, 34 percent in the United States, 37 percent in Spain, 51 percent in Greece, and over 90 percent in the United Kingdom and Ireland.

Nestlé executives identified several consumer trends that could affect the consumption and marketing of coffee in Italy. These included:

- An increase in adult women in the work force to over 30 percent in 1988. This resulted in more food consumption outside the home and increased purchases of ready-to-eat, frozen, and other convenience foods.

- Increased international travel, both into and out of the country, which exposed Italians to the food consumption habits of other cultures.

- Lower birthrates and longer life spans, causing an aging of the population and a reduction in average household size. The number of Italians over 55 years was expected to increase to 31 percent of the population by 1997. The average disposable income of this group was also rising significantly.

- A greater awareness of health issues in the diet. As a result, there was increased interest in consumption of fresh, authentic products, especially among

TABLE A

Coffee Consumption in Italy

Age	% Who Usually Drink Coffee	Average Annual per Capita Consumption (kg)	% of Total Consumption	% of Italian Population[a]
15–24	50	3.04	12.4	16.5
25–34	70	4.36	20.5	14.2
34–45	81	4.60	23.0	13.1.
45–54	83	4.90	24.0	12.6
55–69	67	3.13	15.1	15.6
70+	60	1.86	5.0	9.7

[a]18.3% of the population was under 15 years in 1988.

better-educated young people. For example, fruit and vegetable consumption increased 12 percent from 1986 to 1988. Similarly, nonalcoholic beverage consumption increased by over 30 percent between 1983 and 1988, with mineral water up 35 percent soft drinks up 32 percent, and fruit juices up 40 percent.

Many younger, more health-conscious Italian consumers perceived coffee as an unhealthy beverage. In 1988, the highest level of coffee consumption was among the 45–54 age group, as shown in Table A.

INDUSTRY STRUCTURE AND COMPETITION

The structure of the Italian coffee market is shown in chart form in Exhibit 1. Around 750 firms produced their own blends of roast and ground coffee, buying raw coffee beans either directly from growers or, in the case of the smaller producers, from importers or agents. The coffee roasters sold their blends through retailers to the end consumer (the "family segment") and/or through coffeehouses, restaurants, and other institutional outlets (the "CHR segment"). As shown in Exhibit 2, the CHR segment accounted for 31 percent of the coffee volume consumed in Italy in 1988 but 80 percent of the associated consumer expenditures. Consumption of instant and decaffeinated coffee was minimal. The total volume of coffee consumed was expected to grow 2 percent annually.

Factory sales of coffee in Italy in 1988 approached 1,700 billion lire, as indicated in Exhibit 3.[1] Low entry barriers, regional taste preferences, minimal overheads, and entrenched distribution explained the continued survival of many small coffee roasters each serving a town or a region. However, the combined market share of the national producers was increasing. In 1988, the top four national coffee roasters controlled 42 percent of the market, while the next four companies accounted for a further 10 percent. They enjoyed the efficiencies of national advertising and distribution, quantity discounts when purchasing coffee beans on the world market, and greater negotiating power with the trade. They tended to offer more complete product lines than the smaller and medium-sized producers and to initiate packaging innovations such as the vacuum pack. Exhibit 4 summarizes the retail penetration by type of

---

[1] In 1988, $1 was equivalent to 1,500 lira.

EXHIBIT 1

The Structure of the Italian Coffee Market

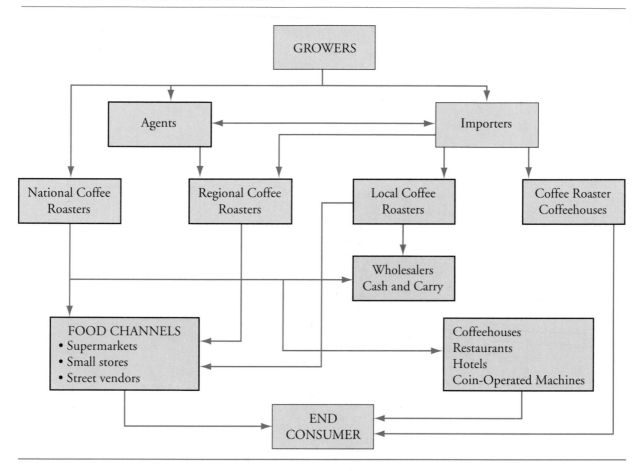

channel and number of items stocked per outlet for the major producers. Exhibit 5 plots the principal competitors on two strategic maps.

With industry consolidation, advertising expenditures on brands of coffee more than doubled between 1985 and 1988, as indicated in Exhibit 6. Likewise, the advertising-to-sales ratios of most major producers also rose, as shown in Exhibit 7.

The principal competitors in the Italian coffee market were as follows:

Lavazza S.p.A., a family-owned company based in Turin, held the largest share of the coffee market, and was the tenth largest food company in Italy. Lavazza was the only company to offer a complete line of nationally distributed products. Lavazza offered 11 brands and blends at different price-quality points but all advertised under the Lavazza umbrella. One of these brands was Bourbon roast and ground, which until 1987, was owned by Nestlé.

Lavazza accounted for 40 percent of coffee advertising in Italy. A well-known television advertisement involved a testimonial by an Italian actor, which reaffirmed the "Italian" quality of Lavazza coffee and concluded with the selling line, "the more

EXHIBIT 2

Italian Coffee Market, 1988 Retail Sales (In Thousands of Tons and Billion Lire)

	Family Segment				CHR Segment				Total			
	Volume (000 tons)	Percent	Value (billion lire)	Percent	Volume (000 tons)	Percent	Value (billion lire)	Percent	Volume (000 tons)	Percent	Value (billion lire)	Percent
Normal	144.9	69%	2,105	20%	65.1	31%	8,267	80%	210.0	97%	10,372	95%
Decaf	2.9	58	48	10	2.2	42	410	90	5.1	2	457	4
Instant	0.7	88	69	49	0.1	12	72	51	0.8	1	141	1
Total	148.5	69%	2,222	20%	67.4	31%	8,749	80%	215.9	100%	10,970	100%

Note: "Normal" refers to regular roast and ground coffee. "Instant" includes decaffeinated instant.

EXHIBIT 3

A. Roast and Ground Coffee: Italian Market Shares of Main Producers by Segment, 1988

	Family Segment				CHR Segment			
	Quantity (000 tons)		Factory Prices (billion lire)		Quantity (000 tons)		Factory Prices (billion lire)	
Lavazza	42.0	30.7%	405	34.6%	3.0	6.5%	35	6.7%
Procter & Gamble	12.3	9.0	108	9.2	-	-	-	-
Café do Brasil	10.2	7.4	83	7.1	0.5	1.1	4	0.8
Illy Caffé	0.4	0.3	6	0.5	1.5	3.2	30	5.7
Segafredo	4.4	3.2	37	3.2	4.3	9.4	45	8.5
Sao Café	7.0	5.1	58	5.0	-	-	-	-
Total Market	137		1,170		45.7		520	

B. Instant Coffee: Italian Market Shares of Main Producers, 1988

	Quantity (tons)	Percent	Value (billion lire)	Percent
Nestlé	650	77.7%	35	80.0%
Crippa & Berger	110	13.1	7	15.9
Others	76	9.2	2	4.1
Total Market	836	100.0%	44	100.0%

you push it down, the more it pulls you up!" The company also sponsored the 1988 World Cup Ski Championships in an effort to present a more youthful image.

2) Segafredo-Zanetti, S.p.A., of Bologna produced roast and ground coffee and was the first company to introduce a combination pack of two 250-gram vacuum-packed bags of coffee for the family segment. Previously, Segafredo had sold only in the CHR segment for which it also produced espresso machines sold under the Segafredo name. The company's communications program concentrated on sponsorships of national and international sporting events.

EXHIBIT 4

Retail Penetration and Average Number of SKUs (Stockkeeping Units) by Channel for Principal Coffee Brands, October 1988

	Hypermarkets		Supermarkets		Convenience Stores	
Lavazza	100.0%	12.2	100.0%	11.1	95.5%	10.9
Procter & Gamble	100.0	5.9	94.6	5.9	95.5	4.7
Nestlé	100.0	5.7	100.0	7.2	100.0	6.1
Crippa & Berger	100.0	5.5	100.0	5.4	95.5	3.6
Café do Brasil	30.4	2.2	8.9	3.0	25.5	1.5
Illy Caffé	10.5	2.0	15.7	2.0	5.5	1.0
Segafredo	69.6	3.9	60.7	3.9	9.1	2.0
Sao Café	69.6	4.5	70.5	4.5	40.5	3.0

EXHIBIT 5

Italian Coffee Market Strategic Groups

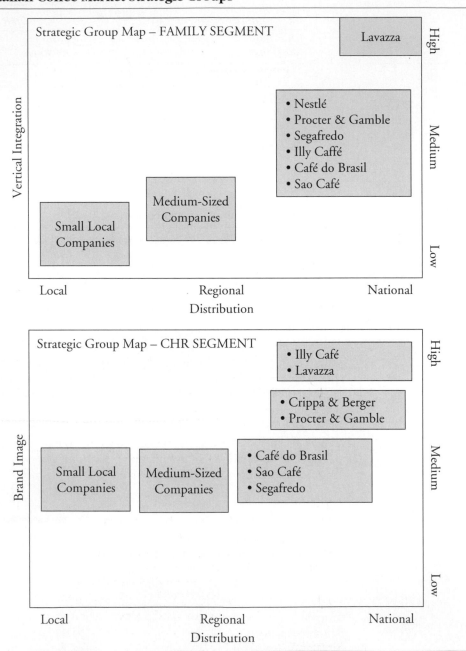

Strategic Group Map – FAMILY SEGMENT

Lavazza   High

Vertical Integration

• Nestlé
• Procter & Gamble
• Segafredo   Medium
• Illy Caffé
• Café do Brasil
• Sao Café

Medium-Sized
Companies

Small Local
Companies   Low

Local   Regional   National
Distribution

Strategic Group Map – CHR SEGMENT

• Illy Café   High
• Lavazza

• Crippa & Berger
• Procter & Gamble

Brand Image

Small Local   Medium-Sized   • Café do Brasil   Medium
Companies   Companies   • Sao Café
                                           • Segafredo

                                                                              Low

Local   Regional   National
Distribution

EXHIBIT 6

Roast and Ground Coffee: Percentages of Total Media Advertising Expenditures in Italy of Major Producers, 1985–1988

Company	1985	1986	1987	1988
Lavazza	36%	46%	34%	40%
Procter & Gamble	24	24	27	20
Nestlé	14	12	-	-
Café do Brasil	-	7	11	14
Illy Caffé	3	4	7	6
Segafredo-Zanetti	1	-	5	7
Sao Café	9	3	4	1
Mauro	3	4	5	6
Altri	10	-	6	6
Total (%)	100%	100%	100%	100%
Billions of lire	48	68	85	129

Source: Company records and AGB.

Note: Nestlé sold its brand of roast and ground coffee in 1987.

3) Crippa and Berger of Milan was the first company to market decaffeinated coffee in Italy. This company competed directly with Nestlé through its own brand of instant coffee, Faemino. Crippa and Berger's other brands were Gah (low caffeine and low fat) and Hag, which held 65 percent of the decaffeinated market compared to 27 percent for Lavazza's decaffeinated brand.

C&B invested 28 percent of sales in advertising in 1988, two-thirds of which was spent on promoting Hag. The advertising was aimed at justifying the premium price of the Hag brand to both the family and the CHR segments. The company did not support Faemino with significant advertising.

4) Procter and Gamble Italia, a subsidiary of the Cincinnati-based company, marketed the Splendid brand. Distribution penetration was excellent thanks to the coverage achieved by P&G's sales force in marketing the company's broad product line. Splendid was promoted through sponsored television programs with high viewer ratings.

In 1988, Splendid Decaffeinato was introduced and allocated an advertising budget of $15 million, more than that for Splendid roast and ground. In 1988, P&G increased its advertising-to-sales ratio to 37 percent compared to 8.5 percent for the category as a whole. Splendid Oro and Classic were advertised as the coffees used in the most prestigious restaurants, while Decaffeinato was targeted at large families.

5) Illy Caffé of Trieste produced a single blend of ground coffee with seven different levels of roasting. Illy Caffé was known for its excellent quality and also marketed a line of decaffeinated and low caffeine coffees under the Mite brand name. Illy advertising emphasized the brand's comparative superiority. "The best, maestro," was the answer of an American patron in an Italian coffeeshop when asked his judgment of Illy coffee.

6) Consorzio Sao Caffé was a consortium of eight local producers formed in 1973 to pool their resources behind a single brand. The consortium advertised its Sao brand on the basis of the quality implied by its Brazilian-sounding name.

EXHIBIT   7

Coffee: Advertising Expenditures as a Percentage of Sales for Major Italian Coffee Brands, 1986–1988

Company	Advertising Investments (billions of lire)			Advertising as Percentage of Total Sales		
	1986	1987	1988	1986	1987	1988
Lavazza	40.0	34.0	62.0	6.6%	6.8%	11.8%
Procter & Gamble	16.0	22.6	40.4	10.2	18.3	36.6
Nestlé	16.8	7.4	4.3	17.7	9.1	5.9
Crippa & Berger	6.0	7.6	13.2	9.2	15.2	28.1
Café do Brasil	5.0	9.4	18.0	4.8	10.1	20.0
Illy Caffé	3.0	6.0	7.4	8.4	15.9	16.8
Segafredo	-	4.3	9.5	NS	4.6	9.0
Sao Café	2.0	3.5	1.3	2.3	5.2	2.2
Mauro	3.0	4.3	7.6	6.0	10.5	22.4

Source: Company records and AGB.

Note: Data included expenditures in support of decaffeinated and instant coffees as well as roast and ground.

Breakdown of Advertising by Product Type for Three Major Producers, 1988

Lavazza	17.4% Decaf
	82.6% Roast and Ground
Nestlé	9.5% Decaf
	90.5% Regular and Instant
Crippa & Berger	68.7% Decaf (HAG)
	31.3% Roast and Ground

Café do Brasil marketed Café Kimbo, a brand favored in southern Italy. Café Kimbo had gained market share rapidly as a result of competitive pricing and memorable advertising. In its television commercial, a well-known anchorperson tasted the coffee in a roasting plant and emphasized the freshness and rich taste of the Kimbo brand.

MARKETING COFFEE

Most of the national brands offered the consumer several blends in a variety of packages. Some producers bought instant and/or decaffeinated coffee from other firms to sell under their own brand names.

During most of the 1980s, a worldwide surplus of coffee beans depressed raw material prices. The consequent cost savings enabled producers to offer higher-quality blends without increasing retail prices. By 1988, 4 million Italian households made coffee at home with restaurant-style espresso machines, and they were particularly interested in premium quality blends.

The major brands were distributed through both the family and CHR segments. It was hard for producers to ensure that coffee served in coffeehouses was identified by brand. However, because many consumers believed that coffee made in a coffeehouse was better than that made at home, a strong brand presence in the CHR segment could help a brand's retail image.

Retailers selected coffees to stock on the basis of brand reputation, margin, and turnover, periodic trade discounts and "three-for-two" consumer promotions. For CHR operators, brand name was less important than consistent quality at a competitive price and, for smaller outlets, the leasing and servicing of espresso machines.

Coffee was sold to the family segment in 200- to 250-gram bags (49 percent volume share), 400- to 500-gram bags (38 percent), 500 gram tins (4 percent) and 1-kg. bags (9 percent). Pliable bags replaced tins in the 1980s as the principal form of packaging. Vacuum-sealed packages with double wrapping were introduced by the leading producers in 1985 to extend the shelf life of ground coffee. Instant coffee including Nescafé was available in small glass jars containing 50 to 125 grams. Research showed that Nescafé's glass jar, large lid, and granular appearance were not associated with "real" coffee.

Details of the cost structures for roast and ground coffee, Nescafé instant coffee, and espresso sold through CHR outlets are presented in Exhibit 8. The average producer price of a kilo of roasted coffee in 1988 was 10,400 lira (including a 6 percent government tax). A kilo of decaffeinated coffee sold for 30,000 lira and a kilo of instant coffee, which produced four times as many servings as the equivalent weight of roast and ground, cost 51,000 lira.

CHR operators paid producers, on average, 18,000 lira (including government tax) for a kilo of roast and ground. The end consumer paid seven to eight times this cost, or 800–900 lira for a cup of espresso coffee using six grams.

EXHIBIT   8

Cost Structures for Roast and Ground Coffee, Nescafé, and Espresso in 1988 (Lire)

	Roast and Ground 250 Gram	Nescafé 125 Gram	Espresso (CHR) 6 Gram
Suggested retailer selling price	3,250	7,500	800
Producer selling price	2,600	6,375	111
Cost of goods sold	2,150	3,160	80
• Manufacturing	1, 490	2,810	56
• Distribution	660	350	24
Contribution margin	450	3,215	31
Sales promotion	45	374	0.3
• Trade	10	250	0.3
• Consumer	35	124	-
Advertising	30	426	0.5
Contribution after marketing expenses	375	2,415	30

NESCAFÉ MARKETING IN ITALY

The flavor of Nescafé in Italy was different from that of Nescafé in other European countries. The roasting and solubilization processes and the raw materials used were specifically adapted to Italian consumer tastes. However, during the 40 years following its launch in Italy in 1938, Nescafé sales grew slowly to only 400 tons by 1978.

Nestlé's main objective when it launched Nescafé was to have the product, although soluble, perceived as "real" coffee. From the outset, Nestlé executives had to combat consumer doubts that a coffee that was easy to prepare could be as good as "real" coffee. Italian consumers aged over 40 perceived Italian espresso as the only "real" coffee flavor and taste, while younger consumers tended to view espresso coffee, like tobacco and alcohol, as "old-fashioned." There was, therefore, a market opportunity for a lighter, good-tasting, and more aromatic coffee. Nescafé advertising aimed to affirm the good taste and quality of Nescafé compared to other Italian coffee. A typical advertisement in the 1970s was, "Hmm, what is it, . . . what's happening . . . smell coffee . . . Nescafé the best of them all." However, most consumers found this direct comparison to "real" coffee unconvincing. Many consumers continued to believe that Nescafé was "missing something" and was no substitute for "real" coffee. Nescafé was viewed as a back-up product for emergency use and best suited for singles and older people.

Image-tracking studies between 1978 and 1988 showed that Nescafé users and nonusers perceived both taste and flavor improvements. However, as indicated in Exhibit 9, Nescafé was often seen as a coffee used by lonely and/or lazy people. From 1979 to 1983, Nescafé tried a more "personal" advertising campaign, which did not focus solely on the product but, rather, showed "typical" people in the work force (a forest ranger, a dockworker, and a train conductor) enjoying Nescafé. The campaign aimed to show that Nescafé was for anyone who "wants something more out of life" and "gives something more to it." A print advertisement from the campaign is presented in Exhibit 10. The advertising campaign was reinforced with sampling programs and displays at the point of purchase.

EXHIBIT 9

Selected Results of Nescafé Image Tracking Study, 1978–1988

	Total Italy				*Total Nescafé Users*			
	1978	*1981*	*1985*	*1988*	*1978*	*1981*	*1985*	*1988*
Nescafé has:								
- a good taste	2.2	2.3	2.5	2.6	2.4	3.1	3.4	3.6
- no flavor	3.4	3.6	3.0	3.0	3.3	3.1	2.4	2.2
Nescafé is:								
- a sad product	3.2	2.9	2.6	2.7	3.0	2.2	1.9	1.7
- coffee with other ingredients	2.9	2.8	2.6	2.5	3.4	4.1	4.2	4.3
- convenient	3.1	3.1	3.2	3.2	3.4	4.1	4.2	4.3
- for lonely people	2.9	2.8	2.9	2.7	3.1	3.4	3.3	3.3
- for lazy people	3.5	3.7	3.5	3.6	3.5	3.5	3.3	3.6

Key: 5 - agree; 1 - disagree.

EXHIBIT 10

Nescafe Print Advertisement, 1980

Despite this effort, the annual tracking study did not show dramatic improvements in the brand's image. Nescafé continued to be widely viewed as inappropriate for those who wanted "gratification" or "a recharge" from their coffee. Nonetheless, sales exceeded 500 tons by 1983.

From 1984 to 1986, a Nescafé advertisement developed in France was also used in Italy. This execution portrayed an exotic train journey interspersed with images of locations where coffee was grown. The ad supported Nescafé's quality claims by highlighting Nescafé's origins without using direct comparisons to traditional Italian coffee. Nescafé's 1985 image-tracking study showed that the brand had gained in perceived quality and reliability. Sales volume increased to 580 tons in 1986 and to 650 tons in 1988.

The results of a 1987 study involving one-on-one interviews with Italian coffee drinkers are reported in Exhibit 11. The study showed that Nescafé's share of usage occasions was greatest among older people who were more sensitive to caffeine. Those aged 55 and over represented 80 percent of Nescafé's consumers, yet their average per capita consumption of Nescafé did not exceed one cup per day. Nescafé was preferred for its ease of preparation during moments of relaxation at home and for its less "aggressive" image. Awareness-tracking studies, reported in Exhibit 12, showed Nescafé brand awareness had reached 83 percent of consumers by 1988. However, despite good distribution, Nescafé's household penetration was only 14 percent. Nescafé sales were disproportionately high in the larger northern Italian cities, as indicated in Exhibit 13, where consumers preferred sweeter blends. Exhibit 14 summarizes the conclusions of a 1988 focus group that asked consumers to compare Nescafé as a milk modifier with mocha coffee.

EXHIBIT 11

Results of Coffee Motivation Study, 1987

- A majority of respondents agreed with the following statements:

    —"Espresso is true coffee."
    —"Nescafé is not as strong as normal coffee."
    —"Espresso coffee is strong, flavorful, and aromatic."
    —"Nescafé is not a real coffee."
    —"Nescafé is easier to handle."
    —"Nescafé is used only in 'emergencies.' "
    —"Nescafé is for older people."

- Nescafé was regarded as "easy to make," especially by Nescafé users. Nonusers more often agreed that "preparing a pot of coffee is not a waste of time."

- "Coffee, tobacco, and alcohol" were commonly regarded by young people as health risks.

- Two-thirds of Nescafé drinkers preferred to consume it with meals or in the afternoon. The remaining one-third used it primarily as a "milk modifier" in the morning.

- The three different formulations of Nescafé were easily distinguished by users.

- Forty-three percent of consumers considered Nescafé "lighter" than an espresso or "mocha" coffee, 20 percent considered it equivalent on this dimension, and 37 percent had no opinion.

EXHIBIT   12

Results of Nescafé Brand Awareness Study, 1978–1988

Base - 100 respondents	1978	1981	1985	1988
Have heard of Nescafé	73%	71%	74%	83%
Have tried Nescafé	29%	33%	38%	39%
Have not tried Nescafé	44%	38%	36%	44%
Have tried Nescafé in past three months	9%	12%	13%	14%
User habits within past three months				
Strong	33%	37%	41%	45%
Average	34%	28%	24%	24%
Weak	33%	36%	35%	31%

Key: Strong = every day or nearly every day; Average = one to three times a week; Weak = within three months.

CONCLUSION

Nescafé needed a revised marketing plan to increase sales. Nescafé already enjoyed excellent distribution penetration, and additional manufacturing capacity was available.

At the management meeting, Mr. Baruffa laid out four options for Nescafé:

1. Focus further on older consumers, already heavy users of Nescafé.
2. Broaden Nescafé's positioning to include its use as a milk modifier, particularly use of Nescafé Classic as a morning beverage with milk.
3. Target younger and more "cosmopolitan" professionals, positioning Nescafé (particularly Gran Aroma) as an international coffee beverage.
4. Try to penetrate the CHR segment of the market.

Mr. Baruffa argued that the first option was the least attractive. He believed that per capita coffee consumption among older consumers could not be increased significantly, though demographic trends indicated that the segment would grow as a percentage of the total Italian population.

EXHIBIT   13

Nescafé versus Roast and Ground Coffee Consumption in Major Italian Cities

	% of Italian Population	% of Total Italian Roast and Ground Consumption	% of Total Italian Nescafé Consumption
Rome	7.0%	9.1%	4.2%
Milan	4.0	5.7	29.5
Turin	2.5	3.1	5.1
Naples	3.2	4.2	0.9
Bologna	2.2	2.7	2.4
Florence	1.8	1.9	2.7
Palermo	1.6	1.8	0.7

EXHIBIT 14

Conclusions of 1988 Focus Group Comparing Nescafé as a Milk Modifier with Mocha/Espresso

Convenience

Nescafé user:	Convenience is one of the most important attributes of Nescafé—it's the easiest way to have milk and coffee.
Nescafé nonuser:	Those who drink mocha coffee do not consider it inconvenient to prepare.

Concentration of Coffee Flavor

Nescafé user:	Both flavor and taste are excellent; the foamy consistency when mixed with milk is closer to cappuccino than normal milk and coffee.
Nescafé nonuser:	Both flavor and taste are good; but why drink Nescafé when one can have mocha and milk?

Caffeine and Stimulating Capability

Nescafé user:	Nescafé is less stimulating than espresso, but caffeine is not a priority.
Nescafé nonuser:	Espresso drinkers want a level of stimulation from coffee that Nescafé does not provide.

Mr. Bechi shifted discussion to the second option. He believed that "youngsters should be the target audience for the next five years." He was concerned about positioning Nescafé as a milk modifier due to Nestlé Italy's leadership in that category with Nesquick and Orzoro. He warned the group about cannibalization and the likely concerns of the milk modifier brand managers.

However, Mr. Baruffa emphasized that younger people's more open-minded attitude toward Nescafé was an important opportunity. Could Nescafé be presented to young people as both a milk modifier and a "new, less-caffeinated alternative to regular coffee."

Mr. Mazzei, the CFO, discouraged further emphasis on the CHR segment. He argued that the trade promotion investment to secure extra distribution would not pay back. He also believed consumers were less likely to switch from espresso or "real" coffee to Nescafé in coffeehouses and restaurants.

Mr. Giuliani argued that Nescafé should be positioned as an international coffee, not as an Italian coffee, to cosmopolitan consumers who populated the larger northern Italian cities. He believed that there was a growing "transnational consumer" segment comprising sophisticated, well-traveled consumers who were developing "universal" consumption habits and who were attracted to international brands, even in food products.

CHAPTER 5

Marketing Research

 Effective management of information is a prerequisite for successful decision making. Put simply, the better the information, the better the decision because information reduces uncertainty, and the less uncertainty, the less risky a decision.

Marketing managers are faced with three information-related tasks. They must first determine the kind and amount of information necessary for making a correct decision. They must then compare the costs of acquiring this information with its value in reducing uncertainty. Finally, managers must be able to organize, interpret, and evaluate information as it relates to the decision at hand.

Marketing research is one source of information for the marketing manager. Although definitions vary, marketing research can be thought of as a systematic procedure for providing marketers with actionable decision-making information. As such, marketing research facilitates decision making by providing information that is useful in both the identification and the solution of marketing problems.

Typically, the marketing manager is not directly involved in the practice of marketing research. Technical functions such as data collection, sampling, scaling, and statistical analysis are more likely to be performed by marketing-research specialists. Still, it is imperative that the marketing manager be familiar with the process, procedures, and techniques of marketing research. Only this familiarity will enable the manager to ascertain the true value of the information provided by marketing research.[1]

Because the decision-making process directly interfaces with the marketing-research process (the latter being a subset of the former), the marketing manager must be able to evaluate the following:

- Value of marketing-research-based information
- Marketing-research information-acquisition process

111

APPRAISING THE VALUE OF INFORMATION

From a conceptual perspective the value of information is reflected by the extent to which information can reduce decision-related uncertainty. Alternatively, the value of information is reflected by the degree to which the chances of making a correct decision are increased by use of information. Implicit in this perspective is the notion that the information being referred to is incremental information. Hence, information value implicitly refers to the value of incremental information—discrete units of information not currently available to the decision maker.

Given this perspective, information is potentially more valuable in certain decision situations than in others. Since the value of information may be defined as information benefits minus information costs, value increases as benefits increase or costs decrease. Additionally, though, information is potentially more valuable in a decision situation in which there is a great deal of uncertainty present and the consequences of an incorrect decision (the amount at stake) are substantial.

Quantitative Appraisal

As indicated in Chapter 3, decision analysis can be used to determine the value of information. Decision analysis is used to link together uncertainties in the environment and the alternatives available to a manager, and it can be extended to identify the upper limit to spend for research information as well.

In the El Nacho example in Chapter 3, decision analysis was used to determine that El Nacho management should maintain its prices, given the subjective probabilities of competitor actions and the attendant outcomes (payoffs) assigned to each alternative competitive reaction linkage. The analysis used to arrive at that decision is reconstructed in Exhibit 5.1.

EXHIBIT   5.1

Decision Analysis and the Value of Information

		Payoff Table Uncertainties	
		Competitors maintain price (probability = 0.9)	Competitors reduce price (probability = 0.1)
Alternatives	A$_1$:Reduce price	$150,000	$110,000
	A$_2$:Maintain price	$175,000	$ 90,000

Calculation of Expected Monetary Value (EMV):

EMV_{A_1} = 0.9($150,000) + 0.1($110,000) = $146,000
EMV_{A_2} = 0.9($175,000) + 0.1($90,000) = $166,500

Calculation of Expected Monetary Value of Perfect Information (EMVPI):

$EMV_{certainty}$ = 0.9($175,000) + 0.1($110,000) = $168,500

$EMVPI = EMV_{certainty} - EMV_{best alternative}$
$EMVPI = $168,500 - $166,500 = $2,000

Exhibit 5.1 also shows how the expected monetary value of "perfect" information (EMVPI) can be calculated. Simply speaking, EMVPI is the difference between what El Nacho would achieve in contribution dollars if its management knew for certain what competitors would do and the average contribution dollars realized without such information. In other words, if El Nacho knew for certain that competitors would maintain their price, the "maintain price" alternative would be selected. If El Nacho management knew for certain that competitors would reduce their price, however, the "reduce price" alternative would be chosen. Assuming El Nacho management faced this decision ten times and knew what competitor reaction would be each time, El Nacho management would make the appropriate decision each time. The result would be an EMV of $168,500. The difference of $2,000 between $168,500 and $166,500 (the best alternative without such information) is viewed as the upper limit to pay for "perfect" information.

Qualitative Appraisal

A question still remains: What constitutes good decision information? Intuitively, certain types of information would seem to be more valuable than others. Therefore, we need to address those explicit characteristics that make information valuable for decision making.

One such characteristic is the cost of information. Although cost (especially absolute cost) may be an overriding concern in determining whether a particular kind or form of information is to be utilized in a specific decision context, cost probably should not be the only characteristic taken into account. The value of information for decision making can also be evaluated according to five other characteristics. To be maximally useful for decision making, information must possess the characteristics of (1) accuracy, (2) currency, (3) sufficiency, (4) availability, and (5) relevancy. The extent to which information possesses these characteristics determines its practical value in the decision-making process.

Accuracy refers to the degree to which information reflects reality. In other words, information must closely approximate the true state of affairs. While no one would disagree with this statement, frequently there is a tendency to overlook the more subtle question "How much accuracy is required for a given decision to be correctly made?" Specifically, the level of accuracy required is best viewed in a relative context: What is the consequence of making an incorrect decision? If a television manufacturer is in the process of launching a new high-definition television (HDTV)—the success or failure of which may determine the future of the firm— there is a need for highly accurate decision information. Alternatively, if the decision relates to whether a restaurant should offer flat or round toothpicks, less accurate information will suffice. Hence, the accuracy criterion should be considered in a relative sense: How accurate must the data be for the specific decision at hand? In brief, information accuracy must be assessed relative to the importance of the decision and the probability and consequences of an incorrect decision.

Currency is the degree to which information reflects events in the present time period. Information must be up to date. Information on clothing styles or automobile travel in the late 1980s may be obsolete for decision making today. The clothing fashion cycle is so rapid that what was in style last fall is "ancient history" this year. Likewise, gasoline and oil price fluctuations can quickly render automobile travel information obsolete. Because of the rapidity with which environmental changes influence marketing, there is little likelihood that stale information will be decision-actionable.

Sufficiency refers to whether there is enough information to make a correct decision. The extent to which information is useful for decision making depends on its completeness and its detail. If information is not sufficient, complete, or detailed enough to permit a decision to be made, it is of little value to a decision maker. Although aggregated information on the existence or size of a market may be available, the lack of detailed information on its geographical, demographic, or attitudinal composition may preclude effective decision making as to what, if any, marketing activities should be directed toward that market.

Availability refers to having information accessible (in hand) when a decision is being made. A marketing manager faced with making a promotion budget decision by the end of July needs appropriate information before then. Even perfect information would be of no value if it was not available until August 1. Information must be available when a decision is being made. Tomorrow is too late.

Relevancy refers to the pertinency and applicability of information to the decision issue at hand. This is perhaps the single most important characteristic of information. Even if information possesses all the other characteristics of good information, it is of no use unless it is relevant. Although trade-offs frequently must be made among the other characteristics—the requirement of accuracy, for example, is often relaxed to ensure availability—relevancy should be the one characteristic immune to compromise. It is the one information ingredient essential for successful decision making.

Bad information—information that does not possess the characteristics just mentioned—may be worse than no information at all. Even if a decision maker does not have information, there is always a chance of making a correct decision. Though good information does not ensure good decisions (judgment is still required), bad information will normally result in poor decisions. The decision maker has little opportunity to make a correct decision if the underlying information is incorrect. The decision to introduce a new recipe for Coca-Cola is a classic example of how bad information can lead to a poor decision. Coca-Cola marketing research focused heavily on taste tests (which favored the new recipe over the old) but failed to consider the emotional bond to the original Coca-Cola. As a result, marketing-research experts have labeled the research effort "bad research," and industry executives have criticized Coca-Cola for neglecting to use a "large dose of judgment" in designing the research and interpreting the results.[2]

MANAGING THE INFORMATION-ACQUISITION PROCESS

The manager should play an active role in the marketing-research information-acquisition process. Specific responsibilities are as follows:

1. Delineating information requirements by defining the problem to be studied
2. Devising the best way to obtain the information
3. Determining the amount to spend for the information
4. Deciding on the types of analysis and interpretation that will best solve the problem
5. Developing actionable marketing strategies from the information

Delineating Information Requirements

The most critical and difficult task a manager faces is the specification of information needed to make a decision. Specification of the kinds and amounts of information needed is based on an understanding of the problem confronting the manager. Consider the situation faced by the Gerber Products Company after it introduced a cereal for infants. Despite optimistic sales forecasts, actual sales performance was disappointing. Was the problem a less-than-expected sales volume, or was this merely evidence of a still more basic problem? If low sales volume was defined as the problem, then a manager would ask the fairly general question "Why has the sales volume failed to meet the forecasts?" Alternatively, if low sales volume was viewed as a result of more basic underlying factors, such as the marketing mix, market capacity, or competitive behavior, information could be gathered on all or any of these factors. Gerber executives chose to begin by examining existing company information on the distribution of the cereal, and they learned that the item was being distributed through only 25 percent of the outlets originally planned for it.[3]

This example illustrates two important points. First, issues facing organizations many times represent the tip of the iceberg; they are symptomatic of more fundamental problems. By addressing the sales-volume question, executives could collect information on a wide variety of topics. However, specification of the problem in terms of factors that could influence sales volume would enable a more disciplined and productive information-collection process to be implemented. This means that a model must be specified that identifies both the factors influencing the problem under investigation and the relationships among these factors. The idea of models and model building should not connote highly sophisticated or mathematical representations of a phenomenon. Simple (not simplistic) models often provide valuable insight and structure for thinking about a problem. For example, sales volume for a new product can be modeled as follows (emphasis in original):

> The number of people in the target market *times* the fraction who become aware of the product *times* the fraction who find it available *times* the share of purchases that triers devote to the new brand *times* the sales rate for the product class.[4]

Second, implicit in the Gerber example is the idea that existing or readily available information is sought out first. Once a problem has been defined, existing sources of information should be examined first. Not only is this information readily available, but it is often the most inexpensive and relevant information available. Only if it is inadequate should additional data be collected.

Devising the Best Means for Obtaining Information

The cost of information will depend on the means for obtaining it. The best means for getting the information necessary for decision making depends on the manager's information requirements, potential or available funds, time constraints, and an appraisal of the usefulness of information once obtained. Managers are often called on to decide whether information should be (1) generated internally, either from available organizational data or from data collected by the organization's personnel, or (2) acquired from external sources, either through standardized information services provided by them or through data collection carried out by them especially for the problem under investigation. Internal and external information sources often complement each other. It is not uncommon to get conflicting information from the two sources, however, and managers sometimes obtain redundant information when both sources are used.

As a generalization, Japanese executives are prone to rely on information gathered by themselves rather than by marketing-research professionals either inside or outside their organizations. Moreover, much of this information is in the form of "soft data," that is, impressions garnered from consumers who have purchased and used the products and from intermediaries (wholesalers and retailers) that sell the products and those of competitors. American and European executives are more likely to rely on marketing-research professionals, either inside or outside their organizations, for "hard data" in numerical form produced by customer surveys and various kinds of syndicated, consumer-tracking data services. Increasingly, these two approaches to gathering information are converging. American and European marketing executives are spending more time with customers and intermediaries; Japanese executives have recognized efficiencies in gathering information through large-scale data collection efforts.[5]

Determining the Cost of Information

Information has a monetary cost in that the acquisition of data must be paid for as a direct expense. The actual amount spent for information is often related to the financial loss of making a poor decision. For instance, it is common for movie studios in the United States to spend upward of $200,000 on test screenings (sneak previews), audience research, and advertising research before a new film is released. Why? The cost of a "flop" is roughly equivalent to the $38 million necessary to produce and market a typical movie today.[6] Information also has a time cost in that the time spent to gather information dictates when the decision can be made. The cost of time is an opportunity cost, described in Chapters 1 and 2. Thus, the expenditure of time in acquiring information is a relevant cost. For example, Campbell Soup Company "spent" 18 months testing a blended fruit juice called Juiceworks. By the time the company had completed its testing, three competing brands had been introduced, so Campbell dropped the product.[7] An important determinant in evaluating expenditures of money and time for information acquisition is the value of the information. Therefore, the manager must evaluate its accuracy, currency, sufficiency, availability, and relevancy to arrive at a decision about the amount of money and time that should be allocated to obtaining it.

Deciding on the Types of Analysis and Interpretation

Since marketing managers must ultimately make a decision based on the information provided by research, they should be involved in specifying the types of analyses performed on it. For example, a manager should specify how the information should be organized. A manager examining the sales of a product might find it useful to have sales data organized by geographical location of the sale, the type of intermediary selling the product, buyer characteristics, and so forth.

An important consideration in specifying the type of analysis is the selection of those factors that best present the information and assist the manager in focusing on critical aspects of the decision to be made. In this way, the manager can ensure that information is relevant—that he or she is not inundated with an impressive volume of meaningless information. Marketing-research practice at Ocean Spray Cranberries, Inc., is a case in point. The Ocean Spray marketing manager for whom research is being conducted is expected to draft a "usage of results" statement when requesting research. This statement is used by the research department in developing a research program to assure that what is expected is ultimately delivered.[8]

Deciding how to interpret marketing-research data is often a difficult task, even after the manager has specified how research data are to be presented. Consider the research conducted by Brown-Forman Distillers Corporation on Frost 8/80, a new brand of whiskey that was clear as opposed to being amber or pale brown like other whiskeys. The firm employed eight research firms and spent $500,000 studying virtually every aspect of the product and its potential market. The product failed despite development and marketing expenditures of $6.5 million. In retrospect, the executive who directed the sales for the brand placed the blame on the interpretation of research data:

> The research we had done probably was all right, but we misread it. The brand came off high on "uniqueness," and we interpreted this to mean the people would be anxious to try it. As it turned out, uniqueness was our biggest problem. The product looked like vodka but tasted like whiskey. It upset people. They didn't know what to make of it. As far as I'm concerned, that was it in a nutshell.[9]

Developing Actionable Strategies

A final responsibility of the manager is the development of actionable marketing strategies based on the information gathered. Even though this responsibility is considered last in this discussion, it follows directly from specifying the information requirements and permeates every aspect of the information-acquisition process. A quote from Mark Twain sums up the importance of knowing in advance the reason for collecting information: "Collecting data is much like collecting garbage. You must know in advance what you are going to do with the stuff before you collect it."[10]

If the information obtained is not actionable, in that it does not lend itself to effective decision making, then its costs have exceeded its value. By specifying in advance, either implicitly or explicitly, what various informational inputs will lead to in terms of specific actions, the manager can ensure that the entire marketing-research, information-acquisition process becomes a worthwhile venture.

NOTES

1. J. Walker Smith, "Beyond Anecdotes: Toward a Systematic Model of the Value of Marketing Research," *Marketing Research* (March 1991): 3–14.

2. "How Coke's Decision to Offer 2 Colas Undid 4½ Years of Planning," *Wall Street Journal* (July 15, 1985): 1ff; and "Coke's Switch a Classic," *Advertising Age* (July 15, 1985): 1ff.

3. "The Low Birthrate Crimps the Baby-Food Market," *Business Week* (July 13, 1974): 44–50.

4. J. D. C. Little, "Decision Support Systems for Marketing Managers," *Journal of Marketing* 43 (1979): 9–27.

5. This discussion is based on Calvin L. Hodock. "The Decline and Fall of Marketing Research in Corporate America," *Marketing Research* (June 1991): 12–22; Johny K. Johansson and Ikujiro Nonaka, "Marketing Research the Japanese Way," *Harvard Business Review* (May–June 1987): 16–18, 22; and "Marketing in Japan: Taking Aim," *The Economist* (April 24, 1993): 74.

   6. "Movie-Research Czar Is Said by Some to Sell Manipulated Findings," *Wall Street Journal* (December 17, 1993): A1, A6; "Putting Movies to the Test," *Dallas Morning News* (May 9, 1992): 1C, 3C.

   7. "A Test for Market Research," *Newsweek* (December 28, 1987): 32–33.

   8. John Tarsa, "Ocean Spray Marketing Research: Delivering Insights in a Customer/Supplier Relationship," *Marketing Research* (September 1991): 5–11.

   9. F. Klein, "An Untimely End," in *Paths to Profit*, ed. J. Barnett (Princeton, NJ: Dow Jones Books, 1973): 36–42.

   10. This quote, attributed to Mark Twain, is found in William Rudelius, W. Bruce Erickson, and William Bakula, Jr., *An Introduction to Contemporary Business* (New York: Harcourt Brace Jovanovich, 1976): 142.

South Delaware Coors, Inc.

Larry Brownlow was just beginning to realize the problem was more complex than he had thought. The problem, of course, was giving direction to Manson and Associates regarding which research should be completed by February 20, 1990, to determine market potential of a Coors beer distributorship for a two-county area in southern Delaware. With data from this research, Larry would be able to estimate the feasibility of such an operation before the March 5 application deadline. Larry knew his decision on whether or not to apply for the distributorship was the most important career choice he had ever faced.

LARRY BROWNLOW

Larry was just completing his M.B.A. and, from his standpoint, the Coors announcement of expansion into Delaware could hardly have been better timed. He had long ago decided the best opportunities and rewards were in smaller, self-owned businesses and not in the jungles of corporate giants. Because of a family tragedy some three years earlier, Larry found himself in a position to consider small business opportunities such as the Coors distributorship. Approximately $500,000 was held in trust for Larry, to be dispersed when he reached age 30. Until then, Larry and his family were living on an annual trust income of about $40,000. It was on the basis of this income that Larry had decided to leave his sales engineering job and return to graduate school for his M.B.A.

The decision to complete a graduate program and operate his own business had been easy to make. Although he could have retired and lived off investment income, Larry knew such a life would not be to his liking. Working with people and the challenge of making it on his own, Larry thought, were far preferable to enduring an early retirement.

Larry would be 30 in July, about the time money would actually be needed to start the business. In the meantime, he had access to about $15,000 for feasibility research. Although there certainly were other places to spend the money, Larry and his wife agreed the opportunity to acquire the distributorship could not be overlooked.

COORS, INC.

Coors's history dated back to 1873, when Adolph Coors built a small brewery in Golden, Colorado. Since then, the brewery had prospered and become the fourth-largest seller of beer in the country. Coors's operating philosophy could be summed up as "hard work, saving money, devotion to the quality of the product, caring about

This case was prepared by Professor James E. Nelson and doctoral student Eric J. Karson, of the University of Colorado, as a basis for class discussion and is not designed to illustrate effective or ineffective handling of an administrative situation. Certain data have been disguised. Copyright by the Business Research Division, College of Business and Administration and the Graduate School of Business Administration, University of Colorado, Boulder, Colorado 80309-0419.

the environment, and giving people something to believe in." Company operation is consistent with this philosophy. Headquarters and most production facilities are still located in Golden, Colorado, with a new Shenandoah, Virginia, facility aiding in nationwide distribution. Coors is still family operated and controlled. The company had issued its first public stock, $127 million worth of nonvoting shares, in 1975. The issue was enthusiastically received by the financial community despite its being offered during a recession.

Coors's unwillingness to compromise on the high quality of its product is well known both to its suppliers and to its consuming public. Coors beer requires constant refrigeration to maintain this quality, and wholesalers' facilities are closely controlled to ensure that proper temperatures are maintained. Wholesalers are also required to install and use aluminum can recycling equipment. Coors was one of the first breweries in the industry to recycle its cans.

Larry was aware of Coors's popularity with many consumers in adjacent states. However, Coors's corporate management was seen by some consumers to hold antiunion beliefs (because of a labor disagreement at the brewery some ten years ago and the brewery's current use of a nonunion labor force). Some other consumers perceived the brewery to be somewhat insensitive to minority issues, primarily in employment and distribution. These attitudes—plus many other aspects of consumer behavior—meant that Coors's sales in Delaware would depend greatly on the efforts of the two wholesalers planned for the state.

MANSON RESEARCH PROPOSAL

Because of the press of his studies, Larry had contacted Manson and Associates in January for their assistance. The firm was a Wilmington-based general research supplier that had conducted other feasibility studies in the south Atlantic region. Manson was well known for the quality of its work, particularly with respect to computer modeling. The firm had developed special expertise in modeling such things as population and employment levels for cities, counties, and other units of area for periods of up to ten years into the future.

Larry had met John Rome, senior research analyst for Manson, in January and discussed the Coors opportunity and appropriate research extensively. Rome promised a formal research proposal (Exhibit 1) for the project, which Larry now held in his hand. It certainly was extensive, Larry thought, and reflected the professionalism he expected. Now came the hard part—choosing the more relevant research from the proposal—because he certainly couldn't afford to pay for it all. Rome had suggested a meeting for Friday, which gave Larry only three more days to decide.

Larry was at first overwhelmed. All the research would certainly be useful. He was sure he needed estimates of sales and costs in a form allowing managerial analysis, but what data in what form? Knowledge of completing operations' experience, retailer support, and consumer acceptance also seemed important for feasibility analysis. For example, what if consumers were excited about Coors and retailers indifferent, or the other way around? Finally, several of the studies would provide information that could be useful in later months of operation, in the areas of promotion and pricing, for example. The problem now appeared more difficult than before!

It would have been nice, Larry thought, to have had some time to perform part of the suggested research himself. However, there just was too much in the way of class assignments and other matters to allow him that luxury. Besides, using Manson

EXHIBIT 1

Research Proposal by Manson and Associates

January 16, 1990

Mr. Larry Brownlow
1198 West Lamar
Chester, PA 19345

Dear Larry:

It was a pleasure meeting you last week and discussing your business and research interests in Coors wholesaling. After further thought and discussion with my colleagues, the Coors opportunity appears even more attractive than when we met.

Appearances can be deceiving, as you know, and I fully agree some formal research is needed before you make application. Research that we recommend would proceed in two distinct stages and is described below.

Stage One Research, Based on Secondary Data and Manson Computer Models:

Study A: National and Delaware Per-Capita Beer Consumption for 1988–1992.
Description: Per-capita annual consumption of beer for the total population and for population age 21 and over in gallons is provided.
Source: Various publications, Manson computer model
Cost: $1,000

Study B: Population Estimates for 1986–1996 for Two Delaware Counties in Market Area.
Description: Annual estimates of total population and population age 21 and over are provided for the period 1986–1996.
Source: U.S. Bureau of Census, Sales Management Annual Survey of Buying Power, Manson computer model
Cost: $1,500

Study C: Estimates of Coors' Market Share for 1990–1995.
Description: Coors' market share for the two-county market area based on total gallons consumed is estimated for each year in the period 1990–1995. These data will be projected from Coors' nationwide experience.
Source: Various publications, Manson computer model
Cost: $2,000

Study D: Estimates of Number of Liquor and Beer Licenses for the Market Area, 1990–1995.
Description: Projections of the number of on-premise sale operations and off-premise sale operations are provided.
Source: Delaware Department of Revenue, Manson computer model
Cost: $1,000

Study E: Beer Taxes Paid by Delaware Wholesalers for 1988 and 1989 in the Market Area.
Description: Beer taxes paid by each of the six presently operating competing beer wholesalers are provided. These figures can be converted to gallons sold by applying the state gallonage tax rate ($.06 per gallon).
Source: Delaware Department of Revenue
Cost: $200

Study F: Financial Statement Summary of Wine, Liquor, and Beer Wholesalers for Fiscal Year 1988.

EXHIBIT 1 (*continued*)

Description: Composite balance sheets, income statements, and relevant measures of performance for 510 similar wholesaling operations in the United States are provided.
Source: Robert Morris Associates Annual Statement Studies, 1989 ed.
Cost: $49.50

Stage Two Research, Based on Primary Data:

Study G: Consumer Study.
            Description: Study G involves focus-group interviews and a mail questionnaire to determine consumers' past experience, acceptance, and intention to buy Coors beer.[a] Three focus-group interviews would be conducted in the two counties in the market area. From these data, a questionnaire would be developed and sent to 300 adult residents in the market area, utilizing direct questions and a semantic differential scale to measure attitudes toward Coors beer, competing beers, and an ideal beer.
            Source: Manson and Associates
            Cost: $6,000

Study H: Retailer Study.
            Description: Group interviews would be conducted with six potential retailers of Coors beer in one county in the market area to determine their past beer sales and experience and their intention to stock and sell Coors. From these data, a personal-interview questionnaire would be developed and executed at all appropriate retailers in the market area to determine similar data.
            Source: Manson and Associates
            Cost: $4,800

Study I: Survey of Retail and Wholesale Beer Price.
            Description: In-store interviews would be conducted with a sample of 50 retailers in the market area to estimate retail and wholesale prices for Budweiser, Miller Lite, Miller, Busch, Bud Light, Old Milwaukee and Michelob.
            Source: Manson and Associates
            Cost: $2,000

Examples of the final report tables are attached [Exhibit 2]. This should give you a better idea of the data you will receive.

As you can see, the research is extensive and, I might add, not cheap. However, the research as outlined will supply you with sufficient information to make an estimate of the feasibility of a Coors distributorship, the investment for which is substantial.

I have scheduled 9:00 A.M. next Friday as a time to meet with you to discuss the proposal in more detail. Time is short, but we firmly feel the study can be completed by February 20, 1990. If you need more information in the meantime, please feel free to call.

Sincerely,

John Rome
Senior Research Analyst

---

[a]A focus-group interview consists of a moderator's questioning and listening to a group of 8 to 12 consumers.

EXHIBIT 2

Examples of Final Research Report Tables

Table A
National and Delaware Residents' Annual Beer Consumption per Capita, 1988–1992 (Gallons)

| Year | U.S. Consumption | | Delaware Consumption | |
	Based on Entire Population	Based on Population Age 21 and Over	Based on Entire Population	Based on Population Age 21 and Over
1988				
1989				
1990				
1991				
1992				

Source: Study A.

Table B
Population Estimates for 1986–1996 for Two Delaware Counties in Market Area

| County | Entire Population | | | | | |
	1986	1988	1990	1992	1994	1996
Kent						
Sussex						

| County | Population Age 21 and Over | | | | | |
	1986	1988	1990	1992	1994	1996
Kent						
Sussex						

Source: Study B.

Table C
Estimates of Coors's Market Share for 1990–1995

Year	Market Share (%)
1990	
1991	
1992	
1993	
1994	
1995	

Source: Study C.

EXHIBIT   2   (continued)

Table D
Estimates of Number of Liquor and Beer Licenses for the Market Area, 1990–1995

Type of License	1990	1991	1992	1993	1994	1995
All beverages						
Retail beer and wine						
Off-premise beer only						
Veterans beer and liquor						
Fraternal						
Resort beer and liquor						

Source: Study D.

Table E
Beer Taxes Paid by Beer Wholesalers in the Market Area, 1988 and 1989

Wholesaler	1988 Tax Paid ($)	1989 Tax Paid ($)
A		
B		
C		
D		
E		
F		

Source: Study E.
Note: Delaware beer tax is $0.06 per gallon.

Table F
Financial Statement Summary for 510 Wholesalers of Wine, Liquor, and Beer in Fiscal Year 1988

Assets	Percentage
Cash and equivalents	
Accounts and notes receivable, net	
Inventory	
All other current	
Total current	
Fixed assets, net	
Intangibles, net	
All other noncurrent	
Total	100.0

EXHIBIT 2 (*continued*)

Table F (continued)

Liabilities	Percentage
Notes payable, short term	
Current maturity long-term debt	
Accounts and notes payable, trade	
Accrued expenses	
All other current	
Total current	
Long-term debt	
All other noncurrent	
Net worth	
Total liabilities and net worth	100.0

Income Data

Net sales	100.0
Cost of sales	
Gross profit	
Operating expenses	
Operating profit	
All other expenses, net	
Profit before taxes	——

Ratios

Quick
Current
Debt/worth
Sales/receivables
Cost of sales/inventory
Percentage profit before taxes, based on total assets

Source: Study F (Robert Morris Associates, © 1989).

Interpretation of Statement Studies Figures:

RMA recommends that Statement Studies data be regarded only as general guidelines and not as absolute industry norms. There are several reasons why the data may not be fully representative of a given industry:

1. The financial statements used in the Statement Studies are not selected by any random or statistically reliable method. RMA member banks voluntarily submit the raw data they have available each year, with these being the only constraints: (a) The fiscal year-ends of the companies reported may not be from April 1 through June 29, and (b) their total assets must be less than $100 million.
2. Many companies have varied product lines; however, the Statement Studies categorize them by their primary product Standard Industrial Classification (SIC) number only.
3. Some of our industry samples are rather small in relation to the total number of firms in a given industry. A relatively small sample can increase the chances that some of our composites do not fully represent an industry.
4. There is the chance that an extreme statement can be present in a sample, causing a disproportionate influence on the industry composite. This is particularly true in a relatively small sample.
5. Companies within the same industry may differ in their method of operations, which in turn can directly influence their financial statements. Since they are included in our sample, too, these statements can significantly affect our composite calculations.
6. Other considerations that can result in variations among different companies engaged in the same general line of business are different labor markets, geographical location, different accounting methods, quality of products handled, sources and methods of financing, and terms of sale.

   For these reasons, RMS does not recommend that Statement Studies figures be considered as absolute norms for a given industry. Rather, the figures should be used only as general guidelines and in addition to the other methods of financial analysis. RMA makes no claim as to the representativeness of the figures printed in this book.

EXHIBIT 2 (continued)

Table G
Consumer Questionnaire Results

	Percentage		Percentage
Consumed Coors in the past:		Usually buy beer at:	
Attitudes toward Coors:	%	Liquor stores	
Strongly like		Taverns and bars	
Like		Supermarkets	
Indifferent/no opinion		Corner grocery	
Dislike			
Strongly dislike			
Total	100.0	Total	100.0
Weekly beer consumption:		Features considered	
Less than 1 can		important when buying beer:	
1–2 cans		Taste	
3–4 cans		Brand name	
5–6 cans		Price	
7–8 cans		Store location	
9 cans and over		Advertising	
Total	100.0	Carbonation	
Intention to buy Coors:		Other	
Certainly will		Total	100.0
Maybe will			
Not sure			
Maybe will not			
Certainly will not			
Total	100.0		

Semantic Differential Scale, Consumers[a]

	Extremely	Very	Somewhat	Somewhat	Very	Extremely	
Masculine	—	—	—	—	—	—	Feminine
Healthful	—	—	—	—	—	—	Unhealthful
Cheap	—	—	—	—	—	—	Expensive
Strong	—	—	—	—	—	—	Weak
Old-fashioned	—	—	—	—	—	—	New
Upper-class	—	—	—	—	—	—	Lower-class
Good taste	—	—	—	—	—	—	Bad taste

Source: Study G.

[a]Profiles would be provided for Coors, three competing beers, and an ideal beer.

EXHIBIT 2 (*continued*)

Table H
Retailer Questionnaire Results

	Percentage		Percentage
Brands of beer carried:		Beer sales:	
Budweiser		Budweiser	
Miller Lite		Miller Lite	
Miller		Miller	
Busch		Busch	
Bud Light		Bud Light	
Old Milwaukee		Old Milwaukee	
Michelob		Michelob	
		Others	
Intention to sell Coors:			
Certainly will		Total	100.0
Maybe will			
Not sure			
Maybe will not			
Certainly will not			
Total	100.0		

Semantic Differential Scale, Retailers[a]

	Extremely	Very	Somewhat	Somewhat	Very	Extremely	
Masculine	—	—	—	—	—	—	Feminine
Healthful	—	—	—	—	—	—	Unhealthful
Cheap	—	—	—	—	—	—	Expensive
Strong	—	—	—	—	—	—	Weak
Old-fashioned	—	—	—	—	—	—	New
Upper-class	—	—	—	—	—	—	Lower-class
Good taste	—	—	—	—	—	—	Bad taste

Source: Study H.
[a]Profiles would be provided for Coors, three competing beers, and an ideal bear.

Table I
Retail and Wholesale Prices for Selected Beers in the Market Area

Beer	Wholesale Six-Pack Price[a] (dollars)	Retail Six-Pack Price[b] (dollars)
Budweiser		
Miller Lite		
Miller		
Busch		
Bud Light		
Old Milwaukee		
Michelob		

Source: Study I.
[a]Price at which the wholesaler sold to retailers.
[b]Price at which the retailer sold to consumers.

and Associates would give him research results from an unbiased source. There would be plenty for him to do once he received the results anyway.

INVESTING AND OPERATING DATA

Larry was not completely in the dark regarding investment and operating data for the distributorship. In the past two weeks he had visited two beer wholesalers in his home town of Chester, Pennsylvania, who handled Anheuser-Busch and Miller beer, to get a feel for their operation and marketing experience. It would have been nice to interview a Coors wholesaler, but Coors management had instructed all of their distributors to provide no information to prospective applicants.

Although no specific financial data had been discussed, general information had been provided in a cordial fashion because of the noncompetitive nature of Larry's plans. Based on his conversations, Larry had made the following estimates:

Inventory		$240,000
Equipment:		
Delivery trucks	$150,000	
Forklift	20,000	
Recycling and miscellaneous equipment	20,000	
Office equipment	10,000	
Total equipment		200,000
Warehouse		320,000
Land		40,000
Total investment		$800,000

A local banker had reviewed Larry's financial capabilities and saw no problem in extending a line of credit on the order of $400,000. Other family sources also might loan as much as $400,000 to the business.

To get a rough estimate of fixed expenses, Larry decided to plan on having four route salespeople, a secretary, and a warehouse manager. Salaries for these people and himself would run about $160,000 annually, plus some form of incentive compensation he had yet to determine. Other fixed or semifixed expenses were estimated as follows:

Equipment depreciation	$35,000
Warehouse depreciation	15,000
Utilities and telephone	12,000
Insurance	10,000
Personal property taxes	10,000
Maintenance and janitorial services	5,600
Miscellaneous	2,400
	$90,000

According to the two wholesalers, beer in bottles and cans outsold keg beer by a three-to-one margin. Keg beer prices at the wholesale level were about 45 percent of prices for beer in bottles and cans.

![MEETING image]

MEETING

The entire matter deserved much thought. Maybe it was a golden opportunity, maybe not. The only thing certain was that research was needed, Manson and Associates was ready, and Larry needed time to think. Today is Tuesday, Larry thought—only three days until he and John Rome would get together for direction.

Ms-Tique Corporation

In January 1991, Phoebe Masters, Product Manager for hand and body lotions, was considering whether to introduce a new package design for the firm's Soft and Silky shaving cream. The major questions were whether a 5½-ounce or an 11-ounce aerosol container should be introduced and whether the cost of additional research could be justified. Timing was critical because the incidence of women's shaving would increase during the spring months and reach its peak during the summer months.

THE COMPANY AND THE PRODUCT

Soft and Silky is marketed by Ms-Tique Corporation, a manufacturer of women's personal-care products. The firm's line of products includes facial creams, hand and body lotions, and a full line of women's toiletries. Products are sold by drug and food-and-drug stores through rack jobbers. Rack jobbers are actually wholesalers that set up retail displays and keep them stocked with merchandise. They receive a margin of 20 percent off the sales price to retailers.

Soft and Silky was introduced in the spring of 1983. The product was viewed as a logical extension of the company's line of hand and body lotions and required few changes in packaging and manufacturing. The unique dimension of the introduction was that Soft and Silky was positioned as a women's shaving cream. The positioning strategy was successful in differentiating Soft and Silky from existing men's shaving creams. Moreover, rack jobbers were able to obtain product placement in the women's personal-care section of drug and food-and-drug stores, thus emphasizing the product's positioning statement. Furthermore, placement apart from men's shaving cream minimized direct price comparisons with men's shaving creams, since Soft and Silky was premium-priced—$2.55 per 5½-ounce tube at retail. Retailers received a 40 percent margin on their selling price.

Soft and Silky was sold in a tube as opposed to an aerosol container. This packaging plan was adopted because the firm did not have the technology to produce aerosol containers in 1983. Furthermore, the firm's policy at that time was to utilize existing manufacturing capacity whenever possible. As of 1991, all products sold by the firm were packaged in tubes, bottles, or jars.

Soft and Silky had experienced a profitable sales growth from the time of its introduction. Although the market for women's shaving cream was small, the premium price and unique positioning had produced a "customer franchise," in Masters's words. "We have a unique product for the feminine woman who considers herself special." The unit sales volume for Soft and Silky for the period 1983–1990 is shown in Exhibit 1.

This case prepared by Professor Roger A. Kerin, of the Edwin L. Cox School of Business, Southern Methodist University, as a basis for class discussion and is not designed to illustrate effective or ineffective handling of an administrative situation. Certain names have been disguised. Copyright © by Roger A. Kerin. No part of this case may be reproduced without written permission of the copyright holder.

EXHIBIT 1

Soft and Silky Unit Sales Volume, 1983–1990

Year	Volume	Year	Volume
1983	220,000	1987	452,237
1984	242,000	1988	565,300
1985	278,700	1989	678,356
1986	347,875	1990	814,028

The Soft and Silky income statement for 1990 is shown in Exhibit 2. Advertising and promotional expenses had increased, as a percentage of sales, each year since 1986.

WOMEN'S SHAVING

Research on women's shaving commissioned by Masters over the past several years had produced a number of findings useful in preparing annual marketing plans for Soft and Silky. The major findings and selected marketing actions prompted by these findings are described below.

Methods of Leg-Hair Removal and Shaving Frequency

Women use a variety of methods for leg-hair removal. The most popular method is simply shaving with soap and water. Shaving with shaving cream is the next most used method, followed by shaving with electric razors. Women typically have their own razors, use double-edge razors, and purchase their own supplies of blades.

Shaving frequency varies by season, with the summer months producing the greatest shaving activity (see Exhibit 3). Over 80 percent of women shave at least once per week, and women who work outside the home shave more frequently than those who do not.

EXHIBIT 2

Soft and Silky Income Statement for the Year Ending December 31, 1990

Sales		$993,114
Cost of goods sold (incl. freight)[a]		325,611
Gross profit		$667,503
Assignable costs:		
Advertising and promotion	$311,648	
Overhead and administrative costs	195,000	506,648
Brand contribution		$160,855

[a]For analysis purposes, treat the cost of goods sold as the only variable cost.

EXHIBIT 3

Seasonality of Women Shaving and Shaving Area (Percentage of U.S. Women)

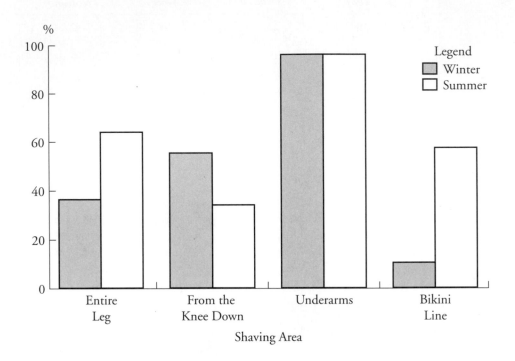

Attitudes toward Shaving

Women view shaving as a necessary evil. When queried about their ideal shaving cream, women typically respond that they want a product that contains a moisturizer, reduces irritation, and makes shaving easier. It appears that four out of five women use a moisturizer after shaving.

These specific findings resulted in a change in the Soft and Silky ingredient formulation in 1987. Prior to 1987, the product contained no moisturizers; however, in 1987, moisturizers were added to the product and were emphasized on the package and in media advertising.

Market Size and Competitive Products

Industry sources estimate the dollar value of women's "wet shaving" products to be over $95 million in 1990, at manufacturer's prices. Razors account for the bulk of this figure.

Typically, only one other shaving cream positioned as a "women's-only" cream is available in the drug and food-and-drug stores served by Ms-Tique. The competitive brand was either S. C. Johnson and Son's Soft Sense or Soft Shave sold by White Laboratories. Masters offered two reasons for this situation. First, the market just isn't that large. I don't think three competing products would or could be profitable. Second, the shelf-space battle in food and food-and-drug stores is increasing. One only has to visit one of these stores to see that the shelves are already congested. I doubt that health-and-beauty-aid buyers in these stores want to add another brand, particularly since shaving cream for women is not a big-turnover item.

"However, since men's shaving creams are a substitute for Soft and Silky, we have to consider them as competitors," she added. The average retail prices per ounce of men's shaving creams packaged in nonaerosol containers and in aerosol containers are shown in Exhibit 4.

NEW PACKAGE DESIGN

The idea for a new package design was provided by Masters's assistant, Heather Courtwright. Courtwright had observed that shaving creams for men were frequently packaged in tubes and aerosol containers. These two packages were frequently displayed side by side in the men's shaving area of drug and food-and-drug stores. The aerosol containers were often more expensive than nonaerosol or tube containers on a container basis, since they were typically 11-ounce cans, but less expensive on a per-ounce basis.

Her observations were brought to Masters's attention in mid-1990. After discussing with her the possibility of changing the package design, Masters directed Courtwright to investigate the idea further. Masters's response was prompted by two recent developments. First, the annual average unit sales volume increase for Soft and Silky had plateaued in recent years. Perhaps a change in packaging might bolster sales volume, she thought. Second, the growth of Soft and Silky had strained manufacturing capacity. Historically, production of Soft and Silky had been easily integrated into the firm's production schedules. However, growth in the entire line of hand and body lotions, coupled with the increase in Soft and Silky sales, had overburdened production scheduling. Given prevailing economic conditions, the firm had no capacity-expansion plans for the next three years.

Courtwright contacted a firm specializing in "contract filling." A contract filler purchases cans, propellants, caps, and valves from a variety of sources and then assembles these components, including the product fill (that is, shaving cream), into the final aerosol product. The production method is called pressure filling. In this method, the cap and valve are inserted in the can and then sealed. At the same time, a vacuum is created in the container. The product fill and propellant are then injected under high pressure through the valve into the can.

EXHIBIT 4

Retail Price Comparisons

Container Type/Size	Average Retail Price per Ounce	Retail Price Range per Ounce
Nonaerosol, 4 oz.	$0.42	$0.32–$0.44
Nonaerosol, 10 oz.	$0.21	$0.18–$0.25
Aerosol, 6 oz.	$0.27	$0.24–$0.30
Aerosol, 11 oz.	$0.16	$0.08–$0.23

The estimated total cost of producing and delivering to retailers an 11-ounce aerosol can of shaving cream was $0.29. A minimum order of 50,000 11-ounce cans would be required. The retail price would be set at $2.85 per 11-ounce can, reflecting Soft and Silky's premium-price strategy. The estimated total cost of producing and delivering to retailers a 5½-ounce aerosol can of shaving cream was $0.20, and the retail price would be $1.85. A 50,000-unit minimum order would be required.

PRELIMINARY TESTS

In November 1990, Courtwright requested $15,000 to assess consumer response to the aerosol container. Masters approved the request on the basis of the cost data provided and the recognition that use of a contract filler would require no incremental investment in manufacturing capability.

Courtwright commissioned a large marketing-research firm to conduct four focus-group studies.[1] Two focus groups would involve current users of Soft and Silky, and two focus groups would involve users of shaving creams other than Soft and Silky. The principal information sought from these focus group studies was as follows:

1. Are present customers and noncustomers receptive to the aerosol can?
2. At what rate would present customers convert to the aerosol can, and would noncustomers switch over to Soft and Silky?
3. Where, in drug and food-and-drug stores, would customers and noncustomers expect to find the aerosol can?
4. Is the price acceptable?

In addition, the marketing-research firm was asked to examine analogous situations of package changes and report its findings.

In late December the marketing-research firm presented its findings:

1. Customers and noncustomers were unanimously in favor of the aerosol can. The 11-ounce can was the favorite, since it would require fewer purchases.
2. Half of Soft and Silky customers said they would convert to the 11-ounce can; 25 percent said they would convert to the 5½-ounce can.
3. One-fourth of the noncustomers said they would switch over to the aerosol can irrespective of can size. These consumers' preference for the aerosol over the tube package was their principal reason (in addition to price) for not buying Soft and Silky previously.
4. Customers expected to find the aerosol can next to the tube container. Noncustomers expected to find the aerosol container next to the men's shaving cream.
5. The pricing was acceptable and actually favored by current customers. Noncustomers thought the price was somewhat high, but liked the moisturizing benefit and would try the product.

In addition to these findings, the marketing-research firm presented ten case histories in which marketers of men's shaving cream had introduced a new package.

---

[1] A *focus-group* interview consists of a moderator's questioning and listening to a group of 8 to 12 con-

(There was no distinction made with respect to size of package, whether the package change was from aerosol to nonaerosol, or vice versa, or previous sales performance.) Two statistics were highlighted: sales growth with the combined packages and the cannibalization rate for the existing package. According to the report,

> It is difficult to draw one-to-one comparisons between the experience of other shaving creams and that of Soft and Silky, given its unique market position. We have tried to do so after examining ten product-design changes. Our estimates [Exhibit 5] are broken down into a "high" and a "low" forecast for each package size. Seven out of the ten products studied experienced the "high" situation presented; three experienced the "low" situation. We see the 11-ounce package as producing the largest increase in ounces sold. Even with the cannibalism effect operating, we believe that an additional package will produce higher sales, in ounces, than the forecasted volume of 5,372,587 ounces (976,834 5½-ounce tubes) for 1991. Only a market test can indicate what will actually occur.

EXHIBIT 5

Soft and Silky Sales Forecasts by Size of Aerosol Container

Forecast A: Low estimate for 5½-ounce aerosol package addition

5½-oz. tube package volume		4,900,000 ounces
5½-oz. aerosol package volume:		
Cannibalized volume	472,587	
Net new volume	250,000	722,587
		5,622,587 ounces

Forecast B: High estimate for 5½-ounce aerosol package addition

5½-oz. tube package volume		5,200,000 ounces
5½-oz. aerosol package volume:		
Cannibalized volume	172,587	
Net new volume	300,000	472,587
		5,672,587 ounces

Forecast C: Low estimate for 11-ounce aerosol package addition

5½-oz. tube package volume		4,500,000 ounces
11-oz. aerosol package volume:		
Cannibalized volume	872,587	
Net new volume	400,000	1,272,587
		5,772,587 ounces

Forecast D: High estimate for 11-ounce aerosol package addition

5½-oz. tube package volume		5,200,000 ounces
11-oz. aerosol package volume:		
Cannibalized volume	172,587	
Net new volume	600,000	772,587
		5,972,587 ounces

JANUARY 1991

Masters and Courtwright studied the research firm's findings carefully. They particularly noted the recommendation that a market test be conducted to determine the best package design.

The test-market recommendation suggested the introduction of the new package design in a limited cross-section of drug and food-and-drug stores, including heavy-volume and low-volume stores. Test stores would be isolated geographically from nontest stores. The new package would be placed among men's shaving creams, and the test would run for three months, beginning April 1, 1991. One-half of the stores would carry the 5½-ounce aerosol container, and the other half would carry the 11-ounce container. The test would include a full complement of promotional aids, including newspaper ads and point-of-purchase displays, and would approximate a full-scale introduction.

Courtwright noted that the estimated cost for the test market would be $22,000, which included the cost of gathering marketing-research data on the cannibalization rate and incremental sales growth. No other incremental costs would be charged against the products. Sales and marketing efforts for the existing package would remain unchanged during the course of the test.

Late in the evening of January 28, 1991, Masters found herself considering whether the 5½-ounce or the 11-ounce aerosol container should be introduced, since she believed it unwise to introduce both sizes, given the uncertainty of market acceptance. She also wondered whether the test-market proposal should be adopted. Masters was confident that, given the product's sales history, the existing package would produce sales of 976,834 units (a 20 percent increase) in 1991. "Perhaps I should have told Heather to forget the whole matter last fall," she thought to herself.

MacTec Control AB

"The choices themselves seem simple enough," thought Georg Carlsson, "either we enter the U.S. market in Pennsylvania and New York, we forget about the U.S. for the time being, or we do some more marketing research." The difficult part was the decision.

Georg was president of MacTec Control AB, a Swedish firm located in Kristianstad. Georg had begun MacTec in 1980 along with his wife, Jessie. MacTec had grown rapidly and boasted some 30 employees and annual revenues of about $2.8 million by 1990. Since 1985, MacTec had been partly owned by the Perstorp Corporation, whose headquarters were located nearby. Perstorp was a large manufacturer of chemicals and chemical products, with operations in 18 countries and annual revenues of about $600 million. Perstorp had provided MacTec with capital and managerial advice, as well as chemical analysis technology.

MACTEC'S AQUALEX SYSTEM

MacTec's product line centered about its Aqualex System, a design of computer hardware and software for the monitoring and control of pressurized water flows. Most often these water flows consisted of either potable water or sewage effluent, as these liquids were stored, moved, or treated by municipal water departments.

The Aqualex System employed MacTec's MPDII microcomputer (see Exhibits 1 and 2) installed at individual pumping stations where liquids are stored and moved. Often these stations were located quite far apart, linking geographically dispersed water users (households, businesses, etc.) to water and sewer systems. The microcomputer performed a number of important functions—it controlled the starts, stops, and alarms of up to four pumps; monitored levels and available capacities of storage reservoirs; checked pump capacities and power consumptions; and recorded pump flows. It could even measure amounts of rainfall entering reservoirs and adjust pump operations or activate an alarm as needed. Each microcomputer could also be easily connected to a main computer to allow remote control of pumping stations and produce a variety of charts and graphs useful in evaluating pump performance and scheduling needed maintenance.

The Aqualex System provided a monitoring function that human operators could not match in terms of sophistication, immediacy, and cost. The system permitted each individual substation to control its own pumping operations; collect, analyze, and store data; forecast trends; transmit data and alarms to a central computer; and receive remote commands. Alarms could also be transmitted directly to a pocket-

---

This case was written by Professor James E. Nelson of the University of Colorado. This case is intended for use as a basis for class discussion rather than to illustrate either effective or ineffective administrative decision making. Some data are disguised. Copyright © by the Business Research Division, College of Business and Administration and the Graduate School of Business Administration, University of Colorado, Boulder, Colorado, 80309-0419. Used with permission.

EXHIBIT 1

Information on the MPDII Microcomputer

MPDII controls and monitors the pumping stations

An MPDII microcomputer is installed at a pumping station and works as an independent, intelligent computer. When required, it can go on-line with the central computer and report its readings there.

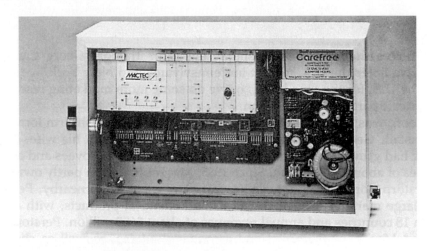

Here are some of the functions of the MPDII:

- It governs the starts, stops, and alarms of up to four pumps, controlled by an integrated, piezo-resistive pressure-level sensor.
- It checks the sump level.
- It checks pump capacity and changes in pump capacity.
- It activates an alarm when readings reach preset deviation limits.
- It registers precipitation and activates an alarm in case of heavy rain.
- It constantly monitors pump power consumption and activates an alarm in case of unacceptable deviation.
- It registers current pump flow by means of advanced calculations of inflow and outfeed from the sump.
- It can register accumulated time for overflow.
- It switches to forward to reverse action, even by remote command.
- It stores locally the last nine alarm instances with time indications. These may be read directly on an LCD display.
- It can be remotely programmed from the central computer.

An MPDII does a great job, day after day, year after year.

sized receiver carried by one or more operators on call. A supervisor could continually monitor pumping operations in a large system entirely via a computer terminal at a central location and send commands to individual pumps, thereby saving costly service calls and time. The system also reduced the possibility of overflows that could produce disastrous flooding of nearby communities.

EXHIBIT 2

Computerized Monitoring and Control of Water Treatment Plants

The Aqualex System cuts operating and maintenance costs for water treatment plants.

The System takes over most of the monitoring and control of the plant by means of computerized controls. This frees resources for use in planned and efficient maintenance work, type of work that cannot be automated.

The Aqualex System is based on a number of intelligent computer sub-stations. These are placed at the pumping stations, sewage treatment plant, waterworks, etc. and are on-line to the central computer.

The computer sub-stations can independently handle local process control, store readings and analyze trends. They carry on advanced communication with the central computer to transmit readings and alarms and receive remote commands.

The central computer has the capacity to process the readings received from the sub-stations and present them in the form of reports and trends. Alarms can also be transmitted to one or more pocket-sized receivers with alarm code displays.

The operator on call can monitor the entire system at home by means of a portable home terminal. This terminal also has the capacity for remote commands, which saves many costly service calls.

The Aqualex System does the job of many people with high precision and reliability.

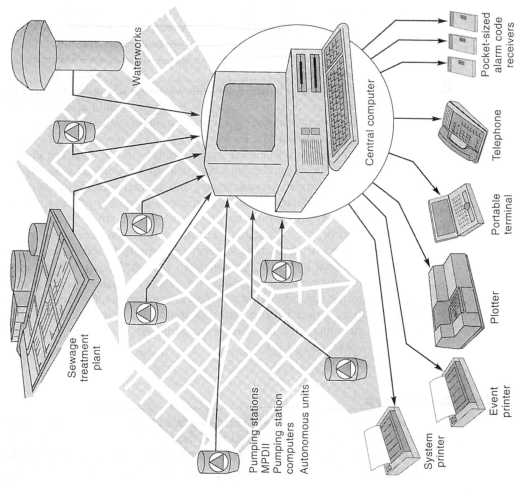

Waterworks

Sewage treatment plant

Pumping stations
MPDII
Pumping station computers
Autonomous units

Central computer

Pocket-sized alarm code receivers

Telephone

Portable terminal

Plotter

Event printer

System printer

139

MacTec personnel would work with water and sewage engineers to design and install the desired Aqualex System. Personnel would also train engineers and operators to work with the system and would be available 24 hours a day for consultation. If needed, a MacTec engineer could be physically present to assist engineers and operators whenever major problems arose. MacTec also offered its clients the option of purchasing a complete service contract whereby MacTec personnel would provide periodic testing and maintenance of installed systems.

An Aqualex System could be configured a number of ways. In its most basic form, the system would be little more than a small "black box" that monitored two or three lift station activities and, when necessary, transmitted an alarm to one or more remote receivers. An intermediate system would monitor additional activities, send data to a central computer via telephone lines, and receive remote commands. An advanced system would provide the same monitoring capabilities but add forecasting features, maintenance management, auxiliary power backup, and data transmission and reception via radio. Prices to customers for the three configurations in early 1989 were about $1,200, $2,400, and $4,200.

AQUALEX CUSTOMERS

Aqualex customers could be divided into two groups—governmental units and industrial companies. The typical application in the first group was a sewage treatment plant having some 4 to 12 pumping stations, each station containing one or more pumps. Pumps would operate intermittently and—unless an Aqualex or similar system were in place—be monitored by one or more operators who would visit each station once or perhaps twice each day for about a half hour. Operators would take reservoir measurements, record running times of pumps, and sometimes perform limited maintenance and repairs. The sewage plant and stations typically were located in flat or rolling terrain, where gravity could not be used in lieu of pumping. If any monitoring equipment were present at all, it typically would consist of a crude, on-site alarm that would activate whenever fluid levels rose or fell beyond a preset level. Sometimes the alarm would activate a telephone dialing function that alerted an operator some distance from the station.

Numerous industrial companies also stored, moved, and processed large quantities of water or sewage. These applications usually differed little from those in governmental plants except for their smaller size. On the other hand, there were a considerably larger number of industrial companies having pumping stations, and so, Georg thought, the two markets often offered about identical market potentials in many countries.

The two markets desired essentially the same products, although industrial applications often used smaller, simpler equipment. Both markets wanted their monitoring equipment to be accurate and reliable, the two dominant concerns. Equipment should also be easy to use, economical to operate, and require little regular service or maintenance. Purchase price often was not a major consideration—as long as the price was in some appropriate range, customers seemed more interested in actual product performance than in initial outlays.

Georg thought that worldwide demand for Aqualex Systems and competing products would continue to be strong for at least the next ten years. While some of this demand represented construction of new pumping stations, many applications were replacements of crude monitoring and alarm systems at existing sites. These existing systems depended greatly on regular visits by operators, visits that often continued even after new equipment was installed. Most such trips were probably not necessary. However, many managers found it difficult to dismiss or reassign monitoring personnel that were no longer needed; many were also quite cautious and conservative, desiring some human monitoring of the new equipment "just in case." Once replacements of existing systems were complete, market growth would be limited to new construction and, of course, replacements of more sophisticated systems.

Most customers (as well as noncustomers) considered the Aqualex System to be the best on the market. Those knowledgeable in the industry felt that competing products seldom matched Aqualex's reliability and accuracy. Experts also believed that many competing products lacked the sophistication and flexibility present in Aqualex's design. Beyond these product features, customers also appreciated MacTec's knowledge about water and sanitation engineering. Competing firms often lacked this expertise, offering their products somewhat as a sideline and considering the market too small for an intensive marketing effort.

The market was clearly not too small for MacTec. While Georg had no hard data on market potential for Western Europe, he thought that annual demand here could be as much as $9 million. About 40 percent of this came from new construction, while the rest represented demand from replacing existing systems. Industry sales in the latter category could be increased by more aggressive marketing efforts on the part of MacTec and its competitors. Eastern European economies represented additional, new potential. However, the water and sewer industries in these countries seemed less interested than their Western counterparts in high-technology equipment to monitor pumping operations. Additionally, business was often more difficult to conduct in these countries. In contrast, the U.S. market looked very attractive.

MACTEC STRATEGY

MacTec currently marketed its Aqualex System primarily to sewage treatment plants in Scandinavia and other countries in Northern and Central Europe. The company's strategy could be described as providing technologically superior equipment to monitor pumping operations at these plants. The strategy stressed frequent contacts with customers and potential customers to design, supply, and service Aqualex Systems. The strategy also stressed superior knowledge of water and sanitation engineering along with up-to-date electronics and computer technology. The result was a line of highly specialized sensors, computers, and methods for process controls in water treatment plants.

This was the essence of MacTec's strategy, having a special competence that no firm in the world could easily match. MacTec also prided itself on being a young, creative company without an entrenched bureaucracy. Company employees generally worked with enthusiasm and dedication; they talked with one another, regularly, openly, and with a great deal of give and take. Most importantly, customers—as well as technology—seemed to drive all areas in the company.

MacTec's strategy in its European markets seemed to be fairly well decided. That is, Georg thought that a continuation of present strategies and tactics should continue to produce good results. However, an aspect that would likely change would be to locate a branch office having both sales and manufacturing activities somewhere in the European Community (EC), most likely the Netherlands. The plan was to have such an office in operation well before 1992, when the 12 countries in the EC (Belgium, Denmark, France, Germany, Greece, Ireland, Italy, Luxembourg, the

Netherlands, Portugal, Spain, United Kingdom) would mutually eliminate national barriers to the flow of capital, goods, and services. Having a MacTec office located in the EC would greatly simplify sales to these member countries. Moreover, MacTec's presence should also avoid problems with any protective barriers the EC itself might raise to limit or discourage market access by outsiders.

Notwithstanding activities related to this branch office, Georg was considering a major strategic decision to enter the U.S. market. His two recent visits to the United States had led him to conclude that the market represented potential beyond that for Western Europe, and that the United States seemed perfect for expansion. Industry experts in the United States agreed with Georg that the Aqualex System outperformed anything used in the U.S. market. Experts thought that many water and sewage engineers would welcome MacTec's products and knowledge. Moreover, Georg thought that U.S. transportation systems and payment arrangements would present few problems. The system would be imported under U.S. Tariff Regulation 71249 and pay a duty of 4.9 percent.

Entry would most likely be in the form of a sales and service office located in Philadelphia. The Pennsylvania and New York State markets seemed representative of the United States and appeared to offer a good test of the Aqualex System. The two states together probably represented about 18 percent of total U.S. market potential for the system. The office would require an investment of some $200,000 for inventory and other balance sheet items. Annual fixed costs would total upward of $250,000 for salaries and other operating expenses—Georg thought that the office would employ only a general manager, two sales technicians, and secretary for at least the first year or two. Each Aqualex System sold in the United States would be priced to provide a contribution margin of about 30 percent. Georg wanted a 35 percent annual return before taxes on any MacTec investment, to begin no later than the second year. At issue was whether Georg could realistically expect to achieve this goal in the United States.

MARKETING RESEARCH

To this end, Georg had commissioned the Browning Group in Philadelphia to conduct some limited marketing research with selected personnel from the water and sewage industries in the city and surrounding areas. The research had two purposes: to obtain a sense of market needs and market reactions to MacTec's products and to calculate a rough estimate of market potential in Pennsylvania and New York. Results were intended to help Georg interpret his earlier conversations with industry experts and perhaps allow a decision on market entry.

The research design itself employed two phases of data collection. The first consisted of five one-hour interviews with water and sewage engineers employed by local city and municipal governments. For each interview, an experienced Browning Group interviewer scheduled an appointment with the engineer and then visited his office, armed with a set of questions and a tape recorder. Questions included:

1. What procedures do you use to monitor your pumping stations?
2. Is your current monitoring system effective? Costly?
3. What are the costs of a monitoring malfunction?
4. What features would you like to see in a monitoring system?
5. Who decides on the selection of a monitoring system?
6. What is your reaction to the Aqualex System?

Interviewers were careful to listen closely to the engineers' responses and to probe for additional detail and clarification.

Tapes of the personal interviews were transcribed and then analyzed by the project manager at Browning. The report noted that these results were interesting in that they described typical industry practices and viewpoints. A partial summary from the report appears below:

> The picture that emerges is one of fairly sophisticated personnel making decisions about monitoring equipment that is relatively simple in design. Still, some engineers would appear distrustful of this equipment because they persist in sending operators to pumping stations on a daily basis. The distrust may be justified because potential costs of a malfunction were identified as expensive repairs and cleanups, fines of $10,000 per day of violation, lawsuits, harassment by the Health Department, and public embarrassment. The five engineers identified themselves as key individuals in the decision to purchase new equipment. Without exception, they considered MacTec features innovative, highly desirable, and worth the price.

The summary noted also that the primary use of the interview results was to construct a questionnaire that could be administered over the telephone.

The questionnaire was used in the second phase of data collection, as part of a telephone survey that had contacted 65 utility managers, water and sewage engineers, and pumping station operators in Philadelphia and surrounding areas. All respondents were employed by governmental units. Each interview took about ten minutes to complete, covering topics identified in questions 1, 2, and 4 above. The Browning Group's research report stated that most interviews found respondents to be quite cooperative, although 15 people refused to participate at all.

The telephone interviews had produced results that could be considered more representative of the market because of the larger sample size. The report had organized these results about the topics of monitoring procedures, system effectiveness and costs, and features desired in a monitoring system:

> All monitoring systems under the responsibility of the 50 respondents were considered to require manual checking. The frequency of operator visits to pumping stations ranged from monthly to twice daily, depending on flow rates, pumping station history, proximity of nearby communities, monitoring equipment in operation, and other factors. Even the most sophisticated automatic systems were checked because respondents "just don't trust the machine." Each operator was responsible for some 10 to 20 stations.
>
> Despite the perceived need for double-checking, all respondents considered their current monitoring system to be quite effective. Not one reported a serious pumping malfunction in the past three years that had escaped detection. However, this reliability came at considerable cost—the annual wages and other expenses associated with each monitoring operator averaged about $40,000.
>
> Respondents were about evenly divided between those wishing a simple alarm system and those desiring a sophisticated, versatile microprocessor. Managers and engineers in the former category often said that the only feature they really needed was an emergency signal such as a siren, horn, or light. Sometimes they would add a telephone dialer that would be automatically activated at the same time as the signal. Most agreed that a price of around $2,000 would be reasonable for such a system. The latter category of individuals contained engineers desiring many of the Aqualex System's features, once they knew such equipment was available. A price of $4,000 per system seemed acceptable. Some of these respondents were quite knowledgeable about computers and computer programming while others were not.

Only four respondents voiced any strong concerns about the cost to purchase and install more sophisticated monitoring equipment. Everyone demanded that the equipment be reliable and accurate.

Georg found the report quite helpful. Much of the information, of course, simply confirmed his own view of the U.S. market. However, it was good to have this knowledge from an independent, objective organization. In addition, to learn that the market consisted of two, apparently equal-sized segments of simple and sophisticated applications was quite worthwhile. In particular, knowledge of system prices considered acceptable by each segment would make the entry decision easier. Meeting these prices would not be a major problem.

A most important section of the report contained an estimate of market potential for Pennsylvania and New York. The estimate was based on an analysis of discharge permits on file in governmental offices in the two states. These permits were required before any city, municipality, water or sewage district, or industrial company could release sewage or other contaminated water to another system or to a lake or river. Each permit showed the number of pumping stations in operation. Based on a 10 percent sample of permits, the report had estimated that governmental units in Pennsylvania and New York contained approximately 3,000 and 5,000 pumping stations for waste water, respectively. Industrial companies in the two states were estimated to add some 3,000 and 9,000 more pumping stations, respectively. The total number of pumping stations in the two states—20,000—seemed to be growing at about 2 percent per year.

Finally, a brief section of the report dealt with the study's limitations. Georg agreed that sample was quite small, that it contained no utility managers or engineers from New York, and that it probably concentrated too heavily on individuals in larger urban areas. In addition, the research told him nothing about competitors and their marketing strategies and tactics. Nor did he learn anything about any state regulations for monitoring equipment, if indeed any existed. However, these shortcomings came as no surprise, representing a consequence of the research design proposed to Georg by the Browning Group some six weeks ago, before the study began.

THE DECISION

Georg's decision seemed a difficult one. The most risky option was to enter the U.S. market as soon as possible; the most conservative was to stay in Europe. In between was the option of conducting some additional marketing research.

Discussion with the Browning Group had identified the objectives of this research as to rectify limitations of the first study as well as to provide more accurate estimates of market potential. (The estimates of the numbers of pumping stations in Pennsylvania and New York were accurate to around plus or minus 20 percent.) This research was estimated to cost $40,000 and take another three months to complete.

Bateson Battery Chargers

Ed Warren left his office early, filled with enthusiasm. His meeting with Mark Mercer had gone well, the field test of a Rejuvenator prototype had exceeded everyone's expectations, and the project now appeared to be back on schedule. "Rejuvenator" was the name chosen by the project team for an innovative battery charger two years ago, in October 1990, when Warren was still working in Corporate Marketing. Mercer, too, was an original team member, having left his job as Manufacturing Engineer in the Bateson Battery Division. Charlene Becker became the third and last team member, coming to the team from Corporate Finance in November 1990.

The three team members had volunteered for an assignment to design several Rejuvenator models and investigate marketing feasibility. Each saw the project as a splendid opportunity to advance his or her own career at Bateson. If the project was a "go," team members would undoubtedly remain with the new division, at high levels of responsibility. On the other hand, if the project was abandoned, each would still have gotten a great deal from a challenging experience—not to mention numerous contacts with and widespread visibility among high-level Bateson executives.

Initial efforts related to the project had involved the concurrent design, testing, product costing, and market analysis for the Rejuvenator. The first three activities had taken place largely inside the company, but market analysis had consisted mostly of studies prepared by commercial marketing research firms. These studies, which ranged in price from $2,000 to $5,000, had helped Warren and his fellow team members "decipher the multitude of applications for battery chargers and the numerous routes available for marketing such a product." Nevertheless, a decision concerning the choice of market targets and subsequent market research was yet to be made as of December 1992.

BATESON CORPORATION

Bateson Corporation is a large manufacturer of automotive and related products with its headquarters in Cleveland, Ohio. Sales revenues for 1991 were over $2.2 billion. Subsidiaries and divisions of the company are located primarily in the United States, with major manufacturing facilities at several locations in California, Florida, Ohio, Michigan, and Indiana. Total employment in December 1992 was over 20,000 people. Major product lines include automotive headliners, carpeting, hoses, interior paneling, seals, and batteries. Almost 70 percent of Bateson's sales revenues come from automotive products.

This case was written by Associate Professor James E. Nelson, of the University of Colorado at Boulder. He thanks Professor Roger A. Kerin, of the Southern Methodist University, for his helpful comments in writing this case. The case is intended for educational purposes rather than to illustrate either effective or ineffective decision making. Some data as well as the identity of the company are disguised. © 1992 by James E. Nelson.

Bateson's strategy in the United States for many of its automotive products could be described as defensive, oriented toward maintaining market share and controlling fixed and variable costs. The U.S. market for automotive parts has reached maturity, with limited growth forecast for the future. Still, the market is characterized by a good deal of change based on emerging technologies and on styling and design modifications initiated by automobile manufacturers.

In contrast to the U.S. market, Europe and eastern Asia were seen by senior Bateson executives as opportunities for growth. The company had joint-venture or licensee agreements with several companies located in several countries in Europe. These firms manufactured and marketed Bateson products under their own brand name and paid Bateson a fee for the privilege. However, with the coming of the new European Community in 1992, Bateson had decided in late 1989 to let these agreements expire at the end of December 1991. Construction of a Bateson manufacturing facility in Frankfurt, Germany, was completed in the summer of 1991, and an office and sales staff were in place soon thereafter. Bateson Europe was fully operational on January 1, 1992.

Bateson also had manufacturing plants and sales offices in Malaysia and Korea. Similar operations were tentatively planned for Mexico and, perhaps, Brazil. In total, almost 30 percent of Bateson's 1991 sales revenues came from international operations, with about one-half coming from foreign production and one-half from U.S. exports. International revenues were expected to grow steadily as the company became increasingly global in its orientation and culture.

Product strategy at Bateson was evolving as well. Early products (pre–World War II) were simple in design and manufacture and had rather long life cycles. Mercer described the six-volt battery on his bookshelf as a mainstay of the Bateson product line for over 20 years. He had found it in his grandfather's 1948 Plymouth. Bateson products had become much more complex and sophisticated, and most new models have a life cycle of between two and five years. Opinions varied, but most industry experts viewed Bateson products as "about average" in terms of quality and price. Although this position was barely acceptable in the United States, the company had found it necessary to raise its design and production standards in Europe.

Bateson Battery Division

The Battery Division (where work on the Rejuvenator had begun) generated almost $200 million in sales for 1991. Over 2,000 employees work as production operators, engineers, accountants, salespeople, and managers in the division. Over 1,000 different models of batteries are manufactured and marketed. Most models are the conventional, lead-acid batteries that are commonly found under the hoods of automobiles and light trucks. Most of these batteries are sold as "replacement" batteries to large retail chains (automotive specialty stores and mass merchandisers) and to wholesalers. About 10 percent of Bateson's models are used in agricultural, construction, and marine applications. Another 10 percent are nickel-cadmium batteries used in a variety of applications.

Much of Bateson's revenues from the entire line of automotive products come from sales made directly to original equipment manufacturers such as Ford, Nissan, Honda, and Hyundai. However, a majority of battery revenues came from after-market sales to chain retailers such as Northern Automotive, AutoZone, and Western Auto, to mass merchandisers such as Sears and JCPenney, and to wholesale distributors that sell to smaller, independent retailers. Price and sales terms have seemed to be the most influential factors when the large retailers select suppliers. Most of the division's 60 sales-people were formerly engineers. Most are experienced and capable, with average tenure with Bateson being about ten years. All are paid a salary plus a commission (based on sales volume and averaging about 60 percent of a salesperson's total compensation).

Bateson Battery Charger

In 1988, a Bateson engineer had developed a microchip design for a battery charger whose performance was based directly on properties of the discharged battery. The design incorporated a pulsing current that changed in magnitude and direction over the charging time period. The consequence was that electrochemical processes in the battery were much improved—the lives of working batteries could be greatly extended, and, in fact, many batteries thought to be worn out could be brought back to normal operation. The design was granted a U.S. patent in 1989. As of December 1992, similar patents were pending in the European Community (under its European Patent Treaty), Spain, India, and Japan.

As Warren saw it, the charger's ability to extend (perhaps even double) the lives of operational batteries and to recondition old batteries were its two primary advantages. He had roughed out a short promotion piece using a simple graphics package that stressed these points (Exhibit 1).

"Our advantage is unlikely to be in costs," said Warren when Becker had summarized her product cost estimates. Each battery charger model was projected to cost about $150,000 in tools and fixtures in order to begin production. Bateson policy required that this investment be recovered within two years after the product entered the market. Fixed costs for each model were estimated at $100,000, exclusive of marketing expenditures and tools depreciation. Variable costs for each model would be between $12 and $500, depending on the charger's size and features, as long as production runs of 2,000 were scheduled. Becker and Mercer had concluded that runs of this size would be feasible. They had also concluded that Bateson's investments and its fixed and variable costs for each model would be little different from those faced by existing competitors. "Our chip for the charger adds only a dollar or so over a conventional design in terms of variable costs, as long as we sell 50,000 units over the model's life cycle," Becker had estimated.

Apart from investments and costs, the selling price for a Bateson charger would depend on many factors. Competitors' prices at the retail level varied "all over the map" according to Becker. For example, a small, conventional battery charger for motorcycles sold to consumers for about $18, while a typical model for automobiles sold for $30. At the middle of the spectrum, high-capacity chargers for electric-powered golf carts retailed for almost $400. At the top end were very high-capacity chargers used by automobile dealers and repair shops that were priced at $800 to $2,000. Bateson's prices for any application would be near competing prices, although the team thought that their charger's technological advantage should command some sort of price premium.

BATTERY CHARGER MARKETS

In December 1992, the team faced a decision: Which market or markets should Bateson focus on for purposes of making a later, go/no-go decision on the product? The issue was extremely complex because of the enormous diversity of battery use. Rechargeable batteries are used in products ranging from electric toothbrushes to

EXHIBIT 1

Mock-Up of Rejuvenator Promotional Piece

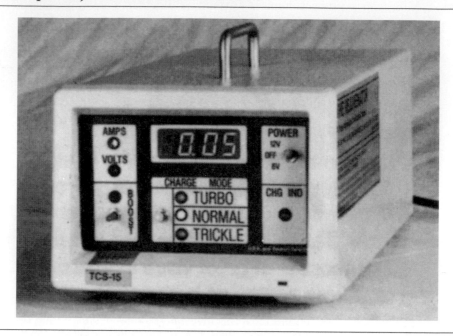

golf carts to space shuttles. The team had already ruled out applications in the first and last categories, focusing initially on seven disparate markets. For the sake of analysis, Warren divided all potential buyers into two groups: end users and commercial markets.

End Users

End users consist of consumers who purchase battery chargers for their own, personal use. A research study conducted by a marketing-research firm and purchased by the team described this market as follows:

> End users buy battery chargers from mass merchandisers and specialty stores, primarily for automotive applications. The purchase often is made based on an emergency (a dead battery), in winter, and in snowbelt states. Purchasers tend to be unaware of product features and product performance and instead rely on clerks or on package information in making their choice. Purchasers usually buy one or two battery chargers over a 20-year period.

The same study went on to describe distribution channels for battery chargers sold to end users as follows. The channel with the largest sales volume consists of automotive specialty stores. These stores sell parts and accessories for almost all makes and models of automobiles. Trade association data identified the largest chain in terms of number of stores to be Northern Automotive, with almost 900 retail stores in operation in 1991. The largest in terms of sales volume was Pep Boys, Inc., which had 1991 sales of over $900 million (from only 300 stores). Other major chains include Autozone,

Chief, and Western Auto. In addition to these large chains, there are numerous independent automotive specialty stores. These stores usually buy parts and accessories from wholesalers who service market areas as large as several states. Because of wholesalers' margins and other factors, prices in independent stores are often slightly higher than prices in the chains. In 1991, chains and independents totaled almost 50,000 stores and sold almost $32 billion in automotive parts and accessories.

About 40 percent of the end user market comes almost completely from large mass merchandisers such as Kmart, Sears, Wal-Mart, and JCPenney. Stores in these chains usually contain an automotive department or section that sells merchandise similar to the products offered in specialty stores. However, mass merchandisers usually offer a larger selection of products, including battery chargers. Mass merchandisers often carry three or four brands of battery chargers, while specialty stores usually carry only one or two. Mass merchandisers might devote two or three times more shelf space to chargers than specialty stores do. Mass merchandisers generally consider automotive departments as attractive operations, with sales growth rates twice that of the average department and with equally attractive gross profit margins.

The marketing-research report concluded that both types of channels expect about a 33 percent retail margin based on their selling price. Both types of channels expect battery chargers to turn over about six times per year. Chain members in both channels usually buy their merchandise directly from manufacturers, often on the basis of an annual, blanket purchase order that guarantees a minimum purchase quantity. Negotiations for these contracts are quite intense, as Bateson's existing salesforce could attest. Independent stores usually buy from wholesalers. Bateson's sales personnel consider wholesalers easier to deal with because they generally represent a much smaller sales volume than the chains.

Commercial Markets

The picture was more complicated on the commercial side. A second research study conducted by another marketing-research firm and purchased by the team divided this market into five smaller markets: transportation fleets (automobiles and trucks), golf carts, boats, light aircraft and helicopters, and automobile dealers and repair shops. However, each market is characterized by its purchase of battery chargers as part of a business activity.

Transportation fleets include public and private buses, over-the-highway tractors, delivery vehicles, rental cars, rental trucks, corporate cars, police cars, school buses, and taxis—a diverse group to say the least. Secondary data were used to conclude that the largest single segment is rental cars and corporate cars with approximately 7 million vehicles estimated to be on the road. The remaining segments contain upward of 3 million vehicles. Fleets usually buy vehicles at least once each year and generally sell their vehicles after one to three years of use. Purchases of battery chargers are usually made directly from a manufacturer or a wholesaler. The chargers themselves might be identical to those used by end users; however, they are more likely to be high-capacity models that are capable of charging a fully discharged battery in ten minutes or less.

Golf cart owners, including golf courses, represent another market. About one-half of the 700,000 golf carts in operation in the United States are estimated to be electric. These split into two equal-sized groups: those owned by individuals and those owned by public and private golf courses. The study described the application as follows:

> An individual owner of an electric golf cart almost always owns a battery charger for the vehicle. Golf courses typically own one charger for every four carts. Carts themselves generally required charging after one or perhaps two rounds of golf. Batteries used in carts often are light duty units purchased in used condition from a golf cart dealer. In addition to the batteries and the carts themselves, dealers also sell battery chargers at the rate of one per cart. The total number of dealers and courses that provide electric carts is about 10,000.

These battery chargers are much different from those for the end-user market. To charge the six or eight batteries in a golf cart requires a high-capacity charger and four to ten hours of uninterrupted charging. Chargers used by golf courses usually have an even higher capacity and can complete a charge cycle on several carts at once in much less time.

Boat owners, including marinas, constitute another market. Secondary data estimated the number of boats in the United States that require a battery to be about 10 million; the number of marinas, boat dealers, and marine motor repair shops total about 10,000. Battery chargers used in marine applications are often the same models used in the end-user market. However, some large marinas and dealers located near large bodies of water also use one or more high-capacity chargers identical to those used by transportation fleets and by automobile dealers and repair shops.

Private or civil aircraft, small commercial airlines (fixed wing passenger and freight and helicopters), airports and heliports, aircraft service and repair facilities, and other aviation services comprise yet another market. The U.S. market contains about 350,000 privately owned and small commercial aircraft. The number of airports and heliports totals about 20,000; the number of repair and other aviation services also totals about 20,000. In addition, a field test in Texas had demonstrated the Bateson charger's performance in the aircraft market. The test report summary read:

> A total of 39 batteries were brought in for testing. All had failed standard maintenance inspections. Eight had obvious physical damage such as cracked cases and were discarded. All of the remaining 31 batteries were charged with the Rejuvenator system and then returned to the maintenance hangar for a full Federal Aviation Authority "deep-cycle" test. Every one of the 31 batteries passed the test and was returned to full service.

The test concluded with the service manager asking to purchase the prototype charger!

The last commercial market—automobile dealers and repair shops—is clearly the largest. The U.S. market contains about 100,000 new and used car dealers and about 300,000 repair shops. Dealers and repair shops usually own several high-capacity chargers, each capable of rapid recharging of dead batteries on as many as ten vehicles at once. Dealers and shops also might own one or two end-user models. Almost all dealers and many of the larger repair shops stock and sell replacement batteries. In contrast to the other commercial markets, the number of automobile dealers and repair shops has been slowly declining.

MOTOR VEHICLE BATTERIES

The number of motor vehicle batteries shipped in the United States in 1991 was estimated by the team to be around 80 million units. About 65 million units were known to be replacement batteries, sold because an existing battery on a car, truck, bus, or other motor vehicle had failed. Battery failures were growing in number because vehicle owners were keeping their vehicles for longer periods of time before disposal—the average age of a vehicle on U.S. highways increased from 4.8 years in 1970 to 6.9 years in 1991. The average life of an automobile battery is about three years.

The cost to the owner for a replacement battery varies "all over the map," according to Becker. Depending on application, battery quality, retail outlet, and other factors, the cost of a replacement battery for a car or light truck could range from $30 to $80. "The only thing I can say for sure," Becker had said, "is that this cost is almost always important to the vehicle's owner. If we can restore the old battery, we come off as a hero."

Bateson could also look like a hero to state governments environmentalists in the United States who were worried about the disposal each year of some 65 million batteries. A data-base search undertaken by a Bateson librarian found numerous environmentally oriented articles addressing battery disposal. The 1990 Clean Air Act, other national legislation, and over 2,000 bills introduced into state legislatures in 1991 also evidenced the nation's concern over hazardous automotive waste. The primary issue related to discarded batteries is water pollution caused by the batteries' lead plates and terminals. If half of the 65 million wornout batteries could be restored and the other half recycled, this pollution problem could be eliminated.

Increasing pressure for restoring and recycling motor vehicle batteries is likely to come from the state of California. The state's Air Resources Board—comparable to the federal Environmental Protection Agency—adopted a regulation that requires 2 percent of all new-car sales in California in 1998 to be "zero emissions vehicles." The requirement rises to 5 percent in 2001 and to 10 percent in 2003 and beyond. The only way to meet the quota is for automobile manufacturers to develop and market battery-powered vehicles. Consequently, General Motors, Ford Motor Company, Toyota, Nissan, BMW, and almost all major automobile manufacturers began extensive research and development efforts for zero emission vehicles in 1990. The Bateson technology would be applicable to charger designs for these vehicles.

BATTERY CHARGER COMPETITORS

A third study commissioned from an outside marketing-research firm had researched battery charger competitors. The resulting report described competing products in the end-user market as "almost indistinguishable" from one another in terms of performance, price, packaging, and warranty. Quite simply, most battery charger designs had not changed in years. In addition, products on the commercial side that are targeted to fleets, boats, aircraft, and auto repair shops are often almost identical to one another, differing only in terms of capacity and durability. The report described the situation as follows:

> Conventional battery chargers utilize an extremely simple concept, which is considered common domain. A few patents have been granted worldwide for design modifications that purport to extend lead-acid battery life. More patents have been granted for designs that reduce charging time.

Given this relatively primitive technology, the team thought that the Bateson battery charger should be quite appealing.

Most battery charger manufacturers in the end-user market compete on the basis of offering "standard" product performance at a low price, the latter feature assured by the use of established designs, long production runs, and limited marketing activities. No competitor advertises to end users. Instead, competitors rely on their salesforces to promote products to automotive specialty chains, mass merchandisers, and wholesalers.

All battery charger manufacturers in the United States are smaller than Bateson in terms of sales revenues and employees. The study estimated that upward of several hundred companies actually manufacture battery chargers in the United States, with about 70 firms competing in the markets described earlier. Many firms target only one or two specialized niches. For example, Rolls Battery Engineering and American Monarch are well known for their golf cart chargers. Kussmaul Electronics Company and Vanner specialize in high-capacity chargers used in the automobile dealer and repair shop market. Teledyne Battery Products targets the aircraft market. Numerous other firms promote their expertise in specialized applications in any market—on the basis of custom engineering, minimum orders of ten units or more, and delivery within four weeks.

The largest manufacturer of chargers for lead-acid batteries was thought by the team to be Schauer Manufacturing Company. Schauer was founded in 1907 and had its headquarters in Cincinnati, Ohio. Schauer employed about 250 people and was expected to sell around $12 million worth of battery chargers in 1991. The company was recognized by industry experts as a full-line manufacturer of chargers, listing 42 standard models in its 1991 catalog. Five models were targeted to end-user markets and sold in numerous automotive specialty and mass-merchandiser stores; the balance serviced a number of customers in the automobile dealer and repair shop market, transportation fleet market, and marine market.

The report concluded with a short section summarizing market size. The discussion began with a caveat stating that because of the diversity and fragmentation of the battery charger industry, any sales estimate was bound to be approximate at best. The report's sales estimate for 1991 was $220 million at manufacturer prices, for charger applications in the seven markets. Sales were thought to be growing at 4 percent per year.

DECISIONS

Ed Warren's meeting with Mark Mercer had begun with a short discussion of the $220 million figure. Clearly the number represented sufficient potential for Bateson—a 10 percent market share would increase sales for the Battery Division by 11 percent. However, just as clearly, a failed market entry consisting of, say, a half-dozen models would have a disastrous effect on Bateson's bottom line. Moreover, a failed entry might upset Bateson's existing customers and could produce negative repercussions for current products.

Warren and Mercer had roughed out their estimates of the numbers of models needed to cover 90 percent of the units sold in the seven markets under consideration. Five models would cover 90 percent of the end-user market (automotive specialty stores and mass merchandisers). Eight models were thought to be enough to satisfy the needs of 90 percent of both the transportation fleet market and the automobile dealer and repair shop market, because the same models could be used for both. Golf carts would require five models (however, these could duplicate those intended for the end-user markets and the automotive markets). The marine and aircraft markets would each require five different models.

They had placed these estimates against a schedule prepared by Charlene Becker that summarized her estimates of manufacturers' sales revenues, Bateson's contribution margins per unit, and Bateson's marketing costs for the seven markets (Exhibit 2). Her estimates of Bateson unit contribution margins reflected a weighted average or composite of the models that Bateson would offer to each market. Estimates of Bateson's marketing costs consisted primarily of salesforce and other promotion expenditures, all of which could be considered fixed for purposes of analysis. The existing salesforce would be used if Bateson targeted only the end-user markets; another salesforce or independent sales representatives would be needed if Bateson entered any commercial market.

Warren and Becker had agreed that these numbers were quite crude and had concluded that more marketing research was needed. However, before additional research could be undertaken, the team would have to narrow the number of markets to no more than two or three. Once they felt comfortable with specific market opportunities for the Rejuvenator, they would commission additional studies.

An outside supplier or suppliers would again be called on to design and execute these additional studies. Warren had described several possibilities to Mercer, as follows:

1. *Focus groups of users.* This research would gather qualitative data from small groups of either end users or mechanics, depending on the market. Some five to seven groups from each market would be needed, each group costing about $5,000. Data would consist of group members' reactions to the

EXHIBIT 2

Estimates for Battery Charger Markets (Dollars at Manufacturer Level)

Markets	1991 Market Sales (thousands)	1991 Market Unit Sales (thousands)	Bateson's Average Unit Contribution Margin	Bateson's Marketing Costs (thousands)	Number of Bateson Models
Specialty shops	$ 48,000	2,400	$ 5	$1,500	5[a]
Mass merchandisers	32,000	1,600	5	1,100	5[a]
Fleets	50,000	140	200	500	8[b]
Golf carts	14,000	50	200	300	5
Marine	12,000	70	50	500	5
Aircraft	4,000	15	200	200	5
Automotive	60,000	170	200	1,000	8[b]
Total	$220,000				

[a]Same models used in specialty shop and mass-merchandiser markets.

[b]Same models used in fleets and automotive markets.

Rejuvenator name and product concept, their knowledge of and likes and dislikes concerning existing chargers, their beliefs about product performance and price, and their purchase and usage behaviors.

2. *Focus groups of corporate buyers.* This research would gather qualitative data from small groups of corporate buyers in each market under consideration. Some three or four groups from each market would be needed, each group costing about $7,000. Data would consist of group members' reactions, much as described for end users.

3. *Surveys of users.* This research would use a probability sample of 300 to 400 users (either end users or mechanics, depending on the market). Each survey would cost about $15,000 for a nationally representative sample. For end users, a telephone survey would be used; for mechanics, personal interviews. Data would consist of respondents' attitudes and beliefs about battery chargers, interest in purchasing a Rejuvenator charger, usage and purchase behaviors, and demographic characteristics.

4. *Surveys of corporate buyers.* This research would use a probability sample of 200 to 300 purchasing agents employed by large retailers and wholesalers in the seven markets. The survey would use personal interviews and cost about $15,000. Data would consist of reactions on the topics described in the preceding study.

5. *Use tests.* This research would place approximately 100 Rejuvenator chargers in the field with either end users or mechanics, depending on the market. Chargers would be used for a four-month period, and data would be collected on actual product performance as well as on user reaction, likes and dislikes, and so forth. The cost would be about $200 per user, not including the chargers themselves.

6. *Test markets.* This research would test actual end-user market reaction under competitive conditions for a four-month period. Two or three market areas would be chosen. Placement of the Rejuvenator charger in retail stores would be guaranteed by the research supplier. Bateson would supply shelf tags, other promotional materials, and limited training for retail salespeople. Data would be collected on actual sales and market share, competitive reaction, and buyer reaction to three different price points, buyer satisfaction, and demographics. The cost would be approximately $100,000 per market, excluding costs of the chargers themselves.

7. *Competitive analysis.* This research would identify major competitors and their marketing strategies in each chosen market and would describe their relative strengths and weaknesses and their expected reactions to a Rejuvenator market introduction. The cost would be about $15,000.

"All things considered," Warren thought as he opened his car door, "the week could hardly have gone better. We've got a great product, good results from the field, and fine numbers from Charlene." His thoughts were interrupted by a question from out of nowhere.

It was his boss, Noah Reddy. "Have you guys decided on markets for that battery charger yet?" The tone was supportive, with no overtones of "What are you doing leaving the office at four on a Friday?"

"Not yet. But we should have an answer by Tuesday," he replied. Warren knew that Reddy expected not only a decision but the team's reasoning behind it. The weekend would be an ideal time for the team to choose markets and support its choice and also rough out a research program for the chosen markets. Noah would like that.

"See if we can't set something up for around 3:00 on Tuesday," was Noah's only response.

CHAPTER 6

Product and Service Strategy and Management

 The fundamental decision in formulating a marketing mix concerns the offering of an organization. Without something to satisfy target market wants and needs, there would be nothing to price, distribute, or communicate. In essence, the ultimate profitability of an organization depends on its product or service offering(s). Accordingly, issues in the development of a product and service strategy are of special interest to all levels of management in an organization.

The three basic kinds of offering-related decisions facing the marketing manager concern (1) modifying the offering mix, (2) positioning offerings, and (3) branding offerings.

In certain ways, offering decisions are extensions of product-market matching strategies described in Chapter 1. Like other marketing-mix decisions, offering decisions must be based on consideration of organization and marketing objectives, organization resources and capabilities, and competitive forces in the marketplace.

THE OFFERING PORTFOLIO

The Offering Concept

Before proceeding to a discussion of offering-related decisions, we should define the term *offering*. In an abstract sense, an *offering* consists of the benefits or satisfaction provided to target markets by an organization. More concretely, an offering consists of a tangible product or service (a physical entity) plus related services (such as delivery and setup), warranties or guarantees, packaging, and the like.

Use of the term *offering* rather than *product* or *service* has numerous benefits for strategic marketing planning. By focusing on benefits and satisfaction offered, it establishes a conceptual framework. This framework is potentially useful in analyzing competing offerings, identifying the unmet needs and wants of target markets, and developing or designing new products or services. It forces a marketer to go beyond the single tangible entity being marketed and to consider the entire offering, or extended product or service.

In a broader view, an organization's offerings characterize its business. Offerings illustrate not only the buyer needs served, but also the types of customer groups sought and the means (technology) for satisfying their needs.

The Offering Mix

Seldom do organizations market a solitary offering; rather, they tend to market many product or service offerings. The typical supermarket contains over 30,000 different products; General Electric offers over a quarter million. Banks provide hundreds of services to customers, including computer billing, automatic payroll deposits, checking accounts, and loans of numerous kinds. Similarly, hospitals maintain a complete "inventory" of services ranging from pathology to obstetrics to food services. The totality of an organization's offerings is known as its product or service *offering mix* or *portfolio*. This mix usually consists of distinct offering lines—groups of offerings similar in terms of usage, buyers marketed to, or technical characteristics. Each offering line is composed of individual offers or items.

Offering decisions concern primarily the width, depth, and consistency of the offering portfolio. Marketing managers must continually assess the number of offering lines (the width decision) and the number of individual items in each line (the depth decision). Although these decisions depend, in part, on the existing competitive or industry situation, as well as organizational resources, they are perhaps most often determined by overall marketing strategy. The options are many. At one extreme, an organization can concentrate on one offering; at the other, it can offer complete lines to its customers. In between, it can specialize in high-profit and/or high-volume offerings. Furthermore, managers must consider the extent to which offerings satisfy similar needs, appeal to similar buyer groups, or utilize similar technologies (the consistency decision).

Increasingly, organizations have turned to "bundling" as a means to enhance their offering mix. *Bundling* involves the marketing of two or more product or service items in a single "package." For example, AT&T sells computer hardware, software, and maintenance contracts together. Bundling is based on the idea that consumers value the package more than the individual items. This is due to benefits received from not having to make separate purchases and enhanced satisfaction from one item given the presence of another. Moreover, bundling often provides a lower total cost to buyers and lower marketing costs to sellers. For instance, Lotus Development Corporation sells a "bundle" of spreadsheet and word-processing software in its Microsoft Office package for $750. Priced separately, items in the bundle could cost a buyer $2,190.[1]

MODIFYING THE OFFERING MIX

The first offering-related decision confronting the manager is whether to modify the offering mix. Rarely, if ever, will an organization's offering mix stand the test of changing competitive actions and buyer preferences, or satisfy an organization's desire for growth. Accordingly, the marketing manager must continually monitor target markets and offerings to determine when new offerings should be introduced and existing offerings modified or eliminated.

Additions to the Offering Mix

Additions to the offering mix may take the form of a single offering or of entire lines of offerings. An example of adding a complete line of offerings is General Mills's introduction, several years ago, of salty snack items called Whistles, Bugles, and Daisies.

Whatever the reason for considering new offerings, three questions should direct the evaluation of this action:

- How consistent is the new offering with existing offerings?
- Does the organization have the resources to adequately introduce and sustain the offering?
- Is there a viable market niche for the offering?

First, in evaluating the consistency of the new offering with existing offerings, offering interrelationships—whether substitute, complementary, or whatever—must be carefully taken into account. This is necessary to avoid situations where sales of the new offering may excessively cannibalize those of other offerings. Eastman Kodak did not originally introduce 35mm cameras and camcorders because of the potential for cannibalizing its core products—cameras. Today, a similar situation exists with electronic imaging cameras, which could cannibalize sales of existing cameras.[2] Determining a new offering's consistency also involves considering the degree to which the new offering fits the organization's existing selling and distribution strategies. For example, will the new offering require a different type of sales effort, such as new sales personnel or selling methods? The Metropolitan Life Insurance Company faced such a situation when it added automobile insurance to its line of life and health insurance, since the sales task for auto insurance differs from that for life insurance. Or will the new offering require a different marketing channel to reach the target market sought? Both the cannibalization question and the question of fit with sales and distribution strategies raise a fundamental third question relating to the buyers sought for the new offering. Will the new offering satisfy the target markets currently being served by the existing offering mix? If it will, then the sales and distribution issue may be settled, but the cannibalization question remains. If it will not, then the situation is just the opposite.

The second issue arising from the addition of new offerings relates to the adequacy of an organization's resources. In particular, the financial strength of the organization must be objectively appraised. New offerings often require large initial cash outlays for research, development, and introductory marketing programs. Gillette, for example, spent $200 million on research and development alone to produce the Sensor razor; introductory marketing programs for grocery products often approach $20 million.[3] Other costs of sustaining the new offering before it returns a profit to the organization must also be measured. These costs will be determined, in part, by the speed and magnitude of competitive response to new offerings in the market and by market growth itself. The experience of Minnetonka, Inc., is a case in point. This firm was the first to introduce bathroom soap in pump dispensers (Softsoap) and antiplaque toothpaste (Check-Up). Both products achieved sizable market shares, only to lose them when larger competitors such as Procter and Gamble entered the market.[4]

Finally, one must determine whether a market niche exists for the new offering. Important questions here are whether the new offering has a relative advantage over existing competitive offerings and whether a distinct buyer group exists for which no offering is satisfactory. Careful market analysis is necessary to answer these questions.

New-Offering Development Process

Marketing managers are often faced with new-offering decisions. In dealing with the often-chaotic process of developing and marketing new offerings, most managers attempt to follow some sort of structured procedure. This procedure typically includes four multifaceted steps: (1) idea generation/idea screening, (2) business analysis, (3) testing, and (4) commercialization.

Briefly, the process is as follows. New-offering ideas are obtained from many sources—employees, buyers, and competitors—through formal (marketing research) and informal means. These ideas are screened, both in terms of organizational definition and capability and from the viewpoint of prospective buyers. Ideas deemed incompatible with organizational definition and capability are quickly eliminated. The match between prospective buyers and offering characteristics is assessed through questions such as the following. First, does the offering have a *relative advantage* over existing offerings? Second, is the offering *compatible* with buyers' use or consumption behavior? Third, is the offering *simple* enough for buyers to understand and use? Fourth, can the offering be *tested* on a limited basis prior to actual purchase? Fifth, are there *immediate benefits* from the offering, once it is used or consumed? If the answers to these questions are yes and the offering satisfies a felt need, then the new-offering idea passes on to the next stage. At that point, the idea is subjected to a business analysis to assess its financial viability in terms of estimated sales, costs, and profitability. Those ideas that pass the business analysis are then developed into prototypes, and various testing procedures are implemented. Marketing-related tests may include product concept or buyer preference tests in a laboratory situation, or even field market tests. Offering ideas that pass through these stages are commercially introduced into the marketplace in the hope that they will become profitable to the organization. A study by Booz, Allen, and Hamilton, Inc., an internationally recognized management consulting firm, indicated that it takes an average of seven ideas to generate one successful new product. This study also reported that the two major factors contributing to the success of new offerings were (1) a fit with market needs and (2) a fit with the internal strengths of the organization.[5]

Although the stages just outlined are relatively straightforward from a managerial perspective, two require further elaboration: the business analysis and testing stages. Sales analysis and profit analysis are two fundamental aspects of the business analysis stage. Forecasting sales volume for a new offering is an enormously difficult task; nevertheless, preliminary forecasts must be made before further investigation of the offering is warranted. For the most part, profitability analyses are related to investment requirements, break-even procedures, and payback periods. Break-even procedures can be used to determine estimates of the number of units that must be sold to cover fixed and variable costs. An extension of this procedure—and one that is frequently used in evaluating new offerings—is to compute the payback period of the new offering. *Payback period* refers to the number of years required for an organization to recapture its initial offering investment. The shorter the payback period, the sooner an offering will prove profitable. Usually the payback period is computed by dividing the fixed costs of the offering by the estimated incoming cash flows from it. Though widely used, the method is limited in that it does not distinguish among offering investments according to their absolute sizes. A final method often used is to calculate the common return on investment (ROI). ROI equals the ratio of average annual net earnings (return) divided by average annual investment, discounted to the present time. Like the payback method, the ROI method does not distinguish among offering alternatives according to their riskiness. Risk must still be subjectively assessed.

Test marketing is a major consideration in the development and testing stage. A test market is a scaled-down implementation of one or more alternative marketing strategies for introducing the new offering. Test markets provide several benefits to managers. First, they generate benchmark data for assessing sales volume when the product is introduced over a wider area. Second, if alternative marketing strategies are tested, the relative impacts of the two programs can be examined under actual market conditions. In a similar vein, test markets allow the manager to assess the incidence of offering trial by potential buyers, repeat-purchasing behavior, and quantities purchased. A manager should remember, however, that test markets of new offerings inform competitors of the organization's activities and thus may increase the magnitude and speed of competitive response. This happened to the Clorox Company. Its Wave laundry detergent with bleach was test-marketed for five years, only to be dropped after competitors introduced their own detergents with bleach supported by extensive marketing resources.[6]

Life-Cyle Concept

An important managerial tool related to the development and management of offerings is the concept of the life cycle. A *life cycle* plots sales of an offering (such as a brand of coffee) or a product class (such as all coffee brands) over a period of

EXHIBIT 6.1

General Form of a Product Life Cycle

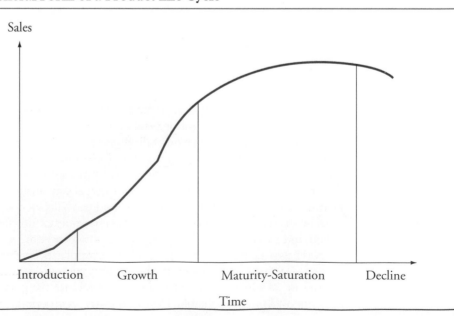

time. Life cycles are typically divided into four stages: (1) introduction, (2) growth, (3) maturity-saturation, and (4) decline. Exhibit 6.1 shows the general form of a product life cycle and the corresponding stages.

The sales curve can be viewed as being the result of offering trial and repeat-purchasing behavior. In other words,

$$\text{Sales volume} = (\text{number of triers} \times \text{average purchase amount} \times \text{price})$$
$$+ (\text{number of repeaters} \times \text{average purchase amount} \times \text{price})$$

Early in the life cycle, management efforts focus on stimulating trial of the offering by advertising, giving out free samples, and obtaining adequate distribution. The vast majority of sales volume is due to trial purchases. As the offering moves through its life cycle, an increasing share of volume is attributable to repeat purchases, and management efforts focus on retaining existing buyers of the offering through offering modifications, enhanced brand image, and competitive pricing.

Anticipating and recognizing movement into advanced stages of the life cycle are crucial to managing the various stages. Movement into the maturity-saturation stage is often indicated by (1) an increase in the proportion of buyers who are repeat purchasers (that is, few new buyers or triers exist), (2) an increase in the standardization of production operations and product-service offerings, and (3) an increase in the incidence of aggressive pricing activities of competitors. As the offering enters into and moves through this stage, management efforts typically focus on finding new buyers for the offering, significantly improving the offering, and/or increasing the frequency of usage among current buyers. Ultimately, the decline stage must be addressed. The decision criteria at this stage are outlined in the following discussion on modifying, harvesting, and eliminating offerings.

Services often follow a life cycle very similar to the product life cycle described above. As a service firm approaches maturity, it typically modifies its operations to attract new buyers. Examples include McDonald's with its expanded menu and barbershops that evolve into hair-stylist operations featuring hair-cutting services for men and women. Often service firms expand their geographical scope by reproducing a limited number of facilities through franchising and licensing agreements to become multisite operators.

Modifying, Harvesting, and Eliminating Offerings

Modifying offerings is a common practice. Firms must always be on the lookout for new ways to improve the value their offerings provide consumers in terms of quality, functions, features, and/or price.

Modification decisions typically focus on trading up or trading down the offering. *Trading up* involves a conscious decision to improve an offering—by adding new features and higher-quality materials or augmenting the offering with attendant services—and raise the price. Examples of augmenting products with services are found in the computer industry. Manufacturers of computers enhanced the image and suitability of their products through programming services, information-system assistance, and user training. *Trading down* is the process of reducing the number of features or quality of an offering and lowering the price.

The dichotomy between trading up and trading down has been blurred in recent years as a result of competitive and cost pressures. In particular, many organizations have modified their offering downward while maintaining or increasing the price. For example, many distillers have reduced the alcohol content of their beverages without changing prices. Some airlines have added more seats, thus reducing leg room, and eliminated certain extras without lowering fares. Consumer-packaged-goods firms have reduced the content of packages without reducing prices—a practice called *downsizing*.

Although modification decisions typically arise in the maturity-saturation stage of the life cycle, modifications might be appropriate earlier in the life cycle to stimulate trial. For example, several producers of microwave ovens recognized early in the introduction phase that the oven had to be augmented with cookbooks to assist buyers in scheduling meals and preparing a variety of foods.

The elimination of offerings as a specific decision is given less attention than new-offering or modification decisions. However, the elimination decision has grown in importance in recent years because of the realization that some offerings may be an unnecessary burden in light of potential opportunities. As an alternative to total elimination, management might consider harvesting the offering when it enters the late-maturity or decline stage of the life cycle. *Harvesting* is the strategic management decision to reduce the investment in a business entity in the hope of cutting costs and/or improving cash flow.[7] In other words, the decision is not to abandon the offering outright but, rather, to minimize human and financial resources allocated to it. Harvesting should be considered when (1) the market for the offering is stable, (2) the offering is not producing good profits, (3) the offering has a small or respectable market share that is becoming increasingly difficult or costly to defend from competitive inroads, and (4) the offering provides benefits to the organization in terms of image or "full-line" capabilities, despite poor future potential.

Outright abandonment, or elimination, means that the offering is dropped from the mix of organizational offerings. Generally speaking, if the answer to each of the following questions is "very little" or "none," then an offering is a candidate for elimination.

1. What is the future sales potential of the offering?
2. How much is the offering contributing to the overall profitability of the offering mix?
3. How much is the offering contributing to the sale of other offerings in the mix?
4. How much could be gained by modifying the offering?
5. What would be the effect on channel members and buyers?

POSITIONING OFFERINGS

A second major offering-related decision confronting the manager concerns the positioning of offerings. *Positioning* typically involves the creation of impressions about a product, service, or organization.[8] The positioning decision therefore involves choosing associations to be emphasized. There are a variety of positioning strategies available, including positioning by (1) attribute or benefit, (2) use or application, (3) product or service user, (4) product or service class, and (5) competitors. Positioning is important both in the introductory stage of the life cycle and in the maturity stage, when sales volume reaches a plateau.

Positioning an offering by attributes or benefits is the strategy most frequently used. Positioning an offering by attributes requires determining which attributes are important to target markets, which attributes are being emphasized by competitors, and how the offering can be fitted into this offering–target market environment. This kind of positioning may be accomplished by designing an offering that contains appropriate attributes or by stressing the appropriate attributes if they already exist in the offering. This latter tactic has been employed by a number of cereal manufacturers, who have emphasized the "naturalness" of their products in response to the growing interest in nutrition among a sizable number of buyers.

In practice, operationalizing the positioning concept requires the development of a matrix relating attributes of the offering to market segments. Using toothpaste as an example, Exhibit 6.2 shows how particular attributes may vary in importance for different market segments.[9] Several benefits accrue from viewing the market for toothpaste in this manner. First, the marketing manager can spot potential opportunities for new offerings and determine if a market niche exists. (We might note here that the elderly market segment has not yet been exploited and might be a viable one for an existing or new offering.) Second, looking at offering attributes and their importance to market segments permits subjective estimation of the extent to which a new offering might cannibalize existing offerings. If two offerings emphasize the same attributes, then they can be expected to compete with each other for the same market segment. Alternatively, if the offerings have different mixes of attributes, they probably will appeal to different segments. For this reason, Procter and Gamble's introduction of Crest tartar-control-formula toothpaste for adults did not have a major adverse effect on its sales of the existing Crest toothpaste for children. Third, the competitive response to a new offering can be judged more effectively using this framework. By determining which brands serve specific markets, one can evaluate offerings in terms of financial strength and market acceptance.

Organizations can also position their offerings by use or application. Arm and Hammer used this approach to reposition its baking powder as an odor-destroying agent in refrigerators and a water softener in swimming pools. Public television was originally positioned as a source of educational and cultural programming.

EXHIBIT 6.2

Attributes and Marketing Segment Positioning

| | Market Segments | | | |
| | Children | Teens, Young Adults | Family | Adults |
Toothpaste Attributes				
Flavor	*			
Color	*			
Whiteness of teeth		*		
Fresh breath		*		
Decay prevention			*	
Price			*	
Plaque prevention				*
Stain prevention				*
Principal brands for each segment	Aim, Stripe	Ultra Brite, McCleans	Colgate, Crest	Check-up, Pearl Drops

Note: An asterisk (*) indicates principal benefits sought by each market segment.

Positioning by user is a third strategy. This strategy typically associates a product or service with a user group. Federal Express positions its delivery service for the busy executive. Certain deodorant brands position themselves for females (Jean Naté by Charles of the Ritz), whereas others focus on males (Brut by Fabergé).

Products and services can be positioned by product or service class as well. For example, margarine brands position themselves against butter. Savings associations position themselves as "banks."

Finally, an organization can position itself or its offerings directly against competitors. Avis positions itself against Hertz in the rental car business. Sabroso, a coffee liqueur, positions itself against Kahlua. For many years, the National Pork Producers Council positioned their product as being like poultry: "Pork: The Other White Meat." Often a political candidate will position himself or herself against the opponent.

The success of a positioning strategy depends on a number of factors. First, the position selected must be clearly communicated. Industry observers argue that General Motors's failure to communicate distinct positions for its different automobile lines was detrimental to the firm's competitive position in the 1980s.[10] Second, as the development of a position is a lengthy and often expensive process, rapid changes in the position should be avoided. Studies of the marketing of political candidates, in particular, emphasize the importance of establishing a position and holding that position throughout a campaign. Finally, and perhaps most important, the position taken in the marketplace should be sustainable and profitable.

BRANDING OFFERINGS

Branding is a third offering-related decision made by marketing managers. A brand is used to identify an offering and set it apart from competing offerings. The major managerial implication of branding offerings is that goodwill, derived from buyer satisfaction with an offering, can lead to *brand equity*—the added value a brand name bestows on a product or service beyond the functional benefits provided.[11] This value has two distinct advantages for the brand owner. First, brand equity provides a competitive advantage, as enjoyed, for example, by the Jell-O label. Second, brand equity allows firms to engage in *brand leveraging*, that is, applying the brand name to new entries in different product-service categories. For example, equity in the Tylenol name as a trusted pain reliever allowed Johnson and Johnson to successfully introduce Tylenol Cold & Flu and Tylenol P.M.

Two branding decisions commonly confront marketing managers. The first relates to the strategy used to assign brands to multiple offerings or multiple lines of offerings. A manufacturer must decide whether to assign one brand name to *all* of the organization's offerings (such as General Electric), to assign one brand name to *each line* of offerings (Sears's appliances are Kenmore, and Sears's tools are Craftsman), or to assign individual names to *each offering* (Tide, Cheer, and Oxydol are all laundry detergents sold by Procter and Gamble). The branding strategy selected will depend on the consistency of the offering mix. If the offerings are related in terms of needs satisfied, then a common (family) brand strategy is often favored. A common brand name for offerings is also likely to be selected if the organization wishes to establish dominance in a class of offerings, as in the case of Campbell's soups. The decision to use a single brand name has certain advantages and disadvantages. Among the advantages is the fact that it is usually easier to introduce new offerings when the brand name is familiar to buyers—an outgrowth of brand equity. However, a single brand name strategy can have a negative effect on existing offerings if a new offering is a failure.

The second branding decision relates to supplying an intermediary with its own brand name. From the intermediary's perspective, the decision is whether or not to carry its own brands. Distributors favor carrying their own brands for a number of reasons.[12] By carrying a private brand, a distributor avoids price competition to some extent, since no other distributor carries an identical brand that consumers can use for comparison purposes. Also, any buyer goodwill attributed to an offering accrues to the distributor, and buyer loyalty to the offering is tied to the distributor, not the producer. If a distributor desires a private brand, it must locate a producer willing to manufacture the brand. A marketing manager is then placed in the position of having to decide whether to be the producer. A potential producer of private brands, or distributor brands, should consider a number of factors when making this decision. If a producer has excess manufacturing capacity and the variable costs of producing a distributor's brand do not exceed the sale price, the possibility exists for making a contribution to overhead and utilizing production facilities. Even though a distributor's brand will often compete directly with a producer's brand, the combined sales of the brands and the profit contribution to the producer may be greater than if a competitor obtained the rights to produce the distributor brand. For these reasons and others, firms such as H. J. Heinz, Borden, and Ralston Purina produce private brands of pet foods, dairy products, and cereals for their distributors.[13] However, a great danger in producing private brands is the possibility of becoming too reliant on private-brand revenue, only to have it curtailed when a distributor switches suppliers or builds its own production plant. Overreliance on distributor brands will also affect trade relationships between a producer and distributor. As a generalization, the influence of a producer, in terms of price and channel leadership, is inversely related to the proportion of its output or revenue obtained from a distributor's brand.

NOTES

1. "It's Not as Easy as 1-2-3 Anymore," *Business Week* (October 14, 1991): 112–114.

2. J. Rigdon, "Kodak Tries to Prepare for Filmless Era without Inviting Demise of Core Business," *Wall Street Journal* (April 18, 1991): B1, B5.

3. "Pinning Down Costs of Product Introductions," *Wall Street Journal* (November 26, 1990): B1; "Blade Runner," *The Economist* (April 10, 1993): 68.

4. Roger Kerin, P. Rajan Varadarajan, and Robert Peterson, "First-Mover Advantage: A Synthesis, Conceptual Framework, and Research Propositions," *Journal of Marketing* (October 1992): 33–52.

5. *New Products Management for the 1980s* (New York: Booz, Allen, and Hamilton, 1982). Also see, "FLOPS," *Business Week* (August 16, 1993): 76–82.

6. B. Johnson, "Wash-day Washout," *Advertising Age* (June 3, 1991): 24.

7. Philip Kotler, *Marketing Management*, 8th ed. (Englewood Cliffs, NJ: Prentice Hall, 1994): 371.

8. David Aaker, Rajeev Batra, and John Myers, *Advertising Management*, 4th ed. (Englewood Cliffs, NJ: Prentice Hall, 1992): 131–139.

9. This example is adapted from Russell Haley, "Benefit Segmentation: A Decision-Oriented Research Tool," in *Marketing Classics*, 7th ed., B. Enis and K. Cox (Boston: Allyn and Bacon, 1991): 208–215.

10. "They're Still Groping," *Business Week* (July 9, 1990): 31.

11. For an extended discussion on brand equity, see David Aaker, *Managing Brand Equity* (New York: Free Press, 1991); and Kevin Keller, "Conceptualizing, Measuring, and Managing Customer-Based Brand Equity," *Journal of Marketing* (January 1993): 1–22.

12. For an extended discussion of distributor brands, see W. Salmon and K. Cmar, "Private Labels Are Back in Fashion," *Harvard Business Review* (May–June 1987): 99–106.

13. "Big Companies Add Private-Label Lines That Vie with Their Premium Brands," *Wall Street Journal* (May 21, 1993): B1.

Frito-Lay, Inc.
Sun Chips™ Multigrain Snacks

In mid-1990, Dr. Dwight R. Riskey, Vice President of Marketing Research and New Business at Frito-Lay, Inc., assembled the product management team responsible for Sun Chips™ Multigrain Snacks. The purpose of the all-day meeting was to prepare a presentation to senior Frito-Lay executives on future action pertaining to the brand.

Sun Chips™ Multigrain Snacks is a crispy textured snack chip consisting of a special blend of whole wheat, corn, rice, and oat flours with a lightly salty multigrain taste and a slightly sweet aftertaste. The product contains less sodium than most snack chips and is made with canola or sunflower oil. The chip is approximately 50 percent lower in saturated fats than chips made with other cooking oils and is cholesterol-free. According to a Frito-Lay executive, it is "a thoughtful, upscale classy chip."

The product had been in test market for ten months in the Minneapolis–St. Paul, Minnesota, metropolitan area. Even though it appeared consumer response was extremely favorable, Riskey and his associates knew their presentation to senior Frito-Lay executives would have to be persuasive. In addition to presenting a thorough assessment of test–market data, Riskey added:

> We will have to do heavy-duty selling [to top executives] because Sun Chips™ Multigrain Snacks required a new manufacturing process, carried a new brand name, and pioneered a new snack chip category. There is a huge capital investment and a huge marketing investment that could be financially justified only with a product that could be sustainable for an extended time period.

FRITO-LAY, INC.

Frito-Lay, Inc. is a division of PepsiCo, Inc., a New York–based diversified consumer goods and services firm. Other PepsiCo, Inc. divisions include Pizza Hut, Inc., Taco Bell Corporation, Pepsi-Cola Company, Kentucky Fried Chicken, and PepsiCo Foods International. PepsiCo, Inc. recorded net income of $1.077 billion on net sales of $17.8 billion in 1990.

Company Background

Frito-Lay, Inc. is a worldwide leader in the manufacturing and marketing of snack chips. Well-known brands include Lay's® brand and Ruffles® brand potato chips, Fritos®

The cooperation of Frito-Lay, Inc., in the preparation of this case is gratefully acknowledged. This case was prepared by Professor Roger A. Kerin, the Edwin L. Cox School of Business, Southern Methodist University, and Kenneth R. Lukaska, Product Manager, Frito-Lay, Inc., as a basis for class discussion and is not designed to illustrate effective or ineffective handling of an administrative situation. Certain company information is disguised and not useful for research purposes. Copyright © Roger A. Kerin. No part of this case may be reproduced without written permission of the copyright holder.

EXHIBIT 1

Frito-Lay, Inc.:   Major Brands

Introduced: 1981
Estimated 1990 Retail Sales:
$143 Million

Introduced: 1938
Estimated 1990 Retail Sales:
$726 Million

Introduced: 1958
Estimated 1990 Retail Sales:
$1.1 Billion

Introduced: 1986
Estimated 1990 Retail Sales:
$136 Million

Introduced: 1932
Estimated 1990 Retail Sales:
$629 Million

Introduced: 1966
Estimated 1990 Retail Sales:
$1.2 Billion

Introduced: 1948
Estimated 1990 Retail Sales:
$638 Million

Source: 1990 PepsiCo, Inc., Annual Report.

brand corn chips, Doritos® brand, Tostitos® brand, and Santitas® brand tortilla chips,
Chee·tos® brand cheese-flavored snacks, and Rold Gold® brand pretzels. The company's major brands are shown in Exhibit 1 along with estimated worldwide retail sales.
Other well-known Frito-Lay products include Baken-Ets® brand fried pork skins,
Munchos® brand potato crisps, and Funyuns® brand onion-flavored snacks. In addition, the company markets a line of dips, nuts, peanut butter crackers, processed beef
sticks, Smartfood® brand ready-to-eat popcorn, and Grandma's® brand cookies.

Frito-Lay, Inc., accounts for 13 percent of sales in the United States snack-food industry, which includes candy, cookies, crackers, nuts, snack chips, and assorted other

items. The company is the leading manufacturer of snack chips in the United States, capturing nearly one-half of the retail sales in this category. Eight of Frito-Lay's snack chips are among the top ten best-selling snack chip items in U.S. supermarkets (see Exhibit 2). Doritos® brand tortilla chips and Ruffles® brand potato chips have the distinction of being the only snack chips with $1 billion in retail sales in the world.

Frito-Lay's snack-food business spans every aspect of snack-food production, from agriculture to stacking supermarket shelves. During 1990 in the United States alone, Frito-Lay used 1.6 billion pounds of potatoes, 600 million pounds of corn, and 55 million pounds of seasonings. The company has 39 manufacturing plants, more than 1,600 distribution facilities, and a 10,000-person route-sales team who call on more than 400,000 retail store customers each week in the United States. Frito-Lay, Inc., recorded U.S. sales of $3.5 billion in 1990.

Product-Marketing Strategies

Frito-Lay pursues growth opportunities through four product-marketing strategies.

1. *Grow established Frito-Lay brands through line extension.* Recognizing that consumers seek variety in snack tastes and sizes without compromising quality, Frito-Lay marketing executives use line extensions to satisfy these wants. Recent examples of line extension include Tostitos® brand bite-sized tortilla chips and Chee·tos® brand Flamin' Hot Cheese Flavored Snacks.

2. *Create new products to meet changing consumer preferences and needs.* Continuous marketing research at Frito-Lay is designed to uncover changing snacking needs of customers. A recent result of these efforts is evident in the launch of a low-oil light line of snack chips.

EXHIBIT   2

**Top-Selling Snack Chip Items in U.S. Supermarkets
(Retail Sales in $ millions)**

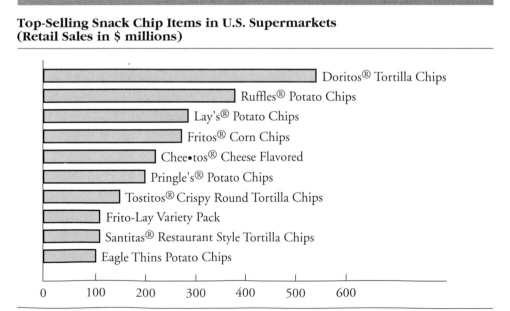

Source: 1990 PepsiCo, Inc., Annual Report.

3. *Develop products for fast-growing snack-food categories.* Recognizing that snack-food categories experience different growth rates, Frito-Lay marketing executives continually monitor consumption patterns to identify new opportunities. For example, Frito-Lay acquired Smartfood® brand popcorn in 1989. In 1990, this brand became the number one ready-to-eat popcorn brand in the United States.

4. *Reproduce Frito-Lay successes in the international market.* Initiatives pursued in the United States often produce opportunities in the international arena. Primary emphasis has been placed in large, well-developed snack markets such as Mexico, Canada, Spain, and the United Kingdom. Innovative marketing coupled with product development efforts produced $1.6 billion in international snack-food sales in 1990.

THE SNACK CHIP CATEGORY

The United States snack-food industry recorded retail sales of $37 billion in 1990, representing a 5 percent increase over 1989. Dollar retail sales of snack chips consisting of potato, corn, and tortilla chips, pretzels, and ready-to-eat popcorn were estimated to be $9.8 billion—a 5 percent increase over 1989. A major source of growth in the snack chip category results from increased per capita consumption. In 1990, consumers in the United States bought 3.5 billion pounds of snack chips, or nearly 14 pounds per person; in 1986, snack chip per capita consumption was slightly less than 12 pounds.

Competitors

Three types of competitors serve the snack chip category: (1) national brand firms, (2) regional brand firms, and (3) private brand firms. National brand firms, which distribute products nationwide, include Frito-Lay, Borden (Guys brand potato and corn chips, and Wise brand potato chips, cheese puffs, and pretzels), Procter and Gamble (Pringles® brand potato chips), RJR Nabisco (several products sold under the Nabisco name as well as Planter's brand pretzels, cheese puffs, and corn and tortilla chips), Keebler Company (O'Boisies brand potato chips), and Eagle Snacks (a division of Anheuser-Busch Companies, Inc., which sells Eagle brand pretzels and potato and corn chips). A second category of competitors are regional brand firms, which distribute products in only certain parts of the United States. Representative firms include Snyder's, Mike Sells, and Charles Chips. Private brands are produced by regional or local manufacturers on a contractual basis for major supermarket chains (for example, Kroger and Safeway).

Competition

The snack chip category is very competitive. As many as 650 snack chip products are introduced each year by national and regional brand companies. Most of the products are new flavors for existing snack chips. The new-product failure rate for snack chips is high, and industry sources report that fewer than 1 percent of new products generate more than $25 million in first-year sales.

Snack chip competitors rely heavily on electronic and print media advertising, consumer promotions, and trade allowances to stimulate sales and retain shelf space in supermarkets. Pricing is very competitive, and snack chip manufacturers often rely on price deals to attract customers. The nature of the technology used to produce snack chips allows snack chip manufacturers to react swiftly to new product (flavor) introductions by competitors. Extensive sales and distribution systems employed by national brand competitors, in particular, allow them to monitor new product and promotion activities and place competing products quickly in supermarkets.

DEVELOPMENT OF SUN CHIPS™ MULTIGRAIN SNACKS

Sun Chips™ Multigrain Snacks resulted from Frito-Lay's ongoing marketing research and product development program. However, its taste and name heritage can be traced to the early 1970s.

Product Heritage

Frito-Lay product development personnel first explored the possibility of a multigrain product in the early 1970s when corporate marketing research studies indicated consumers were looking for nutritious snacks. A multigrain snack chip called Prontos® was introduced in 1974 with the following positioning statement: "The different, delicious new snack made from nature's own corn, oats, and whole grain wheat all rolled into own special recipe, together in a snack for the first time from Frito-Lay." The product was only mildly successful despite advertising and merchandising support. The product was subsequently withdrawn from national distribution in 1978 due to declining sales and manufacturing difficulties. According to Frito-Lay executives, the demise of Prontos® in 1978 was driven by "non-committal" copy, a confusing name, and a product that generated appeal among too narrow a target market. Reflecting on this experience, Riskey added, "I'm not sure there were dramatic things wrong with the product design so much as difficulty with the manufacturing process. It may have been invented and introduced before its time."

The brand name for the product had an equally arduous past. The Sun Chips™ name was originally assigned to a line of corn chips, potato chips, and puffed corn snacks in the early 1970s. In 1976, the brand name was given to a line of corn chips, but by 1985, this line was also withdrawn from distribution due to poor sales performance.

Product Development: The "Harvest" Project

Early 1980s. Interest in a multigrain snack was revisited in the early 1980s when Frito-Lay marketing executives began to worry whether the aging baby boomers (people born between 1946 and 1964) would continue to eat salty snacks such as potato, corn, and tortilla chips. According to Riskey:

> The aging baby boomers were a significant factor [in our thinking]. We were looking for new products that would allow them to snack. But we were looking for "better-for-you" aspects in products and pushing against that demographic shift.

In 1981, Frito-Lay marketing research and product development personnel instituted the "Harvest" project with an objective of coming up with a multigrain snack that would have consumer appeal. After several product concept tests and in-home product use tests failed to generate any consumer excitement, it was concluded that the market for wholesome snacks was not yet fully developed to accept such products. Other evidence seemed to support this view. In 1983, Frito-Lay test marketed O'Grady's™ brand potato chips. The results had been phenomenal. Projections based on test market performance indicated the brand would produce $100 million in annual sales, which it did in 1984 and 1985.

Mid-1980s. The "Harvest" project continued in the mid-1980s, albeit at a slower pace due to staff changes and other responsibilities of project team members. At about this time, a change in top management and corporate objectives focused product development efforts on traditional snacks with an emphasis on flavor line extensions for established Frito-Lay brands (for example, Cool Ranch Doritos® brand tortilla chips) and low-fat versions of its potato, corn, and tortilla chips. In addition, attention was placed on cost-containment measures coupled with continuous quality-improvement initiatives using existing manufacturing facilities and existing product and process snack chip technology.

Late 1980s. Development efforts on a multigrain product were renewed in early 1988. Over the following 13 months, different product formulations (for example, low oil vs. regular oil; salt content; chip shape), alternative positionings, and branding options (extension of an existing Frito-Lay brand vs. a new brand name) were extensively studied using consumer taste tests and product concept tests. The combined results of these tests yielded a multigrain rectangular chip with ridges and an exceptional taste. Further testing on brand names and flavors revealed consumer preferences for two names (one of which was Sun Chips™) and three flavors (original/natural, French onion, and mild cheddar).

Further consumer research revealed that the multigrain product concept and assorted flavors were perceived as a "healthier product." This research also indicated that consumer expectations prior to use (that is, before initial trial of the product) were that the product would not be an "everyday snack" item. Consumers who tried the product, however, perceived the multigrain product to be an "everyday snack," at least for the natural and French onion flavors. Exhibit 3 shows a plot of pretrial consumer expectations and postuse perceptions of different flavors and representative snack chip brands and crackers. Concurrent research on brand names indicated a decided preference for the Sun Chips™ name. The name evoked positive consumer imagery and attributes of "wholesomeness, great taste, light and distinctive, and fun," according to a Frito-Lay executive.

Premarket Test

Positive consumer response to the product concept and brand name prompted an initial assessment of the commercial potential of Sun Chips™ Multigrain Snacks. A simulated test market or premarket test (PMT) was commissioned in April 1989 and conducted by an independent marketing research firm.

A PMT involves interviewing consumers about attitudes and usage behavior concerning a product category (for example, snack chips). Consumers would be exposed to a product concept using product descriptions or mock-ups of advertisements, and their responses would be assessed (see Exhibit 4). These consumers would then be given an opportunity to receive the product if interested. After

EXHIBIT 3

Consumer Expectations and Perceptions of Snack Chips and Multigrain Snacks

PRE-TRIAL PRODUCT EXPECTATIONS

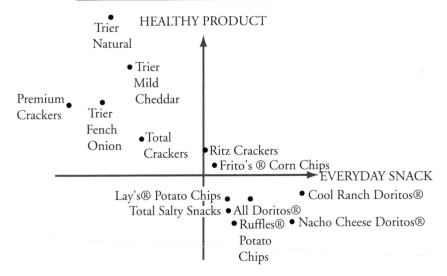

POSTUSE PERCEPTIONS: TRIER REPEATERS VS. TRIER NONREPEATERS

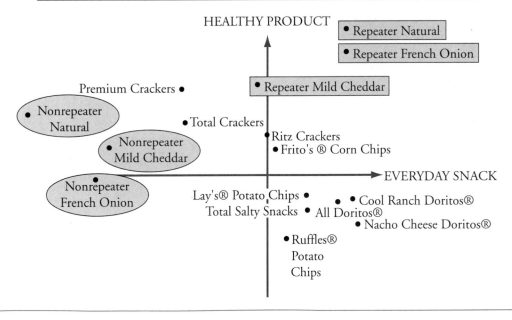

EXHIBIT 4

Concept Board for the Premarket Test

Introducing new SUN CHIPS™ multigrain snacks from Frito-Lay®

The great tasting snack chip for people who care about what they eat.

More and more people care about what they eat because they know that eating habits affect overall health and fitness. SUN CHIPS™ are a special blend of whole wheat, golden corn and other natural great tasting grains. These wholesome grains combined make a uniquely delicious chip with the golden goodness of corn and the nut-like flavor of wheat. They're cooked 'till lightly crisp and crunchy. Then they're lightly salted to let all that naturally good flavor come through. SUN CHIPS™ are a unique combination of great taste, great crunch, and natural goodness, all rolled into one remarkable chip.

So, try new SUN CHIPS™, the chip with the uniquely delicious taste for people who care about what they eat.

Available in these two delicious flavors:

- Natural • French Onion

an in-home usage period of several weeks, they would be contacted by telephone and asked about their attitude toward the product, use of the product, and intention to repurchase. These data would be incorporated into computer models that would include elements of the product's marketing plan (price, advertising, distribution coverage). The output provided by the PMT would include estimates of household trial rates, repeat rates, average number of units purchased on the initial trial and subsequent repeats in the first year, product cannibalism, and first-year sales volume.[1]

The product concept tested in the PMT was priced at parity with Doritos® brand tortilla chips. Planned distribution coverage was set at levels comparable for Frito-

EXHIBIT 5

Simulated Test-Market Results (Selected Statistics)

	Product and Promotion Strategy[a]			
	Natural & Mild Cheddar Combination		*Natural & French Onion Combination*	
	A&M Budget $17 million	*A&M Budget $22 million*	*A&M Budget $17 million*	*A&M Budget $22 million*
Purchase Dynamics				
Brand awareness (% of households)	40	48	40	48
Cumulative first-year trial rate (%)[b]	23	27	21	25
Cumulative first-year repeat rate (%)[c]	61		57	
Number of purchases in first-year per repeating household	5.9		6.2	
Volume Projections ($ millions)				
Pessimistic	87	102	86	102
Most likely	96	113	95	113
Optimistic	106	125	106	125
Incremental annual volume (%)	50		58	
Cannibalized pound volume (%) (from Frito-Lay products)	50		42	

[a]The $11 million advertising and merchandising (A&M) budget for the two flavor combinations produced lower figures than those shown. For example, brand awareness was 35 percent and the cumulative first-year trial rate was 19 percent regardless of flavor combination.

[b]*Cumulative first-year trial* refers to the percentage of households that would try the product.

[c]*Cumulative first-year repeat* refers to the percentage of trier households that repurchased the product.

---

[1]Published validation data on premarket test models indicate that 75 percent of the time they are plus or minus 10 percent of actual performance when a product was introduced (see, for example, A. Shocker and W. Hall, "Pretest Market Models: A Critical Evaluation," *Journal of Product Innovation Management* 3, 1986): 86–107.

Lay potato, corn, and tortilla chips. Two flavor combinations (natural and French onion and natural and mild cheddar) and three advertising and merchandising expenditure levels ($11 million, $17 million, and $22 million) were tested.[2]

Results from the PMT indicated that Sun Chips™ Multigrain Snacks would produce a most likely first-year sales volume of $113 million at manufacturer's prices given the marketing plan set for the product, including a $22 million advertising and merchandising expenditure. The estimated first-year sales volume exceeded the $100 million Frito-Lay sales goal for new products. The natural and French onion flavor combination produced the lowest cannibalization (42 percent) of other Frito-Lay brands. Summary statistics for the simulated test market are shown in Exhibit 5.

TEST MARKET

Positive results from consumer research and the simulated test market led to a recommendation to proceed with Sun Chips™ Multigrain Snacks and implement a test market under Dwight Riskey's direction. The Minneapolis–St. Paul, Minnesota, metropolitan area was chosen as the test site because Frito-Lay executives were confident it had a social and economic profile representative of the United States. Furthermore, Minneapolis–St. Paul, in general, represented a typical competitive environment in which to test consumer acceptance and competitive behavior. The Minneapolis–St. Paul metropolitan area contained 1.98 million households that were identified as users of snack chips, or 2.2 percent of the 90 million snack chip user households in the United States. Discussion among Frito-Lay marketing, sales, distribution, and manufacturing executives and the company's advertising agency indicated that the test market could begin October 9, 1989. Accordingly, a test-market plan and budget were finalized. The test market was scheduled to run for 12 months, with periodic reviews scheduled throughout the test.

Snack-food industry analysts became aware of Frito-Lay's development efforts on a multigrain snack chip soon after the company began preparation for the test market. According to one industry analyst:

> This is a departure from corn or potatoes. Wheat is different. Remember they departed from corn and potatoes a few years ago with Rumbles®, Stuffers® and Toppels®, and it was a distasteful business. I'm sure they will take their time and really test it. It's not like they don't have other products, so there's no hurry.[3]

Test-Market Plan

Product Strategy. Frito-Lay executives decided to introduce both the natural and French onion flavors given consumer research and simulated test-market results. Sun Chips™ Multigrain Snacks would be packaged in two sizes: a 7-ounce package

---

[2]Advertising and merchandising expenditures included electronic and print media advertising, consumer promotions, and trade allowances.

[3]"New Multigrain Chip Being Readied for Test," _Advertising Age_ (June 26, 1989): 4. The products referred to were Stuffers® cheese-filled snacks, Rumbles® granola nuggets, and Toppels® cheese-topped crackers. These products were introduced in the mid-1980s, failed to meet sales expectations, and were subsequently withdrawn from the market.

and an 11-ounce package. These package sizes were identical to Doritos® brand tortilla chips. A 2½-ounce trial package would be used as well.

Package design was considered to be extremely important. According to a Frito-Lay executive, "We wanted distinctive, contemporary graphics which would communicate new, different and fun amidst positive images—sun and a sprig of wheat." This view materialized in a metalized flex bag with primary colors of black (natural flavor) and green (French onion flavor). Exhibit 6 shows the packages used in the test market.

Pricing Strategy. Sun Chips™ Multigrain Snacks would have the same suggested retail prices as Doritos® brand tortilla chips. Research indicated these price points were consistent with consumer reference prices for snack chips and represented a good value. Suggested retail prices and Frito-Lay's selling prices to retailers are shown in Exhibit 7.

Advertising and Merchandising Strategy. The primary audience for Sun Chips™ Multigrain Snacks television advertising was adults between the ages of 18 and 34, since this target audience is the principal purchasers and heavy users of snack chips. A secondary audience expanded the age bracket to 49 years of age, since 34- to 49-year-olds appeared to be receptive to healthier snacks. Household members under 18 years of age would be exposed to the product through in-home usage. The advertising message would convey subtle messages, including wholesomeness, fun, and simplicity. One of the television commercials to be shown in the test market is reproduced in Exhibit 8. In addition to television advertising, the brand would be supported by in-store displays and free-standing inserts (FSIs) in newspapers (see Exhibit 9).

Coupons placed in newspaper FSIs were to be used during the test market to stimulate trial and repeat sales. In addition, free samples would be distributed in supermarkets. Trade allowances were provided to retailers as well.

Distribution and Sales Strategy. Distribution and sales of Sun Chips™ Multigrain Snacks would be handled through Frito-Lay's store-door delivery system, in which the duties of a delivery person and a salesperson are combined. Under this system, a delivery/salesperson solicits orders, stocks shelves, and introduces merchandising programs to retail store personnel. Sun Chips™ Multigrain Snacks would be sold through supermarkets, grocery stores, convenience stores, and other retail accounts that already stocked Frito-Lay's snack products.

Manufacturing Considerations. Frito-Lay manufacturing personnel worked concurrently with marketing personnel on matters related to mass production of a multigrain product. While prototypes were easily developed in limited quantities, large-scale manufacturing would require a production line capable of delivering an adequate product for a market test. Since a multigrain product required different product and process technology than corn or potato products, an investment in one new production line would be necessary. Approval was granted to create a production line to produce and package 1 million pounds of the multigrain snack per year at full theoretical capacity. The production line could be in operation to ship the product in two flavors and three package sizes for the test market in September 1989.

E X H I B I T   6

Sun Chips™ Multigrain Snacks Packaging

E X H I B I T   6   (*continued*)

EXHIBIT 7

Sun Chips™ Multigrain Snacks Price List

Package Size	Suggested Retail Price	Frito-Lay Selling Price to Retailer
2¼ ounce	$0.69	$0.385
7 ounce	$1.69	$1.240
11 ounce	$2.39	$1.732

Test-Market Budget

The advertising and merchandising budget for the test market was equivalent to a $22 million expenditure on a nationwide distribution basis. Approximately 70 percent of the budget would be spent during the first six months of the test market.

Test-Market Results

Consumer response was monitored by an independent research firm from the beginning of the test market. Data gathered by the research firm was submitted to Frito-Lay monthly and consisted of the types of purchases, the incidence of trial and repeat-purchase behavior, and product cannibalization in the test market.

Type of Purchase. Data supplied by the research firm indicated that the coupon program had a major impact on trial activity and approximately 90 percent of purchases were made in supermarkets and convenience stores. After ten months in test market, the 2¼-ounce package accounted for 15 percent of purchases, the 7-ounce package accounted for 47 percent of purchases, and the 11-ounce package accounted for 38 percent of purchases. Fifty-five percent of purchases were for the French onion flavor; 45 percent of purchases were for the natural flavor.

Trial and Repeat Rates. Of critical concern to Frito-Lay executives were the incidences of household trial and repeat-purchase behavior for Sun Chips™ Multigrain Snacks. Exhibit 10 shows the cumulative trial and repeat rates for both flavors combined during the first ten months of the test market. Almost one in five households in the test market had tried the product, and 41.8 percent of these trier households had repurchased the product.

Equally important to Frito-Lay executives were the "depth of repeat" data supplied by the research firm. *Depth of repeat* is the number of times a repeat purchaser buys a product after an initial repeat purchase. Repeat purchasers of Sun Chips™ Multigrain Snacks purchased the product an average of 2.9 times. An estimated average purchase amount for triers was 6 ounces. Repeaters purchased an average of 13 ounces per purchase occasion.

Product Cannibalization. The independent research firm also identified the incidence of product cannibalization. The research firm's tracking data indicated that 30 percent of Sun Chips™ Multigrain Snack pound volume resulted from consumers switching from Frito-Lay's potato, tortilla, and corn snack chips. About one-third of

EXHIBIT 8

Sun Chips™ Multigrain Snacks Television Commercial

LEVINE, HUNTLEY, SCHMIDT
& BEAVER, INC.
CLIENT: FRITO-LAY, INC.
PRODUCT: SUNCHIPS

TITLE: "POLLY"
LENGTH: 30 Seconds
COMM'L NO.: PESU–9013

(Music under) GUY: Polly
want one?

AVO: It seems everyone who tries
new SUNCHIPS feels smarter
eating them.

POLLY: Polly wants another one.

AVO: Smarter because
they're multigrain.

POLLY: Polly wants you to fill her
water cup.

AVO: Smarter because of
the taste.

POLLY: Polly thinks you should
paint this room and this time
pick a better color.

AVO: Smarter because they're
naturally delicious.

POLLY: Polly wants to know why
one species feels it's OK to
imprison another

purely for its own entertainment.

AVO: New SUNCHIPS.

You'll feel smarter eating them.

EXHIBIT   9

Sun Chips Multigrain Snacks Free-Standing Insert (FSI)

EXHIBIT 10

Household Trial and Repeat Rates for Sun Chips™ Multigrain Snacks

	Tracking (4-week) Period									
	1	2	3	4	5	6	7	8	9	10
Cumulative trial[a] (%)	4.7	8.2	9.8	11.3	14.1	15.7	16.5	17.4	18.5	19.9
Cumulative repeat[b] (%)	8.0	22.5	27.1	31.0	32.7	36.5	39.0	39.7	41.8	41.8

[a] *Trial* refers to the percentage of households that tried the product.
[b] *Repeat* refers to the percentage of trier households that repurchased the product.

the cannibalized volume from Frito-Lay's products came from Doritos® brand tortilla chips.

The 30 percent cannibalism rate was not uncommon in new product introductions in the snack food industry. For example, when Frito-Lay introduced O'Grady's™ brand potato chips, one-third of its pound volume came from its Ruffles® brand and Lay's® brand potato chips. Even though cannibalization was an issue to be considered in evaluating test-market performance, Frito-Lay executives noted that the gross profit for Sun Chips™ Multigrain Snacks was higher than that for its other snack chips.[4]

TEST-MARKET REVIEW

Riskey's presentation to senior Frito-Lay executives would conclude with his recommendation for the future marketing of Sun Chips™ Multigrain Snacks. He could recommend that the test be continued for another six months, or be expanded to other geographical areas with the same introductory strategy or some modification. Alternatively, he could recommend that Sun Chips™ Multigrain Snacks be readied for a national introduction with the strategy used in the test market or some modification in the strategy.

Planning Considerations

Numerous topics were raised in his meeting with the product management team responsible for Sun Chips™ Multigrain Snacks. Timing and competitive reaction were important issues. Riskey believed that national and regional competitors were monitoring Frito-Lay's test market. There was also a high probability that these competitors were examining the chip with the intention of developing their own version. Timing was a concern for a variety of reasons. First, if Riskey continued testing the

---

[4]Frito-Lay, Inc. does not divulge profitability data on individual products and product lines. However, for case analysis and class discussion purposes, a multigrain snack chip can be assumed to have a gross profit of $1.30 per pound, while other snack chips (potato, tortilla, and corn) can be assumed to have a gross profit of $1.05 per pound. Gross profit is the difference between selling price and the cost of materials and manufacturing (ingredients, packaging/cartons, direct labor, other assignable manufacturing expenses, and equipment depreciation).

EXHIBIT   11

Cumulative Trial and Repeat Rates for O'Grady's™ Potato Chips and Sun Chips™ Multigrain Snacks: 40-Week Test Market

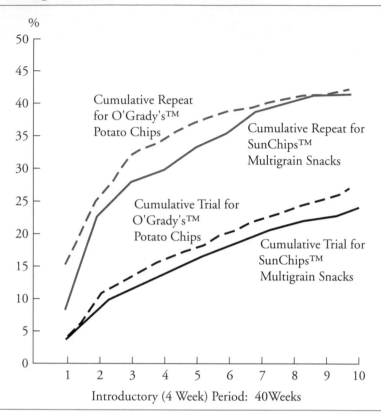

Introductory (4 Week) Period: 40 Weeks

product, a competitor might launch a similar product nationally or regionally and upstage Frito-Lay. The opportunity to be first-to-market would be lost. Second, if an expanded test market or a national introduction was considered, a decision would be needed quickly to assure adequate manufacturing capacity was in place and operating efficiently. Manufacturing capacity expansion would require a significant capital investment. Although preliminary figures represented rough estimates, manufacturing capacity capable of serving 25 percent and 50 percent of snack chip households in the United States would involve a capital expenditure recommendation of $5 million and $10 million, respectively. A full-scale national introduction would require a capital expenditure of $20 million.

Recommendations related to manufacturing capacity expansion would require a justification of the magnitude and sustainability of Sun Chips™ Multigrain Snacks sales over time. Accordingly, Riskey requested marketing research personnel to supply him with comparative brand awareness and cumulative household trial and repeat rate data for O'Grady's™ brand potato chips, since this brand was the most recent Frito-Lay product introduction to achieve $100 million in first-year sales.

Brand-awareness studies on the two brands indicated that O'Grady's™ brand potato chips achieved brand awareness among 28 percent of snack chip households during its market test compared with 33 percent for Sun Chips™ Multigrain Snacks. Exhibit 11 charts trial and repeat data for comparable test-market periods for Sun Chips™ Multigrain Snacks and O'Grady's™ brand potato chips. His interest in the sustainability of sales over time prompted a request for additional data on depth of repeat statistics for the two brands. The depth of repeat, or "repeats per repeater" for O'Grady's™ brand potato chips was 1.9 times, or about twice on an annual basis, compared with 2.9 times for Sun Chips™ Multigrain Snacks, or about three times on an annual basis.

Strategy Considerations

Several strategy options were also discussed. Some product management team members advocated increased advertising and merchandising spending if the brand was tested further or launched nationally. They believed that brand awareness would increase with additional spending and felt that spending the national introduction equivalent of $30 million could stimulate brand trial as well. Others interpreted the purchase data to mean that additional volume was possible by introducing a larger package size (for example, a 15-ounce package). They believed that a fourth, larger package could add about one-half ounce to the average annual purchase amount per repeat (and repeater) purchase occasion. Priced at the same price per ounce as the 11-ounce size, this action would not have a material effect on the brand's gross profit per pound. Others believed that another package size made more sense after the brand was established in the marketplace. Furthermore, the manufacturing and marketing of four sizes could stretch the production capacity, increase inventory, and challenge Frito-Lay sales personnel to get retailer shelf and display space.

Some discussion was also directed toward building the household repeat and depth of repeat business. For example, a flavor extension (for example, mild cheddar) was proposed. An advocate of this approach suggested that a flavor extension could increase the "repeats per repeater" to an average of $3\frac{1}{2}$ times per year given greater variety for consumers. However, the addition of another flavor could increase the cannibalization rate to 35 percent some thought. Also, the mild cheddar flavor still needed to be perfected in large-scale production. Others noted that if a larger package and a flavor extension were simultaneously pursued, the number of stock-keeping units would double from six (2 flavors × 3 sizes) to twelve (3 flavors × 4 sizes). It was agreed by everyone that this action would cause severe manufacturing difficulties, since the multigrain snack process technology was still untested.

Price Waterhouse

The 1980s witnessed widespread innovation in the public accounting industry in the United States. To better serve client needs, public accounting firms expanded their client services to include management consulting and industry-based specialties in addition to their traditional auditing and tax services, and they also broadened the international scope of their operations. Another innovation has been the addition of investment banking–related capabilities to further position public accounting firms as full-service financial counselors for their clients. Specifically, some public accounting firms have begun to assist their clients in assessing the merits of using and pursuing different forms of debt and/or equity financing and to conduct merger, acquisition, and divestiture analyses and negotiations. The latter function consists of bringing a potential seller and buyer together and helping them negotiate an agreement relating to the sale or purchase of securities or sometimes firms or divisions of companies.

The inclusion of investment banking-related services represents a significant change in the role public accounting firms have played. Historically, when it came to the buying and selling of companies, public accounting firms provided due diligence services, assisted their clients in assessing the accounting and tax implications of sale and purchase decisions, and provided postacquisition services including post-merger integration of accounting and management systems.[1] By offering direction and assistance in the strategy and negotiation phase that precedes the actual sale and purchase decision and on subsequent integration issues, public accounting firms have entered territory traditionally occupied by investment bankers.

Interest in providing investment banking–related services to its clients emerged at Price Waterhouse in the late 1980s. After considerable study, the firm decided in mid-1989 to offer these services and formed the Corporate Finance Group in early 1990. In early 1991, senior management was focusing attention on making these services achieve their potential and relating them to existing services offered by Price Waterhouse.

THE PUBLIC ACCOUNTING INDUSTRY

The public accounting industry in the United States can trace its roots to the early nineteenth century. At that time, British industrialists hired accountants who were given responsibility for overseeing their commercial interests in America. This responsibility for establishing checks and balances and assessing the accuracy of financial statements has remained an important function performed by the accounting profession.

---

[1]*Due diligence* refers to the practice of examining a company's records, financial statements, and other aspects of its operation prior to a sale or purchase decision.

The assistance of Price Waterhouse in the preparation of this case is gratefully acknowledged. This case was prepared by Angela Bullard and Lawrence Cervetti, graduate students, under the supervision of Professor Roger A. Kerin, of the Edwin L. Cox School of Business, Southern Methodist University, as a basis for class discussion and is not designed to illustrate effective or ineffective handling of an administrative situation. Selected information has been disguised and is not useful for research purposes. Copyright © by Roger A. Kerin. No part of this case may be reproduced without written permission of the copyright holder.

Nature of Public Accounting

The purpose of accounting is to provide quantitative information, primarily financial in nature, that concerns economic entities and is intended to be useful in making economic decisions. Public accounting is an aspect of accounting that primarily focuses on the rendering of an opinion by an independent auditor as to whether an entity's financial statements are fairly presented. That is, the auditor attests that the accounting practices used in the preparation of financial statements are (or are not) in accordance with generally accepted accounting principles proposed by the Financial Accounting Standards Board.

The public accounting profession is composed of certified public accountants (CPAs), who have met certain educational requirements and have satisfied the statutory and administrative requirements to be registered or licensed as a public accountant. In addition, these individuals have successfully completed the Uniform CPA Examination administered by the American Institute of Certified Public Accountants. There are approximately 307,000 practicing certified public accountants in the United States.

Public Accounting Firms and Services

There are thousands of public accounting firms in the United States. Many of these firms are small professional corporations whose certified public accountants provide a variety of services (bookkeeping, tax preparation, and so forth) for small businesses and individuals. However, public accounting is typically associated with what is termed the "Big Six." The six largest public accounting firms in the United States are Arthur Andersen and Company, Ernst and Young, Deloitte Touche, KPMG Peat Marwick, Coopers and Lybrand, and Price Waterhouse. These six firms combined produced U.S. revenues of approximately $10.9 billion and worldwide revenues in excess of $25 billion in 1990. Exhibit 1 profiles the Big Six accounting firms.

Public accounting firms, and particularly the Big Six, provide their clients with a wide range of services. Even though these firms still perform their traditional role of attesting to the fairness of financial statements through the auditing function, they have expanded their services to include a variety of other activities, such as management consulting of various kinds, tax consulting and preparation, employee compensation and benefit studies, and various types of litigation support work. The expanded mix of services has broadened the appeal of public accounting firms by making many firms a "one-stop" source of business expertise. In 1990, almost one-half of the revenues generated by the Big Six firms arose from services other than auditing.

Several factors have fueled the addition of new services. First, the audit business, which had been the mainstay of public accounting firms and a continuing source of revenue and profit, has become an undifferentiated service in the eyes of many clients. This perception has resulted in the practice of competitive bidding, whereby the lowest bid for auditing services generally wins a proposal. While still a valued service and profit center in 1990, auditing services were no longer generating the same profit margins as existed as recently as the mid-1980s. Second, the incidence of mergers and acquisitions in the 1980s shrank the client base for larger public accounting firms. Third, public accounting firms began to recognize that their clients needed assistance in a variety of areas and that many of these areas were allied with the skill and technical competence presently available within public accounting firms.

EXHIBIT 1

Overview of the Big Six Accounting Firms: 1990

	Arthur Andersen & Co.	Coopers & Lybrand	Deloitte Touche	Ernst & Young	KPMG Peat Marwick	Price Waterhouse
Revenues (billions)						
U.S. revenues	$2.28	$1.40	$1.92	$2.24	$1.83	$1.20
Worldwide revenues	$4.16	$4.10	$4.20	$5.01	$5.40	$2.90
U.S. professional staff (including partners)	19,992	10,898	18,800	16,911	15,000	9,560
Total number of partners	1,344	1,301	1,670	2,025	1,876	920
Number of U.S. offices	87	99	110	125	135	100
Percentages of revenue by function						
Auditing/advisory	35%	60%	57%	53%	53%	47%
Tax	23	20	23	25	27	29
Management consulting	42	20	20	22	20	24

Source: Based on company publications and *Public Accounting Report* (February 15, 1991). Information on Arthur Andersen and Company is both Arthur Andersen and Company public accounting and Arthur Andersen Consulting. Coopers and Lybrand revenue estimates are from *Public Accounting Report*, since the company does not disclose revenues.

PRICE WATERHOUSE

Price Waterhouse was formed in 1860 in England by two chartered accountants, Samuel Lowell Price and Edwin Waterhouse. The firm opened its first office in the United States in 1890 under the name Jones, Caesar and Company. By 1990, Price Waterhouse operated 100 offices in the United States and had a total of 400 offices in 103 countries and territories worldwide. The U.S. firm reported fiscal 1990 net revenues of $1.2 billion.

Price Waterhouse is considered by many in the public accounting industry to be the most prestigious of the Big Six firms and lists more Fortune 500 firms among its clients than any other firm. In fiscal 1990, the U.S. firm was the auditor for 93 of the Fortune 500 companies. Current major clients include such well-known companies as IBM, Exxon, USX, DuPont, W.R. Grace, Borden, Walt Disney, Hewlett-Packard, Bristol-Myers, and Shell Oil. The firm also had a sizable client base among companies with annual sales under $150 million.

Client Services

The emphasis Price Waterhouse places on delivering exceptional client service is evident in the firm's "Client Bill of Rights," which encapsulates the client credo for all Price Waterhouse employees (see Exhibit 2). This credo applies to every service provided. Exhibit 3 lists and briefly describes the 16 prime service categories provided by Price Waterhouse.

Even though Price Waterhouse offers a wide variety of professional services, the firm in fiscal 1990 dedicated professional and financial resources to specific markets and services that offered the greatest potential for profitable growth. These included

EXHIBIT 2

Price Waterhouse's Client Bill of Rights

1. The Right to Professional Excellence

We will be technically proficient in all areas in which we provide advice. We will stay current on business and technical developments and seek counsel from appropriate firm professionals when in doubt about a course of action. We will keep abreast of all issues affecting our client so we can anticipate challenges and provide appropriate advice.

2. The Right to Be Served by Professionals Who Understand Our Business

We will learn all we can about our client's industry and business. We will get to know people within the client organization and outside it who have in-depth knowledge of the client's business, its culture, and its strategic objectives, and we will listen to our client to understand its needs. Being in the thick of our client's business—not on the sidelines—will allow us to identify and anticipate issues of concern to our client. While others may learn on the job, we will strive to know as much as possible about the client and its industry before we ever begin working with a client.

3. The Right to Proactive Advice and Creative Business Ideas

We will take the initiative in proposing actions to enhance our client's success, striving always to offer the innovative recommendations our client expects from its business advisers. We will demonstrate to our client that we expect to be and are qualified to be among those who are consulted about significant client events at the planning stage. We will be thought of as the "idea people." When asked for creative ways to help our client achieve its objectives, we will be the firm that says "Yes, can do. . . ."

4. The Right to Independent Viewpoints and Perspectives

We will advise our client about actions that are in its best long-term interests. Although we will keep client objectives clearly in mind as we aid in decision-making, we will not be sycophants. We will have the independence of spirit, the courage, and the confidence to discourage the client from pursuing a course of action that we believe to be ill-advised.

5. The Right to Effective Communication

We will keep our client contacts informed about the progress of our work and any issues that require their attention. Our written communication will be literate and clear, and our oral communication equally articulate. We will treat our client contacts as professional equals, extending to them and their staffs the same courtesy and respect we ourselves expect. In our communications with client executives and staff, we will demonstrate that we are well-rounded people they can relate to on levels other than the professional one; clients like to do business with people who are interesting and personable, just as we do.

6. The Right to a Wide Range of Professional Resources

We will tap the extensive resources of Price Waterhouse to provide our client with the most experienced and savvy business advice available. We will introduce our colleagues to our client contacts and, when relevant, involve them in client service planning and delivery. To promote well-coordinated services, we will ensure that all appropriate PW professionals are kept informed about services proposed and provided to a client.

7. The Right to Dependable Service

We will never miss a deadline or renege on a commitment. We will do it right the first time and complete the assignment better and faster than the client expects. We will avoid surprises about technical and reporting issues, fees, and staff turnover. When we are the best, we will let the client know; if we do not have the required depth in a particular area, we will have the confidence to direct the client elsewhere.

EXHIBIT   2   *(continued)*

8. The Right to Service Anytime and Anyplace

We will always be available to our client, anytime and anyplace we are needed. That means spending more time in our client's office than in our own, being "on call" for our client at all times, and keeping in close touch with client contacts when we are not on the premises. And it means bringing the worldwide resources of the firm to bear on client issues, providing the services needed across town or across the globe.

9. The Right to State-of-the-Art Technology

We will take advantage of the vast technological resources the firm has created to benefit PW professionals and clients. We will use internal tools to enhance the efficiency and cost-effectiveness of our services. And we will implement PW proprietary software and customize other products that will help our client attain better management information and more effective operations.

10. The Right to Value Added Service

We will always be thinking about how our client can be more successful and of ways we can help it achieve its business goals. We will make our client's concerns our concerns and put its needs ahead of our own. We will challenge ourselves and our client, asking the tough questions, not being afraid to be wrong. We will be ever vigilant in identifying additional ways we can strengthen our client's competitive edge, ways in which we can offer even more than the client expects.

---

multinational corporations, the financial services industry, information technology consulting, specialized tax services, and services for rapidly growing and middle-market companies (those with annual revenues in the range from $10 million to $150 million). Special emphasis was placed on services for which business conditions created demand. These included services related to litigation consulting, reorganization and bankruptcy, and corporate finance.

A central figure in rendering client service is the "engagement partner." This person is typically the senior professional who, along with a team of professionals, is assigned to a client to deliver the services desired. Engagement partners have other responsibilities beyond providing their technical knowledge. Increasingly, these individuals are responsible for identifying new clients and uncovering opportunities to match client needs with other Price Waterhouse services. For example, in fiscal 1990, Price Waterhouse was engaged to assist a long-term client, a commercial bank, in laying the groundwork for successful management of a troubled bank it had acquired in a neighboring state. The firm helped to establish management and control systems, including employee training, for a multibillion-dollar portfolio of loans. In addition, the engagement partner recognized other opportunities, and Price Waterhouse was contracted to provide personal financial planning services to the senior executives of the acquired bank.

Corporate Finance Services

Price Waterhouse has provided numerous services related to the merger and acquisition (M&A) activities of its clients since the early 1900s. Early on, the firm typically became involved in the M&A process only after a client decided to purchase or sell its business or a division. According to a senior Price Waterhouse official, the M&A

EXHIBIT 3

Price Waterhouse Services

Audit and Business Advisory Services

Assist companies by enhancing management, strengthening financial controls, and improving competitiveness. In order to accomplish these goals, Price Waterhouse takes an approach based on an in-depth study of a business, its management philosophy and goals, and the environment in which it operates.

Middle-Market and Growing Companies (MMG)

Assist small and middle-market companies in all aspects of their operations. A group of specially trained business advisers provide services including tax assistance, compensation planning, audit procedures, and management training.

Employee Benefit Services

Assist companies in designing and implementing compensation and benefits programs that are both cost-effective and competitive, as well as fair. These programs include retirement plans, executive compensation programs, and employee benefit plans.

Government Services

Provide foreign, federal, state, and local governments and their respective quasi-governmental agencies with assistance in meeting their goals of reducing costs, increasing productivity, and improving services. Services include statistical and economic analyses, rate structures and strategies, and design and implementation of productivity improvement programs.

Industry Services

Monitor industry developments and participate in industry association activities in several industries in order to produce publications that explore business trends and conduct seminars and inform industry members of emerging issues.

International Business Development Services

Assist U.S. companies with operations abroad and foreign companies with operations in the United States. Services include trade and customs consulting, tax planning, and marketing and strategic planning.

International Trade Services

Help improve the profitability and efficiency of an organization's international operations in areas that are directly related to trade at international levels. The focus lies in two areas, trade and investment development and trade information.

Inventory Services

Assist companies in managing inventory size, mix, pricing, cost, and value. Services include accounting and tax advisory and internal planning and implementation of systems.

Investment Management and Securities Operations Consulting

Work with organizations that sponsor, manage, and support securities and investment companies to provide assistance with systems development and implementation, operational efficiency evaluations, and business feasibility studies for new products and services. Also work closely with the accounting and tax services arms of PW to provide a comprehensive range of investment management services.

Management Consulting Services

Attempt to take advantage of new business technologies, implement innovative business strategies to improve operating efficiency, identify cost-effective solutions to business problems, and successfully implement changes that will solve these problems

EXHIBIT 3 *(continued)*

PW operates the Technology Center to help identify and promote new technologies and develop strategies that can effectively take advantage of these technologies.

Corporate Finance Services

Assist middle-market clients in the sale of their business or the purchase of an additional business. Services include identification of buyers or acquisition candidates, financial analyses and projections, development of a negotiating strategy, private placement assistance, and acting as an agent in placing debt and/or equity securities with institutional investors.

Partnership Services

Offer experienced assistance in systems and tax accounting as well as determine the appropriateness of a Master Limited Partnership or syndication for a company and assist in developing and operating this type of partnership.

Personal Financial Services

Help executives with personal financial planning decisions and provide similar assistance to large populations of employee groups in order to help meet company objectives while offering employees financial peace of mind through financial and retirement planning, flexible benifits development, and benefits communication.

Litigation and Reorganization Consulting

Assist debtors, creditors, and other parties in Chapter 11 bankruptcy proceedings in order to successfully rehabilitate debtors and protect creditors' rights by evaluating debtor operations and developing solutions to their operating problems.

Tax Services

Attempt to minimize taxes and increase profitability by alerting clients to the tax consequences of their business decisions, informing them of legislative developments affecting their taxes, and advising them as to their best tax strategies.

Valuation Services

Determine the current value of assets, stock, and business interests for corporations and individuals for use in tax and business planning, mergers and acquisitions, financing, recapitalization, insurance, and litigation purposes.

---

process can be distilled into three sequenced phases: (1) strategy, (2) execution, and (3) finalization and integration (see Exhibit 4). This official noted:

> We were often engaged to offer assistance in the execution and finalization and integration phase of the M&A process. We were rarely engaged to participate in the earlier strategy phase. Investment bankers were usually involved there, almost as a matter of tradition.

He added:

> The strategy phase is not only the starting point, but also lucrative in financial terms. In addition, it is a service that should have naturally occurred as a result of our auditing and management consulting business. Too often an engagement partner did not pursue this business, while investment bankers did.

The process of mergers and acquisitions is very complex and frequently conducted over a lengthy time period. It also often involves a great deal of personal and professional attention by the parties involved. "Deals aren't made easily," said a Price

EXHIBIT 4

Anatomy of the Merger and Acquisition Process

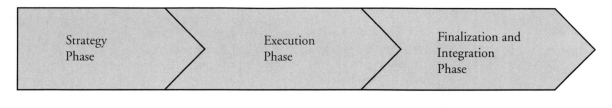

Strategy Phase	Execution Phase	Finalization and Integration Phase

•Identify objectives
•Strategy development
•Valuation analysis
•Candidate identification
•Financing strategy

•Descriptive memorandum
•Strategy implementation
•Alternatives evaluation
•Negotiation assistance
•Due diligence
•Technical accounting and tax
•Operations and systems evaluation

•Purchase price adjustments
•Post-completion integration: operational, organizational, systems, financial
•Asset disposal planning

Waterhouse M&A specialist, "and companies require a significant amount of counseling not only in terms of technicalities, but in terms of strategic implications as well. A CEO wants to know and have confidence in the people giving the advice on whether to buy or sell and how best to do it."

Recognizing that the nature of corporate finance and the nuances of investment banking–related services require unique skills and abilities, particularly in the strategy phase of the M&A process, Price Waterhouse elected to recruit professionals with such qualities and experience in early 1990 and to form the Corporate Finance Group, which also included accounting, tax, and consulting professionals who had experience with mergers and acquisitions. The decision to recruit corporate finance professionals, many of whom held MBA degrees with a corporate finance specialization and had extensive experience in the investment banking industry, was a departure from what other Big Six accounting firms had done. Other Big Six firms had tended to reassign accounting professionals to advance their corporate finance initiatives. According to some industry observers, these two different approaches regarding corporate finance initiatives resulted in an interesting situation in public accounting firms. One such observer commented:

Both approaches have merit and will probably work, but the subtleties of how they will work present some fascinating professional and interpersonal dynamics. First, accounting and finance people are different in both their training and orientation. Surprisingly, few accountants have extensive formal training in finance, and few financial people are well-versed in accounting. This means that accountants in those firms that reassign them will have to learn the techniques and terminology of finance. On the other hand, firms that recruit corporate finance people will benefit quickly from the expertise and experience they bring. However, these corporate finance professionals may be looked at as outsiders and not be easily accepted into the public accounting culture. It is still the case in many public accounting firms that the non-CPA professionals often employed as management consultants are looked upon differently by their accountant colleagues.

INVESTMENT BANKING INDUSTRY

The movement by public accounting firms into the domain of investment banking–related services represented a significant departure from past practices. According to one industry observer,

> By moving "upstream" and becoming involved in decisions previously considered sacred territory by investment bankers, public accounting firms will have to develop or acquire new competencies. Advising on matters of capital structure, managing sensitive negotiations related to acquisitions, divestitures, and financing, assessing strategies for creating shareholder value, and a host of traditional activities upon which investment bankers have built reputations for many years will require new skills and possibly a new cultural orientation for accountants and public accounting firms. Investment banking is transaction-oriented, and investment bankers pride themselves on structuring deals. Many are effective salespeople, some view themselves as marriage brokers, and still others see their function as building relationships and becoming confidants of their clients. Some accountants will feel comfortable performing these roles and tasks, but many will not. For example, a partner with a long-term auditing client isn't likely to actively promote the notion that the client sell its business, since that would be running the risk of losing the client to the buyer's auditing firm.

Scope of Investment Banking

Simply put, an investment banker is an agent who joins buyers and sellers of money. Many investment bankers view themselves as facilitators of the flow of financial capital. Investment bankers are usually experts in financial markets and essentially provide their expertise to firms that wish to raise funds. For example, most of them have specific knowledge of potential buyers of financial securities. Since the role of investment bankers is primarily advisory in nature, building and sustaining relationships play a large part in their day-to-day activities.

Investment bankers perform several important services for their client firms. Specific services fall into three general categories:

1. *Assistance in raising capital.* Investment bankers are engaged to assist companies in raising capital to fund growth. These efforts divide into two categories: public security issues and private placements. *Public security issues* represent the most well-known investment banking function. Initial and secondary public offerings, as they are commonly known, consist of public offerings of debt or equity. Investment bankers may underwrite an issue and assume the risk of selling it in the open market. *Private placements* involve sales of new issues of debt (and occasionally equity) to a limited number of firms such as banks or insurance companies without a public offering. The issuing firm can be public or private.

2. *Merger and acquisition services.* When two firms want to merge their operations or when one firm acquires another, investment bankers are customarily asked to consult for the parties to the transaction. Their function often entails issuing opinions regarding the value of the acquired company or the fairness of the negotiated contract. Some larger investment banking firms often take a more active role and commit capital to help finance a merger or acquisition.

3. *General financial advisory services.* Investment bankers are paid for their knowledge of and access to capital markets. While they are predominantly involved directly in the capital-raising process, they may be engaged to as-

sist in the valuation of a particular issue of securities or a company. Their advice is also sought in areas concerning the use of equity (for example, stock) and debt to fund company growth.

Investment Banking Firms

There are over 200 investment banking firms in the United States. However, industry observers typically recognize six firms as being industry leaders: Merrill Lynch, Pierce, Fenner and Smith; Lehman Brothers; Goldman Sachs; Morgan Stanley; First Boston; and Salomon Brothers. Other well-known firms are Dean Witter Reynolds; Alex Brown and Sons; Prudential Securities; and Smith Barney, Harris Upham and Company. Some firms are primarily regional. For example, Rauscher Pierce Refsnes, Inc., is prominent in the southwestern United States, William Blair in the upper Midwest, and Robinson Humphrey in the southeastern states. Even though investment banking firms provide a variety of services for their clients, they often differ in the extent to which they provide specific services. For example, in 1990, Alex Brown and Sons led the industry in initial public offerings, that is, securities issued for the first time to the public. Merrill Lynch and Goldman Sachs were industry leaders in the issuance of overall corporate debt and equity.[2] Morgan Stanley, First Boston, Lehman Brothers, and Goldman Sachs are typically viewed as leaders in the area of mergers and acquisitions. In addition, larger, national investment-banking firms tend to work with larger clients, while smaller or regional investment banking firms work with smaller clients.

Credibility, reliability, and a history of past successes benefit established investment banking firms. For these reasons and others, established firms typically experience a high incidence of repeat business from existing clients. Nevertheless, these firms are constantly seeking new clients through referrals and missionary efforts (for example, "cold calling"). Referrals often arise from existing clients and from other professionals (law firms and public accounting firms), financial institutions, and private investors.

Many larger banks in the United States are also involved in some investment banking–related activities. Although these banks are prohibited from issuing new securities by the Glass-Steagall Act of 1933, some of them have circumvented this prohibition by establishing foreign subsidiaries that operate in countries that allow banks to enter the securities field.[3] Moreover, there is evidence that the regulatory prohibitions on issuing new securities are being relaxed.

CORPORATE FINANCE INITIATIVE AT PRICE WATERHOUSE

The corporate finance initiative at Price Waterhouse prompted an extensive recruiting effort during much of 1990. By early 1991, about 35 corporate finance professional were working out of six Price Waterhouse offices in the United States. These offices were located in New York, Chicago, Dallas, Los Angeles, San Francisco, and Atlanta.

Client Focus

The Corporate Finance Group was to focus primarily on what Price Waterhouse considered "middle-market" companies, or those companies with annual sales revenue between $10 million and $150 million. Companies in this category could already be clients of Price Waterhouse or not currently availing themselves of Price Waterhouse

---

[2]*Institutional Investor* (February 1991).
[3]"Glass-Steagall Act Repeal: An Issue for 'Everybank,' " *American Banker* (July 6, 1990): 4.

services. The decision to focus on "middle-market" companies was based on the view that larger, national investment banking firms typically directed their efforts toward larger companies, many of which were Fortune 1000 corporations. Furthermore, statistics on merger and acquisition activity indicated that approximately 45 percent of all such transactions were undertaken by "middle-market" companies.[4] However, Price Waterhouse officials acknowledged that by targeting such companies, they would be in direct competition with smaller, regional investment banking firms.

Service Focus

The Corporate Finance Group would provide a variety of services for new and prospective Price Waterhouse clients, including merger and acquisition advisory services, private placement advisory services, and general financial advisory services. According to a presentation made by one corporate finance professional, a sampling of services that could be provided included (1) exclusive sale assignments, (2) development and implementation of acquisition strategies, (3) structuring and financing of corporate recapitalizations, and (4) advice on financial restructuring options. Exhibit 5 details aspects of these four types of services. The mix of services provided by the Corporate Finance Group was intended to complement and expand the currently available expertise and services provided by Price Waterhouse.

Global Reach

The Corporate Finance Group would also benefit from the worldwide presence of Price Waterhouse in 103 countries and territories. This presence, involving thousands of clients, access to financing sources, and knowledge of foreign and domestic firms, affords information and technical resources that could strengthen the corporate finance initiative. A recent example involving an acquisition illustrates the benefits of Price Waterhouse's global reach:

> Learning that a major U.S. firm planned overseas acquisitions, a corporate finance specialist proposed to qualify an acquisition candidate in Western Europe. Given the mandate to act, the specialist drew on Price Waterhouse Europe's network to develop a list of targets with the right characteristics. Eventually, this search resulted in a successful offer for a company that happened to be audited by Price Waterhouse Europe.

Implementation

Field implementation of the corporate finance initiative at Price Waterhouse began in earnest in mid-1990 as the Corporate Finance Group began to take shape. According to a corporate finance specialist, "much of the first few months were devoted to making our presence and purpose known at Price Waterhouse." In this regard, corporate finance specialists often made presentations to the Price Waterhouse staff to introduce themselves and the services they could offer to present and prospective clients. Corporate finance specialists also spent time with auditing and management-consulting engagement partners to discuss opportunities for joint work on behalf of existing clients and opportunities for reaching new clients. During this period, corporate finance specialists occasionally accompanied an engagement partner on a visit to an existing client. Firms that were not Price Waterhouse clients were typically called on exclusively by corporate finance specialists. No advertising was employed. However, the Corporate

---

[4] *Mergers & Acquisitions* (March–April, 1991): 40.

EXHIBIT 5

Representative Sampling of Service Opportunities for Corporate Finance Group

Opportunity	Services provided by CFG

Exclusive sale assignment: Client wishes to sell all or a portion of its business.	1. Identify and evaluate financial alternatives, including
	  • selling off the entire business
	  • divestiture of operating unit(s) or significant assets
	2. Assess likely range of value for business, operating unit, or assets
	3. Identify interested buyers
	4. Prepare descriptive memorandum
	5. Evaluate proposals and negotiate with qualified buyers

Acquisition: Client believes the value of its business can be enhanced with a strategic acquisition.	1. Identify acquisition candidates 2. Perform a valuation analysis 3. Advise on bidding strategies 4. Approach target acquisition on behalf of client 5. Negotiate on behalf of client 6. Assist in financing if necessary

Recapitalization: Client wishes to realize a portion of the values of its business.	1. Identify and evaluate alternatives, including
	  • leveraged recapitalization
	  • leveraged employee stock ownership plan (ESOP)
	  • strategic alliance
	2. Assess debt capacity
	3. Identify appropriate financing sources
	4. Prepare descriptive memorandum
	5. Evaluate proposals and negotiate with lenders or investors

Financial restructuring: Client has a sound business but has inappropriate capitalization.	1. Identify and evaluate the strategic and financial alternatives to improve the client's financial strength and capital structure 2. Prepare descriptive memorandum for use in negotiations with lenders or investors

Finance Group used brochures and formal presentation materials to communicate the nature and scope of its services. "These initial efforts were very useful in introducing our capabilities," said a corporate finance specialist. "However, interest in our services was dealt a blow in August [1990] by the invasion of Kuwait by Iraq and the subsequent threat of international turmoil. Companies were not disposed toward buying and selling businesses and pursuing private placements given the economic and political uncertainty during the fourth quarter of 1990."

Integration of the Corporate Finance Group

Even though potential demand for corporate finance services was negatively affected by the Persian Gulf conflict, efforts to build internal linkages within Price Waterhouse continued. A corporate finance specialist estimated that about 20 percent of the Price Waterhouse partners had embraced the Corporate Finance Group and its services by early 1991 and had actively communicated its capabilities to prospective clients. An engagement partner in the auditing area noted that this new service area was a "real plus" but added:

> Very often you have little time to describe the many services that Price Waterhouse provides. Most of a typical one-hour client meeting is spent listening to the client. If corporate finance service opportunities are not indicated by something the client says, they, like some other services, are put on a "second priority list" to be raised at a later time.

Another engagement partner, also in the auditing function, recounted an experience related to the Corporate Finance Group. He said:

> People in the CFG had been talking to my client about its business and had recommended that my client buy another company. However, our auditors had identified an underperforming division and recommended to the company president that it be sold. What started out as acquisition mindset ended up as a program for a divestiture.

A corporate finance specialist noted a missed opportunity for the Corporate Finance Group's private placement services:

> A few weeks ago our group read about a private placement by one of our blue chip clients after the placement happened. It seemed that the engagement partner was either not aware of the opportunity or did not bring it to our attention.

Some members of the Corporate Finance Group acknowledge that integration of their capabilities will take time, given the nature of their services. "What will be needed are a few large engagements," said a corporate finance specialist. "However," he added, "since acquisitions, divestitures, and private placements take months and sometimes a year or more to plan and execute, results are not immediately seen. And sometimes, the effort does not produce tangible financial results if the deal fails."

Service Mix

One member of the Corporate Finance Group believed that the efforts of the group were "moderately successful" in that both external and internal relationships were being built and service proposals and engagements were being produced. No discernible pattern of service engagements had yet emerged, however.

Business conditions in early 1991 continued to indicate that corporate finance services were in demand and that these services offered significant potential for profitable growth. Given the nature of the services, exclusive sale assignments appeared to provide the greatest profit potential for Price Waterhouse, followed by private placements (including aspects of financial restructuring and recapitalization of companies). Private placements also had the potential for continuing repeat business. Acquisition assignments and engagements and general financial advisory services were next in order of profitability. However, as one engagement partner noted, "A client can buy and buy again, but it can only sell itself once."

Manor Memorial Hospital

In mid-April 1986, Sherri Worth, Assistant Administrator at Manor Memorial Hospital (MMH) in charge of MMH's Downtown Health Clinic (DHC), uncovered an unsettling parcel of news. During a call on the employee benefits director at a downtown department store, she was told that a firm was conducting a study to determine whether sufficient demand existed to establish a clinic five blocks north of MMH's Downtown Health Clinic. The description of the clinic's services sounded similar to those offered by the DHC, and the planned opening date was May 1987.

As Worth walked back to her office, she could not help but think about the possible competition. Upon arriving at her office, Worth called Dr. Roger Mahon, MMH's administrator, to tell him what she had learned. He asked her to contact other employee benefits directors and query patients to see whether they had been surveyed. He expressed concern for two reasons. First, a competitive clinic would attract existing and potential patients of the Downtown Health Clinic. Second, a clinic that provided similar services could hamper the DHC's progress toward achieving its service and profitability objectives. Mahon suggested that Worth summarize the DHC's performance to date so that he could speak to members of the board of trustees' executive committee on what action, if any, the DHC should take to compete for patients. He concluded their discussion by saying, "Who would have thought ten years ago that a hospital administrator would be making decisions not unlike those faced by a retail chain store executive. But I guess it comes with the territory these days."

HEALTH CARE AND THE HOSPITAL INDUSTRY

Health care, and specifically the hospital industry, has undergone a dramatic transformation in the past few decades. Until the 1960s, hospitals were largely charitable institutions that prided themselves on their not-for-profit orientation. Hospitals functioned primarily as workshops for physicians and were guided by civic-minded boards of trustees.

Federal legislation introduced in the 1960s created boom times for the hospital industry. The Hill-Burton Act provided billions of dollars for hospital construction, to be repaid by fulfilling quotas for charity care. Additional funds were poured into expansion and construction of medical schools. Medicare and Medicaid subsidized health care for the indigent, disabled, and elderly. These programs reimbursed hospitals for their incurred costs plus an additional return on investment. The 1960s also saw dramatic increases in commercial insurance coverage, offered as employee fringe benefits and purchased in additional quantities by a more affluent public. Accordingly, health care became accessible to an overwhelming majority of U.S. citizens, regardless of where they lived or their ability to pay. Federal intervention had changed the concept of health-care services from privilege to entitlement.

By the mid-1970s, however, skyrocketing health-care costs had forced the federal government to reassess its role in health care. Stringent controls were placed on hospital construction and expansion, and utilization- and physician-review programs were implemented to ensure against too-lengthy inpatient stays. By the end of the decade, hospitals were initiating voluntary cost-cutting programs to stave off additional government intervention. Despite all efforts, however, health-care expenditures continued to outpace the Consumer Price Index. In 1981 Americans spent close to 10 percent of the gross national product on health care, and the government's portion was 43 percent of the $287 billion tab. Only 11 percent of all hospital services were paid for by individuals; the balance was financed by third-party payors, such as insurance companies.

The 1980s ushered in a very different health-care environment, and hospitals particularly were hard hit by the changes. On the one hand, the federal government sought to reduce health-care costs through cutbacks in subsidy programs and cost-control regulations. On the other hand, innovations in health-care delivery severely reduced the number of patients serviced by hospitals.

One such innovation was preventive health-care programs. These fall into two categories: health maintenance organizations (HMOs) and preferred provider organizations (PPOs). HMOs surfaced in the mid-1970s. An HMO encourages preventive health care by providing medical services as needed for a fixed monthly fee. HMOs typically enter into contractual relationships with designated physicians and hospitals and have been successful in reducing hospital inpatient days and health-care expenditures. PPOs, which emerged in the early 1980s, establish contractual arrangements between health-care providers (physicians and/or hospitals) and large employer groups. Unlike HMOs, PPOs generally offer incentives for using preferred providers rather than restricting individuals to specific hospitals or physicians. PPOs are likely to have the same effect on inpatient days and health-care expenditures as HMOs have, and Mahon had planned to design a PPO for Manor Memorial Hospital using the Downtown Health Clinic as a link to large employers in the downtown area.

A second and farther-reaching innovation that had an impact on health-care delivery in the 1980s was ambulatory health-care services and facilities. Ambulatory health-care services consist of treatments and practices that consumers use on an episodic or emergency basis. Examples include physical examinations, treatment of minor emergencies (such as cuts, bruises, and minor surgery), and treatment of common illnesses (such as colds and flu).

Ambulatory health-care facilities are split into two categories: (1) minor emergency centers, known by acronyms such as FEC (Free-Standing Emergency Clinic) and MEC (Medical Emergency Clinic) and (2) clinics that focus on primary or episodic care.[1] Although regulation is nominal, if a clinic positions itself as an emergency-care center, expressing this focus in its name, it generally is required (or pressured by area physicians) to be staffed 24 hours a day by a licensed physician and to have certain basic life-support equipment.

---

[1]*Primary care* is the point of entry into the health-care system. It consists of a continuous relationship with a personal physician who takes care of a broad range of medical needs. Primary-care physicians include general practitioners, internal medicine and family practice specialists, gynecologists, and pediatricians.

Ambulatory health-care services are the fastest-growing segment of health services.[2] The first no-appointment, walk-in clinic opened in Newark, Delaware, in 1975. By 1985 there were at least 2,500 similar facilities in the United States, not including group-practice physician arrangements and HMOs. Ambulatory health-care services have siphoned away a large portion of the care offered by primary-care physicians and have forced hospitals to deal increasingly with only the most acutely ill and severely injured patients.

Three factors have accounted for the growth of ambulatory health-care services. First, advances in medical technology, miniaturization, and portable medical equipment have made more diagnostic and surgical procedures possible outside the traditional hospital setting. Second, consumers have adopted a more proactive stance on where they will receive their health and medical care. Consumers are choosing the hospital at which they wish to be treated, and the incidence of "doctor shopping" is on the rise. Third, the mystique of medical and health care has been altered with the growth of paramedical professionals and standardized treatment practices.

Most of the early centers emphasized quick, convenient, minor emergency care. Many new centers have positioned themselves as convenient, personalized alternatives to primary-care physicians' practices. These operations typically employ aggressive, sophisticated marketing techniques, including branding, consistent logos and atmospherics, promotional incentives, and mass-media advertising (giving rise to vernacular designations such as "Doc-in-the-Box" and "McMedical"). Although ambulatory-care facilities vary considerably among communities and owners, the following characteristics appear to be universal: (1) branding, (2) extended hours, (3) lower fees than emergency rooms, (4) no appointments necessary, (5) minor emergencies treated, (6) easy access and parking, (7) short waiting times, and (8) credit cards accepted.

Even though these facilities have tapped a market need, not all have been successful. Failure rates are as high as 25 percent in some areas of the country. Many areas were already saturated with many MECs fighting aggressive market-share battles.[3] According to one industry estimate, the average MEC is open 16 hours a day, 7 days a week, with two physicians on each 8-hour shift. The average visit is 15 minutes, and the average break-even volume lies between 30 and 45 visits per day.

MANOR MEMORIAL HOSPITAL

Manor Memorial Hospital is a 600-bed, independent, not-for-profit, general hospital located on the southern periphery of a major western city. It is one of six general hospitals in the city and twenty in the county. It is financially stronger than most of the metropolitan-based hospitals in the United States. It is debt-free and has the highest overall occupancy rate among the city's six general hospitals. Nevertheless, the hospital's administration and board of trustees have serious concerns about its patient mix, which reflects unfavorable demographic shifts. Most of the population growth in the late 1970s occurred in the suburban areas to the north, east, and west. These suburban areas attracted young, upwardly mobile families from the city. They also attracted thousands of families from other states—families drawn to the area's dynamic, robust business climate.

---

[2]"FECs Pose Competition for Hospital EDs," *Hospitals* (March 1984): 77–80; *Immediate Care Centers: Fast Medicine for the '80s* (Washington, DC: U.S. Department of Health and Human Services, November 1984).

[3]See, for example, "Urgent Care Centers Seek Niches," *Modern Healthcare* (April 1984): 110–112.

As hospitals sprang up to serve the high-growth suburban areas, MMH found it-self becoming increasingly dependent on inner-city residents, who have a higher median age and higher incidence of Medicare coverage. Without a stronger stable inflow of short-stay, privately insured patients, the financial health of the hospital would be jeopardized. Accordingly, in the summer of 1984, the board of trustees authorized a study to determine whether to open an ambulatory facility in the downtown area about ten blocks north of the hospital.

DOWNTOWN HEALTH CLINIC

The charter for the Downtown Health Clinic contained four objectives:

1. To expand the hospital's referral base
2. To increase referrals of privately insured patients

EXHIBIT   1

Present and Planned Locations of Downtown Health Clinics and Service Areas

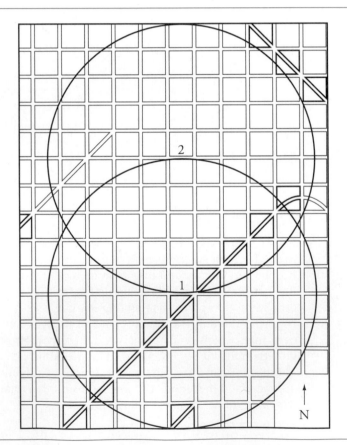

Key:
1. Original DHC and five-block service radius.
2. Planned location of competitor and five-block service radius.

3. To establish a liaison with the business community by addressing employers' specific health needs

4. To become self-supporting three years after opening

The specific services to be offered by the DHC would include (1) preventive health care (for example, physical examinations and immunizations), (2) minor-emergency care, (3) referral for acute and chronic health-care problems, (4) specialized employer services (for example, preemployment examinations and treatment of worker's compensation injuries), (5) primary health-care services (for example, treatment of common illnesses), and (6) basic X-ray and laboratory tests. The DHC would be open 260 days a year (Monday–Friday) from 8:00 A.M. to 5:00 P.M.

The location for the DHC would be in the Greater West Office and Shopping Complex, situated on the corner of Main and West Streets (see Exhibit 1). This location was chosen because a member of the board of trustees owned the Greater West Complex and was willing to share construction, design, and equipment expenses with the hospital.

During the fall of 1984, construction plans for erecting the DHC were well under way, and the expense budget was developed (see Exhibit 2). During the winter months, MMH commissioned a study to determine the service radius of the DHC, estimate the number of potential users of the DHC, assess responsiveness to the services to be offered by the DHC, and review the operations of suburban ambulatory-care clinics. The results indicated that the service area would have a five-block radius, since this was the longest distance office workers would walk. Discussions with city planners indicated the service area contained 11,663 office workers during the 9:00–5:00 Monday–Friday work week. The population in the area was expected to grow 6 percent per year, given new building and renovation activity. Personal interviews with 400 office workers, selected randomly, indicated that 50 percent would use or try the DHC if necessary and that 40 percent of these prospective users would visit the DHC at least once per year (see Exhibit 3 for additional findings). Finally, the study of suburban ambulatory-care facilities revealed the data shown in Exhibit 4. Given their locations in suburban areas, these facilities were not considered direct competition, but their existence indicated that "the city's populace was attuned to ambulatory health care facilities," remarked Worth.

EXHIBIT 2

Downtown Health Clinic: 12-Month Expense Budget

Item	Expenditure
Physician coverage: 260 days times 8 hr/day at $33/hr	$68,640
Professional fees	21,360
Lease	38,250
Supplies	23,447
Utilities	3,315
Personnel, including fringe (director, nurse, laboratory assistant, X-ray technician, receptionist)	84,188
Amortization	15,324
Annual expenditure	$254,524

Note: Expenditures were based on the assumption that the DHC would have 4 visits per hour, or 32 visits per day, when operating at full capacity.

E X H I B I T   3

Profile of DHC Service Area, Based on City and Survey Data

1984 Population Estimate (Source: City Planning Department)

Total office worker population in five-block radius	11,663
Expected annual growth, 1984–1989	6.0%/yr
Sex breakdown in five-block radius:	
Male	40%
Female	60%

Results from Personal Interviews (January 1984)

Would use/try DHC if necessary for personal illness/exams	50%
Expected frequency of DHC use for personal illness/exams among those saying would use/try if necessary:[a]	
Once every other year	60%
Once per year	25%
Twice per year	10%
Three or more times per year	5%

Selected Cross-Tabulations	*Sex*		
	Male	*Female*	*Total*
Would you use or try DHC if necessary?			
Yes	88[b]	168	256
No	72	72	144
Total	160	240	400

	Have Regular Physician (Excluding Gynecologist)		
	Yes	*No*	*Total*
Would you use or try DHC if necessary?			
Yes	58	198	256
No	130	14	144
Total	188	212	400

[a]No difference between males and females on frequency of use.

[b]Of the 160 males interviewed 88 (55 percent) said they would use the DHC; 88 of the 256 interviewees (34 percent) who said they would use the DHC were male.

These results were viewed favorably by the board of trustees and "confirmed our belief that an ambulatory facility was needed downtown," noted Worth. The DHC was formally opened May 1, 1985. Except for the publicity surrounding the opening, however, no advertising or other types of promotion were planned. "Several members of the hospital staff shied away from advertising or solicitation, since it hinted at crass commercialism," said Worth.

EXHIBIT 4

Suburban Ambulatory-Care Clinics: Operations Profile

Operations	EmerCenter #1	EmerCenter #2	Adams Industrial Clinic	Health First	Medcenter
Opening	March 1980	November 1982	June 1980	May 1982	June 1983
Patients/year	9,030	6,000	8,400	5,700	8,661
Hours of operation	10:00 A.M.–10:00 P.M. Monday–Friday	10:00 A.M.–10:00 P.M. Monday–Sunday	8:00 A.M.–5:00 P.M Monday–Friday	5:00 P.M.–11:00 P.M. Monday–Friday; 10:00 A.M.–10:00 P.M. Saturday–Sunday	8:00 A.M.–8:00 P.M. Monday–Sunday
Physicians/8-hr shift	2	2	2	2	2
Estimated patient visits/hour	3.8/hr	3.4/hr	5.0/hr	3.0/hr	3.0/hr
Estimated average charge per visit	$30.00	$31.00	$38.00	$31.00	$32.00
Services provided:					
Preventive health care			✓	✓	✓
Minor emergencies	✓	✓	✓	✓	✓
Employer services			✓		
X-ray/lab tests	✓	✓	✓	✓	✓
Miscellaneous	✓	✓	✓	✓	✓
Use direct-mail advertising	✓	✓	✓	✓	✓

EXHIBIT 5

Downtown Health Clinic Financial Summary

	1985								1986			Total Year to Date
	May	June	July	Aug.	Sept.	Oct.	Nov.	Dec.	Jan.	Feb.	March	
Gross revenue	4,075	8,387	8,844	9,697	11,206	11,406	11,672	11,758	12,846	13,879	14,715	118,485
Variable expenses:												
Bad debt	163	355	354	388	448	456	467	470	513	555	588	4,757
Medical/surgical supplies	6,591	798	935	643	1,063	1,213	1,661	612	976	1,580	1,078	17,150
Drugs	159	54	65	52	305	93	0	56	186	253	76	1,299
Office supplies	647	222	596	718	315	(190)	24	281	467	0	64	3,144
Total variable expense	7,560	1,429	1,950	1,801	2,131	1,572	2,152	1,419	2,142	2,388	1,806	26,350
Contribution	(3,485)	6,958	6,894	7,896	9,075	9,834	9,520	10,339	10,704	11,491	12,909	92,135
Fixed expenses:												
Personnel	7,816	7,459	6,670	5,900	6,816	11,490	7,320	6,249	6,705	8,995	7,644	83,064
Professional services[a]	10,009	6,945	7,732	7,158	7,385	6,800	7,200	7,450	7,242	7,078	7,187	82,186
Facility[b]	3,222	2,537	2,890	2,905	2,622	2,655	2,620	2,613	2,836	2,622	2,719	30,241
Miscellaneous	705	107	133	140	238	45	111	76	106	123	57	1,841
Amortization	1,277	1,277	1,277	1,277	1,277	1,277	1,277	1,277	1,277	1,277	1,277	14,047
Total fixed expense	23,029	18,325	18,702	17,380	18,338	22,267	18,528	17,665	18,166	20,095	18,884	211,379
Net gain (loss)	(26,514)	(11,367)	(11,808)	(9,484)	(9,263)	(12,433)	(9,008)	(7,326)	(7,462)	(8,604)	(5,975)	(119,244)
Number of patient visits	109	231	275	277	322	320	321	366	383	463	423	3,490
Number of working days	22	21	21	22	20	23	22	20	22	21	23	237

[a]Includes professional fees paid (see Exhibit 2).

[b]Includes lease payments, utilities, and maintenance.

Performance: May 1985–March 1986

A financial summary of DHC performance through March 1986 is shown in Exhibit 5. According to Mahon:

> We are pleased with the performance to date and hope the DHC will be self-supporting by April 1987. We are getting favorable word of mouth from satisfied patients that will generate both new and repeat patients. We expect 410 patient visits in April [1986]. In addition, we have taken steps to improve our financial standing. For example, our bad debts have been costing us 4 percent of gross revenue. With a better credit and collection procedure established just last month, we will reduce this figure to 2 percent. We plan to initiate an 8 percent across-the-board increase in charges on May 1 and will experience only a 5 percent increase in personnel and professional services expenses next year.

Records kept by MMH revealed that the DHC was realizing its objectives. For example, the referral objective was being met, since the DHC had made 105 referrals to MMH and produced slightly over $189,000 in revenue and an estimated $15,000 in net profit. Almost all of these patients were privately insured. The service mix, though dominated by treatment of common illnesses and examinations, did indicate that the DHC was being used for a variety of purposes. A breakdown of the reasons for patient visits for the first 11 months of operations is as follows:

Personal illness exams	53%
Worker's compensation exam/treatment	25
Employment/insurance physical exams	19
Emergency	3
Total	100%

Patient records indicated that 97 percent of all visits were by first-time users of the DHC and 113 visits were by repeat patients. Approximately 5 percent of the visits in each month from October 1985 through March 1986 were repeat visits. "We are pleased that we are already getting repeat business because it shows we are doing our job," Worth commented. The average revenue per patient visit during the first 11 months was $33.95.[4] A breakdown of the average charge by type of visit follows. The average charge was to increase 8 percent on May 1, 1986.

Personal illness/exam	$25 per visit
Worker's compensation exam/treatment	$39 per visit
Employment/insurance physical examination	$47 per visit
Emergency	$67 per visit

In an effort to monitor the performance of the DHC, patients were asked to provide selected health-care information as well as demographic information. This information was summarized monthly, and Exhibit 6 shows the profile of patients visiting the DHC for the first 11 months of operation. In addition to this information, patients were asked for suggestions on how the DHC could serve the downtown area. Suggestions typically fell into three categories: service hours, services offered, and waiting time. Thirty percent of the patients suggested expanded service hours, with an opening time of 7:00 A.M. and a closing time of 7:00 P.M. One-half of the fe-

---

[4]The average charge per patient visit includes the charge for basic X-ray and laboratory tests when appropriate.

E X H I B I T   6

**Profile of Downtown Health Clinic Patients:
Personal Illness/Exam Visits Only**

Occupation	
Clerical	48%
Professional/technical/managerial	23
Operator	19
Other	10
	100%

Sex	
Male	30%
Female	70
	100%

Referral Source	
Friend/colleague	35%
Employer	60
Other	5
	100%

Patient Origin

Distance:

One block	25%
Two blocks	28
Three blocks	22
Four blocks	15
Five blocks	8
More than five blocks	2
	100%

Direction:

North of DHC	10%
South of DHC	25
Northeast of DHC	5
Southwest of DHC	15
East of DHC	20
West of DHC	10
Southeast of DHC	10
Northwest of DHC	5
	100%

Have Regular Physician	
Yes	18%
No	82
	100%

male patients requested that gynecological services be added.[5] A majority of the patients expressed concern about the waiting time, particularly during the lunch hours (11:00 A.M.–2:00 P.M.). A check of DHC records indicated that 70 percent of patient visits occurred during the 11:00 A.M.–2:00 P.M. period and that one-half of the visits were for personal illnesses.

Worth believed all three suggestions had merit, and she had already explored ways to expand the DHC's hours and reduce waiting time. For example, the reason for her call on the employee benefits director at a local department store was to schedule employee physical examinations in the morning or late afternoon hours to minimize crowding during the lunch hour. Nevertheless, she believed a second licensed physician might be necessary, with one physician working the hours from 7:00 A.M. to 3:00 P.M. and the other working between 11:00 A.M. and 7:00 P.M. The overlap during the lunch period would alleviate waiting times, she thought. Expanding from 9- to 12-hour days would entail a 33 percent increase in personnel costs, however, as well as the cost of another physician.[6]

Worth believed that scheduling was more of a problem than she or the MMH staff had expected. "You just can't schedule the walk-ins," she said, "and pardon me for saying it, but the people coming in with personal care needs have really caused the congestion." She added that the problem would get worse because the mix of patient needs was moving toward personal illnesses and examinations. "If the trend continues, we should have 20 percent more personal illness visits next year than last year."

Worth believed that gynecological services would be a plus, since 70 percent of the visits were made by women and almost all were under 35 years of age. She said:

> Women should see a gynecologist regularly at least once a year and often twice a year. We could add an additional 2,000 visits per year by having a hospital gynecologist work at the DHC two eight-hour days a week by appointment. An average charge per visit would be about $52 including lab work, and the physician cost would be $35 per hour.

Worth had also given some thought to how the DHC could improve its relations with the business community. Currently, business-initiated visits (worker's compensation examinations and treatments and employment/insurance physical examinations) accounted for 44 percent of the visits to the DHC. Construction in the downtown area had stimulated worker's compensation activity, and growth in employment in the five-block service radius had contributed to employment physicals. Worth believed worker's compensation visits would stabilize at about 81 per month and then decline with slowed building activity. Employment physicals accounted for 50 visits per month and were expected to remain at this level with the current operating hours. Insurance physicals were not expected to increase beyond current levels, nor were emergency visits.

Commenting on her calls on businesses, Worth remarked:

> I have actively called on businesses under the guise of community relations because the MMH staff has not sanctioned solicitation. My guess, after talking with businesspeople, is that we could get virtually every new employment physical if we didn't interfere with employment hours and scheduled them before 8:00 A.M. or after

---

[5]*Gynecology* is that branch of medicine dealing with the female reproductive tract.
[6]Expanded hours would be staffed by part-time personnel, who would receive the same wages as full-time personnel.

5:00 P.M. Given net new employment in the area and new employees due to turnover, I'd guess we could schedule an additional 65 employment physicals every month–that is, a total of 115 a month.

Worth added that she had also received approval to run an "informational advertisement" in the downtown weekly newspaper each week next year provided that the advertisement did not feature prices or appear to be commercial in its presentation. The weekly advertisement would cost $5,200 per year.

The Possibility of Competition

Worth's calls on local businesses and patient interviews indicated that someone was conducting a survey. She believed that Medcenter, a privately owned suburban ambulatory facility, was the sponsor. Medcenter appeared to be successful in its suburban location (see Exhibit 4) and had a reputation for being an aggressive, marketing-oriented operation. Even though Medcenter did not provide employer services at its suburban location, Worth thought the fact that an employee benefits director had been interviewed suggested that such services might be offered.

The proposed location for the new clinic was five blocks directly north of the DHC. Based on the research for the DHC, Worth estimated that the number of office workers within a five-block radius of the competitive clinic would be 11,652 in 1987 and 13,590 in 1988, and would grow at an annual rate of 7 percent through 1995 because of new construction and building renovation. Worth believed the competitor's service area had the same socioeconomic profile and the same usage and employment characteristics as the DHC's service area.

The overlap in service areas was due to the layout of the downtown area and the availability of high-quality street-level space. According to Worth, "It is possible that a third of our current personal illness/exam patients from the northern portion of our service area will switch to the new clinic and about 40 percent of potential personal illness/exam patients in this area will go to the new location." Worth went on to say that the overlap in service areas would cover 3,424 office workers in 1986.

The effect of the competing clinic on the volume of emergency, worker's compensation, and employment/insurance exam work was more difficult to assess. Worth felt that worker's compensation visits would not be materially affected because most construction was being undertaken in areas south, east, and west of the DHC. Emergency visits were so random that it was not possible to assess what effect the competing clinic would have. The projected volume of employment and insurance physicals could change with the addition of a competing clinic, however. Worth guessed, "At worst, we would see no increase in these types of visits over last year since we have not gotten many visits from this area."

A week after she first heard about the possibility of competition, Worth and Mahon met to review the information on the DHC. Just before Worth finished giving her overview, Mahon's administrative assistant interrupted to tell him he had to leave to catch a plane for a three-day conference dealing with health-care marketing. As he left the room, Mahon asked Worth to draft a concise analysis of the DHC's position. He also asked her to specify and evaluate the alternatives for the DHC assuming Medcenter either did or did not open a facility. "Remember," Mahon said, "Manor Memorial has a lot riding on the DHC. Making it work involves not only dollars and cents, but our image in the community as well."

Swisher Mower and Machine Company

In early 1990, Max Swisher, President of Swisher Mower and Machine Company (SMC), received a certified letter from a major national retail merchandise chain inquiring about a private branding arrangement for his company's line of riding mowers. He thought the inquiry presented an opportunity worth consideration, since unit volume sales of the SMC riding mower had eroded in recent years. However, details concerning the inquiry would have to be studied more closely.

COMPANY BACKGROUND

The origins of Swisher Mower and Machine Company can be traced to the mechanical aptitude of its founder, Max Swisher. He received his first patent for a gearbox drive assembly when he was 18 years old. Shortly thereafter, he developed a self-propelled push mower utilizing this drive assembly. He began selling these mowers to neighbors after converting his parents' garage into a small manufacturing operation and formed Swisher Mower and Machine Company in 1949. In the early 1950s, Swisher decided to integrate his drive mechanism into a riding mower and began selling these mowers under the Ride King name in 1956.

In 1966, unit volume for SMC riding mowers peaked at 10,000 units with sales of $2 million. In the early 1970s, sales volume began a downward trend as a result of poor economic conditions in the geographic markets served by SMC. From 1975 to 1989, unit volume remained relatively constant and averaged 4,335 units per year. In 1989, the company sold 4,100 riding mowers and recorded sales of $3.5 million. Exhibit 1 shows the company's unit sales history for riding mowers since 1956.

SMC has 17 employees—3 managers, 1 administrative assistant, and 13 production workers. The company manufactures mowers at its plant in Warrensburg, Missouri, but utilizes outside suppliers for some machine tool work and subassembly. Its facilities have an annual production capacity of 10,000 riding mower units on a single 40-hour-per-week shift. The company's production facility and office space are rented from a related firm.

Max Swisher has always insisted that his company be customer-oriented in recognizing and providing for both dealer and end-user needs. Maintaining a "small

The cooperation of Swisher Mower and Machine Company in the preparation of this case is gratefully acknowledged. This case was prepared by Professor Roger A. Kerin, of the Edwin L. Cox School of Business, of the Southern Methodist University, and Wayne Swisher, Swisher Mower and Machine Company, as a basis for class discussion and is not designed to illustrate effective or ineffective handling of an administrative situation. The case benefited from the assistance of Derek Siewert and Bennet Grayson, graduate students. Certain financial and operating data are disguised and not useful for research purposes. Copyright © by Roger A. Kerin. No part of this case may be reproduced without written permission of the copyright holder.

EXHIBIT 1

Unit Sales History for SMC Riding Mowers

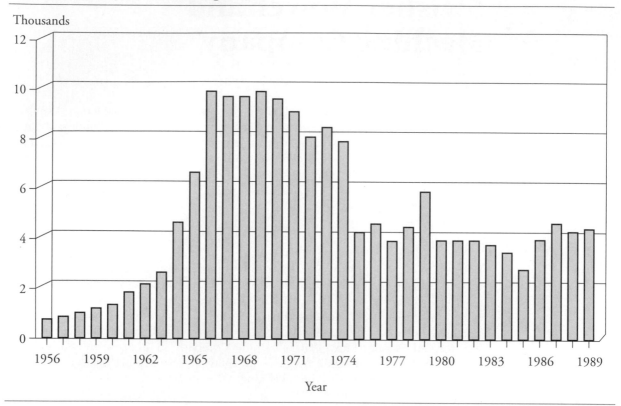

company" image has also been an important aspect of Swisher's business philosophy, which in turn has resulted in personal relationships with dealers and customers alike. A special loyalty has been demonstrated to the original SMC dealers and distributors that helped build the sales foundation of the company. SMC continues to guarantee protection of these and other dealers' trade territories whenever possible.

Product Line

SMC produces three types of lawn mower units. Its flagship product, the Ride King, is a three-wheel riding mower that has a zero turning radius. Developed by Swisher in the 1950s, this design is distinct from competitors' in that the single steerable front wheel is also the drive unit. This feature allows the mower to be put in reverse without changing gears and by simply turning the steering wheel 180 degrees. The company is credited with producing the first zero-turning-radius riding mower.

The manufacturer's list price for the standard Ride King model is $550. Manufacturer gross profit margin on this unit is approximately 17 percent. The cost of goods sold for this product is approximately $100 for labor and $356.50 for parts.

SMC has a reputation for producing high-quality riding mowers that have a simple design allowing for ease of customer use and maintenance. These features and benefits are prominently displayed in the product literature for Ride King (see Exhibit

EXHIBIT 2

Ride King Product Literature

E X H I B I T   2   (*continued*)

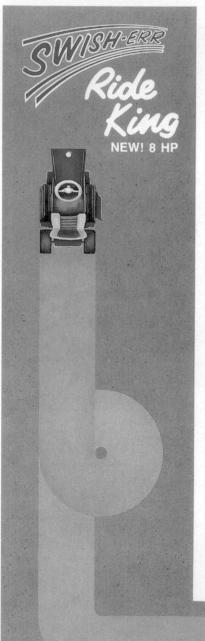

THE ORIGINAL ZERO TURNING RADIUS

32" cut
REVERSES WITHOUT CHANGING GEARS OR BELTS

The Ride King pulls by a single, steerable front wheel which pivots 360° for sharp turns or reverse. Turning of the steering wheel gives you reverse without changing gears or belts. This eliminates complicated transmission, differentials, etc.,therefore less maintenance and initial cost.

Ride King trims with 3/8", turns square corners, makes a clean cut around trees and poles with one pass.

Exclusive patented front wheel drive provides full 360° steering and maximum maneuverability. This front wheel drive prevents tipping over backward. Equipped with automatic brake for stopping on any terrain when clutch is released. Blade stops automatically when blade clutch is released.

Powerful, dependable four cycle engine. "Stops on a Dime—Turns on a Nickel" . . . with change to spare!

OUTSTANDING FEATURES

- Zero Turning Radius.
- All Steel Construction.
- Ball Bearings throughout.
- 8 HP Briggs & Stratton Synchro-Balanced.
- Front Wheel Drive—360°Steering reverses by turning the steering wheel.
- Trims close to objects and obstructions.
- 2 Speed Drive, Optional.
- Allows you to shift up or down without disengaging clutch.
- Saf-Lok Clutch, Disengages Blade. Use as tractor.
- Wide Wheelbase. Big Tires. Superior traction, all air.
- Powerful automatic brake prevents coasting.
- Available with recoil, 12V, 110V starter.
- Belt drive blades (means no sprung crankshaft).
- Extra large and well padded seat suspended on springs on both sides for utmost comfort.
- Large one gallon fuel tank separate from engine for greater safety and durability.
- Steering wheel slanted and designed for the greatest comfort and ease of operation.
- Less moving parts than any other riding mower on the market.

SPECIFICATIONS

MODEL A32

Cut	32"
Length	48"
Width	33"
New Weight	210 lbs.
Rear Tires	3.50 x 6 air
Front Tires	3.50 x 6 air
Engine	8 HP Briggs & Stratton Synchro-Balanced Also Available 6 HP Tecumseh
Blade	Austempered twin blades
Clutch	Positive Lok-Over
Wheels	Ball-Bearing
Deck	11 ga. steel
Blade spindle ball bearing lubricated for life.	

SWISHER MOWER AND MACHINE CO., INC.
BOX 67   WARRENSBURG, MISSOURI 64093
PHONE: 816-747-8183
OUTSIDE MISSOURI: 800-222-8183
FAX: 816-747-8650

2). The reliability and ruggedness of the riding mower are demonstrated by the product's longevity. SMC mowers often run for more than 25 years before having to be replaced. The company provides a one-year warranty on all parts and labor. Riding mowers accounted for 63.6 percent of SMC's total sales and 57.8 percent of total gross profit in 1989.

Most current mowers' parts are interchangeable with the parts of older models that date back to 1956. Even though the patent for the zero-turning-radius drive unit has expired, no competitors have copied this design.

SMC also produces a "trailmower" called T-40. This unit consists of a trailer-type mower that has a cutting width of 40 inches. When hitched to any riding lawn mower this unit effectively increases the cutting width by 40 inches. The "trail-mower" can also be pulled behind all-terrain vehicles. The T-40 was introduced in 1985 and accounted for 8.2 percent of SMC's total sales and 13.2 percent of total gross profit in 1989. Exhibit 3 shows the product literature for the T-40.

SMC deemphasized the sale of its self-propelled push mower in the early 1960s due to lagging sales and increased demand for the riding mower. When it phased out these units, the company began offering push lawn mower "kits." There are three different push mower kits available, and each consists of all the component parts necessary to assemble push mowers. They do not bear the SMC name and are sold under dealers' labels. Kits are sold only to satisfy dealer demand and do not provide a material contribution to the company's gross profit. Kits accounted for 8.2 percent of SMC's total sales in 1989.

The replacement parts business for mowers accounts for the remainder (20 percent) of SMC sales. Since little standardization exists among mower parts in the industry, SMC must provide customers with replacement parts for its mowers. Replacement parts accounted for 29 percent of the company's total gross profit in 1989.

Distribution and Promotion

SMC distributes its lawn mowers through farm supply stores, lawn and garden stores, home centers, and hardware stores located primarily in nonmetropolitan areas. About 75 percent of company sales are made in nonmetropolitan areas.

SMC sells the Ride King mower through wholesale distributors that supply independent dealers and directly to dealers. Wholesalers that represent SMC are located throughout the country, but they mainly supply dealers situated in the south central and southeastern United States. Wholesalers account for 30 percent of riding mower sales; direct-to-dealer sales account for 25 percent of sales.

Private-label riding mower sales account for 40 percent of SMC sales. Its private-label Big Mow mowers are produced for two buying networks: Midstates (Minneapolis, Minnesota) and Wheat Belt (Kansas City, Missouri). These two organizations represent independent farm supply stores and home centers in the upper and central midwestern United States and provide a central purchasing service. Even though these buying groups operate in roughly the same territory, their stores are not generally located in the same towns.

The company's other private label. Big O, is produced for Orgill Brothers wholesale hardware supply center located in Memphis, Tennessee. Orgill acts as a warehousing distributor for its network of hardware stores throughout the upper southeastern United States. Exhibit 4 shows the geographic scope of SMC's distribution in the United States by brand name.

EXHIBIT 3

T-40 Product Literature

THE NEW T-40 TRAILMOWER

- Universal Hitch
- 8 hp Briggs & Stratton or 10 hp Tecumseh
- 40" Cut
- Belt-driven blades (No sprung crankshaft)
- Center mounted wheels to eliminate scalping
- Independent/Quick height adjuster (for fine tuning cut)

- Rear discharge
- 11 gauge All steel construction
- Sealed bearings
- Idler clutch (for easy starting)
- Pneumatic tires 3.50 × 6
- Weight — 225 lbs.

The new T-40 Trailmower is a totally universal pull-behind lawnmower. It has a fully adjustable hitch so that it can be pulled behind any make ATV or offset with any lawn tractor for an additional 40" of cutting width.

The T-40 has a well-balanced design and its center mounted wheels give a smooth cut even on the roughest terrain. The Trailmower features belt-driven twin blades and is available with either the 8 hp Briggs & Stratton or 10 hp Tecumseh engine.

This unit provides a perfect way to use your ATV as a lawn tractor or to expand the cutting width of your present tractor.

Offset for mowing around ponds or low hanging trees

SWISHER MOWER AND MACHINE CO., INC.
BOX 67, WARRENSBURG, MO 64093
PHONE: 816-747-8183
TOLL FREE: 800-222-8183

EXHIBIT   4

Geographic Scope of SMC Distribution

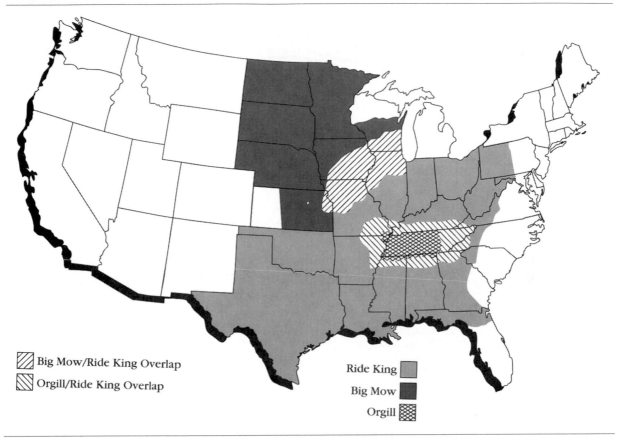

Big Mow/Ride King Overlap

Orgill/Ride King Overlap

Ride King

Big Mow

Orgill

   In recent years the company has developed distributor arrangements in parts of Europe and in the South Pacific. These arrangements produce 5 percent of total company sales.

   Prior to 1985, SMC advertising focused on trade-oriented promotion to wholesalers and dealers. Since 1985, SMC has used consumer advertising to promote Ride King through a co-op advertising program with its dealers utilizing radio, television, and newspapers. A representative newspaper advertisement is shown in Exhibit 5.

Financial Position

SMC has remained a profitable company despite reduced sales volume. The company has consistently generated a net profit return on sales of 10 percent or more annually. Moreover, SMC has been able to produce cash flow at levels large enough to minimize the need for any major short-term or long-term financing. During 1989, accounts receivable and inventory had turns of 8.1 and 5.8, respectively. Nevertheless, Max Swisher was concerned with the availability and cost of short-term financing, since inventory and accounts receivable annual carrying costs were estimated to be 17 percent. Exhibit 6 shows financial statements for 1989.

EXHIBIT 5

Ride King Print Advertisement

SWISH-ERR Ride King

Your lawn deserves the best, not the most expensive. It deserves SWISH-ERR Ride King!

Here's a low-cost mower with features some of the big dollar machines don't even offer! Compare Ride King's . . .

- 8 HP Briggs & Stratton Synchro-Balanced engine
- Front wheel drive
- Zero turning radius
- No transmission or differential — fewer moving parts, less maintenance, greater reliability

PLUS . . . top quality construction throughout, all at an affordable price!

One test drive is all it will take to convince you it doesn't cost a lot to keep a well manicured lawn! *See your Swisher Ride King dealer today for a demonstration.*

DEALER IMPRINT AREA

RIDING LAWN MOWER INDUSTRY

Riding lawn mowers are classified as lawn and garden equipment. This category is composed of numerous products, including walk-behind rotary mowers, riding mowers and tractors, garden tillers, snow throwers, and other outdoor power equipment designed primarily for the consumer market.

A survey by the Outdoor Power Equipment Institute (OPEI) estimated that the lawn and garden equipment industry produced sales of $4.5 billion in 1989, at manufacturers' prices. Of this amount, $3.3 billion was for finished goods and $1.1 billion was for engines. Components, including parts, accounted for the remainder of industry sales.

Sales Trends

Industry statistics show that riding mower unit volume peaked in 1973, when 1.2 million units were sold. Following the decline in the economy in 1975, volume fell to 790,000 units. By 1979, unit shipments had gradually risen to 1 million, but with

EXHIBIT 6

SMC Financial Statements

Income Statement
(Year ended September 30, 1989)

Sales		$3,547,644
Cost of goods sold		2,885,086
Gross profit		$ 662,558
Expenses		
Administrative salaries	$75,000	
Commissions	13,000	
Advertising	53,000	
Travel	7,500	
Insurance for employees	16,500	
Professional services	17,000	
Office expense	10,500	
Bad debts	9,500	
General taxes	1,600	
Depreciation	2,000	
Other	13,200	
Total expenses		$218,800
Income from continuing operations		$443,758
Other income (expenses)		(6,350)
Net income[a]		$437,408

Balance Sheet
(September 30, 1989)

Current assets	
Cash	$ 95,000
Accounts receivable	205,434
Notes receivable	16,430
Inventories	612,540
Prepaid insurance	7,055
Total current assets	$936,459
Net property plant and equipment	43,878
Other assets	4,300
Total assets	$984,637
Liabilities and owner's equity	
Current liabilities	
Accounts payable	$165,490
Accrued sales and payroll taxes	10,400
	$175,880
Owner's equity	
Common stock	$100,000
Retained earnings	717,147
	$817,147
Less: Treasury stock	($8,400)
Total owner's equity	$808,747
Total liabilities and owner's equity	$984,637

[a]SMC is an "S" Corporation and therefore pays no federal and state income taxes.

the slowed economic conditions in the early 1980s, unit shipments again declined. From 1983 to 1987, shipment volume increased each year by an average of 6.7 percent, but the average increase tapered off to 2 percent from 1987 to 1989. Sluggish unit sales have been attributed to drought conditions prevalent in the midwestern United States. Industry estimates indicated that residential riding mower sales would be flat in 1990 and 1991. Commercial and export sales were expected to exhibit modest growth during this period.

The riding lawn mower industry is highly seasonal and cyclical. About one-third of riding lawn mower retail sales occur in March, April, and May. Over half of manufacturer shipments of these products occur in the four-month period from January to April. Industry sales patterns mirror cyclical patterns in the U.S. economy.

Product Configuration

Riding lawn mowers are usually designed in two basic configurations: (1) front-engine lawn tractors and (2) rear-engine riding mowers. However, there are some mid-engine riding mowers on the market, such as those produced by SMC. Lawn tractors with larger engines (20 horsepower or more) are classified as garden tractors.

Riding lawn mowers are targeted at consumers who have large mowing areas, usually composed of an acre or more. Front-engine lawn tractors are the most popular design, with unit sales of 812,000 in 1988, up 1.5 percent from 1987. Rear-engine riding mower unit sales were unchanged from 1987 to 1988, with sales of 375,000 units. Garden tractors posted a 13 percent increase in unit sales for 1988, with a volume of 170,000 units. Statistics for mid-engine mowers are unavailable but are believed to be included in the above figures.

According to industry surveys, the front-engine configuration (lawn tractors and garden tractors) is perceived to be more powerful than the rear-engine configuration and capable of handling bigger jobs. Since the physical dimensions of the front-engine configuration tend to be larger than the rear-engine configuration, consumers tend to perceive lawn tractors and garden tractors as stronger and more durable.

Competition

Sixteen manufacturers comprise the major competitors in the riding lawn mower market. They are American Yard Products (formerly Roper), Ariens, Honda, John Deere, Kubota, Lawn Boy, Lawn Chief Manufacturing, MTD, Inc. (formerly Modern Tool and Die), Murray of Ohio, Noma, Power King, Snapper, Toro, Troy-Bilt, Wheelhorse, and White.

Ariens, Honda, John Deere, Kubota, Lawn Boy, Power King, Snapper, Toro, Troy-Bilt, Wheelhorse, and White sell their products through lawn and garden stores and specialty retailers. Kubota and Troy-Bilt also sell to national mass-merchandise stores. All of these companies manufacture riding mowers only under a nationally branded name. None engage in private-label production.

MTD, Inc., produces the Cub Cadet brand mower sold exclusively in lawn and garden stores and by specialty retailers. MTD also manufactures mowers for JCPenney and Sears under the GrassHandler and Craftsman names, respectively. Kmart sells an MTD nationally branded lawn mower under the MTD name. Murray of Ohio produces private-label mowers for Sears and JCPenney and also manufactures mowers for Kmart, Wal-Mart, and Home Depot under the Murray brand name. However,

EXHIBIT 7

Retail Distribution of Outdoor Power Equipment

	Percentage of Sales23 by Year		
Outlet type	1988	1983	1978
OPE/Farm equipment stores	10	19	7
Hardware stores	13	12	16
Lawn/garden stores	16	17	17
Home centers	5	3	1
National merchandisers	24	22	35
Discount stores	7	8	5
Farm supply stores	4	0	0
Department stores	3	1	2
Other	18	18	17
Total	100	100	100

each of these retailers has different specifications for its mowers. American Yard Products manufactures a nationally branded mower called the Yard Pro, which is sold through specialty retailers. However, a significant portion of its production (70 percent or more) is sold to Sears under the Craftsman label. Noma produces private-label mowers for Kmart, Western Auto, Lowes (a hardware chain), and TSC (Tractor Supply Company). The TSC mower is named Huskee; the Lowes mower is called Turfmaster. Dynamark, the Kmart private label, is produced by Noma. Lawn Chief Manufacturing (a division of Cotter and Company) produces mowers exclusively for True Value Hardware stores and is the only manufacturer that produces a private-label mower for one retail chain.

Private-label riding mowers have captured a growing percentage of unit sales in the industry. It is estimated that private-label mowers currently account for 60–70 percent of total industry sales.

Each of the major competitors produces several riding mowers at different price points. Although retail prices very by type of retail outlet, representative retail prices for national and private label riding mowers typically range from $700 to $5,000.

Retail Distribution

Outdoor power equipment (OPE), including riding mowers, is distributed through a variety of retail outlets. National retail merchandise chains such as JCPenney and Sears account for the largest percentage of sales. However, the percentage of sales captured by national merchandisers has declined in the past decade from 35 percent in 1978 to 24 percent in 1988. Lawn and garden stores, hardware stores, and OPE/farm equipment stores represent the three largest retail distributors after national merchandisers. Exhibit 7 shows the breakdown of sales by type of retailer for 1978, 1983, and 1988.

THE PRIVATE-LABEL PROPOSAL

The inquiry received by SMC concerning a private-label arrangement requested a sample order of 700 standard riding mower units to be delivered in February 1991. The national retail merchandise chain expected to make an annual order of approximately 8,200 units. The proposed arrangement had features that made it quite different from SMC's typical manner of doing business with its other private-label organizations. The chain wanted to purchase the mowers at a price 5 percent lower than SMC's manufacturer's list price for its standard model. They also wished to be a house account without manufacturer's representatives or company sales representatives calling on them. They did not want any seasonal or promotional discounts but only a single guaranteed low price. Reorders would be at the same price. The mowers would be shipped FOB factory (that is, the chain would pay for all freight charges).

The chain wanted to carry inventories in its regional warehouses, but did not want title to transfer to itself until the mowers were shipped to a specific company store. From that point, payment would be made in 30 days. However, the chain agreed to take title to mowers that had been in one of its warehouses for two months. A 30-day payment period would follow the title transfer.

There would be small changes in the appearance of the mower to help differentiate it from SMC's Ride King. The chain requested a different seat and a particular color and type of paint and specified that all parts be American-made or that the mower at least display an "American name" as its producer. The chain would supply all decals displaying its brand name.

The chain did not specify any mechanical specifications for the mower. The letter expressed satisfaction with the design and performance of the machine and noted that only minor cosmetic changes were necessary. SMC's standard warranty would be required for all mower parts. The chain expected SMC to reimburse them for any labor costs resulting from warranty work at $22.00 per hour. Replacement parts would be purchased at present price points and shipped FOB factory.

A two-year contract was offered, which could be automatically extended on a year-to-year basis. Either party could terminate the contract with a six-month notice. A new price would be negotiated at the end of the original two-year period. The contract would be negotiated annually thereafter. The chain also required SMC to assume liability for personal injury that might result from the use and maintenance of the mowers. The chain would supply all advertising related to the product and would not allow SMC to mention its relationship with the chain in any of its advertising or promotion.

EVALUATING THE PROPOSAL

The private-label proposal required careful consideration, according to Swisher. The opportunity to expand production, given excess capacity, coupled with the added benefit of broadened distribution in metropolitan areas seemed inviting. Moreover, increased sales of parts were likely, and the potential for selling the "trail-mower" was possible. At the same time, other factors would have to be considered. For example, SMC was self-insured and had not experienced any significant product-liability claims with some 150,000 units having been sold or used since 1956. However, if the private-label proposal was pursued, greater exposure to liability claims was possible. According to industry sources, manufacturer product-liability insurance premiums for riding mowers could cost as much as $500,000 per year for $1 million in coverage. Insurance companies writing these policies generally required a minimum sales volume of 10,000 units.

Furthermore, although increased production could be handled by paying overtime to SMC production workers, the cost of overtime, reflected in the direct labor cost, would represent about 4 percent of the current manufacturer's sales price for riding mowers. Other direct materials costs could represent another 1 percent of the current manufacturer's price. Additional overhead costs were estimated to be another 1 percent, and other related costs, including additional inventory insurance, pilferage and breakage, additional wear and maintenance on machines, and a county property tax based on inventory, would account for an additional 1.5 percent.

A production agreement would create some one-time added costs for SMC. These costs would include arranging sources for specified materials that differed from those used in standard production and a rearrangement of production facilities to accommodate the new output levels. These one-time costs would be in the range from $10,000 to $12,000.

The added financing costs were of particular importance. Normally, SMC obtained short-term funds from local banks at 2.5 percentage points above the prime rate (currently 10 percent). These funds were used to finance accounts receivable and riding mower inventories, both of which would increase substantially with the new arrangement.

Sales of SMC mowers by the national merchandiser could cannibalize some existing sales. Although the chain's outlets were located in metropolitan areas, there would be some overlap in trade areas with SMC's current dealers. Swisher felt that, as a result, SMC could initially lose approximately 200 units a year of Ride King sales volume. In addition, dealers directly affected would not welcome the added competition, and Swisher believed that a small percentage of independent dealers would be likely to drop the SMC line.

Swisher felt that some aspects of the proposal might be negotiable, such as the title transfer and payment dates. From his experience, he knew that the unit price in the proposal was probably fixed and that the cosmetic changes were not negotiable. He knew that his bargaining position was limited because the chain would be approaching other manufacturers with the same opportunity. However, he also knew that SMC offered a highly differentiated and proven riding mower. This would be an advantage, since many other manufacturers' mowers were indistinguishable.

Swisher had been concerned for several years about SMC's future prospects. The private-label arrangement might offer numerous benefits to SMC, but he wondered if other actions might be even more attractive. For example, a more aggressive advertising and sales effort to recruit new dealers and assist current dealers was being considered. He leaned back in his chair, which he had purchased when he founded SMC, and pondered the possibilities.

American Airlines, Inc.
Proposal for a Three-Class Transcon Service

"We first proposed a three-class service on the JFK-LAX [John F. Kennedy Airport, New York–Los Angeles] route in January 1990; it's now January 1991, and we still don't have formal Planning Committee approval." Bill Crown, Manager, Domestic Pricing Strategy, was voicing his frustration to Barbara Amster, Vice President, Pricing and Yield Management (see Exhibit 1 for a chart of the reporting relationships of Crown, Amster, and others mentioned in the case). Crown continued: "We've already missed the spring and fall '91 introduction windows; if we don't get a go-ahead soon, we won't even be ready for spring '92. Meanwhile, MGM Grand Air offers superior first- and coach-class services, TWA and Pan Am already fly aircraft with a business-class section on this route, and the word is United is planning a three-class product. Then there is the issue of our AAdvantage Gold members upgrading from coach to first class, filling up the first-class cabin, and displacing full-fare first-class passengers—something that would not occur if the aircraft had a business-class cabin to which the Gold members could upgrade."

"I understand your frustration," replied Amster. "We are due to make a presentation before the Planning Committee early next week. Mike [Gunn, Senior Vice President, Marketing] assures me there will be a decision then."

BACKGROUND

American Airlines, Inc. ("American"), principal subsidiary of Dallas/Fort Worth–based AMR Corporation, was the largest airline in the United States. At year-end 1990, American operated 552 aircraft, flying 2,248 flights daily to 182 cities in 42 countries in North and South America, the Caribbean islands, Europe, the Far East, and Australasia. Exhibit 2 gives a five-year summary of the airline's operating results and related statistics.

American achieved its largest-in-the-industry status through a mix of pioneering initiatives and aggressive expansion. In 1976 it initiated the use of sophisticated analytical tools to track booking trends and manage revenue yields on specific flights; in 1977 it revolutionized air-travel pricing by offering deeply discounted Super Saver fares to leisure travelers; in 1981 it introduced AAdvantage, the industry's first frequent-flyer program, offering upgrade privileges and free-travel awards to loyal trav-

EXHIBIT 1

American Airlines, Inc.: Organization Chart as of January 1991 (Selective)

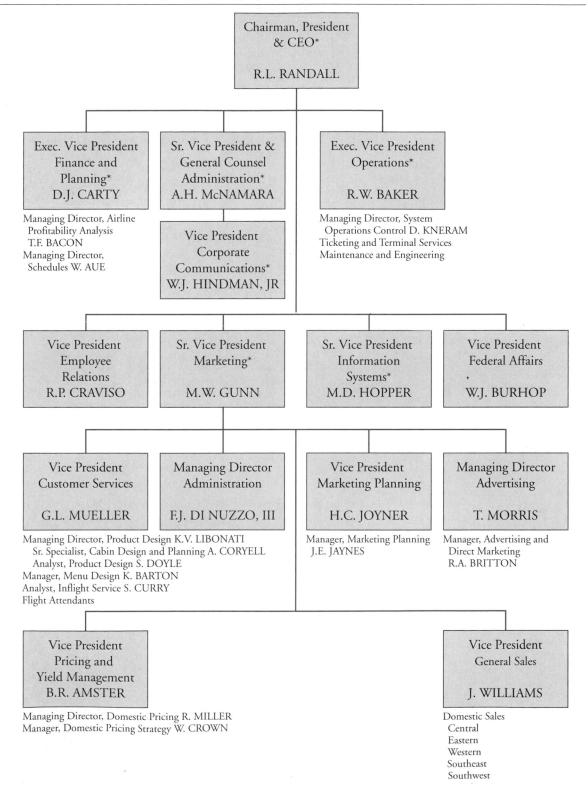

Chairman, President & CEO*

R.L. RANDALL

Exec. Vice President Finance and Planning*
D.J. CARTY

Managing Director, Airline Profitability Analysis
T.F. BACON
Managing Director, Schedules W. AUE

Sr. Vice President & General Counsel Administration*
A.H. McNAMARA

Vice President Corporate Communications*
W.J. HINDMAN, JR

Exec. Vice President Operations*
R.W. BAKER

Managing Director, System Operations Control D. KNERAM
Ticketing and Terminal Services
Maintenance and Engineering

Vice President Employee Relations
R.P. CRAVISO

Sr. Vice President Marketing*
M.W. GUNN

Sr. Vice President Information Systems*
M.D. HOPPER

Vice President Federal Affairs
W.J. BURHOP

Vice President Customer Services
G.L. MUELLER

Managing Director, Product Design K.V. LIBONATI
Sr. Specialist, Cabin Design and Planning A. CORYELL
Analyst, Product Design S. DOYLE
Manager, Menu Design K. BARTON
Analyst, Inflight Service S. CURRY
Flight Attendants

Managing Director Administration
F.J. DI NUZZO, III

Vice President Marketing Planning
H.C. JOYNER

Manager, Marketing Planning
J.E. JAYNES

Managing Director Advertising
T. MORRIS

Manager, Advertising and Direct Marketing
R.A. BRITTON

Vice President Pricing and Yield Management
B.R. AMSTER

Managing Director, Domestic Pricing R. MILLER
Manager, Domestic Pricing Strategy W. CROWN

Vice President General Sales
J. WILLIAMS

Domestic Sales
  Central
  Eastern
  Western
  Southeast
  Southwest

EXHIBIT 2

American Airlines, Inc.: Five-Year Summary of Operating Results and Statistics

Five Years Ended December 31, 1990

	1990	1989	1988	1987	1986
Operating Results ($ in millions)					
Revenues					
Passenger	9,742.8	8,839.2	7,555.1	6,150.9	4960.5
Cargo	428.9	361.7	287.8	260.9	220.4
Other	837.0	760.0	707.7	712.7	675.6
Total operating revenues	11,008.7	9,960.9	8,550.6	7,124.5	5,856.5
Expenses					
Wages, salaries and benefits	3,608.7	3,233.6	2,820.8	2,399.8	2,053.3
Aircraft fuel	1,898.8	1,367.1	1,094.1	1,008.5	837.3
Other	5,433.2	4,629.4	3,834.7	3,243.0	2,573.8
Total operating expenses	10, 940.7	9,230.1	7,749.6	6,651.3	5,464.4
Operating Income (Loss)	68.0	730.8	801.0	473.2	392.1
Operating Statistics					
Available passenger seat miles (in millions)	123, 773	115,222	102,045	88,743	75,087
Revenue passenger miles (in millions)	77,085	73,503	64,770	56,794	48,792
Passenger load factor	62.3%	63.8%	63.5%	64.0%	65.0%
Breakeven passenger load factor	61.8%	57.9%	56.0%	58.5%	59.3%
Revenue yield per passenger mile	12.64¢	12.03¢	11.66¢	10.83¢	10.17¢
Operating expenses per available passenger seat mile	8.84¢	8.01¢	7.59¢	7.50¢	7.28¢

Source: AMR Corporation 1990 Annual Report (Dallas/Fort Worth Airport, TX: AMR Corporation, 1991).

elers; and in 1983 it instituted an innovative two-tier wage structure that preserved the wages and benefits of existing employees, but allowed new employees to be hired at lower levels of wages and benefits.[1] Following the Airline Deregulation Act of 1978,[2] American expanded its number of hubs from two (Chicago, Dallas/Fort Worth) to seven (Chicago, Dallas/Fort Worth, Miami, Nashville, Raleigh/Durham, San Jose [California], and San Juan [Puerto Rico]); it developed new routes and purchased existing ones; and it acquired quieter and more efficient aircraft to serve the growing domestic and international route network. Finally, throughout the 1980s, the airline consolidated its position as the provider of the industry's largest computerized reservation system.

[1]"Twenty Years at American," *Business Week* (July 6, 1992): 50–51.

[2]The act established a timetable for the removal of restraints on market entry and pricing and set in motion a process that led to the rise and fall of airlines, the evolution of "hub-and-spoke" route networks, the reconstitution of aircraft fleets (to match capacity with the demand for travel between hubs and along spokes), and the institution of complex and volatile pricing schemes.

As American spread its wings, its operating revenues grew nearly threefold—from $3.71 billion in 1980 to $11.01 billion in 1990. Operating income, however, did not fare nearly as well: It was negative in 1980 and 1982, it increased from 1983 through 1985, it declined in 1986, it grew in 1987 and 1988, and it fell in 1989 and 1990. The decline in 1990 was particularly sharp and was attributed to three factors: the economic recession, which took its toll on air travel; Iraq's invasion of Kuwait, which led to a sharp escalation in the price of aviation fuel; and the possibility of a Persian Gulf war, which shook public confidence and made people wary of air travel.

American operated in a highly competitive industry, the locus of competition shifting steadily as new carriers entered the market, ailing carriers exited or sought bankruptcy protection, and survivors strived to define the world after deregulation. Prior to the Airline Deregulation Act, routes, schedules, and fares were relatively stable and carriers competed on the basis of service and operating costs; following deregulation, the competitive dimensions expanded to include routes, schedules, on-time departures and arrivals, fares, frequent-flyer programs, product distribution, and the use of sophisticated tools for yield management. Competitive advantage along these dimensions was, however, difficult to sustain: It was a given that the major players would match one another's price changes; after an initial adjustment period, the big carriers had competitive route structures and flight schedules; any advantage that might be enjoyed in the arena of product distribution on account of ownership of computerized reservation systems was subject to litigation and governmental scrutiny; and frequent-flyer programs of the healthier airlines offered comparable benefits. By 1990, service quality and operating costs emerged once again as the major dimensions of competition. American believed it offered superior service and that it was at a disadvantage when it came to operating costs.

"Three-class transcon"—a proposal to replace American's current two-class (coach and first) product on the transcontinental John F. Kennedy Airport, New York–Los Angeles (JFK-LAX) route with a premium-quality three-class (coach, business, and first) product—was aimed at improving American's competitive advantage in product and service.[3]

WHY A THREE-CLASS TRANSCON SERVICE?

Flagship Product for a Flagship Market

JFK-LAX was one of American's most important routes: It accounted for around 2 percent of the airline's operating revenues; it often had the highest operating margins; and it attracted some of the most influential and glamorous travelers. Ron Miller, Managing Director, Domestic Pricing, commented on the need for a distinctive product offering for this market:

> Price wars come and go. Airlines come and go. But one thing does not change: American's position as the dominant carrier in this unique market. The only way to sustain this position is by offering the best possible product—and improving it even further. The proposed three-class transcon American Flagship Service—with a distinguished first-class cabin, a new spacious business-class cabin, and upgraded coach-class service—will be a significant product improvement.

---

[3]The description "three-class transcon" for the product-change proposal applies only to the JFK-LAX route, even though American flew several transcontinental routes out of JFK airport—JFK–Los Angeles, JFK–San Francisco, JFK–San Jose, and JFK–San Diego—and each route was flown with three-class aircraft from time to time.

Three-class transcon and American Flagship Service were not new concepts. In the late 1970s, American had toyed with the idea of introducing a three-class transcontinental service, but without reconfiguring the aircraft into three distinct cabins. The concept was not implemented: the airline did not believe it could satisfactorily isolate the "smoking" and "nonsmoking" sections for each class. As for American Flagship Service, American first used the term in 1984 to describe the service on its transcontinental product, but the branding applied only to food service; nothing else about the product was distinctive. The three-class transcon proposal under consideration in 1990–1991 called for the reconfiguration of the aircraft into three (first, business, and coach) cabins and for the design of a distinctive "new-and-improved" product.

A Product Consistent with American's International Flagship Service

In April 1990, American launched International Flagship Service (IFS), an on-board service designed to give the airline parity with established international carriers:

> IFS goes far beyond great food and fine wines. It means a larger Business Class compartment with extra seat padding, as well as plumper pillows, tucked pillowcases, and larger, softer blankets. It includes redesigned china, glassware, flatware and linens and menus created by some of America's finest chefs. Fresh flowers, improved amenity kits, special ticket jackets and bag tags and a host of other details are also part of the product offering.
>
> And there is more to come. We are now installing personal video units . . . in our First Class cabins, and have added people to provide a highly customized concierge service in our international cities and at our U.S. hubs.
>
> International Flagship Service is a quality strategy that is working. It is helping earn us a larger share of First and Business Class customers. And perhaps most gratifying of all, it is bringing us a growing share of the passengers traveling to the U.S. from overseas.[4]

The proposed three-class American Flagship Service (AFS) would allow JFK-LAX passengers—some of whom may be connecting with American's international flights—to experience the comfort and convenience of IFS. Michael Gunn, Senior Vice President, Marketing, argued for consistency between the airline's international and transcontinental products:

> With AFS, we will be catering to travelers who appreciate premium service and are willing to pay for it—whether flying from New York to London or to Los Angeles, both of which, by the way, take about the same travel time. These people place a high value on comfort on international travel; why shouldn't we provide them the same comfort on long-haul domestic routes?

Meeting First-Class Demand without Depriving AAdvantage Gold Members of Upgrade Opportunities

The three-class transcon proposal was first made in January 1990 by Bill Crown and his colleagues in American's Domestic Pricing Strategy group after a set of studies revealed the following findings:

---

[4]*AMR Corporation 1990 Annual Report* (Dallas/Fort Worth Airport, TX: AMR Corporation, 1991): 24.

1. JFK-LAX first-class cabin load factor averaged 88.6 percent for the 12 months ending December 1989.

2. While first-class demand on the JFK-LAX route was the highest in the American system, the contribution of full-fare first-class passengers to total first-class cabin revenue passenger miles declined from 58.5 percent in fourth quarter 1988 to 44.1 percent in fourth quarter 1989.

3. During the 12 months ending December 1989, nearly 12,000 AAdvantage Gold members upgraded to first class in the JFK-LAX market.[5] The contribution of these upgrades to total first-class cabin revenue passenger miles increased from just over 20 percent in fourth quarter 1988 to over 25 percent in fourth quarter 1989

4. While bookings for all fare groups in the JFK-LAX market increased by 5.9 percent from fourth quarter 1988 to fourth quarter 1989, first-class bookings fell by 5.1 percent—in contrast to historical trends, when first-class bookings grew faster than all fare groups taken together.

5. MGM Grand Air, a competitor with a superior first-class product in the JFK-LAX market (see section on "Competitive Considerations") increased capacity in 1989, suggesting strong first-class demand.

The above findings led to a growing concern that, while first-class demand was strong, American was not capturing its share of the demand because AAdvantage Gold upgrades were filling up the first-class cabin and displacing full-fare first-class customers. This conclusion was reinforced by anecdotal evidence and retrospective studies of first-class bookings, which suggested that some AAdvantage Gold members were locking out full-fare first-class passengers by gaming the system.

The Domestic Pricing Strategy group had developed models to estimate the number of full-fare first-class passengers who were either downgrading to coach class or being "spilled" (turned away) because of inadequate capacity. These models suggested that, on average, two first-class passengers were downgrading to coach class and three first-class passengers were being spilled per operation (one flight in either direction).

The proposed three-class JFK-LAX service would allow AAdvantage Gold members to upgrade only to the next class of service—from coach to business—and free up the first-class cabin for full-fare first-class passengers.[6] At the same time, it would continue to provide Gold members—valuable customers in their own right—the opportunity to upgrade. The importance of this opportunity was underscored by the results of four focus-group studies conducted in New York and Los Angeles by American's Marketing Planning group in October 1989. These studies suggested that some Gold members were not allowed to purchase first-class tickets, but "wanted out" of the coach cabin. While these members were not insistent on first-class travel,

---

[5]American designated the top few percent of its AAdvantage frequent-flyer program members as "Gold" members; Gold membership had its privileges, in particular the ability to upgrade from coach to first class beginning 24 hours prior to flight departure.

[6]Since AAdvantage members could cash in their frequent-flyer miles for awards entitling them to travel first class in this market, the first-class cabin would not be occupied exclusively by full-fare first-class passengers. An *award* was different from an *upgrade*. The former was awarded in exchange for miles accumulated in a member's frequent-flyer account; the latter was a reward an AAdvantage Gold member could claim, either by using a sticker (the number of stickers issued depended on the amount of travel in the previous year) or by paying a nominal charge (typically $50) prior to departure.

they had a preference for an environment that was less cramped, quieter, and more "professional" than coach class. The proposed business class would provide such an environment.

Meeting Demand for a Business-Class Product

As a rule, business-class service—an established product in international travel—was not available within the United States.[7] The proposed three-class transcon service would change that. Crown and his colleagues believed there was a latent demand for domestic business-class travel, and they saw the JFK-LAX market as a test case to define the demand and to gauge its extent.

The most important source of this demand was business-related travel where the traveler did not qualify for Gold-member status (and was not eligible for an upgrade from coach class), but wanted out of the coach cabin. While this traveler was willing to pay a premium over full-coach fare for a product that was better than the coach-class product and allowed a more flexible travel schedule, he or she was unwilling or unable to pay full-fare first-class fares (the October 1989 focus-group studies had revealed that some corporate-travel policies allowed for "anything other than first class"). The Domestic Pricing Strategy group felt that the new business class could be positioned and priced to meet the demand for an intermediate product.

Competitive Considerations

Competitive considerations provided an important impetus to the three-class transcon proposal. First, American was concerned about the increasing threat from MGM Grand Air, which, while it had a two-class service and a lower flight frequency, nevertheless offered a superior-quality product. MGM Grand Air had come into being in the mid-1980s with the express intent of creating a market niche for a first-class-only product in the JFK-LAX market. Charging the same price as American and other carriers, MGM Grand Air offered luxurious and spacious seating,[8] gourmet food and beverage catering, and private terminal lounges and special-service amenities. In August 1990 MGM Grand Air introduced a "Grand" coach class, which was priced at the same level as the other carriers' coach class, but offered a quality of service comparable to other carriers' first class. Not surprisingly, superior service attracted customers: American estimated that MGM Grand Air's market share for first-class travel increased from 13.8 percent in the fourth quarter of 1988 to 17.5 percent in the fourth quarter of 1989—mainly at the expense of American and United Airlines, and in spite of a lower flight frequency and a smaller seat share (see Exhibit 3 for a comparison of fares, flight frequencies, fleets, and aircraft configurations).

---

[7]There were exceptions: on some routes (or flights), airlines offered a three-class service, either to facilitate the optimal use of international aircraft (which were configured for three-class service; TWA and Pan Am routed some of their transatlantic JFK-Europe flights on to Los Angeles, while American routed its Tokyo–San Jose, California, flight on to Boston), or to route these aircraft to dedicated maintenance facilities. International aircraft were also deployed on domestic routes at times of emergencies (for example, a regional rain or snow storm), when the priority was to get traffic flowing again.

[8]The cabin had swivel chairs and tables, and was configured like a lounge. In addition, there were two staterooms, each with four seats that could be converted into sleeping berths.

EXHIBIT 3

Competitive Product Offerings for the JFK-LAX Market

	American	*MGM*	*Pan Am*	*TWA*	*United*
Fares					
First	$1,071	$1,071	$1,071	$1,071	$1,071
Business	$713		$713	$713	
Coach	$656	$656	$656	$656	$656
Frequency (in each direction)	6	2	4	3	4
Aircraft					
Aircraft type	DC-10	DC-8	Boeing 747/ Airbus A310	Boeing 747/ L1010/1011	Boeing 767
# aircraft in type	6	2	2/1	1/2/1	4
Aircraft Configuration					
First class					
Number of seats	34	39	21/12	21/28/18	24
Pitch	44″	Varies	60″	60″	38″
Sleeper?	No	Yes	Yes	Yes	Yes
Legrest	None	Hydraulic	Hydraulic	Hydraulic	Hydraulic
Seat config.	2/2/2	Varies	2/2	2/2/2	2/2/2
Business class					
Number of seats			44/30	52/48/40	
Pitch			40″	40″	
Legrest			None	Hydraulic	
Seat config.			2/2/2	2/2/2	
Coach class					
Number of seats	256	40	347/154	358/199/214	180
Pitch (most/some)	32/31″	37/38″	n/a	n/a	n/a
Seat config.	2/5/2	2/2	n/a	n/a	n/a

Notes

1. The fares are as of September 1990. American charged a higher, "peak" first-class fare ($1,124) on 6 of its 12 daily flights between JFK and LAX. The business-class fare for American was for pro rating revenues for international business-class ticketholders traveling with the airline on the JFK-LAX sector.

2. MGM Grand Air's first-class service was superior to other carriers' first-class service; the airline's "Grand" coach service was comparable to other carriers' first-class service.

3. Pan Am and TWA operated their international aircraft on the JFK-LAX sector. "L1010/1011": Lockheed 1010/1011.

TWA and Pan Am offered a different type of competition: Both airlines operated their three-class international aircraft on this route. Furthermore, TWA allowed unlimited upgrades to business class for anyone flying 5,000 miles or more with the airline over a 12-month period—a more liberal upgrade policy than American's. Pan Am's upgrade policy, while not as generous, was also more liberal.

Finally, there was United Airlines.[9] Even though American and United offered comparable products, American enjoyed a market-share advantage for first-class travel (46.5 percent *vs.* 11.5 percent in fourth quarter 1989)—even after adjusting for American's higher flight frequency and capacity. Still, United posed a challenge, both because of its size (United was second only to American in the United States) and the resources at its disposal. Indeed, American had heard rumors that United might announce a three-class JFK-LAX service.

THE THREE-CLASS TRANSCON SERVICE PROPOSAL

Product

Three groups—Product Design, Food and Beverage Service, and Inflight Service—were responsible for defining the proposed three-class transcon product.

Product Design   The Product Design group was headed by Kathy Libonati, an ex-MGM Grand Air executive, and consisted of the following functions: Cabin Design and Planning, Amenities (pillows, blankets, and so on), Inflight Entertainment, Admirals Club (premium-class lounges at terminals), and Special Services (quasi-concierge services at terminals).

In December 1989 Avery Coryell, Senior Specialist, Cabin Design and Planning, issued a "Request for Service" (RFS) asking Maintenance and Engineering (M&E) to estimate the cost, on a per-aircraft basis, of converting some domestic DC-10s or Boeing 767s to a three-class configuration.[10] M&E was requested to explore a number of options for each aircraft type. Thus, for the DC-10, M&E was asked to consider three different alternatives for total-number-of-seats and pitch for the first-class cabin:[11] 34 nonsleeper seats with the existing domestic 44″ pitch, 22 sleeper seats with the existing international 62″ pitch, and 28 sleeper seats with a new, intermediate 53″ pitch. The pitch in business class was fixed at the international business-class level, 40″, and the initial plans were for a coach-class pitch of 33″ (most seats)/34″ (some seats)—two inches more than the existing pitch in domestic and international coach classes. As for the seat configuration in each row, the first- and coach-class configurations were fixed at 2 seats–aisle–2 seats–aisle–2 seats ("2/2/2") and 2/5/2, respectively; for the business class, however, M&E was asked to evaluate two alternatives: 2/3/2 (existing international business class), or 2/2/2.

The final choice of seat configuration was an iterative process that continued through most of 1990 and involved the following groups: Cabin Design and Planning, Food and Beverage Service (responsibility: food and beverage service design, with implications for galley location, food/beverage cart flows, and flight attendant procedures), Inflight Service (flight attendant procedures), Marketing Planning (AAdvantage award and upgrade rules), Pricing and Yield Management (price, de-

---

[9]Delta, another major carrier, did not fly JFK-LAX. It flew Newark, New Jersey–LAX, however, and for some travelers Newark Airport was a close substitute for JFK Airport.

[10]While the three-class transcon proposal was first presented to the Planning Committee in January 1990, the concept had been in incubation for some time. As early as May 1989, the Domestic Pricing Strategy group had conducted a study to examine the impact of introducing international-style first- and business-class service on the airline's long-haul routes. Later, the LAX-JFK route was selected as the most suitable market for implementing the concept; Coryell's RFS followed soon thereafter.

[11]The pitch is the distance between two consecutive rows of seats.

mand, and revenue impact of different aircraft configurations), Airline Profitability Analysis, and M&E. These groups considered a number of factors.

First, the Boeing 767 option was ruled out in April 1990: The aircraft was too small to meet the total JFK-LAX demand. Second, the new first-class product had to be competitive with, if not better than, MGM Grand Air's first class. This meant that the existing 44"-pitch nonsleeper seats configuration was not acceptable. Third, it was felt that a 62" pitch in the first-class cabin would leave too few seats for full-fare passengers; this would defeat one of the principal goals of the reconfiguration exercise: to have adequate capacity to meet full-fare first-class demand. Fourth, it was decided that the new three-class transcon business class should not be superior to the international business class. This ruled out a 2/2/2 configuration in the business-class cabin. Finally, a 33/34" pitch in the coach class was ruled out because that, too, would have resulted in an unacceptable reduction in the total number of coach-class seats.

Coryell commented on the cabin-configuration decision process and the competitive advantages of the configuration that was finally chosen (see Exhibit 4 for a comparison of the two-class transcon, the three-class international, and the proposed three-class transcon products):

> We must have tried at least fifty different combinations. We had to decide whether to reuse some of the existing international seats in the new business class, or to order new ones—an important decision given the six- to seven-month lead time for new seats. In the coach cabin, we had the choice of new seats that had the same pitch as existing seats, but provided two more inches of knee and shin room. Should we install these seats at the time of the reconfiguration, or given the system-wide implication, put off their installation to some future date?
>
> Then, there was the issue of galleys. The DC-10s we were considering for reconfiguration had some galleys below the coach cabin. To accommodate the planned changes in the food and beverage service, we had to provide special access from these galleys to coach class; otherwise, flight attendants would have had to wheel service carts through the business-class cabin. Even considerations such as whether passengers would be served freshly brewed coffee had important implications: the lead time for wet galleys required for coffee makers is fourteen months; for dry galleys, it is seven months. I even exchanged memos with M&E and Inflight Service about closets and the amount of closet rod per passenger.
>
> I am not saying all the toing-and-froing was not necessary: because of it, we are proposing a really competitive product. No other airline offers electronic legrests in the first-class cabin. United offers a 38" pitch in its first-class cabin; even our business-class cabin will have a 40" pitch. In addition, we will have, for example, improved passenger controls, separate lavatories in the business-class cabin, and dedicated closets.

M&E estimated that the total cost of reconfiguring a DC-10 aircraft would be $1.2 million, with materials accounting for over $900,000 (major expense categories: $650,000 for new seats, $120,000 for video units in the first-class cabin, and $70,000 for two new wet galleys).[12] The reconfiguration would require over 1,600 hours of labor. At $45 per hour, the estimated labor costs were $72,000.

---

[12]This investment will be depreciated over twelve years according to the following depreciation schedule: 4.7 percent in Year 1, 9.2 percent in Year 2, 8.8 percent in Year 3, 8.5 percent in Year 4, 8.2 percent in Year 5, and 8.1 percent in each of Years 6 through 12.

E X H I B I T   4

Product Comparison: Two-Class Transcon, International, and Three-Class Transcon

	Existing Two-Class Transcon Service	*International Service*	*Proposed Three-Class Transcon Service*
Frequency	6	n/a	7
Number of Aircraft (DC-10s)[a]	6	n/a	10
Aircraft Configuration			
First class			
Number of seats	34	22	28
Pitch	44″	62″	53″
Sleeper?	No	Yes	Yes
Legrest	None	Electronic	Electronic
Seat config.	2/2/2	2/2/2	2/2/2
Recline[b]	24°	60°	30°
Lighted digital passenger control units (PCUs), swingarm tray tables, movable headrests		✔	✔
Business class			
Number of seats		56	52
Pitch		40″	40″
Legrest		Hydraulic	Hydraulic
Seat config.		2/3/2	2/3/2
Recline[b]		23°	23°
Lighted digital PCUs, swing arm tray tables, moveable headrests		✔	✔
Coach class			
Number of seats	256	149	157
Pitch (most/some)32/31″	32/31″	32/31″	
Seat config.	2/5/2	2/5/2	2/5/2
Recline[b]	21°	21°	21°
Lavatories (fwd + mid + aft)	2+2+4	2+2+4	2+2+4
Overhead bins (cu. ft./passenger)	1.89	2.25	2.31
Number of closets	7	6	8
Inches of closet rod/passenger	0.99″	0.88″	1.24″

[a]American operates aircraft other than DC-10s on international (as well as domestic nontranscon) routes.
[b]Degrees from vertical.

Cabin configuration was only one aspect of product design. A second group in the Product Design organization was responsible for deciding on (1) all contacts other than ticketing with passengers at airport terminals, and (2) everything other than food and beverages that passengers get on board the aircraft. Susan Doyle, an-

EXHIBIT 5

Proposed Three-Class Transcon Service: Special Product Features

	First Class	Business Class
Cabin, Amenities, Inflight Entertainment, and Service		
International Flagship Service (IFS) seats, pillows, blankets, screen covers, cabin plaques, curtains, and carpeting	✓	✓
Personal video units (with videotape library)	✓	
Electronic headsets	✓	✓
Daily newspapers, playing cards, etc.	✓	✓
Lavatory-cleaning kits, loose amenities, etc.	✓	✓
Incremental flight-attendant staffing	✓	✓
Other: closets labeled by cabin and purpose (to ensure adequate hanging bag and coat closet space for first- and business-class passengers); auxiliary galley units in coach cabin with warming capability and additional work and storage area.		
Food and Beverage Service		
MGM Grand Air level of service	✓	
Existing transcon first-class service level		✓
China and linen	IFS business class	Existing transcon first class
Printed menus and wine inserts	✓	✓
Premium American wines and champagne	✓	✓
Food items with distinct California/New York specialties with executive-meal option	5 entrees	4 entrees
Warm mixed nuts; cookies baked on-board	✓	✓
Caviar and sundaes	✓	
Ground Service		
Dedicated check-in positions	✓	✓
Special ticket jackets and baggage tags	✓	✓
Carry-on baggage service	✓	
Priority baggage delivery	✓	✓
Special parking services; limo service arranged	✓	✓
Incremental special-service staff	IFS first-class level	

alyst, Product Design, commented on this aspect of product design (see Exhibit 5 for a summary of product features):

> We wanted a distinctive product from the moment first- or business-class passengers arrive at one terminal to the moment they leave the other terminal—a product competitive with MGM and others and, at the same time, consistent with IFS [American's International Flagship Service]. At the two [JFK and LAX] terminals, we propose dedicated check-in positions, IFS ticket jackets and baggage tags, carry-on baggage ser-

vice, priority baggage delivery, and so on. Once passengers are on board, everything—pillows, blankets, carpeting, curtains, screen covers, even cabin plaques—will be IFS-level. In the first-class cabin, there will even be personal video units, with a library of videotapes to choose from. Of course, passengers will also have access to programmed entertainment, but we want to give them as much control as possible.

Food and Beverage Service   The Food and Beverage Service group decided what passengers ate and drank on board the aircraft. Kathy Barton, Manager, Menu Design, was responsible for designing this aspect of the proposed three-class product. An analyst in Domestic Pricing Strategy until mid-1989, Barton was relatively new to Food and Beverage Service. She joined the group as a financial analyst, but soon took over the planning of food and beverage services on American's South American routes. When American launched the International Flagship Service in May 1990, she assumed overall responsibility for IFS food and beverage services. Barton saw the three-class transcon proposal as a logical extension of the IFS concept to long-haul U.S. markets:

> We started with three goals. First, we wanted a product consistent with—but not better than—IFS. We knew we couldn't deliver all IFS concepts, but those that we could deliver, we wanted to perfect them for the JFK-LAX market's special character. Second, our food and beverage service had to be better than MGM's. We had our chefs fly with MGM to really understand the competition. And third, the service couldn't be so elaborate that it would confuse passengers.
>
> In business class, we didn't want people who previously flew first class to be disappointed. So the new business-class food and beverages service had to be comparable to the existing domestic first-class service. Even in coach, we thought about service improvements such as warm breads and frozen yogurt.
>
> The whole process was time-consuming. It probably took one-half year of an analyst's time to work out all the options. We had to work with the chefs, who came up with basic concepts; kitchens and caterers, who would deliver on the concepts; Coryell in Cabin Design; and Sean Curry in Inflight Service. Sean is responsible for designing the procedures for flight attendants. We can't simply tell a flight attendant, "Here's our new product. Go run with it." Careful documentation and training are required to ensure consistent product and service quality on every flight.
>
> We are still working on the details of the new menu. If a decision is made to go ahead with the new product, it will take close to six months to train flight attendants in the revised procedures.

Exhibit 5 summarizes the improvements in food and beverage services that were proposed for the new three-class JFK-LAX product. The annual incremental cost of all service improvements (food and beverage services plus all the improvements Susan Doyle talked about) was estimated at $10 million: $4.1 million for existing first-class service in the new business-class cabin, $3.2 million for incremental flight-attendant and terminal-support staffing; $.75 million for the proposed service enhancements; $1.2 million for additional pillows and blankets, videofilms, and loose amenities; and $.75 million for other miscellaneous expenses.

Flight Frequency and the Number of Aircraft to be Reconfigured

In January 1991 American offered 12 flights a day (6 in each direction) between New York JFK and Los Angeles. The three-class transcon proposal called for increasing the frequency in each direction to seven.[13] An important question was how many aircraft would have to be reconfigured to provide a dependable three-class operation on the route.

For the existing two-class service, American used six DC-10-10 aircraft.[14] This fleet size was satisfactory in terms of dependability because the airline had a total of 14 such aircraft, and some substitution was possible in case of an emergency, a mechanical problem, or scheduled maintenance.[15] With the proposed reconfiguration for a three-class transcon product, an aircraft fleet would have to be dedicated to the JFK-LAX market and isolated from the rest of the domestic DC-10 fleet.

Two groups played an important role in determining a suitable fleet size for the reconfigured aircraft: Capacity Planning (responsibility: aircraft scheduling and optimizing aircraft fleet for systemwide passenger flows) and System Operations Control (managing systemwide operations on a day-to-day basis). Walter Aue, Managing Director, Schedules, commented on the three-class fleet-size decision:

> The decision was particularly difficult because of the implications for service dependability and aircraft scheduling and substitutability—not only for the JFK-LAX route (which would be served by the dedicated aircraft), but also for the other domestic routes that are served by DC-10s. We lose several elements of flexibility when we isolate a fleet of aircraft.
>
> First, New York JFK and Los Angeles are major DC-10 maintenance facilities, and it helps to be able to route aircraft such that they end up at either of these two destinations at the time of a scheduled maintenance check. Since the reconfigured aircraft will be dedicated to the JFK-LAX route, it will be easier to schedule them for maintenance, but we will lose a lot of flexibility for the rest of the DC-10 fleet. Second, the aircraft that will be reconfigured are the domestic DC-10-10s. These are not equipped for over-water flights. So, we will not be able to use them on Caribbean flights out of New York JFK, or Hawaiian flights out of Los Angeles. It's not only that we cannot use the reconfigured aircraft on other routes. We also can't use other aircraft on the JFK-LAX route—at least not without loss of the three-class product. That's a third element of flexibility loss. And fourth, with several wide-body aircraft dedicated to only one route, our ability to deploy our fleet optimally throughout the system will be significantly restricted.
>
> What I am saying is, isolating a fleet for the JFK-LAX route is going to be expensive—operationally and financially. You can talk to Don [Kneram, Managing Director, Systems Operations Control] about the operational difficulties; I'll focus on the financial cost of lost flexibility—the isolation cost. There are two elements to this cost: the cost of not being able to use our fleet optimally, and the cost of passengers spilled because of inadequate capacity resulting from aircraft substitution.

---

[13]These are frequencies for Monday through Friday; there was one flight fewer in either direction on Saturday and Sunday.

[14]American had 59 DC-10s in its fleet. Of these, 45 were DC-10-OWs and were equipped for over-water flights; 13 DC-10-OWs were used for international flights, while 32 were used in special markets such as the Caribbean and Hawaiian routes. The remainder of the DC-10 fleet consisted of 14 DC-10-10 aircraft, which were not suitable for over-water use and were dedicated to domestic flights; some DC-10-10s would be reconfigured for the three-class transcon service.

[15]A DC-10-10 required a 10-hour "A" maintenance check every three days, a 16-hour "B" maintenance check every month, and a three-week "C" maintenance check every 15 or 16 months. The "A" and "B" checks could be carried out at the airline's maintenance facilities at New York JFK and Los Angeles (these were the only two facilities at American where "A" and "B" maintenance checks could be carried out for a DC-10 aircraft); the "C" check could be carried out only at a maintenance facility in Tulsa, Oklahoma.

Pricing and Yield Management want to offer seven flights a day in each direction. Systems Operations Control feels that we'll need ten aircraft to support this frequency level with acceptable levels of dependability. That's ten out of fourteen aircraft in its class. What will be the isolation cost? We don't yet have an exact estimate, but the numbers that I have seen so far range from as low as a couple of million dollars a year to as high as ten to twelve million dollars a year. Part of the problem is that passenger spillage depends on aircraft availability—which is difficult to predict—and systemwide load factors—which are difficult to forecast with any degree of accuracy.

Don Kneram, managing director, System Operations Control (SOC), talked about the difficulty of isolating a fleet and ensuring an acceptable level of dependability:

> As a member of the three-class JFK-LAX service task force, I was asked to give SOC's view on the three-class concept. While I agreed that the idea of a three-class product was a good one, I voiced my one major concern, and that was the wisdom of taking several planes and making them unique to a route. As it is, we operate a very complex system. Suppose we have an "event," say, a major snow storm in the New York–New Jersey–New England area. The whole system breaks down and we have to put it back together. The reconfigured DC-10 fleet will restrict our ability to juggle aircraft around on such occasions.
>
> That's one problem. The other problem is the reconfigured fleet itself. Our studies suggest that with ten aircraft, we should be able to offer a dependable level of service. Still, we cannot ban events. I requested that specific marketing guidelines be developed for the acceptable lengths of delays, the substitution of aircraft, and the criteria for flight cancellation. SOC would then be in a better position to select the correct option in case of an off-schedule operation. We're still working out the details.

Changes in AAdvantage Program Rules for Awards and Upgrades

The Marketing Planning organization was responsible for designing and administering American's AAdvantage frequent-flyer program. With a three-class JFK-LAX service, at least two changes were necessary in the program rules. First, upgrade rules had to be changed to allow AAdvantage Gold members to upgrade only to the next class of service—from coach to business. Second, a new award level had to be created to allow AAdvantage members with sufficient program miles to claim an award for first-class travel on the JFK-LAX route (the standard domestic first-class award level would allow only business-class travel). Taken together, these changes would free up a large section of the first-class cabin for full-fare first-class passengers.

John Jaynes, Manager, Marketing Planning, talked about the above changes and their likely impact on AAdvantage Gold members:

> When Pricing and Yield Management first brought up the issue of the first-class cabin being closed out to full-fare passengers, one suggestion was to tighten up on upgrades, but we couldn't do that: AAdvantage Gold members are valuable customers, and we can't be too restrictive with them; as it is, Pan Am and TWA offered more liberal upgrades. We had to find some other alternative.
>
> We talked to focus groups in New York and Los Angeles to understand the nuances of corporate travel policies and to ascertain the Gold members' upgrade needs. I think the new business class will be an acceptable upgrade alternative. Yes, it won't be "first class," but Gold members will get what they really want: quiet, personal space, and special attention. Furthermore, given the size of the business-class cabin, there will be increased opportunity to upgrade.

Should we be as generous as TWA and Pan Am in offering upgrades? No. We offer a better product and a higher level of service. We also believe that a number of AAdvantage members will choose to purchase business-class tickets.

Pricing

The Domestic Pricing Strategy group was responsible for formulating a pricing plan for the new service. When the group presented the three-class proposal to the Planning Committee in January 1990, first-class fares were about 155 percent of full-coach fares on transcon flights. While competing airlines offered similar fares, American was different in that it charged a premium in the first-class cabin for peak-time transcon flights (three out of six flights in each direction). As for business class, only TWA and Pan Am offered this product on the transcon route, and they priced a business-class seat at $50–$60 above the full-coach fare. American used TWA's and Pan Am's business-class fare when prorating revenues for international business-class ticketholders.

In its January 1990 proposal, the Domestic Pricing Strategy group recommended a 10 percent increase in the first-class fare, a 35 percent increase in the business-class fare, and no change in the coach-class fare. The group thought the proposed increases in premium-class fares were justified, but there was no telling what the passengers might think. Also, it was not clear how other airlines would react to American's move.

The Domestic Pricing Strategy group's pricing recommendations in a September 1990 Planning Committee presentation are reproduced in Exhibit 6.

Impact on Demand

While it was impossible to predict exactly how the above changes would affect American's demand on the JFK-LAX route, some demand-impact estimates were nevertheless necessary for planning and investment analysis purposes.[16]

The Domestic Pricing Strategy group was responsible for examining the demand implications of the proposed three-class transcon service. Adopting an average operation (a flight in either direction) as the unit of analysis, and assuming 12 operations a day (the existing frequency, and the only available basis of comparison), the group considered the following factors in its analysis: possible load factors in the three cabins, the likely fare mix in each cabin, the potential recapture of full-fare first-class passengers, the chances of the new business-class product cannibalizing some full-fare first-class demand, and the stimulative and competitive impact of the proposed product enhancements. The principal results of the demand-impact analysis are presented in Exhibit 6.

Communications Strategy

A comprehensive communications strategy had to accompany the new product launch. Several audiences had to be informed, and each had to receive a well-crafted message.

---

[16]The investment analysis was done assuming a 22 percent tax rate.

EXHIBIT 6

JFK-LAX: Existing and Proposed Fares; Existing and Expected Demand per Operation

Cabin	Fare Group	Two-Class Fares 09/90	Proposed Three-Class Fares	Change
First	Peak	$1,124	$1,236	+10%
	Full F	$1,071	$1,178	+10%
Business	Full C	$713	$963	+35%
Coach	Full Y	$656	$656	No change

	Existing Two-Class Transcon Service	Proposed Three-Class Transcon Service
First-class cabin		
Number of seats	34	28
Number of passengers		
Full F fare	14.5	16.5
Full C fare	0.9	0.0
AAdvantage awards—no fare	4.1	4.1
AAdvantage upgrades—discount Y fare	11.5	0.0
Total passengers	31.0	20.6
Business-class cabin		
Number of seats	0	52
Number of passengers		
Full C fare	0.0	2.0
AAdvantage upgrades—discount Y fare	0.0	40.1
Total passengers	0.0	42.1
Coach-class cabin		
Number of seats	256	157
Number of passengers		
Full Y fare	5.4	5.4
Discount Y fare	155.0	119.9
Total passengers	160.4	125.3
Total aircraft		
Number of seats	290	237
Number of passengers	191.4	188.0

Notes

1. On average, 0.9 international business-class ticketholders travel with American on the JFK-LAX sector.
2. On average, discount Y fare = 32 percent of full Y fare.
3. The average travel-agent commission is 10 percent.

Inside American, the audience consisted of sales personnel, ticket and reservation agents, terminal staff, pilots, flight attendants, and maintenance and ground crew. Their enthusiasm for the three-class concept and their dedication to its implementation were critical to its success. The internal communications package would consist of the following: product fairs in New York and Los Angeles, audiovisual presentations, information packages, announcements in internal publications, and comprehensive flight-attendant and terminal-staff training.

Outside American, there were three audiences: travel agents and corporate travel departments, AAdvantage members and key business prospects, and securities analysts. The external communications effort would consist of media advertising, advertising collateral, and direct marketing. Robert Britton, Manager, Advertising and Direct Marketing, talked about the communications strategy:

> The new product will be announced in press conferences in New York and Los Angeles. Press kits will be issued at this time, and senior American executives will be on hand to answer questions. Displays at the press conference will include first- and business-class seats to be installed in the reconfigured aircraft, first-class personal video systems, new electronic headsets, blankets and pillows, and actual samples of the first- and business-class meal services. Securities analysts will attend a separate briefing in New York the same day.
>
> As for advertising, it will focus almost completely on New York and Los Angeles, and will consist of a mix of 60-second television spots, newspaper advertisements, local magazine support, billboard announcements, and New York transit-system posters. Rather than edit and blend existing video footage, the television spots will be custom-produced to highlight the new transcon product. Advertising collateral—full-color brochures, pocket folders, press and sales kits, and promotional merchandise such as notepads and buttons—will be sent directly to corporate accounts, travel agents, and sales representatives. The total advertising budget may exceed $10 million.
>
> We have yet to decide on the basic advertising concept. Should we focus on "place"—the space and environments in the new first- and business-class cabins; should we portray the new services as the implementation of a bold idea; should we emphasize that the new American Flagship Service will continue American's heritage of innovation on this legendary route; or should we capitalize on customer perception of international service as fundamentally better and position the three-class transcon service as a domestic version of our international product?
>
> Finally, direct marketing. We have three objectives. One, to introduce the new first- and business-class products to travel professionals and key prospects, mainly in New York and Los Angeles. Two, to create awareness among frequent travelers, emphasizing the increased opportunity to upgrade to business class. And three, to position the new business-class product to the AAdvantage upgrade audience as a service equivalent to the existing transcon first-class service. We are planning a direct mailing of a brochure to over 20,000 AAdvantage members who might be good upgrade candidates. About 5,000 key travel agents and corporate accounts will also receive an elaborate direct-mail package including apples (California recipients) and oranges (New York recipients).

A Cautionary Note

Thomas Bacon, Managing Director, Airline Profitability Analysis, headed a group responsible for monitoring the profit-and-loss performance of all routes in the American system. Bacon talked about the proposed changes in the JFK-LAX product:

> I appreciate the need for a competitive product and the discussions surrounding the AAdvantage upgrades. Also, with all the airline consolidation that is going on, United could soon have three-class Boeing 747s flying out of JFK. But here's the problem. JFK-LAX is one of our best markets. Why take away seats [the reconfigured DC-10 will have 53 fewer seats] in a situation where the load factors are high

and spillage expensive? Also, Pricing and Yield Management says we are spilling full-fare first-class passengers. But look at the load factors in the first-class cabin. They are nowhere near 100 percent.

DECISION TIME

When the three-class transcon service proposal was first presented to American's Planning Committee in January 1990, the goal was to obtain a quick approval and begin reconfiguring aircraft by September 1990. Given the long lead times for procuring seats and galleys, and the preference for scheduling reconfiguration when the DC-10s are in Tulsa for a "C" maintenance check, the new service could be launched in spring 1991. That date was no longer feasible. A launch in summer 1991 was ruled out because summer was the peak travel season, and pulling out aircraft for reconfiguration would be too expensive. The next product-launch window was fall 1991; but with no decision by year-end 1990, even that window had closed. If the proposal were approved in the January 1991 Planning Committee meeting, seats and galleys could be ordered in time, and a product launch would be possible in early 1992. Unfortunately, none of the aircraft would be reconfigured at the time of a scheduled "C" class maintenance check.

Procter and Gamble, Inc.
Scope

As Gwen Hearst looked at the year-end report she was pleased to see that Scope held a 32 percent share of the Canadian mouthwash market for 1990. She had been concerned about the inroads that Plax, a prebrushing rinse, had made in the market. Since its introduction in 1988, Plax had gained a 10 percent share of the product category and posed a threat to Scope. As Brand Manager, Hearst planned, developed, and directed the total marketing effort for Scope, Procter and Gamble's (P&G) brand in the mouthwash market. She was responsible for maximizing the market share, volume, and profitability of the brand.

Until the entry of Plax, brands in the mouthwash market were positioned around two major benefits: fresh breath and killing germs. Plax was positioned around a new benefit—as a "plaque fighter"—and indications were that other brands, such as Listerine, were going to promote this benefit. The challenge for Hearst was to develop a strategy that would ensure the continued profitability of Scope in the face of these competitive threats. Her specific task was to prepare a marketing plan for P&G's mouthwash business for the next three years. It was early February 1991, and she would be presenting the plan to senior management in March.

COMPANY BACKGROUND

Based on a philosophy of providing products of superior quality and value that best fill the needs of consumers, Procter and Gamble is one of the most successful consumer goods companies in the world. The company markets its brands in more than 140 countries and had net earnings of $1.6 billion in 1990. The Canadian subsidiary contributed $1.4 billion in sales and $100 million in net earnings in 1990. It was recognized as a leader in the Canadian packaged-goods industry, and its consumer brands led in most of the categories in which the company competed.

Between 1987 and 1990, worldwide sales of P&G had increased by $8 billion and net earnings by $1.3 billion. P&G executives attributed the company's success to a variety of factors including the ability to develop truly innovative products to meet consumers' needs. Exhibit 1 contains the statement of purpose and strategy of the Canadian subsidiary.

P&G Canada has five operating divisions, organized by product category. The divisions, and some of the major brands, are:

1. *Paper products*: Royale, Pampers, Luvs, Attends, Always
2. *Food and beverage*: Duncan Hines, Crisco, Pringles, Sunny Delight

---

This case was prepared by Professors Gordon H. G. McDougall and Franklin Ramsoomair, of the Wilfrid Laurier University, as a basis for class discussion and is not designed to illustrate effective or ineffective handling of an administrative situation. Used with permission.

EXHIBIT 1

A Statement of Purpose and Strategy: Procter and Gamble, Canada

We will provide products of superior quality and value that best fill the needs of consumers.

We will achieve that purpose through an organization and a working environment which attracts the finest people, fully develops and challenges our individual talents; encourages our free and spirited collaboration to drive the business ahead; and maintains the Company's historic principles of integrity, and doing the right thing.

We will build a profitable business in Canada. We will apply P&G worldwide learning and resources to maximize our success rate. We will concentrate our resources on the most profitable categories and on unique, important Canadian market opportunities. We will also contribute to the development of outstanding people and innovative business ideas for worldwide company use.

We will reach our business goals and achieve optimum cost efficiencies through continuing innovation, strategic planning and the continuous pursuit of excellence in everything we do.

We will continuously stay ahead of competition while aggressively defending our established profitable businesses against major competitive challenges despite short-term profit consequences.

Through the successful pursuit of our commitment, we expect our brands to achieve leadership share and profit positions and that, as a result, our business, our people, our shareholders, and the communities in which we live and work, will prosper.

Source: Company records.

3. *Beauty care*: Head & Shoulders, Pantene, Pert, Vidal Sassoon, Clearasil, Clarion, Cover Girl, Max Factor, Oil of Olay, Noxzema, Secret
4. *Health care*: Crest, Scope, Vicks, Pepto Bismol, Metamucil
5. *Laundry and cleaning*: Tide, Cheer, Bounce, Bold, Oxydol, Joy, Cascade, Comet, Mr. Clean

Each division had its own Brand Management, Sales, Finance, Product Development and Operations line management groups and was evaluated as a profit center. Typically, within each division a Brand Manager was assigned to each brand (for example, Scope). Hearst was in the Health Care division and reported to the Associate Advertising Manager for oral care, who, in turn, reported to the General Manager of the division. After completing her business degree (B.B.A.) at a well-known Ontario business school in 1986, Hearst had joined P&G as a Brand Assistant. In 1987 she became the Assistant Brand Manager for Scope, and in 1988 she was promoted to Brand Manager. Hearst's rapid advancement at P&G reflected the confidence that her managers had in her abilities.

THE CANADIAN MOUTHWASH MARKET

Until 1987, on a unit basis the mouthwash market had grown at an average of 3 percent per year for the previous 12 years. In 1987, it experienced a 26 percent increase with the introduction of new flavors such as peppermint. Since then, the growth rate had declined to a level of 5 percent in 1990 (Exhibit 2).

The mouthwash market was initially developed by Warner-Lambert with its pioneer brand Listerine. Positioned as a therapeutic germ-killing mouthwash that eliminated bad breath, it dominated the market until the entry of Scope in 1967. Scope, a green, mint-tasting mouthwash, was positioned as a great tasting, mouth-refreshing brand that provided bad-breath protection. It was the first brand that offered

EXHIBIT 2

Mouthwash Market

	1986	1987	1988	1989	1990
Total retail sales (000,000)	$43.4	$54.6	$60.2	$65.4	$68.6
Total factory sales (000,000)	34.8	43.5	$48.1	$52.2	$54.4
Total unit sales (000)[a]	863	1,088	1,197	1,294	1,358
(% change)	3	26	10	8	5
(% change—"breath only")[b]	3	26	0	3	5
Penetration (%)[c]	65	70	75	73	75
Usage (Number of times per week)[d]	2.0	2.2	2.3	2.4	3.0

[a]One unit or statistical case equals 10 liters or 352 fluid ounces of mouthwash.
[b]Excludes Plax and other prebrushing rinses.
[c]Percent of households having at least one brand in home.
[d]For each adult household member.

Source: Company records.

both effective protection against bad breath and a better taste than other mouthwashes. Its advertising focused, in part, on a perceived weakness of Listerine—a medicine breath (for example, "Scope fights bad breath. Don't let the good taste fool you")—and in 1976, Scope became the market leader in Canada.

In 1977, Warner-Lambert launched Listermint mouthwash as a direct competitor to Scope. Like Scope, it was a green, mint-tasting mouthwash and positioned as a "good tasting mouthwash that fights bad breath." Within a year it had achieved a 12 percent market share, primarily at the expense of Listerine, and smaller brands in the market.

In the 1970s Merrell Dow, a large pharmaceutical firm, launched Cepacol, which was positioned very close to Listerine. It achieved and held approximately 14 percent of the market in the early 1980s.

During the 1980s, the major competitive changes in the Canadian mouthwash market were:

- Listerine, which had been marketed primarily on a "bad breath" strategy, began shifting its position and in 1988 introduced the claim "Fights plaque and helps prevent inflamed gums caused by plaque." In the United States, Listerine gained the American Dental Association seal for plaque but, as yet, did not have the seal in Canada.

- Listermint added fluoride during the early 1980s and added the Canadian Dental Association seal for preventing cavities in 1983. More recently, Listermint had downplayed fluoride and removed the seal.

- In early 1987, flavors were introduced by a number of brands including Scope, Listermint, and various store brands. This greatly expanded the market in 1987 but did not significantly change the market shares held by the major brands.

- Colgate Fluoride Rinse was launched in 1988. With the seal from the Canadian Dental Association for cavities, it claimed that "Colgate's new fluoride rinse fights cavities. And, it has a mild taste that encourages children to rinse longer and more often." Colgate's share peaked at 2 percent and then declined. There were rumours that Colgate was planning to discontinue the brand.

- In 1988, Merrell Dow entered a licensing agreement with Strategic Brands to market Cepacol in Canada. Strategic Brands, a Canadian firm that markets a variety of consumer household products, had focused its efforts on gaining greater distribution for Cepacol and promoting it on the basis of price.
- In 1988, Plax was launched on a new and different platform. Its launch and immediate success caught many in the industry by surprise.

THE INTRODUCTION OF PLAX

Plax was launched in Canada in late 1988 on a platform quite different from the traditional mouthwashes. First, instead of the usual use occasion of "after brushing," it called itself a "prebrushing" rinse. The user rinses before brushing, and Plax's detergents are supposed to help loosen plaque to make brushing especially effective. Second, the product benefits were not breath-focused. Instead, it claimed that "Rinsing with Plax, then brushing normally, removes up to three times more plaque than just brushing alone."

Pfizer Inc., a pharmaceutical firm, launched Plax in Canada with a promotion campaign that was estimated to be close to $4 million. The campaign, which covered the last three months of 1988 and all of 1989, consisted of advertising estimated at $3 million and extensive sales promotions including (1) trial-size display in three drugstore chains ($60,000), (2) co-op mail couponing to 2.5 million households ($160,000), (3) an instantly redeemable coupon offer ($110,000), (4) a professional mailer to drug and supermarket chains ($30,000), and (5) a number of price reductions ($640,000). Plax continued to support the brand with advertising expenditures of approximately $1.2 million in 1990. In 1990, Plax held a 10 percent share of the total market.

When Plax was launched in the United States, it claimed that using Plax "removed up to 300% more plaque than just brushing." This claim was challenged by mouthwash competitors and led to an investigation by the Better Business Bureau. The investigation found that the study on which Plax based its claim had panelists limit their toothbrushing to just 15 seconds—and didn't let them use toothpaste. A further study, where people were allowed to brush in their "usual manner" and with toothpaste, showed no overall difference in the level of plaque buildup between those using Plax and a control group that did not use Plax. Plax then revised its claim to "three times more plaque than just brushing alone." Information on plaque is contained in Appendix 1.

THE CURRENT SITUATION

In preparing for the strategic plan, Gwen Hearst reviewed the available information for the mouthwash market and Scope. As shown in Exhibit 2, in 1990, 75 percent of Canadian households used one or more mouthwash brands, and, on average, usage was three times per week for each adult household member. Company market research revealed that users could be segmented on frequency of use; "heavy" users (once per day or more) comprised 40 percent of all users, "medium" users (two–six times a week) comprised 45 percent, and "light" users (less than once a week) comprised 15 percent. No information was available on the usage habits of prebrushing rinse users. Nonusers currently don't buy mouthwash because they either (1) don't believe they get bad breath, (2) believe that brushing their teeth is adequate, and/or (3) find alternatives like gums and mints more convenient. The most important reasons why consumers use mouthwash are:

Most important reason for using a mouthwash:	%
It is part of my basic oral hygiene	40*
It gets rid of bad breath	40
It kills germs	30
It make me fell more confident	20
To avoid offending others	25

*Multiple reasons allowed.

During 1990, a survey was conducted of mouthwash users image of the major brands in the market. Respondents were asked to rate the brands on a number of attributes, and the results show that Plax had achieved a strong image on the "removes plaque/healthier teeth and gums" attributes (Exhibit 3).

Market share data revealed there was a substantial difference in the share held by Scope in food stores, 42 percent (for example, supermarkets) versus drugstores,

EXHIBIT 3

Consumer Perceptions of Brand Images

All Users[a]

Attributes	Cepacol	Colgate	Listerine	Listermint	Plax	Scope
Reduces bad breath	...	...	...	...	−	...
Kills germs	+	...	+	...	...	−
Removes plaque	...	...	...	...	+	−
Healthier teeth and gums	...	...	...	...	+	−
Good for preventing colds	...	...	+	...	...	...
Recommended by doctors/dentists	...	−	..	.. ...	+	...
Cleans your mouth well	...	...	...	...	...	...

Brand Users[b]

Attributes	Cepacol	Colgate	Listerine	Listermint	Plax	Scope
Reduces bad breath	+	−	+	+	−	+
Kills germs	+	...	+	−	−	...
Removes plaque	−	+	+	−	+	−
Healthier teeth and gums	...	+	+	−	+	−
Good for preventing colds	+	−	+	−	−	−
Recommended by doctors/dentists	+	+	+	−	+	−

[a]Includes anyone who uses mouthwash. Respondents asked to rate all brands (even those they haven't used) on the attributes. A "+" means this brand scores *higher than average*. A "..." means this brand scored *about average*. A "−" means this brand scored *below average*. For example, Cepacol is perceived by those who use mouthwash as a brand that is good/better than most at "preventing germs."

[b]Includes only the users of that brand. For example, Cepacol is perceived by those whose "usual brand" is Cepacol as a brand that is good/better than most at "reducing bad breath."

Source: Company records.

27 percent (Exhibit 4). Approximately 65 percent of all mouthwash sales went through drugstores, while 35 percent went through food stores. Recently, wholesale clubs, such as Price Club and Costco, were accounting for a greater share of mouthwash sales.[1] Typically, these clubs carried Cepacol, Scope, Listerine, and Plax.

Competitive data were also collected for advertising expenditures and retail prices. As shown in Exhibit 5, total media spending of all brands in 1990 was $5 million, with Scope, Listerine, and Plax accounting for 90 percent of all advertising. Retail prices were calculated based on a 750 ml bottle, both Listerine and Plax were priced at a higher level in food stores, and Plax was priced at a premium in drugstores.

Information on the U.S. market for 1989 was also available (Exhibit 6). In contrast to Canada, Listerine held the dominant share in the U.S. market. Since early 1989, Listerine had been advertised heavily in the United States as "the only non-prescription mouthwash accepted by the American Dental Association for its significant help in preventing and reducing plaque and gingivitis." In clinical tests in the United States, Listerine significantly reduced plaque scores by roughly 20 to 35 percent, with a similar reduction in gingivitis. In Canada, the 1990 advertising campaign included the claim that Listerine has been clinically proven to "help prevent inflamed and irritated gums caused by plaque build-up." Listerine's formula relied on four essential oils—menthol, eucalyptol, thymol, and methyl salicylate—all derivatives of phenol, a powerful antiseptic.

Listerine had not received the consumer product seal given by the Canadian Dental Association (CDA) because the association was not convinced a mouthrinse could be of therapeutic value. The CDA was currently reviewing American tests for several products sold in Canada. In fact, any proposed changes to the formulation of mouthwashes or advertising claims could require approval from various regulatory agencies.

EXHIBIT   4

Canadian Mouthwash Market Shares

	Units			1990 Average	
	1988	*1989*	*1990*	*Food*	*Drug*
Scope	33.0%	33.0%	32.3%	42.0%	27.0%
Listerine	15.2	16.1	16.6	12.0	19.0
Listermint	15.2	9.8	10.6	8.0	12.0
Cepacol	13.6	10.6	10.3	9.0	11.0
Colgate oral rinse	1.4	1.2	0.5	0.4	0.5
Plax	1.0	10.0	10.0	8.0	11.0
Store brands	16.0	15.4	16.0	18.0	15.0
Miscellaneous other	4.6	3.9	3.7	2.6	4.5
Total	100.0%	100.0%	100.0%	100.0%	100.0%
Retail sales (000,000)	$ 60.2	$ 65.4	$ 68.6	$ 24.0	$ 44.6

Source: Company records.

---

[1]Wholesale clubs were included in food store sales.

EXHIBIT 5

Competitive Market Data, 1990

Advertising Expenditures (000)

Scope	$1,700
Listerine	1,600
Plax	1,200
Listermint	330
Cepacol	170

Media Plans

	Number of Weeks on Air	*GRPs*[a]
Scope	35	325
Listerine	25	450
Plax	20	325

Retail Price Indices

	Food Stores	*Drugstores*
Scope	98	84
Listerine	129	97
Listermint	103	84
Colgate	123	119
Plax	170	141
Store brand	58	58
Cepacol	84	81
Total Market[b]	100	100

---

[a]GRP (Gross Rating Points) is a measurement of advertising impact derived by multiplying the number of persons exposed to an advertisement by the average number of exposures per person. The GRPs reported are monthly.

[b]An average weighted index of the retail prices of all mouthwash brands is calculated and indexed at 100 for both food stores and drug stores. Scope is priced slightly below this index in food stores and about 16 percent below in drugstores.

Source: Company records.

THE REGULATORY ENVIRONMENT

1. **Health Protection Branch**: This government body classifies products into "drug status" or "cosmetic status" based on both the product's action on bodily functions and its advertising claims. Drug products are those that affect a bodily function (for example, prevent cavities or prevent plaque buildup). For "drug status" products, all product formulations, packaging, copy, and advertising must be pre-cleared by the Health Protection Branch (HPB), with guidelines that are very stringent. Mouthwashes like Scope that claim to only prevent bad breath are considered as "cosmetic status." However, if any claims regarding inhibition of plaque formation are made the product reverts to "drug status," and all advertising is scrutinized.

EXHIBIT 6

Canada-U.S. Market Share Comparison, 1989 (% units)

Brands	Canada	United States
Scope	33.0	21.6
Listerine	16.1	28.7
Listermint	9.8	4.5
Cepacol	10.6	3.6
Plax	10.0	9.6

Source: Company records.

2. **The Canadian Dental Association**: Will, upon request of the manufacturer, place its seal of recognition on products that have demonstrated efficacy against cavities or against plaque/gingivitis. However, those products with the seal of recognition must submit their packaging and advertising to the CDA for approval. The CDA and the American Dental Association (ADA) are two separate bodies and are independent of each other and don't always agree on issues. The CDA, for example, would not provide a "plaque/gingivitis" seal unless clinical studies demonstrating actual gum health improvements were done.

3. **Saccharin/Cyclamate sweeteners**: All mouthwashes contain an artificial sweetener. In Canada, cyclamate is used as the sweetener, as saccharin is considered a banned substance. In contrast, the United States uses saccharin because cyclamate is prohibited. Thus, despite the fact that many of the same brands competing in both Canada and the United States, the formula in each country is different.

THE THREE-YEAR PLAN

In preparing the three-year plan for Scope, a team had been formed within P&G to examine various options. The team included individuals from Product Development (PDD), Manufacturing, Sales, Market Research, Finance, Advertising, and Operations. Over the past year, the team had completed a variety of activities relating to Scope.

The key issue, in Hearst's mind, was how P&G should capitalize on the emerging market segment within the rinse category that focused more on "health-related benefits" than the traditional breath strategy of Scope. Specifically with the launch of Plax, the mouthwash market had segmented itself along the "breath-only" brands (like Scope) and those promising other benefits. Plax, in positioning itself as a prebrushing rinse, was not seen as, nor did it taste like, a "breath refreshment" mouthwash like Scope.

Gwen Hearst believed that a line extension positioned against Plax, a recent entry into the market, made the most sense. If the mouthwash market became more segmented, and if these other brands grew, her fear was that P&G would be left with a large share of a segment that focused only on "breath" and hence might decline. However, she also knew that there were questions regarding both the strategic and financial implications of such a proposal. In recent meetings, other ideas had been proposed, including "doing nothing" and looking at claims other than "breath" that might be used by Scope instead of adding a new product. Several team members questioned whether there was any real threat, as Plax was positioned very differently from Scope. As she considered the alternatives, Hearst reviewed the activities of the team and the issues that had been raised by various team members.

Product Development

In product tests on Scope PDD had demonstrated that Scope reduced plaque better than brushing alone because of antibacterial ingredients contained in Scope. However, as yet P&G did not have a clinical database to convince the HPB to allow Scope to extend these claims into the prevention of inflamed gums (as Listerine does).

PDD had recently developed a new prebrushing rinse product that performed as well as Plax but did not work any better than Plax against plaque reduction. In fact, in its testing of Plax itself, PDD was actually unable to replicate the plaque reduction claim made by Pfizer that "rinsing with Plax, then brushing normally removes up to three times more plaque than brushing alone." The key benefit of P&G's prebrushing rinse was that it did taste better than Plax. Other than that, it had similar aesthetic qualities to Plax—qualities that made its "in-mouth" experience quite different from that of Scope.

The Product Development people in particular were concerned about Hearst's idea of launching a line extension because it was a product that was only equal in efficacy to Plax and to placebo rinses, for plaque reduction. Traditionally, P&G had only launched products that focused on unmet consumer needs—typically superior performing products. However, Gwen had pointed out, because the new product offered similar efficacy at a better taste, this was similar to the situation when Scope was originally launched. Some PDD members were also concerned that if they couldn't replicate Plax's clinical results with P&G's stringent test methodology, and if the product possibly didn't provide any greater benefit than rinsing with any liquid, that P&G's image and credibility with dental professionals might be impacted. There was debate on this issue, as others felt that as long as the product did encourage better oral hygiene, it did provide a benefit. As further support they noted that many professionals did recommend Plax. Overall, PDD's preference was to not launch a new product but, instead, to add plaque-reduction claims to Scope. The basic argument was that it was better to protect the business that P&G was already in than to launch a completely new entity. If a line extension was pursued, a product test costing $20,000 would be required.

Sales

The Sales people had seen the inroads Plax had been making in the marketplace and believed that Scope should respond quickly. They had one key concern, as stock-keeping units (SKUs) had begun to proliferate in many categories, the retail industry had become much more stringent regarding what it would accept. Now, to be listed on store shelves, a brand must be seen as different enough (or unique) from the competition to build incremental purchases—otherwise retailers argued that category sales volume would simply be spread over more units. When this happened, a retail outlet's profitability was reduced because inventory costs were higher, but no additional sales revenue was generated. When a new brand was viewed as not generating more sales, retailers might still list the brand by replacing units within the existing line (for example, drop shelf facings of Scope), or the manufacturer could pay approximately $50,000 per stock-keeping unit in listing fees to add the new brand.

Market Research

Market Research (MR) had worked extensively with Hearst to test the options with consumers. Its work to date had shown:

1. A plaque reassurance on current Scope (that is, "Now Scope fights plaque") did not seem to increase competitive users' desire to purchase Scope. This meant that it was unlikely to generate additional volume, but it could prevent current users from switching

    MR also cautioned that adding "reassurances" to a product often takes time before the consumer accepts the idea and then acts on it. The issue in Hearst's mind was whether the reassurance would ever be enough. At best it might stabilize the business, she thought, but would it grow behind such a claim?

2. A "Better-Tasting Prebrushing Dental Rinse" product did research well among Plax users, but did not increase purchase intent among people not currently using a dental rinse. MR's estimate was that a brand launched on this positioning would likely result in approximately a 6.5 percent share of the total mouthwash and "rinse" market on an ongoing basis. Historically, it has taken approximately two years to get to the ongoing level. However, there was no way for them to accurately assess potential Scope cannibalization. "Use your judgment," they had said. However, they cautioned that although it was a product for a different usage occasion, it was unlikely to be 100 percent incremental business. Hearst's best rough guess was that this product might cannibalize somewhere between 2 and 9 percent of Scope's sales. An unresolved issue was the product's name—if it were launched, should it be under the Scope name or not? One fear was that if the Scope name was used it would either "turn off" loyal users who saw Scope as a breath refreshment product or confuse them.

    MR had questioned Hearst as to whether she had really looked at all angles to meet her objective. Because much of this work had been done quickly, they wondered whether there weren't some other benefits Scope could talk about that would interest consumers and hence achieve the same objective. They suggested that Hearst look at other alternatives beyond just "a plaque reassurance on Scope" or a "line extension positioned as a 'Better-Tasting Prebrushing Rinse.' "

Finance

The point of view from Finance was mixed. One the one hand, Plax commanded a higher dollar price/liter and so it made sense that a new rinse might be a profitable option. On the other hand, they were concerned about the capital costs and the marketing costs that might be involved to launch a line extension. One option would

EXHIBIT 7

Scope Historical Financials

Year	1988		1989		1990	
Total market size (Units) (000)	1,197		1,294		1,358	
Scope market share	33.0%		33.0%		32.4%	
Scope volume (Units)(000)	395		427		440	
	$ (000)	**$/Unit**	**$ (000)**	**$/Unit**	**$ (000)**	**$/Unit**
Sales	16,767	42.45	17,847	41.80	18,150	41.25
COGS	10,738	27.18	11,316	26.50	11,409	25.93
Gross margin	6,029	15.27	7,299	15.30	6,741	15.32

Scope Marketing Plan Inputs
Scope "Going" Marketing Spending

Year	1990	1989	1988
Advertising (000)	$1,700	———	———
Promotion (000)	1,460	———	———
Total (000)	3,160	3,733	2,697

Marketing Input Costs

Advertising:		(See previous table)
Promotion:	Samples	(Including Distribution): $0.45 / piece
	Mailed couponing	$10.00 per 1,000 for printing distribution
		$ 0.17 handling per redeemed coupon (beyond face value)
		redemption rates: 10% to 15%
	In-store promotion	$200 / store (fixed)
		$0.17 handling per redeemed coupon (beyond face value)
		redemption rates: 85%+

Source: Company records.

be to source the product from a U.S. plant where the necessary equipment already existed. If the product was obtained from the U.S. delivery costs would increase by $1 per unit. Scope's current marketing and financial picture is shown in Exhibits 7 and 8 and an estimate of Plax's financial picture is provided in Exhibit 9.

Purchasing

The Purchasing Manager had reviewed the formula for the line extension and had estimated that the ingredients cost would increase by $2.55 per unit due to the addition of new ingredients. But, because one of the ingredients was very new, Finance felt that the actual ingredient change might vary by ± 50%. Packaging costs would be $0.30 per unit higher owing to the fact that the setup charges would be spread over a smaller base.

EXHIBIT 8

Scope 1990 Financials

	$ (000)	$/Unit
Net sales[a]	18,150	41.25
Ingredients	3,590	8.16
Packaging	2,244	5.10
Manufacturing[b]	3,080	7.00
Delivery	1,373	3.12
Miscellaneous[c]	1,122	2.55
Cost of goods sold	11,409	25.93
Gross margin	6,741	15.32

[a]Net sales = P&G revenues.

[b]Manufacturing: 50 percent of manufacturing cost is fixed of which $200,000 is depreciation; 20 percent of manufacturing cost is labor.

[c]Miscellaneous: 75 percent of miscellaneous cost is fixed. General office overheads are $1,366,000. Taxes are 40 percent. Currently the plant operates on a five-day one-shift operation. P&G's weighted average cost of capital is 12 percent. Total units sold in 1990 were 440,000.

Source: Company records.

Advertising Agency

The Advertising Agency felt that making any new claims for Scope as a huge strategic shift for the brand. They favored a line extension. Scope's strategy had always been "breath refreshment and good tasting" focused, and they saw the plaque claims as very different, with potentially significant strategic implications. The one time they had focused advertising only on taste and didn't reinforce breath efficacy, share fell. They were concerned that the current Scope consumer could be confused if plaque

EXHIBIT 9

Plax Financial Estimates (Per Unit)

Net Sales	*65.09*
COGS	
Ingredients	6.50
Packaging	8.30
Manufacturing	6.50
Delivery	3.00
Miscellaneous	1.06
Total	25.36

Notes: General overhead costs estimated at $5.88/unit.

Source: P&G estimates.

or any "nonbreath" claims were added and that Scope could actually lose market share if this occurred. They also pointed out that trying to communicate two different ideas in one commercial was very difficult. They believed the line extension was a completely different product from Scope with a different benefit and use occasion. In their minds, a line extension would need to be supported on a going basis separately from Scope.

WHAT TO RECOMMEND?

Hearst knew the business team had thought long and hard about the issue. She knew that management was depending on the Scope business team to come up with the right long-term plan for P&G—even if that meant not introducing the new product. However, she felt there was too much risk associated with P&G's long-term position in oral rinses if nothing was done. There was no easy answer—and compounding the exigencies of the situation was the fact that the business team had differing points of view. She was faced with the dilemma of providing recommendations about Scope, but also needed to ensure that there was alignment and commitment from the business team, or Senior Management would be unlikely to agree to the proposal.

APPENDIX 1

Plaque

Plaque is a soft, sticky film that coats teeth within hours of brushing and may eventually harden into tartar. To curb gum disease—which over 90 percent of Canadians suffer at some time—plaque must be curbed. Research has shown that, without brushing, within 24 hours a film (plaque) starts to spread over teeth and gums and, over days, becomes a sticky, gelatinous mat, which the plaque bacteria spin from sugars and starches. As the plaque grows it becomes home to yet more bacteria— dozens of strains. A mature plaque is about 75 percent bacteria; the remainder consists of organic solids from saliva, water, and other cells shed from soft oral tissues.

As plaque bacteria digest food, they also manufacture irritating malodorous byproducts, all of which can harm a tooth's supporting tissues as they seep into the crevice below the gum line. Within 10 to 21 days, depending on the person, signs of gingivitis—the mildest gum disease—first appear; gums deepen in color, swell, and lose their normally tight, arching contour around teeth. Such gingivitis is entirely reversible. It can disappear within a week after regular brushing and flossing are resumed. But when plaque isn't kept under control, gingivitis can be the first step down toward periodontitis, the more advanced gum disease in which bone and other structures that support the teeth become damaged. Teeth can loosen and fall out— or require extraction.

The traditional and still best approach to plaque control is careful and thorough brushing and flossing to scrub teeth clean of plaque. Indeed, the antiplaque claims that toothpastes carry are usually based on the product's ability to clean teeth mechanically, with brushing. Toothpastes contain abrasives, detergent, and foaming agents, all of which help the brush do its work.

Source: "The Plaque Debate," *Canadian Consumer*, no. 9 (1990): 17–23.

Logitech

Early in the spring of 1990, Pierluigi Zappacosta, CEO of Logitech, reflected on the changing market conditions in North America and Europe and wondered what would be required to maintain and expand Logitech's position in the computer peripherals marketplace. Logitech had become one of three companies that dominated the global market for pointing devices for computers. While Logitech had captured a large unit share of the OEM (original equipment manufacturer) mouse market, Microsoft was the clear leader in terms of industry standards and dollar share of the retail market, and KYE (Genius), having a strong retail presence in Europe, was poised to compete aggressively in North America.

Pierluigi recognized that Logitech had been slow to react to changes in market conditions, such as the 1987 introduction of Microsoft's "white mouse," a shapely design that had developed considerable consumer appeal. This, combined with eroding margins on the OEM mouse business, had left Pierluigi wondering whether Logitech could maintain a leadership position in the pointing device market. Logitech had been successful in developing leadership positions in other niches, such as scanners, and other opportunities existed. Committed to their mission of "connecting the computer to the world" by giving it "senses," Pierluigi wondered what direction(s) the company should take and what the priorities should be.

COMPANY BACKGROUND

Logitech SA was founded in October 1981 by Zappacosta and Daniel Borel in Switzerland after Bobst Graphics, the company with which the two had been developing a European word processing/DTP package, was sold and the new owners did not want to continue the project. Pierluigi had met Daniel at Stanford University, while they were completing their MS (in computer science) degrees. After an initial attempt to bring U.S. technology to Europe with their own software company, Daniel, and then Pierluigi, had joined Bobst to gain industry contacts. They had then formed their own software company with Bobst as the major client. Giacomo Marini, a software manager at Olivetti and a friend of Pierluigi's from the time when they had both worked in Pisa, Italy, joined in founding Logitech together with a group of young engineers.

Two contracts set the stage for the initial growth and development of the organization. First, they won a $1 million contract with Ricoh to develop hardware and software for use with Ricoh printers and scanners. Shortly thereafter, Logitech won

This case was prepared by Brock Smith under the supervision of Professor Adrian B. Ryans for the sole purpose of providing material for class discussion at the Western Business School. Certain names and other identifying information may have been disguised to protect confidentiality. It is not intended to illustrate either effective or ineffective handling of a managerial situation. Any reproduction, in any form, of the material in this case is prohibited except with the written consent of the school. Copyright 1992 © The University of Western Ontario.

a contract with Swiss Timing to develop hardware and software for use at the Olympic Games. Wanting to be close to Ricoh and developments in Silicon Valley, Pierluigi, and later Daniel, and then Giacomo, moved to Palo Alto, California, and created Logitech Inc. In March 1982, Logitech Inc. learned of a Swiss watch company, Depraz, that had developed a mouse. Recognizing the advantages of the mouse relative to other pointing devices such as cursor keys, light pens, and touch screens, Logitech secured the rights to market the Depraz mouse in the United States and packaged it with software for the operation of text and graphics programs.

A major turning point in the strategic direction of the organization came after Logitech secured a contract with Hewlett-Packard to supply 25,000 mice under an OEM contract. It quickly became evident that Hewlett-Packard's price and quality requirements could not be met by Logitech's initial strategy of contracting out manufacturing to Depraz. Adhering to a philosophy of having direct control of the critical elements of the business, Logitech bought the rights to manufacture and market a mouse designed by CC Corporation. With help from Hewlett-Packard, Logitech redesigned the mouse for mass production and set up a manufacturing operation in Redwood City, California, in 1984. Production was moved to Fremont, California, in 1987 in a facility across the street from Logitech's U.S. headquarters.

Control over manufacturing and a commitment to quality led to rapid growth in the OEM mouse market with contracts from Apollo, Olivetti, AT&T, and other key computer manufacturers. However, Apple and IBM were wary of Logitech's manufacturing expertise and continued to buy most of their mice from Alps, a Japanese company operating in California, which had purchased Apple's keyboard and mouse facility and was the exclusive supplier to Microsoft.

In 1986 two events took place that would help solidify Logitech's future in the mouse market. First, due to slow growth in OEM sales, Logitech entered the retail market with the Series 7 mouse, a product that had been successful in the OEM market. Then, to win a piece of the Apple business and to satisfy the demands of OEM customers for Logitech to lower the cost of mice, Logitech set up a manufacturing base in Hsinchu, Taiwan, with an initial production capacity of 1 million mice per year, but potentially expandable to ten times that volume. In retrospect, Pierluigi thought they had been a bit lucky. For a $300,000 investment, they had secured a high-volume, state-of-the-art manufacturing plant in Taiwan's "Silicon Valley" just before Taiwan became a leader in manufacturing technology and a hot-bed of design creativity, and just as the mouse industry took off under the combined forces of Apple's Macintosh, desktop publishing, Microsoft's Windows, and other applications using graphical user interfaces.

In 1988, anticipating a unified Europe in 1992, and wanting to be close to Apple and potential customers such as IBM and Compaq in Europe, Logitech opened another manufacturing facility in Cork, Ireland, which had a capacity, similar to that of the Fremont plant, of about 1.5 million mice per year. At the same time, it broadened its product line with the introduction of a hand-held scanner, a product that shared some technological features with the mouse, that capitalized on Logitech's experience in software development, and that could be marketed through established retail channels.

By the end of 1989, Logitech had reached sales of over $100 million, employed about 1,000 people, had manufacturing facilities on three continents, and had sales offices in England, Germany, Italy, France, Japan, Sweden, Switzerland, the United States, and Taiwan.

CULTURE

The culture at Logitech reflected the global nature and operations of the organization. Because employees had varied life and educational experiences from around the globe, they were appreciative and accepting of differences in backgrounds, perspectives, and styles. As Fabio Righi, Vice President Sales and Marketing, put it: "Our greatest strength as well as our biggest challenge is that Logitech is an international company. It is difficult to be international and local at the same time. Local flavor affects/impacts everything."

Deeply rooted in the Logitech culture was a strong product/technical orientation. Employees gained considerable job satisfaction from being on the leading edge and working on bold, exciting projects. Fabio, for example, talked of the elusive "atomic mouse" like a Grail that helps define the common purpose of the employees. As senior executives admitted, employees tended to be quite internally focused and did not make a great effort to have their beliefs validated before launching a new product into the marketplace. As Ron McClure, Vice President Strategic Marketing, put it: "We are the most critical users of our products. Customer-need recognition is limited by their understanding of technology—they don't know what is possible!"

Related to this technical orientation was a strong design and production orientation. According to Chip Smith, Production Manager in Fremont, "Everything revolves around production. The floor, receiving and shipping, traffic, and order processing are key processes by which we satisfy consumers." Therefore, manufacturing was seen as a key marketing success factor.

There was also a strong spiritual component to the culture at Logitech. This was supported in part by the personal philosophies of the founders, but also by the shared vision that employees had for shaping the future. For example, aesthetics were a high priority, not only in the products, but also in the workplace itself. One might infer that if there was a Logitech company handbook, it would probably be *Zen and the Art of Motorcycle Maintenance*.

Working relationships at Logitech tended to be very informal, flexible, open, and close. Employees were genuinely excited to be on the leading edge and found their jobs and the "family" atmosphere fun. This "family" atmosphere was reinforced by Logitech's policy of hiring talented young professionals from around the world and relocating them to enrich their own and others' perspectives. Dislocated from their own families and culture, employees often relied on one another for social, emotional, and cultural support.

Consistent with the informal, close working relationships, there were few formal procedures and structures within Logitech. Executive decisions were generally made by consensus after seeking employee input. Worldwide interaction of management and staff was maintained on a daily basis by an electronic mail system.

BUSINESS STRATEGY

Pierluigi explained the long-term Logitech vision by saying: "Only if the computer becomes a little more human will it become an effective tool for the mind. And evolution of our own brain through computers is our long-term vision. Our more immediate mission is to connect the computer with the world by giving it 'senses,' humanize the interface to the computer, and help people turn data into meaningful information. Our goals are to maintain/attain the number one position in whatever markets we play in by redefining and continually changing the products and markets we compete in. We want to have a Logitech product on every computer desk."

To achieve its mission and objectives, Logitech's business strategy was to recognize major trends and technologies early, move fast in bringing quality products to market (forming alliances if necessary), develop in-house expertise for product extensions, become effective and efficient manufacturers, have the best salesforce and channels to sell the products, and keep ahead of the competition by an accelerated pace of innovation.

Logitech competed aggressively in both the OEM and retail sides of the personal computer accessory business. On the OEM side of the business, it competed using innovation and skill in manufacturing and design that allowed it to bring new technology to market at very competitive prices (see estimated manufacturing costs in Exhibit 1). Toward this end, Logitech had achieved an experience curve in mouse manufacturing of about 70 percent. On the retail side of the business, Logitech focused on image management. It wanted to be perceived in the marketplace as an innovator that developed neat products that were fun to use and were easy to sell.

About 60 percent of Logitech's unit sales were in the OEM segment, but more than 60 percent of its revenue came from the retail segment. In both the OEM and retail markets, Logitech's financial success (see Exhibit 2) had been, and would continue to be, tied to the development and growth of the PC marketplace and recognition of the need to "humanize" the computer.

PRODUCT DEVELOPMENT

Product development at Logitech involved finding or developing technologies that required Logitech's skills in design, mass manufacturing, and distribution to bring them to market. Logitech had three basic development strategies: Start from scratch, evolve current in-house technology, or buy required technology at an advanced development stage from others. Starting from scratch added about a year to the product development process, since employees had to learn about a technology, decide

EXHIBIT 1

Estimated Manufacturing Costs and Selling Prices

Mouse	Estimated Manufacturing Cost (January 1990)	Estimated Average Selling Price to Channel
Logitech S9	$25.00	$60.00
Microsoft mouse	27.00	75.00
Pilot mouse	17.40	33.00
Dexxa	16.30	19.50
Logitech OEM	15.20	22.00
Taiwanese OEM	13.10	16.50
Ergonomic (corded)	19.60	Not on the market
Ergonomic (cordless)	64.30	Not on the market

Source: Company records.

what to develop, and test product concepts. Building on current expertise to extend or develop new generations of products was the most common approach taken. If required technology was not available internally, then Logitech would buy it, make minor adjustments to bring it to market, then develop internally the skills required or product evolution.

Decisions on product development were usually based on consensus among senior managers and tended to be emotional and based on "gut feel" rather than extensive analysis and research. Some of the decision criteria that were considered, however, included licensing or development costs, manufacturing cost, margins, a six-month payback, whether it was going to be fun to work on, and whether the product could gain a 40 percent share of its market. Focus groups were sometimes used late in the process to validate the "gut feelings." However, Pierluigi recognized that more effort was needed to get qualitative feedback at earlier stages of the product-development cycle.

EXHIBIT 2

Selected Financial Data for Logitech SA (In Swiss Francs)

	Full Year Ending			
	3/31/87	3/31/88	3/31/89	3/31/90 (projected)
Consolidated revenue	$ 33,543,351	$ 62,806,740	$ 124,110,684	$ 180,000,000
Net income after tax	$ 1,459,888	$ 7,032,066	11,206,922	$ 14,000,000
Percentage of revenues	4.35%	11.20%	9.03%	7.78%
Cash flow	$ 2,136,959	$ 9,413,623	$ 14,290,273	$ 17,500,000
Percentage of revenues	6.37%	14.99%	11.51%	9.72%
Earnings per bearer share	—	$54	$76	$96
Dividend per bearer share	—	—	$12	$16
Engineering, research and development expenses	$ 2,579,023	$ 4,663,430	$ 8,396,799	$ 13,700,000
Percentage of revenues	7.69%	7.43%	6.77%	7.61%
Number of personnel	240	442	731	1,000
Current assets	$ 12,117,422	$ 27,026,936	$ 75,526,814	$ 108,000,000
Property, plant, and equipment gross less accumulated depreciation	6,212,338 (1,412,316)	8,843,297 (2,139,330)	22,421,727 (5,222,681)	30,600,000 (8,500,000)
property, plant, and equipment net	4,800,022	6,703,967	17,199,046	22,100,000
Other noncurrent assets	328,775	2,273,945	1,184,542	3,900,000
Goodwill	0	14,214,241	13,093,605	11,200,000
Total assets	$ 17,246,219	$ 50,219,089	$ 107,004,007	$ 145,280,000
Current liabilities	8,945,618	18,701,970	36,775,490	37,200,000
Long-term debt and deferred taxes	3,858,044	5,517,119	10,541,326	43,500,000
Stockholders' equity	4,442,557	26,000,000	59,687,191	69,500,000
Total liabilities and stockholders' equity	$ 17,246,219	$ 50,219,089	$ 107,004,007	$ 145,200,000

EXHIBIT 2 (*continued*)

	1988	*1989*
Net sales	$ 62,806,740	$ 124,110,684
Cost of goods sold	30,921,004	71,493,833
Gross profit	$ 31,885,736	$ 52,616,851
Operating expenses		
Marketing, sales, and support	10,070,523	21,081,432
General and administration	5,553,719	10,276,622
Research, development, and engineering	4,663,430	8,396,799
	$ 20,287,672	$ 39,754,853
Income from operations	$ 11,598,064	$ 12,861,998
Other expenses, net	191,569	59,656
Income before income taxes	11,406,495	12,802,342
Provision for taxes on income	4,374,429	1,595,420
Net income	$ 7,032,066	$ 11,206,922

At any given time there were 20–30 official projects in various stages of development, as well as others that were "unofficial." The major projects were managed by multifunctional new product teams. Currently, there was no central authority on any particular project, but Pierluigi recognized the need to have someone who knew how the whole picture was coming together. Logitech was spending over 7 percent of sales on R&D and money could be found for important projects. Pierluigi thought the biggest problem that Logitech faced in new product development was not getting caught up in "the fun of it."

PERSONAL COMPUTER INDUSTRY

After five years of rapid growth, the PC industry was in turmoil in early 1990. The initial standards established by IBM and Apple had given way to a confusing array of technologies, including IBM's Micro-Channel, EISA (the Micro-Channel alternative offered by Compaq and six other major vendors), RISC (various versions of reduced instruction set computing used primarily by engineering/scientific workstations running under the Unix operating system), and Apple's Macintosh. Confusing matters even more were competing operating systems such as DOS, OS/2, and Unix and competing graphical user interfaces such as Microsoft's Windows (version 2), IBM's Presentation Manager, the Open Systems Foundation's "X," AT&T's Unix System 5, and NeXT's "NeXtStep." All of these competing operating system and user interfaces, however, used mice or another pointing device to control the operating environment. While it was expected that graphical user interfaces would be adopted on most, if not all, systems, the rate of adoption would depend heavily on the success of Microsoft's newly announced Windows 3.0 for DOS and IBM's OS/2.

The industry itself exhibited characteristics of the maturity phase of the product life cycle. Competition was intense, and a shakeout of the market was under way, which affected even some relatively large companies. Consumers were generally even more sophisticated and knowledgeable and did not require the same level of support and sales assistance that they had a few years earlier. Consequently, manufacturers were beginning to make inroads through alternative channels such as mail order, price clubs, and superstores, while traditional full-service retailers such as ComputerLand and Business Land were refocusing their efforts on organizations using outbound direct salesforces. Personal computers themselves were quickly becoming commodity items as limited product differentiation, short technology life cycles, and steep experience curves combined to put substantial downward pressure on prices. With the early mystique of computers wearing off, users, and in particular corporations, were beginning to question and evaluate the impact of computer technology on employee productivity, health, and other aspects of organizational life. Stress injuries, for example, were gaining prominence and were being linked to workplace computer operation. One of these was carpal tunnel syndrome, which involved painful damage to the nerve that runs through the arm as a result of repetitive strain from the use of typewriters, computers, and other arm- or hand-operated equipment. Carpal tunnel syndrome had received considerable media attention (see example in Exhibit 3) and a recent ordinance in California required corporations to take measures to reduce this type of workplace injury. Other concerns were also being raised about cathode ray tubes in terms of possible harmful emissions from computer screens and in terms of eye strain. Thus, while unit growth in the PC industry was expected to be in the 10–15 percent range, profits were eroding and consumers were becoming more critical and discerning.

THE MOUSE MARKETPLACE

In the computer sense, "mice" are hand-held mobile devices that use a combination of hardware and software to translate physical movement into digital signals that control cursor movement on a computer screen and execute commands. Named for their basic shape, mice (and trackballs) were more precise and flexible than other pointing devices such as light pens, touch screens, and cursor keys and were generally more intuitive and easier to use. While the first mice developed in the 1960s were mechanical in design and were used predominantly by engineers, mice were now mostly opto-mechanical in technology and were used by a wide variety of users, including children, for a variety of applications ranging from drawing to interacting with most business software.

Market Development

In December 1985, Logitech entered the retail mouse market, first in North America and then in Europe, with the Logitech mouse, a retail version of its successful Series 7 OEM mouse. Adopting a penetration strategy for the more knowledgeable and price-sensitive North American market, Logitech priced the Logitech mouse at $99 (U.S. currency), about half the suggested price of both the Microsoft mouse and the mouse offered by Mouse Systems Corporation (the first into the U.S. market). Targeting the computer "techies," Logitech initially sold the Logitech mouse directly

EXHIBIT 3

Carpal Tunnel Syndrome

Repetitive Strain Repetitive Pain: Carpal Tunnel Becomes Major Workplace Hazard

By HIMANEE GUPTA

. . . Throughout the country and in Puget Sound, companies are realizing the painful, often crippling condition [carpal tunnel syndrome] has grown into a major workplace hazard. No one's sure just when and how hard it will hit, but any worker who types at computers, works with electronic scanners or regularly performs other repetitive tasks on automated equipment is at risk.

Carpal tunnel syndrome, one of several ailments known as repetitive strain injuries, occurs when constant bending of the hands, wrists and arms inflames tendons that squeeze the main nerve that runs through the arm. . . . The problems start with swelling, tingling and discomfort, and can wind up causing numbness, severe pain and paralysis. Treatment often means slow, painful therapy or surgery followed by therapy. And in terms of treatment, therapy and disability claims, the costs for employers can be enormous . . .

In 1988, the state Department of Labor and Industries paid $6.5 million for 1,910 workers' compensation claims filed for carpal tunnel syndrome. That compares with 1,228 claims in 1986 and 123 in 1979.

Source: Seattle Times, September 18, 1989, Section F, p. 1.

Pressing for New Ways to Type

By RONALD ROEL

. . . Hodges is one of a handful of iconoclasts promoting radical alternatives to today's conventional keyboard designs. Their devices, which so far have been roundly rejected by the big U.S. keyboard makers, range from variations on Hodges' split keyboard to keys that are moved much like a computer mouse. Like Hodges, most keyboard inventors say their passion for change has been spurred, in part, by an interest in reducing hand and wrist injuries, known as repetitive strain injuries, or RSI, experienced by thousands of computer users each year. Some medical experts believe that conventional flat keyboard designs may contribute to RSI . . .

IBM and other major manufacturers say they have no plans to radically change the keyboards used by 25 million office workers. If big changes are made within the next decade, it will probably be to eliminate the keyboard altogether, substituting them with other inputting devices that convert handwriting or human speech directly to computer print, says Maryann Karinch, a spokeswomen for the Computer and Business Equipment Manufacturers' Association, a Washington D.C.–based trade group.

Source: Newsday, October 22, 1989, Section 1, p. 71.

to consumers by soliciting phone and mail orders in trade publications. Initial success generated sufficient market pull to enable Logitech to establish a dealer network and increase the price of mouse by 10–20 percent. In the less-sophisticated European market, Logitech followed Microsoft's lead and used a skimming price strategy, charging about 30 percent more than it did in the United States. Instead of using mail order for distribution, Logitech developed relationships with a strong dealer network in Europe, who were able to support higher prices and margins by meeting the full-service needs of customers with high quality and prestige image products. In 1987, Microsoft launched its new ergonomic "white mouse," for $200 in the United States but $350 in Europe. Logitech were slow to react and did not bring out their Microsoft-compatible Series 9 mouse until 1988. This new mouse was priced about 20 percent below Microsoft in North America and Europe. At this time, Logitech also introduced a "low-end" mouse under the Dexxa brand name to compete against the more than 20 Taiwanese manufacturers, who were pricing their mice in the $20–$35 range. These Taiwanese manufacturers had captured about 40 percent unit market share, compared to the 30 percent unit share of both Logitech and Microsoft in the United States and Europe.

Supporting their R&D efforts from their high margins in Europe, both Logitech and Microsoft were slow to react to changes in the increasingly sophisticated and price-conscious European market. KYE (Genius), the largest of the Taiwanese manufacturers, had introduced a high-quality mouse at $50 in mid-1988 and had captured a major share of the European market. In response, Microsoft and Logitech lowered their prices to $200 and $180, respectively, and Logitech began developing a new mouse at a price of $50–$60. This new "Pilot Mouse" was introduced in Europe at the end of 1989. Microsoft had unbundled its "paint" software from its mouse in the United States, and had lowered the price to within 20 percent of Logitech's. KYE (Genius) had just bought Mouse Systems Corporation and was poised to bring its "Genius" product into the United States under the Mouse Systems brand name, which had a strong user recognition despite its decreasing market share.

The positioning of the major mouse vendors in Europe and North America in early 1990 is shown in Exhibit 4. Worldwide dollar market shares were approximately 40–45 percent of Microsoft, 30 percent for Logitech, and 20 percent for KYE/Mouse Systems. Demand for mice was expected to grow about 50 percent in 1990 and only slightly less in the foreseeable future due to trends toward graphical user interfaces. Sales of portables and laptops were expected to grow 22 percent in 1990 to 1.2 million units (14 percent of the PC market) and were expected to account for almost half of PC sales within a few years. Manufacturers of these computers would have to offer a built-in pointing device. Mice or trackballs seemed to be the logical choice for these pointing devices, but other technologies involving track pens and pen-based computing would likely play an increased role. Moreover, there would be increasing retail demand for replacement products and upgrades. Industry observers expected KYE (Genius) to experience unit sales growth of 60 percent in 1990. Microsoft was expected to experience 50 percent growth, and Logitech was expected to experience slightly lower growth. Logitech's retail sales were expected to remain at 40 percent of total unit sales in 1990. Previous years' unit sales are presented in Exhibit 5.

Buyer Behavior

The mouse marketplace could be segmented into home/personal users, home/business users, and corporate and educational users. Home/personal buyers, who accounted for about 48 percent of Logitech retail sales, were thought to be more price-sensitive than other segments and were less concerned about compatibility with software that they did not yet own. These consumers tended to buy from discount houses or no-frills dealers and would choose among the alternative mice avail-

EXHIBIT 4

Positioning of Products in the Retail Market in January 1990

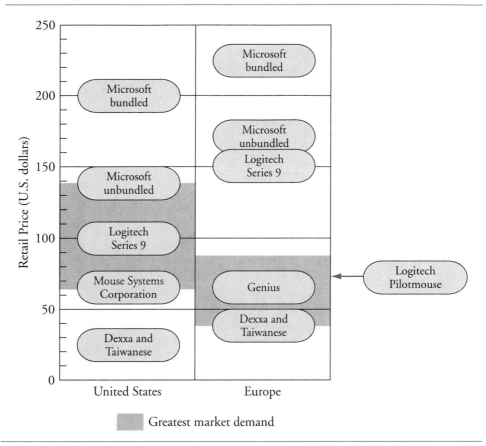

able at the most convenient location. Home/business buyers, representing about 26 percent of Logitech's retail sales, were thought to be value- and brand-conscious, but less concerned about compatibility than corporate users. These consumers were thought to be influenced by articles in *PC World, Byte*, and other trade magazines, and to a lesser extent, advertisements in those magazines. Word-of-mouth and sales

EXHIBIT 5

Estimated World Retail Sales (In Thousands of Units)

Calendar year	Logitech	Microsoft	Mouse Systems	Other	Total Retail	Percentage of Total Market
1988	577	803	630	361	2,371	35
1989	883	1,321	554	400	3,158	40

Source: Company records.

representative recommendations were thought to have the most influence of all. Finally, corporate buyers, representing 25 percent of Logitech's retail sales but 50 percent of Microsoft's, were thought to be more concerned with the brand name of a mouse and its likely compatibility with future hardware and software products. If use of the mouse was "mission critical" in the sense of being tied to productivity or used extensively, corporate buyers tended to play it safe and bought Microsoft.

While the profile of the Logitech mouse buyer was not completely understood, Logitech did keep track of who its retail customers were. Some 82 percent were desktop users and 48 percent of buyers were also the users. For 60 percent, the Logitech mouse was the second mouse they had purchased, and 27 percent bought the mouse "bundled" with a paint program. Some 50 percent purchased the product at a retail store, 26 percent at a superstore, and 13 percent through mail order. Forty percent made the brand decision at the store. In terms of demographics, 80 percent were male, 55 percent were aged 30–45, and over 60 percent had five or more years of computer experience.

Competition

On the retail end of the business, the major competitors were Microsoft, Logitech, and Mouse Systems/Genius. Microsoft was positioned as the compatibility leader for both hardware and software and marketed its product to the premium, brand-conscious segment. It used its software reputation to help sell mice, and often bundled its mouse with Microsoft programs that required one. The second major competitor, Mouse Systems, was a bit of an enigma. It traditionally competed aggressively on price and promotions, but had limited resources and product quality was not believed to be as high as Logitech's or Microsoft's. However, with KYE's purchase of Mouse Systems, KYE was now claiming to be the largest mouse producer in the world (in terms of units) and was expected to become a force in North America.

On the OEM end of the business, Logitech's main competitors were Alps and Mitsumi (the two Japanese companies that supplied Microsoft), KYE/Mouse Systems, Z-nix, Truedox, and Primax and Silitec (Taiwanese manufacturers). Primax and Silitec were suppliers to Packard Bell, the fourth-largest PC vendor. All these competitors competed aggressively on price, resulting in low margins and profits. While Logitech felt it had a superior product both technically and in terms of quality, new users often could not tell the difference and most products met their basic needs.

LOGITECH'S POSITIONING AND MARKETING STRATEGY

Logitech's overall mouse strategy was to compress technology life cycles and give consumers more options for increasing productivity. It competed by developing innovative designs and technologies, producing high-quality products, and pricing the products to deliver good customer value. It aggressively managed its costs and tried to maintain strong relationships with its distributors. Traditionally, its products had been positioned to attract the serious and technically oriented user, but were now also attracting creative and aesthetically oriented users looking for fun, form, and function. This overall strategy had led to an increase in unit sales of over 74 percent in 1989, but because the average selling price had decreased 22 percent, revenues increased at only about half the rate of unit sales.

Product Strategy

Logitech's product strategy was to develop products that were consistent with, but not obvious extensions of, current offerings. The image it was attempting to develop was that Logitech offered neat products that were fun to use. Marketed under the theme "tools for the imagination," Logitech's current retail product offering included the Logitech (Series 9) mouse, the Pilot (Series 15) mouse (in Europe only), the Dexxa brand mouse, Trackman (a trackball pointing device), ScanMan (a hand-held scanner), and utility software (desktop publishing, a DOS management shell, a paint program, and character recognition). The mice were sold unbundled or bundled with popular software such as Microsoft's Windows (Exhibit 6). On the OEM side,

EXHIBIT 6

Illustrative Product Literature

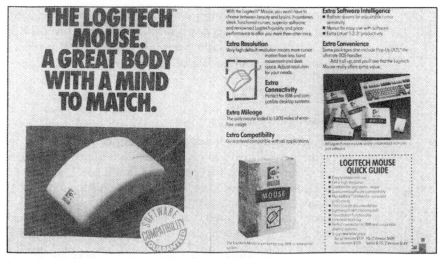

it offered the Series 9 mouse (a three-button, Microsoft-compatible mouse), the Series 14 mouse (a uniquely shaped two-button, Microsoft-compatible mouse that was expected to be very popular), and the new Series 15 mouse.

Pricing Strategy

Logitech's pricing strategy was to support a street price $10–$20 below Microsoft by differential channel pricing. This involved starting with a target street price and working back to the manufacturer's selling price using the margins expected by different channels. This was particularly tricky, since different channels had very different expectations. Electronic superstores and price clubs worked with 8–25 percent margins, while traditional dealers and department stores worked with 30–40 percent margins, and stores would carry the Logitech product only if they could get their margin. Pricing was further complicated by grey marketing and cross-channel ownership. The former would arise if differential pricing in different countries created opportunities for the product to be bought by distributors in one market to be sold at a profit in another. The latter arose if a holding company owned more than one type of Logitech distributor and was able to supply a superstore, for example, with a product bought for a full-service dealer. Estimated average wholesale prices for Logitech's and Microsoft's mice products are presented in Exhibit 1.

Distribution and Sales Strategy

Logitech used a mix of direct sales, telemarketing, and distributors to achieve its objective of intensive distribution. Six OEM sales reps backed by 11 support staff managed ongoing relationships with key customers. On the retail side, Logitech had four retail channel groups: major retail and corporate accounts, education/government, international corporate accounts, and other retail chains or independents. While traditionally Logitech's salesforce had focused on developing channel relationships, management had increasing concerns about the lack of inroads made into corporate markets. Where Microsoft marketed directly to major corporations, Logitech had tried to reach the corporations through dealers.

Logitech's distribution goals were to be everywhere it could be, to have as many stock-keeping units as possible in each store to maximize its shelf space, and to maintain strong distributor relationships. This required utilizing a mix of wholesaling intermediaries and retailers ranging from small independent computer stores to major international chains. Logitech believed it had successfully covered 98 percent of the market with its distribution strategy and led the industry with 50 percent coverage in the rapidly growing channel of consumer electronic superstores. However, it actively sought alternative channels of distribution, such as mail-order and telemarketing, as the industry matured and evolved toward commodity products.

Communication Strategy

Logitech's communication strategy had traditionally been a no-nonsense cognitive feature-function-benefit approach designed to present solutions to customer needs. Wanting to develop an upscale image and develop greater affective appeal, Logitech created a new avant-garde visual identity and logo in January 1989. Although Logitech wanted to create an image of being a market leader in design and quality, and to communicate core product benefits of fun, creative freedom, and solution uniqueness, change was not achieved overnight. By the spring of 1990, some Logitech executives were concerned that they had not yet achieved a consistent feeling with their communication strategy. They had used a wide variety of communication media to spread their messages, but relied heavily on print advertising in trade magazines as well as point-of-purchase materials and packaging. Logitech also paid particular attention to cooperative advertising and special channel programs to motivate and support distributors.

THE SITUATION IN EARLY 1990

While Pierluigi was happy with the performance of Logitech, he was concerned with Logitech's ability to maintain margins in the mouse marketplace and wondered how he could maintain the current rate of growth and profitability into the 1990s. The Series 9 mouse had been a success, but it had been a quick response to Microsoft's sleek redesign and was not perceived internally as leading edge. As most mice now provided the same level of productivity, Pierluigi felt that a move toward ergonomic differentiation might be appropriate. Shortly after the launch of the Series 9 mouse, Logitech had begun developing two versions of a new ergonomic mouse based on the technology of the Series 9. One of these was designed specifically for right-handed users and the other for left-handed users. These new designs were shaped to fit the curve of the hand at rest and would help reduce repetitive stress problems, such as carpel tunnel syndrome. Prototypes of the ergonomic mouse had been completed (Exhibit 7) and had been received well in focus groups. In a second mouse development, Logitech engineers had developed a radio "cordless" mouse that could be used to control a computer without the impediment of a cord and without the line-of-sight requirement of an infrared mouse. This technology could be packaged in the Series 9 mouse shape or the new ergonomic mouse shape at a price about $100 higher than a corded mouse. Finally, Logitech had developed technology for

EXHIBIT 7

Mouse Prototypes

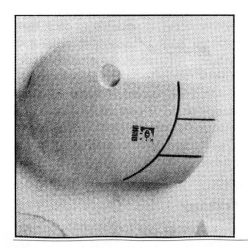 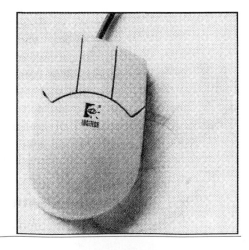

a three-dimensional mouse that showed promise for high-end CAD/CAM and design applications.

Pierluigi had to decide whether to launch one, two, or all of these new products, and if so, how. The cordless mouse and the 3-D mouse were "neat" from a technological perspective and had generated some excitement among the engineers. The ergonomic mouse was not particularly exciting from a technological perspective, but it might help differentiate the Logitech product in the marketplace. In addition, it might provide a "foot in the door" for attracting corporate business. However, from a strategic perspective, not everyone was comfortable with the right- and left-handed approach. Ron McClure, Vice President Strategic Marketing, had expressed concerns about the potential reception for the product among corporate customers and resellers. Corporate buyers would probably not know whether the user would be left-handed or right-handed, and many mice would be shared by multiple users. It was not clear, for example, how a purchaser for a school lab would decide how many right-handed versions and how many left-handed versions to buy. Corporate users also might not have much input into the purchase decision to specify brand preference. The "safe" corporate strategy would be to buy a generic "one type fits all" mouse. Ron had a similar concern about OEM customers. An OEM usually bundled the Logitech mouse with the OEM's software or hardware and would probably not want to package left-handed and right-handed versions. Resistance to the new ergonomic mouse was also based on three other factors. Distributor representatives said it could be an SKU nightmare for resellers if they had to carry left- and right-handed, corded and cordless mice as well as the current bus, serial port, mouseport, serial and mouseport, IBM and Apple versions, bundled or unbundled. Many employees were concerned that it would be the first Logitech product launched that was not based purely on a technological innovation/advantage. Finally, for many of the reasons outlined above, Logitech SA did not think they would want to launch the product in Europe.

While Logitech had been built on mouse technology, there were other directions that seemed to have great long-term potential. Scanner technology was similar to mouse technology, and Logitech's handheld ScanMan had been a great success in terms of market share, margins, and product image. Driven by increased demand for desktop publishing and multimedia solutions, the scanner market was expected to grow 25–30 percent per year, and opportunities existed to produce better greyscale or even color scanners. Another opportunity related to scanners would be to develop a digital camera that captured black and white images and downloaded them to a computer. Finally, the interactive gloves developed for computer games might be improved on to use with computers.

There were lots of neat products to develop, but Pierluigi knew he needed to act strategically. Personally, he was a strong champion of the new ergonomic mouse, but he recognized that it might be risky. The product was ready to launch and he could not put off the decision much longer. He wondered, if they did launch, how it should be done. Would this be an addition to the line or a replacement? How could Europe be convinced to carry the product? Should the cordless mouse be launched as part of the new ergonomic product line, or separately, or not at all? How should the products be priced? How would Microsoft react? Would pursuit of other opportunities be a better use of resources? Pierluigi thought the best place to start looking for answers and directions was in their mission statement and long-term vision. He wondered whether "humanizing the computer" by giving senses to the computer adequately reflected their current and potential operation.

CHAPTER 7

Marketing Communication Strategy and Management

 Marketing communication is the process by which information about an organization and its offerings is disseminated to selected markets. Given the role communication plays in facilitating mutually beneficial exchange relationships between an organization and prospective buyers, its importance cannot be overstated. The goal of communication is not just to induce initial purchases; it is also to achieve postpurchase satisfaction, thus increasing the probability of repeat sales. Even if prospective buyers possessed a pressing need and an organization possessed an offering that precisely met that need, no exchange would occur without communication. Communication is necessary to inform buyers of the following:

- The availability of an offering
- The unique benefits of the offering
- The where and how of obtaining and using the offering

Exactly how potential buyers are to be informed—the actual message communicated—is one of the most subjective communication decisions. Although message development can be somewhat aided by research, there are no guaranteed message strategies available for all offerings, markets, or organizations. Each individual situation must determine whether the message is to be hard-sell, fearful, humorous, or informational. Whatever message format is chosen, the message communicated should be desirable to those to whom it is directed, exclusive or unique to the offering being described, and believable in terms of the benefit claims made for the offering.

It is the task of the marketing manager to manage the communication process most effectively. Marketing managers have at their disposal specific communication activities, often called *elements, functions, tools,* or *tasks.* These include advertising, personal selling, and sales promotion. Collectively, the activities are termed the *marketing communication mix.*[1] Elements of the communication mix range from very flexible (for example, personal selling) to very inflexible (for example, mass advertising), and each has a unique set of characteristics and capabilities. To a certain ex-

271

tent, however, they are interchangeable and substitutable. It is the responsibility of the marketing manager to find the most effective communication mix at the least possible cost.

Marketing managers should not limit their thinking to which communication activity to use when designing communication strategies. Rather, the real issue is which activity should be emphasized, how intensely it should be applied, and how communication activities can be most effectively combined and coordinated. Rare is the organization that employs only one form of communication. In a single communication strategy, all three communication activities might be used simultaneously. For instance, advertising activities might be employed to develop offering awareness and comprehension; sales promotion might be used to increase purchase intention; and personal selling might be utilized to obtain final conviction and purchase.

ANALYTICAL COMMUNICATION STRATEGY FRAMEWORK

From a managerial perspective, the formulation of a marketing communication strategy requires six major decisions. Once the offering and target markets have been defined, the manager must consider the following decisions:

1. What are the information requirements of target markets as they proceed through the purchase process?
2. What objectives must the communication strategy achieve?
3. Which specific mix of communication activities should be employed in conveying information to target markets?
4. How much should be budgeted for communicating with target markets, and in what manner should resources be allocated among various communication activities?
5. How should the communication be timed and scheduled?
6. How should the communication process be evaluated as to its effectiveness, and how should it be controlled?

Theoretically, these questions are distinct and thus can be approached in a sequential manner. In practice, however, they are likely to be approached simultaneously, since they are closely interrelated.

INFORMATION REQUIREMENTS IN PURCHASE DECISIONS

The first step in designing a communication strategy is to determine how buyers purchase a particular offering and to define the role of information in the purchase process.[2] This often requires use of a purchase-process (or adoption-process) model. Usually, such a model treats buyers as though they were moved through a series of sequential stages in their purchase processes, such as

Unawareness → Knowledge → Preference → Purchase

At any point in time, different buyers are in different stages of the model, and each stage requires a different communication strategy.

Most models allow the marketing manager to distinguish between solitary and joint decision making. In any purchase decision, the person or persons involved can play several possible roles—purchaser, influencer, decision maker, and or consumer. In certain purchase situations, one individual may play more than one role. In other purchase situations, such as a joint purchase decision, the roles may be played by different individuals. Whereas a mother may be the family member who purchases breakfast cereal, her children may influence the brand purchased, and the father may consume the product. A similar situation could exist in an industrial setting. A purchasing agent may be the buyer, an engineer the influencer and decision maker, and a technician the user. Understanding who is playing the roles is a prerequisite for successfully determining what the communication message should be, as well as to whom it should be directed and how it should be communicated.

Similarly, the process used by buyers to purchase an offering influences the role of information, and hence the most effective communication strategy. For example, in industrial settings purchasing procedures are often prescribed. Therefore, understanding when, where, how, and what information is employed in the purchase decision will enable an organization to direct the proper communication to the proper individual at the proper time.[3] These remarks also apply to communication directed toward consumers. Consider the case of consumers making a decision to buy a house. To communicate effectively, an organization must know *what* information these consumers think is necessary (price, location, size), *where* they will seek it (newspapers, brokers, friends), *when* they will seek it (how far in advance, on what days), and *how* they will apply the information once obtained. Advances in database direct marketing, which enable identification of prospective buyers who have a predisposition to purchase certain products and services and who are accessible through mail and telephone solicitation, have made the communication process even more effective. For instance, Kimberly-Clark Corporation, the maker of Huggies diapers, buys mailing lists of new mothers and sends coupons, child-care tips, and new-product information to them during their babies' diaper-wearing stage.[4]

Finally, the way in which buyers perceive an organization and its offering is closely related to their information needs. The perceived importance of the offering and the perceived risk in making an incorrect purchase decision influence the extent to which buyers receive information, as well as their choice of information source(s). The more important or risky an offering is perceived to be (because of large dollar outlays, ego involvement, or health and safety reasons), the more likely it is that buyers will seek information from sources other than the organization providing the offering.

REASONABLE COMMUNICATION OBJECTIVES

The objectives set for communication programs will depend on the overall offering-market strategies of the organization and the stage of the product's life cycle. Communication objectives will differ according to whether the strategy being employed is market penetration, market development, or product development. For instance, a penetration strategy will suggest communication objectives that emphasize more frequent offering usage or that build preference for or loyalty to the offering. On the other hand, a market development strategy will encourage communication that will stimulate awareness and trial of the offering.

Life-cycle stage plays a role in determining whether communication objectives should stimulate primary demand or selective demand. Early in the life cycle, communication efforts focus on stimulating primary demand—demand for the product or service category, such as dairy products, personal computers, or family planning. Typically, the message conveyed focuses on introducing the benefits of a product or service or overcoming objections to the product or service. Later in the life cycle, when substitute products or services exist, communication efforts focus on stimulating selective demand—demand for a particular brand or product/service. Typically, the message conveyed extols the benefits of a particular competitive offering and seeks to differentiate that offering from others.

Objectives must also be delineated for individual communication tools. Both general and specific communication objectives need to relate directly to the tasks that the tools are to accomplish. Communication objectives and the tasks must be reasonable—*consistent* both among themselves and with other marketing elements, *quantifiable* for measurement and control purposes, and *attainable* with an appropriate amount of effort and expenditure.

COMMUNICATION MIX

Development of an appropriate communication activities mix requires the assignment of relative weights to particular communication activities, based on communication objectives. Although no established guidelines exist for designing an optimal communication mix, several factors that influence the mix need to be considered. These factors are:

- The information requirements of potential buyers
- The nature of the offering
- The nature of the target markets
- The capacity of the organization

Information Requirements of Buyers

As a starting point in determining the communication mix, an analysis of the relative value of the communication tools used at various stages in the purchase-decision process ought to be undertaken. Consider the purchase-decision process for a new automobile. Through advertising, manufacturers seek to stimulate awareness of the new models and to indicate where they can be purchased. Sales personnel provide information on specific options available, financing, and delivery. Sales promotion brochures and catalogs provide descriptions of performance characteristics and other salient features. Which communication tool has the greatest impact on prospective buyers? The answer to this question, while admittedly difficult to arrive at, will lead to a weighing of the importance of the communication tools. The manager will achieve an effective communication mix only by understanding the information requirements of potential buyers and by meeting those requirements with the appropriate communication-mix elements.

Nature of the Offering

A major consideration in developing the communication mix is the organization's offering. A highly technical offering, one with benefits not readily apparent (such as performance or quality), or one that is relatively expensive is likely to require personal selling. On the one hand, advertising is a potent communication tool when the offering is not complex, is frequently purchased, is relatively inexpensive, or has benefits that readily differentiate it from competing offerings. Sales promotion lends itself to nearly every offering type because of the wide variety of forms it can assume. Its main use, however, is to induce immediate action on frequently purchased products.

Target-Market Characteristics

The nature of the target market is another consideration. A target market comprising a small number of potential buyers, existing in close proximity to one another and each purchasing in large quantities, might suggest a personal selling strategy. In contrast, a mass market that is geographically scattered generally calls for an emphasis on advertising. However, firms are finding that direct marketing also can be used to reach a geographically dispersed target market. This realization has led many firms to substitute mail and telephone solicitations for media (radio, print, and television) advertising.[5]

Organizational Capacity

A fourth consideration is the ability or willingness of the organization to undertake certain communication activities. The organization is continually faced with *make-or-buy decisions*. If an organization decides to employ a particular communication activity, should it perform the activity internally (that is, make it) or contract it out (in other words, buy it)?

One such make-or-buy decision is the choice between a company sales force and independent sales representatives.[6] The decision has both economic and behavioral dimensions. The economic dimension relates to the issue of fixed versus variable costs. The cost of independent representatives is variable; they are paid on sales commission only. A company sales force, on the other hand, typically includes a variable-cost element *and* a fixed-cost component. If independent representatives fail to sell, no costs are incurred; however, if a company sales force fails to sell, the fixed costs still have to be paid. These concepts are useful in determining whether independent representatives or company representatives are more cost-effective at different sales levels.

Suppose independent representatives received a 5 percent commission on sales and company sales personnel received a 3 percent commission in addition to incurring a salary and administration cost of $500,000. At what sales level would company representatives become more or less costly than independent representatives? This question can be resolved by setting the cost equations for both types of representatives equal to each other and solving for the sales level amount, as follows:

$$\underset{0.03(x) + \$500,000}{\text{Cost of company reps}} = \underset{0.05(x)}{\text{Cost of independent reps}}$$

where x = sales volume. Solving for x, we get $25 million as the sales volume at which the costs of company and independent reps are equal.

The calculation indicates that if the sales volume were below $25 million, the independent representative would be cheaper; above that amount, the company sales force would be cheaper. Of course, a fundamental issue is the likelihood of achieving a $25 million sales level, which in turn depends on effective sales forecasting.

Behavioral dimensions of this decision focus on issues of control, flexibility, effort, and availability of independent and company sales representatives. There is considerable difference of opinion as to the relative advantages and disadvantages of company and independent representatives with respect to each factor. Proponents of a company sales force argue that this strategy offers greater control, since the company selects, trains, and supervises sales personnel. The sales effort is enhanced because sales personnel are representing only one company's product line. Flexibility exists because the firm can change sales-call patterns and customers and can transfer personnel. Finally, availability of sales personnel is superior, since an independent representative might not exist in a geographical area, whereas a company representative can be relocated. Proponents of independent sales representatives argue that selection, training, and supervision of sales personnel can be done equally well by sales agencies and at no cost to the firm. Flexibility is improved, since fixed investment in a sales force is minimal. Effort is increased, since independent representatives live on their commissions. Finally, availability is no problem, since the entrepreneurial spirit of these individuals will take them wherever effective demand exists. These economic and behavioral dimensions were carefully considered when Apple Computer, Inc., ultimately decided to replace its network of independent representatives with its own 350-person sales force. Using these same criteria, however, Coca-Cola's Food Division recently decided to eliminate 110 sales positions and sell through independent agents (food brokers).[7]

Another make-or-buy decision relates to advertising. Often it is advantageous to have intermediaries (such as wholesalers, retailers, and dealers) assume advertising costs and placement responsibilities. Cooperative advertising, where a manufacturer shares the costs of advertising or sales promotion, is an example of this type of strategy.

Push versus Pull

Two approaches that incorporate the topics just discussed are termed push and pull communication strategies.[8] A *push communication strategy* is one in which the offering is pushed through a distribution channel in a sequential fashion, with each channel level representing a distinct target market. A push strategy concentrates on channel intermediaries, building relationships that can have long-term benefits. With such a strategy, advertisements are likely to appear in trade journals and magazines, and sales aids and contests are likely to be used as incentives to gain shelf space and distribution. A principal emphasis, however, is on personal selling to wholesalers and retailers. This strategy is typically used when (1) an organization has easily identifiable buyers, (2) the offering is complex, (3) buyers view the purchase as being risky, (4) a product or service is early in its life cycle, or (5) the organization has limited funds for direct-to-consumer advertising.

A *pull communication strategy* seeks to create initial interest among potential buyers, who in turn demand the product from intermediaries, ultimately pulling the offering through a channel. A pull strategy normally employs heavy end-user (consumer) advertising, free samples, and coupons to stimulate end-user awareness and interest. Consumers might be encouraged to ask their favorite retailer for the offering to pressure retailers into carrying the product. Pennzoil Motor Oil's "Ask for Pennzoil" and General Motors's "Ask for Genuine GM parts" advertising campaigns are prime examples of a pull communication strategy in practice.

The conditions favoring a pull strategy are virtually opposite to those favoring a push strategy. A central issue in choosing a push strategy is the ability and willingness of wholesalers and retailers to implement selling and sales promotion programs advocated by manufacturers. An important consideration in using a pull strategy is whether an *advertising opportunity* exists for a product or service. Such an opportunity exists when (1) there is a favorable primary demand for a product or service category, (2) the product or service to be advertised can be significantly differentiated from its competitors, (3) the product or service has hidden qualities or benefits that can be portrayed effectively through advertising, and (4) there are strong emotional buying motives involved, such as buyers' concern for health, beauty, and safety. The value of an advertising opportunity decreases if one or more of these conditions are not met. Nonprescription drugs and cosmetics often satisfy most of these conditions and are frequently advertised. Commodities such as unprocessed foods (for example, corn, oat, and wheat) are rarely advertised; however, when they are processed and dietary supplements and flavors are added to produce cereals, they are advertised effectively.

Nevertheless, push and pull communication strategies are often used together.[9] Investment in end-user advertising stimulates consumer demand and hence product or service sales volume. Investment in efforts to gain display space for products, promote specific services, and educate retail salespeople builds channel relationships that have long-term benefits.

COMMUNICATION BUDGETING

As you might expect, the question of how much to spend on communication is difficult to answer. Many factors, including those previously mentioned, must be considered in communication budget determination.[10] In general, the greater the geographical dispersion of a target market, the greater the communication expenditure required; the earlier an offering is in its life cycle, the greater the necessary expenditure, and so forth.

The primary rule in determining a communication budget is to *make the budget commensurate with the tasks required of the communication activities.* The more important communication is in a marketing strategy, the larger the amount of funds that should be allocated to it. Conceptually, budget determination is straightforward—set the budget so that the marginal costs of communication equal the marginal revenues resulting from it. This, though, requires an assessment of the effectiveness of communication.

Because it is difficult to evaluate communication effectiveness, attempts to establish a relationship between budget size and communication effectiveness have generally proven unproductive. For this reason, there is no widely agreed-on criterion for establishing the size of a communication budget. Instead, numerous guidelines have been suggested. These guidelines can be roughly grouped as *formula-based* or *qualitatively based.*

The most widely used formula-based approach has been to set the communication budget as a percentage of sales. Most frequently, past sales are employed, but anticipated sales are also occasionally used. Hence, when sales increase, communication activity increases. Although it creates certain conceptual problems (for example, which should come first—sales or communication?), this approach is commonly used as a starting point because of its simplicity. A second formula-based method is to allocate for communication a fixed dollar amount per offering unit, and then to calculate the communication budget by multiplying this per-unit allocation by the number of units expected to be sold. This method is most often used by durable-goods manufacturers such as automobile companies.

In practice, the formula-based approaches tend to be rather inflexible and not marketing-oriented, so they are often supplemented by qualitatively based approaches. Management may use the *competitive-parity approach*, whereby an organization attempts to maintain a balance between its communication expenditures and those of its competitors. Another approach is to use *all available funds* for communication. This strategy might be employed in introducing a new offering for which maximum exposure is desired; it is also sometimes used by nonprofit organizations. A final approach is termed the *task approach*. Here, an organization budgets communication as a function of the particular marketing task that is to be accomplished.

Although all of these approaches are useful, each has decided limitations. More often than not, managers use these approaches in conjunction with one another.

Communication Budget Allocation

Once a communication budget has been settled on, it must be allocated across the communication activities. This can be accomplished by using guidelines similar to those discussed previously for general communication budget determinations.[11] Advertising and personal selling will be used to illustrate necessary budgetary allocation decisions.

Advertising Budget Allocation   Decisions about advertising budget allocation revolve around media selection and scheduling considerations. Basically, there are five mass media—television, radio, magazine, newspaper, and outdoor (billboard)— that an organization can use in transmitting its advertising messages to target markets. Each of these media, or *channels*, consists of *vehicles*—specific entities in which advertisements can appear. In magazines, the vehicles include *Newsweek* and *Mechanics Illustrated*. *Newsweek* can be thought of as a mass-appeal vehicle, whereas *Mechanics Illustrated* might be considered a selective-appeal vehicle. Moreover, media can be *vertical* (reaching more than one level of a distribution channel) or *horizontal* (reaching only one level of a channel).

Media selection is based on numerous factors, the most important of which are cost, reach, frequency, and audience characteristics. Cost frequently acts as a constraint—for example, a 30-second national television commercial (spot) during the Superbowl costs approximately $1 million, not including associated production costs. *Cost* is usually expressed as cost per thousand (CPM) readers, viewers, and so on, to facilitate cross-vehicle comparisons. *Reach* refers to the number of buyers potentially exposed to an advertisement in a particular vehicle. *Frequency* refers to the number of times the consumption units are exposed in a given time period; total exposure equals reach multiplied by frequency. The more closely the characteristics of the target market match those of a vehicle's audience, the more appropriate the vehicle.

Other considerations include the purpose of the advertisement (image building, price, and so on), product needs, and the editorial climate of the vehicle. Whereas price advertisements (those emphasizing an immediate purchase) are more likely to be found in newspapers than in magazines, the opposite is true for advertisements of products requiring color illustration and detailed explanation. Finally, audience characteristics determine which advertisements are acceptable, as well as which are appropriate. For example, Van Heusen advertises its men's shirts in *Vogue, Cosmopolitan,* and *Glamour* magazines because 70 percent of men's shirts are purchased by women.[12]

The timing, or scheduling, of advertisements is critical to their success. Purchases of many offerings (such as skis, snowblowers, and swimsuits) are seasonal or are limited to certain geographical areas. Thus, the advertising budgeting must take into account purchasing patterns. For example, advertising snowblowers in Ohio during the month of July is probably not a worthwhile endeavor.

There are numerous timing strategies that a marketing manager can employ when undertaking an advertising campaign. One alternative is to concentrate advertising dollars in a relatively short time period—a *blitz strategy*. Another alternative is to spend small amounts over the long term to maintain continuity. A *pulse strategy* might be employed, whereby an organization periodically concentrates its advertising but also attempts to maintain some semblance of continuity.

Sales-Force Budget Allocation The sales-force budgeting problem is two-faceted: How many salespeople are needed, and how should they be allocated? A commonly used formula is

$$NS = \frac{NC \times FC \times LC}{TA}$$

where

NS = number of sales people
NC = number of customers (actual or potential)
FC = necessary frequency of customer calls
LC = length of average customer call, including travel time
TA = average available selling time per salesperson (less time spent on administrative duties)

In most instances, the time period is one business year. Although this formula can be used for nearly all types of salespeople, from retail clerks to highly creative salespeople, it is more likely used with the latter.

Assume that the number of potential customers is 2,500 and four calls should be made per customer per year. If the length of the average call and travel time is two hours and there are 1,340 working hours per year available for selling (50 weeks × 40 hours × 67 percent available selling time per week), then

$$NS = \frac{2,500 \times 4 \times 2}{1,340} = 15 \text{ salespeople needed}$$

The formula is flexible. It is possible to create several different strategies simply by varying (1) how the various elements in this formula are defined and (2) the elements themselves, such as the frequency of calls with actual customers and potential customers.

A related decision concerns the allocation of salespeople. Every salesperson must have a territory, whether defined as square feet of selling space, a geographical area, or a delivery route. In determining how large the sales territory should be, decision makers should attempt to equate selling opportunities with the work load associated with each sales territory.

The question of how the sales force should be organized is perhaps more difficult to answer, as it directly relates to organization and marketing objectives, offering characteristics, competitor and industry practices, and the like. The alternatives include having salespeople specialize in certain offerings or in customer types or in a combination of offerings and customer types. For instance, Procter and Gamble has a sales force that sells household cleaning products and another that sells food items. Firestone Tire and Rubber has a sales force that calls on its own dealers and another that calls on independent dealers, such as gasoline stations.

EVALUATION AND CONTROL OF THE COMMUNICATION PROCESS

As part of every communication strategy, there must be mechanisms for evaluation and control. Without them, a marketing manager would be hard-pressed to manage the communication process effectively. There would be no way to determine whether a strategy had achieved its objectives, nor would there be a way to make changes in a strategy in response to competitive activities or environmental occurrences, whether fortuitous or not.

Implicit in both mechanisms is the concept of *continuousness*. The marketing manager must continuously monitor the execution of any communication plan or strategy to ensure that the communication objectives are being attained.

Ideally, evaluation and control should incorporate some measure of sales or profits. Although this is possible for certain communication tools (the sales effectiveness of a direct-mail program can be judged in a relatively straightforward way), for others, it is not. It is nearly impossible to isolate the contribution of institutional advertising to any individual sales transaction.

Budgeting is the ultimate form of control because slashing or adding to the budget of a communication activity effectively eliminates or accentuates the activity itself. The budgeting element is illustrated by the decision to add an additional sales representative at a salary of $50,000 or to allocate the same amount to a direct-mail sales promotion program, when the product mix contribution margin is 25 percent. A simple break-even calculation ($50,000 ÷ 0.25) reveals that $200,000 in additional sales must be generated to cover the incremental cost. The issue is therefore whether the new sales representative or the sales promotion is more likely to achieve this break-even sales volume. Incremental analysis of this type is increasingly being viewed as the appropriate approach for evaluating and controlling expenditures for sales promotion, advertising, and personal selling.[13]

NOTES

1. Publicity is a fourth element often included in the communication mix, but it is not considered here for two reasons. First, publicity is often uncontrollable except through the broader public relations function of an organization; hence, it is not typically the responsibility of the marketing manager. Second, even if publicity is the responsibility of the marketing manager, it is often managed as a mixture of advertising and personal selling, and thus does not require separate treatment.

2. Don E. Schultz and Stanley I. Tannenbaum, *Essentials of Advertising Strategy*, 2nd ed. (Lincolnwood, IL: NTC Business Books, 1988).

3. "Consumer Cycle Is Clue to Ad Timing," *Advertising Age* (September 24, 1990): 30.

4. Gary Levin, "Data Bases Loom Large for '90s," *Advertising Age* (October 21, 1991): 21, 24.

5. "What Happened to Advertising?" *Business Week* (September 23, 1991): 66–72.

6. Independent representatives are autonomous individuals or firms paid commissions for selling a manufacturer's product. These individuals or companies represent several non-competing products that are sold to one or several categories of customers. They do not carry product inventories or take legal title to goods. Their functions vary from selling only a firm's products to broader activities including applications engineering, in-store merchandising support (point-of-purchase displays, stocking), and product maintenance. Independent representatives go by a variety of names, including broker, manufacturer's representative, and sales agent.

7. "Coca-Cola Foods' Teasley Focuses Marketing on Minute Maid Juices," *Wall Street Journal* (June 23, 1988): 32.

8. Debate on push versus pull strategies can be found in Alvin Achenbaum and F. Kent Mitchel, "Pulling Away from Push Marketing," *Harvard Business Review* (May–June 1987): 38–42.

9. Portions of this discussion are based on Robert C. Blattberg and Scott A. Neslin, *Sales Promotion: Concepts, Methods, and Strategies* (Englewood Cliffs, NJ: Prentice Hall, 1990): 466–471.

10. For an extensive discussion of promotional budgeting with an emphasis on advertising, see Simon Broadbent, *The Advertiser's Handbook for Budget Determination* (Lexington, MA: Lexington Books, 1988).

11. An alternative approach to budget determination is to build up a communication budget. By first determining individual budgets for various communication activities and then summing them, it is possible to arrive at an overall communication budget.

12. "Women Help Van Heusen Collar Arrow," *Wall Street Journal* (May 22, 1992): B1, B5.

13. Magid Abraham and Leonard Lodish, "Getting the Most Out of Advertising and Promotion," *Harvard Business Review* (May–June 1990): 50–58.

Morgantown Furniture, Inc. (A)

Late in the evening of August 8, 1993, Charlton Bates, President of Morgantown Furniture, Inc., called Dr. Thomas Berry, a marketing professor at a private university in the Northeast and a consultant to the company. The conversation went as follows:

Bates: Hello, Tom. This is Chuck Bates. I'm sorry to call you this late, but I wanted to get your thoughts on the tentative 1994 advertising program proposed by Mike Hervey of Hervey and Bernham, our ad agency.

Berry: No problem, Chuck. What did they propose?

Bates: The crux of their proposal is that we should increase our advertising expenditures by $200,000. They suggested that we put the entire amount into our consumer advertising program for ads in several shelter magazines.[1] Hervey noted that the National Home Furnishings Foundation has recommended that furniture manufacturers spend 1 percent of their sales exclusively on consumer advertising.

Berry: That increase appears to be slightly out of line with your policy of budgeting 5 percent of expected sales for total promotion expenditures, doesn't it? Hasn't John Bott [Vice President of Sales] emphasized the need for more sales representatives?

Bates: Yes, John has requested additional funds. You're right about the 5 percent figure too, and I'm not sure if our sales forecast isn't too optimistic. Your research has shown that our sales historically follow industry sales almost perfectly, and trade economists are predicting about a 3 percent increase for 1994. Yet, I'm not too sure.

Berry: Well, Chuck, you can't expect forecasts to be always on the button. The money is one thing, but what else can you tell me about Hervey's rationale for putting more dollars into consumer advertising?

Bates: He contends that we can increase our exposure and tell our quality and styling story to the buying public—increase brand awareness, enhance our image, that sort of thing. He also cited industry research data that showed that as baby boomers [consumers between the ages of 29 and 47] age they are becoming more home-oriented and are replacing older, cheaper furniture with more expensive, longer-lasting pieces. All I know is that my contribution margin will fall to 25 percent next year because of increased labor and material cost.

Berry: I appreciate your concern. Give me a few days to think about the proposal. I'll get back to you soon.

After hanging up, Berry began to think about Bates's summary of the proposal, Morgantown's present position, and the furniture industry in general. He knew that

---

[1]Shelter magazines feature home improvement ideas, new ideas in home decorating, and so on. *Better Homes and Gardens* is an example of a shelter magazine.

Bates expected a well thought out recommendation on such issues and a step-by-step description of the logic used to arrive at that recommendation.

THE COMPANY

Morgantown Furniture is a manufacturer of medium- to high-priced wood bedroom, living room, and dining room furniture. The company was formed at the turn of the century by Charlton Bates's grandfather. Bates assumed the presidency of the company upon his father's retirement. Forecasted year-end net sales in 1993 were $75 million with a before-tax profit of $3.7 million.

Morgantown sells its furniture through 1,000 high-quality department stores and independent furniture specialty stores nationwide, but all stores do not carry the company's entire line. The company is very selective in choosing retail outlets. According to Bates, "Our distribution policy, hence our retailers, should mirror the high quality of our products." As a matter of policy, Morgantown does not sell to furniture chain stores or discount outlets.

The company employs ten full-time salespeople and two regional sales managers. Sales personnel receive a base salary and a small commission on sales. A company sales force is atypical in the furniture industry; most furniture manufacturers use sales agents or representatives who carry a wide assortment of noncompeting furniture lines and receive a commission on sales. "Having our own sales group is a policy my father established years ago," noted Bates, "and we've been quite successful in having people who are committed to our company. Our people don't just take furniture orders. They are expected to motivate retail salespeople to sell our line, assist in setting up displays in stores, and give advice on a variety of matters to our retailers and their salespeople." He added, "It seems that my father was ahead of his time. I was just reading in the *Standard & Poor's Industry Surveys* for household furniture that the competition for retail floor space will require even more support, including store personnel sales training, innovative merchandising, inventory management, and advertising."

In 1992, Morgantown allocated $3,675,000 for total promotional expenditures for the 1993 operating year, excluding the salary of the Vice President of Sales. Promotion expenditures were categorized into four groups: (1) sales expense and administration, (2) cooperative advertising programs with retailers, (3) trade promotion, and (4) consumer advertising. Sales costs included salaries for sales personnel and sales managers, selling-expense reimbursements, fringe benefits, and

EXHIBIT 1

Allocation of Morgantown's Promotion Dollars, 1993

Sales expense and administration	$ 995,500
Cooperative advertising allowance	1,650,000
Trade advertising	467,000
Consumer advertising	562,500
	$3,675,000

Source: Company records.

clerical/office assistance, but did not include salespersons' commissions. Commissions were deducted from sales in the calculation of gross profit. The cooperative advertising budget is usually spent on newspaper advertising in a retailer's city. Cooperative advertising allowances are matched by funds provided by retailers on a dollar-for-dollar basis. Trade promotion is directed toward retailers and takes the form of catalogs, trade magazine advertisements, booklets for consumers, and point-of-purchase materials, such as displays, for use in retail stores. Also included in this category is the expense of participating in trade shows. Morgantown is represented at two shows per year. Consumer advertising is directed at potential consumers through shelter magazines. The typical format used in consumer advertising is to highlight new furniture and different bedroom, living room, and dining room arrangements. The dollar allocation for each of these programs in 1993 is shown in Exhibit 1.

THE HOUSEHOLD FURNITURE INDUSTRY

The household furniture industry is divided into three general categories: wood, upholstered, and metal. Total furniture industry sales in 1993 were forecasted to be $20 billion at manufacturers' prices.

The household wood furniture industry is made up of over 1,000 manufacturers, of which major well-known ones include Ethan Allen, Thomasville, Bassett, Drexel Heritage, and Henredon. No one firm in the wood furniture industry captures over 5 percent of industry sales. Wood furniture industry sales were projected to be $10 billion in 1993 and $10.3 billion in 1994 at manufacturers' prices.

Consumer Expenditures for Furniture

Consumer spending for wood furniture is highly cyclical and closely linked to the incidence of new housing starts, consumer confidence, and disposable personal income. Since wood furniture is expensive and often sold in sets, such as a dining room table and chairs, consumers consider these purchases deferrable.

Expenditures for furniture of all kinds have declined as a percentage of consumer disposable personal income since 1979. It has been estimated that about 1 percent of a U.S. household's disposable income was spent for household furniture and home furnishings in 1992. The expected absolute growth in consumer disposable income has led industry economists to forecast an average annual industry growth in furniture in the range from 2.7 percent to 3 percent from 1994 through 1996. Exhibit 2 shows annual furniture sales at retail prices for the period 1980 to 1992.

Furniture Buying Behavior

Even though industry research indicates many consumers consider the furniture shopping process to be enjoyable, consumers acknowledge that they lack the confidence to assess furniture construction, make judgments about quality, and accurately evaluate the price of furniture. Consumers also find it difficult to choose among the many styles available, fearing they will not like their choice several years later, or that their selection will not be appropriate for their home and they will be unable to return it.

EXHIBIT 2

Total Retail Furniture Sales in the United States, 1980–1992 (In Billions of Dollars at Retail Prices)

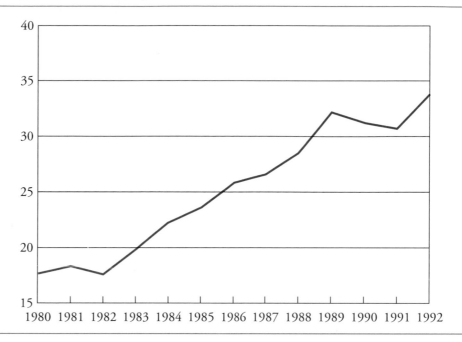

Source: U.S. Department of Commerce.

Results of a consumer panel sponsored by *Better Homes and Gardens* and composed of its subscribers provide the most comprehensive information available on furniture-buying behavior. Selected findings from the *Better Homes and Gardens* survey are reproduced in the appendix following this case. Other findings arising from this research are as follows:

- 94 percent of the subscribers enjoy buying furniture somewhat or very much.
- 84 percent of the subscribers believe "the higher the price, the higher the quality" when buying home furnishings.
- 72 percent of the subscribers browse or window-shop furniture stores even if they don't need furniture.
- 85 percent read furniture ads before they actually need furniture.
- 99 percent of the subscribers agree with the statement "When shopping for furniture and home furnishings, I like the salesperson to show me what alternatives are available, answer my questions, and let me alone so I can think about it and maybe browse around."
- 95 percent of the subscribers say they get redecorating ideas or guidance from magazines.
- 41 percent of the subscribers have written for a manufacturer's booklet.
- 63 percent of the subscribers say they need decorating advice to "put it all together."

Consumer research data have prompted both furniture retailers and manufacturers to stress the need for well-informed retail sales personnel to work with customers. For example, many manufacturers have established education centers where they train retail salespersons in the qualitative and construction details of the furniture they sell. Some manufacturers also distribute product literature to customers via retailers. Drexel Heritage, for instance, provides a series of books entitled *Living with Drexel Heritage* to its authorized retailers, who then give them to customers.

Distribution

Furniture is sold through over 110,000 specialty furniture and home furnishings stores, department stores, and mass-merchandise stores in the United States. Exhibit 3 shows the breakdown of furniture sales by type of retail outlet. Industry trends indicate that the number of independently owned furniture stores has declined, while furniture store chains have grown in popularity. Also, mass merchandisers and department stores such as JCPenney and Sears are moving their furniture lines to free-standing furniture stores. The most significant recent trend among independent and chain furniture stores, department stores, and mass merchandisers is the movement toward the "gallery concept"—the practice of dedicating an amount of space and sometimes an entire free-standing retail outlet to one furniture manufacturer. There are currently 6,500 galleries, and it is estimated this number will reach 11,000 by 1997. Commenting on the gallery concept, Charlton Bates said:

> The gallery concept has great appeal for a furniture manufacturer, since product is displayed in a unique and comfortable setting without the lure of competitive brands. We have galleries in a small number of our furniture stores. The fact that we are not getting our full line in all of our retailers galls me because the opportunity to even discuss the gallery concept with many of our retailers doesn't exist.

EXHIBIT 3

Retail Distribution of Furniture

| | Percent of Sales by Year | |
Outlet Type	*1992*	*1987*
Furniture stores (chains and sole proprietorships)	45	52
Specialty stores and home centers	28	23
Galleries	5	4
Department stores (e.g., Macy's)	5	4
Mass merchants (e.g., Sears, JCPenney, and Montgomery Ward)	5	6
Interior designers and decorators	4	5
Discount department stores (e.g., Target)	3	3
Warehouse clubs	2	1
Catalogs	2	2
	100	100

Source: Company records.

According to a recent study in *Furniture/Today*, the 100 largest furniture retailers in the United States accounted for 32 percent of all furniture sales. The top ten furniture store chains commanded 15 percent of total furniture sales in 1992.

The selling of furniture to retail outlets centers on manufacturers' expositions held at selected times and places around the country. The major expositions occur in High Point, North Carolina, in October and April. Regional expositions are also scheduled during the June–August period in locations such as Dallas, Los Angeles, New York, and Boston. At these *marts*, as they are called in the furniture industry, retail buyers view manufacturers' lines and often make buying commitments for their stores. However, Morgantown's experience has shown that sales efforts in the retail store by company representatives account for as much as one-half of the company's sales in any given year.

Advertising Practices

Manufacturers of household furniture spend approximately 4 percent of annual net sales for advertising of all types (consumer, trade, and cooperative advertising). This percentage has remained constant for many years. The typical vehicles used for consumer advertising are shelter magazines such as *Better Homes and Gardens, House Beautiful*, and *Southern Living.* Trade advertising directed primarily toward retailers includes brochures, point-of-purchase materials to be displayed on a retailer's sales floor, and technical booklets describing methods of construction and materials. Cooperative advertising, shared with retailers, usually appears in newspapers, but there are also some television and radio spots featuring the brands carried by retailers.

Since 1990, the Home Furnishings Council has conducted an advertising campaign designed to promote home furnishings in general. This effort was undertaken to stimulate demand and halt the decline in the percentage of consumer disposable income devoted to furniture purchases. The campaign slogan "Home Is Where the Heart Is," focused on the importance of a home to families and their quality of life (see Exhibit 4).

THE BUDGET MEETING

At the August 8 meeting attended by Hervey and Bernham executives and Morgantown executives, Michael Hervey proposed that the expenditure for consumer advertising be increased by $200,000 for 1994. Cooperative advertising and trade advertising allowances would remain at 1993 levels. Hervey further recommended that shelter magazines account for the bulk of the incremental expenditure for consumer advertising.

John Bott, Morgantown's Vice President of Sales, disagreed with the budget allocation and noted that sales expenses and administration costs were expected to rise by $50,000 in 1994. Moreover, Bott believed that an additional sales representative was needed to service Morgantown's accounts, since 50 new accounts were being added. He estimated that the cost of the additional representative, including salary and expenses, would be at least $70,000 in 1994. "That's about $120,000 in additional sales expenses that have to be added into our promotional budget for

EXHIBIT 4

Home Furnishings Council Print Advertisement

Home Furnishings Tips From Kathie Lee Gifford.

Second In A Series:
"How Do I Start?!" My Answer: Don't Panic, Breathe Easy, And Read This.

Nobody ever said that decorating a room, or a whole house, was a piece of cake. But it's definitely *not* hard, and can actually be fun—especially if you start off right.

You can do that by following the terrific "Getting Started" tips found in Haven. It's the incredibly easy to use, complete decorating guide that's *free* at home furnishings stores everywhere that display the "heart and home" sign of the Home Furnishings Council.

Here are a few of Haven's time-saving, money-saving, sanity-saving ideas on starting off right.

1. For Step One, you don't even have to step out of your home, just go through all the decorating magazines you've been saving to find the rooms, the home furnishings, the colors and styles you like. Then take a grand tour of your own home, to see what you like, and what you'd like to never see again. Put all your thoughts on paper.

2. Next comes my favorite part, visiting home furnishings stores and galleries.

3. Take advantage of all the help and advice that these stores' sales experts have to offer you. Tell them your budget (don't be timid about it!) so they can help you get the best value for your dollar. Show them the pictures you tore out of magazines, bring along your room dimensions, your likes and dislikes—the more they know, the more they can help.

> For the store nearest you offering free copies of Haven, please call 1-800-521-HOME, ext. 345

4. And, most important, work with them to realistically plan your decorating in phases—no one expects you to buy *everything* you want at once.

See, making a beautiful home for the most wonderful family in the world *is* a whole lot easier than you thought.

HOME
FURNISHINGS
COUNCIL

Home Is Where The Heart Is.

Source: Courtesy of the Home Furnishings Council.

1994," Bott noted. He continued:

> We expect sales of about $75 million in 1993 if our sales experience continues throughout the remainder of the year. If we assume a 3 percent increase in sales in 1994, that means our total budget will be about $3,862,500, if my figures are right— a $187,500 increase over our previous budget. And I need $120,000 of that. In other words, $57,500 is available for other kinds of promotion.

Hervey's reply to Bott noted that the company planned to introduce several new styles of living room and dining room furniture in 1994 and that these new items would require consumer advertising in shelter magazines to be launched successfully. He agreed with Bott that increased funding of the sales effort might be necessary and thought that Morgantown might draw funds from cooperative advertising allowance and trade promotion.

Bates interrupted the dialogue between Bott and Hervey to mention that the $200,000 increase in promotion exceeded the 5 percent percentage-of-sales policy by $12,500. He pointed out that higher material costs plus a recent wage increase were forecasted to squeeze Morgantown's gross profit margin and threaten the company objective of achieving a 5 percent net profit margin before taxes. "Perhaps some juggling of the figures is necessary," he concluded. "Both of you have good points. Let me think about what's been said and then let's schedule a meeting for a week from today."

As Bates reviewed his notes from the meeting, he realized that the funds allocated to promotion were only part of the question. How the funds would be allocated within the budget was also crucial. A call to Tom Berry might be helpful in this regard, too.

APPENDIX A: SELECTED FINDINGS FROM THE BETTER HOMES AND GARDENS CONSUMER PANEL REPORT—HOME FURNISHINGS[2]

Question: If you were going to buy furniture in the near future, how important would the following factors be in selecting the store to buy furniture? (Respondents: 449)

Factor	Very Important	Somewhat Important	Not Too Important	Not at All Important	No Answer
Sells high-quality furnishings	62.6%	31.0%	3.8%	1.1%	1.5%
Has a wide range of different furniture styles	58.8	29.2	8.2	2.9	0.9
Gives you personal service	60.1	29.9	7.8	0.9	1.3
Is a highly dependable store	85.1	12.7	1.1	—	1.1
Offers decorating help from experienced home planners	26.5	35.9	25.4	10.9	1.3

[2]Reprinted courtesy of the *Better Homes and Gardens* ® Consumer Panel.

Factor	Very Important	Somewhat Important	Not Too Important	Not at All Important	No Answer
Lets you "browse" all you want	77.1	17.8	3.3	0.7	1.1
Sells merchandise that's a good value for the money	82.0	15.6	0.9	0.2	1.3
Displays furniture in individual room settings	36.3	41.2	18.7	2.4	1.3
Has a relaxed, no-pressure atmosphere	80.0	17.1	1.6	—	1.3
Has well-informed salespeople	77.5	19.8	1.6	—	1.1
Has a very friendly atmosphere	68.2	28.1	2.4	—	1.3
Carries the style of furniture you like	88.0	10.0	0.9	—	1.1

Question: Please rate the following factors as to their importance to you when you purchase or shop for case-goods furniture, such as a dining room or living room suite, *1* being the most important factor, *2* being second most important, and so on, until all factors have been ranked. (Respondents: 449)

Factor	1	2	3	4	5	6	7	8	9	10	NA
Construction of item	24.1%	16.0%	18.5%	13.1%	10.5%	6.9%	4.9%	1.6%	0.2%	1.1%	3.1%
Comfort	13.6	14.7	12.9	12.3	12.7	10.9	8.2	4.5	4.0	2.4	3.8
Styling and design	33.6	19.8	11.1	9.6	4.7	7.3	4.5	1.6	2.9	1.6	3.3
Durability of fabric	2.2	7.6	9.8	14.5	15.1	14.7	12.9	5.6	5.8	7.8	4.0
Type and quality of wood	10.9	17.8	16.3	15.8	14.7	5.8	5.3	3.1	4.9	2.0	3.4
Guarantee or warranty	1.6	3.8	1.6	5.3	8.7	10.0	13.8	25.2	14.5	11.1	4.4
Price	9.4	6.2	8.7	8.5	10.0	12.5	14.2	11.8	6.9	8.0	3.8
Reputation of manufacturer or brand name	6.2	3.6	4.7	5.6	6.2	6.2	12.7	17.1	22.7	11.6	3.4
Reputation of retailer	1.6	1.8	1.6	2.4	4.0	7.3	7.4	13.6	22.0	34.5	3.8
Finish, color of wood	4.7	7.6	10.2	8.0	8.9	13.4	10.7	10.0	10.2	12.7	3.6

Question: Below is a list of 15 criteria that may influence what furniture you buy. Please rate them from *1* as most important to *5* as least important. (Respondents: 449)

Criterion	1	2	3	4	5	No Answer
Guarantee or warranty	11.4%	11.1%	26.3%	16.9%	5.3%	29.0%
Brand name	9.1	6.5	14.3	25.6	11.6	32.9
Comfort	34.7	27.8	14.5	8.5	4.7	9.8
Decorator suggestion	4.0	2.4	2.7	8.2	44.8	37.9
Material used	14.9	24.1	14.9	13.4	6.2	26.5

Criterion	1	2	3	4	5	No Answer
Delivery time	0.7	0.5	1.3	2.9	55.2	39.4
Size	7.6	10.7	13.6	30.9	4.0	33.2
Styling and design	33.4	17.8	21.8	13.6	2.2	11.2
Construction	34.3	23.6	13.1	11.4	2.9	14.7
Fabric	4.0	25.6	24.9	14.0	4.5	27.0
Durability	37.0	19.4	13.6	6.9	4.9	18.2
Finish on wooden parts	5.8	14.7	16.7	10.7	16.7	35.4
Price	19.4	21.8	16.0	10.9	15.4	16.5
Manufacturer's reputation	4.2	9.1	15.4	22.9	14.3	34.1
Retailer's reputation	2.2	4.7	10.5	21.2	26.5	34.9

Question: Listed below are some statements others have made about shopping for furniture. Please indicate how much you agree or disagree with each one. (Respondents: 449)

Statement	Agree Completely	Agree Somewhat	Neither Agree nor Disagree	Disagree Somewhat	Disagree Completely	NA
I wish there were some way to be really sure of getting good quality in furniture	61.9%	24.7%	4.7%	4.2%	3.6%	0.9%
I really enjoy shopping for furniture	49.2	28.3	7.6	9.8	4.2	0.9
I would never buy any furniture without my husband's/wife's approval	47.0	23.0	10.9	9.8	7.1	2.2
I like all pieces in the master bedroom to be exactly the same style	35.9	30.7	12.7	11.1	7.6	2.0
Once I find something I like in furniture I wish it would last forever so I'd never have to buy again	36.8	24.3	10.0	18.9	9.1	0.9
I wish I had more confidence in my ability to decorate my home attractively	23.1	32.3	12.5	11.6	18.7	1.8
I wish I knew more about furniture styles and what looks good	20.0	31.0	17.1	13.4	16.7	1.8
My husband/wife doesn't take much interest in the furniture we buy	6.5	18.0	12.3	17.8	41.4	4.0
I like to collect a number of different styles in the dining room	3.3	10.5	15.2	29.8	38.3	2.9
Shopping for furniture is very distressing to me	2.4	11.6	14.3	18.0	51.9	1.8

Question: Listed below are some factors that may influence your choice of furnishings, Please rate them with *1* being most important, *2* being second most important, and so on, until all factors have been rated. (Respondents: 449)

Factor	1	2	3	4	5	No Answer
Friends and/or neighbors	1.3%	16.9%	15.8%	22.1%	41.7%	2.2%
Family or spouse	62.8	9.4	14.3	9.8	2.0	1.7
Magazine advertising	16.3	30.3	29.6	17.6	4.2	2.0
Television advertising	1.1	6.7	14.7	32.5	42.3	2.7
Store displays	18.9	37.2	22.1	14.0	5.6	2.2

Question: When you go shopping for a *major piece* of furniture or smaller pieces of furniture, who, if anyone, do you usually go with? (Respondents: 449—multiple responses)

Person	Major Pieces	Other Pieces
Husband	82.4%	59.5%
Mother or mother-in-law	6.2	9.1
Friend	12.0	18.9
Decorator	4.2	1.6
Other relative	15.6	15.4
Other person	2.9	3.3
No one else	5.1	22.3
No answer	0.9	3.1

Question: When the time comes to purchase a *major* item of furniture or other smaller pieces of furniture, who, if anyone, helps you make the final decision about which piece to buy? (Respondents: 449—multiple responses)

Person	Major Pieces	Other Pieces
Husband	86.0%	63.5%
Mother or mother-in-law	2.4	4.5
Friend	3.6	8.0
Decorator	3.1	2.7
Other relative	10.0	12.9
Other person	1.6	1.8
No one else	7.1	24.3
No answer	0.9	2.2

Morgantown Furniture, Inc. (B)

In November 1993, Morgantown Furniture, Inc., merged with Lea-Meadows Inc., a manufacturer of upholstered furniture for living and family rooms. The merger was not planned in a conventional sense. Charlton Bates's father-in-law died suddenly in early August 1993, leaving his daughter with controlling interest in Lea-Meadows. The merger proceeded smoothly, since the two firms were located on adjacent properties and the general consensus was that the two firms would maintain as much autonomy as was economically justified. Moreover, the upholstery line filled a gap in the Morgantown product mix, even though it would retain its own identity and brand names.

The only real issue that continued to plague Bates was merging the selling effort. Morgantown had its own sales force, but Lea-Meadows relied on sales agents to represent it. The question was straightforward, in his opinion: "Do we give the upholstery line of chairs and sofas to our sales force, or do we continue using the sales agents?" John Bott, Morgantown's Vice President of Sales, said the line should be given to his sales group; Martin Moorman, National Sales Manager at Lea-Meadows, said the upholstery line should remain with sales agents.

LEA-MEADOWS INC.

Lea-Meadows Inc. is a small, privately owned manufacturer of upholstered furniture for use in living and family rooms. The firm is more than 75 years old. The company uses some of the finest fabrics and frame construction in the industry, according to trade sources. Net sales in 1993 were $5 million. Total estimated industry sales of 1,100 upholstered furniture manufacturers in 1993 were $5.6 billion. Forecasted 1994 industry sales for upholstered furniture were $5.8 billion. Company sales had increased 7 percent annually over the past five years, and company executives believed this growth rate would continue for the foreseeable future.

Lea-Meadows employed 15 sales agents to represent its products. These sales agents also represented several manufacturers of noncompeting furniture and home furnishings. Often a sales agent found it necessary to deal with several buyers in a store in order to represent all the lines carried. On a typical sales call, a sales agent first visited buyers to discuss new lines, in addition to any promotions being offered by manufacturers. New orders were sought where and when it was appropriate. The sales agent then visited the selling floor to check displays, inspect furniture, and inform salespeople about furniture styles and construction. Lea-Meadows paid an agent

This case was prepared by Professor Roger A. Kerin, of the Edwin L. Cox School of Business, Southern Methodist University, as a basis for class discussion and is not designed to illustrate appropriate or inappropriate handling of administrative situations. All names and data are disguised. Copyright © by Roger A. Kerin. No part of this case may be reproduced without written permission from the copyright holder.

commission of 5 percent of net company sales for these services. Moorman thought sales agents spent 10 to 15 percent of their in-store time on Lea-Meadows products.

The company did not attempt to influence the type of retailers that agents contacted, although it was implicit in the agency agreement that agents would not sell to discount houses. Sales records indicated that agents were calling on specialty furniture and department stores. An estimated 1,000 retail accounts were called on in 1993. All agents had established relationships with their retail accounts and worked closely with them.

MORGANTOWN FURNITURE, INC.

Morgantown Furniture, Inc., is a manufacturer of medium- to high-priced wood bedroom, living, and dining room furniture.[1] Net sales in 1993 were $75 million; before-tax profit was $3.7 million. Total estimated industry sales of wood furniture in 1993 were $10 billion at manufacturers' prices. Projected sales for 1994 were $10.3 billion.

The company employed ten full-time sales representatives, who called on 1,000 retail accounts in 1993. These individuals performed the same function as sales agents but were paid a salary plus a small commission. In 1993, the average Morgantown sales representative received an annual salary of $70,000 (plus expenses) and a commission of 0.5 percent on net company sales. Total sales administration costs were $130,000.

Morgantown's salespeople were highly regarded in the industry. They were known particularly for their knowledge of wood furniture and willingness to work with buyers and retail sales personnel. Despite these advantages, Bates knew that all retail accounts did not carry the complete Morgantown furniture line. He had therefore instructed Bott to "push the group a little harder." At present, sales representatives were making ten sales calls per week, with the average sales call running three hours. Salespersons' remaining time was accounted for by administrative activities and travel. Bates recommended that the call frequency be increased to seven calls per account per year, which was consistent with what he thought was the industry norm.

MERGING THE SALES EFFORTS

Through separate meetings with Bott and Moorman, Bates was able to piece together a variety of data and perspectives on the question of merging the sales efforts. These meetings also made it clear that Bott and Moorman differed dramatically in their views.

John Bott had no doubts about assigning the line to the Morgantown sales force. Among the reasons he gave for this view were the following. First, Morgantown had developed one of the most well respected, professional sales forces in the industry. The representatives could easily learn the fabric jargon, and they already knew personally many of the buyers who were responsible for upholstered furniture. Second, selling the Lea-Meadows line would require only about 15 percent of present sales

---

[1]Additional background information on the company and industry can be found in the case titled "Morgantown Furniture, Inc. (A)."

call time. Thus, he thought that the new line would not be a major burden. Third, more control over sales efforts was possible. Bott noted that Charlton Bates's father had created the sales group 30 years earlier because of the commitment it engendered and the service "only our own people are able and willing to give." Moreover, the company salespeople have the Morgantown "look" and presentation style, which is instilled in every one of them. Fourth, Bott said that it wouldn't look right if both representatives and agents called on the same stores and buyers. He noted that Morgantown and Lea-Meadows overlapped on all their accounts. He said, "We'd be paying a commission on sales to these accounts when we would have gotten them anyway. The difference in commission percentages would not be good for morale."

Martin Moorman advocated keeping sales agents for the Lea-Meadows line. His arguments were as follows. First, all sales agents had established contacts and were highly regarded by store buyers, and most had represented the line in a professional manner for many years. He, too, had a good working relationship with all 15 agents. Second, sales agents represented little, if any, cost beyond commissions. Moorman noted, "Agents get paid when we get paid." Third, sales agents were committed to the Lea-Meadows line: "The agents earn a part of their living representing us. They have to service retail accounts to get the repeat business." Fourth, sales agents were calling on buyers not contacted by the Morgantown sales force. Moorman noted, "If we let Morgantown people handle the line, we might lose these accounts, have to hire more sales personnel, or take away 25 percent of the present selling time given to Morgantown product lines."

As Bates reflected on the meetings, he felt that a broader perspective was necessary beyond the views expressed by Bott and Moorman. One factor was profitability. Existing Morgantown furniture lines typically had gross margins that were 5 percent higher than those for Lea-Meadows upholstered lines. Another factor was the "us and them" references apparent in the meetings with Bott and Moorman. Would merging the sales effort overcome this, or would it cause more problems? The idea of increasing the sales force to incorporate the Lea-Meadows line did not sit well with him. Adding new salespeople would require restructuring of sales territories, involve potential loss of commissions by existing salespeople, and be "a big headache." Finally, there was the subtle issue of Moorman's future. Moorman, who was 50 years old, had worked for Lea-Meadows for 25 years and was a family friend and godfather to Bates's youngest child. If the Lea-Meadows line was represented by the Morgantown sales force, Moorman's position would be eliminated.

Cadbury Beverages, Inc.
CRUSH® Brand

In January 1990, marketing executives at Cadbury Beverages, Inc. began the challenging task of relaunching the CRUSH, HIRES, and SUN-DROP soft drink brands. These brands had been acquired from Procter and Gamble in October 1989.

After considerable discussion, senior marketing executives at Cadbury Beverages, Inc., decided to focus initial attention on the CRUSH brand of fruit-flavored carbonated beverages. Three issues were prominent. First, immediate efforts were needed to rejuvenate the bottling network for the CRUSH soft drink brand. Second, according to one executive, "[we had] to sort through and figure out what the Crush brand equity is, how the brand was built . . . and develop a base positioning."[1] Third, a new advertising and promotion program for CRUSH had to be developed, including setting objectives, developing strategies, and preparing preliminary budgets.

Kim Feil was assigned responsibility for managing the relaunch of the CRUSH soft drink brand. She had joined Cadbury Beverages, Inc., on December 12, 1989, as a Senior Product Manager, after working in various product management positions at a large consumer goods company for five years. Recounting her first day on the job, Feil said, "I arrived early Wednesday morning to find 70 boxes of research reports, print ads, sales and trade promotions and videotapes stacked neatly from the floor to the ceiling." Undaunted, she began to sift through the mountains of material systematically, knowing that her assessment and recommendations would soon be sought.

CADBURY BEVERAGES, INC.

Cadbury Beverages, Inc. is the beverage division of Cadbury Schweppes PLC, a major global soft drink and confectionery marketer. In 1989, Cadbury Schweppes PLC had worldwide sales of $4.6 billion, which were produced by product sales in more than 110 countries. Cadbury Schweppes PLC headquarters are located in London, England; Cadbury Beverages, Inc., worldwide headquarters are in Stamford, Connecticut. Exhibit 1 shows the product list sold worldwide by Cadbury Beverages, Inc. Exhibit 2 details the product list for the United States.

---

[1]Patricia Winters, "Fresh Start for Crush", *Advertising Age* (January 6, 1990): 47.

The cooperation of Cadbury Beverages, Inc., in the preparation of this case is gratefully acknowledged. This case was prepared by Professor Roger A. Kerin, of the Edwin L. Cox School of Business, Southern Methodist University, as a basis for class discussion and is not designed to illustrate effective or ineffective handling of an administrative situation. Certain information has been disguised and is not useful for research purposes. Crush is a registered trademark used by permission from Cadbury Beverages, Inc. Copyright © by Roger A. Kerin. No part of this case may be reproduced without written permission of the copyright holder.

E X H I B I T   1

Worldwide Product List for Cadbury Beverages, Inc.

Carbonates	Waters	Still Drinks/Juices
Canada Dry	Schweppes	Oasis
Schweppes	Canada Dry	Atoll
Pure Spring	Pure Spring	Bali
Sunkist	Malvern	TriNaranjus
Crush		Vida
'C' Plus		Trina
Hires		Trina Colada
Sussex		Red Cheek
Old Colony		Allen's
Sun-Drop		Mitchell's
Gini		Mott's
		Clamato
		E. D. Smith
		Rose's
		Mr & Mrs "T"
		Holland House

History

Cadbury Schweppes PLC has the distinction of being the world's first soft drink maker. The company can trace its beginnings to 1783 in London, where Swiss national Jacob Schweppe first sold his artificial mineral water. Schweppe returned to Switzerland in 1789, but the company continued its British operations, introducing a lemonade in 1835 and tonic water and ginger ale in the 1870s. Beginning in the 1880s, Schweppes expanded worldwide, particularly in countries that would later form the British Commonwealth. In the 1960s, the company diversified into food products.

In 1969, Schweppes merged with Cadbury. Cadbury was a major British candy maker that traced its origins to John Cadbury, who began his business making cocoa in Birmingham, England, in the 1830s. By the middle of this century, Cadbury had achieved market presence throughout the British Commonwealth, as well as other countries.

In 1989, Cadbury Schweppes PLC was one of the world's largest multinational firms and was ranked 457 in *Business Week*'s Global 1000. Beverages accounted for 60 percent of company worldwide sales and 53 percent of operating income in 1989. Confectionery items accounted for 40 percent of worldwide sales and produced 47 percent of operating income.

Soft Drinks

Cadbury Schweppes PLC is the world's third largest soft drink marketer behind Coca-Cola and PepsiCo. The company has achieved this status through consistent marketing investment in the SCHWEPPES brand name and extensions to different

EXHIBIT 2

U.S. Product List for Cadbury Beverages, Inc.

Schweppes	Canada Dry	Sunkist	Crush, Hires, Sun-Drop	Mott's, Red Cheek, Holland House, Mr & Mrs "T," Rose's
Tonic Water	Tonic Water	Sunkist Pineapple Soda	Crush Orange	Mott's 100% Pure Apple Juices
Diet Tonic Water	Sugar Free Tonic Water	Sunkist Grape Soda	Crush Diet Orange	Mott's 100% Pure Juice Blends
Club Soda	Club Soda	Sunkist Fruit Punch	Hires Root Beer	Mott's Juice Drinks
Seltzer Water	Seltzer Waters	Sunkist Strawberry Soda	Hires Diet Root Beer	Mott's Apple Sauce
Sparkling Waters	Sparkling Mineral Waters	Sunkist Orange Soda	Hires Cream Soda	Mott's Apple Sauce Fruit Snacks
Grapefruit Soda	Barrelhead Root Beer	Sunkist Diet Orange Soda	Hires Diet Cream Soda	Mott's Prune Juice
Collins Mix	Barrelhead Sugar-Free	Sunkist Sparkling	Crush Strawberry	Clamato
Grape Soda	Root Beer	Lemonade	Crush Grape	Beefamato
Ginger Ale	Wink	Sunkist Diet Sparkling	Crush Cherry	Grandma's Molasses
Diet Ginger Ale	Ginger Ale	Lemonade	Crush Pineapple	Rose's Lime Juice
Raspberry Ginger Ale	Diet Ginger Ale		Crush Cream Soda	Rose's Grenadine
Diet Raspberry Ginger Ale	Cherry Ginger Ale		Sun-Drop Cherry Citrus	Red Cheek Apple Juice
Bitter Lemon	Diet Cherry Ginger Ale		Sun-Drop Diet Citrus	Red Cheek Juice Blends
Lemon Sour	Bitter Lemon			Mr & Mrs "T" Margarita Salt
Lemon Lime	No-Cal Brand Soft Drinks			Mr & Mrs "T" Bloody Mary Mix
	Cott Brand Soft Drinks			Mr & Mrs "T" Liquid Cocktail Mixers
	Lemon Ginger Ale			Mr & Mrs "T" Rich & Spicy
	Diet Lemon Ginger Ale			Holland House Cooking Wines
				Holland House Dry Mixers
				Holland House Wine Marinades
				Holland House Smooth & Spicy
				Holland House Coca Casa
				Cream of Coconut
				Holland House Liquid Mixers

beverage products such as tonic, ginger ale, club soda, and seltzer in various flavors. In addition, the company has acquired numerous other brands throughout the world, each with an established customer franchise. For example, Cadbury Schweppes PLC acquired the CANADA DRY soft drink brands and certain rights to SUNKIST soft drinks in 1986. In 1989, the company acquired certain soft drink brands and associated assets (for TriNaranjus, Vida, Trina, and Trina Colada) in Spain and Portugal and purchased the GINI brand, which is the leading bitter lemon brand in France and Belgium. Also, in October 1989, the company acquired all the CRUSH-brand worldwide trademarks from Procter and Gamble for $220 million.

Cadbury Schweppes PLC (Cadbury Beverages, Inc.) was the fourth largest soft drink marketer in the United States in 1989 with a carbonated soft drink market share of 3.4 percent. (The three leading U.S. soft drink companies, in order, were Coca-Cola, PepsiCo, and Dr. Pepper/7Up.) Nonetheless, the company's brands were often the market leader in their specific categories. For example, CANADA DRY is the top-selling ginger ale in the United States, SCHWEPPES is the leading tonic water, and CANADA DRY Seltzers top the club soda/seltzer category. The combined sales of SUNKIST and CRUSH brand orange drinks lead the orange-flavored carbonated soft drink category.

According to industry analysts, the 1989 acquisition of CRUSH meant that CANADA DRY would account for 39 percent of Cadbury Beverages soft drink sales in the United States. SUNKIST, CRUSH, and SCHWEPPES would account for 22 percent, 20 percent, and 17 percent of U.S. sales, respectively. The remaining 2 percent of U.S. sales would come from other soft drink brands.[2]

CARBONATED SOFT DRINK INDUSTRY

American consumers drink more soft drinks than tap water. In 1989, the average American consumed 46.7 gallons of carbonated soft drinks, or twice the 23 gallons consumed in 1969. Population growth compounded by rising per capita consumption produced an estimated $43 billion in retail sales in 1989.

Industry Structure

There are three major participants in the production and distribution of carbonated soft drinks in the United States. They are concentrate producers, bottlers, and retail outlets. For regular soft drinks, concentrate producers manufacture the basic flavors (for example, lemon-lime and cola) for sale to bottlers, which add a sweetener to carbonated water and package the beverage in bottles and cans. For diet soft drinks, concentrate producers include an artificial sweetener, such as aspartame, with their flavors.

There are over 40 concentrate producers in the United States. However, about 82 percent of industry sales are accounted for by three producers: Coca-Cola, PepsiCo, and Dr. Pepper/7Up.

Approximately 1,000 bottling plants in the United States convert flavor concentrate into carbonated soft drinks. Bottlers are either owned by concentrate producers or franchised to sell the brands of concentrate producers. For example, roughly

---

[2]Patricia Winters, "Cadbury Schweppes' Plan: Skirt Cola Giants," *Advertising Age* (August 13, 1990): 22–23.

one-half of Pepsi-Cola's sales are through company-owned bottlers; the remaining volume is sold through franchised bottlers. Franchised bottlers are typically granted a right to package and distribute a concentrate producer's branded line of soft drinks in a defined territory and not allowed to market a directly competitive major brand. However, franchised bottlers can represent noncompetitive brands and decline to bottle a concentrate producer's secondary lines. These arrangements mean that a franchised bottler of Pepsi-Cola cannot sell Royal Crown (RC) Cola but can bottle and market orange CRUSH rather than PepsiCo's Mandarin Orange Slice.

Concentrate producer pricing to bottlers was similar across competitors within flavor categories. Exhibit 3 shows the approximate price and cost structure for orange concentrate producers and bottlers.

The principal retail channels for carbonated soft drinks are supermarkets, convenience stores, vending machines, fountain service, and thousands of small retail outlets. Soft drinks are typically sold in bottles and cans, except for fountain service. In fountain service, syrup is sold to a retail outlet (such as McDonald's), which mixes the syrup with carbonated water for immediate consumption by customers. Supermarkets account for about 40 percent of carbonated soft drink industry sales. Industry analysts consider supermarket sales the key to a successful soft drink marketing effort.

EXHIBIT 3

Approximate Price and Cost Structure for Concentrate Producers and Bottlers

| | Concentrate Producers | | | |
| | Regular (Sugar) | | Diet (Aspartame) | |
	$/Case	Percentage	$/Case	Percentage
Net selling price	$0.76	100%	$0.92	100%
Cost of goods sold	0.11	14	0.12	13
Gross profit	$0.65	86%	$0.80	87%
Selling and delivery	0.02	3	0.02	2
Advertising and promotion	0.38	50	0.38	41
General and administrative expense	0.13	17	0.13	14
Pretax cash profit/case	$0.12	16%	$0.27	30%

| | Bottlers | | | |
| | Regular (Sugar) | | Diet (Aspartame) | |
	$/Case	Percentage	$/Case	Percentage
Net selling price	$5.85	100%	$5.85	100%
Cost of goods sold	3.16	54	3.35	57
Gross profit	$2.69	46%	$2.50	43%
Selling and delivery	1.35	23	1.35	23
Advertising and promotion	0.40	7	0.40	7
General and administrative expense	0.05	1	0.05	1
Pretax cash profit/case	$0.89	15%	$0.71	12%

Soft Drink Marketing

Soft drink marketing is characterized by heavy investment in advertising, selling and promotion to and through bottlers to retail outlets, and consumer price discounting. Concentrate producers usually assume responsibility for developing national consumer advertising and promotion programs, product development and planning, and marketing research. Bottlers usually take the lead in developing trade promotions to retail outlets and local consumer promotions. Bottlers are also responsible for selling and servicing retail accounts, including the placement and maintenance of in-store displays and the restocking of supermarket and convenience store shelves with their brands.

Flavor and Brand Competition Colas account for slightly less than two-thirds of total carbonated soft drink sales. Other flavors, such as orange, lemon-lime, cherry, grape, and root beer, account for the remaining sales. Estimates of market shares for flavors in 1989 were as follows:

Flavor	*Market Share*
Cola	65.7%
Lemon-lime	12.9
Orange	3.9
Root beer	3.6
Ginger ale	2.8
Grape	1.1
Others	10.0
	100.0%

Diet soft drinks represented 31 percent of industry sales in 1989. Industry trend data indicate that sales of diet drinks accounted for a large portion of the overall growth of carbonated soft drink sales in the 1980s.

There are more than 900 registered brand names for soft drinks in the United States. Most of these brands are sold only regionally. Exhibit 4 shows the top ten soft drink brands in 1989. Six of these brands were colas, and all ten brands were marketed by Coca-Cola, PepsiCo, or Dr. Pepper/7Up.

Soft Drink Purchase and Consumption Behavior Industry research suggests that the purchase of soft drinks in supermarkets is often unplanned. Accordingly, soft drink purchasers respond favorably to price (coupon) promotions, in-store (particularly end-of-aisle) displays, and other forms of point-of-sale promotions (such as shelf tags). The importance of display is evidenced in the view held by an industry analyst who estimated that a brand is "locked out of 60 percent of the [supermarket soft drink] volume if it can't get end-aisle displays."[3] The typical supermarket purchaser of soft drinks is a married woman with children under 18 years of age living at home.

Soft drink buying is somewhat seasonal, with consumption slightly higher during summer months than winter months. Consumption also varies by region of the country. Per capita consumption in the East South Central states of Kentucky, Tennessee, Alabama, and Mississippi was highest in the United States in 1989, with 54.9 gallons compared with the national per capita average of 46.7 gallons. In the Mountain states of Montana, Idaho, Wyoming, Colorado, New Mexico, Arizona, Utah, and Nevada, per capita consumption was 37.1 gallons—the lowest in the nation.

[3]Patricia Winters, "Crush Fails to Fit on P&G Shelf," *Advertising Age* (July 10, 1989): 1, 42–43.

EXHIBIT 4

Market Share of Top Ten Soft Drink Brands in the United States, 1989

Brand	Market Share
1. Coca-Cola Classic	19.8%
2. Pepsi-Cola	17.9
3. Diet Coke	8.9
4. Diet Pepsi	5.7
5. Dr Pepper	4.5
6. Sprite	3.7
7. Mountain Dew	3.6
8. 7Up	3.2
9. Caffeine-free Diet Coke	2.5
10. Caffeine-free Diet Pepsi	1.6
Top Ten Brands	71.4
Other Brands	28.6
Total Industry	100.0%

Consumption of diet beverages was more pronounced among consumers over 25 years of age. Teenagers, and younger consumers generally, were heavier consumers of regular soft drinks.

ORANGE CATEGORY

Orange-flavored carbonated soft drinks recorded sales of 126 million cases in 1989, or 3.9 percent of total industry sales sold through supermarkets.[4] Prior to 1986, annual case volume had hovered in the range from 100 to 102 million cases. In the mid-1980s, PepsiCo introduced Mandarin Orange Slice, and Coca-Cola introduced Minute Maid Orange. Entry of these two brands, supported by widespread distribution and heavy advertising and promotion, revitalized the category and increased supermarket sales to 126 million cases. Annual supermarket case volume for the period 1984–1989 was as follows:

Year	Annual Supermarket Case Volume of Orange-Flavored Soft Drinks
1984	102,000,000
1985	100,000,000
1986	126,000,000
1987	131,000,000
1988	131,000,000
1989	126,000,000

---

[4]*Case author's note:* The soft drink industry uses supermarket sales and market shares as a gauge to assess the competitive position of different brands and flavors, since supermarket volumes affect sales through other retail outlets and fountain service. As an approximation and for analysis purposes, *total case* volume for a brand or flavor can be estimated as 2.5 times supermarket case volume. Therefore, total sales of orange-flavored soft drinks are 2.5 × 126,000,000 = 315 million cases.

EXHIBIT 5

Orange Carbonated Soft Drink Brand Market Shares, 1985–1989 (Rounded)

Brand	Year				
	1985	1986	1987	1988	1989
SUNKIST	32%	20%	13%	13%	14%
Mandarin Orange Slice	NA	16	22	21	21
Minute Maid Orange	NA	8	14	13	14
CRUSH	22	18	14	11	8
Total Top Four Brands	54%	62%	63%	58%	57%
Others	46%	38%	37%	42%	43%

Major Competitors

Four brands captured the majority of orange-flavored soft drink sales in 1989. Mandarin Orange Slice marketed by PepsiCo was the category leader with a market share of 20.8 percent. SUNKIST, sold by Cadbury Beverages, Inc., and Coca-Cola's Minute Maid Orange had market shares of 14.4 percent and 14 percent, respectively. Orange CRUSH had a market share of 7.5 percent. Other brands accounted for the remaining 43.3 percent of sales of orange-flavored soft drinks. Exhibit 5 shows the market shares for the major competitors for the period 1985–1989.

The major competitors sold both regular and diet varieties of orange-flavored drink. As shown in Exhibit 6, slightly over 70 percent of sales in this category were regular soft drinks. Orange CRUSH sales mirrored this pattern. SUNKIST, however, exceeded the category average with 82 percent of its case volume sales being the regular form. For Mandarin Orange Slice and Minute Maid Orange, case volume was almost evenly split between regular and diet drinks.

Major competitors also differed in terms of market coverage in 1989. SUNKIST was available in markets that represented 91 percent of total orange category sales. By comparison, orange CRUSH was available in markets that represented only 62 percent of orange category sales. Mandarin Orange Slice and Minute Maid Orange were available in markets that represented 88 percent of orange category sales. Exhibit 7 shows the market coverage by the four major competitors for the period 1985–1989.

EXHIBIT 6

Case Volume in 1989 by Type of Drink: Regular versus Diet

Type	Total Soft Drinks	Total Orange	CRUSH	SUNKIST	Mandarin Orange Slice	Minute Maid Orange
Regular	68.9%	73.2%	71.3%	82.1%	49.0%	53.1%
Diet	31.1	26.8	28.7	17.9	51.0	46.9
	100.0%	100.0%	100.0%	100.0%	100.0%	100.0%

EXHIBIT   7

Market Coverage of Orange Category by Major Competitors, 1985–1989

| | Year | | | | |
Brand	1985	1986	1987	1988	1989
CRUSH	81%	81%	78%	78%	62%
SUNKIST	95	83	79	86	91
Mandarin Orange Slice	10	68	87	88	88
Minute Maid Orange	10	60	87	88	88

Competitor Positioning and Advertising

Each of the four major competitors attempted to stake out a unique position within the orange category. For example, Minute Maid Orange appeared to emphasize its orange flavor, while SUNKIST focused on the teen lifestyle. Mandarin Orange Slice and Minute Maid Orange appeared to be targeted at young adults and households without children. These brands also appeared to be emphasizing the "better for you" idea. CRUSH and SUNKIST targeted teens and households with children at home. Exhibit 8 summarizes the apparent brand positionings of the major competitors and selected performance data compiled by the CRUSH marketing research staff.

   Slightly over $26 million was spent on advertising by the four major brands in 1989. Mandarin Orange Slice and Minute Maid Orange accounted for 84 percent of all advertising expenditures in the orange category. Although both brands were advertised on network and cable television and both used spot television commercials

EXHIBIT   8

Competitive Positioning and Performance, 1989

	SUNKIST	Mandarin Orange Slice	Minute Maid Orange	CRUSH
Positioning	"Teens on the Beach"; "Drink in the Sun"	"Who's Got the "Juice?"; Contemporary youth culture	The orange, orange" orange flavor, taste of real orange	"Don't just quench it, CRUSH it"; bold user imagery with thirst quenching benefit
Target	Teens, 12–24	Young adults, 18–24	Young adults, 18–34	Teens, 13–29
Household size of purchaser	3–4 (children at home)	1–2 (no children)	1–2 (no children)	3–5 (children at home)
Package sales mix	Two-liter 51% Cans 42% Other 9%	Two-liter 54% Cans 42% Other 4%	Two-liter 54% Cans 41% Other 5%	Two-liter 64% Cans 31% Other 5%
Loyalty (percentage of brand buyer's orange volume)	36%	55%	48%	46%

Source: CRUSH Marketing Research Staff Report. Based on trade publications and industry sources.

in local markets, their advertising differed in other respects. Minute Maid Orange used outdoor billboards and network radio for advertising, but Mandarin Orange Slice did not. In comparison, Mandarin Orange Slice was advertised in magazines and newspapers, but Minute Maid Orange was not.

CRUSH and SUNKIST spent less on advertising and used fewer advertising vehicles than did Minute Maid Orange and Mandarin Orange Slice. CRUSH was promoted most frequently on spot television and in newspaper and outdoor signage. SUNKIST used newspapers, spot television, outdoor billboards, and some syndicated television.

Two advertising trends were evident in the orange category since 1986. First, total expenditures for measured print and broadcast media declined each year since 1986, when $52.2 million was spent for advertising. In that year, Mandarin Orange Slice and Minute Maid Orange were introduced nationally. Second, competitors increased the variety of media used for advertising. In 1986, spot television and outdoor billboards were used almost exclusively. By 1989, a broader spectrum of vehicles was used, including broadcast media (network, spot, syndicated, and cable television and network radio) and print media (outdoor, magazines, and newspapers). Exhibit 9 shows advertising expenditures for the four major brands for the period 1985–1989.

Competitor Pricing and Promotion

Concentrate pricing among the four major competitors differed very little. Typically, no more than a one-cent difference existed. The price differential between regular (with sugar) and diet (with aspartame) concentrate was virtually the same across competitors. The similarity in pricing as well as in raw material costs resulted in similar gross profit margins across competitors in the orange category. However, as noted in Exhibit 3, the gross profit margin differs between regular and diet soft drink concentrate.

EXHIBIT 9

Concentrate Producers' Advertising Expenditures for Broadcast and Print Media for Major Orange Soft Drink Brands, 1985–1989 (In Thousands of Dollars)

Brand	1985	1986	1987	1988	1989
Mandarin Orange Slice (Total)	$17,809.4	$32,079.9	$29,555.8	$15,001.3	$11,388.1
Regular	12,739.4	27,704.2	20,123.2	10,247.9	11,199.5
Diet	5,070.0	4,375.7	2,676.4	1,881.9	
Regular and Diet			6,756.2	2,872.5	188.6
SUNKIST (Total)	$ 7,176.2	$ 4,013.0	$ 910.7	$1,719.3	$ 2,301.9
Regular	4,816.5	1,340.6	887.2	309.4	281.5
Diet	2,316.0	1,269.5	1.3		
Regular and Diet	43.7	1,402.9	22.2	1,409.9	2,020.4
CRUSH (Total)	$ 4,371.2	$ 7,154.9	$ 4,296.7	$ 6,841.1	$ 1,853.6
Regular	3,282.7	4,712.9	2,729.8	2,561.6	1,382.2
Diet	1,004.6	2,413.1	959.4	1.2	127.7
Regular and Diet	83.9	28.9	607.5	4,278.3	343.7
Minute Maid Orange (Total)	$ 174.4	$ 7,952.3	$ 9,027.2	$12,811.3	$10,463.1
Regular	174.4	7,508.2	7,211.6	9,252.5	10,191.9
Diet			1,745.1	3,450.2	
Regular and Diet		444.1	70.5	108.6	271.2

EXHIBIT 10

Example of CRUSH Trade Promotion

HAVE A CRUSH ON US!
DEALER LOADERS

Item

- A   Crush Adventure Back Pack
- B   Beach Bag/Blanket
- C   Neon Cap
- D   Sony® Walkman
- E   Dirty Dunk®

Advertising and promotion programs were jointly implemented and financed by concentrate producers and bottlers. Concentrate producers and bottlers split advertising costs 50-50. For example, if $1 million were spent for television brand advertising, $500,000 would be paid by the brand's bottlers and $500,000 would be paid by the concentrate producer. Bottlers and concentrate producers split the cost of retail-oriented merchandise promotions and consumer promotions 50-50.

A variety of merchandising promotions are used in the soft drink industry. One kind of promotion, called a "dealer loader," is a premium given to retailers. A common form is a "display loader" such as ice chests, insulated can coolers, T-shirts, or sweatshirts, which are part of an in-store or point-of-purchase display. After the display is taken down, the premium is given to the retailer. End-of-aisle displays and other types of special free-standing displays are also provided, as are shelf banners. Concentrate producers will often allocate 10 cents (for shirts) to 20 cents (for displays) per case sold to bottlers who implement these merchandising promotions. Consumer promotions include sponsorship of local sports and entertainment events, plastic cups and napkins with the brand logo, and stylish baseball caps, T-shirts, or sunglasses featuring the brand name. Assorted other promotions are also used, including coupons, on-package promotions, and sweepstakes. Concentrate producers will offer anywhere from 5 cents (for cups, caps, or glasses) to 25 cents (for local event marketing including cups, caps, or glasses) per case sold to bottlers who use these promotions. Examples of trade and consumer promotions are shown in Exhibits 10 and 11.

Concentrate producers occasionally offer bottlers price promotions in the form of distribution incentives. These incentives are typically based on case sales and are frequently used to stimulate bottler sales and merchandising activity. These incentives are often in the range from 15 to 25 cents per case depending on the amount of effort desired or needed.

CRUSH MARKETING PROGRAM

In January 1990, several strategic marketing decisions were made concerning the CRUSH brand. Most notably, a decision was made to focus initial attention on the orange flavor. Even though the CRUSH line featured several flavors, orange (regular and diet) accounted for almost two-thirds of total CRUSH case volume. (Exhibit 12 shows the CRUSH product line.) Second, marketing executives at Cadbury Beverages, Inc., decided to focus immediate attention and effort on reestablishing the bottling network for the CRUSH line, particularly orange CRUSH. Third, it was decided that careful consideration of CRUSH positioning was necessary to build on the existing customer franchise and provide opportunities for further development of the CRUSH brand and its assorted flavors. Finally, the executives agreed to the development of an advertising and promotion program, including the determination of objectives, strategies, and expenditures.

Bottler Network Development

Recognizing the traditional and central role that bottlers play in the soft drink industry, company marketing and sales executives immediately embarked on an aggressive effort to recruit bottlers for the CRUSH line. The CRUSH bottling network had gradually eroded in the 1980s due in part to Procter and Gamble's decision to test a distribution system for selling CRUSH through warehouses rather than through

EXHIBIT 11

Example of CRUSH Consumer Promotion

EXHIBIT 12

CRUSH Product Line

bottlers. This action, which centralized bottling in the hands of a limited number of bottlers that shipped product to warehouses for subsequent delivery to supermarkets and other retail outlets, had led many in the CRUSH bottler network to question their future role with CRUSH. An outgrowth of this action was that CRUSH had the lowest market coverage of orange category sales potential among major competitors.

Recruitment efforts in early 1990 broadened the bottler network. By mid-1990, new bottling agreements had been arranged, and trade relations with 136 bottlers were established. The revitalized bottler network meant that CRUSH would be available in markets that represented 75 percent of total orange category sales in time for the CRUSH relaunch. The broadened bottler network would also require promotional support. According to Kim Feil, "We knew that reestablishing trade relations was an important first step. However, we also knew that new and existing bottlers would be gauging the kind and amount of advertising and promotional support we would provide when we relaunched CRUSH."

Positioning Issues

Numerous issues related to positioning were being addressed while the bottler recruitment effort was under way. First, since the company already marketed SUNKIST, questions arose concerning the likely cannibalization of SUNKIST sales if a clearly differentiated position for orange CRUSH in the marketplace was not developed and

EXHIBIT 13

Positioning of CRUSH, 1954–1989

Year	Positioning	Target	Campaign
1954	Natural flavor from Valencia oranges	All-family	"Naturally—it tastes better, Orange-CRUSH"
1957–Late 1960s (est.)	Good for you; fresh juice from specially selected oranges	All-family"	Tastes so good . . . so good for you!"
1963–1964 (est.)	Introduced full line of flavors: grape, strawberry, grapefruit, root beer, cherry	All-family	No clear introduction effort: • "Thirsty? CRUSH that thirst with Orange CRUSH" • "Delicious, refreshing, satisfying—Grape CRUSH" • "Clean fruit taste—Grapefruit CRUSH" • "Mellow CRUSH Root Beer"
Early 1970s (est.)	Unique taste, the "change of pace" drink	All-family directed toward purchaser who is female HH 18–35, promotions targeted child/young adults	"Ask for CRUSH, the taste that's all its own."
1979–1980	Competitive taste superiority	Maintained early 1970s TV but focused on young males with sports	Added "There is no orange like orange CRUSH . . ." to "Ask for CRUSH, the taste that's all its own."
1980	Competitive taste superiority in fruit flavors	Added new radio for 10–19 target	Same as above
1981	100% natural flavors, contemporary wholesome brand	13–39 Teens and young adults	"Orange lovers have a CRUSH on us"
1980–1985	Great, irresistible taste	13–39	"Orange lovers have a CRUSH on us"
1983	More orangery taste	13–39	"Orange lovers"
1981–1982	Great taste	13–39	Test: "First CRUSH"
1984	Sugar-free CRUSH, great taste of Nutrasweet	13–49	"Celebrate"
1986–1987	Taste with 10% real juice	Teens, 12–17	"Peel Me a CRUSH"
1987	The drink that breaks monotony	Teens, 12–17	Test: "Color Me CRUSH"
1987–1989	Bold user imagery with thirst-quenching benefit	Teens, 13–29	"Don't just quench it, CRUSH it"

successfully executed. A second issue concerned the relative emphasis on regular and diet CRUSH with respect to Mandarin Orange Slice and Minute Maid Orange. These two competitors had outpaced CRUSH and SUNKIST in attracting the diet segment of orange drinkers. Third, viable positions had to be considered that did not run contrary to previous positionings and would build on the customer franchise currently held by orange CRUSH. In this regard, a historical review of CRUSH positioning was conducted. The results of this effort are reproduced in Exhibit 13.

Company executives recognized that issues relating to positioning needed to be addressed in a timely manner. Without a clear positioning statement, the creative process underlying the advertising program could not be initiated.

Advertising and Promotion

CRUSH marketing executives were pleasantly surprised to learn that the CRUSH brand had high name awareness in the markets served by existing and new bottlers. According to the company's consumer awareness tracking research, of the four major brands, CRUSH had the highest orange-brand awareness in Seattle, San Francisco, New York, Miami, Los Angeles, Chicago, and Boston. Nevertheless, numerous issues had to be addressed concerning the CRUSH advertising and promotion program.

In particular, objectives for the advertising and promotion had to be established and communicated to the advertising agency that would represent CRUSH. Next, the relative emphasis on consumer advertising and on types of trade and consumer promotion had to be determined. Specifically, this meant setting the budget for advertising expenditures and the amounts to be spent on a per case basis for promotions. Ultimately, a *pro forma* statement of projected revenues and expenses would be necessary for presentation to senior management at Cadbury Beverages, Inc. Implicitly, this required a case volume forecast for orange CRUSH that realistically portrayed market and competitive conditions and "the quality of my marketing program," said Feil.

Godiva Europe

In July 1991, Charles van der Veken, President of Godiva Europe, examined with satisfaction the financial results of Godiva Belgium for the last period, which showed an operating profit of 13 million Belgian francs. "We've come a long way," he thought to himself, remembering the financial situation he inherited just one year ago, which showed a loss of 10 million francs.[1] Over the course of the past year van der Veken had completely restructured the company. He started by firing the Marketing and Sales staff and then changed the retail distribution network by removing Godiva's representation from numerous stores. He then completely rethought the decoration and design of the remaining stores, and established precise rules of organization and functioning applicable to those stores. These changes made the Godiva-Belgium network of franchises comparable to those in the United States and Japan. For, while in all other countries Godiva stores conveyed an image of luxury and of high scale products, in Belgium, where the Godiva concept was originally conceived, this image was scarcely maintained. Fearing what he called the "boomerang effect," van der Veken had first focused on restructuring the Godiva retail network, an objective that was today on the road to realization. "It is time," thought van der Veken, "to communicate the desired image of Godiva more widely, now that we have a retail network capable of maintaining that image on the level of the Triad Countries."[2]

THE GODIVA EUROPE COMPANY

Godiva has its roots in Belgium, where the hand crafting of chocolates stems from a long tradition. Joseph Draps, founder of Godiva in the 1920s, took control of the family business upon the death of his father and created an assortment of prestigious chocolates for which he lacked a name. He finally chose the name "Godiva" because it had an international sound and a history, that of Lady Godiva:

> Lady Godiva is the heroine of an English legend. She was the wife of Leofric, Count of Chester in the 11th century, whom she married around 1050. Roger de Wendower (13th century) tells that Godiva implored Leofric to lower the taxes that were crushing Coventry. The Count would not consent unless his wife would walk through the town completely naked, which she did, covered only by her long hair. John Brompton (16th century) added that nobody saw her. According to a ballad from the 17th cen-

---

[1]In 1991, 34 Belgian franc (bf) = $1.00 U.S.
[2]The Triad Countries include the United States, Japan, and countries in Western Europe.

This case study has been prepared by Professeur Jean-Jacques Lambin, of Louvain University, Louvain-la-Neuve, Belgium, with the cooperation of Jean-François Buslain and Sophie Lambin. Certain names and data have been disguised, and the case cannot be used as a source of information for market research. Used with permission.

tury, Godiva ordered all the inhabitants to remain at home. The only one to see her was an indiscreet Peeping Tom. Since 1678, every three years in Coventry, a Godiva Procession is held. (Grand Larousse, Vol. 5, p. 522).

Godiva was purchased in 1974 by the multinational Campbell Soup Company. Godiva International is made up of three decision centers: Godiva Europe, Godiva USA, and Godiva Japan, as shown in Exhibit 1. An essentially Belgian company in the beginning, Godiva has become an almost entirely triadic enterprise with a presence in the United States, Japan, and Western Europe.

Godiva Europe is headquartered in Brussels, Belgium. The company's factory, which has 3,000 tons of annual production capacity, is also situated in Brussels, from where products are exported to more than 20 countries throughout the world, including Japan. There is another production unit in the United States, which can provide about 90 percent of the needs of the U.S. market, with the remainder being imported from Belgium.

In 1990, Godiva Europe had annual sales of 926 million Belgian francs. The company is well placed to serve Belgium, its largest market. After Belgium, the principal European markets are France, Great Britain, Germany, Spain, and Portugal. Godiva USA and Godiva Japan distribute Godiva products to their respective markets and constitute the two other most important markets.

The largest part of European production volume (55 percent) is sold under the Godiva brand name, about 10 percent is sold through private labels arrangements, and another 10 percent is sold under the brand Corné Toison d'Or; 25 percent of Godiva Europe's production is sold directly to Godiva Japan and Godiva USA at a company transfer price. Thus, only 65 percent of the total sales are made in Europe, under the brand name Godiva. A significant share of Godiva Europe's sales are made through more than 20 airport duty-free shops throughout the world. Those sales,

EXHIBIT 1

Campbell Soup Organizational Structure

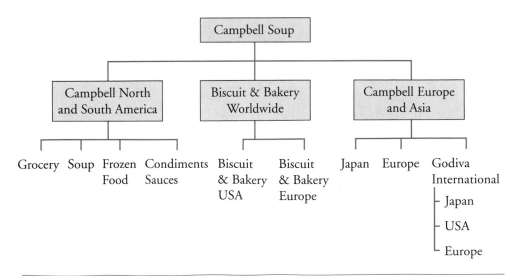

free of a value-added tax (VAT), are made at the expense of local country sales, but they help to establish the international image of Godiva.[3]

Godiva Europe also owns the Corné Toison d'Or brand, which is distributed through 40 stores in Belgium, which are mostly located in the Brussels area. This brand has an image very similar to Godiva: a refined, hand-made, luxury product. The acquisition of Corné Toison d'Or was made in 1989 to fully exploit the production capacity of the Brussels plant modernized two years earlier. The original objective was to differentiate the positioning of the brand Corné Toison d'Or from Godiva, but this objective was never pursued by management. A further complication stemmed from the fact that another Corné brand, Corné Port Royal, also exists in the Belgian market with a retail network of 18 stores.

Godiva USA has a factory in Pennsylvania that serves the U. S. market. Godiva Japan, which is solely concerned with marketing, distribution, and sales of Godiva chocolates, imports the product from Belgium. The Japanese market is very important for Godiva International because of the high price level, 4,000 bf per kilogram compared to 2,000 bf in the United States, and 1,000 bf in Belgium.[4]

The reference market of Godiva International consists of the Triad Nations. As a branch of Campbell Soup Company, Godiva benefits from a privileged position. Godiva International is directly attached to the Campbell Soup Company Vice President Europe-Asia without an intermediary who facilitates communication.

THE WORLD CHOCOLATE MARKET

Unlike coffee or tea, chocolate lends itself to multiple preparations. It can be eaten or drunk, munched, or savored. The official journal of the European Community divides chocolate into four categories: bars of chocolate that are filled or not filled, chocolate candies or chocolates (called "pralines" in Belgium) such as Godiva's chocolates, and other chocolate preparations.

Chocolate consumption stabilized in the mid-1980s as a result of increasing raw material costs and an ensuing price rise of finished products. As depicted in Exhibit 2, the past three years have shown very good performances with worldwide consumption of confectionery chocolate (all categories included) of just over 3 million tons in 1989, or an increase of 30.7 percent compared with 1980 consumption. Overproportional consumption were observed in Japan (+54.2 percent), Italy (+102.1 percent), Australia (+45.1 percent) and the United States since 1980.

EXHIBIT 2

Chocolate Confectionery World Consumption (In Thousands of Tons)

Years	1980	1985	1986	1987	1988	1989
Tons	2,359.6	2,778.1	2,780.2	2,862.0	2,990.8	3,083.6
Index	100	118	118	121	127	131

Source: IOCCC, December 1990, p. 45.

---

[3]A value-added tax is a government tax levied upon the value that is added to products as they progress from raw material to consumer goods.
[4]1 kilogram = 2.205 pounds.

A distinction is made between industrial and chocolate pralines within the chocolate candies category. Industrial chocolates are sold in prewrapped boxes with or without brand names. The generic boxes are mostly sold through large retail chains at Christmas or Easter; brand boxes are luxurious, offer a high-quality assortment of chocolates, and emphasize the brand name in the package and through mass-media advertising. Typical of this subcategory is the brand Mon Chéri from Ferrero. The sales of generic boxes are stable in Europe, while sales of brand boxes are increasing. This suggests that consumers pay attention to brand names and to the quality image communicated by chocolate packaging and advertising.

Chocolate pralines, on the other hand, designate chocolate products that are hand-made or decorated by hand. The distinctive characteristics of pralines are their delicate flavor and luxurious packaging. They are also highly perishable and fragile with regard to conservation and transport. Typically, Godiva chocolates belong to this last product category.

Chocolate Consumption per Country

The per capita consumption of chocolate varies among countries as shown in Exhibit 3. Chocolate consumption is higher in the northern part of Europe and lower in the Mediterranean region. In 1990, Switzerland had the highest per capita consumption with 9.4 kilograms per person. The lowest per capita consumption rate is observed in Spain with 1.2 kilograms per person.

Exhibit 3 also shows that the share of chocolate candies (namely, pralines) with respect to total chocolate confectionery consumption, is strongest in Belgium with 44 percent against 41 percent in Great Britain, 37 percent in France, 35 percent in Italy, and 34 percent in Switzerland. Switzerland is the largest consumer of chocolate candies, followed closely by the United Kingdom and Belgium, while the other countries are found far behind these three leaders.

EXHIBIT 3

Chocolate Confectionery Consumption per Country

	Per Capita Consumption in Kilograms in 1989		Share of Chocolates in Confectionery Chocolate
Country	Chocolate Candies	Chocolate Confectionery	
Belgium	2.65	6.09	43.5%
Denmark	1.17	5.61	20.9%
France	1.69	4.59	36.8%
Spain	0.14	1.21	11.6%
Italy	0.65	1.84	35.3%
Japan	0.44	1.59	27.8%
Germany, Federal Republic	1.64	6.81	24.1%
Switzerland	3.17	9.41	33.9%
United Kingdom	2.96	7.15	41.4%
United States	1.14	4.77	23.9%

Source: IOCCC, Statistical bulletin, Brussels, December 1990. Chocolate candies: candy bars, pralines, and other chocolate products. Solid and filled bars and chocolate products.

In examining the level of consumption reached in countries such as Switzerland, the United Kingdom, and Belgium, it is possible to get an idea of the enormous potential that the world chocolates market holds. In fact, countries like Spain, Italy, and Japan are susceptible to one day reaching such a level of consumption roughly comparable to Switzerland, the United Kingdom, and Belgium provided effective marketing programs are implemented. Available industry statistics do not allow more precise estimates of the share of "chocolate pralines" in the category of chocolate candies.

Evolution of Consumption

Growth rates of chocolate confectionery are also very different among countries as shown in Exhibit 4. Countries experiencing the highest growth rates are Italy, Japan, United Kingdom and the United States. With the exception of the United Kingdom, these are the countries where the per capita consumption are the lowest. The largest consumer countries like Belgium, Germany, and Switzerland have probably reached a plateau in terms of per capita consumption.

Purchase Behavior of the Chocolate Consumer

Chocolate was imported to Europe by the Spanish at the time of the exploration of the New World. At that time, only the wealthy ate chocolate.

Today, chocolate is a mass-consumption product, accessible to everyone. Consumers are demanding and desire variety. In making chocolate a luxury product, chocolatiers have given chocolates a certain nobleness. The hand-worked character of production and refined decoration give chocolates their status. Chocolates are offered at holidays and other special occasions, and are eaten among friends in

EXHIBIT 4

Evolution of Chocolate Confectionery Consumption: Average Yearly Growth Rate, 1980–1989

| Country | Consumption (Kilogram per Person) | | Average Growth | |
	1980	1989	1980 = 100	Average Growth Rate
Belgium	6.04	6.09	100.8	1.76%
Denmark	4.80	5.61	116.9	1.79%
France	3.96	4.59	115.9	1.65%
Spain	nd	1.21	nd	-
Italy	0.92	1.84	200.0	8.00%
Japan	1.09	1.59	145.9	4.28%
German Federal Republic	6.56	6.81	103.8	0.42%
Switzerland	8.44	9.41	111.5	1.22%
United Kingdom	5.48	7.15	130.5	3.00%
United States	3.69	4.77	129.3	2.89%

nd = no data
Source: IOCCC, December 1990, p.49.

an atmosphere of warmth. They are not purchased like bars of chocolate; the behavior of the consumer of chocolate pralines is much more deliberate and involved. The higher prices of chocolate pralines with respect to the other categories of chocolate do not inhibit the consumer but limit more impulsive purchases.

The consumption of chocolate of all categories is associated with pleasure. A qualitative study of the Belgian market shows that this pleasure is associated with the ideas of refinement, taste pleasure and gift: ". . . chocolate pralines are offered as a gift while chocolate bars are purchased for self-consumption. A praline would be mainly feminine, . . . women seem to appreciate them more and pralines are described by them as refined and fine." In addition, the strong and powerful taste, a particular form, the consistency of chocolate that melts in the mouth, and the feel of the chocolate to the touch are also factors to which the consumer is sensitive. Finally, the idea of health, of a pure product devoid of chemicals, is also in the consumer's mind.

GODIVA CHOCOLATES IN THE WORLD

The ancestry of chocolates can be traced to the chef of the Duke of Choiseul de Plessis-Praslin, an ambassador of Louis XIII of France, when he prepared almonds browned in caramelized sugar. However, chocolates as we know them today, a filling surrounded by chocolate, were born in Belgium. It was at the end of the nineteenth century that Jean Neuhaus, son of a confectioner from Neuchatel living in Brussels, created the first chocolates that he named "pralines."

The current concern of Godiva International is to convey a similar image of Godiva chocolates across the world: the image of a luxury chocolate that is typically Belgian. In what follows, the main characteristics of consumers in each country where Godiva is distributed will be briefly presented.

Belgium

Belgium is the birthplace of chocolates and where their consumption is strongest. While there are no significant differences in the consumption rate among the different Belgian regions, differences do exist among the four main socioprofessional categories, as shown in Exhibit 5.

In 60 percent of purchases, chocolates are offered as gifts and consumers make a clear distinction between a purchase for self-consumption and for a gift. The customer prefers a package where he or she may select the assortment. However, the image of chocolate pralines has aged; chocolates have become a product more com-

EXHIBIT 5

The Demand for Pralines in Belgium: Average Expenditures per Household in 1988 (bf)

Regions	Belgium	Brussels	Wallonie	Flanders
	814	884	812	793
Households	Independent	White Collar	Blue Collar	Inactive
	1,239	800	567	755

Source: INS, *Enquête sur less budgets des ménages* (1988). The total population includes 3,876,549 households.

parable to flowers than to a luxury product. The results of a brand image study conducted in the Brussels area (see Appendix A) shows that, while Godiva is strongly associated with the items "most expensive," "nicest packaging," and "most beautiful stores," it is not clearly perceived as very different from its main competitors, Neuhaus namely, on items associated with superior quality or a significant quality differential. Neuhaus and Corné, two directly competing brands, are perceived in a very similar way as shown in the perceptual map presented in Exhibit 6.

In Belgium, Godiva holds a 10 percent market share and Léonidas 43 percent. Léonidas also has a large international coverage with more than 1,500 outlets throughout the world and a production capacity of 10,000 tons, or three times that of Godiva Europe. In 1991, the size of the total Belgian market for chocolate pralines is estimated to be 3.6 billion Belgian francs (VAT included) or about 8,800 tons. This estimate is based on the data presented in Exhibit 5.

France

French chocolate is darker, dryer, and more bitter than Belgian chocolates. Belgian chocolates are however well-known and appreciated due to Léonidas, which introduced chocolates in France and today holds the largest market share and sells through 250 boutiques. Belgian chocolates are represented as well by Jeff de Bruges, which

EXHIBIT 6

Brand Image Study: Chocolate Pralines in Belgium, Bubble Area = Awareness

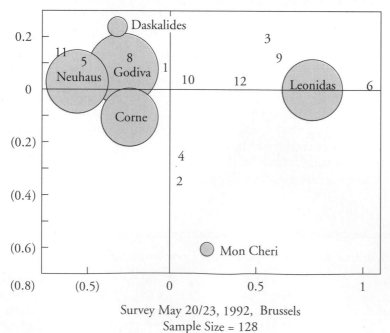

1. Queen of chocolate
2. Ideal for gift
3. For self-indulgence
4. Special occasions
5. Beautiful boutique
6. Attrative price
7. Nice packaging
8. Refined chocolate
9. Belgian chocolate
10. Taste I like best
11. Expensive chocolate
12. Wordly known brand

Survey May 20/23, 1992, Brussels
Sample Size = 128

belongs to Neuhaus. Godiva has a share in a small niche, which is also occupied by several French chocolatiers, none of whom have national market coverage. In France, chocolates are above all regarded as a gift that is offered on certain special occasions, and their purchase is very seasonal (60 percent of all purchases are made at Christmas), which poses problems of profitability during periods of lower sales. Estimates of market size are presented in Exhibit 7.

United Kingdom

An assortment of confectionery products, in which different types of chocolate are mixed, is most appreciated in the United Kingdom. Godiva is currently being introduced to the British market and seeks to create the concept of high-quality and more refined Belgian chocolates. The change of mentality is progressing, but the British are viewed as rather conservative and the economic climate is not very favorable for a luxury product. Mark and Spencer, an upscale British retailer, is selling Belgian chocolates under the private brand name Saint Michael. The Belgian origin of the chocolates is clearly indicated in the packaging, however.

Spain and Portugal

In Spain and Portugal, chocolate pralines are a completely new concept. Godiva was the first to introduce chocolates a few years ago, and the reception was excellent. Godiva chocolates immediately acquired the image of a refined, luxury product. In Spain, Godiva is sold through the upscale department store Corte Inglese and by several franchises. Consumers' attitudes toward chocolate is very positive. Chocolates are principally offered as gifts and most often in luxurious boxes.

Germany

In Germany, a "chocolates culture" does not really exist. Germans appear to be satisfied with a classic chocolate bar and do not yet place much importance on the distinctive qualities of fine chocolates. Godiva pralines are distributed through five franchised dealers.

EXHIBIT 7

Estimated Consumption of Chocolates in France; 1988–1990 (In Tons)

Year	1988	1989	1990
Production	44,302	47,660	50,720
Imports (+)	9,677	10,478	11,546
Exports (−)	3,788	5,739	7,970
Total Consumption	50,191	52,399	54,365
Per capita Consumption	0.900 kg	0.935 kg	0.965 kg

Source: "Production des IAA," SCEES (Décembre 1991): 61 (bonbons de chocolat); Eurostat "Foreign Trade"—Categories: 1806.90.11 and 1806.90.19. The category "bonbons de chocolat" includes other products than chocolate pralines: Thus, total consumption is overestimated.

Other European Countries

In Holland, chocolate pralines are perceived as too expensive. In Italy and in the Nordic countries, chocolate pralines consumption is still a very marginal phenomenon.

United States

Chocolates are very popular in the United States. Chocolates are given as presents on special occasions such as birthdays, Valentine's Day, and Christmas. Chocolates are typically offered in prewrapped packages, with an interior form to house them. The output of the Godiva facility in Pennsylvania almost suffices to cover the needs of present domestic consumption. A small proportion of the Brussels plant output is exported to the United States. The Belgian factory delivers only new products or some products that cannot be produced by the Pennsylvania plant, such as the Godiva golf balls and the chocolate cartridges. In addition to 95 company-owned stores, 800 outlets carry Godiva chocolates in the United States. These outlets are generally located in upscale department stores situated in suburban shopping malls, like Lord & Taylor, Neiman Marcus, Saks Fifth Avenue, Filenes, and I Magnin.

Japan

In Japan, the Godiva chocolate is perceived foremost as European (60 percent as Belgian and 40 percent as Swiss or French). Chocolates are a prestigious and luxury gift. A large problem of seasonality exists in Japan as 75 percent of purchases take place near Valentine's Day. A unique feature of this market is that Japanese women give Japanese men chocolates on Valentine's Day. The Japanese market is a very attractive market for Godiva International and is still expanding.

The Duty-Free Market

In addition to these countries, one must also include the duty-free market, which represents a very significant market segment in terms of output. The number of duty-free stores is still increasing, and sales are closely linked to the development of passenger traffic. Godiva holds a very strong position in this market where Léonidas is not present.

Generally speaking, the annual growth potential in Europe is very different and varies from country to country. In the United States, growth varies between 5 and 10 percent annually, while in Japan growth is very strong varying between 20 to 25 percent annually.

GODIVA'S MARKETING STRATEGY

Godiva pralines are produced by four means of fabrication: those that are formed in a mold, those that are hollowed then filled, those where a solid filling is coated with chocolate, and finally those that are produced entirely by hand: hand-made chocolates. Seventy percent of Godiva pralines are machine-made, and 30 percent are hand-made. However, 60 percent of the 70 percent machine-made chocolates must be decorated by hand. Hand decoration is necessary to assure the quality level and the look of the praline.

Godiva strives to find an optimal compromise between automation and hand-work, hoping both to ensure the profitability and to perpetuate the name of Godiva as a producer of hand-made luxury chocolates. However, the difference in production costs between machine-made and hand-made chocolates is considerable (hand-made chocolates can cost up to seven times more than machine-made). Charles van der Veken often had second thoughts about the wisdom of maintaining this product policy. He thought:

> Isn't the investment in making hand-made chocolates disproportional to the expectations of our customers? Do they really perceive the added value of these hand-made chocolates? Aren't these chocolates just a bit too sophisticated?

Whatever the case, the objective pursued by Godiva is to convert the European market to the quality level of the Godiva praline. The Belgium consumer is the reference point: "Shouldn't a product that has passed the test of the Belgian consumer, a fine connoisseur of chocolate and a demanding customer, be assured of success throughout the world?"

The Godiva facility in Belgium produces chocolates for the entire world, with the exception of the United States. Products exported from Belgium are identical for all countries, but sales by items are different. For example, in France, the demand for drier and more bitter chocolates is stronger while in the United Kingdom, cream and white chocolates are more popular. The production capacity of the Belgian factory is not fully utilized, and there is a significant available capacity. Today, the U.S. factory still produces a slightly different and more limited assortment of chocolate pralines. These differences will progressively vanish, and the trend is toward similar production. The planning of production is particularly complex, however, because of the high seasonality of consumption combined with the emphasis on chocolate freshness.

Packaging Policy

Only packaging will distinguish one country from another in order to better meet national and local chocolate consumption habits. In the United States, the tradition is to purchase chocolates prewrapped, while in Europe and Japan the custom-made assortment dominates. What's more, in Japan, chocolates are purchased in very small quantities (given the price); thus the beauty of the packaging becomes predominant, whereas in Europe and more precisely in Belgium, the value of the gift is more often related to the judicious assortment of chocolates that were chosen. As stated by a Godiva dealer, "Customers have very precise ideas on the type of assortment they want, even for gifts, and they don't like to buy prewrapped standard assortments."

Currently, the trend in packaging at Godiva is packaging by themes called "collections." With these "collections," Godiva leaves the food industry for the luxury products sector. These hand-made creations constitute a research and development activity that ensures continuous innovation, and provides renewed promotional displays in the Godiva boutiques. In these "collections," beautiful fabric boxes, hand-crafted according to the principles of "haute couture," will illustrate through the calendar Valentine's Day, Spring, Easter, Mother's Day, Christmas, etc. In Belgium, the price of such a box (1,000 bf) is exorbitant with respect to the price of the chocolates; thus these boxes serve more often for in-store decoration than for sales.

For several years, Godiva has also tried to develop tea rooms attached to Godiva boutiques where customers can eat fine pastries or ice cream. The people who stop here see these rooms as havens of peace where they can rest between purchases while shopping and buy a few chocolates or even a box of chocolates.

Pricing Policy

Making a Godiva chocolate incorporates an enormous amount of manual labor and the gross margins are modest (35 to 40 percent on average), while top management of Campbell Soup requires a 15 percent rate of return on capital invested for Godiva, a normal rate of return for a luxury product.

From one country to another, the price differences are great as shown in Exhibit 8. One of the main preoccupations of Godiva Europe is to standardize retail prices at the European level, in view of the unified European Community in 1993.

Previously, Godiva franchisees were held to a contract with the Godiva national and had to be supplied within that country. From 1993 on, it will no longer be possible to keep French franchisees from getting their supplies directly from the Belgian factory, which sells its chocolates at a much lower price. This is why prices must be modified. This adaptation has been started in Belgium with a 10 percent increase in prices effective August 1, 1991. The price of one kilo of Godiva chocolates is 1,080 bf, whereas the average market price for chocolates in Belgium is 450 bf per kilo.

This price policy, however, has not been easily accepted by the market, particularly in Belgium, where the price gap between the high and the low end of the market is already very large (see Exhibit 9). Charles van der Veken observed that, in Belgium, a 10 percent price increase has generated a loss in volume of about 7 percent. He is also aware that this lost volume goes to Léonidas for the most part.

Distribution Policy

The ultimate goal that Godiva is pursuing in its distribution policy is to obtain across the world something akin to the Benetton model: boutiques with a uniform look. This

EXHIBIT 8

Price of One Kilo of Godiva Pralines (bf)

Country	Price to Franchisees	Retail Price (VAT Included)	VAT (%)
Belgium	640	1,080	6.0
France	763	1,920	18.6
Spain	640	2,145	6.0
United Kingdom	757	1,782	17.5
Italy	640	2,009	9.0
Holland	640	1,261	6.0
Germany	640	1,641	7.0
Portugal	640	2,408	16.0
United States	n.a.	2,040	-
Japan	n.a.	4,000	-

Source: Trade publications.

EXHIBIT 9

Retail Price Comparison among Brands

Belgium		France		United Kingdom	
Brands (bf/kg)	Price	Brands (ff/kg)	Price	Brands (£/lb)	Price
Godiva	1,080	Godiva	320	Godiva	13.50
Neuhaus	980	Hédiard	640	Gérard Ronay	20.00
Corné PR	880	Fauchon	430	Valrhona	16.80
Corné TO	870	Maison ch.	390	Charbonel	14.00
Daskalidè	680	Le Notre	345	Neuhaus	12.00
Jeff de Bruges	595	Fontaine ch.	327	Léonidas	6.75
Léonidas	360	Léonidas	120	Thornton's	5.80

Source: Trade publications.

"look" includes a logo with golden letters on a black background, a facade incorporating these same colors, interior fixtures in pink marble, glass counters, and so forth.

The current retail distribution problem lies in the great disparity between the Godiva boutiques in different countries, mainly in Europe and even more particularly in Belgium (Exhibit 10 shows the Godiva distribution network). Through the years the boutiques in Belgium have become less and less attractive. As a consequence, the Godiva brand image has aged. Abroad, however, Godiva benefits from an extremely prestigious image, and the boutiques merit their name. Nevertheless, Charles van der Veken fears the worst:

> If we don't react quickly, we could compromise the world brand image of Godiva. What would a Spanish tourist think in comparing the boutique of a local distributor

EXHIBIT 10

The Godiva Distribution Network

Country	Company-Owned Stores	Franchised Dealers	Department Stores and Others	Total Outlets
Belgium	3	54	-	57
France	1	19	-	20
Spain	-	6	18	24
United Kingdom	2	-	15	17
Italy	-	2	-	2
Holland	-	2	-	2
Germany	-	4	1	5
Portugal	-	3	7	10
Total Europe	**6**	**90**	**41**	**137**
United States	95	-	800	895
Japan	-	22	67	89

Source: Trade publications and yellow pages.

in Brussels to the refined boutiques that he finds in Spain, although Belgium is the birthplace of chocolates?

Godiva's retail distribution action plan for Belgium covers a period of 18 months. A contract has been made with the franchises in which Godiva imposes both exclusivity and design; all the boutiques must have completed renovation. Once the movement is well established in Belgium, Godiva hopes this will create a spillover effect to all of Europe, because the new boutiques will constitute a reference for the recruitment of new franchises or for spontaneous requests for renovations.

This renovation movement has already begun and every two weeks a "new" boutique is inaugurated. The renovated boutiques have been transformed so that everything is in black and gold, and the entire interior decoration is redone according to the same single standard of luxury.

Generally, consumer reactions in Belgium seem favorable, although in certain respects consumers find the stores almost too beautiful. As for the franchisees, they feel as though they have a new business, and appear to be changing some of their former bad habits. If the effects remain favorable in the medium term, van der Veken said he will increase the margin provided to franchises, which is still different from one country to the other (see Exhibit 8).

The Chairman of Godiva International, Mr. Partridge, has frequently questioned the wisdom of this costly exclusive distribution system because he believes chocolate is not really a destination purchase. In Europe, the adoption of a broader distribution system is difficult, however, because of the reluctance of consumers vis-à-vis prewrapped assortments of chocolates. van der Veken is convinced, however, that the Godiva boutique is a key component of the Godiva image of a luxury good.

The Competitive Environment

The hand-made luxury chocolate segment is occupied by many other brands. Exhibit 11 presents a ranking of the specialty brands for Belgium, France, and Germany, in descending order of market share. The strength of the Léonidas competitive position in Europe is clearly shown by this comparison. Léonidas was created in 1910. It did for chocolate pralines what Henry Ford did for the car: a mass-consumption product sold at a low price. Their recipe is simple: a price of 360 bf per kilograms,

EXHIBIT 11

Main European Competitors

Belgium		France		United Kingdom	
Brands	Share	Brands	Share	Brands	Tons
Léonidas	42.8%	Léonidas	62.0%	Tornton's	1,200
Godiva	10.3	Thornton's	18.0	Léonidas	300
Neuhaus	7.1	Jeff de Bruges	14.0	Godiva	40
Mondose	5.4	Godiva	3.0		
Corné TO	2.7	Le Notre	1.0		
Others	31.7	Others	2.0		

Source: Industry trade publications (market shares are calculated on sales revenues).

8,600 square meters of industrial space, a production capacity of 10,000 tons. Léonidas is a very important competitor for Godiva. With total sales of over 2.6 billion Belgian francs, and a 32 percent operating profit margin, Léonidas has 1,500 stores world-wide, and is now expanding rapidly in the international market. The next major competitor is Neuhaus, which recently merged with Mondose and Corné Port Royal and which is also pursuing an international development strategy. The "others" include the many small confectionery-chocolatiers who nibble at the market share of the larger companies in offering fresh, original products made from pure cocoa.

However, given its broad market coverage, Charles van der Veken believes that Godiva has a significant competitive advantage due to its integration into Campbell Soup 13 years ago, which provided Godiva with an opportunity for global expansion much more quickly than its competitors. Thus Godiva is present everywhere, and even if it often skirts a competitor in a particular market, it is rarely the same one across the world. Godiva can thus currently be considered the global leader in the luxury chocolate segment.

Only in Belgium is Godiva having difficulties making use of its competitive advantage. The volume growth has proven important everywhere, except in Belgium. According to Charles van der Veken, the market is already too saturated, and it is up to the best to make the difference.

Advertising Strategy

Today Godiva does not need to make itself known on the international level: Its brand name is already globally recognized. Its current concern, in line with the policy that has been pursued for the past several months, is to create a common advertising message for the entire world. However, this will not be an easy task as evidenced by a comparison of the situation in Belgium, the United States, and Japan. In the United States and Japan the product is relatively new, and has a strong image inasmuch as there is no direct competitor. In Belgium the consumer has followed the evolution of Godiva chocolates, and the progressive commoditization of the brand. It is therefore more difficult to impress Belgians with a product that is already well-known. What's more, Belgians are in daily contact with other brands of chocolates, with which they can easily compare Godiva.

Thus, as van der Veken pointed out, Godiva finds itself faced with very different worlds. Up until now, in the United States, advertising was focused on prestige, luxury, refinement, with a communication style similar to the one adopted by Cartier, Gucci, or Ferrari. These advertisements were presented in magazines well adapted to the desired positioning: gourmet, fashion, or business magazines that cater to higher-income echelons (see Exhibit 12).

In Belgium, however, this type of advertising tended only to reinforce the aged, grandmotherish image of Godiva chocolates. What's more, the gap between the "perceived image" (a food item interchangeable with others of the same type) and the "desired image" (an exceptional luxury product) was so large that spectacular results could not be expected.

A study performed by Godiva seems to show that nobody could remember these advertisements, nor the promises that were made. In Belgium, Godiva had also made use of event marketing: being represented at events at which the target population had a large chance of being present. Thus two years ago, Godiva was the sponsor of a golf competition in Belgium that held its name (Godiva European Master). Such

EXHIBIT 12

Typical Godiva Print Advertisement in the United States

actions are however extremely costly, and their effectiveness is difficult to measure. The total advertising budget of Godiva Europe is 31 million Belgian francs per year.

THE ADVERTISING DECISION

Aware of this problem, Godiva Europe is in the process of evaluating its advertising strategy. The following situation had to be solved: creating a common advertising message targeted at the three main markets while taking into consideration the inevitable cultural differences among countries.

Godiva USA had just sent Charles van der Veken the briefing of an international advertising campaign, which is summarized in the Exhibit 13. He said that adopting this advertising style on the European market worried him to a certain degree:

> The least one can say is that differences of mentality exist between our two continents. We certainly need to wake up our old-fashioned Godiva, but we should also be careful of overly radical changes.

Reflecting with his marketing staff, van der Veken tended to define the advertising objective in the following manner.

> The objective of Godiva USA is to increase the frequency of the purchase of chocolates for gifts as well as for self consumption, whereas Belgium wants to make its brand image more youthful. Thus, the United States should adjust its advertising slightly "downward," in making the product more accessible through convivial advertising and less "plastic beauty." While Belgium should strive, jointly with other marketing efforts (redesign of boutiques, increased quality of service, creation of "collections"), to adjust its advertising slightly "upward," in affirming itself as a prestigious luxury product, only younger.

The upward adjustment for Belgium was a daring challenge. Charles van der Veken wondered if it would not be preferable to pass through a transitory period before beginning a global marketing campaign, which would take into consideration the historical and cultural context of Belgium.

Just then, Mrs. Bogaert, van der Veken's assistant, entered his office holding a fax from Godiva International:

> The campaign cannot be launched in time for Christmas; prepare as quickly as possible your advertising campaign for Belgium and contact your agencies. Meeting in five weeks in New York for the confirmation of our projects.

Charles van der Veken immediately called his Director of Marketing, informed her of the freshly arrived news, and asked her to submit for the Belgian market a campaign project based upon the American model, targeted in a first step to the Belgian market, but which could be extended to the other European markets, if not to the entire world. Together they agreed upon objectives in three main categories:

1. Qualitative objectives:
   - Rapidly reinforce the luxury image of Godiva
   - Make visibility a priority
2. Quantitative objectives:
   - Increase the frequency of purchase

EXHIBIT   13

The Briefing from Godiva International

1. **Current Positioning**
   - To adults who want a quality product for special moments, Godiva is an accessible luxury branded by Godiva Chocolatier and distinguished by superior craftsmanship.

2. **Consumer Benefit**
   - Whether you give Godiva or consume it yourself, you will relish its uniquely sensual pleasures: taste and presentation.

3. **Promise**
   - Using the finest ingredients and Belgian recipes for a remarkable taste experience.
   - Godiva heritage of fine chocolate making.
   - Beautifully crafted packaging.
   - Handcrafted in fine European heritage/style.
   - Created by an expert chocolatier.

4. **Psychographic Characteristics**
   - Godiva purchasers are discerning and driven by quality expectations. While they are value-oriented, they will pay a higher price if a significant quality differential exists, since they aspire to have or share the best.
   - Godiva men and women are sensual individuals, enjoying the pleasures that things of exceptional look, feel taste, sound and smell can offer them.

5. **Competitive Frame**
   - Gift: flowers, perfume, wine, other fine chocolates, giftables of the same price range.
   - Self-consumption: any item meant to provide a range of self-indulgences at Godiva's basic price-points.

6. **Target Audience**
   - The Godiva target covers a range of demographic characteristics:
   - Broad age range (25–54 primarily)
   - Women and men
   - Across a breadth of income levels, but with reasonable to high disposable incomes.

7. **Advertising Objectives**
   - To revitalize Godiva's worldwide premium position most specifically as it pertains to the superior quality of the chocolate product.
   - To motivate our current Godiva franchise to purchase on more frequent occasions (gifting and self-consumption).
   - To motivate current purchasers of competitive chocolates and nonchocolate giftables to convert to the Godiva franchise.

8. **Message**
   - Godiva chocolates are expertly crafted to provide an unparalleled sensory experience.

9. **Tone and Manner**
   - Luxurious—Energetic—Modern—Upscale—Emotionally involving.

---

3. Other objectives:
   - Concentrate all efforts on Belgium during several months (months of peak sales)
   - Synergy of all other methods of promotion and advertising

An additional 13 million (bf) advertising budget would be allocated to the campaign. After some thought, it seemed possible to Mr. van der Veken that a triad campaign would, on a long-term basis, be feasible in spite of cultural differences. He did not believe, however, that business generated in the other European countries would be high enough today to justify the same advertising budget as for Belgium. This became even more obvious when one considered that, in terms of media costs and for a same impact, 1 bf in Belgium is equivalent to 1.6 bf in France and 1.9 bf in the United Kingdom.

Charles van der Veken was also convinced that an European advertising campaign is useless without having first improved and reinforced the Godiva European distribution.

APPENDIX A: RESULTS OF THE BRAND IMAGE STUDY IN THE BRUSSELS MARKET AREA

Aided Brand Awareness

Brand Name	Not at all	Only by name	By experience	Total
Corné	24.2%	28.9%	46.9%	100%
Corné Toison d'Or	31.3%	25.8%	43.0%	100%
Corné Port Royal	69.3%	16.5%	14.2%	100%
Daskalides	54.3%	26.0%	19.7%	100%
Godiva	2.3%	19.5%	78.1%	100%
Léonidas	2.3%	10.9%	86.7%	100%
Mon chéri	4.7%	23.6%	71.7%	100%
Neuhaus	13.3%	25.0%	61.7%	100%

Don't know any of brands Corné, Corné Toison d'Or, Corné Port Royal: 22.7%. Known "by name" or "by experience" at least one of the following brands: Corné, Corné Toison d'Or, Corné Port Royal: 77.3%

Brand Image Analysis

	Brand associated most with each attribute									
Attribute	Corné (1)	Corné Toison D'or (2)	Corné Port Royal (3)	Corné Total (1+2+3)	Daska Lides	Godiva	Léoni-Das	Mon Chéri	Neu-Haus	Total
The queen of chocolates	7.1%	5.5%	0.8%	(13.4)		37.8%	27.6%	1.6%	19.7%	100%
Ideal for gift	11.0%	3.1%		(14.1)		29.1%	26.8%	10.2%	19.7%	100%
For self-indulgence	4.8%	3.2%	0.8%	(8.8)	0.8%	26.4%	48.0%	1.6%	14.4%	100%
For special occasions	6.5%	8.9%	0.8%	(16.2)	0.8%	26.8%	28.5%	8.1%	19.5%	100%
The most beautiful boutique	6.0%	9.4%		(15.4)		40.2%	12.0%	0.9%	31.6%	100%
The most attractive price	3.3%	2.5%		(5.8)	0.8%	5.7%	81.1%	4.9%	1.6%	100%
The nicest packaging	7.2%	7.2%	0.8%	(15.2)	0.8%	49.6%	6.4%	3.2%	24.8%	100%
The most refined chocolate	8.8%	7.2%	1.6%	(17.6)	0.8%	35.2%	18.4%	0.8%	27.2%	100%
Typically Belgian chocolate	6.5%	2.4%		(8.9)		30.1%	48.1%	2.4%	10.6%	100%
Taste I like best	5.6%	4.0%	1.6%	(11.2)		32.3%	37.9%	3.2%	15.3%	100%
The most expensive chocolate	6.7%	8.4%		(15.1)	2.5%	40.3%	5.9%	0.8%	35.3%	100%
Worldly known brand	4.0%	0.8%		(4.8)	0.8%	42.7%	39.5%	4.8%	7.3%	100%

Brand Preferences by Situation

For self-consumption		For gift	
Corné:	2.4%	Corné:	3.9%
Corné Toiuson d'Or:	4.1%	Corné Toison d'Or:	3.9%
Corné Port Royal:	0.8%	Corné Port Royal:	0.8%
Daskalides:		Daskalides:	0.8%
Godiva:	24.4%	Godiva:	29.1%
Léonidas:	48.0%	Léonidas:	27.6%
Mon chéri:	2.4%	Mon chéri:	5.5%
Neuhaus:	12.2%	Neuhaus:	25.2%
Other:	5.7%	Other:	3.2%
	100%		100%

Honeywell, Inc.

SPECTRONICS DIVISION

In early January 1981, Gary Null, Marketing Manager for Fiber Optics, scheduled a meeting with members of his management team to discuss the promotion program prepared by the division's advertising agency. The program represented the first comprehensive advertising, sales-promotion, and publicity campaign for the line of fiber-optics products manufactured by the Spectronics Division of Honeywell, Inc.

The consensus of Null's team was that the proposed campaign was thorough and exciting. Nevertheless, Null realized that the campaign would have to be approved by top management. Therefore, in the memo to his management team, he outlined the topics to be addressed:

1. Should we adopt the 1981 promotion campaign as presented to us?
2. If yes, how can we justify it, and at what expenditure level?
3. If no, what changes, if any, might we make in the program?

In addition, he asked each member of the group to prepare written arguments to support the position favored.

THE FIBER-OPTICS INDUSTRY, FALL 1980

The concept of fiber optics can be traced to the nineteenth century, when an English physicist demonstrated that light can be transmitted through a stream of water by internal reflection. Years later, others observed that two optically dissimilar materials could be assembled to form a fiber that would transmit light. Research on optical fibers continued through the mid-twentieth century, when such other transparent fibers as glass and plastic were found to be superior conductors of light.

Although technologically complex, fiber optics can be described as the technique of transmitting light through long, thin, flexible fibers of glass, plastic, and other transparent material. When fiber optics is used in a commercial application, a light source emits infrared light flashes corresponding to data. Millions of light flashes per second send streams of light through a transparent fiber. Because of a mirror effect, the fiber accelerates the movement of light. A light sensor at the other end of the fiber "reads" the data transmitted.

Fiber-optics technology has been heralded as a replacement for copper wires as a means for transmitting data. Four major benefits of optical fibers over copper

This case was made possible through the cooperation of the Spectronics Division of Honeywell, Inc. The case was prepared by Professor Roger A. Kerin and Angela Schuetze, graduate student, of the Edwin L. Cox School of Business, Southern Methodist University, as a basis for class discussion and is not designed to illustrate effective or ineffective handling of an administrative situation. Certain names and data have been disguised. Copyright © by Roger A. Kerin. No part of this case may be reproduced without the written permission of the copyright holder.

wire have been cited. First, they save space, since optical fibers can carry more information than copper wire. Second, optical fibers do not create magnetic fields and are immune to electromagnetic fields. Third, optical fibers do not conduct electricity and thus can be used when electrical cables would be hazardous. Finally, optical fibers are small and lightweight relative to copper wire. These benefits prompted scientists to proclaim that fiber-optics technology would replace copper wire in the second half of the twentieth century, and a new industry developed.

Fiber-Optics Components and Systems

Fiber-optics products are divided into two categories: fiber-optics components and fiber-optics systems. Components are the individual products necessary to emit, transmit, and detect light. There are five types of components: emitter or transmitter, fiber or cable, detector or receiver, connector, and coupler. An *emitter* is a light source. A *detector* receives the light sent by the emitter. The *fiber* or *optical cable* is a glass fiber through which light is transmitted from the emitter to the detector. A *connector* acts as a link between the emitter or the detector and the optical cable. *Couplers* enable a large number of emitters and detectors to be joined into a single optical connector. When several components are assembled to form a complete, self-contained unit capable of data transmission, a fiber-optics system exists.

Market for Fiber-Optics Technology

The market for fiber-optics technology was in its infancy in 1981. Although estimates varied, most industry forecasters believed the sales of fiber-optics components and systems would exceed $100 million in 1981 and reach $1.9 billion by 1990.

EXHIBIT 1

U.S. Fiber-Optics Component Consumption by Application

Application	1981	1986	1990
Telecommunications (including telephone)	34%	38%	43%
Adjustments	27	21	19
Government/military	25	27	22
Automotive	—	—	1
Business/retail	1	2	2
Instruments	1	1	1
Satellite earth	1	1	1
Industrial	3	4	4
Cable T.V.	5	3	2
Computer	3	3	3
Total (millions of dollars)	$135	$814	$1,868

Note: "Adjustments" include U.S.-manufactured components and systems not used in U.S. equipment, minus imported parts—that is, the trade balance (exports minus imports) plus inventory change plus nonproduction use. Nonproduction uses include replacement parts, scrappage, and parts for R&D. The concept of adjustment is important in order to reconcile U.S. application requirements and U.S. production.

Source: Gnostic Concepts, Inc., Menlo Park, California. Printed with permission.

EXHIBIT 2

U.S. Fiber-Optics Production by Component Type

Component Type	1981	1986	1990
Cable	57%	53%	60%
Transmitter, receiver, repeater	38	37	30
Connector, coupler	5	10	10
Total (millions of dollars)	$135	$814	$1,868

Note: A "repeater" is a regenerative component that allows the restoration of signal after degradation due to transmission over an optical cable. Repeaters are most frequently used in medium-to-long cables. Virtually all cable production is devoted to telecommunications, cable TV, and satellite earth applications.

Source: Gnostic Concepts, Inc., Menlo Park, California. Printed with permission.

The application of fiber-optics technology varies by end users and by type of component. Gnostic Concepts, Inc., a major electronics research firm, made the volume estimates by user segment and component type shown in Exhibits 1 and 2.

Competitive Activity

The appeal of fiber-optics technology had attracted a host of firms involved in various applications, and numerous firms entered the industry as component and system suppliers. Corning Glass Works, ITT, and AT&T's Western Electric division represent major manufacturers of fiber-optics cable for use in telecommunications. General Electric, AMP, Motorola, and Amphenol North America represent major firms pursuing the fiber-optics component and system market. In addition, selected computer manufacturers such as IBM, DEC, and Sperry-Univac were developing fiber-optics technology. Overall, competitive activity was great, as the fiber-optics industry evolved. The various competitors were each seeking a technological advantage while actively seeking to stimulate volume through marketing efforts. Cost considerations also loomed as a critical determinant of competitive activity. Although costs varied among component and system suppliers, gross margins in the industry fell in the range from 25 to 30 percent.

SPECTRONICS DIVISION

Spectronics is a division of Honeywell, Inc., a Minneapolis, Minnesota–based Fortune 500 company. Honeywell, Inc., is a high-technology company engaged in a variety of businesses that produce computers and controls for information processing, energy management, environmental control, industrial processes, and aerospace and defense. Honeywell, Inc., revenues in 1979 were $4.2 billion; operating profit was $478.1 million.

Spectronics is engaged in the business of optoelectronics. Optoelectronics is a branch of electronics that deals with solid-state and other electronic devices for generating, modulating, transmitting, and sensing electromagnetic radiation in ultraviolet, visible-light, and infrared portions of the light spectrum. Products produced by

Spectronics include light-emitting and light-sensing devices, optical switches, fiber-optics devices, and a variety of optic data-transmission ports and components for use in computers, office equipment, automobiles, and aircraft systems. Spectronics was acquired by Honeywell, Inc., in August 1978. Spectronics's total product sales prior to the acquisition exceeded $11 million.

Sales and Marketing Efforts

Spectronics markets its full line of products through its own sales force and selected distributors. International sales are handled through the international sales offices of Honeywell, Inc. "The term *sales* is sort of a misnomer," said Null. "Our people are actually problem solvers in the truest sense. The majority of our sales volume arises from custom optoelectronic components, assemblies, and systems to meet exact customer requirements." He continued:

> We work closely with design engineers, and virtually all of our sales and advertising effort is directed toward this audience. We advertise in technical publications and try to communicate state-of-the-art applications of optoelectronics. I'd say the total advertising budget for Spectronics is modest, and a good share of that goes to updating product catalogs and other product-related information.

Null added, "Design engineers play an instrumental role in developing technical specifications for optoelectronic devices. Although they do not necessarily make the final decision on the type and source of these devices, their views carry considerable weight, given the nature of the technology. But fiber optics is different. Optoelectronics is a mature technology; fiber optics is an emerging technology. Our sales and advertising effort may have to be modified."

Fiber Optics

Spectronics had been developing fiber optics data-transmission systems for more than six years prior to its acquisition by Honeywell, Inc. Principal efforts during this developmental period had focused on applying the division's engineering skills to special applications of fiber optics for use in the military. Spectronics's largest Department of Defense contract for fiber optics was a $2.1 million army contract for light-emitting diode (LED) modules for forward-looking infrared systems. Secondary emphasis was placed on custom applications of fiber optics for commercial use.

Present product-development efforts for commercial use have focused on short- to medium-distance applications (under two miles) of fiber-optics technology for local area networking in the computer industry. A "local network" is a data communications system for connecting terminals and computers that are within one building, in several buildings on the same property, or in close proximity, as opposed to long-haul networks for public switching networks such as telephone lines. However, Spectronics's products also have industrial applications and can be used in the instrumentation industry.

In May 1980, Spectronics, in conjunction with DuPont and ITT Cannon, announced a point-to-point data link called the HDC Interface. This link is suitable for short-range data transmission between computers and uses Spectronics source and detector pairs, DuPont plastic core cables, and electrical connectors from ITT Cannon. The HDC Interface link is shown in Exhibit 3. By late 1980, Spectronics's line of fiber-

EXHIBIT 3

HDC Interface Link

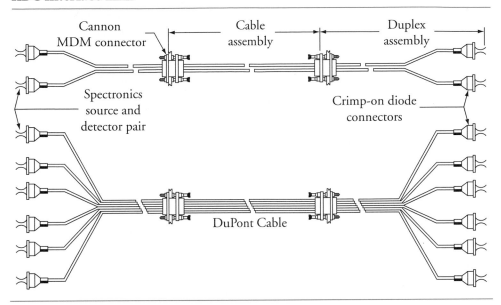

optics products included fiber–optics connectors, transmitters, receivers, and couplers among other fiber–optics assemblies and systems.

Success in product development prompted Null to give increased attention to
the marketing aspects of fiber optics for commercial use. Null noted:

> Fiber optics will take us into new markets and require us to deal with different peo-
> ple than we have in the past. Our present customers in the computer and instru-
> mentation markets and industrial users should be receptive to the fiber optics
> technology. But fiber optics will necessitate expanding into new segments of each
> market, such as robotics in the industrial segment. Our people who are now re-
> sponsible for our other optoelectronic products will have to come up with a new
> customer list and develop contacts.

After talking with top management, he was given approval to commission the division's advertising agency to prepare a comprehensive promotion program for fiber
optics directed at commercial (nonmilitary) uses. The next section describes the campaign recommended to Null in late October 1980.[1]

PROPOSED 1981 PROMOTION CAMPAIGN

The proposed campaign consists of two complementary components: (1) Fiber-
Optics Corporate Campaign and (2) Fiber-Optics Product Campaign.

---

[1]The section presents a highly condensed version of the actual program. The main points of the campaign are reported in their entirety, however. Selected creative work has been omitted because of
space limitations.

Fiber-Optics Corporate Campaign

Situation Analysis and Corporate Campaign The present fiber-optics market is characterized by a healthy amount of activity by a variety of participants, yet no company has forged ahead to establish itself as the industry leader. For this reason, the market appears to be primed for just such a campaign as we are proposing. The number-one "leader" position is there for the taking. It is important to note that although there are few companies that have the technology and the commitment of resources to that technology that Honeywell/Spectronics does, the leader position is open only until someone claims it.

The target firms in this campaign are North American computer and control system original equipment manufacturers (OEMs). The targeted audiences in order of priority are (a) operating management, (b) engineering management, and (c) design engineers.

The objectives for the campaign are (1) to build a leadership identity and reputation in fiber optics for Honeywell/Spectronics, (2) to promote "currency" of fiber optics as a "today" production technology, (3) to generate awareness of affordability, ease of use, and availability of fiber optics, and (4) to further solidify perception of Honeywell/Spectronics as a single entity.

Campaign Strategy Approaches to leadership promotion vary greatly according to the taste, style, and resources of the advertiser. The most obvious and least effective is often the unabashed "We're Number One" technique. Very closely aligned is the product-comparison technique, which usually sacrifices impact and communicates a more subtle "We're Number One." A more prestigious approach is what we call the "Speaking for the Industry" approach. The formula is simple. By generating above-par awareness through higher-impact advertising, the market size can be increased, and Honeywell/Spectronics's market share will increase accordingly. The company with the technology and production capacity to best satisfy the market derives the greatest benefit. As Honeywell/Spectronics's marketing efforts stimulate the market, the same marketing efforts do double duty in generating awareness of Honeywell/Spectronics as the most capable fiber-optics supplier and thereby increasing its market share. Thus we recommend a program that promotes fiber optics rather than one that compares our products with those of competitors.

Media Effort The media effort will concentrate on carefully chosen publications.

Targets   Target audiences fall into four subcategories, as follows:

1. *Primary target audience—operating management.* Direct advertising impressions toward managerial/administrative professionals throughout the industrial community to establish awareness of fiber optics in general and Honeywell/Spectronics in particular. Communication with these decision makers is an important support to the sales effort.

2. *Secondary target audience—engineering.* Direct advertising impressions toward engineers within the computer and control/instrumentation systems industry who are responsible for the design and specification of equipment and devices. Emphasize coverage of those engineers within the engineering management and procurement committee areas.

3. *Geographic target audience.* Advertise nationally, with primary emphasis on centers of electronic activity.

4. *Seasonal targets.* Schedule advertising for maximum weight and impact to begin the campaign. Thereafter, schedule for consistent exposure throughout the year.

Media strategy   To achieve the media objectives, we recommend the following strategy. Advertise in print media for a more detailed explanation of Honeywell/Spectronic's message and the most comprehensive and cost-effective coverage of the target audience.

1. Utilize business and industry trade magazines (1) targeted by title/function to the industry management professional or design engineer, (2) edited to be of business interest to their readers, (3) providing coverage of the target in the total United States, and (4) covering the target in the computer and controls environment conducive to the positive communication of our message.

2. Be flexible in scheduling execution to take advantage of all communication opportunities (that is, special sections/editorial emphasis on fiber optics in selected publications).

3. Utilize two-page spread ads in four colors for maximum impact and effectiveness.

Media recommendations and cost   The publications recommended in Exhibit 4 were selected on the basis of their (1) impact in the marketplace, (2) total coverage of the target audience, (3) editorial quality and compatibility (value to reader), and (4) media efficiency.

The recommended media/insertion/cost schedule is shown in Exhibit 5. Also shown is an alternative lower-cost schedule.

Publicity and Sales Promotion   Publicity and sales promotion have been neglected by the fiber-optics industry.

Objectives and audience   The objectives of publicity and sales promotion are (1) to position fiber optics as a current or "now" technology and (2) to position Honeywell/Spectronics as the leader of the fiber-optics industry. The primary audience for publicity and sales promotion efforts includes (1) engineering management, (2) design management, and (3) design engineers. The secondary audience for these efforts includes (1) the business community and (2) the general public.

Publicity effort   Fiber optics has not received the level of media exposure normally accorded a developing technology with such current and potential scope, particularly within business and mass media. The lack of coverage seems largely due to an inadequate flow of information from the companies involved in fiber-optics research. In order to provide media with sufficient information to maximize Spectronic's position, the recommended public relations program focuses on (1) media symposia, (2) feature stories, and (3) trade shows.

1. *Media symposia.* In order to gain immediate, widespread exposure for fiber–optics and Honeywell/Spectronics, the public relations program begins with a series of four media symposia across the country. Various aspects of fiber-optics technology will be addressed by company spokespeople as well as by invited experts. The agency recommends a division of invited guests and company spokespeople between audiences composed of (1) technical news and trade writers and (2) those associated with general or business news. An

EXHIBIT 4

Recommended Publications for Corporate Campaign

Business Week/Industrial is an edition for subscribers in industry, specifically those employed in manufacturing as well as mining, construction, transportation, communications, and utilities. Its paid circulation of 350,000 is the largest available to us. Published weekly, *Business Week* has earned and enjoys a unique leadership role as "the" weekly consumer business magazine.

Industry Week is published on alternate Mondays for the management (both corporate and operations) of industrial firms. *IW* reaches every industrial firm in the United States with 100 + employees. This circulation is also qualified by management function and company size.

Control Engineering is published monthly for engineers who design, develop, and apply control and instrumentation systems. Editorial is technical, informing control engineers of automatic control and data-handling systems about the practical application of new instrumentation and analytical and systems-design techniques. Special attention is given to the processing industry, machinery, and manufacturing, with emphasis on the exchange of information between industries. *CE* is considered the leading publication serving the control and instrumentation systems market. *CE* should be considered the basic media vehicle for this market.

Computer Design is published monthly for the digital electronics market. Editorial is devoted to designers of digital equipment and systems. Circulation covers design engineers and engineering management throughout the total electronics OEM—circuits, components, computer equipment, subsystems, computer-based systems, and computers. We feel *CD* should be a basic buy for coverage of our target in the computer area.

EDN is published semimonthly for specifying designers of electronic products, equipment, and systems. Qualified recipients are engineers and engineering management in the electronics OEM. Editorial is technical and in depth. *EDN* offers the most efficient coverage of our target engineer.

Electronic Design is published bimonthly for the traditional EOEM design engineer and engineering management. Editorial covers new technology and products. *ED* provides the largest total EOEM, engineering, and engineering management circulation of candidate publications.

Electronics Products Magazine is published monthly and reports on new products, systems, and subassemblies for specifiers of electronics products in the EOEM. In terms of circulation, *EPM* resembles *ED* and *EDN*.

Electronics is published on alternate Thursdays for manufacturers and users of electronics products and equipment worldwide. *Electronics* reports and interprets new industry development/technological changes in electronics. *Electronics* is recognized as the leading publication in this field and is recommended as a basic vehicle.

Machine Design is published on alternate Thursdays for individuals performing a design engineering function. Technical editorial covers the following: (a) design and development; (b) current news; (c) design problem-solving ideas; (d) personal, professional, and management information; and (e) new product announcements. *MD* is the acknowledged leader in the product design engineering field in both circulation and editorial coverage. *MD* has a full-time electronics editor and includes an electronics feature section in each issue. *MD* has the greatest share of total, electronics, and exclusive advertisers of the design engineering publications.

Design Engineering is a technical magazine published monthly for engineers engaged in the design and development of products for resale and specialized in-plant equipment. Editorial covers (a) research and technology, (b) electrical/electronic power and control, (c) fluid power and control, (d) mechanical design and power transmission, and (e) materials and manufacturing. Because of the cost efficiency, *DE* would effectively add impact. However, it should not be considered as a replacement for *MD* or *DN*.

EXHIBIT 5

Media/Insertion/Cost Schedules

Publication	Recommended Media/Cost Schedule		
	One-Time Cost (1981 est.)	Number of Insertions	Total Cost
Business Week/Industrial	$31,648	13	$411,424
Control Engineering	5,500	12	66,000
Computer Design	6,465	10	64,650
Electronics	7,073	10	70,730
Machine Design	9,396	10	93,960
Total		55	$706,764

Publication	Alternative Media/Cost Schedule		
	One-Time Cost (1981 est.)	Number of Insertions	Total Cost
Industry Week	$17,472	13	$227,136
Control Engineering	5,500	12	66,000
Computer Design	6,465	10	64,650
Electronics	7,073	10	70,730
Total		45	$428,516

exhibit of items utilizing fiber–optics should be developed to serve as examples of the technology.

2. *Feature development.* Through the symposia, Honeywell/Spectronics will create its own informed and receptive media audience. This audience should not be left with only the remembrance of its learning experience. Thus, the agency will develop an ongoing program of feature stories. These will be for placement in trade, business, and general mass-media publications.

3. *Trade shows.* In keeping with the leadership positioning, Honeywell/Spectronics will design its own high-quality exhibit for trade shows. The exhibit does not need to be large, nor does it need to alter the current exhibit policy.

A special effort will be made to gain editorial attention during major trade shows. A press kit will be developed for and distributed to the media attending each show. The agency will serve as press contact, inviting media to visit the Spectronics exhibit and arranging interviews with Spectronics spokespeople. A simple, low-cost card included in each kit will allow media people to ask for information on Honeywell/Spectronics by requesting all subsequent news releases or by detailing the kinds of data that would most benefit the individual writer.

Seal program promotion   As the computer and control OEM industries are analyzed for sales promotion opportunities, the greatest area of opportunity rests in the marketing rather than in the engineering and specification ends of their businesses. These businesses sell their products largely on the basis of technology and

EXHIBIT 6

Fiber-Optics Quality Seal

benefits. The marketing of fiber optics as a value-added feature of their products would serve to promote the currency of fiber–optics for these user systems.

The first step in the development of fiber–optics as an OEM merchandising tool is the production of promotional vehicles available to the computer and control systems manufacturers. To this end, the agency recommends the formation of a "Fiber-Optics Quality Seal." The first pass at an execution of this seal may be "We've Seen the Light." Everything from camera-ready logo art to literature and lapel buttons could be provided to the manufacturer free or on a very low-cost basis. Exhibit 6 shows the logo/seal. Marketing of the merchandising program should, from that point forward, be an integral part of the Spectronics sales call, supported by explanatory literature and examples of other participating manufacturers.

The fee for publicity and sales promotion efforts is $63,000, which includes the out-of-pocket costs for trade shows, the four media symposia, and the seal program promotion.

Creative Directions   Creative materials will concentrate on promoting a leadership image.

Media advertising   Four-color print advertisements have been chosen to portray the leadership look. The quality and assertiveness of the advertisements will

EXHIBIT 7

Two-Page Print Advertisement

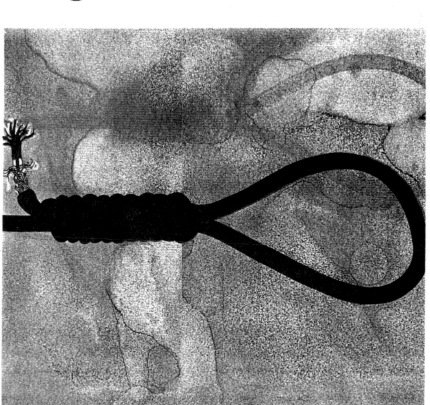

EXHIBIT 8

Two-Page Print Advertisement

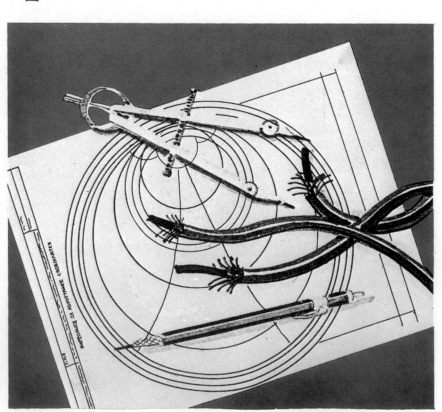

If you're still designing with copper wire,
you're probably still designing.

Honeywell
Spectronics

EXHIBIT 9

Fiber-Optics Corporate Campaign Budgets

	Alternative A	*Alternative B*
Media	$706,764	$428,516
Public relations/sales promotion	63,000	63,000
Creative materials:		
Media advertising	40,000	40,000
Collateral advertising	30,000	30,000
Agency fee	12,000	12,000
Total	$851,764	$573,516

speak to the resources and commitment of a leader. The first-year campaign will promote the use of fiber–optics over copper wire. The first ad will dramatically announce that the era of the old technology is over. Subsequent ads will position Honeywell/Spectronics as the leader of the new technology and make the reader aware that fiber–optics is here now, affordable, and practical. A dramatic visual will arrest the reader. Further reading will be provoked by headlines that tease the reader's intelligence. Body copy will play off the headline, visual, and "leader identity." Sample print advertisements (without copy) are shown in Exhibits 7 and 8.

Collateral materials The agency will design and develop an eight-page four-color brochure. The quality of the literature will attest to the resources and commitment required of a leader. The literature will be impactful, concise, and informative. The brochure will be used in addition to available technical literature, not as a replacement.

Budget The fiber-optics corporate campaign budget is shown in Exhibit 9. The budget shows the alternative media spending levels in the context of the overall campaign.

Fiber-Optics Product Campaign

Objectives The objectives of the product campaign are

1. To increase top-of-mind awareness of Spectronics as a supplier of a full line of fiber-optics products.
2. To support Spectronics's leadership position promoted in the Honeywell campaign.

Strategy Use four-color full-page ads in selected trade publications to speak directly to the design engineer. Each ad will be accompanied by an additional black-and-white one-third vertical page listing distributors and their telephone numbers. One ad will feature simplicity and ease of use, and the other ad will promote Spectronics's full-line capabilities.

EXHIBIT 10

Product Campaign Budget

	Recommended Media/Cost Schedule		
Publication	*One-Time Cost*	*Number of Insertions*	*Total Cost*
Electronics	$4,869	4	$ 19,476
Control Engineering	4,925	5	24,625
Computer Design	4,605	6	27,630
Electronic Design	4,440	5	22,200
EDN	4,305	6	25,830
Electronics Products Magazine	3,960	4	15,840
Total		30	$135,601
	Alternative Media/Cost Schedule		
Publication	*One-Time Cost*	*Number of Insertions*	*Total Cost*
Electronics	$4,869	3	$ 14,607
Control Engineering	4,925	3	14,775
Computer Design	4,605	4	18,420
Electronic Design	4,440	3	13,320
EDN	4,305	4	17,220
Electronics Products Magazine	3,960	2	7,920
Total		19	$ 86,262

These executions will complement the Honeywell program both by gaining from its heavy exposure and, in turn, by providing an added depth targeted to the design engineer. The product campaign is designed to complement the corporate campaign and will run in parallel with it.

Media and Budget The media chosen are technical in orientation and thus complement the copy of the advertisements. The media expenditure levels are slightly higher than those now practiced. A recommended and alternative media budget are shown in Exhibit 10.

Club Med España

Jean-Michel Landau, the newly appointed managing director of Club Med Spain, was eager to proceed with his plans to launch a full-scale marketing and sales effort for the Spanish market. It was February 3, 1992, and in less than two weeks Club Med would be holding a press conference in Madrid to announce its first major communications campaign aimed at Spanish holiday travelers. With vacation spending rising at an annual rate of 32 percent, Spain was one of Europe's fastest-growing markets for package holidays. In fact, some managers at "The Club" feared that they had waited too long to exploit the Spanish market and that sales opportunities had been lost; consequently, there were high expectations that, once a formal communication campaign was launched, sales in Spain would quickly blossom.

Jean-Michel's communications budget for the Spanish market was limited. Jean-Michel knew that he would have to employ an effective mix of communication techniques in order to promote the product, while at the same time generating enough sales over the next few seasons to continue funding his marketing efforts. Should he emphasize the unique Club Med concept through media advertising? Or should he focus directly on his distributors and target customers? What was the most effective means of reaching his target audience? How effectively would he be able to measure the results as the season progressed so that he could modify his strategy appropriately for the next season?

As he considered these issues, Jean-Michel thought back on his successful years as marketing manager for Club Med's biggest market—France. "Spain is a different kind of challenge," he said, "but here in Spain, I have a brand new market, and there are no constraints on how I operate. I can build this organization from the bottom up."

BACKGROUND

Club Méditerranée was founded in 1950 by George Blitz, who, along with a group of friends, developed the Club as an association devoted to sports and seaside vacations. Originally, the Club was a nonprofit organization, and during their travels the members adhered to a set of principles encompassing rustic, communal life. By 1954, as the organization grew increasingly popular, Blitz asked Mr. Gilbert Trigano, whose family business supplied the Club with tents, to take over management of the Club. Trigano accepted, and sensing the commercial potential of the Club's concept, he transformed the organization into a profitable enterprise.

This case was prepared by Research Associate Alex Bloom, under the supervision of Professor Dominique Turpin, as a basis for class discussion rather than to illustrate either effective or ineffective handling of a business situation. Copyright © 1993 by the International Management Development Institute (IMD), Lausanne, Switzerland. Not to be used or reproduced without permission directly from IMD.

The Club Med Concept

The Club's venue began to evolve when, in 1954, Club Med under Trigano's management opened its first straw hut village. Social life at the village also took its formal shape customers were named *Gentils Membres* (GMs) or "nice members," and staff were referred to as *Gentils Organizateurs* (GOs) or "nice organizers." The GO's role in the village was, in the words of the Club, that of a "friend rather than a servant." Much of the Club's appeal stemmed from the daily games and sports activities, which the GOs would organize, and the nightly amateur entertainment, which the GOs would perform, often with the GMs themselves participating. Each resort was run by a "chef de village" who was responsible for village operations as well as for hosting and entertaining the GMs. These "chefs de village," who would move from village to village each season, soon attained fame both within Club Med and among its loyal GMs.

The Club Med vacation was sold as an all-inclusive package, including transportation, food, entertainment, sports, and activities. This was integral to the Club's principles of egalitarianism and communal interaction at the village. For example, instead of using money, GMs would pay for any extras (usually drinks) with beads taken from a necklace; and at mealtimes, GMs and GOs alike would sit together at tables of eight. Furthermore, the "hassles" of modern civilization—such as telephones, televisions, and even newspapers—were not provided or allowed in the villages.

Globalization

As Club Med's unique vacation concept attained fame and success, the company expanded its operations by opening new villages at prime locations around the world. The first snow village was opened in Switzerland in 1956, and over the next decade villages were opened throughout Europe and North Africa. In 1968, a village was opened in Guadeloupe in the Caribbean; in 1979, villages opened in South America, New Caledonia, and Malaysia. The first village in the United States was opened in 1980, and the first one in Japan was opened in 1987. By 1990, Club Med operated over 100 villages in 33 countries around the world and employed over 24,000 people.

Sales had also expanded around the world. Countries like Belgium, Italy and Germany had provided strong customer bases from early on in the Club's history; North and South American markets were cultivated during the 1970s, and, more recently, sales had been growing rapidly in Japan and the Far East. Club Med's target in Japan was ambitious: 200,000 members by 1999 from 50,000 in fiscal year 1989. By 1990, with sales offices in 26 countries, Club Med's global revenues had reached FF 8.2 billion.[1] Sixty-two percent of their customers came from Europe, 20 percent from North America; and 12 percent from Japan and the Far East. France, with 431,700 GMs, was still the Club's largest single market, providing over 35 percent of its total customer base.

Global expansion was not painless, however. As sales grew outside of France, it became apparent that village operations had to be modified to accommodate the demands of non-French GMs. Consequently, GOs were hired from different nationalities in order to address any cultural or language problems that might arise, menus were modified to cater to non-French tastes when necessary (Japanese GMs, for example, expected seaweed for breakfast rather than croissants), and bookings were controlled in order to balance the mix of nationalities at the villages. GOs and GMs from around the world mixing together in Club Med villages gave the product an "international" character, but created a complex logistical tangle between marketing and operations.

---

[1]1990 average market exchange rate: 1 US$ = FF 5.4453.

Sales and Marketing

New markets were typically launched by opening a Club Med agency (or "boutique"), which would sell directly to the public while serving as a base for operations. In the larger, more highly penetrated markets, the bulk of the sales were made through independent travel agents; the boutiques continued to play an important role, however, serving as information outlets and reinforcing the Club's image through their presence in metropolitan centers. Besides, sales made through the boutiques normally yielded better margins than those made through travel agencies.

Club Med focused on providing outstanding service to its GMs. A sophisticated customer feedback survey, known internally as the *baromètre* (or "barometer"), was used to monitor GM satisfaction, and the results of the survey were used to measure the performance of the village managers and their GO teams. Consequently, the repeat purchase rate for Club Med products was typically high (the repeat purchase rate in France, for example, was 70 percent), and many GMs returned to the Club year after year for their holidays.

Product Evolution and Diversification

While much of the early Club Med concept remained as an integral part of the village experience, attention to GM satisfaction and changing tastes had led to an evolution of the product. 'Upscale' activities (such as golf) were added, special facilities were created to accommodate children, and the product line now ranged from straw-hut villages and bungalows to luxury resorts. Most villages now had locks on the rooms, and the Club had become sensitive to criticisms of being "overorganized."

In addition to its village holidays, Club Med had begun to diversify into other, related activities. Club Med villages were marketed to corporate customers for seminars, conferences, and incentive trips through the "Club Med Business" program; a luxury yacht (the "Club Med One" and "Club Med Two") offered cruise packages in the Mediterranean and the Caribbean, or the Pacific. A "City Club" was opened in downtown Vienna, and Club Med subsidiaries operated timeshare holiday villas.

CLUB MED IN SPAIN

Club Med's presence in Spain began in 1962 when the company opened a hut village in Cadaqués on the Costa Brava, a resort area on the Mediterranean Sea. Since then, four more villages were opened, bringing total capacity to over 4,000 beds. The most recent village, an upscale resort hotel in Ibiza, was opened in 1990. Two of the villages were operated during both the summer and winter seasons, while the remaining three operated as summer villages only.

Club Med began selling its holiday packages to Spanish vacationers in the mid-1970s through Club de Vanguardia, a local tour operator. In 1982, the Club opened a boutique in Barcelona, where most of its customers were concentrated. The boutique sold Club Med holidays directly to the Spanish public, while at the same time serving as a base for managing village operations in Spain. Parallel to the opening of the Barcelona boutique, Club Med made its products available for distribution by most leading travel agencies in Spain. Promotion of the product was left to word of mouth and to the travel agents, who received a standard commission (5–8 percent on the retail price) for every sale.

Sales during the 1990–91 season alone totaled 2,200 bookings, representing about 8,000 customers with revenues reaching Pta 450 million.[2] Thirty-nine percent of these

---

[2] 1990 average market exchange rate: 1 US$ = Pta 101.90.

revenues were from group sales to companies using Club Med villages for conferences, seminars, or incentive trips. Awareness of the product (1.5 percent in 1990) remained low in Spain, but the unfostered growth in sales led Club Med management in Paris to conclude that the Club Med vacation should be marketed more actively to the Spanish market. Italy was cited as an example of a country where, some years earlier, conditions had been similar to those currently existing in Spain; Italy had since grown to become Club Med's largest market in Europe outside France.

Jean-Michel Landau

Jean-Michel Landau, 42, was a veteran Club Med manager. Born in southern France, he grew up in North Africa where he joined Club Med at the age of 19. He soon became a *chef de village* and eventually moved into management, heading Club Med country offices in Mexico, Tunisia, Italy, and Canada. Prior to taking over the Spanish office in October 1991, he had spent six years as head of marketing and sales activities in France. Under Jean-Michel, sales in France were the highest they had ever been for Club Med, reaching revenues of FF 2.3 bilion in 1989.

"As marketing manager in France," explained Jean-Michel, "you are not allowed any mistakes. One percent loss of market share in France represents a tremendous amount of money to the Club." In contrast to the 300-person organization he managed in France, Club Med's office in Spain employed only 25 people; but Jean-Michel felt this gave him the freedom and flexibility he needed to tackle a new market launch. Because of his success in France, Club Med senior management felt that Jean-Michel was ideal for building up the marketing organization in Spain. Sales potential in Spain was felt to be high, and Paris wanted to develop the Spanish market as quickly as possible. Christian Remoissenet, who had been with Club Med in Spain since 1989, was appointed sales and marketing manager by Jean-Michel, and together the two of them would oversee the day-to-day activities of marketing the product (refer to the organization chart in Exhibit 1).

THE SPANISH TOURIST INDUSTRY

By 1990, more than half of Spain's population of 39 million traveled on holiday each year. While this figure had not changed dramatically through the 1980s, holiday spending had increased at an average yearly rate of 32 percent, with 1989 expenditures (excluding international transportation) reaching Pta 365 billion. Spaniards were thus among the fastest-growing holiday spenders (average growth around the world was only 18 percent for the same period), and by 1990 Spain ranked fifteenth among nations in terms of overall vacation spending.

Most Spaniards spent their holidays in Spain. By the late 1980s, however, the number of Spaniards traveling abroad for their holidays began to increase rapidly, growing from 7 percent of vacationers in 1985 to 19 percent by 1990. (Exhibit 2 shows a breakdown of foreign destination by geographical origin for Spanish travelers and lists the key travel incentives for Spanish holiday makers.)

Club Med's Spanish GMs represented the upper end of the vacation market. An analysis of the 1987 season showed that over 75 percent of Spanish GMs were professionals or executives, most were between the age of 30 and 50, and most traveled as singles or couples, with less than 20 percent of the bookings consisting of families. In contrast to the overall market, Club Med customers preferred to vacation abroad, with nearly two-thirds of the GMs choosing non-Spanish destinations (although only one-third chose destinations outside the Mediterranean basin—refer to

EXHIBIT   1

Organization Chart of Club Med Spain

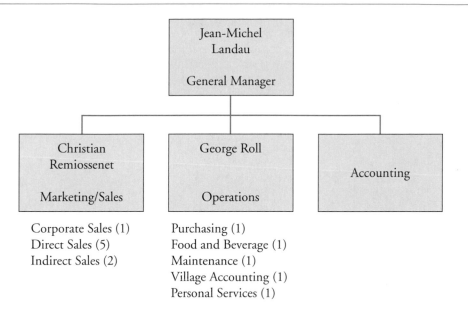

Corporate Sales (1)   Purchasing (1)
Direct Sales (5)   Food and Beverage (1)
Indirect Sales (2)   Maintenance (1)
                          Village Accounting (1)
                          Personal Services (1)

*Numbers in parantheses denote number of employees.

*Numbers in parantheses denote number of employees

Exhibit 3). The Club also achieved a higher than average volume of low-season sales, with 26 percent of its GM's travelling during the winter.

In preparation for the marketing campaign, Jean-Michel commissioned a customer satisfaction study with Metra-Seis, a market research firm in Barcelona. The study, which was based on interviews with selected GMs, indicated that certain aspects of Club Med's products conflicted with Spanish expectations. Complaints focused on the quality of accommodations, the inflexibility of time schedules, the high degree of organization and the fact that French was the principal language of the Club; some also felt that the Club concept was not adequately explained in either the brochure or at the point of sale. However, overall satisfaction with the Club was high. Positive comments particularly emphasized the sports activities, the children's activities, and the food.

Competitive Package Holiday Products

Club Med's principal competitors in Spain were the major tour operators who developed and sold inclusive package holiday products. Sales of package holiday products had been growing in Spain, from 900,000 packages sold in 1985 to 1.5 million packages in 1990. (Travel agent revenues for 1990, *including* transportation, reached Pta 900 billion; with nearly one-third of this amount estimated to be attributed to package holiday sales.) The typical package holiday was comprised of transportation and accommodation, often including one or more meals and sometimes consisting of excursions to multiple destinations. The most common package holiday

EXHIBIT   2

Excerpts from a Survey of the Spanish Tourist Market

Motivations for Tourist Travel within Spain:	
Diversion and change of environment	41.6%
Visit family and friends	31.5%
Health and relaxation	16.1%
Visit new places	13.6%
Motivations for Tourist Travel to Foreign Countries:	
Tourism	49.3%
Tourism and other	31.5%
Visit family	13.8%
Cultural curiosity	10.5%
Preferred Activities:	
Cultural activities	86.0%
Relaxation	49.4%
Night life	27.4%
Cuisine	25.6%
Rural tourism	14.0%
Principal Foreign Destinations (Note: some respondents listed two destinations—total may be greater than 100%):	
France	30.3%
Italy	19.0%
Portugal	17.8%
Andores	14.0%
Germany	7.2%
Switzerland	6.1%
United Kingdom	6.0%

Source: Le Marché Touristique Espagnol—Guide Pratique (Maison de la France, 1990)

products sold to Spanish vacationers were to local sun/sea destinations in Spain, followed by European and North African sun/sea destinations during the summer and winter seasons, and European snow destinations during the winter; less common were excursions to the Americas and the Far East.

By 1990, there were 284 tour operators developing package holiday products in Spain. Tour operators distributed their products through independent travel agencies that operated more than 3,000 travel agency outlets throughout the country (an "independent" typically owned an average of one to three outlets, all in one particular city or region, and sold holiday packages on behalf of the tour operators on a commission basis). The larger tour operators, however, generally operated their own outlets as well. Wagons-Lits and Viajes Melia, the two largest such companies, operated 150 and 120 outlets, respectively. Both of these companies were typical of the large international travel groups that had been expanding globally, primarily through acquisition of local travel agent chains. Wagons-Lits, a French conglomerate, had worldwide revenues of FF 16.1 billion in 1990, while Viajes Melia, a Spanish company that had been bought by an Italian group in 1987, had revenues of Pta 33.9 billion.

Jean-Michel estimated that the retail price of Club Med holidays averaged 30 percent higher than those of available package holidays to comparable destinations.

EXHIBIT   3

Customer Profile

1. Club Med Spain customer profile, summer 1989 season

Sales by destination—individuals:

Spain	35%
Mediterranean basin (Morocco 19%, Tunisia 7%, Turkey 5%, Greece 4%, others)	35%
Nearby destinations (France 6%, Portugal 4%, Italy 3%)	13%
Exotic islands (Caribbean 6%, Polynesia 2%, Mauritius 1%, Maldives 1%, Phuket 0.7%, Bali 0.7%)	13%
Long-distance destinations (Mexico 2.5%, Brazil 1%, Malaysia 0.25%, Senegal 0.25%)	4%

2. Survey of current and potential customers who contacted the Barcelona boutique, November, 1989

First heard of Club Med through:

Friends, acquaintances	70%	(80% for potential customers)
Brochure	22%	
Media	4%	
Mailing	4%	

Principal motivations for purchase of Club Med:

Sports activities	35%	(40% for potential customers)
Meet new friends	19%	
Rest/relaxation	16%	
Social activities	16%	
Destination country	11%	
Exoticism	3%	

Travel status:

Couple	30%
Family	26%
Couple with children	18%
Friends	15%
Alone	11%

3. Club Med Customer analysis, 1987 season

Profession:

Heads of enterprises	36%
Executives	19%
Liberal professions	27%
Employees	11%
Students	5%
Other	2%

Departure status:

Alone	44%
Couple	38%
With family or friends	18%

Source: Evaluation du Marchá du Tourisme Espagnol et Stratágie de Dáveloppement (Charles Riley Consultants International).

Club Med believed that this premium price reflected the unique characteristics of the product, and that the organized activities, the entertainment, and the GO spirit at a Club Med village were features that were not to be found in the standard inclusive packages. In other countries, Club Med often justified its higher prices by claiming that the additional activities at the Club yielded higher value for money, and that just the transportation, accommodation, food, and activities would cost the consumer much more if purchased separately than through a Club Med package.

CLUB MED'S STRATEGY FOR SPAIN

Jean-Michel's goal was to build up the GM customer base in Spain from the current 8,000 customers to 50,000 customers and to raise national awareness for the Club from 1.5 percent to 40 percent over a five-year period. According to Club Med Espana's estimates, a target of 50,000 customers represented about 10 percent of the 500,000 Spaniards who took package holidays comparable in value to the average Club Med product. Jean-Michel expected marketing efforts to result in a doubling of both group and individual sales for the 1991–92 season, and for growth to continue steadily over the next few years as the product gained recognition.

An advertising and public relations campaign would be launched within the month. This, along with the Club Med brochure, would be critical in building the Club's image in Spain. An effective distribution network would also have to be created. Selected travel agencies would have to develop a good understanding of the product, and incentives would have to be provided to sell Club Med over other package holiday products.

Target

Club Med España aimed at targeting the most affluent segment of the Spanish population, particularly liberal professionals—doctors, lawyers, property owners, business people, etc. Charles Riley Consultants International had estimated Club Med's potential market in Spain in 1990 to be 375,000 customers.

Product Offering

In 1991, Club Med Espana wanted to offer its Spanish customers a whole range of products and destinations through three versions of the Trident:

- The winter ski catalogue offered 10 destinations to French ski resorts—1 in Italy and 9 in Switzerland.

- The winter sun catalogue destinations introduced: 12 destinations in Europe and Africa—Spain, France, Israel, Ireland, Morocco, Portugal, Senegal, Tunisia, and the Caribbees (Antilles); 13 in the Caribbean or America— Bahamas, the French Caribbean, Haiti, Brasil, Mexico, and the United States; 8 in Asia, Polynesia, and other far away places—Indonesia, Malaysia, the Maldives, Tahiti, New Caledonia, Mauritius, and Thailand.

- The summer catalogue introduced: 32 villages in Europe and Africa—4 in Spain and Turkey, 5 in France and Morocco, 3 in Greece, Tunisia and Italy, 1 in Ireland, Israel, Portugal, and Senegal; 16 destinations in the Americas— 5 in Mexico, 3 in the French Caribbean, 2 in Brazil and the Bahamas, 1 in the United States, the Turks and Caicos, and Haiti; and 6 destinations in Asia and Polynesia—Indonesia, Malaysia, the Maldives, Mauritius, Thailand, and Tahiti.

Communication

A poll conducted by Dym S.A. (a market research organization that had developed a holiday and travel-oriented omnibus) found that only 1.5 percent of the population in Spain had heard of Club Med. (In contrast, the awareness level for France was 90 percent; results of the Spanish survey are shown in Exhibit 4).

Advertising would be developed by the local offices of RSCG, an international advertising agency based in Paris that handled all of Club Med's advertising for Europe. RSCG planned to use existing Club Med material from its archives in Paris, but to design advertisements specifically targeted to a Spanish audience. Jean-Michel had run two series of trial tactical advertisements in Barcelona's daily "La Vanguardia" in December of 1991. The test, which was timed to coincide with the Christmas holidays, seemed to have produced successful results, with more bookings requested than could be accommodated.

RSCG would also be used to produce the Club Med brochure: the "Trident" as it was called within the company, in reference to the Club's logo. The Trident was distributed to travel agents, who displayed it on shelves, redistributed it to customers, and used it as a reference to the Club's products. Brochures were also distributed to customers directly by Club Med, both at the boutique, and, when new brochures were printed, through direct mailings to previous GMs. Historically, Club Med gave away four brochures for every direct booking and ten brochures for every indirect booking. A total of 50,000 brochures had been printed and distributed in Spain during the two 1990–91 seasons, and another 30,000 brochures had already been printed for the winter season of 1991–92.

A major decision that Jean-Michel had to make was to determine the size of the communications budget. Since Club Med España was spending very little on communications before he took over his new position, Jean-Michel had to start from "scratch" to figure out an appropriate budget for the Spanish market. During 1990–91, Club Med España had spent the equivalent of FF 26,000 in advertising, FF 132,000 in promotion, FF 975,000 in brochures, and FF 352,000 in commissions to travel agents. He knew that his major local competitor had spent Pta 300 million on communications during the past year. However, such a budget was well over what he could afford. In any case, any budget he would present to the Paris headquarters had to be fully justified.

Distribution

By 1990, only one-third of Club Med's individual sales in Spain were made through 40 travel agents. Club Med España expected that agents would make about two-thirds of its sales by 1995–96. Jean-Michel's objective was to obtain national coverage by increasing this number to 150–200 agents. Travel agents would be key to a successful marketing effort, however, and because of his experience as marketing manager for France, Jean-Michel was particularly concerned about developing the distribution channels properly in Spain. "In France," he explained, "99 percent of our indirect sales are made by one agency—a competitor of ours, Havas Voyages. We account for 30 percent of their gross turnover, and they account for 30 percent of ours. We fight a lot, but we can't live without them, and they can't live without us. I don't want a situation like this in Spain—it leaves you with no control over the distribution."

Consequently, Jean-Michel planned to spread the risk of indirect distribution over several of the more prestigious independent travel agents in Spain, which would

EXHIBIT 4

Results of the DYM Survey, November–December 1991

Questions:

Q1: "Have you ever had the occasion to hear about Club Med?"

Q2: "If yes,' tell me please, what is the principal activity of Club Med?"

Results:

	Total	Age			Status (see below)				Sex	
		16–30	31–45	46–50	A+B	C1	C2	D	M	F
Q1:										
Yes	1.5	1.3	2.1	1.1	3.3	0.8	1.6	0.9	1.5	1.5
No	98.5	98.7	97.9	98.9	96.7	99.2	98.4b	99.1	98.5	98.5
Q2:										
Vacation club	10.6	-	25.3	-	12.9	53.7	-	-	13.2	8.0
Travel agency	3.7	11.6	-	-	12.1	-	-	-	-	7.5
Club Mediterranáe*	3.3	-	7.9	-	10.7	-	-	-	6.6	-
Residences w/activities	-	-	-	-	-	-	-	-	-	-
Conglomerate	2.5	-	-	9.5	-	-	6.4	-	-	5.0
Sports facilities	11.9	26.8	7.9	-	27.8	-	8.6	-	6.6	17.3
Sports/football	4.3	13.4	-	-	13.9	-	-	-	-	8.6
Food company	9.7	9.5	9.7	10.0	8.4	24.9	10.5	-	13.3	6.1
Other	26.9	11.0	33.2	36.4	7.9	21.4	48.1	17.8	12.3	41.5
Don't know	31.3	41.0	15.9	44.0	20.4	-	26.4	82.2	47.8	14.7

The socioeconomic status classification is defined as follows:

	Social Status	Head Of Household's Occupation
A	Upper middle class	Higher managerial, administrative, or professional
B	Middle class	Intermediate managerial, administrative, or professional
C1	Lower middle class	Supervisory, clerical, junior managerial, administrative, or professional
C2	Skilled working class	Skilled manual workers
D	Working class	Semi-and unskilled manual workers
E	Others	

*Club Med had recently changed its name in Spain from "Club Mediteranáe" to "Club Med."

be selected based on gross turnover (candidates should average about Pta 400 million per year), geographical location, and their previous track record selling Club Med. Selected agents would be groomed as "Club Med Experts." Employees from "Expert" agencies would be sent to Club Med villages, would receive extensive training on Club Med's products and selling techniques, and would eventually be granted more favorable commissions than normal travel agencies.

The boutique was still the most critical point of sale, with two-thirds of the GMs currently booking their trips directly through Club Med. Jean-Michel was preparing to open a second boutique in downtown Madrid by the end of February, in time for the beginning of summer bookings. Startup costs for the Madrid boutique had been budgeted at Pta 36 million, of which Pta 25 million represented a one-time "rental rights" payment, while the remaining Pta 11 million had been used for construction and decorating. With a rent of Pta 300,000 per month, Jean-Michel estimated that the direct costs of operating the Madrid boutique would amount to about 5 percent of its gross sales within two years of operation. A third boutique was planned for Valencia, the third largest city in Spain, but no time frame had been set; boutiques located outside Madrid, however, were expected to incur significantly lower rental and rights costs.

OPTIONS

Commercial activity for Club Med Spain was measured by headquarters in Paris on a sales-driven system whereby the Spanish office received a 15 percent commission for each booking. "Profitability" of the office was then effected by two main factors: transportation margins and the cost of sales. Since transportation was included in every Club Med booking, the office bought seats on charter flights and resold them to its GMs; profit margins from this activity averaged 20–25 percent for the Spanish office, and Jean-Michel estimated that transportation would soon be accounting for 35–40 percent of gross revenues. Cost of sales were comprised of travel agent commissions, overhead for boutiques, and the cost of advertising and promotion. (Village operations for Spain, which also fell under Jean-Michel's management, did not represent a factor in measuring "commercial activity of the Spanish office; Spanish villages were booked worldwide, and Jean-Michel was only responsible for their cost of operations.) Line items in a pro forma income statement for planning purposes are shown in Exhibit 5.

The communications budget would be based on loss-making sales during the initial years of the marketing plan. As a budgetary guideline, Jean-Michel had agreed with Club Med headquarters in Paris to maintain gross operation costs (not including village operations) at 30–35 percent of revenues for about three years—beginning with the 1991–92 season—until operations could become profitable. Line items for the communication budget are shown in Exhibit 6.

While Spain showed every indication of providing Club Med with a strong market, Jean-Michel faced the dilemma of allocating his limited budget between promoting the product and pushing it through the distribution channels. Furthermore, the right products had to be sold to the right customers; otherwise the initial marketing effort could backfire through client dissatisfaction.

The Cost of Advertising

Advertising represented the most expensive component of the communications campaign. RSCG proposed an advertising schedule that focused on print media in Barcelona and Madrid and that would cost the Club an estimated Pta 34 million, including Pta 2.3 million for design and layout (the schedule and a summary of advertising rates are shown in Exhibit 7). The RSCG proposal was for a series of double-page, color advertisements to be run in selected daily and weekly newspapers during the summer season. The proposal also included periodic tactical advertisements for promoting specific destinations and included advertisements in two travel-oriented specialty magazines (see Exhibit 8). Lead times for reserving advertising space limited the extent to which advertising could be modified as the season progressed. Jean-Michel also

EXHIBIT 5

Proforma Income Statement

	A	B	C	D	E	F	G
1							
2							
3		90/91	91/92	92/93	93/94	94/95	95/96
4	Number of Customers (GM)						
5	Number of Bookings						
6							
7							
8	Revenues (Millions Ptas)						
9	Of Which:						
10	*Transport. (35%)*						
11	*Transport. Margins (23%)*						
12							
13	*Villages (100%–35%)*						
14	*Villages Margins (15%)*						
15							
16	Total Gross Margins						
17	Cost of Sales (%)						
18	Cost of Sales						
19	Net Profit/(Loss)						

planned to repeat the Dym survey at least once per year (at a cost of Pta 200,000 per poll) in order to monitor the awareness level as the advertising campaign proceeded.

The advertising campaign would be coordinated with public relations activities, including a press conference scheduled for mid-February to announce the launch of Club Med's advertising campaign. A public relations firm, Gene Associates, had been contracted to manage all of Club Med's public relations activities in Spain for a fee of Pta 500,000 per month; the firm's responsibilities included organizing press conferences and feeding stories to the press, as well as organizing any special events. Jean-Michel was considering sponsoring some events (such as golf tournaments) that would promote the Club and generate news coverage; in addition to the public relations firm's fee, such activities typically cost the Club about Pta 400,000 per event.

A New Brochure

Since Spaniards were unfamiliar with the Club, the Trident would play a critical role in promoting the product and generating sales. The current Spanish Trident was sim-

EXHIBIT 6

Communications Budget

A	B	C	D	E	F	G
20						
21						
22						
23						
24	90/91	91/92	92/93	93/94	94/95	95/96
25 Customers						
26						
27 SALES (Million Pta.)						
28 Of Which:						
29 Boutique (%)						
30 *Of Which*:						
31 *Barcelona* (%)						
32 *Madrid* (%)						
33 Total Boutique (Mill. Pta)						
34 Travel Agency (Mill. Pta.)						
35						
36 EXPENSES (Million Pta.)						
37 Overheads Boutique Barcelona						
38 Overheads Boutique Madrid						
39 Indirect Commissions (8%)						
40						
41 PR Agency (Fees/year)						
42 No. of PR Events/Year						
43 Cost/Event						
44 Total PR						
45						
46 Advertising Layout (Pta)						
47 Advert. Space (Summer)						
48 Advert. Space (Winter)						
49 Total Advertising						
50						
51 No. of brochures/year						
52 Brochure Layout (Pta.)						
53 No. of copies						
54 Printing cost/brochure						
55 Total Printing						
56 Total Cost for Brochures						
57						
58 Market Survey (once/year)						
59						
60 No. of Direct Mailings						
61 Cost of Direct Mailings						
62 Total Direct Mail						
63						
64 Other Expenses:						
65						
66						
67						
68						
69						
70 Total Expenses						
71 Budgeted Cost of Sales (%)						
72 Projected Cost of Sales						
73 Budget Surplus (Overrun)						

EXHIBIT 7

RSCG Proposed Advertising Schedule

Double–page, color, image advertisements, newspapers:

Sunday Supplements	Weeks of	Total Cost (pta '000,000)
La Vanguardia	16/3, 4/5, 18/5, 1/6	10.0
El Periodico	16/3, 22/5	4.5
ABC	18/5, 1/6	5.3
El Mundo	16/3, 25/5	4.0
El Paris	4/5	6.4

Double–page, color, image advertisements, magazines:

Sunday Supplements	Month of	Total Cost (pta '000,000)
GEO	May	1.5
Viajar	June	1.2

Quarter page, tactical advertisements, newspapers:

Leading Dailies	No. Ads	Total Cost (pta '000,000)
La Vanguardia	8	3.3
El Paris	8	3.9

ilar to the "European" Trident produced every season in Paris and translated into the appropriate languages for Club Med's other marketing organizations in Europe. A brief introduction described the Club, after which the villages were listed by country, with one to two pages and a few photographs used to describe each village.

Three decisions had to be taken on the Trident: the number of different Tridents, the number of copies, and the content. RSCG estimated the cost of producing three separate brochures (summer, winter-sun, and winter-ski) to be Pta 3 million for layout and design, plus Pta 173.7 per copy for printing. As with advertising, RSCG would use photographs from Paris in the production of the new Spanish Tridents. Layout and text would be different, however, with the aim of targeting Spanish GMs and better explaining the Club concept. Targeting included the emphasis placed on the individual villages Popular Club Med destinations for Spaniards, for example, could be displayed more prominently, and the least visited villages would have their description omitted entirely (although the full product line would be included in the price list).

Finally, direct mailings to previous customers were conducted to distribute newly published brochures and to announce special offerings. A direct mailing to the current customer base costed approximately Pta 600,000; several mailings would have to be conducted during the 1991–92 season.

EXHIBIT 8

Tactical Advertisements developed by RSCG for Club Med, Spain (Published in "La Vanguardia," December 1991)

EXHIBIT 8 (*continued*)

Indice

1	**La vida en el Club**
3	**La mayor escuela de deportes del mundo**
4	**El paraiso de los niños**
5	**Enriquecer sus conocimientos, descubrir**
6	**Club Med 1**

Europa-Africa

					Ouarzazate
12	**Costa de Marfil**	19	**Israel**	26	**Portugal**
	Assinie		Coral Beach		Da Balaïa
14	**España**	20	**Irlanda**	28-29	**Senegal**
	Don Miguel		Waterville		Les Almadies
					Cap Skirring
16-18	**Francia**	22-25	**Marruecos**	30	**Túnez**
	Opio		Agadir		Monastir
	Pompadour		Marrakech		

America-Oceana

34-36	**Antillas**	39	**República de Haiti**	43	**Turks and Caicos**
	La Caravelle		Magic Haiti		Turquoise
	Les Boucaniers	40-41	**Brasil**	44-45	**Méjico**
	Saint Lucie		Itaparica		Cancun
37-38	**Bahamas**		Rio das Pedras		Huatulco
	Eleuthera	42	**República Dominicana**	46	**EE.UU.**
	Paradise Island		Punta Cana		Sandpiper

Asia-Oceano-Indico

50	**Indonesia**	54-56	**Polinesia**	58	**Isla Mauricio**
	Bali		Moorea		La Pointe aux Canonniers
52	**Malasia**		Bora Bora		
	Cherating	57	**Nueva Caledonia**	59	**Tailandia**
53	**Maldivas**		Chateau Royal		Phuket
	Faru				

60	**Vivamos**
62	**Egipto**
64	**City Club**
68-79	**Tarifas**

Prices and Quotas

Each village had a basic price that was set by Club Med's headquarters in Paris. Jean-Michel could adjust the price seasonally, so long as the basic price remained the annual average. In addition to setting prices based on time of year, special promotions were often used to fill certain destinations or if bookings were slow (promotions could be in the form of price discounts, or special deals such as free accommodation for children, etc.).

Price setting, however, had to be balanced between Spanish seasonal holiday patterns and a complex quota system imposed by Paris, which limited the bookings that Jean-Michel could make for each village. Club Med attempted to manage the mix of GMs at the villages by assigning each country a fixed number of booking slots for each destination, and countries like Spain did their best to fill these slots by adjusting their marketing efforts. These quotas were primarily in place to ensure adequate supply for France, Club Med's biggest market; consequently, quotas during the high season months were rarely adequate for the other countries. Jean-Michel did not expect this to affect 1991–92 sales, but he did expect the quota system to become problematic relatively soon, since Spanish holiday patterns were heavily concentrated in the month of August.

The Travel Agent Network

The standard travel agent commission in Spain was 5–8 percent of the retail price. Club Med Experts were expected to promote the Club because of the training they received and because of the expected volume that Club Med sales would generate for them (Jean-Michel expected Experts to eventually reach 10 percent of their gross turnover through Club Med sales). Initial training costs were minimal—about Pta 5,600 per agent. Commissions could be adjusted, however, either temporarily as an incentive to fill specific destinations, or on a permanent basis to push the Club through specific agencies (above-average commissions were typically set at 10 percent).

While travel agent incentives were particularly critical during the initial stages of the marketing strategy, the demand for Club Med could be expected to increase on its own once the product gained notoriety. Thus, Jean-Michel had to determine the optimal number of agencies to include in the Club Med Expert program and set an incentive policy that would generate sales effectively until the advertising campaign began to pay off.

The next three years, then, would be a busy time for Jean-Michel and his staff, as they faced the intricacies of growing their customer base as quickly as possible with a limited budget and within the constraints imposed by Club Med headquarters. Would the advertising campaign be successful in conveying a positive image of the Club? What should Jean-Michel's communications budget be? Would awareness increase fast enough? Would distribution be effective? The upcoming season's sales—by which Paris would ultimately judge them—would go a long way in answering these questions.

CHAPTER 8

Marketing Channel Strategy and Management

 Marketing channels play an integral role in an organization's marketing strategy. Channels not only link a producer of goods to the goods' buyers, but also provide the means through which an organization implements its marketing strategy. Marketing channels determine whether the target markets sought by an organization are reached. The effectiveness of a promotional strategy is determined, in part, by the number of channel intermediaries, their geographical concentration, and their ability and willingness to perform promotion-related functions. Moreover, an organization's price strategy is influenced by the markup and discount policies of intermediaries. Finally, product strategy is affected by intermediaries' branding policies, willingness to stock a variety of offerings, and ability to augment offerings through installation or maintenance services, the extension of credit, and so forth.

To the extent that a marketing manager has alternative channels available for reaching chosen target markets, the task facing the manager is to select those channels that meet three objectives. First, of all channel options, the chosen channel should provide the best coverage of the target markets sought. This means that the channel will place the organization's offerings in the right location, in the right quantity, at the right price, and at a time when buyers wish to purchase them. Second, the channel should satisfy the buying requirements of the target markets sought. Buying requirements refer to buyers' needs for information about the offering, convenience of purchase, and services such as delivery that are incidental to purchasing. Finally, the chosen channel should maximize potential revenues returned to the organization while minimizing the costs of achieving adequate market coverage and satisfying buyer requirements. Channel profitability is determined by the profit margins earned (revenues minus cost) for each channel member and for the channel as a whole.

THE CHANNEL-SELECTION DECISION

Making the channel-selection decision is not so much a single act as it is a process of making various component decisions. The process of channel selection involves specifying the type, location, density, and functions of intermediaries, if any, in a marketing channel. However, before addressing these decisions, the marketing manager must conduct a thorough market analysis in order to identify the target markets that will be served by a prospective marketing channel. The target markets sought and their buying requirements form the basis for all channel decisions. In other words, the marketing manager needs answers to fundamental questions such as these: Who are potential customers? Where do they buy? When do they buy? How do they buy? What do they buy? By working backward from the ultimate buyer or user of an offering, the manager can develop a framework for specific channel decisions and can identify alternative channel designs.[1] For example, managers of Ricoh Company Ltd. studied its market, the serious (as opposed to recreational) camera user, and concluded that a change in marketing channels was necessary. The company terminated its contract with a wholesaler who sold to mass-merchandise stores and began using manufacturer's agents who sold to photo specialty stores. These stores agreed to stock and display Ricoh's full line and promote it prominently, and sales volume tripled within 18 months.[2]

Direct versus Indirect Distribution

Exhibit 8.1 illustrates common channel designs for consumer and industrial offerings. Also indicated is the number of levels in a marketing channel, which is determined by the number of intermediaries between the producer and the ultimate buyers

EXHIBIT   8.1

Marketing Channel Designs

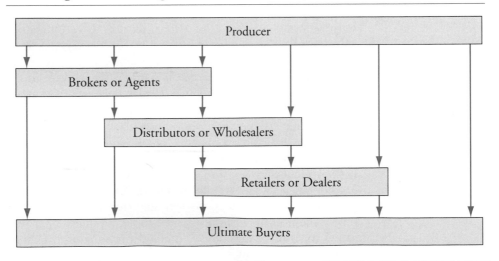

or users. As the number of intermediaries between the producer and the ultimate buyer increases, the channel increases in length.

The first decision facing a manager is whether the organization should use intermediaries to reach target markets or contact ultimate buyers directly through its own sales forces or distribution outlets.[3] If the manager elects to use intermediaries, then the type, location, density, and number of channel levels must be determined.

Organizations usually elect to contact ultimate buyers directly rather than through intermediaries when the following conditions exist. Direct distribution is usually employed when target markets are composed of a limited number of buyers who are easily identifiable and are geographically concentrated, when personal selling is a major component of the organization's communication program, when the organization has a wide variety of offerings for the target market, and when sufficient resources are available to satisfy target market requirements that would normally be handled by intermediaries (such as credit, technical assistance, delivery, and post-sale service). Direct distribution must be considered when intermediaries are not available for reaching target markets, or when intermediaries do not possess the capacity to service the requirements of target markets. For example, Procter and Gamble sells its soap and laundry detergents direct, door to door in the Philippines because there are no other alternatives in many parts of the country. Also, when Ingersoll-Rand first introduced pneumatic tools, a direct channel was used because considerable buyer education and service was necessary. As buyers became more familiar with these products, the company switched to using industrial distributors. Certain characteristics of offerings also favor direct distribution. Typically, sophisticated technical offerings such as mainframe computers, unstandardized offerings such as custom-built machinery, and offerings of high unit value are distributed directly to buyers. Finally, the overall marketing strategy might favor direct distribution. An organization might seek a certain aura of exclusivity not generated by using intermediaries, or an organization might want to emphasize the appeal of "buying direct," presumably important to certain target markets. Direct distribution may also be appropriate if the organization seeks to differentiate its offering from others distributed through intermediaries.

Even though a variety of conditions favor direct distribution, an important caveat must be noted. The decision to market directly to ultimate buyers involves the absorption of all functions (contacting buyers, storage, delivery, and credit) typically performed by intermediaries. The marketing principle "You can eliminate intermediaries, but not their functions" is particularly relevant to the manager considering direct distribution. This point is occasionally overlooked by marketing managers when they elect to distribute directly. The costs of performing these functions can be prohibitive, depending on the organization's financial resources and the opportunity cost of diverting financial resources from other endeavors. Therefore, even though all signs favor direct distribution, the capacity of the organization to perform tasks normally assigned to intermediaries may eliminate this alternative from final consideration. A similar caveat must be noted with respect to intermediaries who consider acquiring functions typically performed by channel members above or below them in the channel (for example, a retailer who wishes to perform wholesaling functions). Recently, Southland Corporation (7-Eleven) eliminated its warehousing of merchandise in favor of using independent wholesalers. Two of the reasons cited for this decision were that independent wholesalers could perform these functions more efficiently and at a lower cost than Southland.[4]

Channel Selection at the Retail Level

In the event that intermediaries are chosen as the means for reaching target markets, the channel-selection decision then focuses on the type and location of intermediaries at each level of the marketing channel, beginning with the retail level.

Consider the case of a manufacturer of sporting goods. If retail outlets are chosen, the question becomes, What type of retail outlet? Should hardware stores, department stores, sporting goods stores, or some combination be selected to carry the line of sporting goods? Also, where should these retail outlets be located? Should they be in urban, suburban, or rural areas, and in what parts of the country?

Type and location decisions depend on the buying requirements of the target markets and the potential profitability of the outlets to the manufacturer. If retail outlets are to play a role in providing information about the offering to potential buyers, which of the retail outlets will most actively promote the line through point-of-purchase displays, store-sponsored advertising (including cooperative advertising), and/or knowledgeable sales personnel? Which of the stores will carry a reasonable inventory to attract buyers interested in selection and variety? Which outlets carry competing or complementary products? Which outlets are conveniently located for buyers? The profitability of a retail outlet relates to the potential volume in the trade area served by the outlet, the merchandising skill of store management, and the store's competitive environment. Each of these factors must be evaluated before a decision on the type and location of retail outlets is finalized. Consideration of these factors prompted IBM and Apple Computer to broaden their distribution of personal computers beyond traditional dealers to include mass merchandisers and warehouse-like computer superstores.[5]

Next, the density of intermediaries at the retail level of distribution must be determined. *Density* refers to the number of intermediaries carrying the organization's offering in a particular geographical area. Three degrees of density at the retail level are intensive distribution, exclusive distribution, and selective distribution.

1. *Intensive distribution* at the retail level means that a manager attempts to distribute the organization's offerings through as many retail outlets as possible. More specifically, a manager may seek to gain distribution through as many outlets of a specific type (such as drugstores) as possible. In its extreme form, intensive distribution refers to gaining distribution through almost all types of retail outlets, as cigarette manufacturers do.

2. *Exclusive distribution* is the opposite of intensive distribution in that typically *one* retail outlet in a geographical area carries the manufacturer's line. Usually, the geographical area constitutes the defined trade area of the retailer. Magnavox Corporation used this approach for some of its products when it utilized only 3,000 dealers among the several thousand retail outlets available. Automobile distribution is another familiar example of exclusive distribution.

   Occasionally, the exclusive-distribution strategy involves a contractual arrangement between a retailer and manufacturer that gives the retailer exclusive rights to sell a line of products or product in a defined area in return for performing specific marketing functions. A common form of an exclusive agreement is a franchise agreement.

3. *Selective distribution* is between these two extremes. This strategy calls for a manufacturer to select a few retail outlets in a specific area to carry its offering. This approach is often used for marketing furniture, some brands of

men's clothing, and quality women's apparel. Selective distribution weds some of the market coverage benefits of intensive distribution to the control over resale evident with the exclusive distribution strategy. For this reason, selective distribution has become increasingly popular in recent years among marketers.

The popularity of selective distribution has come about also because of a phenomenon called effective distribution. *Effective distribution* means that a limited number of outlets at the retail level account for a significant fraction of the market potential. An example of effective distribution is a situation in which a marketer of expensive men's wristwatches distributes through only 40 percent of available outlets, but these outlets account for 80 percent of the volume of the wristwatch market. Increasing the density of retail outlets to perhaps 50 percent would probably increase the percentage of potential volume to 85 percent; however, the attendant costs of this action might lead to only a marginal profit contribution at best.

The decision as to which of the three degrees of density to select rests on how buyers purchase the manufacturer's offering, the amount of control over resale desired by the manufacturer, the degree of exclusivity sought by intermediaries, and the contribution of intermediaries to the manufacturer's marketing effort.

Intensive distribution is often chosen when the offering is purchased frequently and when buyers wish to expend minimum effort in its acquisition. Almost by definition, convenience goods such as tobacco products, personal-care products, and gasoline fall into this category. Limited-distribution strategies (exclusive and selective) are chosen when the offering requires personal selling at the point of purchase. Major appliances and industrial goods are typically distributed exclusively or selectively.

The density of retail distribution varies inversely with the amount of control over resale desired by the manufacturer. As the density of retail outlets increases, the number of intermediary levels increases, further removing the manufacturer from the ultimate consumer. A manufacturer's control over resale declines sharply in these cases. If control over resale is important, then a strategy of more limited distribution is used. Interests of intermediaries in improving their own competitive advantage also limit distribution. If the nature of the offering demands considerable investment by an intermediary in terms of service capabilities, specialized selling at the point of sale, or unique display methods, limited distribution in the retailer's trade area may be required.

Channel Selection at Other Levels of Distribution

After having determined the nature of retail distribution, the marketing manager must then specify the type, location, and density (if any) of intermediaries that will be used to reach retail outlets. These specific selection decisions closely parallel the retail network decisions made earlier.

If a second-level intermediary (wholesaler, broker, or industrial distributor) is decided on, the question becomes, What type of wholesaler? Should the manager select a specialty wholesaler, which carries a limited line of items within a product line; a general-merchandise wholesaler, which carries a wide assortment of products; a general-line wholesaler, which carries a complete assortment of items in a single retailing field; or a combination of wholesalers? Obviously, an important consideration is what types of wholesalers sell to the retail outlets desired. When Mr. Coffee decided to use supermarkets to sell its replacement coffee filters, it had to recruit food brokers to call on these retailers. Often, the decision is based on what is available. If the available wholesalers do not meet the requirements of the manufacturer in terms of satisfying retailers' requirements for delivery, inventory assortment and volume, credit, and so forth, then direct distribution to retailers becomes the only viable alternative. However, careful study of a wholesaler's role in distribution should precede any decision to bypass them, particularly in countries outside the United States. The Gillette Company's experience in Japan is a case in point.[6] Gillette attempted to sell its razors and blades through company salespeople in Japan as it does in the United States, thus eliminating wholesalers traditionally involved in marketing toiletries. Warner-Lambert Company sold its Schick razors and blades through the traditional Japanese channel involving wholesalers. The result? Gillette holds 10 percent of the Japanese razor and blade market and Schick holds 62 percent.

The location of wholesalers is determined by the location of retail outlets to the extent that geographical proximity affects logistical considerations such as transportation costs and fast delivery service. The density of wholesalers is influenced by the density of the retail network and wholesaler service capabilities. Generally, as the density of retail outlets increases, the density of wholesalers necessary to service them also increases.

Similar kinds of decisions are required for each level of distribution in a particular marketing channel; their determination will depend on the extent of market coverage sought and the availability of intermediaries. Suffice it to say that the number of levels in a marketing channel varies directly with the breadth of the market sought.

DUAL DISTRIBUTION

The discussion thus far has focused on the selection of a single marketing channel. However, many organizations use multiple channels simultaneously, a practice called dual distribution.[7] *Dual distribution* occurs when an organization distributes its offering through two or more different marketing channels that may or may not compete for similar buyers. For example, General Electric sells its appliances directly to house and apartment builders but uses retailers to reach consumers.

Dual distribution is adopted for a variety of reasons. If a manufacturer produces its own brand as well as a private store brand, the store brand might be distributed directly to that particular retailer, whereas the manufacturer's brand might be handled by wholesalers. Or a manufacturer may distribute directly to major large-volume retailers, whose service and volume requirements set them apart from other retailers, and may use wholesalers to reach smaller retailer outlets. Finally, geography itself may affect whether direct or indirect methods of distribution are used. The organization might use its own sales group in high-volume and geographically concentrated markets but use intermediaries elsewhere.

The viability of the dual-distribution approach is highly situational and will depend on the relative strengths of the manufacturer and retailers. If a manufacturer decides to distribute directly to ultimate buyers in a retailer's territory, the retailer may drop the manufacturer's line. The likelihood of this depends on the importance of the manufacturer's line to the retailer and the availability of competitive offerings. If a retailer accounts for a sufficiently large portion of the manufacturer's volume in a market, elimination of the line could have a negative effect on manufacturer's sales volume.

SATISFYING INTERMEDIARY REQUIREMENTS AND TRADE RELATIONS

The role of intermediaries in channel selection has been cited several times; however, a number of specific points require elaboration. The impression given so far may be that intermediaries are relatively docile elements in a marketing channel. Nothing could be further from the truth!

Even though reference has been made to "selecting" intermediaries, selection in actual practice is a two-way street. Accordingly, the marketing manager must be sensitive to possible requirements of intermediaries that must be met in order to establish profitable exchange relationships. Intermediaries are concerned with the adequacy of the manufacturer's offering in improving its product assortment for its own target markets. If the product line or individual offering is inadequate, then the manufacturer must look elsewhere. Intermediaries also seek marketing support from manufacturers. For wholesalers, support often involves promotional assistance; for industrial distributors, it includes technical assistance. As noted previously, intermediaries concerned with competition usually seek a degree of exclusivity in handling the manufacturer's offering. The ability of the intermediary to provide adequate market coverage, given an exclusive agreement, will determine whether this interest can be satisfied by the manufacturer. Finally, intermediaries expect a profit margin on sales consistent with the functions they are expected to perform. In short, trade discounts, fill-rate standards (that is, the ability of the manufacturer to supply quantities requested by intermediaries), cooperative advertising and other promotional support, lead-time requirements (that is, the number of working days from order placement to receipt), and product-service exclusivity agreements each contribute to the likelihood of long-term exchange relationships. A manager who fails to recognize these facts of life often finds that the functions necessary to satisfy buyer requirements, such as sales contacts, display, adequate inventory, service, and delivery, are not being performed.

Conflicts often arise in trade relations. *Channel conflict* arises when one channel member (such as a manufacturer or an intermediary) believes another channel member is engaged in behavior that is preventing it from achieving its goals. Three sources of conflict are most common.[8] First, conflict arises when a channel member bypasses another member and sells or buys direct. When Wal-Mart elected to purchase products direct from manufacturers rather than through manufacturers' agents, these agents picketed Wal-Mart stores and placed ads in the *Wall Street Journal* critical of the company. Second, there can be conflict over how profit margins are distributed among channel members. This happened when Businessland and Compaq Computer Corporation disagreed over how price discounts were applied in the sale of Compaq's products. Compaq stopped selling to Businessland for 13 months, and sales of both companies suffered. A third source of conflict arises when manufacturers believe wholesalers or retailers are not giving their products adequate attention. For example, H.J. Heinz Company became embroiled in a conflict with supermarkets in Great Britain because the supermarkets were promoting and displaying private brands at the expense of Heinz brands.

Conflict can have destructive effects on the workings of a marketing channel. To reduce the likelihood of conflict, one member of the channel sometimes seeks to coordinate, direct, and support other channel members. This channel member assumes the role of a *channel captain* because of its power to influence the behavior of other channel members.

This type of power can take four forms. First, economic power arises from the ability of a firm to reward or coerce other members, given its strong financial position or customer franchise. IBM and Toys "R" Us have economic power. Expertness is a second source of power. For example, American Hospital Supply helps its customers—hospitals—manage order processing for hundreds of medical supplies. Identification with a particular channel member may also bestow power on a firm. For instance, retailers may compete to carry Ralph Lauren, or clothing manufacturers may compete to be carried by Neiman-Marcus or Bloomingdale's. Finally, power can arise from the legitimate right of one channel member to dictate the behavior of other members. This would occur under contractual arrangements (such as franchising) that allow one channel member to legally direct how another behaves.

CHANNEL-MODIFICATION DECISIONS

An organization's marketing channels are subject to modification, but less so than product, price, and promotion. Shifts in geographical concentration of buyers, the inability of existing intermediaries to meet the needs of buyers, and the costs of distribution represent external reasons for modifying existing marketing channels. Sanyo Electric, Inc., eliminated many of its distributors when managers observed that 20 distributors could cover the same market that 90 had in previous years.[9] An organization might initiate a channel-modification program if the product-market strategy changed with the adoption of a market development or diversification strategy. General Motors (Saturn), Honda (Acura), Toyota (Lexus), and Nissan (Infiniti) created separate dealer networks to sell their new luxury models designed for upscale consumer markets.[10] Whatever the reason for modifying an organization's marketing channels, at the base of the channel-modification decision should lie the marketing manager's intent to better achieve the three channel objectives cited earlier. The approach taken in making these decisions involves an assessment of both the benefits and the costs of making a change.

Qualitative Consideration in Modification Decisions

The qualitative assessment of a modification decision can be based on a series of questions. These questions imply that the modification decision involves a comparative analysis of the existing and new channels.

1. Will the change improve the effective coverage of the target markets sought? How?
2. Will the change improve the satisfaction of buyer needs? How?
3. Which marketing functions, if any, must be absorbed in order to make the change?
4. Does the organization have the resources to perform the new functions?
5. What effect will the change have on other channel participants?
6. What will be the effect of the change on the achievement of long-range organizational objectives?

Quantitative Assessment of Modification Decisions

A quantitative assessment of the modification decision considers the financial impact of the change in terms of revenues and expenses. Suppose an organization is considering replacing its wholesalers with its own distribution centers. Wholesalers receive $5 million annually from the margin on sales of the organization's offering. The organization's cost of servicing the wholesalers is $500,000 annually. Therefore, the cost of using wholesalers in this instance is the margin received by wholesalers plus the $500,000 devoted to servicing them, for a total of $5.5 million. Stated differently, the organization would save this amount if the wholesalers were eliminated.

If it eliminated the wholesalers, however, the organization would have to assume their functions, including the costs of sales to retail accounts formerly assumed by the wholesalers. Sales administration costs would be incurred also. In addition, since the wholesalers carry inventories to service retail accounts, the cost of carrying the inventory would have to be assumed, as well as the expenses of delivery and storage. Finally, since wholesalers extend credit to retailers, the cost of carrying the accounts receivable must be included.

Once the costs incurred by eliminating the wholesaler have been estimated, an evaluation of the modification decision from a financial perspective is possible. Such an evaluation is shown below with illustrative dollar values.

Cost of Wholesalers		*Cost of Distribution Centers*	
Margin to wholesalers	$5,000,000	Sales to retailers	$1,500,000
Service expense	500,000	Sales administration	250,000
Total cost	$5,500,000	Inventory cost	935,000
		Delivery and storage	1,877,000
		Accounts receivable	438,000
		Total cost	$5,000,000

Since using wholesalers costs $5.5 million and the cost of distribution centers would be $5 million, a cost perspective suggests selection of the latter option. However, the effect on revenues must be considered. This effect can be determined by first addressing the questions noted earlier and then translating market coverage, the satisfaction of buyer needs, and channel-participant response into dollar values.

NOTES

1. Louis W. Stern and Frederick D. Sturdivant, "Customer-Driven Distribution Systems," *Harvard Business Review* (July–August 1987):34–41.

2. "Distributors: No Endangered Species," *Industry Week* (January 24, 1983): 47–52.

3. For a comprehensive review on direct versus indirect distribution, see V. Kasturi Rangun, Melvyn A. J. Menezes, and E. P. Mair, "Channel Selection for New Industrial Products: A Framework, Method, and Application," *Journal of Marketing* (July 1992): 69–82.

4. "Southland Loses $39 Million after Charge for Closures," *Dallas Morning News* (February 20, 1993): C3.

5. "A Surprise Lift for Computer Retailers," *Business Week* (October 4, 1992): 63–64.

6. "Gillette Tries to Nick Schick in Japan," *Wall Street Journal* (February 4, 1991): B3, B4.

7. For an extended discussion of dual distribution, see John A. Quelch, "Why Not Exploit Dual Marketing?" *Business Horizons* (January–February 1987): 52–60.

8. These examples of channel conflict are found in "Bloody, Bowed, Back Together," *Business Week* (March 19, 1990): 42–43; "Sales Representatives Group to Stage Protest at Wal-

Mart," *Dallas Times Herald* (July 2, 1987): C2; and "Heinz Struggles to Stay at the Top of the Stack," *Business Week* (March 11, 1985): 49.

9. "Sanyo Sales Strategy Illustrates Problems of Little Distributors," *Wall Street Journal* (September 10, 1985): 31.

10. "Here Comes GM's Saturn," *Business Week* (April 9, 1990): 56–62; and "Japanese Firms Push Posh Car Showrooms," *Wall Street Journal* (October 18, 1989): B1.

Zoëcon Corporation
Insect Growth Regulators

In January 1986, Zoëcon Corporation executives met to assess future growth and profit opportunities for its Strike® brand insect growth regulator (IGR) called Strike ROACH ENDER®. The meeting was prompted by a recent change in top management and corporate objectives, which now emphasized a focus on high-financial-return businesses and products.

The first item on the agenda was the marketing program for Strike ROACH ENDER. This product had been in a consumer test market for six months in four cities: Charleston, South Carolina; Beaumont, Texas; Charlotte, North Carolina; and New Orleans, Louisiana. The results of the test market and future directions for the product were to be discussed. Ideas had already surfaced in informal meetings, however. Some executives believed Zoëcon (pronounced Zoy-con) should expand distribution of Strike ROACH ENDER to 19 cities in April 1986, with the intent of distributing the product nationally in April 1987. Other executives felt that Zoëcon should concentrate its effort on opportunities in the professional pest control market. Still other executives held the view that Zoëcon should reconsider any plans to market the product itself. Rather, these executives said, Zoëcon should sell its IGR compound to firms actively engaged in reaching the consumer insecticide market. These firms included d-Con Company, S.C. Johnson and Son (Raid), and Boyle-Midway Division of American Home Products (Black Flag).

Further discussions indicated that some alternatives were mutually exclusive and others were not. For example, Zoëcon could sell to the consumer market under the Strike name or through other firms and also distribute its IGR to professional pest control operators. However, if Zoëcon was able to sell its IGR compound to, say, d-Con, then selling Strike ROACH ENDER would be infeasible. According to one Zoëcon executive, "The decision is basically how can we best allocate our technical, financial, and marketing resources for our IGR compounds."

ZOËCON CORPORATION

Zoëcon Corporation was founded in 1968 in Palo Alto, California, by Dr. Carl Djerassi to research endocrinological methods of insect population control. Djerassi was a pioneer in the development of chemical methods for human birth control, which subsequently led to the introduction of the birth control pill. The name Zoëcon is a combination of the Greek words *zoe* for life and *con* for control.

This case was prepared by Dr. Larry Smith, graduate student, under the supervision of Professor Roger A. Kerin, of the Edwin L. Cox School of Business, Southern Methodist University, as a basis for classroom discussion and is not designed to illustrate effective or ineffective handling of an administrative situation. Certain names and data have been disguised. The cooperation of Zoëcon Corporation in the preparation of this case is gratefully acknowledged. Copyright © by Roger A. Kerin. No part of this case may be reproduced without written permission of the copyright holder.

Zoëcon Corporation was acquired in 1983 by Sandoz, Ltd., a Swiss-based producer of pharmaceuticals, agrichemicals, and colors and dyes. Zoëcon's mission was to be the marketing arm of Sandoz, Ltd, in the animal health and insect control areas. Zoëcon sells (1) animal health products to small-animal veterinarians and clinics, (2) pest control chemicals for farm animals, (3) insecticides for household pets and pest control to supermarkets, pet stores, veterinarians, and pest control companies, and (4) products and chemical compounds to firms engaged in marketing pest control products to the consumer market. For example, Zoëcon produces the chemicals for the Black Flag Roach Motel sold by Boyle-Midway. The company recorded $100 million in sales from these products and a 25 percent pretax profit on sales. A partial list of company products and applications is shown in Exhibit 1.

EXHIBIT 1

Selected Zoëcon Products and Applications

Brand/Product	Target Insects
Consumer	
Strike ROACH ENDER®	Cockroaches, fleas, ticks, mosquitoes,
Strike FLEA ENDER®	spiders, crickets
VAPORETTE® flea collars	
Methoprene	
Roach traps	
Insect strips	
Animal Health	
VET-KEM®—flea collars, dips, flea, aerorols and foggers, flea powders, flea shampoos	Fleas, ticks, sarcoptic mange
ZODIAC®—flea collars, dips, flea aerosols and foggers, flea powders, flea and regular shampoos	
STARBAR®—flybait; cattle dusts, sprays, and dips; swine dusts, sprays, and dips; insect strips; rodenticides; pet products; Altosid® feed-through	Houseflies, cattle hornflies, grubs, lice, mosquitoes, rats and mice, fleas, ticks, and sarcoptic mange
Pest Control	
SAFROTIN®	Cockroaches, fleas, houseflies, pharoah's ants, stored-product pests, tobacco moths, cigarette beetles, mosquitoes, and blackflies
PRECOR®	
GENCOR®	
FLYTEK®	
PHARORID®	
DIANEX®	
KABAT®	
ALTOSID®	
TEKNAR®	

Source: Company records. STRIKE, ROACH ENDER, FLEA ENDER, VAPORETTE, VET-KEM, ZODIAC, STARBAR, SAFROTIN, PRECOR, GENCOR, FLYTEK, PHARORID, DIANEX, KABAT, ALTOSID, and TEKNAR are trademarks of Sandoz, Ltd.

INSECT CONTROL

The use of chemical toxins to control insect pests is commonplace. Although these toxins are potentially harmful to people as well as insects, recent advances in chemistry have reduced the threat to people. Surviving insects, however, may produce successive generations that are resistant to toxins.

Public concern over the toxic effect of agricultural and household insecticides has remained widespread despite the advances in chemistry. In particular, consumers have evidenced increasing concern that safer household insecticides be used where children and pets might come in contact with the residual chemicals. The demand for safer compounds caused a change in the focus of research and development from new insect adulticides, which kill adult insects, to chemical compounds that disrupt insect reproduction.

Insect Life Cycles

Insect reproduce by laying eggs. The life patterns after hatching from the egg vary among different insect species. The flea has a complete metamorphic cycle, passing in sequence through the egg, larval, and pupal stages to the adult stage in 23 days. Cockroach metamorphosis is incomplete. Wingless nymphs hatch from eggs and grow by shedding their exoskeletons, molting six times through six nymphal stages, called instars. Molting of the sixth instar produces winged, sexually mature adult roaches in 74 days.

Metamorphosis is controlled by the insect's endocrine system. In fleas, hormones regulate development and transition from larval to pupal to adult stages. Analogously, in roaches, molting is initiated when the brain produces a neurohormone that activates prothoracic gland production of a molting hormone. Additionally, a juvenile hormone is produced by the brain in decreasing amounts, until at the sixth and final molt no juvenile hormone is produced. This molting produces sexually mature adult cockroaches up to two inches long.

The life cycle of the cockroach is shown in Exhibit 2. It begins with formation of about 40 eggs in a capsule called an ootheca. The adult female produces one ootheca every 23 days over an average life span of 150 days, for a total of about 260 roaches. Research on cockroaches indicates that a roach population will increase geometrically if ample food, water, and shelter are available. Research also indicates that roaches are omnivorous and have a particular liking for beer.

Insect Growth Regulators

Insect growth regulators are effective against insects that are problems as adults, such as cockroaches. Roaches have been shown to carry bacteria, viruses, fungi, and protozoa, which cause diseases such as food poisoning, diarrhea, dysentery, hepatitis B, polio, and encephalitis. They are also capable of carrying organisms causing cholera, plague, typhus, leprosy, and tuberculosis. Furthermore, in susceptible individuals cockroach contaminations may produce allergic reactions similar to hay fever, asthma, food allergies, and dermatitis.

Insect growth regulators are synthetic analogs of the natural insect juvenile hormones produced in the normal sequence of metamorphosis. The concentration of juvenile hormone produced decreases with each molting, to permit emergence of

EXHIBIT 2

Normal Life Cycle of the Cockroach

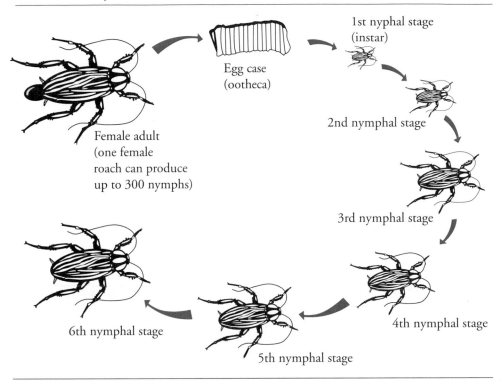

Female adult
(one female
roach can produce
up to 300 nymphs)

Egg case
(ootheca)

1st nyphal stage
(instar)

2nd nymphal stage

3rd nymphal stage

4th nymphal stage

5th nymphal stage

6th nymphal stage

an adult insect after the pupal stage (for fleas) or after the last nymph stage (for roaches). If the larva or nymph is exposed to an IGR during the stage prior to molting, however, subsequent development into an adult is prevented or altered. Fleas exposed to an IGR during the larval stage pupate but fail to emerge to continue the reproductive cycle. Similarly, cockroaches exposed to an IGR in the sixth instar molt will become deformed, sexually immature adults incapable of reproducing.

As chemicals, IGRs are much less toxic than compounds typically used in household insecticides. Because they are synthetic chemical analogs of juvenile hormones specific to insects, they are not physiologically active in human or animal endocrine systems.

IGRs are extremely effective in eliminating insect populations. Only a few tenths of a milligram per square foot is required for effective control of insect reproduction. When an IGR is combined with an adulticide, many insects are killed and those that survive are prohibited from reproducing. In time, an insect infestation is controlled and, ideally, eliminated.

A unique feature of IGRs is that the immediate effects of an application are not observable. That is, since an IGR affects the reproductive cycle of an insect, it does not kill insects that come in contact with the compound. Controlled tests of a cockroach IGR indicate that a significant reduction in roach population occurs after 120 days and continues with applications spaced at 120-day intervals. When the IGR is combined with an adulticide, adult roaches and nymphs are killed upon contact with the adulticide. Short-term residual effects of the adulticide can repel roaches from treated areas, however. Therefore, the adulticide can hamper the effect of an IGR, since insects avoid treated areas.

PREMISE INSECTICIDE MARKET

The premise insecticide market is divided into two segments: the consumer market and the professional pest control market. The distinction is based on distribution systems and product forms. Insecticides for the consumer market are packaged in easy-to-use, do-it-yourself containers sold mostly through supermarkets. The professional pest control market consists of sales of insecticides, often in diluted form, to professional applicators. Orkin and Terminix are examples of professional applicators.

Consumer Market

Estimated annual sales for all consumer-disbursed insecticides in 1985 were $400 million at manufacturers' prices. Sales were forecasted to grow at an average rate of 10 percent per year through 1990. S. C. Johnson and Son, Inc. captured 45 percent of this market with its Raid brand. The Boyle-Midway Division of American Home Products accounted for 12 percent of the market with Black Flag, and d-Con Company captured 10 percent. No other company had a market share greater than 8 percent.

Supermarkets accounted for 70 percent of insecticide sales, followed by drugstores (9 percent) and a host of other retailers such as home improvement centers and house and garden outlets (21 percent). Aerosol sprays, including foggers, were the preferred method for applying insecticides and accounted for 74 percent of retail sales. Liquid sprays followed with 14 percent. Solids, strips, pastes, traps, and baits generated 12 percent of retail sales. Differences in packaging were based on consumers' preferences for quick-kill, residual control, or a margin of safety. Quick-kill dominated the consumer mindset, hence the popularity of aerosols and liquids that allowed for a "chase and squirt" routine when a roach was seen.

The consumer market was further subdivided into insect-specific insecticides. Ant and roach killers captured 40 percent of the market, flying insect killers 20 percent, flea killers 11 percent, and other insect-specific products 29 percent.

As expected, household insecticide sales were seasonal and varied by geography. The six-month period from May through October was the prime sales time for insecticides; 75 percent of annual sales were made during this period. The southern tier of 14 states (from the East Coast to the West Coast) accounted for 50 percent of annual sales.

Insecticides sold to the consumer market are heavily promoted. In 1983, the most recent year for which advertising expenditures were available, manufacturers spent $28.6 million for magazine, newspaper, television, radio, and outdoor advertising. For example, it was estimated that S. C. Johnson and Son spent $1.4 million to advertise Raid Ant & Roach Killer, Roach and Flea Killer, and Roach Traps. Boyle-Midway spent almost $3 million to advertise its Black Flag Roach & Ant Killer and Roach Motel. Past history of product introductions indicated that a minimum $10 million promotion investment was required to successfully launch a new product when consumers were familiar with the brand name.

Professional Pest Control Market

The professional pest control market produced revenues of $2.5 billion in 1985. Revenues were forecasted to be $3.7 billion in 1990, representing an annual average growth rate of 8 percent. About 6 percent of the revenues produced by pest control operators (PCOs) were accounted for by chemical compound cost.

The majority (52 percent) of professional pest control revenues resulted from general insect control (for example, of cockroaches, fleas, or ants). Termite control accounted for 21 percent of professional pest control revenues. The remaining 27 percent were from specialty pest control applications, especially rodent control.

This market was dominated by many small PCOs. There were an estimated 14,000 PCOs, of which only two (Orkin and Terminix) had annual sales greater than $100 million. About 28 PCOs had annual sales greater than $3 million, whereas over 6,000 had revenues under $50,000 annually.

Insecticides were sold to PCOs through distributors. These distributors purchased insecticides in bulk quantities (cases and pallets) from producers and then sold them to PCOs in smaller quantities. These distributors typically received an average gross margin of 27 percent on the selling price to PCOs. Although percentages varied, industry sources estimated that the producer's average gross profit on chemicals sold to the professional pest control market was 51 percent. By comparison, the average gross profit on insecticides sold to the consumer market was 55 percent.

Producer marketing expenses associated with selling to the professional pest control market were small in comparison to the costs of selling to the consumer market. As a general rule, about 27 percent of sales were spent for marketing to PCOs. Most of these expenses were for trade advertising and sales efforts.

ZOËCON PRODUCT DEVELOPMENT AND MARKETING

From its beginning, Zoëcon made a large commitment to ongoing research on IGRs. By the mid-1970s, Zoëcon research scientists, who comprised more than 25 percent of the company's employees, had synthesized more than 1,250 IGRs, and 175 patents had been issued for these inventions.

Development and Marketing of Flea Compound

The first commercialized IGR, methoprene, was introduced in 1974 for mosquito control. This IGR was made available in a variety of product forms over the years for multiple control uses. In 1980, Zoëcon obtained EPA approval for the use of methoprene under the trade name PRECOR® as a flea control compound. Given the company's already established trade relations with PCOs, veterinary clinics, and pet stores, Zoëcon began selling its flea control compound to these outlets. By 1985, Zoëcon executives estimated that the company had captured 80 percent of all flea product sales made through these outlets. Some company executives attributed the success of PRECOR to the fact that PCOs, veterinarians, and pet store sales personnel could explain the unique benefits and application of methoprene.

The early success of PRECOR led Zoëcon to look for opportunities outside of PCOs, animal clinics, and pet stores. Market analysis revealed that supermarkets accounted for a rapidly growing percentage of flea product sales volume. Since Zoëcon had no significant experience dealing with supermarkets, it approached the makers of d-Con,

Black Flag, and Raid products about including PRECOR in their products. Only d-Con expressed interest. In 1981, d-Con introduced Flea Stop, a fogger for fleas containing only PRECOR—no adulticide was included among the ingredients. Flea Stop sold well in supermarkets, given the sales and marketing support provided by d-Con.

PRECOR's success prompted Zoëcon to again approach the makers of Black Flag and Raid in 1982. No agreement could be reached, however. This setback resulted in the decision by Zoëcon to develop its own brand for sales through supermarkets. In early 1983, Zoëcon introduced Strike FLEA ENDER, which includes PRECOR and an adulticide, in 19 cities that accounted for the majority of flea product sales. By late 1983, Strike FLEA ENDER had captured 11 percent of flea product sales in those cities. This success led to an agreement with S. C. Johnson and Son, in December 1983, to include PRECOR in its Raid Flea Killer Plus. This agreement allowed Zoëcon to continue marketing PRECOR under the STRIKE brand name. Strike FLEA ENDER had an 18 percent market share in 1985; however, the product had not yet achieved its profit objective.

Development and Marketing of Roach Compound

Continuing research efforts resulted in the development of hydroprene, an IGR that was particularly useful for preventing normal cockroach maturation. This discovery was viewed as a major breakthrough in the creation of synthetic chemical analogs of naturally occurring insect juvenile hormones. In early 1984, Zoëcon obtained EPA registrations for hydroprene. By late 1984, the company was marketing hydroprene under the GENCOR® trade name only to PCOs, since pet stores and veterinary clinics had little or no use for this compound.

In late 1984, Zoëcon executives responsible for Strike FLEA ENDER proposed that a hydroprene-based product with the name Strike ROACH ENDER be introduced to supermarkets. This proposal requested that Strike ROACH ENDER, which would contain hydroprene and an adulticide, be introduced in the same 19 cities where Strike FLEA ENDER was being sold. Top management believed that an opportunity existed but that Strike ROACH ENDER should be test-marketed before an investment in all 19 markets was made. Accordingly, a test market plan was drafted in early 1985.

Test-Marketing Strike Roach Ender

Two objectives were set for the test market: to determine consumer acceptance of the product and to qualify the trade and consumer marketing program. The four cities chosen for the test were Charlotte, North Carolina; Charleston, South Carolina; Beaumont, Texas; and New Orleans, Louisiana. These cities were considered representative of the 19-city market where 80 percent of roach insecticides were sold. The cities contained 1.17 million households, or 5.3 percent of the 22 million households in that market area. The test market ran from May through October 1985. Product shipments to supermarkets in the four cities began in April.

Segmentation and Positioning Research on roach insecticide users indicated that three segments existed, based on the primary benefit sought. The primary target market for Strike ROACH ENDER was the "end problem permanently" segment. A secondary market was the "product that lasts" segment. The "convenience/low cost" segment was not considered a primary or secondary target.

EXHIBIT   3

Strike ROACH ENDER Print Advertisement

Strike ROACH ENDER was positioned as a scientific breakthrough with unique qualities desired by the targeted segments. A print advertisement for the product is shown in Exhibit 3.

Product Packaging and Price Strike ROACH ENDER was packaged in a 10-ounce aerosol spray and a 6-ounce fogger. The retail price for the aerosol was $4.49 and for the fogger was $3.99. These prices were 50 to 75 percent higher than those of existing roach insecticides. The premium price was justified on the basis of the product's unique compound and long-lasting effect. The higher price also provided supermarkets with a higher margin than they received from competitive products. Price and cost data are shown in Exhibit 4.

Consumer and Trade Promotion Television and newspaper advertising was used to build consumer awareness, and cents-off coupons were employed to stimulate product trial. The consumer promotion and media strategy focused on 25- to 54-year-old women living in households of three or more. A "blitz" strategy was used, with the heaviest promotion scheduled for the first three months of the test. A public relations effort was also launched, featuring press kit mailings to newspapers, guest appearances on local radio and television talk shows, and an 800-number consumer hotline to answer consumers' questions.

The trade promotion included discounts for first-time supermarket buyers, a calendar to assist buyers in coordinating store promotion with consumer advertising, freestanding in-store displays, and sales aids. Exhibit 5 shows a Strike ROACH ENDER trade promotion.

Test-Market Expenditures and Results The cost of the test market was $1,478,000. An itemized summary is shown in Exhibit 6.

Results of the test market were tracked by an independent marketing research firm. At the end of the test in November 1985, 57 percent of the households in the test cities had tried the product, and 30 percent of those households that had tried the product had repurchased during the test period. The average number of units purchased by all trier households was 1.3 units. Households that repurchased bought an average of 3.5 units. Sixty-six percent of Strike ROACH ENDER sales were of the aerosol spray; 34 percent were of foggers. This breakdown was identical for first purchases and subsequent purchases. Product shipments data indicated that 11,700 cases (at 12 units per case) of 10-ounce aerosol units and 6,300 cases (at 12 units per case) of 6-ounce fogger units were shipped to supermarket warehouses in the four cities during the test period.

EXHIBIT 4

Strike ROACH ENDER Package Economics

	10-oz. Aerosol	6-oz. Fogger
Price to trade[a]	$3.14	$2.79
Cost of goods sold[b]	1.41	1.26
Zoëcon's gross profit	$1.73	$1.53

[a]Price to trade is the price at which Zoëcon sells directly to the retailer.

[b]Cost of goods sold includes the cost of the can, solvent, propellant, active ingredients, and freight. Note that the cost of goods sold represents virtually all of the variable costs associated with the product forms.

EXHIBIT 5

Strike ROACH ENDER Trade Promotion

JANUARY MEETING

When Zoëcon executives met in January 1986, the first item on the agenda was to review the test-market results and prepare marketing plans for 1986. Different points of view had already been expressed in informal discussions among Zoëcon executives. One position advanced was that Strike ROACH ENDER distribution should be expanded to the 19 cities where Strike FLEA ENDER was being sold. Marketing research indicated that these 19 cities accounted for 80 percent of roach insecticide

EXHIBIT 6

Summary of Marketing Expenses for the Strike ROACH ENDER Test Market

Activity	Expense
Promotion and advertising[a]	$1,016,000
Setup/auditing[b]	377,000
Marketing research[c]	65,000
Miscellaneous[d]	20,000
	$1,478,000

[a]Includes consumer advertising and promotion to supermarket buyers.
[b]Includes point-of-purchase materials, monitoring of shelf placement, sales aids, and free goods.
[c]Includes consumer tracking studies (for example, product awareness and purchase behavior).
[d]Includes public relations campaign.

volume. These executives reasoned that the up-front investment in marketing research, public relations, and set-up/auditing costs would not have to be repeated in the expanded distribution. Rather, the primary direct costs associated with the roll-out to all 19 cities would be for promotion and advertising.

A second view was that Zoëcon should direct its resources to PCOs. These executives noted that GENCOR (hydroprene) had been well received by PCOs in late 1984 and many PCOs were promoting its benefits to their customers. These executives felt that ongoing investment of $500,000 per year above the 27 percent of sales typically budgeted for trade advertising and sales efforts would accelerate its use.

A third opinion was that Zoëcon should pursue opportunities for selling hydroprene to the makers of d-Con, Black Flag, and Raid for use in their products. This strategy had worked in the past for PRECOR (methoprene). A product cost analysis performed on Strike ROACH ENDER indicated that the cost of goods sold for the 10-ounce aerosol package without hydroprene would be $0.80. For the 6-ounce fogger package without hydroprene, the cost of goods sold would also be $0.80. Furthermore, Zoëcon could realize a 50 percent gross margin on hydroprene sold to another insecticide marketer with no investment in marketing or sales. These costs would be absorbed by the marketer of the product—d-Con, Black Flag, or Raid. Executives favoring this option believed the test-market experience could be used to interest insecticide marketers in the product. Specific aspects of the proposal, including the price for hydroprene, would have to be developed if this option was adopted. Executives favoring the continued marketing of Strike ROACH ENDER cautioned that this action could spell the end for Zoëcon's presence in the consumer market.

Zoëcon executives present at the January 1986 meeting were acutely aware of the importance of the decision they faced. Moreover, the peak season for roach insecticides was approaching, and a decision needed to be made quickly.

Hendison Electronics Corporation

The corporate planning process for Hendison Electronics Corporation had just concluded, and Richard Hawly, Vice President of Marketing, was reviewing the corporate goals for 1991. Even though Hawly had participated in the deliberations and the drafting of the final document, he was impressed with the ambitious goals. For example, the corporate plan established a sales goal of $37 million for 1991, when sales volume for 1990 was estimated to be $27 million.

During the planning process, a number of fellow executives had voiced concern over whether the distribution approach used by Hendison Electronics was appropriate for the expanded sales goals. Hawly felt that their concerns had merit and should be given careful consideration. Though he had considerable latitude in devising the distribution strategy, the final choice would have to be consistent with the overall marketing program for the company in 1991. A recommendation and supporting documentation had to be prepared in a relatively short time to permit an integrated marketing program introduction in January 1991.

THE COMPANY

Hendison Electronics Corporation was formed in 1961 by Mark Speerson, who had a Ph.D. in electrical engineering. The company introduced a stereo radio unit in 1964 and a line of television sets in 1966. By the early 1980s, the company had expanded its product line to include a full line of home entertainment equipment.

Hendison Electronics is an assembler rather than a manufacturer of home entertainment equipment. As an assembler, the company purchases components under contract from large (usually foreign) manufacturers. These components are then identified as Hendison Electronics Corporation products and placed in consoles or other packages for sale under the Solartronics brand name.

Hendison Electronics distributes its products directly to 425 independent specialty home entertainment dealers and 50 exclusive dealers which are of standard industry size in terms of selling space. Combined, these 475 dealers service 150 markets in 11 western and Rocky Mountain states. The exclusive dealers, however, are the sole company representatives in 50 markets. According to Hawly, this disparity in market coverage occurred as a result of the company's early difficulty in gaining adequate distribution.[1]

---

[1]Exclusive dealerships had chosen to operate in this manner. This was not the policy of Hendison Electronics Corporation. However, Hendison Electronics did not pursue additional dealers in these markets for the purpose of carrying company products.

This case was prepared by Professor Roger A. Kerin, of the Edwin L. Cox School of Business, Southern Methodist University, as a basis for class discussion and is not designed to illustrate effective or ineffective handling of an administrative situation. Certain names and data have been disguised. Copyright © by Roger A. Kerin. No part of this case may be reproduced without written permission of the copyright holder.

The independent dealers typically carry ten or more brands of home entertainment equipment products, whereas the exclusive dealerships carry only Hendison Electronics products and noncompetitive complementary products. Dealerships are located in market areas with populations of approximately 100,000 or fewer. In contrast, major competitors tend to be national in scope. Partially as a result of that—and partially because of economies of scale in advertising and distribution—these firms had been selling an increasing proportion of their products through mass merchandisers such as chain and discount stores. The overwhelming majority of these stores were located in retail trading areas with 1 million or more inhabitants.

The company employs ten sales representatives, each responsible for a territory that is generally delineated by state borders. These representatives deal primarily with the independent dealers and call on them twice a month on average.

THE HOME ENTERTAINMENT INDUSTRY

The home entertainment industry grew considerably in the 1980s with the rise in consumer disposable income, changes in lifestyles, and product innovation. Estimates of the actual dollar volume of the industry are extremely vague, partly because of the rapidly changing product mix encompassed by the general term *home entertainment* and constant product innovation.

Despite the difficulty in estimating market size, it is generally accepted that Thomson (GE and RCA brands), Zenith, Matsushita (Panasonic and Quasar brands), Sony, and North American Philips (Magnavox, Sylvania, and Philco brands) account for the bulk of total dollar volume. Private brands, produced by several of these firms and many others, are also important in the industry. The total market was estimated to be growing at a rate of 6 percent annually.

Though it is difficult to define specifically the product mix in the industry at any one time, eight general product categories exist: television, compact disc players, video cassette recorders, radios, phonographs, tape recorders, tape decks, and high-fidelity stereo system components. Product categories vary dramatically in terms of saturation. For example, 99 percent of the households in the United States have a television set, 65 percent have a video cassette recorder, and 48 percent have a portable radio or tape player. By comparison, 14 percent of households in the United States have a compact disc player and only 6 percent have a portable compact disc player. Exhibit 1 shows the incidence of first purchase and replacement purchases for selected home entertainment products.

In 1987 the company commissioned a study on the socioeconomic characteristics and purchase behavior of buyers of home entertainment products. Exhibit 2 shows selected demographic characteristics of buyers of selected home entertainment products. The study reported that these purchasers had median household incomes above the median household income of the U.S. population as a whole. The research also revealed the following:

1. In-store demonstration, friend or relative recommendation, dealer or salesperson presentation, and advertising are dominant influences when buyers decide what brand of home entertainment products to purchase.
2. The median number of shopping trips made before purchasing home entertainment products was 2.4.

EXHIBIT 1

First Purchase and Replacement Purchases for Selected Home Entertainment Products

	Percentage of Households Buying			
	For First Time	*As Replacement*	*In Addition to One Now Owned*	*Total Market*
Color console TV	37	49	14	100
Color portable TV	41	30	29	100
Color table-model TV	44	31	25	100
Stereo receiver/amplifier	58	23	19	100
Stereo speakers	55	21	24	100
Tape deck	71	14	15	100
Tape recorder	61	15	24	100
Video cassette recorder	85	10	5	100

Source: Company records.

3. The most frequently shopped outlets for home entertainment products were radio/TV stores.

The vast majority of home entertainment products are distributed through five types of retail outlets: (1) home furnishings/furniture stores, (2) housewares/hardware stores, (3) auto supply stores, (4) department stores/mass merchandisers (such as Circuit City), and (5) radio/TV stores. The volume of home entertainment merchandise sold by these outlets is unknown because of the variety of merchandise offered. However, selected data on the radio/TV store group with a more homogeneous product mix are available (see Exhibit 3). These types of dealers represent all of Hendison Electronics's accounts and operate with a gross margin of 27.5 percent.

HENDISON ELECTRONICS CORPORATE POLICY FOR 1991

The following is an excerpted version of the company's statement of policy.

General Corporate Objective

Our customer is the discriminating purchaser of home entertainment products who makes the purchase decision in a deliberate manner. To this customer we will provide, under the Solartronics brand, quality home entertainment products in the higher-priced brackets that require specialty selling. These products will be retailed through reputable electronics specialists who provide good service.

Marketing Objectives and Strategy

The company's marketing objective is to serve the discriminating purchaser of home entertainment products who approaches a purchase in a deliberate manner with

EXHIBIT 2

Demographic Characteristics of Heads of Households Buying Selected Types of Home Entertainment Products

	For First Time	As Replacement	In Addition to One Now Owned
Color console TV			
Median age	38	50	42
Median number of household members	3.3	3.3	4.3
College graduate	21.3%	15.4%	30.6%
Color table-model TV			
Median age	36	45	46
Median number of household members	3.4	3.2	4.3
College graduate	44.0%	22.5%	30.8%
Color portable TV			
Median age	41	43	43
Median number of household members	3.1	2.9	3.8
College graduate	24.2%	32.2%	33.9%
Stereo receiver/amplifier			
Median age	39	40	46
Median number of household members	3.6	3.3	4.3
College graduate	32.1%	43.8%	46.8%
Stereo speakers			
Median age	37	34	41
Median number of household members	3.5	3.0	4.1
College graduate	34.7%	38.8%	38.7%
Video cassette recorder			
Median age	39	39	NA
Median number of household members	3.2	3.4	NA
College graduate	42.1%	20.1%	NA
Tape recorder			
Median age	43	44	43
Median number of household members	3.7	4.2	3.9
College graduate	28.1%	39.4%	39.1%
Tape deck			
Median age	40	34	49
Median number of household members	3.9	3.5	4.2
College graduate	27.5%	20.5%	29.6%

Source: Company records.

heavy consideration of long-term benefits. We will emphasize home entertainment products with superior performance, style, reliability, and value that require representative display, professional selling, trained service, and brand acceptance—retailed through reputable electronics specialists to those consumers whom the company can most effectively service. This will be accomplished by:

1. A focused marketing effort to serve the customer who approaches the purchase of a home entertainment product as an investment.

EXHIBIT 3

Number and Retail Sales of Radio/TV Stores in the Western and Rocky Mountain States

State	Number	Sales (thousands of dollars)
Arizona	289	$ 164,870
California	2,375	1,581,046
Colorado	331	180,119
Idaho	86	30,029
Montana	81	38,408
Nevada	88	55,397
New Mexico	113	42,749
Oregon	286	132,726
Utah	124	57,204
Washington	457	182,993
Wyoming	59	20,252
11-state total	4,289	$2,485,793

Source: Census of Retail Trade and Hendison Electronics Corporation estimate.

2. Concentration on our areas of differential advantage: high-technology television, audio, and related home entertainment products with innovative features, superior reliability, and high performance levels—products that generally sell for more than $600 at retail.

3. Emphasis on products requiring display, demonstration, and product education, which must be delivered to and serviced in the home, to be sold through reputable merchants that specialize in home entertainment products and provide good service.

4. Concentration on distribution in existing markets, and general exclusion of large core cities with populations of 1 million or more.

5. Developing brand acceptance by obtaining in every market served a market position of at least $6.50 sales per capita, which our research indicates is possible.

Hendison Electronics's 1991 policy statement and marketing strategy represented a significant departure from the company's previous marketing posture. For many years the company had manufactured and marketed good-quality, medium- and promotionally priced home entertainment products. In the last few years, however, the company had begun to emphasize more expensive and more luxurious home entertainment equipment.

Although this was not stated in the overall marketing strategy, the company had also become more aggressive in its advertising. The advertising budget for 1991 included television advertising, which the company had previously eschewed in favor of local newspaper advertising on a cooperative basis with dealers. In 1991, television advertising would be allotted $3 million and would be directed at the 100 highest-potential markets, 50 markets served by exclusive dealers and 50 other current markets that had the next highest potential.

The overall direction of the marketing program had been reaffirmed in the recent corporate planning sessions. The sales target of $37 million was viewed as both ambitious and necessary. Hendison Electronics's senior managers were of the firm belief that the company had to attain a larger, critical mass of sales volume to preserve its buying position with component suppliers, particularly with respect to component prices and discounts.

Even though there was agreement on the marketing effort and the need to expand sales volume, different viewpoints were raised concerning the capacity of present dealers to deliver $37 million in sales. This matter had consumed much of Hawly's time recently.

THE DISTRIBUTION STRATEGY ISSUE

Hawly was well aware of the value that Hendison Electronics placed on its dealers and the importance of developing a close linkage between the company and the dealers. The company had long emphasized that dealers are an asset that must be consistently supported.

Hawly saw his charge as determining the characteristics, the number, and the locations of the dealers Hendison Electronics would need to meet its sales goal of $37 million in 1991. Initially this would involve identifying the types of dealers that would satisfy the needs of the kind of customer the company sought and that would work closely with the company in meeting corporate objectives.

A number of different viewpoints had been voiced by Hawly's fellow executives. One viewpoint favored increasing the number of dealers in the markets currently served by the company. The reasoning behind this position was that it would be difficult for existing dealers to attain the $37 million sales goal specified in the corporate plan. Executives expressing this view noted that even with a 6 percent increase in sales following the industry trend, it would be necessary to add at least another 100 dealers. They said these dealers would be likely to be independent (nonexclusive) dealers located in the 100 markets not served by exclusive dealerships. Hawly believed that adding another 100 dealers over the next year would not be easy and would require increasing the sales force that serviced nonexclusive dealers. Executives acknowledged that this plan had more merit in the long run of, say, three to four years. However, their idea had merit as a long-term distribution policy, they thought. The incremental direct cost of adding a sales representative was $50,000 per year.

A second viewpoint favored the development of an exclusive franchise program, since 27 nonexclusive dealers had posed such a possibility in the last year. Each of these dealers represented a different market and each of these markets was considered to have high potential and be a candidate for the new advertising program. These dealers were prepared to sell off competing lines. They would sell Hendison Electronics home entertainment products exclusively in their market for a specified franchise fee. In exchange for the dealer's contractual obligation to promote, merchandise, and service Hendison Electronics products in a specified manner consistent with corporate objectives, Hendison Electronics would drop present dealers in their markets and not add new dealers. Further, these dealers noted, the company's current contractual arrangements with its independent dealers allowed for cancellation by either party, without cause, with 90-days advance notification. Thus, the program could be implemented during the traditionally slow first quarter of the up-coming year. If adopted, Hendison Electronics executives believed the franchise program in these 27 markets could be served by the television advertising program. The other 50 markets served by exclusive dealers would be unaffected, since this advertising program was already being applied. The remaining 73 markets would also be unaffected, except for increased advertising in 23 high-potential markets.

A third viewpoint called for a general reduction in the number of dealerships without granting any exclusive franchises. Executives supporting this approach cited a number of factors favoring it. First, analysis of dealers' sales indicated that 10.5 percent of Hendison Electronics dealers (all exclusive dealers) produced 80 percent of company sales. Second, an improvement in sales-force effort and possibly increased sales might result if more time were given to fewer dealers. Third, committing Hendison Electronics to an exclusive franchise program would limit its flexibility in the future. Although a number had not been set, some consideration had been given to the idea of reducing the number of dealers in the 150 markets served by the company from 475 to 250. This would mean that the 50 exclusive dealers would be retained and 200 nonexclusive dealers would operate in the remaining 100 markets, of which the top 50 would benefit from the television advertising program.

A fourth viewpoint voiced by several executives was not to change either the distribution strategy or the dealers. Rather, they believed that the company should do a better job with the current distribution system. It was their opinion that additional sales personnel and the expanded television advertising budget should be sufficient. Moreover, they argued that because of a recessionary environment, the early 1990s was not the time for major changes in distribution policy and practices.

Goodyear Tire and Rubber Company

In early 1992, Goodyear Tire and Rubber Company executives were reconsidering a proposal made by Sears, Roebuck and Company. Sears management had approached Goodyear about selling the company's popular Eagle brand tire in 1989. The proposal was declined. At the time, Goodyear's top management believed that such an action would undermine the tire sales of company-owned Goodyear Auto Service Centers and franchised Goodyear Tire Dealers which were the principal retail sources for Goodyear brand tires. However, following a $38 million loss in 1990 and a change in Goodyear top management in 1991, the Sears proposal resurfaced for consideration.

Two factors contributed to the renewed interest in the Sears proposal.[1] First, between 1987 and 1991, Goodyear brand tires recorded a 3.2 percent decline in market share for replacement tires in the United States. This share decline represented a loss of about 4.9 million tire units. It was believed that the growth of warehouse membership club stores and discount tire retail claims coupled with multibranding among mass merchandisers contributed to the market share erosion (see Exhibit 1). Second, it was believed that nearly 2 million worn-out Goodyear brand tires were being replaced annually at some 850 Sears Auto Centers in the United States. According to a Goodyear executive, the failure to repurchase Goodyear brand tires happened by default "because the remarkable loyalty of Sears customers led them to buy the best tire available from those offered by Sears," which did not include Goodyear brand tires.

The Sears proposal raised several strategic considerations for Goodyear. First, as a matter of distribution policy, Goodyear had not sold the Goodyear tire brand through a mass merchandiser since the 1920s, when it sold tires through Sears. A decision to sell Goodyear brand tires again through Sears would represent a significant change in distribution policy and could create conflict with its franchised dealers. Second, if the Sears proposal was accepted, several product policy questions loomed. Specifically, should the arrangement with Sears include (1) only the Goodyear Eagle brand or (2) all of its Goodyear brands? Relatedly, should Goodyear allow Sears to carry one or more brands exclusively and have its own dealers carry certain brands on an exclusive basis? Goodyear presently has 12 brands of passenger and light-truck tires sold under the Goodyear name ranging from lower-priced

[1]Modern Tire Dealer, "Newsfocus," March 1992, p. 13.

This case was prepared by Professor Roger A. Kerin, of Edwin L. Cox School of Business, Southern Methodist University, as a basis for class discussion and is not designed to illustrate effective or ineffective handling of an administrative situation. The case is based on published sources. The author wishes to thank Professor Arthur A. Thompson, Jr., of the University of Alabama, for kindly granting permission to extract information from his industry note, "Competition in the World Tire Industry, 1992," for use in this case, the Goodyear Tire and Rubber Company for comments on a previous draft of the case and permission to reproduce its advertising copy, and Michelin Tire Corporation for permission to reproduce its advertising copy. Copyright © by Roger A. Kerin. No part of this case may be reproduced without written permission of the copyright holder.

EXHIBIT 1

U.S. Market Share of Replacement Tire Sales by Type of Retail Outlet; 1982 and 1992

Type of Retail Outlet	1982	1992*
Traditional multibrand independent dealers	44%	44%
Discount multibrand independent dealers	7	15
Chain stores, department stores	20	14
Tire company stores	10	9
Service stations	11	8
Warehouse clubs	—	6
Other	8	4
	100%	100%

*Estimate.

Source: Goodyear Tire and Rubber Company.

tire brands to a very expensive special high-speed tire for a Corvette that bears the Goodyear name.

THE TIRE INDUSTRY

The tire industry is global in scope, and competitors originate, produce, and market their products worldwide.[2] World tire production in 1991 was approximately 850 million tires, of which 29 percent were produced in North America, 28 percent in Asia, and 23 percent in Western Europe. Ten tire manufacturers account for 75 percent of worldwide production. Groupe Michelin, with headquarters in France, is the world's largest producer and markets the Michelin, Uniroyal, and BF Goodrich brands. Goodyear is the second largest producer with Goodyear, Kelly-Springfield, Lee, and Douglas being its most well known brands. Bridgestone Corporation, a Japanese firm, is the third largest tire producer. Its major brands are Bridgestone and Firestone. These three firms account for almost 60 percent of all tires sold worldwide.

The Original Equipment Tire Market

The tire industry divides into two end-use markets: (1) the original equipment tire market and (2) the replacement tire market. Original equipment tires are sold by tire manufacturers directly to automobile and truck manufacturers. Original equipment tires represent 25 to 30 percent of tire unit production volume each year. Goodyear is the perennial market share leader for original equipment tires capturing 38 percent of this segment in 1991. Exhibit 2 shows the original equipment tire market shares for major tire suppliers.

Demand for original equipment tires is derived; that is, tire volume is directly related to automobile and truck production. Overall original equipment tire demand

[2]Portions of the tire industry overview are based on "Competition in the World Tire Industry, 1992," in Arthur A. Thompson, Jr., and A. J. Strickland III, *Strategic Management: Concepts & Cases*, 7th ed. (Homewood, IL, 1993), pp. 581–614.

EXHIBIT 2

Manufacturer Brand Market Share for Original Equipment Passenger Tires in the United States

Original Equipment (OE) Buyer	Tire Manufacturer (Brand)						
	Goodyear	Firestone	Michelin	`Uniroyal Goodrich	General Tire	Dunlop	Bridgestone
General Motors	33.5%	1.5%	14.5%	32.5%	18.0%	0.0%	0.0%
Ford	26.0	39.0	23.5	0.0	11.5	0.0	0.0
Chrysler	83.0	0.0	0.0	0.0	17.0	0.0	0.0
Mazda	15.0	50.0	0.0	0.0	0.0	0.0	35.0
Honda of U.S.	30.0	0.0	47.0	0.0	0.0	16.0	7.0
Toyota	15.0	40.0	0.0	0.0	3.0	42.0	0.0
Diamond Star	100.0	0.0	0.0	0.0	0.0	0.0	0.0
Nissan	0.0	35.0	22.0	0.0	35.0	8.0	0.0
Nummi (GM-Toyota)	50.0	50.0	0.0	0.0	0.0	0.0	0.0
Volvo	0.0	0.0	100.0	0.0	0.0	0.0	0.0
Saturn	0.0	100.0	0.0	0.0	0.0	0.0	0.0
Isuzu	15.0	35.0	0.0	50.0	0.0	0.0	0.0
Subaru	0.0	0.0	100.0	0.0	0.0	0.0	0.0
Hyundai	35.0	0.0	65.0	0.0	0.0	0.0	0.0
Overall OE market share	38.0%	16.0%	16.0%	14.0%	11.5%	2.75%	1.25%

Source: Modern Tire Dealer, January 1991, p. 27.

is highly price inelastic given the derived demand situation. However, the price elasticity of demand for individual tire manufacturers (brands) was considered highly price elastic, since car and truck manufacturers could easily switch to a competitor's brands. Accordingly, price competition among tire manufacturers was fierce and motor vehicle manufacturers commonly relied upon two sources of tires. For example, General Motors split its tire purchases among Goodyear, Uniroyal/Goodrich, General Tire, Michelin, and Firestone brands in the early 1990s. Even though the original equipment market was less profitable than the replacement tire market, tire manufacturers considered this market strategically important. Tire manufacturers benefited from volume-related scale economics in manufacturing for this market. Furthermore, it was believed that car and truck owners who were satisfied with their original equipment tires would buy the same brand when they replaced them.

The Replacement Tire Market

The replacement tire market accounts for 70 to 75 percent of tires sold annually. Primary demand in this market is affected by the average mileage driven per vehicle. Every 100-mile change in the average number of miles traveled per vehicle produces a 1 million unit change in the unit sales of the replacement market, assuming

EXHIBIT 3

Unit Tire Sales in the United States, 1987–1991

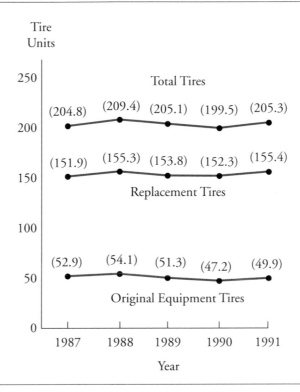

Tire Units

Source: *Modern Tire Dealer,* 1993 Facts/Directory.

an average treadwear life of 25,000 to 30,000 miles per tire.[3] Worldwide unit shipments in this segment have been "flat" due in part to the longer treadlife of new tires. Exhibit 3 shows original equipment and replacement unit sales in the United States for the period 1987 to 1991.

Tire manufacturers produce a large variety of grades and lines of tires for the replacement tire market under both manufacturers' brand names and private labels. Branded replacement tires are made to the tiremaker's own specifications. Some private-label tires supplied to wholesale distributors and large chain retailers are made to the buyer's specifications rather than to the manufacturer's standards.

The major tire producers often used network TV campaigns to promote their brands, introduce new types of tires, and pull customers to their retail dealer outlets. Their network TV ad budgets commonly ran from $10 million to $30 million, and their budgets for cooperative ads with dealers were from $20 million to $100 million. Print media were also used extensively. As an illustration, a Michelin print

---

[3]"Competition in the World Tire Industry, 1992," p. 587.

ad featuring the slogan "Michelin, Because So Much Is Riding on Your Tires" is shown in Exhibit 4. Several tire companies also sponsored auto racing events to promote the performance capabilities of their tires.

Goodyear is the perennial market-share leader in the U.S. replacement tire market. The company holds a leadership position in the passenger car, light-truck, and highway truck product categories (see Exhibit 5).

Retail Distribution. Major brand-name tire manufacturers capitalized on their reputation and experience as producers of original equipment tires by building strong wholesale and retail dealer relationships and networks through which to sell their brand-name replacement tires to vehicle owners. The tire industry uses "retail points of sale" to gauge the retail coverage of tire manufacturers and their brands. Goodyear brand tires have the broadest retail coverage with almost 8,000 "retail points of sale," most of which are company-owned Goodyear Auto Service Centers or franchised Goodyear Tire Store dealers with multiple locations. Groupe Michelin is estimated to have almost 14,000 "points of sale" for its three major brands—Michelin, Goodrich, and Uniroyal. The number of "retail points of sale" for major tire brands is shown in Exhibit 6.

Retail Marketing.[4] Independent tire dealers usually carried the brands of several different major manufacturers and a discount-priced private-label brand so as to give replacement buyers a full assortment of qualities, brands, and price ranges to choose from. Service stations affiliated with Exxon, Chevron, and Amoco marketed Atlas brand tires produced by Firestone (Bridgestone). Other service stations, especially those that emphasized tire sales, stocked one or two manufacturers' brand tires and a private-label brand. Retail tire outlets that were owned or franchised by the manufacturers (that is, Goodyear Tire Stores and Firestone Auto Master Care Centers) carried only the manufacturer's name brands and perhaps a private-label or lesser-known, discount-priced line made by the manufacturer. Department stores and the major retail chains such as Montgomery Ward and Sears Roebuck and Company occasionally carried manufacturers' label tires but usually marketed only their own private-label brands.

Manufacturers found it advantageous to have a broad product line to appeal to most buyer segments to provide tires suitable for many different types of vehicles driven under a variety of road and weather conditions. When vehicle owners went to a tire dealer to shop for replacement tires, they had a variety of tread designs, tread widths, tread durabilities, performance characteristics, and price categories to choose from. Car and light-truck owners were often confused by the number of choices they had; few buyers were really knowledgeable about tires. Many buyers ended up choosing a tire on the basis of price, while others followed the recommendation of the local dealer whom they regularly patronized. The retail prices of replacement tires ranged from retreaded (or recapped) tires selling for under $20 to $35 each to top-of-the-line tires going for $125 to $175 each. Tire dealers ran frequent price promotion ads in the local newspapers, making it easy for price-sensitive buyers to watch for sales and buy at off-list prices. In recent years, consumers had become more price conscious and less brand loyal (thus eroding the importance of securing replacement sales through original equipment sales to vehicle manufac-

---

[4]This material is extracted from "Competition in the World Tire Industry, 1992," pp. 588–591.

EXHIBIT 4

Michelin Print Advertisement

EXHIBIT 5

Estimated U.S. Market Shares of the Top Ten Brands in the Replacement Tire Market, 1991

Passenger Car Tires		Light-Truck Tires		Highway Truck Tires	
Brand	*Share*	*Brand*	*Share*	*Brand*	*Share*
Goodyear	15.0%	Goodyear	11.0%	Goodyear	23.0%
Michelin	8.5	BF Goodrich	10.0	Michelin	15.0
Firestone	7.5	Firestone	5.0	Bridgestone	11.0
Sears	5.5	Michelin	6.0	General Tire	7.0
General	4.5	Cooper/Falls	5.0	Firestone	6.0
BF Goodrich	3.5	Kelly-Springfield	5.0	Kelly-Springfield	6.0
Bridgestone	3.5	Armstrong	4.0	Dunlop	6.0
Cooper	3.5	General Tire	4.0	Yokohama	5.0
Kelly-Springfield	3.0	Bridgestone	3.0	Cooper	4.0
Multi-Mile	3.0	Dunlop	2.0	Toyo	3.0
Others	42.5%	Others	44.0	Others	14.0
	100.0%		100.0%		100.0%

Source: Modern Tire Dealer, January 1991, p. 27; *Market Data Book* 1991; *Tire Business*, January 1992, p. 13.

turers). However, it was often difficult for car owners to comparison shop on the basis of tire quality and tread durability because of the proliferation of brands, lines, grades, and performance features. Manufacturers had resisted the development of standardized specifications for replacement tires, and there was a general lack of common terminology in describing tire grades and construction features.

EXHIBIT 6

Estimated Number of Retail Points of Sale for Major Tire Brands in the United States, 1991

Tire Brand (Parent Company)	Number of Retail Points of Sale
Armstrong (Pirelli)	978
Bridgestone (Bridgestone Corp.)	5,960
Cooper (Cooper Tire and Rubber)	1,518
Dunlop (Sumitomo)	2,046
Firestone (Bridgestone Corp.)	4,208
General (Continental A.G.)	2,107
Goodrich (Groupe Michelin)	4,215
Goodyear (Goodyear Tire and Rubber)	7,964
Kelly-Springfield (Goodyear Tire and Rubber)	2,421
Michelin (Groupe Michelin)	7,169
Pirelli (Pirelli Group)	2,133
Uniroyal (Groupe Michelin)	2,321

Source: Market Data Book 1991, *Tire Business*, January 1992, p, 1992, p. 14.

In most communities, the retail tire market was intensely competitive. Retailers advertised extensively in newspapers, on outdoor billboards, and occasionally on local TV to establish and maintain their market shares. Price was the dominant competitive appeal. Many dealers featured and pushed their private-label "off-brand" tires because they could obtain higher margins on them than they could selling the name-brand tires of major manufacturers. Dealer-sponsored private-label tires accounted for 15 to 20 percent of total replacement tire sales in the United States in 1991. Surveys showed dealers were able to influence a car owner's choice of replacement tires, both as to brand and type of tire. Most replacement tire buyers did not have strong tire brand preferences, making it fairly easy for tire salespeople to switch customers to tire brands and grades with the highest dealer margins. Normal dealer margins on replacement tires were in the 35 to 40 percent range, but many dealers shaved margins to win incremental sales.

Retailer Profitability. Since the mid-1970s, tire retailers' profit margins had been under competitive pressure, partly because of stagnant growth in tire sales and partly because of declining retail prices since 1980. To bolster profitability, tire dealers had expanded into auto repair services (engine tune-ups, shock-absorber and muffler replacement, and brake repair), retreading, and automobile accessories. Some tire retailers were experimenting with becoming "total car care centers." Auto service work was very attractive because gross profit margins were bigger than the margins earned on replacement tire sales. A recent survey of independent tire dealers indicated that 38.2 percent of their sales and 45.8 percent of their earnings came from automobile service.[5]

GOODYEAR TIRE AND RUBBER COMPANY

Goodyear Tire and Rubber Company, headquartered in Akron, Ohio, was founded in 1898 by Frank and Charles Seiberling. The company began as a supplier of bicycle and carriage tires, but soon targeted the fledgling automotive industry. The introduction of the Quick Detachable tire and the Universal Rim (1903) helped make Goodyear the world's largest tire manufacturer by 1916, the same year the company introduced the pneumatic truck tire. Goodyear held the distinction as the world leader in tire production until November 1990, when Groupe Michelin acquired the Uniroyal Goodrich Tire Company (then the second largest U.S. tire manufacturer) for a purchase price of $1.5 billion.

Goodyear's principal business is the development, manufacture, distribution, and sale of tires throughout the world. Tires and tire tubes represented 83 percent of Goodyear's corporate sales of $10.9 billion in 1991. Corporate-wide earnings in 1991 were $96.6 million. In addition to Goodyear brand tires, the company owns the Kelly-Springfield Tire Company, Lee Tire and Rubber Company, and Delta Tire. The company also manufactures private-label tires.

Goodyear controls 20 to 25 percent of the world's tire manufacturing capacity and about 37 percent of U.S. tire-making capacity. Sales outside of the United States accounted for about 42 percent of company revenues.

---

[5]"Dealer Attitude Survey Concerning Automotive Service," *Modern Tire Dealer* (Spring 1992), p. 1.

Market Presence

Approximately 60 percent of Goodyear worldwide sales were in the tire replacement market and 40 percent were to the original equipment market. The Goodyear brand is the market share leader in North America and in Latin America and number two throughout Asia outside of Japan (behind Bridgestone). The Goodyear brand is third in market share in Europe behind Michelin and Pirelli. Goodyear is second to Groupe Michelin (Michelin, Uniroyal-Goodrich) in terms of worldwide market share for auto, truck, and farm tires (see Exhibit 7). The company operates 44 tire products plants in 28 countries and seven rubber plantations.

Tire Product Line and Pricing

Goodyear produces tires for virtually every type of vehicle. It has the broadest line of tire products of any tire manufacturer. The broad market brand names sold under the Goodyear umbrella include the Arriva, Corsa, Eagle, Invicta, Tiempo, Decathlon, Regatta, S4S, T-Metric, Wrangler (light-truck tire), and Aquatred. The Aquatred brand was the most recent introduction and featured a new tread design that prevented hydroplaning (see Exhibit 8). Sales of this brand were expected to reach 1 million units in 1992 based on initial sales figures.

The Goodyear name is one of the best known brand names in the world. Goodyear brand tires have been traditionally positioned and priced as premium quality brands. Nevertheless, the company has recently introduced mid-priced tire brands. These include the Decathlon and T-Metric brands with lower treadwear and traction performance characteristics than its other brands (see Exhibit 9).

Kelly-Springfield Tire Company and Lee Tire and Rubber Company, two Goodyear subsidiaries, also sell some 16 tire brands and engage in private-label manufacturing. For example, Wal-Mart sells the Douglas-brand made by the Kelly-Springfield unit.

Goodyear Advertising and Distribution

Goodyear is one of the leading national advertisers in the United States. The company also has maintained a high profile in auto racing to emphasize the high-per-

EXHIBIT 7

Worldwide Market Shares of Tire Makers, 1990

Tire Manufacturer (Brands)	Market Share
Michelin/Uniroyal-Goodrich	21.5%
Goodyear	20.0
Bridgestone/Firestone	17.0
Continental/General	7.5
Pirelli/Armstrong	7.0
Sumitomo/Dunlop	7.0
Others	20.0
	100.0%

Source: Goodyear Tire and Rubber Company, 1991 Annual Report, p. 5.

EXHIBIT 8

Aquatred Print Advertisement

ONE GALLON PER SECOND.

POURING BUCKETS? GOODYEAR AQUATRED® PUMPS UP TO A GALLON OF WATER AWAY AS YOU DRIVE.

The award-winning* Aquatred, with its deep-groove AquaChannel,™ moves up to one gallon of water away per second at highway speeds. This keeps more of the tire's tread area in contact with the road for superb wet traction. **ONLY FROM GOODYEAR.** For your nearest Goodyear retailer call 1-800-GOODYEAR.

*Which awards? *Popular Science*, 1991 Best of What's New. *Popular Mechanics*, 1992 Design & Engineering Award. *Fortune*, a 1992 "Product of the Year." Industrial Designers Society of America, Gold Industrial Design Excellence IDEA Award. *Discover*, Discover Award for Technological Innovation.

TREADLIFE 60000 WARRANTY

Aquatred features a 60,000-mile treadlife limited warranty. Ask your retailer for details.

THE BEST TIRES IN THE WORLD HAVE GOODYEAR WRITTEN ALL OVER THEM.

Experience Goodyear traction for your high-performance, passenger and multi-purpose vehicles.

EAGLE GS-C.®
Dual tread zone for high-performance traction.

AQUATRED®
Deep-groove design for outstanding wet traction.

WRANGLER GS-A®
"Triple Traction" tread for all-surface traction.

GOODYEAR
#1 in Tires

Source: Courtesy of the Goodyear Tire and Rubber Company.

EXHIBIT 9

Goodyear Brand Passenger-Car Tires
(Including Minimum Assigned Grades for Treadwear, Traction, and Temperature)

Brand	Treadwear[a] Rim Diameter 13"	Treadwear[a] All Others	Traction[b]	Temperature[c]
Aquatred	320	340	A	B
Arriva	260	310	A	B
Corsa GT	280	280	A	B
Decathlon	220	240	B	C
Eagle GA	280	300	A	B
Eagle GA (HNIZ)	280	300	A	A
Eagle GS-C	-	220	A	A
Eagle GS-D	-	180	A	A
Eagle GT (H)	-	200	A	A
Eagle GT II	-	320	A	B
Eagle GT + 4	-	240	A	B
Eagle GT + 4 (HNIZ)	-	240	A	A
Eagle ST IV	280	300	A	B
Eagle VL	-	220	A	A
Eagle VR	-	220	A	A
Eagle ZR	-	220	A	A
Invicta	-	280	A	B
Invicta GA	-	280	A	B
Invicta GA (HN)	-	280	A	A
Invicta GA (L)	-	300	A	B
Invicta GA (L) (HN)	-	220	A	A
Invicta GFE	280	300	A	B
Invicta GL	260	280	A	B
Invicta GL (H)	-	280	A	A
Invicta GLR	260	280	A	B
Invicta GS	320	340	A	B
Regatta	300	320	A	B
S4S	240	280	A	B
Tiempo	240	280	A	B
T-Metric	240	240	B	C

Note: The U.S. Department of Transportation (DOT) requires tire manufacturers to state the size, load and pressure, treadwear, traction and temperature on their tires. This information is provided by manufacturers based on their own tests and not provided by the DOT. Treadwear, traction, and temperature are all useful quality indicators and appear on the tire sidewall.

[a] *Treadwear.* This is an index based on how quickly the tire tread wears under conditions specified by the U.S. Government, relative to a "standard tire." The index does not specify how long a tire tread will last on a car because driving conditions vary. However, a tire with a treadwear index of 200 shows wear about twice as long as a tire with an index of 100 under similar conditions.

[b] *Traction.* This is a measure of a tire's ability to stop on wet pavement under specified conditions. Grades range from A (highest) to C (lowest).

[c] *Temperature.* This is a measure of a tire's resistance to heat buildup under simulated high-speed driving. Grades range from A (highest) to C (lowest).

The source of this information is *Consumer Reports*, "How to 'Read' a Tire" (February 1992); 78.

formance capabilities of its tires and the company's commitment to product innovation. The Goodyear name is prominently featured on the company's well-known blimps frequently seen at special events in communities throughout the United States. The company's advertising slogan, "The best tires in the world have Goodyear written all over them," communicates the Goodyear positioning as a high-quality, worldwide tire manufacturer and marketer.

Goodyear distributes its tire products through almost 8,000 retail points of sale in the United States and some 25,000 retail outlets worldwide. The company operates about 1,000 company-owned Goodyear Auto Service Centers and sells through 2,500 franchised Goodyear Tire Dealers in the United States, many of which are multisite operators. These retail outlets account for a major portion of Goodyear brand annual tire sales. In addition, the company sells its tires through some multibrand dealers. As of early 1992, the company did not typically sell Goodyear brand tires through discount multibrand dealers, mass-merchandise chain stores, or warehouse clubs.[6]

STRATEGIC CONSIDERATIONS IN BROADENING DISTRIBUTION

Interest in reconsidering Sears Auto Centers for selling Goodyear brand tires meant that Goodyear executives would have to revisit the company's long-standing distribution policy. Furthermore, a product policy question relating to which brands might be sold through Sears had to be considered. Decisions on these policy issues were further complicated by Goodyear Tire Dealer franchisee reaction to broadened distribution and estimates of incremental sales possible through expanded distribution.

An immediate reaction was forthcoming from franchised Goodyear tire dealers who heard about the Sears proposal. According to comments appearing in the *Wall Street Journal*,[7] one dealer said, "We went with them through thick and thin, and now they're going to drown us." Other dealers indicated they would add private-label brands to their product line. One dealer said: "We [will] sell what we think will give the customer the best value, and that's not necessarily Goodyear." While it was clear that some franchise dealers were critical of broadened distribution of any kind, the pervasiveness of this view was unknown. Furthermore, it was not readily apparent how many dealers would actually carry competitive brands.

Tire industry analysts expected Sears to benefit from carrying Goodyear brand tires. According to market share estimates made by *Modern Tire Dealer*, an industry trade publication, Sears's share of the U.S. replacement passenger car market had declined from 6.5 percent in 1989 to 5.5 percent in 1991.[8] Goodyear brand tires would certainly enhance the company's product mix and draw tire buyers who were already Sears customers. The extent of the draw, however, would depend on how many or which Goodyear brands were sold through Sears Auto Centers.

---

[6]Goodyear brand tires could sometimes be purchased at discount multibrand dealers because of "diverting." Diverting is the practice whereby a manufacturer's authorized distributors/dealers sell the manufacturer's products to unauthorized distributors/dealers who, in turn, distribute the manufacturer's products to customers. This practice is common for many consumer products, see W. Bishop, Jr., "Trade Buying Squeezes Marketers," *Marketing Communications* (May 1988); pp 52–53.

[7]"Independent Goodyear Dealers Rebel," *Wall Street Journal* (July 8, 1992); p B2.

[8]Statistics reported in *Modern Tire Dealer* (January 1991): 27; "Tire Makers are Traveling Bumpy Road As Car Sales Fall, Foreign Firms Expand," *Wall Street Journal* (October 19, 1990): B1.

Cannibalization of company-owned Goodyear Auto Service Center and franchised Goodyear Tire Dealers tire sales also meant that Goodyear executives had to consider the incremental sales from broadened distribution. In other words, even though distribution through Sears could increase sales of Goodyear brand tires from the manufacturer's perspective, the danger would be that company-owned and franchised Goodyear Tire Dealers might incur a loss in unit sales. This could be particularly evident in communities where Sears had a strong market presence.

Konark Television India

On December 1, 1990, Mr. Ashok Bhalla began to prepare for a meeting scheduled for the next week with his boss, Mr. Atul Singh. The meeting would focus on the distribution strategy for Konark Television Ltd., a medium-sized manufacturer of television sets in India. At issue was the nature of immediate actions to be taken as well as long-range planning. Bhalla was Managing Director of Konark, responsible for a variety of activities, including marketing; Singh was President.

THE TELEVISION INDUSTRY IN INDIA

The television industry in India started in late 1959 when the Indian Government used a UNESCO grant to build a small transmitter in New Delhi. The station soon began to broadcast short programs promoting education, health, and family planning. Daily transmissions were limited to 20 minutes. In 1965, the station began broadcasting variety and entertainment programs and expanded its programming to one hour per day. Programming increased to three hours per day in 1970 and to four hours per day by 1976, when commercials were first permitted. The number of transmission centers in the country grew slowly but steadily during this period as well.

In July 1982, the Indian government announced a special expansion plan, providing Rs. 680 million for extending the television network to cover about 70 percent of India's population. By early 1988, the 245 TV transmitters in operation were estimated to have met this goal. The government then authorized construction of 417 new transmitters, which would extend network coverage to over 80 percent of India's population. By late 1990, daily programming averaged almost 11 hours per day, and television was the most popular medium of information, entertainment, and education in India. The network itself consisted of one channel except in large metropolitan areas, where a second channel was also available. Both television channels were owned and operated by the government.

Despite the huge increase in network coverage, many in the TV industry still described the Indian government's attitude toward television as conservative. In fact, some said that it was only the pressure of TV broadcasts from neighboring Sri Lanka and Pakistan that forced India's rapid expansion. Current policy was to view the industry as a luxury industry capable of bearing heavy taxes. Thus, the government charged Indian manufacturers high import duties on foreign manufactured components that they purchased plus heavy excise duties on sets that they assembled; in addition, state governments charged consumers sales taxes that ranged from 1 per-

This case was written by Fulbright Lecturer and Associate Professor James E. Nelson, of the University of Colorado at Boulder, and Dr. Piyush K. Sinha, Associate Professor, Xavier Institute of Management, Bhubaneswar, India. The authors thank Professor Roger A. Kerin, of the Edwin L. Cox School of Business, Southern Methodist University, for his helpful comments in writing this case. The case is intended for educational purposes rather than to illustrate either effective or ineffective decision making. Some data in the case are disguised. Copyright © 1991 by James E. Nelson.

cent to 17 percent. The result was that duties and taxes accounted for almost one-half of the retail price of a color TV set and about one-third of the retail price of a black-and-white set. Retail prices of TV sets in India were estimated to be almost double the prevalent world prices.

Such high prices limited demand. The number of sets in use in 1990 was estimated to be only about 25 million. This number provided coverage to about 15 percent of the country's population, assuming five viewers per set. Increasing coverage to 80 percent of the population would require over 100 million additional TV sets, again assuming five viewers per set. This figure represented a huge latent demand, equal to several years of production at 1989 levels (see Exhibit 1). Many in the industry expected production and sales of TV sets to grow rapidly, if only prices were reduced. Presently, production exceeded demand.

INDIAN CONSUMERS

The population of India was estimated at approximately 850 million people in 1990. The majority lived in rural areas and small villages. The gross domestic product per capita was estimated at only $450.

In sharp contrast to the masses was the television market, which was concentrated among the affluent middle and upper social classes, variously estimated at some 12 to 25 percent of the total population. Members of this segment exhibited a distinctly urban lifestyle. They owned video cassette recorders, portable radio/cassette players, motor scooters, and compact cars. They earned MBA degrees, exercised in health spas, and traveled abroad. They lived in dual-income households, sent their children to private schools, and practiced family planning. In short, members of this segment exhibited tastes and purchasing behaviors much like their middle-class, professional counterparts in the United States and Europe.

Although there was no formal marketing research available, Ashok Bhalla thought he knew the consumer fairly well. "The typical purchase probably represents a joint

EXHIBIT 1

Production of TV Sets in India (000's)

Year	Black and White 36 cm	Black and White 51 cm	Color	Total
1980	—	310	—	310
1981	—	370	—	370
1982	—	440	—	440
1983	—	570	70	640
1984	180	660	280	1,120
1985	440	1,360	690	2,490
1986	820	1,330	900	3,050
1987	1,700	1,400	1,200	4,300
1988	2,800	1,600	1,300	5,700
1989[a]	3,200	1,800	1,300	6,300

[a]Figures for 1989 are estimated.

decision by the husband and wife. After all, they will be spending over one month's salary for our most popular color model." That model was now priced at retail at Rs. 11,300, slightly less than retail prices of many national brands. However, a majority in the target segment probably did not perceive a price advantage for Konark. Indeed, those in the segment seemed somewhat insensitive to differentials in the range from Rs. 10,000 to Rs. 14,000, considering their TV sets to be valued possessions that added to the furnishing of their drawing rooms. Rather than price, most consumers seemed influenced by promotions and dealer activities.

TELEVISION MANUFACTURERS IN INDIA

Approximately 140 different companies manufactured TV sets in India in 1989. However, many produced fewer than 1,000 sets per year and could not be considered major competitors. Further, Bhalla expected that many would not survive 1990—the trend definitely was toward consolidation to 20 or 30 large firms. Most manufacturers sold in India only, although a few had begun to export sets (mostly black and white) to nearby countries.

Most competitors were private companies whose actions ultimately were evaluated by a board of directors and shareholders. Typical of this group was Videocon. The company was formed only in 1983, yet it was thought to be India's largest producer of color TV sets. A recent trade journal article had attributed Videocon's success to a strategy that combined higher dealer margins (2 percent higher than industry norms), attractive dealer incentives (Singapore trips, etc.), a reasonably good dealer network (about 200 dealers in 18 of India's 25 states), an excellent price range (from Rs. 7,000 to Rs. 18,000), and an advertising campaign that featured a popular Indian film star dressed in a Japanese kimono. Onida, the other leader in color sets, took a different approach. Its margins were slightly below industry standards; its prices were higher (Rs. 13,000 to Rs. 15,000); and its advertising strategy was the most aggressive in the industry. Many consumers seemed sold on Onida before they ever visited a retailer.

Major competitors in the black-and-white market were considered by Bhalla to be Crown, Salora, Bush, and Dyanora. These four companies distributed black-and-white sets to most major markets in the country. (Crown and Bush manufactured color sets as well.) The strengths of these competitors were considered to be high brand recognition and strong dealer networks. In addition, several Indian states had one or two brands, such as Konark and Uptron, whose local success depended greatly on tax shelters provided by state governments.

All TV sets produced by the different manufacturers could be classified into two basic sizes, 51 centimeters and 36 centimeters. The larger size was a console model, while the smaller was designed as a portable. Black-and-white sets differed little in styling. There were differences in picture quality and chassis reliability; however, these differences tended to be difficult for most consumers to distinguish and evaluate. In contrast, differences in product features were more noticeable. Black-and-white sets came with and without handles, built-in voltage regulators, built-in antennas, electronic tuners, audio and video tape sockets, and on-screen displays of channel and time. Warranties differed in terms of coverage and time period. Retail prices for black-and-white sets across India ranged from about Rs. 2,000 to Rs. 3,500, with the average thought by Bhalla to be around Rs. 2,600.

Differences among competing color sets seemed more pronounced. Styling was more distinctive, with manufacturers supplying a variety of cabinet designs, cabinet finishes, and control arrangements. Konark and a few other manufacturers had recently introduced a portable color set in hopes of stimulating demand. Quality and performance variations were again difficult for most consumers to recognize. Differences in features were substantial. Some color sets featured automatic contrast and brightness controls, on-screen displays of channel and time, sockets for video recorders and external computers, remote control devices, high-fidelity speakers, cable TV capabilities, and flat-screen picture tubes. Retail prices were estimated to range from about Rs. 7,000 (for a small-screen portable) to Rs. 19,000 (for a large-screen console), with an average around Rs. 12,000.

Advertising practices varied considerably among manufacturers. Many smaller manufacturers used only newspaper advertisements that tended to be small in size. Larger manufacturers, including Konark, also advertised in newspapers, but used quarter-page or larger advertisements. Larger manufacturers also spent substantial amounts on magazine, outdoor, and television advertising. Videocon, for example, was thought to have spent about Rs. 25 million, or about 4 percent of its sales revenue, on advertising in 1989. Onida's percentage might be as much as twice that. Most advertisements for TV sets tended to stress product features and product quality, although a few were based primarily on whimsy or fantasy. Most ads did not mention price. Perhaps 10 percent of the newspaper advertising was in the form of cooperative advertising, featuring the product prominently in the ad and listing local dealers. Manufacturers would design and place cooperative ads and pay at least 80 percent of media costs.

KONARK TV LTD.

Konark TV Ltd. began operations in 1973 with the objective of manufacturing and marketing small black-and-white TV sets for the Orissa state market. Orissa is located on the east coast of India, directly below the state of West Bengal and Calcutta. Early years of operation found production leveling at about 5,000 sets per year. However, in 1982 the company adopted a more aggressive strategy when it became clear that the national market for TV sets was going to grow rapidly. At the same time, the state government invested Rs. 1.5 million in Konark in order to enable it to produce color sets. Konark also began expanding its dealer network to nearby states and to more distant, large metropolitan areas. Sales revenues in 1982 were approximately Rs. 80 million.

The number of Konark models produced grew rapidly to ten, evenly divided between color and black-and-white sets. (Exhibits 2 and 3 present sales literature describing two Konark models.) Sales revenues increased as well, to Rs. 640 million for 1989, based on sales of 290,000 units. For 1990, sales revenues and unit volume were expected to increase by 25 percent and 15 percent, respectively, while gross margin was expected to remain at 20 percent of revenues. In early 1990, the state government invested another Rs. 2.5 million to strengthen Konark's equity base, despite an expectation that the company would barely break even for 1990. Employment in late 1990 was almost 700 people. Company headquarters remained in Bhubaneswar, the state capital of Orissa.

EXHIBIT 2

Sales Literature for a Konark Color Television

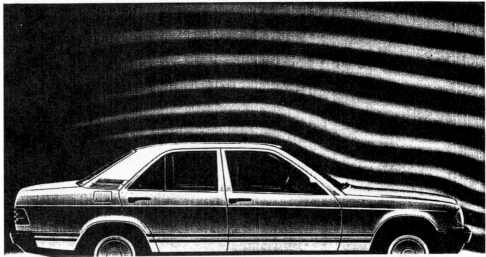

The latest in German technology now comes to India…

Presenting the amazing new colour TV 'Galaxy Plus'

EXHIBIT 2 (continued)

The New Colour TV from Konark. 'Galaxy Plus.'
Incorporating all the sophisticated features likely to be introduced in the next few years.

Superior German technology. That's what sets the new 'Galaxy Plus' apart from all other colour TVs.

One of the latest models of GRUNDIG (W. Germany), world leaders in entertainment electronics. Brought to you by Konark Television Limited.

A symbol of German perfection

The Galaxy Plus combines the best of everything: World-famous German circuitry and components. The latest international TV technology. And the most demanding standards of picture and sound quality.

All of which make it more sophisticated. More dependable.

Features that are a connoisseur's delight.

The Galaxy Plus has several advanced features which offer you an extraordinary audio-visual experience, the like of which you will probably not feel with any other make.

What the Galaxy Plus offers you that other TVs don't

Never-before picture quality

Through the world's latest Colour Transient Improvement (CTI) technology. Which reduces picture distortion. And improves colour sharpness. Giving you a crystal-clear picture and more natural colours.

Programmes from all over the world

The Galaxy Plus is capable of bringing you the best of international TV networks. Thanks to a satellite dish antenna, a unique 7–system versatility, and 99 channels with memory.

These features of the Galaxy Plus also help it play all types of Video Cassettes. Without any picture or sound distortion.

Simultaneous connection with external devices

An exclusive 20 pin Euro AV socket helps you connect the Galaxy Plus simultaneously with all external audio/video devices: Computers, VCRs, Video games. And cable TV.

While its automatic colour and brightness tuning save you the bother of frequent knob-fiddling.

Catch all your favourite programmes. Always.

You can preset the Galaxy Plus to switch itself on and off for your favourite programmes. Or, for worry-free operation by your children, in your absence.

Your own musical alarm clock

An on-screen time display reminds you of an important programme or appointment. While a built-in chimer wakes you up every day. Pleasantly.

Automatic pre-selection and operation

Select specific stations or external functions, code them in the 39+AV programme memory of the Galaxy Plus. And then, get them at the touch of a button. On the full-function Remote Control.

Handles wide voltage fluctuation

From a heart-stopping low of 140V. To a shocking high of 260V. The Galaxy Plus performs merrily through such a large range.

Richer, better TV sound

A higher audio output (8W) brings you all the beauty and power of full-bodied sound and clarity.

Saves power and money

Unlike other TVs, the Galaxy Plus uses only 60W. Besides, it also switches to the stand-by-mode automatically, when there is no TV signal for over 10 minutes.

Both features help you save precious electricity and money.

From Konark Television Limited

The futuristic Galaxy Plus is brought to you by Konark Television Limited. Through its nationwide network of over 500 sales outlets. Each of which also provide you prompt after-sales service. Should you ever need it.

The revolutionary new Galaxy Plus. See it in action at your nearest dealer. Compare it with every other make available in the local market.

And see how, feature by advanced feature, the Galaxy Plus is truly years ahead of its time. And the competition.

A marvel of German Technology

Konark Television Limited
(A Government of Orissa Enterprise)
Electronic Bhawan, Bhubaneswar 751 010. Phone: 53441 Telex: 0675-271

EXHIBIT 3

Sales Literature for a Konark Black-and-White Television

PERFECT CONTRASTS IN B/W

KONARK TV

Rohini Core (51 cm) B&W
The vertical wonder

- Double speakers with 4W output and tape-out facility
- High contrast and brightness ratios
- Better picture resolution (more than 320 lines)
- Built-in voltage stabiliser (150-280V)

EXHIBIT 3 (*continued*)

**Rohini Premier
(51 cm) B&W**

Elegant excitement

- Exquisitely laminated double-shutter cabinet
- Double speakers with 4W output and tape-in and tape-out facility
- High contrast and brightness ratios
- Superior picture resolution (over 320 lines)
- Built-in voltage protection (150-280V)

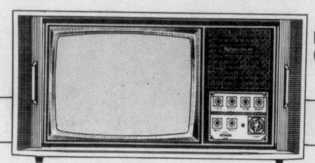

**Rohini Deluxe
(51 cm) B&W**

The classic look

- Exquisitely polished sliding-shutter cabinet
- 4W audio output with 7" speaker
- Audio tape-in and tape-out facility
- Better picture resolution (more than 320 lines)
- Built-in voltage regulator (150-280V)

KONARK TV
(A Govt. of Orissa Enterprise)

Konark Television Ltd.
Electronics Bhavan, Rasulgarh,
Bhubaneswar 751 010.

Manufacturing facilities were also located in Bhubaneswar, although some assembly was performed by three independent distributors. Assembly was done out of state to save state sales taxes and to lower the prices paid by consumers. Many Indian states charged two levels of sales taxes depending upon whether or not the set was produced within the state. The state of Maharashtra (containing Bombay), for example, charged a sales tax of 4 percent for TV sets produced within the state and 16.5 percent for sets produced outside the state. Sales taxes charged by West Bengal (Calcutta) were 6 percent and 16.5 percent, while rates in Uttar Pradesh (New Delhi) were 0 percent and 12.5 percent. State governments were indifferent as to whether assembly was performed by an independent distributor or by Konark, as long as the activity took place inside state borders. Present manufacturing capacity at Konark was around 400,000 units per year. Capacity could easily be expanded by 80 percent with the addition of a second shift.

The Konark line of TV sets was designed by engineers at Grundig, Gmbh., a German manufacturer known for quality electronic products. This technical collaboration saved Konark a great deal of effort each year in designing and developing new products. Also, the resulting product line was considered by many in the industry to be of higher quality than the lines of many competitors. Circuitry was well designed, and production engineers at the factory paid close attention to quality control. In addition, each Konark set was operated for 24 hours as a test of reliability before being shipped. The entire line reflected Konark's strategy of attempting to provide the market with a quality product at prices below those of the competition. In retail stores in Orissa, the lowest-priced black-and-white model marketed by Konark sold to consumers for about Rs. 2,200, while its most expensive color set sold for about Rs. 15,000. Sales of the latter model had been disappointing to date. The premium market for color sets was quite small and seemed dominated by three national manufacturers.

Konark had a well-established network of more than 500 dealers located in 12 Indian states. In nine states, Konark assembled and sold its products directly to dealers through branch offices (Exhibit 4) operated by a Konark area manager. Each branch office also contained two or three salespersons, who were assigned specific sales territories. All together, branch offices were expected to account for about 30 percent of Konark's sales revenues and cost Konark about Rs. 10 million in fixed and variable expenses for 1990. In three states, Konark instead used the services of independent distributors to sell to dealers. The three distributors carried only Konark TV sets and earned a margin of 3 percent (based on cost) on all their activities, including assembly. All dealers and distributors were authorized to service Konark sets. The branch offices monitored all service activities.

In the state of Orissa, Konark used a large branch office to sell to approximately 250 dealers. In addition, Konark used company-owned showrooms displaying the complete line as a second channel of distribution. For these showrooms, Konark leased space at one or two locations in larger cities. The total cost of operating a showroom was estimated at about Rs. 100,000 per year. Prospective customers often preferred to visit a showroom because they could easily compare different models and talk directly to a Konark employee. However, they seldom purchased—only about 5 percent of Orissa's unit sales came from the ten showrooms in the state. Buyers preferred instead to purchase from dealers because dealers were known to bargain and sell at a discount off the list price. In contrast, Konark showrooms were under strict orders to sell all units at list price. About half of Konark's 1990 revenues would come from Orissa.

EXHIBIT 4

Konark's Branch Office Locations and Proposed Distribution

Branch office locations
Proposed distribution

EXHIBIT 5

Terms and Conditions for Dealers of Konark Products

1. The Dealer shall canvass for, secure orders, and affect sales of Konark Television sets to the best of its ability and experience and will guarantee sale of a minimum of sets during a calendar month.

2. The Company shall arrange for proper advertisement in the said area and shall give publicity of its products through newspapers, magazines, cinema slides, or by any other media and shall indicate, wherever feasible, the Dealer's name as its Selling Agent. The cost of such advertisements may be shared by the Company and the Dealer as may be mutually agreed to.

3. The appointment shall be confirmed after 3 months and initially be in force for a period of 1 year and can be renewed every year by mutual consent.

4. The Company reserves the right to evaluate the performance of a Dealer.

5. This appointment may be terminated with a notice of 1 month on either side.

6. The Company shall deliver the Konark Television sets to the Dealer at the price agreed upon on cash payment at the factory at Bhubaneswar. On such delivery, the title to the goods will pass to the Dealer and it will be the responsibility of the Dealer to transport the sets to [its] place at [its] cost and expenses.

7. The Company may, however, at its discretion allow a credit of 30 (thirty) days subject to the Dealer furnishing a Bank Guarantee or letter of credit or security deposit toward the price of Konark Television sets to be lifted by the Dealer at any time.

8. The Company shall not be responsible for any damage or defect occurring to the sets after delivery of the same to the Dealer or during transit.

9. The Dealer shall undertake to sell the sets to customers at prices fixed by the Company for different models. Dealer margins will be added to wholesale prices while fixing the customer's price of the television sets.

10. The Dealer will not deal with similar products of any other company so long as its appointment with Konark Television continues.

11. The Dealer shall not encroach into areas allocated to any other Dealer.

12. Any dispute or difference arising from or related to the appointment of Dealership shall be settled mutually and, failing amicable settlement, shall be settled by an Arbitrator to be appointed by the Chairman of the Company, whose decision shall be final and binding upon the parties. The place of arbitration shall be within the State of Orissa, and the Court in Bhubaneswar (Orissa) only shall have jurisdiction to entertain any application, suit, or claim arising out of the appointment. All disputes shall be deemed to have arisen within the jurisdiction of the Court of Bhubaneswar.

13. Essential requirements to be fulfilled before getting a Dealership:
    a. The Dealer must have a good showroom for display and sale of television sets.
    b. The Dealer should have sufficient experience in dealing with electronics products (consumer goods).

The appointment of dealers either by Konark or its distributors depended on certain conditions (Exhibit 5). Chief among them was the dealer's possession of a suitable showroom for the display and sale of TV sets. Dealers also had to agree to sell Konark TV sets to the best of their ability, at fixed prices, and in specified market areas. Dealers were not permitted to sell sets made by other manufacturers. Dealers earned a margin on every TV set they sold, ranging from Rs. 100 (on a small black-and-white model) to Rs. 900 (on a large color model). Bhalla estimated that the average margin for 1990 would be about Rs. 320 per set.

THE CRISIS

The year 1990 seemed to represent a turning point for the Indian TV industry. Unit demand for TV sets was expected to have grown only 10 percent, compared to almost 40 percent in 1989 and 1988. Industry experts attributed the slowing growth rate to a substantial hike in consumer prices. The blame was laid almost entirely on increases in import duties, excise taxes, and sales taxes, plus devaluation of the rupee—despite election-year promises by government officials to offer TV sets at affordable prices! In addition, Konark was about to be affected by the Orissa state government's decision to revoke the company's sales tax exemption beginning January 1, 1991. "Right now we are the clear choice, as Konark is the cheapest brand with superior quality. But with the withdrawal of the exemption, we will be in the same price range as the 'big boys' and it will be a real run for the money to sell our brand," remarked Ashok Bhalla.

Bhalla was also concerned about some dealer activities that he thought were damaging to Konark. He knew that many dealers played with the assigned margin and offered the same Konark product at differing prices to different customers. Or, equally damaging, different dealers sometimes quoted different prices for the same product to a single customer. Some dealers recently had gone so far as to buy large quantities of TV sets from Konark and sell them to unauthorized dealers in Bhubaneswar or in neighboring districts. This problem was particularly vexing because the offending dealers—while few in number—often were quite large and important to Konark's overall performance. Perhaps as much as 40 percent of Konark's sales revenues came from "problem" dealers.

Early in 1990, Bhalla thought that an increase in the margins that Konark allowed its dealers was all that was needed to solve the problem. However, a modest change in dealer compensation had resulted in several national competitors raising their dealer margins even higher—without an increase in their retail prices. The result was that prices of Konark's models became even closer to those of national competitors and Konark's decline in market share actually steepened. By late 1990, Konark's unit share of the Orissa market had fallen from 80 percent to just over 60 percent. "Unless something is done soon," Bhalla thought, "we'll soon be below 50 percent."

THE DECISION

Some immediate actions were needed to improve dealer relations and stimulate greater sales activity. An example was Konark's quarterly "Incentive Scheme," which had begun in April 1989. The program was a rebate arrangement based on points earned for a dealer's purchases of Konark TV sets. Reaction was lukewarm when the program was first announced. However, a revision in August 1989 greatly increased participation. Other actions yet to be formulated could be announced at a dealers' conference that Bhalla had scheduled for next month.

All such actions would have to be consistent with Konark's long-term distribution strategy. The problem was that this strategy had not yet been formulated. Bhalla saw filling this void as his most pressing responsibility, as well as of great interest to Atul Singh. Bhalla hoped to have major aspects of a distribution strategy ready for discussion at next week's meeting. Elements of the strategy would include recommendations on channel structure (branch offices or independent distributors, company showrooms or independent dealers) in existing markets as well as in markets identified for expansion. The latter markets included Bombay, Jaipur, and Trivandrum, areas that contained some 2 million consumers in the target segment. Most importantly, the strategy would have to address actions to combat the loss of the sales tax exemption in Orissa.

Carrington Carpet Mills, Inc.

In January 1994, Suzanne Goldman was scheduled to meet with Robert Meadows, President of Carrington Carpet Mills, Inc. Goldman knew that the meeting would relate to the recent board of directors meeting. In her position as Special Assistant to the President, or "troubleshooter," as she called herself, Goldman had noticed that such meetings often led to a project of some type. Her expectations were met, as Meadows began to describe what had happened at the board meeting:

> The directors are not pleased with the present state of affairs. The cyclical nature of carpet sales is again proving itself, as disposable personal income and new house construction have plateaued and actually declined in many areas of the country. Our wholesalers are complaining about slow payments from retailers. In many cases, their receivables are taking 60 days to collect, and we are extending our receivables to satisfy them at a 10 percent annual carrying cost. Wholesalers are cutting back on inventory as costs of carrying inventory approach 10 percent annually. Our inventories have increased, and our delivery costs have risen as we attempt to service our wholesalers. Costs of servicing wholesalers are running about 4 percent of sales. I could go on, but you get the picture. The possibility of establishing our own warehouses or wholesale operation was raised, but I was unprepared to discuss it. Needless to say, I was somewhat embarrassed. Would you examine such a program for me and prepare a position paper for the May board meeting? Focus only on the retail sales business, since we handle contract sales on a direct basis, and assume the same sales level as in 1993. Remember that our policy is to finance programs from internal funds. I'd like to see you do the same comprehensive job that you did on the advertising and sales program last November.

THE INDUSTRY

The carpet and rug industry reported sales of $10 billion at manufacturers' prices in 1992. Sales in 1993 would reach $10.5 billion, according to Meadows. Industry sales are evenly divided between "contract," or commercial, sales and retail sales for household use.

The industry is highly concentrated. In 1992, 15 companies out of some 250 carpet and rug manufacturers accounted for approximately 75 percent of total industry carpet and rug volume. Shaw Industries is the industry leader (see Exhibit 1).

Industry trends suggest that continued cost pressures arising from raw material prices will accelerate in the next five years. This trend is likely to compress profit margins, since upward of 80 percent of the typical producer's cost of goods sold is

EXHIBIT 1

Top 15 North American Carpet and Rug Manufacturers in 1992

Manufacturer	Sales ($ in millions, U.S.)
1. Shaw Industries	$ 2,035.9
2. The Beaulieu Group of America	752.0
3. Interface, Inc.	594.0
4. Collins & Aikman	405.0
5. Alladdin Mills	397.0
6. Peerless/Galaxy Carpet	392.0
7. Queen Carpet	390.0
8. Mohawk Carpet	352.5
9. Burlington Industries	346.0
10. Milliken & Company	320.0
11. Diamond Rug & Carpet	290.0
12. World Carpets, Inc.	280.0
13. JPS Textile Group, Inc.	269.6
14. Fieldcrest/Cannon	267.4
15. Horizon Industries	259.0

Source: "The Top North American Carpet & Rug Manufacturers," *Carpet & Rug Industry* (June 1993): 16–68, 85.

Note: Mowhawk Carpet acquired Horizon Industries in July 1992.

for materials. A second trend is the increasing emphasis on olefin fibers (primarily polypropylene) in carpet and rug manufacturing, even though nylon is still the most used fiber. DuPont (the largest nylon carpet producer) introduced its first polypropylene carpet under the brand name *Proselect* in 1989 and also acquired Hercules's olefin carpet fiber business, doubling its olefin carpet fiber business. Amoco introduced in 1989 a polypropylene carpet called *Genesis* for residential use, claiming that it overcame several disadvantages of polypropylene, such as matting and crushing, compared with nylon. In a move demonstrating the growing importance of olefin fibers, Shaw Industries acquired AMOCO's polypropylene manufacturing facilities in July 1992. A third trend is the relatively strong market for higher-quality carpets and rugs. Higher-quality products should experience better sales results than popular-priced lines over the next few years. A fourth trend concerns the mix of sales between commercial sales and retail sales. Retail sales growth for home use are likely to outpace commercial sales due to a projected surplus in commercial office space. A final trend concerns the growth of area rug sales versus broadloom sales. (The term *broadloom* refers to the loom on which a carpet is woven. A broadloom is generally considered to be one capable of weaving in widths of nine feet or more.) Area rug sales grew 12 to 13 percent in 1992 and were projected to grow by 10 percent in 1993. Broadloom sales growth was generally flat.

Three major types of retail outlets account for the vast majority of carpet and rug volume in the retail segment. The latest statistics available indicate that floor covering specialty stores account for 58 percent of industry volume; department stores, 21 percent; and furniture stores, 19 percent. Although no statistics exist, industry observers believe that mass merchandisers and discount stores are increasing their share of carpet and rug sales volume.

Carpet manufacturers have recently placed renewed interest on consumer marketing and brand identification.[1] Consumer research has shown that the carpet purchase for household use is important typically a replacement purchase, and often time-consuming for the buyer. The purchase process is similar to that observed in furniture buying: (1) multiple store shopping, (2) joint decision making between a husband and wife, and (3) considerable ego involvement. Questionnaires completed by *Better Homes and Gardens* Consumer Panel members revealed the following:

1. Almost one-half of panel members purchasing carpet in the past two years bought it to replace another carpet or rug. (*Note*: Industry estimates indicate a carpet replacement cycle of eight years.)

2. About three in five panel members said that the brand name of carpet was a very important or somewhat important consideration in determining quality.

3. Surface appearance, color, durability, and soil resistance/cleanability were designated as very important factors in choosing a carpet/rug by over one-half of panel members responding.[2]

THE COMPANY

Carrington Carpet Mills, Inc., is a manufacturer of a full line of medium- to high-priced carpets for household use. Contract sales to apartment and office builders are also made but account for only 10 percent of total company sales. Total company sales in 1993 were $60 million, with a net profit before tax of $2.4 million. Exhibit 2 shows abbreviated financial statements.

The company currently distributes its line through seven wholesalers located throughout the United States. These wholesalers, in turn, supply 4,000 retail accounts, including department stores, furniture stores, and floor-covering specialty stores. Inspection of distribution records revealed that 80 percent of total company sales are made through 50 percent of its retail accounts. This relationship exists within all market areas served by Carrington Carpet Mills. Meadows commented that these sales-per-account percentages indicate that at the retail level the company is gaining adequate coverage, if not over coverage.

Advertising by Carrington Carpet Mills is primarily in shelter magazines and newspapers. The emphasis in advertisements is on fiber type, colors, durability, and soil resistance. A cooperative advertising program with retailers had been expanded on the basis of Goldman's recommendation. According to Goldman, "The coop program is being well received and has brought us into closer contact with retail accounts." The company employs two regional sales coordinators, who act as a liaison with wholesalers, assist in managing the cooperative advertising program, and make periodic visits to large retail accounts. In addition, they are responsible for handling contract sales.

---

[1] Janet Herlihy, "The Mills' Role in Consumer Marketing," *Carpet & Rug Industry* (December 1993): 12–18ff.

[2] *Inquiry: A Study on Home Furnishings from the Better Homes and Gardens Consumer Panel.* Copyright Meredith Corporation.

E X H I B I T   2

Carrington Carpet Mills, Inc., Abbreviated Financial Statements, 1993

Income Statement

Net sales	$60,000,000
Less cost of goods sold	45,000,000
Gross margin	$15,000,000
Distribution expenses	$1,800,000
Selling and administrative expenses	9,000,000
Other expenses	1,800,000
Net income before tax	$2,400,000

Balance Sheet

Current assets	$21,550,000
Fixed assets	19,200,000
Total assets	$40,750,000
Current liabilities	$ 8,250,000
Long-term debt and net worth	32,500,000
Total liabilities and net worth	$40,750,000

Independent wholesalers play a major role in the company's marketing strategy. Wholesalers maintain extensive sales organizations, with the average wholesaler employing ten salespeople. Carpet manufacturers expect that retail accounts receive at least one call per month. Goldman's earlier evaluation of the sales program revealed that wholesaler sales representatives perform a variety of tasks, including checking inventory and carpet samples, arranging point-of-purchase displays, handling retailer complaints, and taking orders. About 25 percent of an average salesperson's time is spent on nonselling activities (preparing call reports, acting as a liaison with manufacturers, traveling, and so forth). About 40 percent of each one-hour sales call is devoted to selling Carrington Carpet Mills carpeting; 60 percent is devoted to selling noncompeting products, such as furniture accessories and draperies. This finding disturbed company management, who felt that a full hour was necessary to represent them. In addition to making sales, wholesalers also carry carpet inventory. Carrington Carpet Mills's wholesalers typically carry sufficient inventory to keep the number of turnovers at five per year. Carrington Carpet Mills's executives felt that inventory levels sufficient for four turns per year were necessary to service retailers properly. Finally, wholesalers extend credit to retail accounts. In return for these services, wholesalers receive a 22 percent margin on sales billed, at the price to retailers.

DIRECT DISTRIBUTION EXPERIENCE OF COMPETITORS

In February and March, Goldman sought out information on competitors' experience with direct distribution. Despite conflicting information from trade publications and knowledgeable industry observers, she was able to arrive at several important conclusions. First, competitors with their own warehousing operations located them in seven metropolitan areas: Atlanta, Chicago, Cleveland, Dallas–Fort Worth, Los Angeles, New York, and Philadelphia. Carrington Carpet Mills had wholesalers already operating in these metropolitan areas, except for Dallas–Fort Worth and Atlanta.

The company serviced these two areas from wholesalers located in Houston, Texas, and Richmond, Virginia, respectively. Second, approximately $5 million in sales was necessary to operate a warehouse operation economically. The average warehouse operation could be operated at an annual fixed cost (including rent, personnel, operations) of $700,000. Goldman was informed that suitable warehouse space was available in the metropolitan areas under consideration; therefore, the company would not have to embark on a building program. Third, salaries, expenses, and fringe benefits of highly qualified sales representatives would be about $60,000 each annually. One field sales manager would be needed to manage eight sales representatives. Salary, expenses, and fringe benefits would be approximately $70,000 per field sales manager per year. Finally, sales administration costs were typically 40 percent of the total sales force and management costs per year. Though these figures represented rough approximations, in Goldman's opinion and in the opinion of others with whom she conferred they were the best estimates available.

In March Goldman received a disturbing telephone call from a long-time successful wholesaler of the company's products. The wholesaler told her that he and others were aware of her inquiries about direct distribution possibilities. Through innuendo, the wholesaler threatened a mass exodus from Carrington Carpet Mills once the first company warehouse was opened. He implied that plans were already under way to establish a trade agreement with a competitor. This conversation would have significant impact on her recommendation if direct distribution was deemed feasible. In short, a roll-out by market area looked less likely. A rapid transition would be necessary, which would require sizable cash outlays.

$$ROI = \frac{P \cdot Q - C \cdot Q}{g}$$

$$\frac{ROI \times g + C \cdot Q}{Q} = P$$

- Price objectives consistent with marketing objectives.
- Enhancing product / brand image
- Providing customer value
- Adequate return on cash flow
- Price stability in an industry / market.

- Cover unit variable cost.
- Pricing dep. on life cycle of the product
- Effect on profits
- Prices of other goods & services provided
- Price influences consumer's perception of quality
- Subs, use ratio of price - income.
- Old B-E, New B-even sales change
- Full cost price / Variable

$$ROg = \frac{Pr}{Invest\,m}$$

$$ROg = \frac{P \cdot Q - C \cdot Q}{Inv}$$

CHAPTER 9

Pricing Strategy and Management

 Whether or not it is so recognized, pricing is one of the most crucial decision functions of a marketing manager. To a large extent, pricing decisions determine the types of customers and competitors an organization will attract. Likewise, a single pricing error can effectively nullify all other marketing-mix activities. Despite its importance, price rarely serves as the focus of marketing strategy, in part because it is the easiest marketing-mix activity for the competition to imitate.

It can be easily demonstrated that price is a direct determinant of profits (or losses). This fact is apparent from the fundamental relationship

Profit = total revenue − total cost

Revenue is a direct result of unit price times quantity sold, and costs are indirectly influenced by quantity sold, which in turn is partially dependent on unit price. Hence, price simultaneously influences both revenues and costs.

Despite its importance, pricing remains one of the least understood marketing-mix activities. Both its effects on buying behavior and its determination continue to be the focus of intensive study.[1]

PRICING CONSIDERATIONS

Although the respective structures of demand and cost obviously cannot be neglected, other factors must be considered in determining pricing objectives and strategies. Most important, the pricing objectives have to be consistent with an organization's overall marketing objectives. Treating the maximization of profits as the sole pricing objective not only is a gross oversimplification, but may undermine the broader objectives of an organization. Other pricing objectives include enhancing product or brand image, providing customer value, obtaining an adequate return on investment or cash flow, and maintaining price stability in an industry or market.

Exhibit 9.1 shows how numerous factors affect a marketing manager's pricing discretion. Demand for a product or service sets the price ceiling. Costs, particularly direct (variable) costs, determine the price floor. More broadly, consumer value perceptions and buyer price sensitivity will determine the maximum price(s) that can be charged. On the other hand, the price(s) chosen must at least cover unit variable cost; otherwise, for each product sold or service provided, a loss will result.

Although demand and cost structures set the upper and lower limit of prices, government regulations, the price of competitive offerings, and organizational objectives and policies narrow a manager's pricing discretion. Regulations prohibiting predatory pricing, the level of differentiation among competitive offerings, and the financial goals set by the organization are all factors that may affect the price range within broad demand and cost boundaries.

There are still other factors that must be considered in pricing a product or service. The life-cycle stage of the product or service is one factor—greater price discretion exists early in the life cycle than later. The effect of pricing decisions on profit margins of marketing channel members must be assessed. The prices of other products and services provided by the organization must be considered as well; that is, price differentials should exist among offerings such that buyers perceive distinct value differences.

Price as an Indicator of Value

In determining value, consumers often pair price with the perceived benefits derived from a product or service. Specifically, *value* can be defined as the ratio of perceived benefits to price:[2]

EXHIBIT   9.1

Conceptual Orientation to Pricing

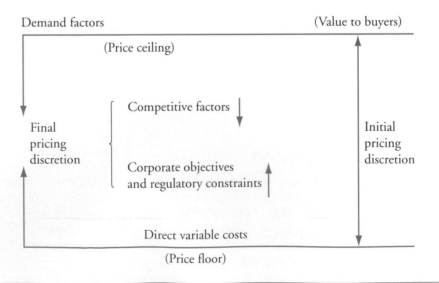

Source: Kent B. Monroe, *Pricing: Making Profitable Decisions*, 2nd ed. (New York: McGraw-Hill, 1990). Reproduced with permission of McGraw-Hill, Inc.

$$\text{Value} = \frac{\text{perceived benefits}}{\text{price}}$$

This relationship shows that for a given price, value increases as perceived benefits increase. Also, for a given price, value decreases as perceived benefits decrease. Seasoned marketers know that value is more than a low price. According to a Procter and Gamble executive, "Value is not just price, but is linked to the performance and meeting expectations of consumers."[3]

For some products, price alone influences consumers' perception of quality—and ultimately value. For example, in a *Better Homes and Gardens* survey of home furnishing buyers, 84 percent agreed with the statement "The higher the price, the higher the quality." For computer software, it has also been shown that consumers believe a low price implies poor quality.

Consumer value assessments are often comparative. In such cases, determining value involves a judgment by a consumer as to the worth and desirability of a product or service relative to substitutes that satisfy the same need. A consumer's comparison of the costs and benefits of substitute items gives rise to a "reference value." Although Equal, a sugar substitute containing Nutrasweet, might be more expensive than sugar, some consumers value it more highly than sugar because it has no calories. Retailers have found that they should not price their store brands 20 to 25 percent below manufacturers' brands. When they do, consumers often view the lower price as signaling lower quality.[4]

Price Elasticity of Demand

An important concept used to characterize the nature of the price-quantity relationship is that of *price elasticity of demand.* The coefficient of price elasticity, E, is a measure of the relative responsiveness of the *quantity* of a product or service demanded to a change in the *price* of that product or service. In other words, the coefficient of price elasticity measures the ratio of the percentage change in the quantity purchased of a product or service to the underlying percentage change in the price of the product or service. This relationship can be expressed as follows:

$$E = \frac{\text{percentage change in quantity demanded}}{\text{percentage change in price}}$$

If the percentage change in quantity demanded is greater than the percentage change in price, demand is said to be *elastic.* In such cases, a small reduction in price will result in a large increase in the quantity purchased; thus, total revenue will rise. Conversely, if the percentage change in quantity demanded is less than the percentage change in price, demand is *inelastic,* and a price reduction will have less of an impact on revenues. Price elasticity of demand is an important factor, for example, in the setting of airline prices for business and leisure fares.[5] Business fares are less price elastic than leisure fares.

A number of factors influence the price elasticity of demand for a product or service. In general,

- The more *substitutes* a product or service has, the greater its price elasticity.
- The more *uses* a product or service has, the greater its price elasticity.

- The higher the *ratio* of the price of the product or service to the income of the buyer, the greater the product's price elasticity.

In practice, it is common to apply the concept of price elasticity simultaneously to more than one product or service. By computing the *cross-elasticity of demand* for product A and product B, it is possible to measure the responsiveness of the quantity demanded of product A to a price change in product B. A negative *cross-elasticity coefficient* indicates that the products are complementary; a positive coefficient indicates that they are substitutes. An understanding of the implications of cross-elasticity is especially important for successful implementation of product-line pricing, in which product demand is interrelated and the goal is to maximize revenue for the entire line and not just for individual products or services.

Consider a marketer of cameras and films (or of copying machines and paper, or of personal computers and software). Should the marketer price cameras very low, perhaps close to or even below cost, in order to promote film sales? Film could then be marketed at relatively high prices. Or should an opposite strategy be employed—selling high-priced cameras but low-priced film? Examples of these alternative tie-in pricing strategies are readily available. For instance, Nintendo, a leader in video games, has traditionally priced its hardware at or near cost and made its profit on its software.[6] The important point is that in most organizations, products are not priced in isolation. In certain instances, individual products may be sold at a loss merely to entice buyers or to ensure that the organization can offer potential buyers complete product lines. In such situations, the price may bear little relationship to the actual cost of a product.

The concept of elasticity, though valuable, is often difficult to quantify in practice. As a framework for appraising the effects of price changes even in a qualitative sense, however, it is invaluable.

Estimating the Profit Impact from Price Changes

In Chapter 2, the basic principles of break-even analysis and leverage were described. These same principles can be applied to assessing the effect of price changes on volume.

The impact of price changes on profit can be determined by looking at cost, price, and volume data for individual products and services. Consider the data shown in the top half of Exhibit 9.2 for two products, alpha and beta. These products have identical prices ($10), unit volumes (1,000 units), and net profits ($2,000), but their cost structures differ. Product alpha has a unit variable cost of $7 and assignable fixed costs of $1,000. Product beta has a unit variable cost of $2 and assignable fixed costs of $6,000. The unit break-even volume for product alpha is 333.3 units ($1,000/$3). Product beta's unit break-even volume is 750 units ($6,000/$8).

The lower half of Exhibit 9.2 illustrates the potential profit impact of price changes for the two products. For product alpha to profit from a 10 percent price cut, its sales volume would have to increase by more than 50 percent. In contrast, sales of product beta, with its larger unit contribution, would only have to increase by slightly more than 14 percent for a profit to be realized.

The same type of analysis can be applied to price increases. For example, if product alpha's price were increased 10 percent, its sales volume could decrease by 25 percent before profits would decline. On the other hand, product beta, with its

EXHIBIT   9.2

Estimating the Effect of Price Changes

	Product Alpha	*Product Beta*
Cost, Volume, and Profit Data		
Unit sales volume	1,000	1,000
Unit selling price	$10	$10
Unit variable cost	$7	$2
Unit contribution	$3 (30%)	$8 (80%)
Fixed costs	$1,000	$6,000
Net profit	$2,000	$2,000
Break-Even Sales Change		
For a 5% price reduction	+20.3%	+6.6%
For a 10% price reduction	+50.0%	+14.3%
For a 20% price reduction	+200.0%	+33.4%
For a 5% price increase	−14.3%	−5.9%
For a 10% price increase	−25.0%	−11.1%
For a 20% price increase	−40.0%	−20.0%

higher unit contribution, could absorb only an 11 percent sales decline with a 10 percent price increase. Other price change effects are shown in Exhibit 9.2 for illustrative purposes.

The procedure for estimating the profit impact from price changes involves three steps:

1. Calculate the break-even volume at the original price.
2. Calculate the break-even volume at the new price.
3. Calculate the change in sales before profits are affected.

$$\text{Sales change (\%)} = \frac{\text{new price break-even} - \text{old price break-even}}{\text{old price break-even}} \times 100$$

PRICING STRATEGIES

Because of the difficulty of estimating demand, most pricing strategies have a decided reliance on cost as a basic foundation.[7] To a great extent, price strategies can be termed either full-cost or variable-cost strategies. *Full-cost price strategies* are those that consider both variable and fixed costs (sometimes termed *direct* and *indirect* costs). *Variable-cost price strategies* take into account only the direct variable costs associated with offering a product or service.

Full-Cost Pricing

Full-cost pricing strategies generally take one of three forms: markup pricing, break-even pricing, and rate-of-return pricing. *Markup pricing* is a strategy in which the selling price of a product or service is determined simply by adding a fixed amount to the (total) cost of the product. The fixed amount is usually expressed as a percentage of either the cost or the price of the product. If it costs $4.60 to produce a product and the selling price is $6.35, the markup on *cost* would be 38 percent, and the markup on *price* would be 28 percent.

Markup pricing is frequently used in routine pricing situations, such as with grocery or clothing items, but it is also sometimes employed in pricing unique products or services—for example, military equipment or construction projects. Markup pricing may well be the most common type of pricing strategy. Although it possesses decided drawbacks (especially if a single percentage is applied across products without regard to their elasticities or competition), its simplicity, flexibility, and controllability make it highly popular.

As noted in Chapter 2 when discussing the financial aspects of marketing management, break-even analysis is a useful tool for determining how many units of a product or service must be sold at a specific price for an organization to cover its total costs (fixed plus variable costs). Through judicious use of break-even analysis, it is also possible to calculate the break-even price for a product or service. Specifically, the break-even price of a product or service equals the per-unit fixed costs plus the per-unit variable costs.

Rate-of-return pricing is slightly more sophisticated than either markup or break-even pricing. Still, it contains the basic ingredients of both of these strategies and can be viewed as an extension of them. In a *rate-of-return pricing strategy*, price is set so as to obtain a prespecified rate of return on investment (capital) for the organization. Since rate of return on investment (ROI) equals profit (Pr) divided by investment (I),

$$\text{ROI} = \text{Pr}/I = \frac{\text{revenues} - \text{cost}}{\text{investment}} = \frac{P \cdot Q - C \cdot Q}{I}$$

where P and C are, respectively, unit selling price and unit cost and Q represents the quantity sold.

By working backward from a predetermined rate of return, it is possible to derive a selling price that will obtain that return rate. If an organization desires an ROI of 15 percent on an investment of $80,000, total costs per unit are estimated to be $0.175, and a demand of 20,000 units is forecast, then the necessary price will be

$$\frac{(\text{ROI}) \times I + CQ}{Q} = P = \frac{(0.15)\$80,000 + \$0.175 \times 20,000}{20,000} = 0.175$$

or roughly $0.78.

This pricing strategy, popularized by General Motors, is most commonly used by large firms and public utilities whose return rates are closely watched or are regulated by government agencies or commissions. Like other types of full-cost pricing strategies, rate-of-return pricing assumes a standard (linear) demand function and insensitivity of buyers to price. This assumption often holds true only for certain price ranges, however.

Variable-Cost Pricing

An alternative to full-cost pricing strategies is a variable-cost, or contribution pricing, strategy. This type of strategy is sometimes used when an organization is operating at less than full capacity and fixed costs constitute a great proportion of total unit costs. The basic idea underlying *variable-cost pricing* is that, in certain short-run pricing situations, the relevant costs to consider are the variable costs, not the total costs. Specifically, in this strategy, variable unit cost represents the minimum selling price at which the product or service can be marketed. Any price above this minimum represents a contribution to fixed costs and profits.

Variable-cost pricing is a form of demand-oriented pricing. As such, it can serve two different purposes: (1) stimulate demand and (2) shift demand. Since variable-cost prices are lower than full-cost prices, the assumption is that they will *stimulate demand* and increase revenues, and hence will lead to economies of scale, lower unit costs, and greater profits. This is why airlines offer different classes of fares, hotels offer special weekend rates, and movie theaters have discounts for senior citizens. Variable-cost pricing also makes sense because fixed costs must be met no matter whether a product or service is sold—the airline must maintain its flight schedule whether or not there are any passengers; the hotel or movie theater has to remain open even if it is only partially filled—and the incremental (variable) costs of serving one more customer are minimal.

Consider a bus line making a daily run from Minot to Fargo, North Dakota. The price of a one-way ticket is $8.00, and on an average trip the bus is 60 percent full. If unit fixed and variable costs are, respectively, $5.50 and $2.00, should the bus line offer a half-price fare for children under five years of age? Ignoring price elasticity and the like for the moment, the answer is yes, the reduced fare should be offered. The reduced fare ($4.00) covers the variable costs ($2.00) and still makes a contribution of $2.00 to fixed costs. Since the bus line will make the trip regardless of how many passengers there are, in the short run every reduced-fare ticket sold contributes $2.00 to fixed expenses. Such a pricing approach always assumes that no more profitable use may be made of the revenue-generating activity.

In addition to stimulating demand, variable-cost pricing can be used to *shift demand* from one time period to another. Movie theaters sometimes have lower matinee ticket prices to encourage customers to switch from evening to afternoon attendance. Likewise, certain utilities (such as telephone companies) have different price schedules to shift demand away from peak load times and smooth it out over extended time periods.

New-Offering Pricing Strategies

Full- and variable-cost pricing strategies are *technical strategies* that can be used when an organization initially sets its prices or when it changes them. When pricing a new product or service, however, a manager also has to consider other, more *conceptual* strategies.

When introducing a new product or service to the marketplace, an organization can employ one of three alternative pricing strategies. With a *skimming pricing strategy*, the price is set very high initially and is typically reduced over time.[8] A skimming strategy may be appropriate for a new product or service if any of the following conditions hold:

1. Demand is likely to be price inelastic.
2. There are different price-market segments, thereby appealing first to buyers who have a higher range of acceptable prices.
3. The offering is unique enough to be protected from competition by patent, copyright, or trade secret.

4. Production or marketing costs are unknown.

5. A capacity constraint in producing the product or providing the service exists.

6. An organization wants to generate funds quickly to recover its investment or finance other developmental efforts.

7. There is a realistic perceived value in the product or service.

Many of these conditions were present when StarSignal, a small California firm, introduced a $26,000 facsimile machine that prints color documents.[9]

At the other extreme, an organization may use a *penetration pricing strategy*, whereby a product or service is introduced at a low price. This strategy may be appropriate if any of the following conditions exist:

1. Demand is likely to be price elastic in the target market segments at which the product or service is aimed.

2. The offering is not unique or protected by patents, copyrights, or trade secrets.

3. Competitors are expected to enter the market quickly.

4. There are no distinct and separate price-market segments.

5. There is a possibility of large savings in production and marketing costs if a large sales volume can be generated.

6. The organization's major objective is to obtain a large market share.

IBM apparently considered these factors and consciously chose a penetration strategy when, in 1990, it introduced a line of high-powered personal computers for business and scientific purposes and priced the computers at roughly half of what competitors were charging. A company spokesperson said, "We've priced these things to go."[10]

Between these two extremes is an *intermediate pricing strategy*. As might be expected, this type of strategy is the most prevalent in practice. The other two types of introductory pricing strategies are, so to speak, more flamboyant; given the vagaries of the marketplace, however, intermediate pricing is more likely to be used in the vast majority of initial pricing decisions.

Competitive Bidding

Although this discussion has centered on administered pricing strategies, one additional form of pricing deserves brief mention. In certain situations, buyers prespecify in contract proposals characteristics of the products or services that they desire to purchase. Potential sellers then bid to obtain the contract. This proposal-bidding procedure, commonly known as *competitive bidding*, is especially prevalent when an organization is marketing to the government or to large industrial concerns.

Competitive bidding requires a highly specialized type of pricing strategy, since (1) demand is known and constant and (2) other marketing-mix elements are virtually uncontrollable or are inconsequential. For this reason, sophisticated mathematical bidding models have been developed to assist organizations in developing winning bids. Most of these models attempt to compute expected profits resulting from different bid prices by associating each price with a probability of winning.

Determination of costs is a vital part of preparing any competitive bidding proposal; depending on organizational goals, either full or variable costs may be used.

Still, the most crucial aspect of competitive bidding is undoubtedly estimating the probabilities of award. Not only must these probabilities take into account the needs of the organization, but they must also reflect what the likely bids of the competitors will be.

NOTES

1. For extensive treatments of pricing, see Kent B. Monroe, *Pricing: Making Profitable Decisions*, 2nd ed. (New York: McGraw-Hill, 1990); and Thomas T. Nagle and Reed K. Holden *The Strategy and Tactics of Pricing*, 2nd ed. (Englewood Cliffs, NJ: Prentice Hall, 1995).

2. For a comprehensive review of the price-quality-value relationship, see Valarie A. Ziethaml, "Consumer Perceptions of Price, Quality, and Value," *Journal of Marketing* (July 1988): 2–22.

3. "Laundry Soap Marketers See the Value of 'Value'!" *Advertising Age* (September 21, 1992): 3, 56.

4. "Store-Brand Pricing Has to Be Just Right," *Wall Street Journal* (February 14, 1992): B1.

5. Robert A. Crandall, "Different Products, Different Prices," *American Way* (November 1, 1991): 12.

6. "Nintendo: Game Over," *The Economist* (November 20, 1993): 74–75.

7. "The Price Is Wrong, and Economists Are in an Uproar," *Wall Street Journal* (January 2, 1991): B1.

8. An extended discussion of skimming and penetration pricing is found in Joel Dean, "Pricing Policies for New Products," *Harvard Business Review* (November–December 1976): 141–153.

9. "U.S. Invents, Japan Profits (Again)," *Fortune* (March 12, 1990): 14–15.

10. "IBM Introduces Line of Workstations; Industry Analysts Impressed by Prices," *Wall Street Journal* (February 16, 1990): B3.

Burroughs Wellcome Company
Retrovir

"I think that Burroughs Wellcome is very interested in getting all their money back as soon as possible, because the sun won't shine forever."[1]

Cofounder of Project Inform,
an AIDS treatment information agency (1987)

"Once the drug is out on the marketplace, the company controls the pricing."[2]

Dr. George Stanley,
Food and Drug Administration (1987)

"To make AZT accessible to everyone who should be on it, Burroughs Wellcome has an obligation to give up a significant amount of money to allow people to get access."[3]

Executive Director,
National Gay and Lesbian Task Force (1989)

"There's no plan to make another price cut."[4]

Sir Alfred Sheppard,
Chairman of the Board, Wellcome PLC (1989)

In January 1990, Burroughs Wellcome executives were under continued pressure to reduce the price of Retrovir. Retrovir brand zidovudine is the trade name for a drug called azidothymidine (AZT), which had been found to be effective in the treatment of acquired immune deficiency syndrome (AIDS) and AIDS-related complex (ARC). AIDS is a disease caused by a virus that attacks the body's immune system and damages the system's ability to fight off other infections. Without a functioning immune system, a person becomes vulnerable to infection by bacteria, protozoa, fungi, viruses, and other malignant agents, which may cause life-threatening illnesses, such as pneumonia, meningitis, and cancer. AIDS is caused by HIV (human immunodeficiency virus), a human virus first discovered in 1983. AZT is classified as an antiviral drug that interferes with the replication of HIV. As such, AZT is a treatment, not a cure, for AIDS.

In 1987, Burroughs Wellcome obtained approval from the U.S. Food and Drug Administration to market Retrovir, the first and, as of 1990, the only drug authorized for the treatment of AIDS. Soon after Burroughs Wellcome made Retrovir available

---

[1]"The Unhealthy Profits of AZT," *The Nation* (October 17, 1987): 407.

[2]Ibid.

[3]"AZT Maker Expected to Reap Big Gain," *New York Times* (August 29, 1989): 8.

[4]"Wellcome Seeks Approval to Sell AZT to All Those Inflicted with AIDS Virus," *Wall Street Journal* (November 17, 1989): B4.

This case was prepared by Professor Roger A. Kerin, of the Edwin L. Cox School of Business, Southern Methodist University, with the assistance of Angela Bullard, graduate student, as a basis for class discussion and is not designed to illustrate effective or ineffective handling of an administrative situation. The case was prepared from published sources. Quotes, statistics, and published operating information are footnoted for reference purposes. Copyright © by Roger A. Kerin. No part of this case may be reproduced without the written permission of the copyright holder.

for prescription sales on March 19, 1987, the company became embroiled in controversy related to the price of the drug. Critics charged that Burroughs Wellcome, which sold the drug to wholesalers at a price of $188 for a hundred 100-milligram capsules, engaged in price gouging of a "highly vulnerable market." The company's President, T. E. Haigler, responded that the high price was due to the "uncertain market for the drug, the possible advent of new therapies, and profit margins customarily generated by significant new medicines."[5]

Nevertheless, the company reduced its price by 20 percent in December 1987, and again by 20 percent in September 1989. Prior to the 1989 price reduction, the Subcommittee on Health and the Environment of the U.S. House of Representatives had launched an investigation into possible "inappropriate" pricing of Retrovir. Soon after the announced price reduction in 1989, the chairman of the House subcommittee said that this was "a good first step. But I think the company can do better."[6] In November 1989, the Chairman of Wellcome PLC, the parent company of Burroughs Wellcome, was quoted as saying, "There's no plan to make another price cut."[7] However, pressure to again reduce the price continued.

ACQUIRED IMMUNE DEFICIENCY SYNDROME

Acquired immune deficiency syndrome can be traced to a blood sample taken and stored in the Central African nation of Zaire in 1959 (see Exhibit 1 for a chronology of important events). It was not until 1982, however, that the Centers for Disease Control

EXHIBIT 1

AIDS Chronology, 1959–1990

1959	Blood sample taken and stored in the Central African nation of Zaire. Retesting the sample in 1986, physicians discover it to be HIV-infected.
1978	Doctors determine that a child in New York died as a direct result of immune system breakdown.
1981	The Centers for Disease Control (CDC) reports breakdowns of the immune systems of several male homosexuals with the resulting occurrence of infectious diseases and cancers.
1982	CDC names the "mystery disease" acquired immune deficiency syndrome (AIDS) and warns that it may be spread by a virus in bodily fluids such as blood and semen.
1983	Scientists at the Pasteur Institute in Paris, France, isolate a suspected AIDS-causing virus.
1984	U.S. researchers identify an AIDS-causing virus as the same one isolated by the French scientists.
1985	A test is licensed to detect an AIDS-causing virus in blood.
1986	The AIDS-causing virus is named human immunodeficiency virus, or HIV.
1987	U.S. Food and Drug Administration permits sale of azidothymidine (AZT), which eases some of the symptoms of AIDS and AIDS-related complex (ARC).
1988–1990	AIDS fatalities continue to increase while the pharmaceutical industry searches for a cure.

[5]"The High-Cost AIDS Drug: Who Will Pay for It?" *Drug Topics* (April 6, 1987): 52.
[6]"How Much for a Reprieve from AIDS?" *Time* (October 2, 1989): 81.
[7]"Wellcome Seeks Approval to Sell AZT . . .," *Wall Street Journal* (November 17, 1989): B4.

in Atlanta, Georgia, labeled the disease and warned that it might be spread by a virus in bodily fluids such as blood and semen. In 1983 and 1984, French and American scientists isolated a suspected AIDS-causing virus that was subsequently named human immunodeficiency virus, or HIV, in 1988. HIV is a retrovirus that can become an extra link in the genetic code, or DNA, of a cell. HIV inhibits and eventually destroys the T-4 cell, which is a key part of a person's immune system that attacks foreign germs. Without T-4 cells, people succumb to all manner of infections. The identification of HIV was a major breakthrough especially since, prior to 1984, it was not established in the scientific community that retroviruses like HIV caused human diseases.

Incidence and Cost of HIV and AIDS

Efforts to track and forecast the incidence and cost of HIV and AIDS began in earnest in 1986. Research focused on identifying high-risk individuals, determining the geographical concentration of the disease, and arriving at estimates of the number of people afflicted with HIV and AIDS.[8] This research found that almost 90 percent of AIDS victims were homosexual men or intravenous drug users. One-half of all reported AIDS cases were in the San Francisco, Miami, New York City, Los Angeles, and Houston metropolitan areas.

Tracking and forecasting the incidence of AIDS cases and HIV infections proved to be more difficult. The CDC reported 5,992 AIDS cases in 1984 and 35,198 cases in 1989. Estimates of HIV infections in 1990 ranged between 800,000 and 1,300,000 Americans depending on the estimation procedure employed. The incidence of AIDS cases in the period 1981–1989 are charted in Exhibit 2. The fatality rate for persons inflicted with AIDS was about 91 percent in 1981 and 46 percent in 1989.

Treating AIDS patients has proved to be extremely expensive. According to a 1987 study by the Rand Corporation, an internationally recognized research organization, the lifetime medical costs of an AIDS patient in his thirties were estimated to be between $70,000 and $141,000. For comparison, the lifetime cost of treating a person in his thirties with digestive tract cancer was $47,000; leukemia, $29,000; and a heart attack, $67,000.

An estimated 40 percent of persons with AIDS have received care under the Medicaid Program, which is administered by the Health Care Financing Administration and funded jointly by the federal government (55 percent) and individual states (45 percent). Estimated annual costs for AIDS care and treatment funded by Medicaid ranged between $700 million and $750 million in 1988. Medicaid spending for AIDS was estimated to reach $2.4 billion in 1992. In addition, private insurers paid $250 million annually in AIDS-related medical payments.

---

[8]Portions of this material are based on statistics reported in Brad Edmundson, "AIDS and Aging," *American Demographics* (March 1990): 28–34; Fred J. Hellinger, "Forecasting the Personal Medical Care Costs of AIDS from 1988 through 1991," *Public Health Reports* (May–June 1988): 309–319; William L. Roper and William Winkenwerder, "Making Fair Decisions about Financing Care for Persons with AIDS," *Public Health Reports* (May–June 1988): 305–308; Centers for Disease Control, "Human Immunodeficiency Virus Infection in the United States: A Review of Current Knowledge," *Morbidity and Mortality Weekly Report* (December 18, 1987): 2–3, 18–19; "Now That AIDS Is Treatable, Who'll Pay the Crushing Cost?" *Business Week* (September 11, 1989): 115–116; Centers for Disease Control, "HIV/AIDS Surveillance Report" (U.S. Department of Health and Human Services, Public Health Services: December 1990).

EXHIBIT   2

AIDS Cases, 1981–1989

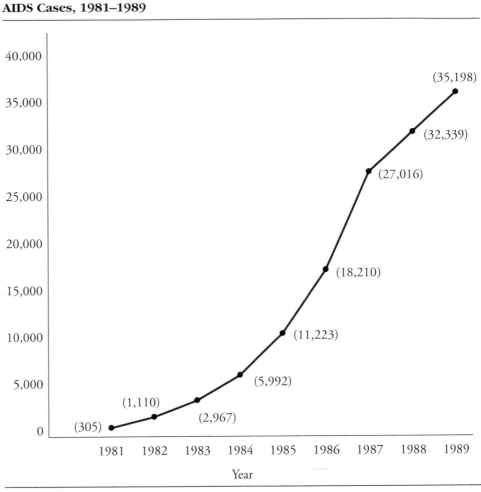

Source: Based on Centers for Disease Control, "HIV/AIDS Surveillance Report" (U.S. Department of Health and Human Services, Public Health Services: December 1990).

Anti-HIV Drug Treatment

The identification of HIV in the mid-1980s prompted numerous pharmaceutical companies to search for antiviral drugs. Burroughs Wellcome led the research effort in part because of its prior development of drugs that combat viral diseases. In addition to AZT supplied by Burroughs Wellcome, other compounds were in various stages of development and commercialization.[9] One antiviral drug has been given limited approval by the FDA and is available to patients who have a negative reaction to AZT. This drug, produced by Bristol Myers and called DDI, is an antiviral drug that appears to inhibit reproduction of HIV and slow the damage it causes. DDI was initially stud-

---

[9]Portions of this material are based on "A Quiet Drug Maker Takes a Big Swing at AIDS," *Business Week* (October 6, 1986): 32; "There's No Magic Bullet, but a Shotgun Approach May Work," *Business Week* (September 11, 1989): 118.

ied for AIDS use by the National Cancer Institute. Like AZT, it interferes with the ability of HIV-infected cells to produce new viruses and slows the progression of HIV infection, but does not eradicate or eliminate the infection. The principal advantage of DDI over AZT is that it appears to be less toxic. DDC, developed by Hoffman-LaRoche, was in clinical trials in 1989. Other drugs produced by Glaxo and Triton Biosciences, Inc., were being tested as well. Industry analysts believed that one or more of these drugs would obtain FDA approval for prescription sales by 1991.

BURROUGHS WELLCOME COMPANY

Burroughs Wellcome is the American subsidiary of Wellcome PLC, an English public limited company with headquarters in London.[10] Wellcome PLC is a multinational firm with manufacturing operations in 18 countries and employs 20,000 people. Approximately 18 percent of the company's employees are engaged in research and development efforts. The company's primary business, which accounts for 89 percent of its fiscal 1989 revenue, is human health-care products, both ethical (prescription) and over the counter (nonprescription). Two ethical products account for 34 percent of its human health-care revenue: Zovirax and Retrovir. Zovirax, which is used in the treatment of herpes infection, is the company's single largest-selling product with annual sales of $492 million in 1989. Retrovir is its second largest-selling product with sales of $225 million in fiscal 1989. In addition, the company markets Actifed and Sudafed, cough and cold preparations, as over-the-counter products. These two products combined account for annual sales of $253 million. Wellcome PLC had an animal health-care business that accounted for about 11 percent of company revenue. This business was divested in late 1989.

North America represents the largest market for the products sold by Wellcome PLC, with annual sales of $997 million. Sales in the United States are roughly equivalent to 42 percent of Wellcome PLC's worldwide sales. The United Kingdom is the company's second largest market and accounts for about 10 percent of worldwide sales.

Wellcome PLC recorded total revenues of $1.75 billion and net profit before tax of $262.1 million in fiscal 1987. Total revenues for fiscal 1989 (fiscal year ended August 31, 1989) were $2.1 billion with net profit before taxes of $475 million.[11] Selected financial and operating ratios for Wellcome PLC for the fiscal years 1987–1989 are shown in Exhibit 3. Exhibit 4 presents comparative statistics for other major firms in the U.S. pharmaceutical industry. Percentage sales and the net income growth since fiscal 1985 for Wellcome PLC are shown below:

Fiscal Years	*Sales Growth*	*Net Income Growth*
1985–1986	0.2%	7.2%
1986–1987	12.6	47.3
1987–1988	10.4	35.1
1988–1989	12.6	42.9

[10]Much of this material is described in Wellcome PLC's 1989 and 1990 *Annual Reports*; "Burroughs Wellcome Company," Burroughs Wellcome news release, December 13, 1990; Brian O'Reilly, "The Inside Story of the AIDS Drug," *Fortune* (November 5, 1990); 112–129. Financial figures and percentages represent approximations, since information is reported in U.S. dollars and the British pound sterling. These figures are not useful for research purposes.

[11]These figures are based on the average exchange rate of $1.55 = £1 in 1987, $1.68 = £1 in 1989 (Wellcome PLC 1990 *Annual Report*).

EXHIBIT 3

Selected Financial and Operating Ratios of Wellcome PLC

	Fiscal Year[a]		
	1989	*1988*	*1987*
Financial Ratios			
Gross profit margin (gross profit/sales)	70.6%	68.1%	67.5%
Return on sales (net income before tax/sales)	20.0	17.7	14.9
Return on assets (net income before tax/total assets)	20.0	18.0	15.0
Return on equity (net income before tax/common equity)	35.0	36.0	32.0
Operating Ratios			
R&D expenditures/sales	13.4	13.1	12.6
Selling, general, and administration costs/sales	36.9	36.5	39.2

Source: Welcome PLC annual reports.

[a]Fiscal Year ends August 31.

DEVELOPMENT OF RETROVIR

Burroughs Wellcome's AIDS research program began in June 1984 with an extensive search for likely drug candidates. According to Philip Furman, head of virus research, "We looked at all our known antivirals on the off chance that one would work against retroviruses."[12]

Laboratory Testing

Burroughs Wellcome scientists examined hundreds of compounds over a period of five months, but none proved acceptable. In November 1984, AZT was found to inhibit animal viruses in a laboratory setting. AZT had been synthesized in 1964 by a researcher at the Michigan Cancer Foundation. It was hoped then that the drug would be useful in the treatment of cancer, but when investigated, it was found to have no potential as an anticancer agent. In the early 1980s, Burroughs Wellcome scientists resynthesized AZT in their exploration of compounds with possible effectiveness against bacterial infection. This research provided information about the spectrum of the drug's antibacterial activity and its toxicity and metabolism in laboratory animals, but intensive development was not pursued. The drug was not examined again

---

[12]This material is based on "The Development of Retrovir," Burroughs Wellcome news release, June 1990; L. Wastila and L. Lasagna, "The History of Zidovudine (AZT)," *Journal of Clinical Research and Pharmacoepidemiology*, Vol. 4 (1990): 25–29; "The Inside Story of the AIDS Drug," *Fortune* (November 5, 1990): 112–129; "AIDS Research Stirs Bitter Fight over Use of Experimental Drugs," *Wall Street Journal* (June 18, 1986): 26.

EXHIBIT 4

Selected Financial and Operating Ratios for Pharmaceutical Firms in the United States, 1989

| | *Pharmaceutical Firm* | | | | | |
	Merck & Co.	*Pfizer, Inc.*	*Abbott Labs*	*Upjohn*	*Schering-Plough*	*Eli Lilly*
***Financial Ratios*[a]**						
Gross profit margin	76.3%	63.6%	52.5%	69.8%	73.8%	69.9%
Return on sales	34.8	16.2	22.2	15.8	20.4	31.9
Return on assets	33.8	11.0	24.6	14.2	17.9	22.7
Return on equity	64.9	20.2	43.8	26.5	33.0	35.4
Operating Ratios						
R&D/sales	11.5	9.4	9.3	14.0	10.3	14.5
SG&A/sales	30.7	37.2	20.5	40.3	42.3	27.5

Source: Company annual reports.

[a]See Exhibit 3 for definitions of ratios.

until late 1984 when it showed promise as an AIDS treatment. (Exhibit 5 details significant events in the development of Retrovir.)

Following *in vitro* demonstration of its potential by Burroughs Wellcome's scientists, 50 coded compounds including AZT were sent to Duke University, the National Cancer Institute (NCI), and the FDA for independent testing to assess their *in vitro* activity against the human retrovirus.[13] Early in 1985 these tests showed that AZT was, in fact, active against HIV in the test tube. The company then began extensive preclinical toxicologic and pharmacologic testing in the spring of 1985. At the same time, work began on scaling up synthesis of the drug in preparation for clinical testing in patients with HIV. On June 14, 1985, Burroughs Wellcome submitted an application to the FDA to obtain Investigational New Drug (IND) status for the compound, which would allow its use in a limited number of severely ill AIDS and ARC patients. A week later, the FDA notified Burroughs Wellcome that the submitted data were sufficient to allow clinical studies in humans to be initiated.

Human Testing

Retrovir was administered to patients for the first time on July 3, 1985, at the Clinical Center of the National Institutes of Health (NIH) in Bethesda, Maryland. This initial (Phase I) study, conducted under a protocol developed by Burroughs Wellcome in collaboration with scientists at the NCI, Duke University, the University of Miami, and UCLA, involved 40 patients infected with HIV. The purpose of Phase I testing was to determine how Retrovir acted in the body, the appropriate dosage, and potential adverse reactions or side effects. Initial results were encouraging. Some of the patients showed evidence of improvement, including an increased sense of well-being, weight gain, and positive changes in various measures of the immune system function. Extended treatment, however, lowered production of red blood cells and certain white blood cells in some patients who had taken high doses.

[13]*In vitro*, a Latin phrase meaning "in glass," is used medically to mean to isolate from a living organism and artificially maintain in a test tube.

EXHIBIT 5

Retrovir Milestones, 1984–1990

June 1984	Burroughs Wellcome begins an AIDS research program to search for chemical compounds that might be effective against HIV.
November 1984	Burroughs Wellcome scientists identify AZT as potentially useful against AIDS.
Spring 1985	*In vitro* activity of AZT against HIV is confirmed by laboratories at Duke University, FDA, and NCI. This confirmatory work, requested by Burroughs Wellcome, is done on coded samples whose chemical identity is not revealed to the outside laboratories.
Spring 1985	Burroughs Wellcome continues toxicologic and pharmacologic testing of AZT. Work begins on scaling up synthesis of the drug, as the compound has never been produced beyond the few grams used for research purposes.
June 1985	FDA permits Burroughs Wellcome to begin clinical trials of AZT in humans.
July 1985	AZT is designated an "orphan drug" for the treatment of AIDS (a designation made when the affected population is less than 200,000).
July 1985	Burroughs Wellcome begins a collaborative Phase I study with NCI and Duke University to assess AZT's safety and tolerance in humans.
December 1985	Enrollment in the Phase I study, eventually involving 40 patients and investigators from NCI, Duke University, University of Miami, and UCLA, continues. Patient responses are encouraging.
February 1986	Burroughs Wellcome initiates and is the sole sponsor of a Phase II study at 12 academic centers, eventually involving 281 patients.
September 1986	The Phase II study is halted when an interim analysis by an independent data safety and monitoring board shows a significantly lower mortality rate in patients receiving AZT compared to those randomized to receive a placebo.
October 1986	Burroughs Wellcome, National Institutes of Health, and FDA establish a Treatment IND (Investigational New Drug) program as a means of providing wider access to AZT prior to FDA clearance.
December 1986	Burroughs Wellcome completes submission of a New Drug Application to FDA.
March 1987	The FDA clears Retrovir brand zidovudine (AZT) as a treatment for advanced ARC and AIDS.
February 1988	Burroughs Wellcome is issued a U.S. patent for the use of Retrovir as a treatment for AIDS and ARC based on the innovative work done by company scientists.
August 1989	Controlled clinical trials indicate that certain HIV-infected early symptomatic and asymptomatic persons can benefit from Retrovir with fewer or less severe side effects.
October 1989	Burroughs Wellcome establishes a Pediatric Treatment IND program, providing wider access to Retrovir for medically eligible children prior to FDA clearance.
January 1989	The FDA clears modified dosage guidelines for therapy with Retrovir patients with severe HIV infection.

Source: Abridged from a Burroughs Wellcome news release, "Retrovir Milestones," dated December 13, 1990.

By early 1986, sufficient data on Retrovir were available to proceed with more extensive human testing. The need now was to prove that the drug could provide useful therapy for AIDS and ARC patients. More volunteers and an objective basis for comparison were essential to the conduct of the Phase II trial. A double-blind, placebo-controlled trial, conducted and financed by Burroughs Wellcome, began on February 18, 1986. A total of 281 patients participated. Safeguards built into the study provided for data to be reviewed periodically by a board of impartial experts convened under the auspices of the National Institute of Allergy and Infectious Diseases (NIAID). If either the placebo or the drug-treated group did either so poorly or so well that it would be unethical to continue the trial, the study would be stopped.

About this time, both the medical community and the general public had heard of the Phase II trial. As publicity about the trial gained momentum, AIDS patient-advocacy groups became impatient with what they perceived as an overly tedious and unnecessary process. They began accusing Burroughs Wellcome and the FDA of delaying the drug's availability. These critics argued that withholding potentially effective therapy from AIDS patients was inhumane and unethical, as was the use of a placebo. David Barry, Vice President and head of the research, medical, and development divisions, defended the trial process, asserting that, if placebo controls were removed, "it could destroy the most modern and rapid clinical research plans ever devised."[14]

In September 1986, the review board recommended that the administration of the placebo be terminated. Analysis of the data had shown a significantly lower mortality rate among those patients who had received Retrovir for an average period of six months. When the trial stopped, there had been 19 deaths among the 137 patients receiving the placebo and 1 death among those patients taking Retrovir. The group receiving Retrovir also had a decreased number of infections. In addition, the weight gain, improvements in the immune system, and ability to perform daily activities noted in the Phase I trial were confirmed. However, patients involved in the Phase II trial also experienced adverse reactions similar to those reported in the earlier trial. Since it was no longer appropriate to withhold drug treatment from placebo-treated patients, all patients who had formerly received the placebo were offered Retrovir treatment with the agreement of the FDA.

Expanded distribution of the drug meant that the company would have to obtain a larger supply of thymidine, a biological chemical first harvested from herring sperm and a key raw material in AZT. In 1986, the world's supply of thymidine was 25 pounds. Recognizing that this supply would be exhausted quickly, the head of technical development at Burroughs Wellcome began a worldwide search for a thymidine supplier, recognizing that it took months and 20 chemical reactions to produce this material. This search uncovered a small German subsidiary of Pfizer, Inc., a New York–based pharmaceutical firm, which had produced thymidine in the 1960s. This company was persuaded to produce thymidine by the ton.

In March 1987, the FDA released Retrovir for treatment for adult patients with symptomatic HIV infection, those patients for whom the drug had been shown to be beneficial in clinical trials. Although no hard figures were available, it was believed that about 50,000 individuals in the United States had symptomatic HIV infection. The recommended dosage for symptomatic HIV patients was 1,200 milligrams every day, administered in 12 100-milligram capsules.

---

[14]David Barry, testimony before the House Committee on Government Operations Subcommittee on Intergovernmental Relations and Human Resources, July 1, 1987.

Research and Development Costs

The direct research and development costs associated with Retrovir were estimated to be about $50 million, according to industry analysts.[15] This cost was considered low, since the typical cost of developing a new drug in the United States is $125 million. Indeed, Wellcome PLC had spent $726 million for research and development on dozens of drugs in the five years preceding approval of Retrovir without producing a major commercial success. However, when the costs of new plant and equipment to produce Retrovir were also considered, total research and development cost estimates ranged from $80 million to $100 million. Furthermore, the company provided the equivalent of $10 million of the drug free to 4,500 AIDS patients and supplied free of charge a metric ton of AZT to the National Institutes of Health's AIDS Clinical Trials Group.

Burroughs Wellcome's research and development effort did benefit from AZT being designated as an "orphan drug" in 1985 under provisions of the Orphan Drug Act of 1983. This act, which applies to drugs useful in treating 200,000 or fewer people in the United States, confers special consideration to suppliers of these drugs. For example, the orphan drug designation for Retrovir provided a seven-year marketing exclusivity after its commercial introduction, tax credits, and government subsidization of clinical trials.

MARKETING OF RETROVIR

Initial distribution of Retrovir was limited because of its short supply in March 1987. A special distribution system was set up to ensure availability of the drug to those patients who had been shown to benefit from its use. This system remained in place until September 1987, when supplies were adequate and broader distribution was possible.

The initial price set for Retrovir to drug wholesalers in March 1987 was $188 for a hundred 100-milligram capsules. This price represented an annual cost to AIDS patients ranging from $8,528 to $9,745 depending upon wholesaler and pharmacy margins, which combined ranged from 5 to 20 percent. An immediate controversy was created, with the public, media, and AIDS patient-advocacy groups seeking justification of the price for Retrovir, a decrease in its price, or federal subsidization. Critics pointed out that, for comparison, the annual cost of Interferon, a cancer-fighting drug, was only $5,000. The cofounder of Project Inform, an AIDS treatment information agency, said, "I think that Burroughs Wellcome is very interested in getting all their money back as soon as possible, because the sun won't shine forever."[16] Congressional hearings resulted in the chairman of the House Subcommittee on Health and the Environment charging that Burroughs Wellcome's "expectation was that those people who want to buy the drug will come up with the money" and that the government would "step in" to subsidize those who could not.[17] Congress subsequently created a $30 million emergency fund for AIDS patients who were unable to afford the cost of AZT.[18]

---

[15]Cost estimates have been made by industry analysts and have not been confirmed or denied by Burroughs Wellcome.

[16]"The Unhealthy Profits of AZT," *The Nation* (October 17, 1987): 407.

[17]FDC Reports—the Pink Sheet 49 (11): 5, 1987.

[18]"Find the Cash or Die Sooner," *Time* (September 5, 1988): 27.

Company officials acknowledged that the pricing decision was difficult to make. According to one official, "We didn't know the demand, how to produce it in large quantities, or what competing drugs would come out in the market. There was no way to find out." Another company official said, "I guess we assumed that the drug . . . would be paid in some manner by the patient himself out of his own pocket or by third-party payers. We really didn't get into a lot of calculation along those lines."[19]

On December 15, 1987, the capsule price of Retrovir was reduced by 20 percent. The company announced that the price reduction was made possible because of cost savings achieved in the production process and an improved supply of synthetically manufactured thymidine. The company continued its research on AZT throughout 1988 into 1989, including treatments for children with HIV infection. In August 1989, this research program indicated that Retrovir produced positive results in postponing the appearance of AIDS in HIV-infected people. This development expanded the potential users of the drug to between 600,000 and 1 million people. (However, industry sources believe that fewer than one-half of the people with HIV have been tested and told of their condition and would thus be seeking treatment.) FDA approval for marketing to this larger population was expected by March 1990.

Recognizing the expanded potential patient population and anticipated production economies, the capsule price of Retrovir was again reduced by 20 percent in September 1989. In reference to this price reduction, Burroughs Wellcome's *1989 Annual Report* noted:

> In arriving at our decision to reduce the price, we carefully weighed a number of factors. These included our responsibility to patients and shareholders, the very real remaining uncertainties in the marketplace, and the vital need to fund our continuing research and development programmes.[20]

The new price to drug wholesalers was set at $120 for a hundred 100-milligram capsules. The retail price to users was about $150 for a hundred 100-milligram capsules. Industry analysts estimated that the direct cost of manufacturing and marketing Retrovir was 30 cents to 50 cents per capsule.[21]

Sales of Retrovir since its introduction are shown in Exhibit 6. Unit volume for Retrovir in fiscal 1990 was forecasted to be 53 percent higher than fiscal 1989 unit volume.

Patient-advocacy groups continued to criticize the pricing of Retrovir. AIDS activists chanted such slogans as "Be the first on your block to sell your Burroughs Wellcome stock" while picketing stock exchanges in London, New York, and San Francisco. The executive director of the National Gay and Lesbian Task Force said, "To make AZT accessible to everyone who should be on it, Burroughs Wellcome has an obligation to give up a significant amount of money to allow people to get access."[22] Members of Senator Edward Kennedy's staff began researching possible ways to nationalize the drug by invoking a law that allows the U.S. government to revoke exclusive licenses in the interest of national security. In addition, there were published reports that the American Civil Liberties Union was considering a suit against Burroughs Wellcome. The suit would challenge the 17-year-use patent awarded Burroughs Wellcome for Retrovir, arguing that government scientists discovered AZT's efficacy against HIV.[23] The Subcommittee on

---

[19] "The Inside Story of the AIDS Drug," *Fortune* (November 5, 1990): 124–125.

[20] Wellcome PLC 1989 *Annual Report*: 13.

[21] "How Much for a Reprieve from AIDS?" *Time* (October 2, 1989): 81.

[22] "AZT Maker to Reap Big Gain," *New York Times* (August 19, 1989): 8.

[23] "A Stitch in Time," *The Economist* (August 18, 1990): 21–22.

EXHIBIT 6

Retrovir Sales Volume, Fiscal 1987–1989

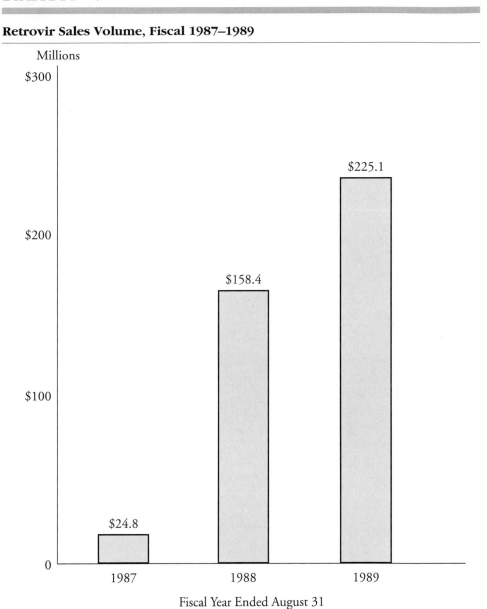

Fiscal Year Ended August 31

Source: Wellcome PLC 1990 *Annual Report.*

Note: U.S. dollar sales volume computed using average exchange rate £1 = $1.55 (1987), £1 = $1.76 (1988), £1 = $1.68 (1989).

Health and the Environment of the U.S. House of Representatives, which had already launched an investigation into possible "inappropriate" pricing of the drug, continued its hearings. However, Sir Alfred Sheppard, the company's Chairman, remained firm, saying "There's no plan to make another price cut." Later in 1990, he added, "If we wrapped the drug in a £10 note and gave it away, people would say it cost too much."[24]

[24]"The Inside Story of the AIDS Drug," *Fortune* (November 5, 1990): 124–125.

In January 1990, the FDA approved modified dosage guidelines for Retrovir. These guidelines reduced the recommended adult dosage to 500 milligrams per day for some symptomatic AIDS patients from the original recommended dosage of 1,200 milligrams per day established in 1987. However, some clinicians warned that lower dosages should be prescribed cautiously. Also in January, congressional lobbyists began a campaign to curb "excessive profits earned by the drug industry as a whole." Industry observers were speculating that the price of Retrovir might have to be cut again sometime in 1990 because of continued pressure from the U.S. Congress, the media, and AIDS patient-advocacy groups.[25]

---

[25]"Profiting from Disease," *The Economist* (January 27, 1990): 17–18.

Augustine Medical, Inc.
The Bair Hugger® Patient Warming System

In July 1987, Augustine Medical, Inc., was incorporated as a Minnesota corporation to develop and market products for hospital operating rooms and postoperative recovery rooms. The first two products the company planned to produce and sell were a patented patient warming system designed to treat postoperative hypothermia in the recovery room and a tracheal intubation guide for use in the operating room and in emergency medicine.

By early 1988, company executives were actively engaged in finalizing the marketing program for the patient warming system named Bair Hugger® Patient Warming System. The principal question yet to be resolved was how to price this system.

THE BAIR HUGGER® PATIENT WARMING SYSTEM

The Bair Hugger® Patient Warming System is a device designed to control the body temperature of postoperative patients. Specifically, the device is designed to treat the hypothermia (a condition defined as a body temperature of less than 36 degrees Centigrade or 96 degrees Fahrenheit) experienced by patients after operations.

Medical research indicates that 60 to 80 percent of all postoperative recovery room patients are clinically hypothermic. Several factors contribute to postoperative hypothermia. They are (1) a patient's exposure to cold operating room temperatures (which are maintained for the surgeons' comfort and for infection control), (2) heat loss due to evaporation of the fluids used to scrub patients, (3) evaporation from the exposed bowel, and (4) breathing of dry anesthetic gases.

The Bair Hugger® system consists of a heater/blower unit and a separate inflatable plastic/paper cover, or blanket. A photo of the system is shown in Exhibit 1. The heater/blower unit is a large, square, boxlike structure that heats, filters, and blows air through a plastic cover. An electric cord wraps around the back of the unit for storage, and the unit is mounted on wheels for easy transport. The blower tubing attaches to the warming cover through a simple cardboard connector strap and can be retracted into the top of the unit for storage. Temperature is set by a dial with four settings on the top of the unit. A top lid opens to a storage bin that holds 12 warming covers for easy access. The disposable warming covers come packaged in 18-inch-long tubes. When unrolled, the plastic/paper cover is flat and covers an average-sized patient from shoulders

This case was prepared by Professor Roger A. Kerin, of the Edwin L. Cox School of Business, Southern Methodist University, Michael Gilbertson, of Augustine Medical, Inc., and Professor William Rudelius, of University of Minnesota, as a basis for class discussion and is not designed to illustrate effective or ineffective handling of administrative situations. Certain names and data have been disguised. The assistance of graduate students Anne Christensen, Joanne Perty, and Laurel Wichman of the University of Minnesota is appreciated. The cooperation of Augustine Medical, Inc., in the preparation of the case is gratefully acknowledged. Copyright © by Roger A. Kerin. No part of this case may be reproduced without the written permission of the copyright holder.

EXHIBIT 1

Bair Hugger ® Patient Warming System

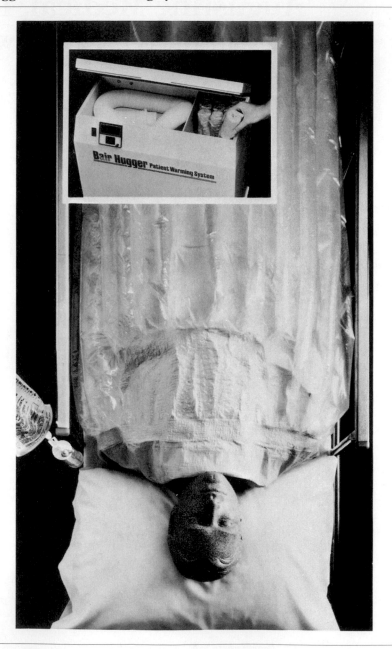

to ankles. The blanket consists of a layer of thin plastic and a layer of plastic/paper material laminated into full-length channels. Small holes punctuate the inner surface of the cover. When inflated through a connection at the feet of the patient, the tubular structure arcs over the patient's body, creating an individual patient environment. The warm air exits through the slits on the inner surface of the blanket, creating a gentle flow of warm air over the patient. The warming time per patient is about two hours.

The plastic cover was patented in 1986; there is no patent protection for the heater/blower unit.

COMPETING TECHNOLOGIES

Many competing technologies are available for the prevention and treatment of hypothermia. These technologies generally fall into one of two broad types of patient warming: surface warming or internal warming.

Surface-Warming Technologies

Warmed hospital blankets are the most commonly used treatment for hypothermia in recovery rooms and elsewhere. An application of warmed hospital blankets consists of placing six to eight warmed blankets in succession on top of a patient. Almost all patients receive at least one application; it is estimated that 50 percent of the postoperative patients require more than one application. The advantages of warmed hospital blankets are that they are simple, safe, and relatively inexpensive. The main disadvantage is that they cool quickly, provide only insulation, and require the patient's own body heat for regenerating warmth.

Water-circulating blankets are the second most popular postoperative hypothermic treatment. Water-circulating blankets can be placed under a patient, over a patient, or both. If a blanket is placed just under the patient, only 15 percent of the body's surface area is affected. However, hospitals typically place water-circulating blankets either just over the patient or over and under the patient, forming an insulated environment that encloses 85 to 90 percent of the body's surface area. The disadvantages of water-circulating blankets are that they are heavy and expensive and can cause burns on pressure points. Moreover, although a widely used and accepted method of warming, especially for more severe cases of hypothermia, water-circulating blankets are considered only slightly to moderately effective.

Electric blankets are generally unacceptable as a hypothermic treatment because of the risk of burns to the patient and of explosion in areas where oxygen is in use.

Air-circulating blankets and mattresses are not in common use in the United States, although variations on this technology have been used in the past. This technology relies on warmed air flowing over the body to transfer heat to the patient. The advantages of warmed-air technology are that it is safe, lightweight, and theoretically more effective than warmed hospital blankets or water-circulating blankets. Products using this technology are not widely found in the U.S. market, however.

Thermal drapes, also known as reflective blankets, have recently been introduced and are gaining acceptance as a preventive measure used in the operating room. They consist of head covers, blankets, and leggings placed on the uninvolved portions of the patient's body. Their use is recommended when 60 percent of a patient's body surface can be covered. The advantages of this technology are that it is simple, safe, and inexpensive and has been shown to reduce heat loss. The disadvantage is that it merely insulates the patient and does not transfer heat to someone who is already hypothermic.

Infrared heating lamps are popular for infant use. When placed a safe distance from the body and shined on the skin, they radiate warmth to the patient. The advantages of heat lamps are that they are effective and illuminate the patient for observation or therapy. A disadvantage is that since the skin needs to be exposed, modesty prevents widespread use among adults. (They are, however, used in adult skin-graft operations.) Nurses dislike radiant heat lamps and panels because they tend to heat the entire recovery room and are uncomfortable to work under.

Partial warm-water immersion has been used in the past, especially in cases where a patient was deliberately cooled to slow down metabolism. With this method, the patient is placed in a bath of warm water and watched carefully. The advantages of this technology are that it transfers heat very effectively and it is simple. The disadvantages are that the system is inconvenient to set up and requires close monitoring of the patient, which increases labor costs. In addition, water baths must be carefully watched for bacterial growth, and they are very expensive to purchase and use.

Increasing room temperature is the most obvious way to prevent and treat hypothermia, but it is seldom used. The advantages of this method are that it is simple and relatively inexpensive and has been proven effective at temperatures of over 70 degrees Fahrenheit. The disadvantage is that warm room temperatures are not acceptable to the nurses and surgeons who must work in the environment. Furthermore, warm temperatures increase the risk of infection.

Internal-Warming Technologies

Inspiring *heated and humidified air* is a fairly effective internal-warming technique currently being used with intubated patients (those having a breathing tube in the trachea). However, delivery of heated and humidified air by mask or tent to nonintubated patients is not acceptable in postoperative situations, because mask or tent delivery would interfere with observation and communication and, in the case of a tent, might increase the chance of infection. The fact that the patient must be intubated is a disadvantage, since the vast majority of postoperative patients are not intubated.

Warmed intravenous (I.V.) fluids are used in more severe hypothermic cases to directly transfer heat to the circulatory system. Warmed I.V. fluids are very effective because they introduce warmth directly into the circulatory system. The disadvantages of this technology are that it requires very close monitoring of the patient's core temperature and high physician involvement.

Drug therapy diminishes the sensation of cold and reduces shivering but does not actually increase body temperature. Although drug therapy is convenient and makes patients feel more comfortable, it does not warm them and in fact slows their recovery from anesthesia and surgery.

COMPETITIVE PRODUCTS

A variety of competitive products that use the above-mentioned technologies are available (see Exhibit 2). A review of competitors' sales materials and interviews with hospital personnel provided the following breakdown of competitive products.

EXHIBIT 2

Representative Competitive Products and Prices

Product	List Price	Company	Estimated Size of Company (sales; employees)	Comments
Blanketrol 200	$2,995/manual unit; $4,895/automatic unit; $165–$305/reusable blanket; $20/disposable blanket	Cincinnati Sub-Zero	$10 million; 90 employees	Hypothermia equipment is a small part of its overall business.
MTA 4700	$4,735/unit; $139/reusable blanket; $24/disposable blanket	Gaymar Industries	$17 million; 150 employees	Hypothermia equipment seems to be a major part of its business.
Aquamatic	$4,479/unit	American Hamilton (division of American Hospital Supply)	$3.3 billion; 31,300 employees	Hypothermia equipment is a very minor part of American Hospital Supply's business.
Climator	$4,000/unit	Hosworth Air Engineering Ltd.	Not available	The company would begin distribution of hypothermia equipment in the United States in 1988.

Warmed Hospital Blankets

For treating adult hypothermia, hospitals use their own blankets, which they warm in large heating units. Many manufacturers produce heating units for hospital use. The cost of laundering six to eight two-pound hospital blankets averages $0.13 per pound. Laundering and heating costs are absorbed in hospital overhead.

Water-Circulating Blankets

Several manufacturers produce water-circulating mattresses and blankets, but Cincinnati Sub-Zero, Gaymar Industries, and Pharmaseal are the major suppliers. Prices of automatic control units that measure both blanket and patient temperatures range from $4,850 to $5,295. Manual control units are priced at about $3,000, although they appear to be discounted by as much as 40 percent in actual practice.

The average life of water-circulating control units is 15 years. Reusable blankets list at from $168 to $375, depending on quality. Disposable blankets list at from $20 to $26. Volume discounts for blankets can reduce the list price by almost 50 percent.

Water-circulating blanket technology has changed little over the past 20 years except for the addition of solid state controls. There is little differentiation among the products of different firms.

Reflective Thermal Drapes

O.R. Concepts sells a product named the Thermadrape, which comes in both adult and pediatric sizes. Adult head covers list for $0.49 each; adult drapes list for $2.50 to $3.98, depending on size; leggings are priced at $1.50.

Air-Circulating Blankets and Mattresses

Two competitors are known to provide an air-circulating product like the Bair Hugger® Patient Warming System; however, neither is currently sold in the United States. The Sweetland Bed Warmer and Cast Dryer was in use 25 years ago but is no longer manufactured. This product consisted of a heater/blower unit that directed warm air through a hose placed under a patient's blanket. The Hosworth-Climator is an English-made product that provides a controlled-temperature micro-climate by means of air flow from a mattress. The Climator comes in a variety of models for use in recovery rooms, intensive care units, burn units, general wards, and patients' homes. The model most suitable for postoperative recovery rooms is priced at $4,000. This product could be distributed in the United States sometime in 1988. A summary of representative competitor products and list prices is shown in Exhibit 2.

THE HOSPITAL MARKET

Approximately 21 million surgical operations are performed annually in the United States, or 84,000 operations per average eight-hour work day. Approximately 5,500 hospitals have operating rooms and postoperative recovery rooms.

Research commissioned by Augustine Medical, Inc., indicated that there are 31,365 postoperative recovery beds and 28,514 operating rooms in hospitals in the United States. An estimated breakdown of the number of postoperative hospital beds and the percentage of surgical operations is shown below:

Number of Postoperative Beds	Number of Hospitals	Estimated Percentage of Surgical Operations
0	1,608	0%
1–6	3,602	20
7–11	1,281	40
12–17	391	20
18–22	135	10
23–28	47	6
29–33	17	2
>33	17	2

Given the demand for postoperative recovery room beds, the research firm estimated that hospitals with fewer than seven beds would not be highly receptive to the Bair Hugger® Patient Warming System. The firm also projected that one system would be sold for every eight postoperative recovery room beds.

Interviews with physicians and nurses, followed by a demonstration of the system, yielded a variety of responses:

1. Respondents believed that the humanitarian ethic "to make the patient feel more comfortable" is important.

2. Respondents felt that the Bair Hugger® Patient Warming System would speed recovery for postop patients.

3. Respondents wanted to test the units under actual conditions in postoperative recovery rooms. They were reluctant to make any purchase commitments without testing. A typical comment was "No one today, in this market, ever buys a pig in a poke.

E X H I B I T   3

Sales Literature for the Bair Hugger ® Patient Warming System

Common Problem: Post-Operative Hypothermia

Practical Solution: Bair Hugger™ Patient Warming System

EXHIBIT   3   (*continued*)

A Warm Welcome for Your Recovery Room Patients

Augustine Medical, Inc.'s new Bair Hugger™ Patient Warming System is the most practical and comforting solution for post-operative hypothermia available today.

Every year more than 10,000,000 hospital patients experience the severe discomfort and vital signs instability associated with post-operative hypothermia. Years later, patients can still vividly recall this discomfort. Augustine Medical's new Patient Warming System is a warm and reliable solution to post-operative hypothermia.

A Practical Solution to Post-Operative Hypothermia

The Bair Hugger™ Patient Warming System consists of a Heat Source and a separate disposable Warming Cover that directs a gentle flow of warm air across the body and provides for safe and comfortable rewarming.

The Bair Hugger Heat Source uses a reliable, high efficiency blower, a sealed 400W heating element, and a microprocessor-based temperature control to create a continuous flow of warm air. There are no pumps, valves or compressors to maintain. Special features include built-in storage space for the air hose, power cord and a convenient supply of disposable Warming Covers. The Heat Source complies with all safety requirements for hospital equipment.

1. PATENTED SELF SUPPORTING DESIGN
As the tubes fill with air, the Warming Cover naturally arches over the patient's body.

2. TISSUE PAPER UNDERLAYER
The tissue paper underlayer of the Warming Cover is soft and comfortable against the patient's skin.

3. AIR SLITS
Tiny slits in the underlayer allow warm air from the Heat Source to gently fill the space around the patient.

4. SHOULDER DRAPE
The shoulder drape is designed to tuck under the chin and shoulders, trapping warm air under the cover and preventing air flow by the patient's face.

5. DISPOSABLE COVERS
The disposable Covers prevent cross contamination and reduce laundry requirements.

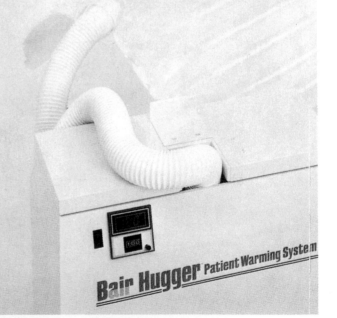

4. Respondents felt that the product was price-sensitive to alternative methods. If the product performed as claimed and demonstrated, purchase was probable by at least one-half of the individuals interviewed. Respondents were very receptive to the notion of using the heater/blower free of charge and only paying for the disposable blankets. Physicians wanted to confer with others who would be responsible for using the product to administer the warming treatment, however, such as the head nurse in postoperative recovery rooms and the chief anesthesiologist.

EXHIBIT 3 (*continued*)

THE BAIR HUGGER™
PATIENT WARMING SYSTEM
IS SO EASY TO USE.
Remove a new Warming Cover
from the storage compartment
and unroll over the patient.

Connect the heater hose to the
inlet of the Warming Cover and
turn on the heater.

6. SIMPLE CONTROLS
A preprogrammed temperature range
and a preset high temperature limit of
110°F, make the Bair Hugger safe and
simple to use.

7. INTERNAL WARMING COVER STORAGE
The storage compartment provides a
convenient supply of Warming Covers
ready for immediate use.

8. INTERNAL HOSE STORAGE
The hose retracts into its own
compartment for ready access.

9. LIGHTWEIGHT, COMPACT DESIGN
The Heat Source is designed for
convenience and portability. While in
use, it tucks under the foot of the gurney.
The unit's light weight and small size
make it simple to move and store.

10. BUILT-IN POWER CORD STORAGE
The power cord storage holds up to 12
feet of cord, making the Heat Source
portable and easy to store.

11. 5µ AIR FILTER
The air filter assures dust-free air
circulation through the Bair Hugger
Warming Cover. The filter is simple to
change when necessary.

The Bair Hugger™ Warming Cover:

The Warming Cover consists of a layer of plastic and a layer of tissue paper laminate bonded together into long tubular channels. The self-supporting Warming Cover is designed to arch over the patient's body creating a warm, comfortable environment.

The Warming Cover is convenient to use because no straps, tapes or other fasteners are required to stabilize the cover and the patient does not have to be disturbed or moved.

When the Warming Cover is completely inflated, warm air from the Heat Source exits the tubular channels through slits in the Cover's soft underlayer, surrounding the patient with a gentle flow of warm air.

---

5. Respondents believed that the pressure to move patients through the operating room and out of postop is greater than in the past. Efficiency is the byword.

6. Capital expenditures in hospitals were subject to budget committee approval. Although the amounts varied, expenditures for equipment over $1,500 were typically subject to a formal review and decision process.

EXHIBIT 3 *(continued)*

A Warm and Practical Discovery: Bair Hugger™ Patient Warming System

Post-Operative Hypothermia– A Common Problem

As a practicing anesthesiologist, Dr. Scott D. Augustine observed that there was no practical treatment for the common problem of post-operative hypothermia. An extensive review of post-operative hypothermia revealed several important facts:

- Post-operative hypothermia (T<36°C or <96.7°F) occurs in 60-80% of all post-operative patients (1). This extremely common problem affects more than 10,000,000 surgical patients every year.

- Several factors contribute to post-operative hypothermia including the patient's exposure to cold operating room temperatures, heat loss due to evaporation of fluids used to scrub the patient, evaporation of moisture from exposed bowels, and the breathing of dry anesthetic gases.

- Unlike environmental hypothermia, post-operative hypothermia is not usually life threatening. However, it can have serious side effects for older or unstable patients. Negative effects include a decrease in cardiovascular stability and an increase in oxygen consumption of up to 400% during unaided rewarming, as well as severe shivering and significant patient discomfort (2).

- Patients with unstable body temperatures require intensive nursing care, which means higher costs. Recovery room time may also be prolonged due to the instability caused by post-operative hypothermia.

Variety of Treatments–Only One Practical Solution

Many methods have been used to try to warm patients after surgery including warmed hospital blankets, water mattresses and heat lamps (3). Studies have shown, though, that these methods are ineffective.

The most common method of treating hypothermia–heated hospital blankets–does not actively heat the patient. The small amount of heat retained by a cotton blanket quickly dissipates, thereby requiring patients to rewarm themselves. Because multiple blankets are typically used, this method is both inconvenient and time-consuming for nursing staff and produces large amounts of laundry.

Another common method used to try to rewarm post-operative hypothermia patients is the use of a water circulating mattress. Water circulating equipment is heavy, complex, expensive and prone to leakage. While water mattresses have been used for many years, there is no clinical evidence that documents their effectiveness (4, 5). This lack of effectiveness can be explained by the minimal body surface area in contact with the mattress, (only 15%) and the lack of blood flow to this area. The weight of the patient creates a pressure which prevents normal cutaneous blood flow. The heat in the mattress cannot be transported away from the skin and the contact surface becomes an insulator effectively minimizing potential heat transfer to the patient.

New Approach Needed

As Dr. Augustine discussed the problem of post-operative hypothermia with doctors, nurses, and industry experts he became convinced that a new approach to warming patients was needed. A survey of anesthesiologists showed that most were dissatisfied with the current technology available for treating hypothermia. A new technology was definitely needed.

As a result of his research, Dr. Augustine developed the Bair Hugger™ Patient Warming System. Numerous studies and reports have shown that increased ambient room temperatures will prevent hypothermia (6-10). Indeed, before the advent of air conditioning, the average ambient temperature of the OR was higher and hyperthermia in the peri-operative period was not uncommon. Surgical patients will predictably lose or gain heat depending on the ambient temperature of the surrounding environment. The Bair Hugger™ System simulates a warm room by surrounding the patient in a gentle flow of warm air–A Focused Thermal Environment™.

The Bair Hugger™ Patient Warming System combines the convenience and effectiveness of warm air to safely rewarm hypothermic patients. The Warming System's minimal cost is rapidly recovered in saved nursing time, reduced linen expenses and lower overall recovery room costs. There is now a practical and cost-effective solution to post-operative hypothermia.

Two-week Free Trial

To arrange for a free two-week trial of the Bair Hugger™ Patient Warming System, fill out the enclosed reply card or call us collect at (612) 941-8866.

SPECIFICATIONS	HEATER/BLOWER UNIT
Size	26" high x 14" deep x 22" wide
Weight	65 lbs.
Power Requirements	110VAC
Temperature Range	Ambient to 110°F Max
Enclosure	Enameled steel
Displayed Variables	Temperature °F
Power Cable	12 Feet long
Display	.5 inch (1.2 cm) Character LCD
COVERS	
Size	54" x 36"
Weight	8 ounces
Material	Polyethylene and tissue paper laminate

AUGUSTINE MEDICAL INC.

PRACTICAL SOLUTIONS TO COMMON PROBLEMS IN ACUTE CARE™

10393 West 70th St., Suite 100 Eden Prairie, Minnesota 55344

References: (1) Vaughan MS, Vaughan RW, Cork RC: Anesthesia and Analgesia 60:746-751, 1981. (2) Bay J, Nunn JG, Prys-Roberts C: British Journal of Anaesthesia 40: 398-406, 1968. (3) Kucha DH, Nichols GH, Christ NM, Bynum JW: Military Medicine 139:388-390, 1974. (4) Morris RH, Kumar A: Anesthesiology 36:408-411, 1972. (5) Goundsouzian NG, Morris RH, Ryan JF: Anesthesiology 39:351-353, 1973. (6) Morris, RH: Annals of Surgery 173:230-233, 1971. (7) Morris RH, Wilkey BR: Anesthesiology 32:102-107, 1970. (8) Clark RE, Orkin LR, Rovenstine EA: JAMA 154:311-319, 1954. (9) Bigler JA, McQuistow WO: JAMA 146:551, 1951. (10) Harrison GG, Bull AB, Schmidt HJ: British Journal of Anaesthesia 40:398-406, 1960.

AUGUSTINE MEDICAL, INC.

Augustine Medical, Inc., was founded in 1987 by Dr. Scott Augustine, an anesthesiologist. His experience had convinced him that hospitals needed and desired a new approach to warming patients after surgery. His medical knowledge, coupled with a technical flair, prompted the development of the Bair Hugger® Patient Warming System.

The Bair Hugger® Patient Warming System has several advantages over water-circulating blankets. First, warm air makes patients feel warm and stop shivering. Second, the system cannot cause burns, and water leaks around electrical equipment are not a problem, as they are with water-circulating blankets. Third, the disposable blankets eliminate the potential for cross-contamination among patients. Finally, the system does not require that the patient be lifted or rolled. Augustine's personal experience indicated that all of these features would be welcome by nurses and patients alike. Features and benefits of the Bair Hugger® Patient Warming System are detailed in the company's sales literature, shown in Exhibit 3.

Investor interest in Augustine Medical and the medical technology it provided produced an initial capitalization of $500,000. These funds were to be used for further research and development, staff support, facilities, and marketing. It was believed that this initial investment would cover the fixed costs (including salaries, leased space, and promotional literature) of the company during its first year of operation. The company would subcontract the production of the heater/blower unit and would manufacture warming covers in-house using a proprietary machine. Only minor assembly would be performed by the company.

The Bair Hugger® Patient Warming System would be sold by and through medical products distributor organizations in various regions around the country. These distributor organizations would call on hospitals, demonstrate the system, and maintain an inventory of blankets. The margin paid to the distributors would be competitively set at 30 percent of the delivered (that is, less discounts) selling price on the heater/blower unit and 40 percent of the delivered (discounted if necessary) price on the blankets.

Preliminary estimates from subcontractors and a time-and-motion study on assembly indicated that the direct cost of the heater/blower unit would be $380. The cost of materials, manufacturing, and packaging of the plastic disposable blankets was estimated to be $0.85 per blanket.

The central issue at this time was the determination of the list price to hospitals for the heater/blower unit and the plastic blankets, given the widespread incidence of price discounting. Immediate attention to the price question was important for at least three reasons. First, it was felt that the price set for the Bair Hugger® Patient Warming System would influence the rate at which prospective buyers would purchase the system. Second, price and volume together would influence the cash flow position of the company. Third, the company would soon have to prepare price literature for its distributor organizations and for a scheduled medical trade show, where the system would be shown for the first time.

U.S. SemiCon Corporation
Facsimile Technology Program

The telephone was ringing as Adrian Bartos, manager of facsimile technology engineering at U.S. SemiCon Corporation (USS), entered his office at 5:00 P.M. on January 7, 1990. The call was from the director of engineering for Mexus, Inc., who told Bartos that a competitor had underbid USS for an order on its digital converter semiconductor device for facsimile (fax) machines. Bartos was confident that the competitor's bid price was unrealistically low, since USS, with all its design and manufacturing experience, could meet the bid only by pricing with profit margins significantly less than those for previously produced devices. While assembling his staff and their group vice president to discuss the ramifications of the competitive bid, Bartos realized that a decision of this importance would significantly affect his company's presence as a supplier to the burgeoning fax machine industry.

THE FACSIMILE MACHINE INDUSTRY

As early as 1983, the facsimile, or fax, machine was an esoteric intercompany communication device. According to industry estimates, some 50,000 fax machines were in operation in 1983, and most were housed in large Fortune 500 corporations. In 1989, 1.4 million fax machines were sold, representing $1.8 billion in sales. Industry forecasters were projecting unit sales of 3.2 million and dollar sales of $2.9 billion in 1993. Exhibit 1 shows the actual and projected unit and dollar sales of stand-alone fax machines for the ten-year period 1984–1993.

Origins of the Technology

The fax machine can trace its origins to 1842 when the first primitive one was designed by a Scottish inventor, Alexander Bain. His machine had a pendulum that created a brown stain as it swung across chemically treated paper. Although not a commercial success, his original ideas sparked a number of subsequent developments in the nineteenth century. In 1902, Arthur Korn devised a photoelectric scanning system for the transmission and reproduction of photography. He developed a commercial picture-transmission system in 1907. By 1934, the Associated Press was

---

This case was prepared by Professor Roger A. Kerin, of the Edwin L. Cox School of Business, Southern Methodist University, as a basis for class discussion and is not designed to illustrate effective or ineffective handling of an administrative situation. Company names and certain market, financial, and price data have been disguised as has the focal product. Fundamental relationships, however, remain intact and are useful for analysis purposes. Copyright © by Roger A. Kerin. No part of this case may be reproduced without written permission of the copyright holder.

EXHIBIT 1

Facsimile Machine Actual and Projected Unit and Dollar Volume, 1984–1993

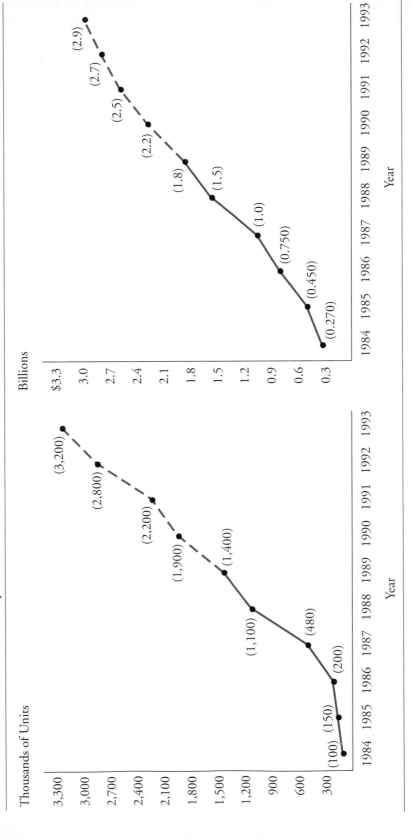

employing a facsimile system to transmit photos and text for newspapers. After extensive use of facsimile technology by the U.S. military in World War II, the Federal Communications Commission authorized its development on a commercial basis in 1948.

Today's facsimile technology is much like the technology envisioned by Bain and successive inventors. Facsimile technology involves a scanning device that converts the optical content of a document into an equivalent electrical signal. This signal is then converted into a series of audio tones to be sent over telephone lines. A receiving fax machine restores the tones to electrical signals and amplifies them in order to drive a printing device that reproduces the document.

Commercial Development

Commercial development of fax machines began in earnest in the 1960s. Xerox and Motorola pioneered the effort to produce commercially successful machines. In 1968, Xerox produced a machine that permitted receipt of documents by an unattended telephone, and in 1970, it introduced a lightweight portable machine that sent and received documents. In the late 1970s, four firms—Xerox, Exxon Information Systems, Burroughs, and Harris/3M (now Lanier Worldwide)—supplied 90 percent of the facsimile machines sold in the United States.

Two technical developments broadened the commercial appeal of fax machines in the early 1980s. First, the Consultative Committee on International Telephone and Telegraph (CCITT), which establishes worldwide standards for data communications, developed uniform standards to regulate transmissions from one fax machine to another. As a result, most fax machines around the world could communicate with each other. A second development was the introduction of electronic circuitry that replaced electromechanical parts in fax machines. The advent of electronics reduced transmission time from 6 minutes per page to 18 seconds, improved print quality, and provided cost savings.

Competitive and Marketing Environment

These two technical developments were followed in rapid succession by a number of changes in the competitive and marketing environments. In 1983, seven producers and nine brands composed the facsimile machine industry. By 1989, some 25 producers selling over 60 different brands competed for facsimile machine sales. The flow of new entrants into the industry resulted in rapid and often sizable fluctuations in producer market shares. Exhibit 2 illustrates the change in membership and market shares of the top five producers.

While U.S. companies dominated the market in the late 1970s and early 1980s, the top five producers in 1989 were Japanese firms. Industry analysts believed that Japanese producers would continue to dominate the industry for two reasons. First, fundamental facsimile technology, namely, printer and scanner technology, had been traditionally controlled by Japanese industry. Second, even though Japanese firms licensed printer and scanner technology, they still controlled the critical component technology. These factors gave Japanese firms a decided cost advantage and technical edge in facsimile machine production. However, industry analysts predicted that South Korean firms, such as Daewoo, Lucky-Goldstar, and Samsung, would enter the facsimile machine market in the early 1990s using Japanese-licensed technology. It was believed that these firms could introduce models priced as low as $300.

EXHIBIT 2

Unit Volume Market Shares of Facsimile Machine Manufacturers

1982		1986		1988		1989	
Company	*Share*	*Company*	*Share*	*Company*	*Share*	*Company*	*Share*
Xerox	30%	Ricoh	16%	Sharp	21%	Sharp	23%
Exxon	24	Canon	13	Murata	15	Murata	17
Burroughs	17	Pitney Bowes	12	Canon	11	Canon	9
3M	14	Sharp	10	Ricoh	10	Panasonic	8
Matsushita	6	Fujitsa	7	Pitney Bowes	6	Ricoh	8
Others	9	Others	42	Others	37	Others	35
	100%		100%		100%		100%

Notable changes in marketing practices also occurred. Fax machines were originally sold exclusively by the producer's salespeople, but in 1989, 60 percent of office machine dealers sold them. Distribution was also expanded to include some discount and department stores. By late 1989, most producers relied upon multiple channels, including direct sales to large corporate accounts and retail outlets for sales to small businesses, including home offices. Investment in advertising also increased with broadened distribution. For the 12-month period ending June 30, 1989, Sharp, which is the present market leader, spent $3.7 million on media advertising, Canon spent almost $4 million, and Ricoh, $1.1 million.[1] These expenditures represented a sizable investment, since little emphasis was placed on advertising by facsimile machine producers as recently as 1985.

Product innovation efforts were also evident. Some of the more noteworthy innovations included (1) models for home office use with built-in telephones, (2) models that used plain, rather than thermal, paper for copies, (3) models that integrated telex for electronic mail purposes, and others that linked facsimile capability with large mainframe computers and minicomputers, and (4) models that allowed for secure (confidential) transmissions. In addition, the industry average price for fax machines declined from approximately $2,700 in 1984 to about $1,300 in 1989.

Market Segmentation

The facsimile machine industry in 1989 was divided into four segments based on product price and features (see Exhibit 3). The fastest-growing segment consisted of stripped-down machines for small businesses priced below $1,500. Murata, Canon, and Ricoh competed in this market segment as well as in the mid-range ($1,500–$3,000) segment. The high-end market segment was less price-sensitive, but more feature-driven. This segment consisted of large corporations with heavy volume needs, and Canon was its leader. Most facsimile machine producers competed in only two of these three market segments, such as low end and mid range or mid range and high end. However, some producers, for example, Sharp and Canon, competed in all three. The fourth market, the deluxe segment, represented an emerging

[1]Brian Bagot, "Brand Report: FAX Facts," *Marketing & Media Decisions* (December 1989): 129–130ff.

E X H I B I T   3

Facsimile Machine Market Segmentation

	Low-End Segment	Mid-Range Segment	High-End Segment	Deluxe Segment
Price Points Description of Segment	Under $1,500 Small businesses and individuals	$1,500–$3,000 Larger businesses with higher fax volume needs	$3,000–12,000 Corporate and multisite buyers with heavy volume and high-quality reproduction needs	$25,000+ Fortune 500 corporations with heavy volume needs as well as information system integration needs
Machine Features	Stripped-down, entry-level models that are operator-fed (operator must feed a single sheet at a time and wait for each sheet to be completed before feeding another)	Automatic sheet feeder, which handles 5- to 50-page transmissions, and often delayed transmission features, which allow for transmission at times when unit is unattended	Automatic sheet feeders for multipage transmissions, half-tone reproduction capability, autodialing, and often simultaneous, multisite transmission with relay broadcasting memory capability to prevent backlogs	Integration of computers and fax technology, color transmissions
Major Competitors	Sharp Canon Toshiba Ricoh Murata	Sharp Canon Toshiba Murata Panasonic	Canon Xerox Pitney Bowes Ricoh Telautograph	Pitney Bowes Xerox

opportunity as fax technology was fused with computer technology in large-scale corporate information systems. Few producers competed in this segment as yet. It was still in the embryonic stage with experimental, customized technology and applications being prominent.

Although estimates varied greatly because of changing model price and feature configurations, some analysts believed that facsimile industry unit volume was divided among the three major segments as follows: low-end machines accounted for 45 to 55 percent of unit volume, mid-range machines for 30 to 45 percent, and high-end machines for 10 to 15 percent.

Industry Suppliers

Over 100 different firms produced products for inclusion in fax machines. These firms included plastic molders, which supplied the cover or "box"; electromechanical firms, which manufactured mechanical controls, electric motors, and printing heads; and semiconductor firms, which produced modems, integrated circuits, analog/digital converters, logic devices, memory devices, signal processors, and other electronic components. Semiconductor devices comprised approximately 25 percent of the total material used to produce a fax machine. The remaining 75 percent of material consisted of electric parts (25 percent) and nonelectric/electronic material and parts (50 percent).

Some 20 firms supplied semiconductor technology for fax machines. Some of these firms were vertically integrated and also produced fax machines (for example, Toshiba and Matsushita). Even though Japanese manufacturers dominated the market for fax machines, most of the semiconductors used in modems, converter chips and devices, data-compression devices, and other electronic parts were made by U.S. firms. For example, Rockwell International Corporation was estimated to supply 60 to 80 percent of the modems used in fax machines. Major well-known U.S. electronics firms that supplied semiconductor technology for other uses included Texas Instruments, Motorola, and National Semiconductor. Other smaller firms, such as U.S. SemiCon Corporation, also competed on a selective basis.

Fax machine producers typically evaluated suppliers using a wide variety of criteria. These criteria included design and technical support capabilities, evidence of product quality, reliability, delivery and production flexibility, and cost. Increasingly, these criteria were being translated into requests for small-volume production to accommodate customization for different fax machine models, shortened cycle time from production agreement to finished product delivery, and compatibility considerations to allow fax machine producers to "second source" products from one or possibly two other suppliers.

U.S. SEMICON CORPORATION

U.S. SemiCon Corporation manufactured a wide variety of electrical and electronic products. The company competed in three industry segments: (1) government aerospace and defense, (2) electrical distribution products and systems, and (3) industrial control products and systems. Sales in 1989 were $263 million; operating profit before taxes was $23.4 million. An internal strategic review of company operations in mid-1989 produced five directives:

1. We will disengage from government aerospace and defense programs.
2. We will emphasize expansion of the electrical and industrial segments and contiguous new segments, taking advantage of synergy.
3. We will self-fund growth.
4. We will pursue growth through internal development of products and markets rather than through acquisitions.
5. We will pursue opportunities related to electronics, particularly when our skills can be decisive.

Operating guidelines, or "must statements," that pertained to management philosophy, budgeting, and profit expectations were also outlined:

1. We must retain and build upon our corporate philosophies and methods to manage profitable growth. Attention to the USS management culture through planning and control mechanisms such as Program Potential Budgeting (PPB) and Cost-Centered Design and Manufacturing (CCDM) will be emphasized.
2. Funds must be invested in major growth thrusts—that is, products that serve markets with a high growth rate and in which USS can develop and sustain a profitable position.

3. We must continue to increase our basic technological strengths, especially in semiconductor technology. This includes not only the design, development, and production of key components and devices, but also the application of these components to new systems.

Program Potential Budgeting System

The PPB system is the action plan for any endeavor at USS. A PPB program states not only what a particular endeavor expects to achieve, but also how it will be achieved and the specific actions necessary to achieve it, including the costs of design, engineering, production, and marketing. Funding is derived from a portion of operating profits intended to support a new business strategy and is controlled at the department (profit-and-loss center) level. Funding for programs is competitive in that division managers obtain input from each of the program managers and subsequently submit funding requests to a budget committee. Programs are ranked according to their growth and profitability potential by the budget committee, with funds allocated accordingly.

The annual budgeting procedure is highly refined and well controlled. Flexibility is retained, however, to modify a program definition. Programs are defined in the fourth quarter for the coming calendar year and are reviewed monthly and quarterly. The flexibility of the process is illustrated by the following reflection of Adrian Bartos on the Facsimile Technology Program:

> In 1987 the Chip Sensor Program was funded at $150,000 and the Facsimile Technology Program was allocated $75,000. In 1988, the Chip Sensor Program was allocated $180,000, while we were allocated $100,000. Then, in December 1988, a group of vice-presidents from a facsimile machine manufacturer visited us. The prospects outlined by these executives allowed for an improved Facsimile Technology Program to be developed. Funds from the Chip Sensor Program were immediately diverted to the Facsimile Technology Program, which marked the beginning of the program as it now stands.

Bartos noted that this episode was not uncommon given the corporate policy that funds should be invested in products that serve growth markets and in which the company could develop a profitable position. In the same vein, existing programs exhibiting poor profit performance could lose funding and personnel could be reassigned. Bartos was very much aware of this fact: "The sequence of events that benefited the Facsimile Technology Program could work against it unless the program sustained its profitability."

Facsimile Technology Program

USS traced its participation in the facsimile machine industry to the early 1980s, when electromechanical parts were being replaced with electronics. "We were involved early in the transition given our semiconductor technology," noted Bartos, "but only in a limited way since we were engaged mostly in the then more lucrative defense industry." At the time, Bartos was a project engineer for missile guidance systems.

Early Development In late 1986, USS was approached by ECI Corporation to prepare a proposal for a digital converter device in the amount of 10,000 units. The proposed unit price was $55. According to a USS executive, "A $550,000 project was relatively small potatoes, but we had excess capacity and available PPB funds. There was a general belief that we could get a footprint in the market. Moreover, technology and production synergies were present with two other programs. All three programs would benefit from the shared experience in design and engineering."

By mid-1987, it became apparent to USS officials that the facsimile market would double in unit volume in 1988. Adrian Bartos was assigned responsibility for the Facsimile Technology Program in late 1987. His assignment was to pursue rather than wait for business from facsimile machine producers. He sought and received PPB funding for design, engineering, marketing, and production support. It was immediately apparent to him after calling on some 15 facsimile machine producers that cost requirements imposed by these increasingly cost-conscious firms would stretch USS's Cost-Centered Design and Manufacturing policy. The CCDM policy required that a product be designed from the start to achieve specific performance, cost, and profit goals. In practice, this meant that design activities would focus on efforts to lower material and labor content so as to reduce the product cost necessary to perform a function.

The general guide used by USS in charting cost reductions was the learning (or experience) curve phenomenon, which is described in the appendix to this case. In effect, Bartos hoped that he could realize a 20 percent reduction in the cumulative average product labor cost per unit each time volume doubled for a new design. Similar curves would be developed for each proposal to facsimile machine producers and would reflect USS's ability to economize on material and labor content for each succeeding generation of digital converter devices. Bartos realized, however, that a practical limit existed to how much he could reduce overall costs.

Building the Business In 1988, Bartos received a call from an AMEX Electronics executive requesting that he produce a digital converter device for them. This proposal included a bid price of $45. In late February, AMEX Electronics placed a confirmed order for 50,000 units. "Suddenly we were a profitable $2 million-plus business," said Bartos.

Bartos received a call from Mexus, Inc., a Japanese firm, on November 28, 1988, asking for a proposal. A new proposal was developed to Mexus's specifications, and a price of $36 per unit was bid. The difference in the ECI, AMEX Electronics, and Mexus prices arose from manufacturing cost savings due to order size (75,000 per year for Mexus) and different product specifications, which included "off-the-shelf technology," according to Bartos.

During this period Bartos consolidated and generated a variety of data pertaining to the facsimile machine market for the purpose of assessing USS's potential market position and identifying possible areas of product superiority and of synergy with the company's other product development efforts. These data would serve as inputs for his PPB funding requests and preparation of financial, marketing, and production plans. It was also during this time that Bartos and his staff were recognized for their design work by the USS Engineering Excellence Committee. The recognition formally acknowledged their contributions to related programs, which had demonstrable effects on lowering costs.

On February 26, 1989, Bartos was notified that Mexus accepted his proposal and bid price, provided the delivery time could be shortened, which was agreed to. During the remaining spring months, Bartos directed an increasing amount of his time toward designing second-generation digital converter devices for USS customers and managing the production and delivery of first-generation devices. Time was also spent preparing PPB funding and planning schedules, interacting with customer engineering staffs, and making presentations to prospective buyers along with USS technical salespeople. During this period, Bartos submitted proposals to two other facsimile machine producers. However, neither proposal was accepted.

Mexus Second-Generation Bid On November 10, 1989, Bartos was asked to bid on a more sophisticated second-generation digital converter device for Mexus. Given the nature of the bid, including customized specifications, quantity (150,000 units), and delivery time, Bartos proposed a price of $44 (see the price-cost schedule in Exhibit 4 and supplementary material). Shortly thereafter, Bartos was advised that the competitive bid level was $42 per unit, which he met after a lengthy discussion with his group vice president and members of his staff. Then, at 5:00 P.M. on January 7, 1990, Bartos was informed that USS had been underbid by a competitor at a price of $37. He met with his staff and group vice president to discuss their options.

Bartos had forecasted an 80 percent labor learning curve for his bid, as shown in Exhibit 4. The labor estimate for the first 1,000 units was about 1.75 hours/unit, but this cumulative average time would decrease to about 0.35 hour/unit at 150,000 units. The cumulative average time at 75,000 units was 0.44 hour/unit. That is, one-half of the unit volume would require more than 0.44 hour/unit to build, and one-half would require less. These labor hour estimates also included time for testing.

Also shown in Exhibit 4 is a 90 percent labor learning curve corresponding to the doubling of unit volume from 150,000 units to 300,000 units without redesign and major change to the configuration. Cumulative average labor hours/unit for 300,000 units would be 0.314 with the midpoint being approximately 0.33 hour/unit at the 225,000th unit produced.

Bartos did not forecast reductions in material or yield cost, since he did not foresee an interim design change that would be fruitful in the short run. Furthermore, labor cost/unit reductions, assuming that he would bid for an additional 150,000 second-generation digital converter devices within the near future, did not look promising.

Overshadowing the entire situation was the question of whether the competitor was also forecasting prices and costs on an 80 percent labor learning curve. This factor would be critical if volume doubled again for the Mexus account.

Bartos was also plagued by other considerations that emerged in his staff meeting. First, the future of cumulative facsimile unit sales volume remained a question. Even though industry forecasters were projecting a 36 percent increase in unit volume for 1990 and another 16 percent increase in 1991, at issue was the market share that Mexus would capture. According to one staff member, "Assuming that our device is used in all units sold by Mexus in 1990, then Mexus is roughly pro-jecting a 1990 market share of 8 percent. This seems high, since Mexus is not one of the top fax machine marketers in market share." Bartos believed that Mexus was using multiple sources and that all Mexus facsimile machine models did contain USS or similar types of digital converter devices. He reminded his staff that the facsimile market was still in flux and Murata, for example, catapulted itself from tenth place in market share in 1985 to second place in 1988 and 1989 on the basis of an aggressive marketing effort. Bartos's contacts with Mexus executives indicated that Mexus had ambitious growth goals, particularly in the low-end and mid-range market segments, where it focused its sales, promotion, and distribution effort.

EXHIBIT 4

U.S. SemiCon Corporation's Second-Generation Bid Price and Cost Estimate for the Digital Converter Device for Mexus, Inc.

Cost and Price Calculation

$26.50   Yielded material cost
  6.36   Labor cost (0.44 hour/unit @ $14.45/hour)

$32.86   Total material, labor, and direct overhead or "manufactured cost"

 11.14   25% gross margin approximation

$44.00   Unit selling price at unit volume of 150,000

Estimated Labor Learning Curve for Second-Generation Digital Converter Device

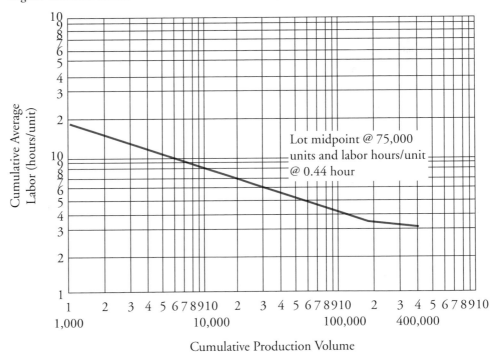

Cumulative Production Volume

Note: 0.44 hour = lot midpoint of the 150,000-unit lot; $14.45 = hourly rate including factory overhead.

A second consideration dealt with delivery. Even if USS was awarded the contract, a possibility existed that all 150,000 units would not be shipped, since contingencies provided that Mexus could stop shipment at any time. In other words, as few as 50,000 to 75,000 units could be shipped and the order stopped. "This hasn't happened to us yet," said Bartos. "However, it has happened to others, and the probability increases as the order size increases," added the group vice president.

Profitability was a third consideration. USS policy held that every project must achieve the corporate net profit before tax objective (8.9 percent of net sales). Exceptions to this policy would be approved provided that (1) extraordinary short-run factors necessitated such action and (2) long-term growth potential and profitability could be demonstrated, based on competitive conditions.

The strategic capability and intent of the competitor proposing the $37 bid was a fourth consideration. Bartos was confident that the competitor was not a major semiconductor firm, such as Texas Instruments, Motorola, or National Semiconductor, but he did not know its identity. "My guess is that it's a niche player like us specializing in one or two electronic components or devices," Bartos said. "It may be buying the business, have a cost advantage, or be prepared to accept lower profitability."

At 9:00 P.M. on January 7, the meeting adjourned. The group vice president asked that Bartos and his staff prepare a recommendation with supporting documentation for his review the next morning.

APPENDIX

It has been observed in many industries and for a variety of products that the average manufacturing cost per unit declines by a constant percentage with every doubling of cumulative production output. This phenomenon is called the experience, or learning, effect and results from a variety of sources. Seven such factors are described below:

1. *Labor efficiency.* As workers repeat a particular production task, they become more dexterous and learn improvements and shortcuts that increase their collective efficiency. The greater the number of worker-based operations, the greater the amount of learning that can accrue from experience. This learning effect may go beyond the labor directly involved in manufacturing. Maintenance personnel, supervisors, and persons in other line and staff manufacturing positions also increase their productivity, as do people in marketing, sales, administration, and other functions.

2. *Work specialization and methods improvements.* Specialization increases worker proficiency at a given task. For instance, when two workers who formerly did both parts of a two-stage operation each specialize in a single stage, they tend to become more efficient in performing the more specialized task. Redesigning work operation methods can also result in greater efficiency.

3. *New production processes.* Process innovations and improvements can be an important source of cost reductions. The semiconductor industry, for instance, achieves learning effects from improved production technology by devoting a large percentage of its research and development effort to process improvements.

4. *Getting better performance from production equipment.* When first designed, a piece of production equipment may have a conservatively rated output. Experience may reveal innovative ways of increasing its output.

5. *Changes in the resource mix.* As experience accumulates, a producer can often incorporate different or less expensive resources in the operation. For instance, less skilled (lower-cost) workers can replace skilled (higher-cost) workers, or automation can replace labor.

6. *Product standardization.* Standardization allows the replication of tasks necessary for worker learning. Even when flexibility and/or a wider product line are important marketing considerations, standardization can be achieved by modularization. For example, by making just a few types of engines, transmissions, chassis, seats, and body styles, an auto manufacturer can achieve experience effects arising from standardization of each part. These parts in turn can be assembled into a wide variety of models.

7. *Product redesign.* As experience is gained with a product, both the manufacturer and customers gain a clearer understanding of its performance requirements. This understanding allows the product to be redesigned to conserve material, to incorporate greater efficiency in its manufacture, and to substitute less costly materials and resources for more costly ones, while at the same time improving performance. The new designs that substitute plastic, synthetic fiber, and rubber for leather in ski boots are examples of this.

The influence of these factors has been seen in reduced prices for many well-known products. For example, prices of CD players have decreased from over $900 when they were first produced to less than $200 today, and cellular telephones that sold for $4,000 are now priced as low as $99.

The Experience, or Learning, Effect

The experience, or learning, effect is amenable to measurement and has proven useful in projecting costs based on the doubling of cumulative unit production. An example of this phenomenon is tabulated in Exhibit 5, where the production growth rate is 20 percent per year, the original unit cost is $100, and the cost per unit is projected to decline at a constant rate of 15 percent with every doubling of cumulative volume. As can be seen, with an annual production growth rate of 20 percent, cumulative volume doubles three times in five years, and cumulative average unit cost, which was $100 for the first 1,000 units, declines to $61.41 for 8,000 units.

EXHIBIT 5

Illustration of the Experience, or Learning, Effect

Year	Annual Production	Cumulative Volume	Times Required for Doublings of Cumulative Volume	Cumulative Average Unit Cost with 15% Constant Decline
1	1,000	1,000		$100.00
			→ 1st doubling	
2	1,200	2,200	(1,000 to 2,000): 1.89 years	$ 85.00
3	1,440	3,640		
			→ 2nd doubling (2,000 to 4,000):	
4	1,728	5,368	3.22 years	$ 75.25
			→ 3rd doubling	
5	2,074	9,930	(4,000 to 8,000): 4.23 years	$ 61.41

EXHIBIT   6

Representations of the Experience, or Learning, Curve

A. A Typical 85 Percent Curve Displayed on Linear Scales

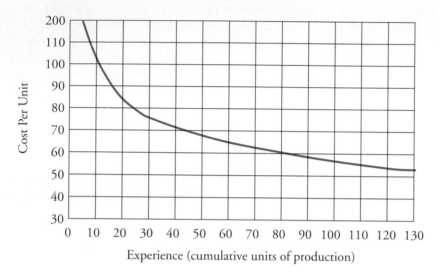

B. A Typical 85 Percent Curve Displayed on Logarithmic Scales

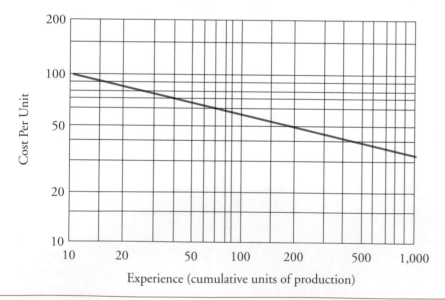

In practice, the learning effect is represented by a curve. Specifically, these curves are charted by plotting cost per unit on a vertical axis and cumulative production volume on a horizontal axle. Thus, if unit cost declines by 15 percent each time the cumulative volume of production doubles, an 85 percent curve is indicated. This means that the cumulative average cost of the 100 units produced will be about 85 percent of the cost to produce 50 units, and 200 units will be about 85 percent of the cost to produce 100 units, and so forth. An 85 percent curve is shown in Exhibit 6. Learning curves are typically drawn on double log paper, in which both the horizontal and vertical axes are charted on a logarithmic scale. When presented in this manner, the "curve" appears as a straight line, also shown in Exhibit 6. The labor learning curve shown in the case (Exhibit 4) is plotted on a logarithmic scale.

Strategic Implications

The strategic implications of the experience, or learning, curve arise from the slope of the curve and the rate of accumulation of experience. Specifically,

Slope of the curve: All things being equal, a firm that fails to achieve cost reductions along an experience or learning curve slope that are at least equivalent to those achieved by its competitors will eventually find itself at a competitive cost disadvantage.

Rate of experience accumulation: All things being equal, a firm that fails to accumulate experience at least as rapidly as its competitors will find itself at a competitive cost disadvantage.

The strategic message of the learning curve is straightforward. The major-volume firm in a product market has the greatest potential for the lowest unit costs and largest profits due to cumulative production volume. As costs decline, opportunities for price reductions become available and give the firm a lower price-cost advantage that is difficult for competitors (with little cumulative volume) to match and remain profitable. Since experience, or learning, effects are most likely to occur in rapidly growing markets, frequent doubling of cumulative volume is most likely to be observed during the early stages of the product life cycle (late introductory and growth stages). These effects are less likely to be observed in later stages of the product life cycle, when unit sales increase at decreasing rates or actually decline.

Procter and Gamble Inc.
Downy Enviro-Park

In February 1989, Grad Schnurr, the brand manager for Downy fabric softener at Procter and Gamble Inc., needed to work fast to develop plans to launch a refill pouch called the Enviro-Pak for the Downy product line. The introduction of such packaging would result in a reduction in the solid waste created by the Downy fabric softener. Several key decisions had to be made regarding pricing and promotion. Senior management had a keen interest in this project, especially after seeing the success of the Green Product line introduced by Loblaws, the largest supermarket chain in Canada. The Green Product line consists of products that are either environmentally friendly or healthy for the body. Some of the products in the line are phosphate-free laundry detergent, low-acid coffee, and biodegradable garbage bags. The environment was clearly a significant concern to consumers, and Procter and Gamble Inc. wanted to be the first major consumer goods company in the market with a response.

COMPANY HISTORY

Procter and Gamble (P&G) was founded in Cincinnati, Ohio, in 1837 when William Procter, a candlemaker, and James Gamble, a soap maker, formed a partnership that grew to become a leading international company. By 1988, P&G was selling more than 160 brands in 140 countries and was a global leader in household cleaning, health care, personal care, and food product markets. Total sales exceeded $20 billion in 1988. P&G's leading brands include Tide laundry detergent, Pampers diapers, Ivory soap, Downy fabric softener, Crest toothpaste, Crisco oil, Duncan Hines baking mixes, and Vicks cold care products.

Procter and Gamble Inc. opened its first Canadian plant in 1915 in Hamilton, Ontario. It subsequently added three manufacturing sites in Belleville and Brockville, Ontario, and Pointe Claire, Quebec. P&G Inc. experienced substantial growth during the 1980s, with net sales doubling between 1978 and 1988; 1988 sales exceeded $1.2 billion, with net income of $78.9 million.

P&G Inc. was organized into four divisions: Laundry and Cleaning Products, Health and Beauty Care, Food, and Paper Products. In an effort to push down decision making and increase responsiveness to the market, the company was organized on a category basis within each division (for example, Fabric Softeners within the Laundry and Cleaning Products division). Each category had managers from Marketing, Finance, Sales, Product Supply, and Marketing Research assigned to it.

This case was written by Janet Lahey, MBA student, and Chris Lane under the supervision of Professor Adrian B. Ryans, of the University of Western Ontario, as a basis for class discussion rather than to indicate either effective or ineffective handling of an administrative situation. Certain nonpublic data in this case have been disguised to protect proprietary information. Copyright © 1990 by the University of Western Ontario. Used with permission.

Marketing was organized on a brand management basis, with a brand manager and one or two assistant managers concentrating on the business of one product/brand, such as Tide detergent or Downy fabric softener. Promotions and projects within a brand were executed by business teams, which involved the other functional managers responsible for the category. During significant new product launches or promotions, these teams would meet every three or four weeks to review the critical path and discuss their progress.

DOWNY

Downy was a popular liquid fabric softener used in the washing machine to soften clothes, remove static from clothes, and leave them with a fresh scent. In early 1989, regular Downy was being sold in 1-liter, 1.5-liter, and 3-liter plastic jugs, and concentrated Downy was being sold in 500-milliliter, 1-liter, and 2-liter sizes. Overall, Downy was the number two brand in Canada in the liquid fabric softener category with a 12 percent share of the market. Its major competition consisted of a similar product called Fleecy, manufactured by Colgate-Palmolive, as well as fabric softener dryer sheets, which Procter and Gamble produced. There was little growth in this market segment, and competition usually took place on a price or incremental improvement (scent, efficacy) basis.

Pricing

The three-liter bottle of Downy generated a contribution margin of 23 percent and was sold directly to the retail trade at $5.99. The average retail shelf price of $7.30 reflected typical retail trade margin levels of 18 percent (calculated on retail price). When Downy was on deal, the retail shelf price would fall to about $5.99 (retailers would still receive an 18 percent margin on the deal price). Downy appeared to be priced at a premium versus its competition, but on a price-per-use basis was on par with the major competitor.

Promotion

The 1989 Downy marketing plan included several promotions and incentives at both the consumer and trade levels. Events were scheduled to take place approximately every two months and would generally last four weeks. Approximately 70 percent of Downy was sold to the retail trade on deal.

ENVIRONMENTAL CONCERN

In 1989, the environment had become a significant issue to Canadian consumers. David Nichols of Loblaws gained celebrity status when he launched an innovative line of Green Products, which were claimed to be "environmentally friendly." In Ontario alone, Loblaws sold more than $5 million of Green Products. It was clear that these products had a wide appeal. Business magazines were running articles concerning environmental management on a regular basis. One environmental concern, which was the primary focus of several lobby groups and which could be most readily addressed by consumers, was solid waste.

Landfill sites in urban communities like Toronto were projected to be full by the mid-1990s. This posed a serious problem for government officials in determining locations for new sites, since "NIMBY" (not in my back yard) protests by the residents close to proposed landfill locations were increasingly effective. People were becoming aware of how much solid waste was being buried in the ground. As a result, some communities had started up "Blue Box" curbside recycling programs, which were run by the government and partially funded by industry. Household residents stored particular types of waste, such as newspapers, soft drink bottles, and tin cans, in blue plastic boxes which were collected and sorted by municipal operators. The overwhelming success of these programs, with participation rates over 80 percent, indicated that citizens were highly concerned about protecting their environment and were willing to make an effort to reduce the amount of solid waste being sent to landfill sites.

Government Action

The Ontario government had legislated new regulations for the soft drink industry, under the Environmental Protection Act, requiring specific percentages of recyclable bottles. It had also stated a goal of a 25 percent reduction in the use of landfill sites by 1992. Other industries were speculating that the provincial government would soon require funding from them for recycling programs and were aware that legislation similar to that for the soft drink industry might also follow. Ontario was seen to be the leading province in dealing with environmental issues. Other provinces were expected to introduce similar programs after they had been proven in Ontario.

Procter and Gamble's Environmental Policy

P&G Inc. considered itself to be a community leader in terms of being a responsible business organization that contributed to the well-being of the environment. By 1989 it had already undertaken a number of environmental initiatives including:

1. Using recycled materials for P&G product cartons and shipping containers (laundry detergent cartons were made of 100 percent recycled paper)
2. Introducing a paper recycling program in the corporate head office
3. Eliminating heavy metals from printing inks to facilitate safer incineration

P&G Inc.'s efforts in the solid waste area were a major responsibility of a division's General Manager and Director of Product Development. The corporate policy followed the generally accepted ranking of waste management priorities: source reduction, reuse, and recycling.

EUROPEAN ENVIRO-PAKS

In early 1989, Procter and Gamble Inc. was receiving consumer complaints regarding solid waste at an increasing rate. Calls about the environment had doubled in frequency over the past few months. P&G subsidiaries in Germany, Switzerland, and France had recently introduced "stand-up" pouches as refills for previously purchased bottles of Downy. These pouches (a type of Enviro-Pak) significantly reduced the solid waste generated by the Downy product. Grad Schnurr decided to review the results of the European launches to help him develop a strategy for a Canadian introduction (see Exhibit 1).

EXHIBIT   1

European Enviro-Pak Results

	Market Share of Downy Enviro-Pak	*Enviro-Pak Share of Downy Business*
Germany	11.2%	26%
France	2.3	14
Switzerland	4.1	19
Austria	3.1	31
Spain	0.7	12
Italy	0.7	8

Source: Company records.

Product

A number of market research studies conducted in Europe indicated that the success of the pouch could be attributed primarily to its convenience and cost relative to the bottled Downy. Packages that reduced the amount of solid waste could generate further savings to German consumers, who were faced with financial penalties for excess garbage disposal.

Promotion

In Germany, the Downy pouch had been launched with substantial consumer and trade promotions including in-store refill demonstrations and give-aways, trade samples followed by telephone calls for orders, shopping bag advertising, trade incentives for display, and direct delivery of display pallets.

Pricing

The most popular package size for Downy in Europe was a four-liter bottle. The European pouch had been originally priced at a 5 percent discount off the price of this bottled version, with very disappointing repurchase results. The problem stemmed from the promotional price of the four-liter bottle, which often made the consumer price of the pouch more expensive. The trade was not reducing the pouch prices because it wished to retain the good margins they provided. P&G conducted a test market in one city with the pouch priced at a 15 percent discount off the bottle on a per-usage basis. This resulted in a significant volume improvement, with the pouch reaching a market share of 17 percent versus its previous share of 10 percent.

Share Results and Cannibalization

The pouch had been introduced in Germany and had achieved an 11 percent market share (see Exhibit 1). Although this was accompanied by a drop in the share of the partner four-liter size, the overall market share for Downy grew, taking Downy's share from 20 percent to 25 percent after the pouch was launched. Schnurr wondered whether the same effect would occur in Canada, and what implications this had for the pricing of the pouch. Recent sales data and forecasts for the spring of 1989 for regular Downy are shown in Exhibit 2.

EXHIBIT   2

Downy Sales to the Trade in Canada

	Shipments (Thousands of Cases)[a]	Market Share
July 1988	79	
August 1988	72	13.8%
September 1988	91	
October 1988	78	12.6
November 1988	95	
December 1988	69	12.5
January 1989	139	
February 1989	96	12.6
March 1989[b]	89	
April 1989[b]	70	14.2
May 1989[b]	73	
June 1989[b]	100	11.8

[a]Three-liter Downy, packed six bottles to a case.
[b]Forecast.
Source: Company records.

THE DOWNY ENVIRO-PAK

The Downy Enviro-Pak provided a significant reduction in solid waste after use, containing 85 percent less plastic than the three-liter bottle it would refill. The pouch was similar to a plastic milk bag, but had a gusseted bottom so it could stand upright on the shelf (see Exhibit 3). A consumer would cut the corner of the pouch off and then pour the product through a funnel into an empty three-liter bottle. He or she would then add two liters of water, shake the bottle, and have three liters of fabric softener ready for use.

Schnurr thought the Downy Enviro-Pak offered benefits for both consumers and the trade. Consumers would be attracted to the product for two reasons. First, by using the Enviro-Pak, they would be reducing the amount of household solid waste they generated. Second, the price could be lower than that of the regular bottle. Schnurr recognized that the pouch represented a small inconvenience to consumers, as they had to do some preparation before they could use the product. Some consumers would also be concerned about spillage when they were refilling the bottle. These factors would need to be addressed through the Enviro-Pak's price and promotion plan.

The trade would also benefit in two ways. The pouches would attract environmentally conscious shoppers to stores, away from competitors that did not carry such products. Also, the unique design of the Enviro-Pak provided more efficient use of space than did the bottled Downy. This second feature would provide decreased retailer handling and inventory costs.

EXHIBIT 3

Proposed Package for Downy

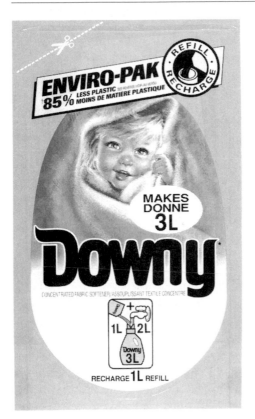
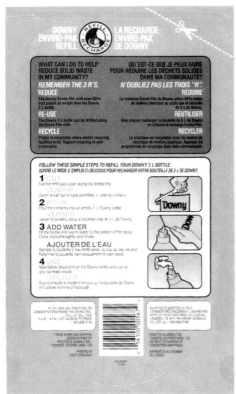

Competitive Activity

Downy's three major competitors had also launched refill versions in Europe. No such activity had taken place in North America, but Canada would be a logical target for the next expansion, given the growing concern about the environment. However, Schnurr was unsure as to how applicable the German market results would be in predicting the response to the new package in Canada.

The logistics of the product launch also remained to be worked out. Given the likelihood of competitive activity in developing a more environmentally friendly fabric softener package, Schnurr wasn't sure whether he should conduct a test market first or launch the Enviro-Pak in parts of Canada immediately. This decision was further complicated by trade rumors that Colgate-Palmolive was about to launch an environmental package. It would be much tougher trying to get retailers to list the Enviro-Paks if they already carried competitive versions. The brand that was able to introduce its environmental package first would gain an enviable reputation as a leading force in fighting the war on solid waste.

Manufacturing Issues

The manufacturing business team members estimated that their production schedule could support an August launch in Ontario and Quebec. These provinces were chosen for a number of reasons, including rising environmental awareness, potential volume, distribution time from plant, and competitive activity. The Hamilton plant estimated that it would take it an additional four months to get enough volume to fill the distribution pipeline and support ongoing shipments for the rest of the country. The annual fixed cost of a packing line capable of producing 300,000 cases annually of Enviro-Paks was estimated at $600,000.[1]

Given the unique nature of this product, there was a high degree of uncertainty about the shipment forecasts. The last thing Grad Schnurr wanted was to have an overwhelming response to the Enviro-Pak, with orders that P&G could not fill due to lack of supply.

Pricing

Schnurr knew it would be vital to maintain the pouch price below the comparable price of the 1.5-liter and 3-liter bottles. The pouch design provided a significant savings in the cost of goods sold. Its total delivered (variable) cost was 10 percent less than that of the three-liter bottle. Schnurr had to consider the total contribution of the brand and how much of this saving should be passed on to the trade and consumers. He was considering two options:

1. *An everyday low retail price ($6.29).* This option would give the Enviro-Pak a discount versus the regular price of the 3-liter size ($7.30), using a cost-per-use comparison. The price to retailers would be either $5.16 or $4.74, depending on whether they were offered an 18 percent or 25 percent margin. The higher margin would help assure fast acceptance, as retailers traditionally received 18 percent margins on the Downy bottle. To gain additional retailer support during the introductory period, retailers would be given a purchase allowance of $1.00 off each case. This amounted to an $.08 saving per bottle.

   In this scenario, there would be no special promotion or discount periods when the regular Downy product was on deal. One concern Schnurr had with this option was that the Enviro-Pak would be priced above the 3-liter bottles when the bottles were featured on promotion at $5.99.

2. *A moderately lower retail price ($7.00), with featuring.* Under this scenario, the trade would be offered discount pricing for the Enviro-Pak coinciding with the regular Downy promotion schedule. The regular retail trade price would be $5.74, while the promotional offers would provide for a 20 percent discount, or a price of $4.59 for the trade and $5.60 for consumers.

Promotion

Grad Schnurr had put together a preliminary promotion plan, including trade discounts and television, radio, and print advertising. He was also considering using displayable shipping containers. These containers enabled retailers to build a dis-

---

[1]Each case would contain 12 Enviro-Paks.

play by cutting off the top portion of each container and stacking them at aisle ends. The incremental cost of this style of container would be $0.95 per case.

Given the unique environmental properties of the Downy Enviro-Pak, the launch would need some extra consideration to ensure that the product was accepted by environmental groups, as well as the trade and consumers. This was evident in the problems Loblaws had faced when the environmental value of some of its Green Products was disputed by environmental groups such as Pollution Probe and Friends of the Earth. Schnurr wanted to make sure that consumers accepted the Enviro-Pak as a valid environmental package without giving the impression that P&G was exploiting this concern for the sake of profits. He wondered how to go about this tactical issue. Should some of the environmental lobby groups be consulted before the launch? What if they did not support the idea? Would early consultation risk the security of the launch plans? Schnurr needed to consult with Barry Smith, P&G Inc.'s Public Relations Manager, to start planning their approach.

Warner-Lambert Ireland
Niconil

Declan Dixon, director of marketing for Warner-Lambert Ireland (WLI), examined two very different sales forecasts as he considered the upcoming launch of Niconil®, scheduled for January 1990. Niconil was an innovative new product that promised to help the thousands of smokers who attempted to quit smoking each year. More commonly known simply as "the patch," Niconil was a transdermal skin patch that gradually released nicotine into the bloodstream to alleviate the physical symptoms of nicotine withdrawal.

Now in October of 1989, Dixon and his staff had to decide several key aspects of the product launch. There were different opinions about how Niconil should be priced and in what quantities it would sell. Pricing decisions would directly impact product profitability as well as sales volume, and accurate sales forecasts were vital to planning adequate production capacity. Finally, the product team needed to reach consensus on the Niconil communications campaign to meet advertising deadlines and to ensure an integrated product launch.

COMPANY BACKGROUND

Warner-Lambert was an international pharmaceutical and consumer products company with over $4 billion in worldwide revenues expected in 1989. Warner-Lambert consumer products (50 percent of worldwide sales) included such brands as Dentyne chewing gum, Listerine mouth wash, and Hall's cough drops. Its pharmaceutical products, marketed through the Parke Davis Division, included drugs for treating a wide variety of ailments, including heart disease and bronchial disorders.

Warner-Lambert's Irish subsidiary was expected to generate £30 million in sales revenues in 1989:[1] £22 million from exports of manufactured products to other Warner-Lambert subsidiaries in Europe and £4 million each from pharmaceutical and consumer products sales within Ireland. The Irish drug market was estimated at £155 million (in manufacturer sales) in 1989. Warner-Lambert was the sixteenth-largest pharmaceutical company in worldwide revenues; in Ireland, it ranked sixth.

Dixon was confident that WLI's position in the Irish market would ensure market acceptance of Niconil. The Parke Davis Division had launched two new drugs successfully within the past nine months: Dilzem, a treatment for heart disease, and

---

[1]In 1989, one Irish pound was equivalent to US$1.58.

Research Associate Susan P. Smith prepared this case under the supervision of Professor John A. Quelch as the basis for class discussion rather than to illustrate either effective or ineffective handling of an administrative situation. Copyright © 1992 by the President and Fellows of Harvard College. No part of this publication may be reproduced, stored in a retrieval system, used in a spreadsheet, or transmitted in any form or by any means—electronic, mechanical, photocopying, recording, or otherwise—without the permission of Harvard Business School. Used with permission.

Accupro, a blood pressure medication. The momentum was expected to continue. The Irish market would be the first country launch for Niconil and thus serve as a test market for all of Warner-Lambert. The companywide significance of the Niconil launch was not lost on Dixon as he pondered the marketing decisions before him.

SMOKING IN THE REPUBLIC OF IRELAND

Almost £600 million would be spent by Irish smokers on 300 million packs of cigarettes in 1989; this included government revenues from the tobacco sales tax of £441 million. Of 3.5 million Irish citizens, 30 percent of the 2.5 million adults smoked cigarettes (compared with 40 percent of adults in continental Europe and 20 percent in the United States).[2] The number of smokers in Ireland had peaked in the late 1970s and had been declining steadily since. Table A presents data from a 1989 survey that WLI had commissioned of a demographically balanced sample of 1,400 randomly chosen Irish adults. Table B shows the numbers of cigarettes smoked by Irish smokers; the average was 16.5 cigarettes.

Media coverage on the dangers of smoking, anti-smoking campaigns from public health organizations such as the Irish Cancer Society, and a mounting array of legislation restricting tobacco advertising put pressure on Irish smokers to quit. Promotional discounts and coupons for tobacco products were prohibited, and to-

TABLE   A

Incidence of Cigarette Smoking in Ireland, 1988–1989

Of adult population (16 and over)	30%	(100%)
By Gender		
Men	32	(50)
Women	27	(50)
By Age		
16–24	27	(17)
25–34	38	(14)
35–44	29	(12)
45–54	29	(9)
55+	27	(19)
By Occupation		
White collar	24	(25)
Skilled working class	33	(30)
Semi- and unskilled	38	(29)
Farming	23	(17)

Note. To be read (for example): 27 percent of Irish citizens aged 16–24 smoked, and this age group represented 17 percent of the population.

---

[2]*Adults* were defined as those over the age of 15, and *smokers* as those who smoked at least one cigarette per day.

TABLE   B

Number of Cigarettes Smoked Daily in Ireland (Based on 400 Smokers in a 1989 Survey of 1,400 Citizens)

More than 20	16%
15–20	42
10–14	23
5–9	12
Less than 5	4
Unsure	3

bacco advertising was banned not only on television and radio but also on billboards. Print advertising was allowed only if 10 percent of the ad space was devoted to warnings on the health risks of smoking. Exhibit 1 shows a sample cigarette advertisement from an Irish magazine.

SMOKING AS AN ADDICTION

Cigarettes and other forms of tobacco contained nicotine, a substance that induced addictive behavior. Smokers first developed a tolerance for nicotine and then, over time, needed to increase cigarette consumption to maintain a steady, elevated blood level of nicotine. Smokers became progressively dependent on nicotine and suffered withdrawal symptoms if they stopped smoking. A craving for tobacco was characterized by physical symptoms such as decreased heart rate and a drop in blood pressure, and later could include symptoms like faintness, headaches, cold sweats, intestinal cramps, nausea, and vomiting. The smoking habit also had a psychological component stemming from the ritualistic aspects of smoking behavior, such as smoking after meals or in times of stress.

Since the 1950s, the ill effects of smoking had been researched and identified. Smoking was widely recognized as posing a serious health threat. While nicotine was the substance within the cigarette that caused addiction, it was the tar accompanying the nicotine that made smoking so dangerous. Specifically, smoking was a primary risk factor for ischaemic heart disease, lung cancer, and chronic pulmonary diseases. Other potential dangers resulting from prolonged smoking included bronchitis, emphysema, chronic sinusitis, peptic ulcer disease, and for pregnant women, damage to the fetus.

Once smoking was recognized as a health risk, the development and use of a variety of smoking cessation techniques began. In *aversion therapy*, the smoker was discouraged from smoking by pairing an aversive event such as electric shock or a nausea-inducing agent with the smoking behavior, in an attempt to break the cycle of gratification. While aversion therapy was successful in the short-term, it did not prove a lasting solution, as the old smoking behavior would often be resumed. Aversion therapy was now used infrequently. *Behavioral self-monitoring* required the smoker to develop an awareness of the stimuli that triggered the desire to smoke and then to systematically eliminate the smoking behavior in specific situations by neutralizing those stimuli. For example, the smoker could learn to avoid particular situations or to adopt a replacement activity such as chewing gum. This method was

EXHIBIT 1

Cigarette Advertisement from an Irish Magazine

successful in some cases but demanded a high degree of self-control. While behavioral methods were useful in addressing the psychological component of smoking addiction, they did not address the physical aspect of nicotine addiction that proved an insurmountable obstacle to many who attempted to quit.

NICONIL

Warner-Lambert's Niconil would be the first product to offer a complete solution for smoking cessation addressing both the physical and psychological aspects of nicotine addiction. The physical product was a circular adhesive patch, 2.5 inches in diameter and containing 30 mg of nicotine gel. Each patch was individually wrapped in a sealed, tear-resistant packet. The patch was applied to the skin, usually on the upper arm, and the nicotine was absorbed into the bloodstream to produce a steady level of nicotine that blunted the smoker's physical craving. Thirty milligrams of nicotine provided the equivalent of 20 cigarettes, without the cigarettes' damaging tar. A single patch was applied once a day every morning for two to six weeks, depending on the smoker. The average smoker was able to quit successfully (abstaining from cigarettes for a period of six months or longer) after three to four weeks.

In clinical trials, the Niconil patch alone had proven effective in helping smokers to quit. A WLI study showed that 47.5 percent of subjects using the nicotine patch abstained from smoking for a period of three months or longer versus 15 percent for subjects using a placebo patch. Among the remaining 52.5 percent who did not stop completely, there was a marked reduction in the number of cigarettes smoked. A similar study in the United States demonstrated an abstinence rate of 31.5 percent with the Niconil patch versus 14 percent for those with a placebo patch. The single most important success factor in Niconil effectiveness, however, was the smoker's motivation to quit. "Committed quitters" were the most likely to quit smoking successfully, using Niconil or any other smoking cessation method.

There were some side effects associated with use of the Niconil patch, including skin irritation, sleep disturbances, and nausea. Skin irritation was by far the most prevalent side effect, affecting 30 percent of patch users in one study. This skin irritation was not seen as a major obstacle to sales, as many study participants viewed their irritated skin areas as "badges of merit" that indicated their commitment to quitting smoking. WLI recommended placement of the patch on alternating skin areas to mitigate the problem. Future reformulations of the nicotine gel in the patch were expected to eliminate the problem entirely.

Niconil had been developed in 1985 by two scientists at Trinity College in Dublin working with Elan Corporation, an Irish pharmaceutical company specializing in transdermal drug delivery systems. Elan had entered into a joint venture with WLI to market other Elan transdermal products: Dilzem and Theolan, a respiratory medication. In 1987 Elan agreed to add Niconil to the joint venture. Warner-Lambert planned to market the product worldwide through its subsidiaries, with Elan earning a royalty on cost of goods sold.[3]

Ireland was the first country to approve the Niconil patch. In late 1989 the Irish National Drugs Advisory Board authorized national distribution of Niconil, but stipulated that it could be sold by prescription only. This meant that Niconil, as a prescription product, could not be advertised directly to the Irish consumer.

---

[3]A royalty of 3 percent on cost of goods sold was typical for such joint ventures.

HEALTH CARE IN IRELAND

Ireland's General Medical Service (GMS) provided health care to all Irish citizens. Sixty-four percent of the population received free hospital care through the GMS, but were required to pay for doctor's visits (which averaged £15 each), and for drugs (which were priced lower in Ireland than the average in the European Economic Community). The remaining 36 percent of the population qualified as either low-income or chronic-condition patients and received free health care through the GMS. For these patients, hospital care, doctor's visits, and many drugs were obtained without fee or co-payment. Drugs paid for by the GMS were classified as "reimbursable"; approximately 70 percent of all drugs were reimbursable in 1989. Niconil had not qualified as a reimbursable drug; although WLI was lobbying to change its status, the immediate outlook was not hopeful.[4]

SUPPORT PROGRAM

While the patch addressed the physical craving for nicotine, Dixon and his team had decided to develop a supplementary support program to address the smoker's psychological addiction. The support program included several components in a neatly packaged box which aimed to ease the smoker's personal and social dependence on cigarettes. A booklet explained how to change behavior and contained tips on quitting. Bound into the booklet was a personal "contract" on which the smoker could list his or her reasons for quitting and plans for celebrating successful abstinence. There was a diary that enabled the smoker to record patterns of smoking behavior prior to quitting and that offered inspirational suggestions for each day of the program. Finally, an audiotape included instruction in four relaxation methods which the smoker could practice in place of cigarette smoking. The relaxation exercises were narrated by Professor Anthony Clare, a well-known Irish psychiatrist who hosted a regular television program on the BBC. The tape also contained an emergency-help section to assist the individual in overcoming sudden episodes of craving. A special toll-free telephone number to WLI served as a hot line to address customer questions and problems. Sample pages from the Niconil support program are presented as Exhibit 2.

While studies had not yet measured the impact of the support program on abstinence rates, it was believed that combined use of the support program and the patch could only increase Niconil's success. It had proven necessary to package the Niconil support program separately from the patch to speed approval of the patch by the Irish National Drug Board. A combined package would have required approval of the complete program, including the audiotape, which would have prolonged the process significantly. If separate, the support program could be sold without a prescription and advertised directly to the consumer. Development of the support program had cost £3,000. WLI planned an initial production run of 10,000 units at a variable cost of £3.50 per unit.

The support program could serve a variety of purposes. Several WLI executives felt that the support program should be sold separately from the nicotine patches.

---

[4]None of the products in the smoking-cessation-aid market was reimbursable through the GMS. Reimbursable items excluded prescriptions for simple drugs such as mild painkillers and cough and cold remedies

EXHIBIT 2

Sample Pages from Niconil Support Program

The first step

Fill in the contract in your own words. Write down all the reasons that are most important to you for beating the smoking habit.

Then write down how your life will be better and more enjoyable without the smoking habit.

Finally, write down how you will reward yourself for your courage and hard work. You will deserve something very special.

Choose the day

Decide when to stop and put a ring round that date on your calendar.

Try to find a time when you are not going to be under pressure for a few days. The start of a holiday is good for two reasons. You will not have the stress of work and you will be free to change your routine.

Countdown

1. In the days leading up to your stop date see if you can get your partner or a friend to stop smoking along with you.

2. Ask a local charity to sponsor you or join a non-smoking group. Having other people to talk to who have kicked the habit can be a lifeline when your willpower gets shaky. They will know and understand what you are going through. Your doctor will be able to tell you what groups are running in your area.

3. The evening before your stop date, throw away **all** your cigarettes and get rid of your lighters and ashtrays. You will not need them again.

4. Read over your smoker's diary entries. Know your habit.
   • What are the most dangerous times?
   • Where are the most dangerous places?
   • What are the most dangerous situations?
   • Who do I usually smoke with?

CONTRACT

1. I,...,
   **HAVE STOPPED SMOKING BECAUSE
   I WANT:**

2. **MY LIFE WILL BE BETTER WHEN I AM FREE
   OF SMOKING BECAUSE:**

3. **AFTER BEATING SMOKING FOR A MONTH
   I WILL CELEBRATE BY:**

SIGNED:

DATE:

COUNT DOWN TO D-DAY — **DAY 1**

Cigarette	Time of day?	Where were you?	Who were you with?	What were you doing?	How did you feel?
1					
2					
3					
4					
5					

WEEK ONE   *THE WINNER'S DIARY*

DAY

1. Today is the greatest challenge. If you succeed today, tomorrow will be easier. You can do it.

2. Well done. The first 24 hours are over. Your lungs have had their first real rest for years.

3. Remember: smoking is for losers. If you find yourself getting tense, use your relaxation tape.

4. Read your contract again. See how much better life is getting now that you are freeing yourself from this unpleasant addiction.

5. Your body says "thank you". It's feeling fitter already.

6. Don't forget to distract yourself at key cigarette times.

7. Well done. You're through your first week. Give yourself a treat. Go out for a meal or buy yourself something you've always wanted.

They considered the support program a stand-alone product that could realize substantial revenues on its own, as well as generating sales of the Niconil patches. Supporting this position, a pricing study completed in 1989 found that the highest mean price volunteered for a 14-day supply of the patches and the support program combined was £27.50, and for the patches alone, £22.00. The highest mean price for the support program alone was £8.50, suggesting a relatively high perceived utility of this component among potential consumers. There was a risk, however, that consumers might purchase the Niconil support program *instead* of the patches, or as an accompaniment to other smoking cessation products—thus limiting sales of the Niconil patches.

Another group of executives saw the support program as a value-added point of difference that could stimulate Niconil patch sales. This group favored wide distribution of the support programs, free of charge, to potential Niconil customers. A third group of WLI executives argued that the support program was an integral component of the Niconil product which would enhance the total package by addressing the psychological aspects of nicotine addiction and improve the product's success rate, thereby increasing its sales potential. As such, these executives believed that the support program should be passed on only to those purchasing Niconil patches, at no additional cost.

Two options, not necessarily mutually exclusive, were under consideration for the distribution of the support programs. One option was to distribute them through doctors prescribing Niconil. A doctor could present the program to the patient during the office visit as he or she issued the Niconil prescription, reinforcing the counseling role of the doctor in the Niconil treatment. Supplying the GPs with support programs could also serve to promote Niconil in the medical community. A second option was to distribute the support programs through the pharmacies, where customers could receive the support programs when they purchased the Niconil patches. A disadvantage of this option was that a customer might receive additional support programs each time he or she purchased another package of Niconil. However, these duplicates might be passed on to other potential consumers and thus become an informal advertising vehicle for Niconil.

PRICING

Because all potential Niconil customers would pay for the product personally, pricing was a critical component of the Niconil marketing strategy. Management debated how many patches to include in a single package and at what price to sell each package. In test trials, the average smoker succeeded in quitting with Niconil in three to four weeks (for example, 21 to 28 patches); others needed as long as six weeks.[5]

As Niconil was essentially a tobacco substitute, cigarettes provided a logical model for considering various packaging and pricing options. The average Irish smoker purchased a pack of cigarettes daily, often when buying the morning newspaper. Fewer than 5 percent of all cigarettes were sold in cartons.[6] Because the Irish smoker rarely purchased a multi-week cigarette supply at once, he or she was thought likely to compare the cost of cigarette purchases with the cost of a multi-week sup-

---

[5]Smokers were advised not to use the patch on a regular basis beyond three months. If still unsuccessful in quitting, they could resume use of the patch after stopping for at least a month.

[6]A carton of cigarettes contained 20 individual packs of cigarettes; each pack contained 20 cigarettes.

ply of Niconil. WLI thus favored packaging just a seven-day supply of patches in each unit. However, Warner-Lambert subsidiaries in continental Europe, where carton purchases were more popular, wanted to include a six-week supply of patches in each package if and when they launched Niconil. Managers at Warner-Lambert's international division wanted to standardize packaging as much as possible across its subsidiaries and suggested as a compromise a 14-day supply per package.

Following the cigarette model, two pricing schemes had been proposed. The first proposal was to price Niconil on a par with cigarettes. The average Irish smoker smoked 16.5 cigarettes per day and the expected retail price in 1990 for a pack of cigarettes was £2.25. WLI's variable cost of goods for a 14-day supply of Niconil was £12.00.[7] Pharmacies generally added a 50 percent retail mark-up to the price at which they purchased the product from WLI. A value-added tax of 25 percent of the retail price was included in the proposed price to the consumer of £32.00 for a 14-day supply. In addition, the consumer paid a £1.00 dispensing fee per prescription.

Under the second pricing proposal, Niconil would be priced at a premium to cigarettes. Proponents argued that if the Niconil program were successful, it would be a permanent replacement for cigarettes and its cost would be far outweighed by the money saved on cigarettes. The proposed price to the consumer under this option was £60.00 for a 14-day supply.

COMPETITION

Few products would compete directly with Niconil in the smoking cessation market in Ireland. Two small niche products were Accudrop and Nicobrevin, both available without a prescription. Accudrop was a nasal spray that smokers applied to the cigarette filter to trap tar and nicotine, resulting in cleaner smoke. Anticipated 1990 manufacturer sales for Accudrop were £5,000. Nicobrevin, a product from the United Kingdom, was a time-release capsule that eased smoking withdrawal symptoms. Anticipated 1990 manufacturer's sales for Nicobrevin were £75,000.

The most significant competitive product was Nicorette, the only nicotine-replacement product currently available. Marketed in Ireland by Lundbeck, Nicorette was a chewing gum that released nicotine into the body as the smoker chewed the gum. Because chewing gum in public was not socially acceptable among Irish adults, the product had never achieved strong sales, especially given that its efficacy relied on steady, intensive chewing. A second sales deterrent had been the association of Nicorette with side effects, such as mouth cancer and irritation of the linings of the mouth and stomach.

Nicorette was sold in 10-day supplies, available in two dosages: 2 mg and 4 mg. Smokers would chew the 2-mg Nicorette initially, and switch to the 4-mg gum after two weeks if needed. In a 1982 study, 47 percent of Nicorette users quit smoking, versus 21 percent for placebo users. A long-term follow-up study in 1989, however, indicated that only 10 percent more Nicorette patients had ceased smoking, compared with placebo users. The average daily treatment cost to Nicorette customers was £0.65 per day for the 2-mg gum and £1.00 per day for the 4-mg gum. Nicorette, like Niconil, was available at pharmacies by prescription only, so advertising had been limited to medical journals. Anticipated 1990 manufacturer sales of Nicorette were £170,000; however, the brand had not been advertised in three years.

7This cost of goods included Elan's royalty.

FORECASTING

Although Nicorette was not considered a successful product, WLI was confident that Niconil, with its less-intrusive nicotine delivery system and fewer side effects, would capture a dominant position in the smoking cessation market and ultimately increase the demand for smoking cessation products. Precise sales expectations for Niconil were difficult to formulate, however, and two different methods had been suggested.

The first method assumed that the percentage of smokers in the adult population (30 percent in 1990) would drop by one percentage point per year through 1994. An estimated 10 percent of smokers attempted to quit smoking each year, and 10 percent of that number purchased some type of smoking cessation product. WLI believed that Niconil could capture half of these "committed quitters" in the first year, selling therefore to 5 percent of those who tried to give up smoking in 1990. Further, they hoped to increase this share by 1 percent per year, up to 9 percent in 1994. Having estimated the number of customers who would purchase an initial two-week supply of Niconil, WLI managers then had to calculate the total number of units purchased. Based on experience in test trials, WLI anticipated that 60 percent of first-time Niconil customers would purchase a second two-week supply. Of that number, 20 percent would purchase a third two-week supply. About 75 percent of smokers completed the program within six weeks.

A more aggressive forecast could be based on WLI's 1989 survey, which showed that of the 30 percent of [the 1,400] respondents who were smokers, 54 percent indicated that they would like to give up smoking, and 30 percent expressed interest in the nicotine patch. More relevant, 17 percent of smokers indicated that they were likely to go to the doctor and pay for such a patch, though a specific purchase price was not included in the question. A rule of thumb in interpreting likelihood-of-purchase data was to divide this percentage by three to achieve a more likely estimate of actual purchasers. Once the number of Niconil customers was calculated, the 100 percent/60 percent/20 percent model used above could then be applied to compute the total expected unit sales.

PRODUCTION

Under the terms of the joint venture with Elan and using current manufacturing technology, production capacity would be 1,000 units (of 14-day supply packages) per month in the first quarter of 1990, ramping up to 2,000 units per month by year-end. WLI had the option to purchase a new, more efficient machine that could produce 14,000 units per month and reduce WLI's variable cost on each unit by 10 percent. In addition, if WLI purchased the new machine and Niconil was launched in continental Europe, WLI could export some of its production to the European subsidiaries, further expanding its role as a supplier to Warner-Lambert Europe. WLI would earn a margin of £2.00 per unit on Niconil that it sold through this channel.[8] Estimated annual unit sales, assuming a launch of Niconil throughout Western Europe, are listed in Table C. Warner-Lambert management aimed to recoup any capital investments within five years; the Niconil machine would cost £1.2 million and could be on-line within nine months.

---

[8]Warner-Lambert's European subsidiaries were likely to consider purchasing this new machine themselves as well.

T A B L E   C

Estimated Unit Sales of Niconil in Western Europe

Year 1	100,000 units
Year 2	125,000 units
Year 3	150,000 units
Year 4	175,000 units
Year 5	200,000 units

MARKETING PRESCRIPTION PRODUCTS

Prescription products included all pharmaceutical items deemed by the Irish government to require the professional expertise of the medical community to guide consumer usage.[9] Before a customer could purchase a prescription product, he or she first had to visit a doctor and obtain a written prescription which specified that product. The customer could then take the written prescription to one of Ireland's 1,132 pharmacies and purchase the product.

The prescription nature of Niconil thus created marketing challenges. A potential Niconil customer first had to make an appointment with a doctor for an office visit to obtain the necessary prescription. Next, the doctor had to agree to prescribe Niconil to the patient to help him or her to quit smoking. Only then could the customer go to the pharmacy and purchase Niconil. This two-step purchase process required WLI to address two separate audiences in marketing Niconil: the Irish smokers who would eventually use Niconil and the Irish doctors who first had to prescribe it to patients.

Niconil's potential customers were the 10 percent of Irish smokers who attempted to give up smoking each year (2 percent of the total Irish population). Market research had shown that those most likely to purchase Niconil were aged 35–44 and in either white-collar or skilled occupations (18 percent of Irish smokers). Smokers under the age of 35 tended to see themselves as "bullet proof": because most were not yet experiencing the negative health effects of smoking, it was difficult to persuade them to quit. Upper-income, better-educated smokers found less tolerance for smoking among their peers and thus felt greater pressure to quit. Research had also indicated that women were 25 percent more likely to try Niconil as they tended to be more concerned with their health and thus more often visited the doctors from whom they could learn about Niconil and obtain the necessary prescription.

The most likely prescribers of Niconil would be the 2,000 General Practitioners (GPs) in Ireland. The average GP saw 15 patients per day and eight out of ten general office visits resulted in the GPs writing prescriptions for patients. Although 10 percent of Irish doctors smoked, virtually all recognized the dangers of smoking and rarely smoked in front of patients. A *Modern Medicine* survey of 780 Irish GPs indicated that 63 percent formally gathered smoking data from their patients. GPs acknowledged the health risk that smoking posed to patient health, but they were usually reluctant to pressure a patient to quit unless the smoker was highly motivated. Unsolicited pressure to quit could meet with patient resistance and result, in

[9]Drugs and other pharmaceutical products that did not require a written prescription from a doctor were called "over-the-counter," or "OTC" drugs.

some cases, in a doctor losing a patient and the associated revenues from patient visits. Smoking cessation was not currently a lucrative treatment area for GPs. Most would spend no longer than 15 minutes discussing smoking with their patients. To the few patients who asked for advice on how to quit smoking, 92 percent of GPs would offer "firm, clear-cut advice." Fewer than 15 percent would recommend formal counseling, drug therapy, or other assistance. GPs were not enthusiastic about Nicorette due to poor results and the incidence of side effects.

WLI was confident that Niconil would find an enthusiastic audience among Irish GPs. As a complete program with both physical and psychological components, Niconil offered a unique solution. In addition, the doctor would assume a significant counseling role in the Niconil treatment. It was anticipated that the GP would initially prescribe a 14-day supply of Niconil to the patient. At the end of the two-week period, the patient would hopefully return to the doctor for counseling and an additional prescription, if needed.

MARKETING COMMUNICATIONS

WLI intended to position Niconil as *a complete system that was a more acceptable alternative to existing nicotine replacement therapy for the purpose of smoking cessation.* Niconil would be the only smoking cessation product to address both the physical dimension of nicotine addiction through the patch and the psychological dimension through the support program. Compared with Nicorette gum, Niconil offered a more acceptable delivery system (Niconil's transdermal system vs. Nicorette's oral system) and fewer, less severe side effects. WLI planned to promote these aspects of the product through a comprehensive marketing program. The Niconil launch

EXHIBIT 3

Niconil First Year Budget (£'000)

Advertising	
Ad creation	£ 4
Media advertising	28
Total advertising	32
Promotion	
Development of support program	3
Production of support programs	35
Training/promotional materials	44
Direct mailing to GPs	2
Total promotion	84
Public Relations	
Launch symposium	5
Round-table meeting	2
Press release/materials	1
Total public relations	8
Market research	3
Sales force allocation	23
Product management allocation	50
Total budget	£200

marketing budget, detailed in Exhibit 3, followed the Warner-Lambert standard for new drug launches. Several WLI executives felt that this standard was inadequate for the more consumer-oriented Niconil and pressed for increased communications spending.

ADVERTISING

Because Irish regulations prohibited the advertising of prescription products directly to the consumer, Niconil advertising was limited to media targeting the professional medical community. Three major publications targeted this audience: *Irish Medical Times, Irish Medical News,* and *Modern Medicine.* WLI planned to advertise moderately in the first year to raise awareness of Niconil in the medical community. After that it was hoped that the initial momentum could be maintained through strong public relations efforts and personal testimony to the product's efficacy. Exhibit 4 summarizes the proposed 1990 media advertising schedule for Niconil.

WLI's advertising agency had designed a distinctive logo for Niconil that would be used on all packaging and collateral materials such as "No Smoking" placards. These would feature the Niconil logo and be distributed to doctors' offices, hospitals, and pharmacies to promote the product. Ideally, the logo would become sufficiently well recognized that it could be used eventually on a stand-alone basis to represent Niconil to the end consumer without the brand name. This would allow some flexibility in circumventing Irish advertising restrictions to reach the end consumer. Sample logos and packaging are illustrated in Exhibit 5. The agency had also developed the following four concepts for a Niconil medical journal advertisement:

- "Day and night I crave cigarettes. I can't stop. I'm hooked." When they ask for help, give them the help they need—new Niconil nicotine transdermal patches.

- Where there's smoke, there's emphysema, throat cancer, angina, lung cancer, sinusitis. Now a way to break this deadly addiction. Introducing Niconil nicotine transdermal patches—all they need to succeed.

- Emphysema, lung cancer, peptic ulcer, angina, sinusitis, throat cancer. Help end their deadly addiction. One-a-day instead of a pack-a-day. Introducing Niconil nicotine transdermal patches.

- "How many of your patients are dying for a smoke?" Help them break the cycle of addiction. Introducing Niconil nicotine transdermal patches. A better way to stop.

EXHIBIT 4

1990 Niconil Media Advertising Schedule

Publication	Frequency	Circulation	Cost/1,000	Placements
Irish Medical Times	Weekly	5,200	£154	13
Irish Medical News	Weekly	5,100	137	11
Modern Medicine	Monthly	3,700	176	5

EXHIBIT 5

Sample Niconil Logo and Packaging

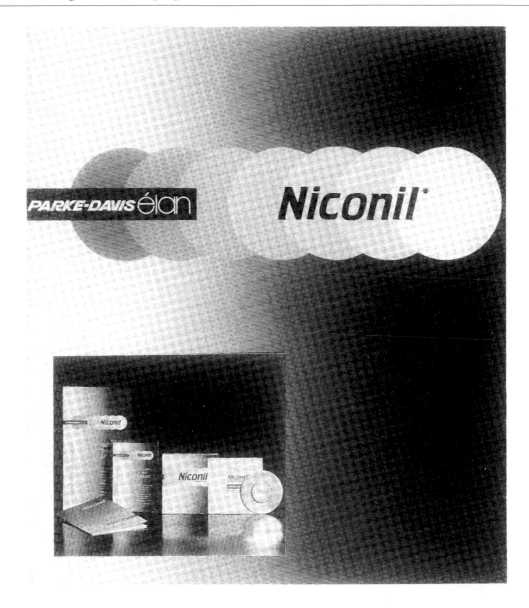

DIRECT MAIL

A direct mail campaign to Ireland's 2,000 GPs was planned in conjunction with the Niconil product announcement. Two weeks prior to launch, an introductory letter would be mailed with a color photo of the product, a reply card offering a support program, and additional product information. The support programs would be mailed in response to the reply cards, arriving just prior to the launch. A response rate of at least 50 percent was anticipated based on past direct mail campaigns.

PUBLIC RELATIONS

The formal Niconil product announcement was scheduled to occur in Dublin at a professional event that WLI had dubbed the "Smoking Cessation Institute Symposium." The symposium would be chaired by Professor Anthony Clare (the narrator of the Niconil audio-tape), Professor Hickey (an expert in preventive cardiology), and Professors Masterson and J. Kelly from Elan Corporation. Open to members of the medical profession and media, the event was intended to focus attention on the dangers of smoking and to highlight Niconil as a ground-breaking product designed to address this health hazard.

WLI had sought endorsements from both the Irish Cancer Society and the Irish Heart Foundation, two national health organizations that actively advocated smoking cessation. Because both nonprofit institutions relied on donations for financing and were concerned that a specific product endorsement would jeopardize their tax-exempt status, they refused to endorse Niconil directly. Representatives from each institution had, however, stated their intention to attend the launch symposium.

In advance of the symposium, a press release and supporting materials would be distributed to the media. Emphasis would be placed on the role that Niconil would play in disease prevention. It would also be noted that Niconil had been developed and manufactured locally and had the potential for worldwide sales. Other planned public relations activities included a roundtable dinner for prominent opinion leaders in the medical community. Publicity in the media was planned to coincide with key "commitment to change" times such as New Year's and Lent.[10]

SALES STRATEGY

WLI Ireland had a sales force of 16 representatives whose average annual salary, bonus, and benefits amounted to £25,000 in 1988. They focused their selling efforts on 1,600 Irish GPs who were most accessible geographically and most amenable to pharmaceutical sales visits. The sales staff was divided into three selling teams of four to six representatives. Each team sold separate product lines to the same 1,600 GPs. The team that would represent Niconil was already selling three other drugs from Elan Corporation that were marketed by WLI as part of their joint venture. These four salespeople would add Niconil to their existing product lines. Sales training on Niconil would take place one month prior to the product launch.

The pharmaceutical salesperson's challenge was to maintain the attention of each GP long enough to discuss each item in his or her product line. Because Niconil was expected to be of great interest to GPs, the salespeople were keen to present Niconil first during the sales visit, followed by the less exciting products. Normally, a new product would receive this up-front positioning. However, Dixon argued that Niconil

---

[10]Lent was an annual penitential period during spring of the Roman Catholic religious calendar that was still observed by many of the 95 percent of the Irish who were Roman Catholic.

should be presented last during the sales call to maximize the time that a salesperson spent with each GP and to prevent the sales time devoted to the other three Elan products from being cannibalized by Niconil. Based on revenue projections for all four products, salespeople would be instructed to spend no more than 15 percent of their sales call time on Niconil. On average, each WLI salesperson called on six to seven doctors per day. The goal was for each sales team to call on the 1,600 targeted GPs once every three months. In the case of Niconil, all 16 sales people would present the new brand during their calls for six weeks after launch.

CRITICAL DECISIONS

With just three months to go before the launch of Niconil, Dixon felt he had to comply with the international division's suggestion to include a 14-day supply of patches in each Niconil package, but he debated whether to price the product on a par with or at a premium to cigarettes. Equally important, he had to decide which sales forecast was more accurate so that he could plan production capacity. And finally, he needed to make decisions on the communications program: which advertising concept would be the most effective, what other efforts could be made to enhance product acceptance, and was the current budget adequate to support Warner-Lambert's first national launch of such an innovative product?

WilTel, Inc.

Three years ago Roy Wilkens, president of WilTel, Inc., had concluded that the world would want ATM (asynchronous transfer mode) communications capabilities. He was proud of the progress that his Advanced Development Center had made in the past two and a half years in developing the software and hardware components for WilTel's next-generation fast-packet platform.

It now appeared highly likely that the internal target date (fourth quarter 1993) could be met for launching the ATM switching platform. What was not clear, however, was how to launch ATM-based services in the marketplace. The ATM market development team had just spent the morning examining two extreme alternatives for early entry into the market. One alternative was to launch a "generic" ATM transport service in much the same fashion that WilTel launched its pioneering frame relay service in 1991—as simply another transmission service. A second alternative was to offer a "packaged" service including equipment required for specific customer applications. Whichever alternative was chosen would determine the positioning and the pricing strategies that would follow.

COMPANY HISTORY

Williams Telecommunications (WilTel) is a wholly owned subsidiary of The Williams Companies, Inc. The Williams Companies, in turn, is a Fortune 500 oil and gas pipeline transmission company. Founded in 1908 by brothers David R. Williams and S. Miller Williams, Jr., and formally incorporated in 1949, The Williams Companies, Inc. had consolidated revenues (including those of WilTel) of nearly $2.5 billion in 1992.

In 1984 The Williams Companies created a task force headed by Roy Wilkens (who was running The Williams Pipe Line Company subsidiary at the time) to investigate possible uses of pipeline that had been decommissioned. One suggestion of the task force was to use the decommissioned pipeline as conduit for a telecommunications system based on fiber-optic cable. It was initially believed that such a telecommunications system would primarily serve the communication needs of The Williams Companies. However, if there was sufficient transmission capacity, the task force thought it might be possible to sell this capacity as a common carrier to regional long-distance telephone carriers such as Teleconnect in Cedar Rapids, Iowa.

Given The Williams Companies's expertise in constructing and maintaining oil and gas pipelines, together with the fact that the company already owned the right of way for hundreds of miles of decommissioned pipeline, the task force thought that a relatively inexpensive, yet very secure, fiber-optic cable system could be con-

This case was prepared by Robert A. Peterson, the University of Texas at Austin, and William R. Wilson, Wiltel, Inc., as a basis for class discussion and is not designed to illustrate effective or ineffective handling of an administrative situation. Certain figures have been disguised; hence the case is not useful for research purposes. Copyright © by Robert A. Peterson. No part of this case may be reproduced without written permission of the copyright holder.

structed. In June 1985, The Williams Companies formed WilTel to deliver long-distance digitized telecommunications by means of fiber-optic cable. By June 1986 the first part of the cable system had been completed. It stretched from Omaha, Nebraska, to Chicago and from Kansas City to Minneapolis. Within the next few years, the cable network expanded rapidly through internal construction projects, acquisitions, and agreements with railroads to use their rights-of-way for laying cable. Presently, WilTel has access to more than 50,000 miles of fiber-optic cable network, of which it owns outright in excess of 9,000 miles. Exhibit 1 shows the WilTel fiber-optic network as of the end of 1992; it is the fourth largest fiber-optic network in the United States.

Initially WilTel positioned itself as a long-distance common carrier (an interexchange carrier). In this capacity it initially provided private line (dedicated network) services at a fixed fee to other common carriers (OCCs). OCCs, many of which were small or regionally based carriers, contracted for capacity on WilTel's network and then resold long-distance services directly to their customers. Currently WilTel has approximately 140

EXHIBIT 1

WilTel Nationwide Digital Network

Note: Major cities have been
identified on map.
Additional cities along
network routes may
be served.

Note: Major cities have been identified on map. Additional cities along network routes may be served.

OCCs as customers that account for about 40 percent of its network services revenue, although through consolidation it is expected that the number of OCCs will decline over time, with one consequence being increased competition among the remaining carriers. Later the company expanded its services to include switched long distance services (primarily voice) targeted at business users. Switched services are typically priced on a time-of-day and distance basis.

At the same time that it was expanding its fiber-optic network, WilTel decided to position itself as a business-to-business telecommunications specialist with particular expertise in data transmission. This was in part because data transmission was expected to increase at a compounded annual growth rate of at least 35 percent for the foreseeable future, whereas voice transmission was expected to grow about 5 percent annually. WilTel's positioning required the development or acquisition of competencies to provide total integrated communications solutions for its customer base. Ultimately, this strategy resulted in WilTel acquiring and integrating several companies that allowed it to move into the overall design, construction, and implementation of digital communication networks for voice, data, and video transmissions. For example, in January 1991 WilTel purchased Centel Communications Systems, one of the country's largest sellers of customer premise equipment (for example, PBX, or private branch equipment, which handles incoming and outgoing telephone calls, voice mail, automatic call distribution, and the like). This gave WilTel the capability to both supply and support customers' telecommunications equipment on-site. Moreover, it allowed WilTel to assume complete management responsibility for other firms' telecommunications systems. For instance, in 1992 the company signed agreements to install, maintain, and administer the telecommunications systems of such firms as Continental Bank, GE Aerospace, and Philadelphia Electric Company. Exhibit 2 briefly describes the four primary WilTel business units.

EXHIBIT 2

Williams Telecommunications Business Units

WilTel Network Services	**WilTel Communications Systems**
Nationwide, comprehensive private line and switched long-distance products and services.	National sales and service infrastructure. Customer premise equipment sales and management.

WilTel Data Network Services	**Vyvx, Inc.**
Custom products and services in data network interconnectivity, management, and implementation.	Nationwide switched video distribution services for television and cable networks, video-conferencing, and business television.

Source: Company records.

By the beginning of 1993, WilTel had in excess of 20,000 customers, including more than half of the Fortune 500 companies. Over time it had evolved into a major provider of telecommunications services and is recognized in the industry as an innovator in providing new technologies and services as well as being a very aggressive marketer. To illustrate, in 1990 WilTel became the first nationwide fiber-optic network to carry broadcast-quality television transmissions (the first of which was Superbowl XXIV) through its Vyvx business unit. Also that year it introduced the industry's first Fractional T3 service (a channelized high-capacity service designed to economically support high-traffic customer network segments). As Exhibit 3 indicates, WilTel's 1992 revenues totaled nearly $758 million, and it is expected that they would approach $1 billion in 1993. The WilTel fiber-optic network stretches across 45 states and serves more than 250 major cities.

Because of its focus on business-to-business marketing, WilTel is not very visible to the general public (less than 2 percent of its network services revenue is derived from residential customers). It does, though, possess a good reputation among its commercial customers. For example, in a survey of businesses conducted in 1992 by *Data Communications* magazine, WilTel received the highest technology ratings of any long-distance carrier. Even so, WilTel does not target all businesses or focus on all possible long-distance services. Rather, as Roy Wilkens repeatedly says, "We are not trying to be everything to everybody, but we're trying to fill certain areas where WilTel can perform very well and try to win in those areas. You have to pick what areas you think you're good at, then focus on them."

Focus on Quality and Reliability

WilTel has always focused on providing the highest-quality service and having a reliable network. For example, the company has generally provided service reliability levels in excess of 99.999 percent. This means that network failures occur less than .001 percent of the time, far less than the industry-accepted standard. The company

EXHIBIT 3

WilTel Financial Data and Operating Statistics[a]

	1992	1991	1990	1989	1988
Revenues	$757.6	$623.1	$376.2	$299.7	$174.6
Network services	478.1	405.8	369.2	299.5	174.6
Communication systems	258.0	205.7	—	—	—
Other	21.5	11.6	7.0	.2	—
Operating profit	$31.2	$82.3	$91.0	$59.5	$20.1
Operating statistics					
Private Line:					
Billable circuits	18,045	15,040	12,531	11,341	8,700
Switched Services:					
Billable calls (millions)	322.7	105.1	59.4	42.6	—

[a]Financial data in millions of dollars.

Source: Company annual reports.

monitors its entire fiber-optic network 24 hours a day through a very sophisticated computer system based in Tulsa, Oklahoma. More than 500,000 individual status and system alarms are monitored continuously to prevent network failures. In addition, WilTel has a comprehensive aerial surveillance program. In this program the entire network is patrolled at least once per month and as frequently as four times per day where there is heavy telecommunications traffic.

If there should be a problem with part of the network, WilTel has a readily available combination of alternative plans, bypass patching, and agreements with other firms for disaster recovery operations that would minimize any inconvenience to its customers. Because of its elaborate monitoring and protection system, WilTel is able to guarantee higher performance specifications to its customers than can any of its competitors.

Products and Services

WilTel, Inc. offers a broad array of products and services to meet its customers' needs. For the most part, these products and services directly relate to WilTel's fiber-optic network. Fiber optics are hair-thin tubes of glass that digitally transmit voice, video, and data at the speed of light. A single fiber can transport up to 48 broadcast-quality video channels. A 144-fiber cable can handle millions of simultaneous two-way telephone calls.

The three major categories of WilTel's network services are (1) private-line services, (2) switched voice (long-distance) services, and (3) packet data services. Illustrative services in each of these categories are presented in Exhibit 4.

Dedicated private-line services allow companies to directly connect their on-site equipment through a local telephone company to a long-distance provider. This access method provides very high quality transmissions on a point-to-point basis. A group of 24 dedicated lines bundled together is known as a DS-1. Companies pay a fixed contractual fee, usually on a monthly basis, for this service, regardless of how much it is used (the average utilization rate of a private line is only 20–30 percent of its capacity). For example, although pricing is very complex—because of widely varying needs and requirements, virtually every customer pays a different fee for its private line(s)—an average (hypothetical) DS-3 private line is priced at $21,500 per month. Long-distance services include 800 numbers, directory assistance, and electronic order processing. Packet data services differ from private-line services in that costumers share the WilTel network (that is, there are no dedicated circuits). They allow customers to only pay for the bandwidth they need when they need it.[1] For example, frame relay is a protocol that permits high-speed transmission of data without having dedicated high-speed private-line facilities. Because the network is shared, transmission costs are usually lower than those associated with a private line in a moderate-sized (for example five-node) or larger network. Exhibit 5 schematically illustrates the difference between private-line circuits connecting a company's sites in five cities and the frame-relay network that would interconnect them.

---

[1]Casewriters' note: Bandwidth is the speed or bit rate at which a signal can be transmitted. Faster speed means more information can be transmitted per second, which means higher bandwidth. Broadband is usually defined as bandwidth greater than 2 Mbps (2 million bits per second).

EXHIBIT 4

Example WilTel Network Services

Private-Line Services	Switched Voice Services	Packet Data Services
DS-3	Off-Net Origination/Termination	Frame Relay
Fractional DS-3 (T-3)	Off-Net Termination	ATM (proposed)
DS-1	Carrier 800 NXX	
Fractional DS-1 (T-1)	WilTel 800 Numbers Origination	
56 kbps Digital Data Service	International Switched Services	
DS-0 with DDS Access	Directory Assistance	
DS-0 with VF Access	Electronic Order/Entry Processing	
	Flexible Billing Cycles for Carriers/Resellers	
	Travel Card	

Source: Company records.

The Frame-Relay Experience

WilTel was a pioneer in developing and offering frame relay. In March 1991, WilTel was the first firm to offer a frame-relay transmission service, which is a fast-packet protocol for moving data from one local-area network (LAN) to another across the fiber-optic network. Frame relay is primarily an interface specification used for high-speed movement of data that are transmitted in bursts rather than at constant rates. Its speed (operating bit range) varies from 56 Kbps (56 thousand bits per second) to 2 Mbps (2 million bits per second). Example applications are imaging, computer-aided design, and document sharing. Frame relay organizes data prior to transmission into frames of variable length (hence, the name "frame relay"). This is ideal for irregular transmission, such as for rapid bursts of data, but is unsuitable for voice and video transmissions, which require constant-rate transmission.

From a publicity and visibility perspective, being the first to offer frame relay was an enormous success. Many businesses that were potential customers of WilTel were not aware of the company prior to the introduction of frame relay, or assumed that WilTel was only a common carrier reselling its services to OCCs. Hence, frame relay identified WilTel as a major technology innovator and an aggressive marketer. It also made WilTel's competitors take notice of the company's technical capabilities.

As a result of being first to the marketplace with frame relay, WilTel was the market leader for more than two years, in spite of having to compete directly against AT&T, MCI, and Sprint. As one of WilTel's customers remarked, "With frame relay,

EXHIBIT 5

Schematic Illustration of Interconnectivity of Private-Line Circuits and Frame-Relay Network

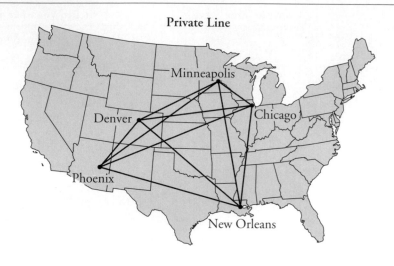

Private Line

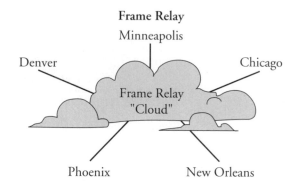

Frame Relay

our company is getting increased flexibility and more bandwidth but is paying $2,700 less per month." As of March 1993, WilTel controls 30 to 40 percent of the market for frame relay.

Unfortunately, despite the favorable publicity and visibility, frame relay has not been a big commercial success for WilTel. Although market analysts and the trade press had predicted a large market for frame relay service, these predictions turned out to be grossly overstated. For example, most sources predicted that frame-relay services would generate approximately $100 million in sales in 1992. Total industry revenues that year were actually less than $10 million. While there has been great enthusiasm for frame relay, and many potential users have tried it, at this point in time WilTel probably has fewer than 100 paying customers, an increase of about 40 from its first complete year of operation. Approximately three-quarters of these customers were new to the company. In part the sluggish demand has been attributed to potential customers waiting for the much-heralded ATM services.

ASYNCHRONOUS TRANSFER MODE

Asynchronous transfer mode is an international standard for processing, multiplexing, switching, and transmitting information streams within a broadband communications network. Essentially ATM allows any type of message, whether voice, video, or data to be "chopped up" into very small pieces. These pieces are then placed in 48-octet segments. (An octet is one byte of information. One byte equals eight bits, which is equivalent to, for example, one print character.) A five-octet header is "pasted" to the front of each segment. The resulting 53-byte segment becomes ATM's basic transportation unit, cell, or packet. (See Exhibit 6 for a schematic representation of an ATM packet.) The cell header contains the address and other information about the cell that allows it be to directed to a particular destination, whereas the remainder of the cell contains its "payload" of information.

Following their configuration, ATM cells enter a multiplexer, which is a device for mixing information from different sources (channels) to make more efficient use of the available bandwidth in a communication system. The cells leave the multiplexer in a single stream and are dropped one at a time on a neverending train of ATM "boxcars" that carry them to their destination. Because the ATM cells are short

E X H I B I T   6

Schematic Representation of ATM Packet

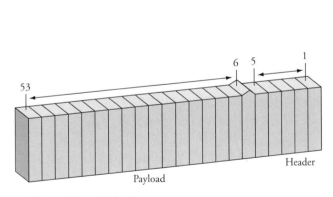
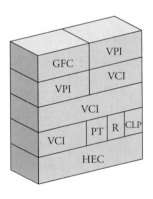

CLP = Cell Loss Priority
GFC = Generic Flow Control (UNI only)
HEC = Header Error Conrol
PT = Payload Type
R = Reserved for future use
VCI = Virtual Circuit Identifier
VPI = Virtual Path Identifier

Source: Company publicity document.

and have a fixed length, ATM switches can handle millions of cells per second and therefore the overall communication can move at a very high speed. The transmission bit rate for ATM begins at 1.5 Mbps and ranges as high as 2.4 Gbps, 2.4 billion bits per second. (See Exhibit 7 for a comparison of different bit rates in terms of the time it would take to transmit one gigabyte of information—1 billion bits per second. One gigabyte is approximately the size of the *Encyclopaedia Britannica*.) When they reach their destination the cells are reassembled for delivery to the receiving party.

At its essence, ATM is a high-bandwidth packet service capable of rapidly transmitting large amounts of information. For instance, ATM allows users to tie together their computer and peripheral equipment for more efficiently sharing, storing, or accessing data even though the equipment might be respectively located in Seattle and Miami.

WilTel's basic alternatives when deciding to market ATM were two. ATM could be marketed as simply a universal transport medium (that is, WilTel could offer the technology as simply one service in its portfolio and allow users to decide on its particular application). Possible applications that have been mentioned for ATM include supporting multimedia traffic, connecting wide-area telecommunications hubs, transmitting high-definition television signals, and connecting mainframe computers, either to each other or to peripherals or storage facilities in different locations, on an as-needed basis. Or WilTel could attempt to market ATM as a part of a total package of products and services for a specific application. Doing so would require that the company partner with other firms that could provide customer premises equipment as well as switching equipment. Doing so would also mean that WilTel would no longer function simply as a common carrier, but would also provide a parallel set of services offering particular solutions to customers' problems. Although any ATM service could potentially increase users' communication flexibility and save considerable sums of money, it is not clear that an ATM "solution" is really required for most current applications. Moreover, if WilTel offers a packaged ATM service

EXHIBIT 7

Time Required to Transmit One Gigabyte of Information

Digital Signal	Channel Capacity (64 Kbps)	Bit Rate[a]	Minutes
DS-0	1	64 Kbps	2,083.33
DS-1	24	1.554 Mbps	86.36
DS-3[b]	672	44.736 Mbps	2.97
OC-3[c]	2,106	155.520 Mbps	0.87
OC-12[c]	8,544	622.080 Mbps	0.22

[a]Kbps is thousands of bits per second and Mbps is millions of bits per second, approved measures of bandwidth (the speed at which a signal can be transmitted).

[b]The WilTel ATM platform would initially function at DS-3 speeds but increase to SONET (synchronous optical network) speeds, SONET being the approved standard for transporting information over optical fiber. OC-1 is the beginning SONET speed, 52 million bits per second (52 Mbps).

[c]Representative SONET level (range is from OC-1 to OC-48).

prematurely, without precisely identifying the particular needs that it will address, it might only be opening the door to its major rivals. Sprint, in particular, was thought to have an ATM service nearly ready to market as a generic service.

THE TELECOMMUNICATIONS INDUSTRY

When someone picks up a telephone receiver to make a long distance call, that person is initially connected to a local exchange carrier (LEC), a firm that services a particular geographical area (a LATA, or local access and transport area). Most likely this carrier is one of the "Baby Bells" or regional Bell operating companies (RBOC) that were formerly owned by AT&T, or an independent local exchange carrier such as GTE. An individual placing a long-distance call from, say, Los Angeles to New York City would initially connect with Pacific Telesis, the RBOC in California. The individual's call would then be switched to an interexchange carrier that he or she would select, such as AT&T, MCI, Sprint, or WilTel. The interexchange carrier would transmit the telephone call to New York City, where it would be handed off to NYNEX, the local exchange carrier, and transmitted to the receiving party. Most local telephone calls are carried by copper wires (for example, twisted-pair copper wires) and cables, whereas most interexchange service is provided by fiber-optic networks.

Exhibit 8 contains the 1992 revenues of the seven RBOCs as well as those of GTE. These eight companies dominate the local exchange telecommunications industry. Because of flat sales in the past few years, they have been searching for new sources of revenue. Presently they are investigating frame relay and ATM and are beginning to offer their own version of a high-speed data-transmission service (SMDS, or switched multimegabit data service).

The long-distance telecommunications industry is comprised of three tiers of interexchange carriers. The first tier consists of AT&T, MCI, and Sprint. Collectively, these three companies dominate the long-distance market and possessed a combined market share of more than 80 percent in 1992. AT&T in particular is the industry cost and price leader and earned $3.8 billion in net income in 1992. Both

EXHIBIT 8

1992 Revenues for RBOCs and GTE

Local Exchange Carrier	1992 Revenues (In Billions)
Ameritech	$11.2
Bell Atlantic	12.6
Bell South	15.2
NYNEX	13.2
Pacific Telesis	9.9
Southwestern Bell	10.0
US West[a]	10.3
GTE[b]	20.0

[a]1991 revenues.

[b]Includes nontelecommunications revenues.

Source: SEC filings.

figuratively and literally AT&T is the dominant interexchange carrier. As industry wags frequently note, "Nobody ever got fired for buying from AT&T." Because of AT&T's position in the industry, many of its competitors, including WilTel, try to position themselves against it (see Exhibit 9).

The second tier consists of WilTel and carriers such as LDDS and Cable & Wireless. Each of these companies has minimum revenues of $250 million annually. The third tier of interexchange carriers consists of more than 400 companies with annual revenues less than $250 million each, with the majority having revenues below $50 million. Virtually all of the third-tier interexchange carriers are regional in nature, are limited by the size of their transmission systems, or are dependent on third parties for their network services and products.

ATM Competitive Overview

When the market development team was considering the viability of the ATM service, it commissioned an analysis of WilTel's three major competitors, AT&T, MCI, and Sprint. In general, AT&T positions itself as "all things to all people," MCI as "lower priced than AT&T," and Sprint as "high-quality network." The analysis produced estimates of the major strengths and weaknesses of these competitors. These strengths and weaknesses are summarized in Exhibit 10.

THE DECISION

Although Roy Wilkens and the ATM market development team were enthusiastic about the ATM switching platform, other WilTel staff members had some reservations. One staff member worried that ATM might bring frame-relay sales to a standstill, especially if the service were offered in an unpackaged form as a universal packet service.

Another staff member was concerned whether the ATM market was large enough to risk pursuing, particularly since Sprint had already announced its intent to enter the market. Some industry sources estimated the ATM market size to be nearly $300 million in 1994 and increasing to $800 million in 1996, and an optimistic WilTel manager had placed the company's possible market share in 1994 at 30–40 percent and 25 percent in 1996 if it were the first to enter the market. Even so, this staff member repeatedly called the team's attention to the frame-relay experience. A third individual was positively disposed toward ATM, but believed that WilTel should take a wait-and-see approach. Specifically, this person, also citing the frame-relay experience, believed that WilTel should not introduce the service at all until one of its major rivals did so. Rather, it should wait and see what specific applications appeared to be the most promising, then pursue them.

One of the most difficult issues confronting the ATM development team was how to price whichever alternative was selected. Part of the problem in determining the appropriate pricing structure was that price would probably determine the type of customers who would use the ATM services, how much they would use the services, and when they would use the services. Because all fiber-optic networks ultimately have a fixed capacity, it is important to accurately predict not only average usage, but peak usage as well. (A network whose capacity was designed to equal or exceed peak demand will be an unprofitable network because it will be over-

EXHIBIT 9

Sample WilTel Advertisement

YOU'RE TIRED. FED UP. AND JUST PLAIN AT&TEED OFF.

SO TELL THE BIG GUYS YOU'RE LEAVING THEM FOR WILTEL.

At WilTel, we've got what they've got, without the attitude problem. It's called WilPower, and it's everything you need – or only the part you need – for total business telecommunications solutions:
• Nationwide fiber-optic network for voice, data, video and broadcast.
• Premises equipment from PBX and intelligent concentrators to routers and multiplexers. • Customized LAN-to-WAN integration and operation.
• Expert outsourcing from interim project managers to full time network engineers.

So call WilTel and get WilPower. Oh, and the lower blood pressure is standard equipment with any purchase.

WILTEL
TURNS UP EVERYTHING

©1993 WilTel

Source: Company records.

EXHIBIT   10

ATM Competitive Analysis Summary

AT&T

Overall Strengths

- Long-time market leader with overwhelming name recognition and a strong, positive reputation for reliability.
- Large imbedded base of customers and broad range of product and service offerings. Probably controls at least 85 percent of the private-line market.
- Substantial sales, marketing, technical, and financial resources. Revenues in 1992 were almost $65 billion ($39.6 billion of which came from telecommunications).

Possible Weaknesses

- Current dominant market position and broad range of product-service mix may inhibit launch of ATM services. Cannibalizing high margin private line services with much more efficient ATM-based services will pose a threat to current earnings. Conflict in promoting new efficient data services was evident in slow frame-relay launch.
- Head-on competition with WilTel if WilTel packages is problematic for two reasons. First, AT&T's Paradyne unit manufactures a poor competitive product for certain ATM applications. Hard for AT&T to abandon its own product for a competititve substitute. Second, potential regulatory conflict if AT&T creates hardware-network service package. In addition, the market niche sought by WilTel may be too small to warrant a deliberate encounter entry.

MCI

Overall Strengths

- A solid marketing company with strong reputation for aggressive service development. Good reputation for customer service.
- Substantial sales, marketing, technical, and financial resources. Revenues in 1992 were $10.6 billion.

Possible Weaknesses

- Historical success is derived from a clear focus on growing long-distance business. May not be able to aggressively pursue business in both voice and data market.
- Little evidence that MCI is prepared in the near term to launch ATM-based services. Public statements endorse a strong focus on a complementary protocol. Ability to create an ATM service package exists, but company lacks strong data-communications position.

Sprint

Overall Strengths

- Is perceived to be the most reliable "all-fiber" network. Strong reputation for technical networking expertise. Substantial data-networking experience with worldwide standards.
- A clear, stated interest in being ATM market leader. Winner of first major ATM broadband government contract (under protest by AT&T with adverse ruling expected from Government Accounting Office).
- Substantial sales, marketing, technical, and financial resources. Revenues in 1992 were $9.2 billion.

Possible Weaknesses

- Is not thriving in long-distance war. May have to redeploy data-communication assets to fight market-share erosion in voice arena. Also, major acquisition of Centel in 1992 will be a drain on top management for many months.
- Is not seen as an aggressive marketing company. Weak reputation for innovative service development. Ability to create ATM service package is high, but is very likely to copy WilTel service model if perceived to be successful.

built.) One way that is used to manage demand by long-distance carriers is to price according to the time of day (time-varying pricing basically decreases usage during peak hours and increases it during those periods when there is little use). For example, long-distance charges are considerably higher between 9 A.M. and 1 P.M. (when demand is high) than from 9 P.M. to 1 A.M. (when demand is low).

Pricing ATM as a universal packet service would be relatively straightforward. Factors that would have to be considered include local access fees, transmission distance, and bandwidth required.[2] More specifically, WilTel would have to determine port charges (the cost of gaining access to the fiber-optic network switches) and usage charges (which would probably be a function of the number of packets to be transported). Hence, the cost of the service to the user would essentially be a direct function of the amount of usage. The packaged version would probably bear an all-inclusive price but also be based on LEC access fees, port charges, access equipment (if the customer leased its premises equipment through WilTel or its partner), and a usage charge (in this instance based on average expected transmission distance and bandwidth usage). Thus the cost of the ATM service would be only one component of the overall price paid by a user. Most likely the packaged price would not be distance-sensitive but would simply provide customers with a 20–40 percent savings over their current service cost.

---

[2]Casewriters' note: LECs charge OCCs origination and termination fees for all long-distance switched services. These charges typically run about 47 percent of the cost of a long-distance call and are passed through to users at an OCC's cost.

CHAPTER 10

Marketing Strategy Reformulation: The Control Process

 Marketing strategies are rarely, if ever, timeless. As the environment changes, so must product-market and marketing-mix plans. Moreover, as organizations strive for gains in productivity, constant attention must be given to improving the efficiency of marketing efforts.

The marketing control process serves as the mechanism for achieving strategic adaptation to environmental change and operational adaptation to productivity needs.[1] Marketing control consists of two complementary activities: strategic control, which is concerned with "doing the right things," and operations control, which focuses on "doing things right." *Strategic control* assesses the direction of the organization as evidenced by its implicit or explicit goals, objectives, strategies, and capacity to perform in the context of changing environments and competitive actions. The ever-present issue of defining the fit between an organization's capabilities and objectives and environmental threats and opportunities is at the core of strategic control. *Operations control* assesses how well the organization performs marketing activities as it seeks to achieve planned outcomes. It is implicitly assumed that the direction of the organization is correct and that only the organization's ability to perform specific tasks needs to be improved.

The distinction between strategic and operations control is important to grasp. It has been noted that a "poorly executed plan can produce undesirable results just as easily as a poorly conceived plan."[2] Though undesirable results (declining sales, eroding market share, or sagging profits) may be identical, remedial actions under the two types of control will differ. Remedial efforts drawn from an operations-control perspective focus on heightening the marketing effort or identifying ways to improve *efficiency*. Alternatively, remedial efforts based on a strategic-control orientation focus on improving the *effectiveness* of the organization in seeking opportunities and mitigating threats in its environment. Improper assessment of the need for strategic versus operations control can lead to a disastrous response in which an organization pours additional funds into an ill-conceived strategy only to realize further declines in profit.

STRATEGIC CHANGE

Strategic change is defined here as change in the environment that will affect the long-run well-being of the organization. Strategic change may represent opportunities or threats to an organization, depending on the organization's competitive posture. For example, the gradual aging of the U.S. population represents a potential threat to organizations catering to children, whereas this change represents an opportunity to organizations providing products for and services to the elderly.

Strategic change can arise from a multitude of sources.[3] One source is *market evolution*, which results from changes in primary demand for a product class and changes in technology. For example, increased primary demand for calcium in diets prompted the marketers of Tums antacid, Total cereal, and Citrus Hill and Minute Maid orange juice to promote the presence of calcium in their products. Technological change often prompts market evolution and changes in marketing techniques, as evidenced by the application of electronics to the watch industry described later in this chapter.

Market redefinition is another source of strategic change. *Market redefinition* results from changes in the offering demanded by buyers or promoted by competitors. For example, firms that provided only automatic teller machines (ATMs) for banks saw the market redefined to electronic funds transfer, with total systems rather than equipment alone being the offering purchased. Firms with systems capabilities, such as IBM and NCR, thus gained a competitive advantage in the redefined market.

Change in marketing channels is a third source of strategic change. Some recent changes in marketing channels have been prompted by *scrambled merchandising*, a trend among intermediaries to carry a wider assortment of merchandise than they did in the past (for example, 7-Eleven stores offer gasoline, and many gasoline stations now sell food items). Scrambled merchandising has led many manufacturers to reevaluate channel relationships and potential outlets for goods and services. For example, in the early 1980s, supermarkets' share of home improvement product sales grew to over 20 percent. Firms seeing this trend benefited from the change; those that did not found themselves struggling to gain access to display space in supermarkets. Similarly, it is not uncommon today to find various electronics products, such as hand-held calculators, television sets, tape recorders, and personal computers, in general-merchandise stores as well as in specialty outlets.

Threat severity or opportunity potential is determined by the organization's business definition. In other words, does the threat or opportunity relate to the type of customer served by the organization, the needs of the customers, the means by which the organization satisfies these needs, or some combination of these factors?

The effects of strategic change are apparent in the transformation of the worldwide watchmaking industry.[4] Although Swiss watchmakers had dominated this industry for a century, market evolution, market redefinition, and marketing channel changes combined to spell disaster for the Swiss. While a technologically motivated market evolution changed the offering from jeweled watches to quartz and electronic watches, the primary marketing channel changed from select jewelry stores to mass merchandisers and supermarkets. Moreover, a redefinition of the term *watch* occurred. No longer was a watch defined solely in terms of craftsmanship or elegance as jewelry. Many people began to think of a watch as an economical and disposable timepiece. These changes, brought about by Timex and such Japanese firms as Seiko and Citizen, severely affected the Swiss watchmakers. Today, Swiss watchmakers have, for the most part, retreated to a highly specialized market niche, which can be identified as the prestige, luxury, artistry watch segment. For example, Swiss watches "tell you something about yourself" (Patek) and are "the most expensive in the world" (Piaget).

This example highlights how strategic change can affect an entire industry and its individual participants. In practice, several options exist for dealing with strategic change:

1. An organization can attempt to marshal the resources necessary to alter its technical and marketing capabilities to fit the market-success requirement. (Swiss watchmakers did not do this but, rather, devoted modest research funds to perfecting the design of mechanical watches, in which they had a distinctive competency. Only Ebauches S.A. invested in electronic technology and pursued the marketing opportunity available for an inexpensive, fashion watch—the Swatch.)

2. An organization can shift its emphasis to product markets where the match between success requirements and the firm's distinctive competence is clear and can cut back efforts in those product markets where it has been outflanked. (Many Swiss watchmakers chose this option.)

3. An organization can leave the industry. (Over 1,000 Swiss watchmakers selected this option, thereby eliminating more than 45,000 Swiss jobs.)

OPERATIONS CONTROL

The goal of operations control is to improve the productivity of marketing efforts. Because cost identification and allocation are central to the appraisal of marketing efforts and profitability, marketing-cost analysis is a fundamental aspect of operations control. This section provides an overview of marketing-cost analysis and selected examples of product-service mix control, sales control, and marketing-channel control.

Nature of Marketing-Cost Analysis

The purpose of *marketing-cost analysis* is to assign or allocate costs to a specified marketing activity or entity (hereafter referred to as a *segment*) in a manner that accurately displays the financial contribution of activities or entities to the organization. Marketing segments are typically defined on the basis of (1) elements of the product-service offering, (2) type or size of customers, (3) sales divisions, districts, or territories, and/or (4) marketing channels. Cost allocation is based on the principle that certain costs are directly or indirectly assignable to every marketing segment.[5]

Several issues arise in regard to the cost-allocation question:

1. How should costs be allocated to separate marketing segments? As a general rule, the manager should attempt to assign costs in accordance with an identifiable measure of application to an entity.

2. What costs should be allocated? Again, as a general rule, costs arising from the performance of a marketing activity or charged to that activity according to administrative policy are the costs that should be allocated.

3. Should all costs be allocated to marketing segments? The answer to this question will depend on whether the manager opts for a "whole equals the sum of parts" income statement. If so, then all costs should be fully allocated. If it appears that certain costs have no identifiable measure of application to a segment or do not arise from one particular segment, however, these costs should not be allocated.

The manager should follow two guidelines in considering the cost-allocation question. First, when costs are allocated, fundamental distinctions between cost behavior patterns should be maintained. Second, the more joint costs there are (costs that have no identifiable basis for allocation or that arise from a variety of marketing segments), the less exact cost allocations will be. In general, greater detail in cost allocation will provide more useful information.[6]

Product-Service Mix Control

Proper control of the product-service mix involves two interrelated tasks. First, the manager must assess the performance of offerings in the relevant markets. Second, the manager must appraise the financial worth of product-service offerings.

Sales volume, as an index of performance, can be approached from two directions. Growth or decline in unit sales volume provides a quantitative indicator of the acceptance of offerings in their relevant markets. Equally important is the proportion of sales coming from individual offerings in the product-service mix and how this sales distribution affects profitability. Many firms experience the "80–20 rule"—80 percent of sales or profits come from 20 percent of the firm's offerings. For example, 20 percent of Kodak's products contribute more than 80 percent to the firm's sales.[7] Such an imbalance in the mix can have a disastrous effect on overall profitability if sudden changes in competitive or market behavior threaten the viability of this 20 percent.

Market share complements sales volume as an indicator of performance. Market share offers a means for determining whether an organization is gaining or losing ground in comparison with competitors, provided it is used properly. Several questions must be considered when market share is used for control purposes. First, what is the market on which the market-share percentage is based, and has the market definition changed? Market share can be computed by geographical area, product type or model, customer or channel type, and so forth. In the Goodyear Tire and Rubber Company case in Chapter 8, the market share for tires was reported by geography (U.S. versus worldwide), product type (passenger car and truck), type of retail outlet (company-owned stores, discount tire stores, etc.), as well as by manufacturers' total sales. Second, is the market itself changing? For example, high market share by itself may be misleading, since overall sales in the market may be declining or growing. Finally, the unit of analysis—dollar sales or unit sales—must be considered. Because of price differentials, it is better to use unit rather than dollar volume in examining market share.

A second aspect of product-service control consists of appraising the financial contribution of market offerings. An important step in this process is the assignment of costs to offerings in a manner that reflects their profitability. However, this step is difficult and often requires astute managerial judgment. Moreover, the definition of an offering is itself illusive. For example, a "red-eye" flight (early morning or late evening) scheduled by an airline might be viewed as an offering. The decision by

McDonald's and Taco Bell to open for the breakfast trade can be viewed as a market offering, the costs of which include not only the cost of producing the menu items but also the cost of being open.

From a control perspective, the manager should examine the financial worth of market offerings using a *contribution-margin approach*, in which the relevant costs charged against an offering include direct costs and assignable overhead.[8] The units by which these costs are broken down should be those that contribute most meaningfully to the analysis.

Consider the situation in which the owner of a chain of gasoline service stations is examining operating performance. Exhibit 10.1 shows the operating performance before and after cost allocation by department. Examination of the total yields little managerially relevant information. When costs are disaggregated by department, however, it becomes apparent that gasoline operates at a net loss, whereas general merchandise and automobile service operate profitably. Fortunately, each department "contributes" to overhead; that is, each department's revenue exceeds its allocated variable costs.

This analysis serves a useful purpose in identifying potential trouble spots. Several alternatives exist for taking corrective action. If the owner decided to drop the unprofitable line and leave the selling space empty, then general merchandise and automobile service would have to cover the total fixed costs, which will continue. It is doubtful that this would occur. (Note that gasoline does contribute to the payment of fixed costs.) Another possibility is that the manager might expand the other departments to use the empty space. Estimates of market demand and forecasts of revenue would be needed for further consideration of this action. Moreover, a commitment of resources would have to occur that would in effect significantly alter the nature of the business.

Sales Control

Sales control directs a manager's attention to both the behavioral and the cost aspects of sales activity. The behavioral element consists of sales effort and allocation of selling time. The cost aspect consists of expenses arising from the performance and administration of the sales function.

EXHIBIT 10.1

Disaggregating Service Station Costs for Product-Service Mix Control (Thousands of Dollars)

		Department		
	Total	Gasoline	General Merchandise	Automobile Service
Sales	$4,000	$2,000	$1,700	$300
Cost of goods sold and variable expenses	3,000	1,600	1,220	180
Contribution margin	1,000	400	480	120
Fixed expenses	900	500	310	90
Net income	$ 100	$ (100)	$ 170	$ 30

Sales control is usually based on a performance analysis by sales territories or districts, size and type of customers or accounts, products, or some combination of these variables. Various measures used to assess sales performance include sales revenue, gross profit, sales call frequency, penetration of accounts in a sales territory, and selling and sales administration expenditures.

Consider a situation in which a district sales manager has requested a quarterly performance review of two sales personnel in a territory within the district. These individuals have failed to achieve their sales, gross profit, and profit quotas. Exhibit 10.2 displays the representatives' performance according to customer-volume account categories. These categories were established by the national sales manager on the basis of industry norms, as were the following expected quarterly call frequencies:

Account Definition	Expected Frequency of Quarterly Calls
A: $1,000 or less in sales	2
B: $1,000–$1,999 in sales	4
C: $2,000–$4,999 in sales	6
D: $5,000 or more in sales	8

Both representatives had an equal number of A, B, C, and D accounts.

Exhibit 10.3 shows various indices prepared by the district sales manager from the performance summary shown in Exhibit 10.2. Among the principal findings evident from Exhibit 10.3 are the following:

1. The representatives' account penetration varied inversely with the size of the account. Whereas representatives had penetrated 75 percent of the smaller A accounts, only 30 percent of the potentially large D accounts were listed as active buyers.

EXHIBIT 10.2

Performance Summary for Two Sales Representatives

Account Category	(1) Potential Accounts in Sales District[a]	(2) Active Accounts[b]	(3) Sales Volume[c]	(4) Gross Profit[d]	(5) Total Calls[e]	(6) Selling Expenses[f]	(7) Sales Administration[g]
A	80	60	$ 48,000	$14,000	195	$18,400	
B	60	40	44,000	15,400	200	17,900	
C	40	10	25,000	12,250	50	11,250	
D	20	6	33,000	16,500	42	9,000	
Totals	200	116	$150,000	$58,550	487	$56,550	$10,000

[a]Based on marketing research data identifying potential users of company products.

[b]Current accounts.

[c]Based on invoices.

[d]Based on invoice price for full mix of products sold.

[e]Based on sales call reports cross-referenced by customer name.

[f]Direct costs of sales including allocated salaries of two sales representatives.

[g]Costs not assignable on a meaningful basis; includes office expense.

EXHIBIT   10.3

Selected Operating Indices of Sales Performance

Sales Volume/ Active Account (Col. 3 ÷ Col. 4)	Gross Profit Active Account (Col. 4 ÷ Col. 2)	Selling Expenses/ Active Account (Col. 6 ÷ Col. 2)	Contribution to Sales Administration (Gross Profit— Selling Expenses)
A: $800	$240	$307	–$67
B: $1,100	$385	$448	–$63
C: $2,500	$1,225	$1,125	$1,375
D: $5,500	$2,750	$1,500	$1,250

Account Penetration (Col. 2 ÷ Col. 3)	Call Frequency/ Active Account (Col. 5 ÷ Col. 2)	Selling Expense per Call (Col. 6 ÷ Col. 5)	Gross Profit %/ Active Account (Col. 4 ÷ Col. 3)
A: 75%	3.25	$94.36	30%
B: 67	5.0	$89.50	35
C: 25	5.0	$225.00	49
D: 30	7.0	214.29	50

2. Part of the reason for this performance appears to lie in the call frequency of the representatives. The representatives exceeded the call norm on the A and B accounts, but fell short on call frequency on the C and D accounts. Moreover, their "effort" level appears questionable (487 calls ÷ 90 days ÷ 2 representatives = 2.7 calls per day).

3. The gross profit percentage derived from sales to smaller accounts was considerably lower than that derived from sales to the larger accounts, which in turn affected profitability.

4. When account sales volume is matched with gross profit and selling expenses, it becomes apparent that the smaller accounts actually produced a net contribution dollar loss.

The sales control process in this instance revealed that the two representatives were not actively calling on accounts (only 2.7 calls per day) and that their allocation of call activity focused on smaller-volume, less profitable accounts that were in fact contributing a *loss* to overhead. Redirection of effort is clearly called for in this situation.

Marketing Channel Control

Marketing channel control consists of two complementary processes. The manager must first assess environmental and organizational factors that may alter the structure, conduct, and performance of marketing channels. These considerations were highlighted in Chapter 8. Second, the manager must evaluate the profitability of marketing channels.

Profitability analysis for marketing channels follows the general format outlined for product-service control. Cost identification and allocation differ, however. Two types of costs—order-getting and order-servicing costs—must be identified and allocated to different marketing channels. *Order-getting costs* include sales expenses and advertising allowances. *Order-servicing expenditures* include packing and delivery costs, warehousing expenses, and billing costs.

Consider a hypothetical marketer of furniture polishes, cleaners, and assorted furniture improvement products. This firm uses its own sales force to sell its products through three marketing channels: furniture stores, department stores, and home improvement stores. Exhibit 10.4 shows income statements for all three channels combined, as well as individually (general and administration costs are not allocated or included). It is apparent that when costs and revenues are allocated by channel, furniture store and department store channels generate equal sales revenue; however furniture stores incur a sizable loss and department stores account for almost all of net income. Why are the returns so different?

Inspection of disaggregated costs suggest the following:

1. The gross margin percentage on the mix of products sold to department stores is 38 percent, whereas the gross margin percentage on products sold to furniture stores and home improvement stores is 30 percent. Thus, lower-margin products are being sold through furniture and home improvement stores on the average.

2. Order-getting costs (selling and advertising) run about 21 percent of sales for furniture stores, but only 7 percent for department stores and 16 percent for home improvement stores.

3. Order-servicing costs are 17 percent of sales for furniture stores, 14 percent for department stores, and about 12 percent for home improvement stores.

EXHIBIT   10.4

Disaggregated Costs of Furniture Improvement Products for Marketing Channel Control (Thousands of Dollars)

		Marketing Channel		
	Total	*Furniture Stores*	*Department Stores*	*Home Improvement Stores*
Sales	$12,000	$5,000	$5,000	$2,000
Cost of goods sold	8,000	3,500	3,100	1,400
Gross margin	4,000	1,500	1,900	600
Expenses				
Selling	1,000	617	216	167
Advertising	750	450	150	150
Packing and delivery	800	370	300	130
Warehousing	400	200	150	50
Billing	600	300	250	50
Total expenses	3,550	1,937	1,066	547
Net channel income (loss)	$450	$(437)	$834	$53

In short, a manager can conclude that the effort (reflected in costs) necessary to generate sales and service in the furniture store channel is much greater than that needed for department and home improvement stores. Moreover, furniture stores purchase products with a lower gross margin. Once these problems have been identified, efforts to remedy the situation can be explored in a more systematic fashion.

CONSIDERATIONS IN MARKETING CONTROL

Proper implementation of strategic and operations control requires that the manager be aware of several pertinent considerations. Three of these considerations follow.

Problems versus Symptoms

Effective control, whether at the strategic or the operations level, requires that the manager recognize the difference between root problems and surface symptoms. This means that the manager must develop causal relationships between occurrences. For example, if there is evidence of a sales decline or poor profit margins, the manager must "look behind" the numbers to identify the underlying causes of such performance and then attempt to remedy them. This diagnostic role is similar to that of a physician, who must first establish patient symptoms in order to identify the ailment.

Effectiveness versus Efficiency

A second consideration is the dynamic tension that exists between effectiveness and efficiency. Effectiveness addresses the question of whether the organization is achieving its intended goals, given environmental opportunities and constraints and organizational capabilities. Efficiency relates to productivity—the levels of output, given a specified unit of input. Suppose a sales representative has a high call frequency per day and a low cost-per-call expense ratio. The individual might be viewed favorably from an efficiency perspective. If the emphasis of the organization is on customer service and problem solving, however, this person might be viewed as ineffective.

Data versus Information

A third consideration is the qualitative difference between data and information. Data are essentially *reports* of activities, events, or performance. Information, on the other hand, may be viewed as a *classification* of activities, events, or performance designed to be interpretable and useful for decision making. The distinction between data and information was illustrated in the discussion of marketing-cost analysis techniques, where data were organized into meaningful classifications and operating ratios.

NOTES

1. For a review of the marketing control literature, see Bernard J. Jaworski, "Toward a Theory of Marketing Control: Environmental Context, Control Types, and Consequences," *Journal of Marketing* (July 1988): 23–29.

2. R. Paul, N. Donavan, and J. Taylor, "The Reality Gap in Strategic Planning," *Harvard Business Review* (May–June 1978): 126. See also Thomas Bonoma, "Making Your Marketing Strategy Work," *Harvard Business Review* (March–April 1984): 68–76.

3. These concepts were drawn from D. Abell, "Strategic Windows," *Journal of Marketing* (July 1978): 21–26.

4. This example is adapted from D. Landes, "Time Runs Out for the Swiss," *Across the Board* (January 1984): 46–55; and L. Rukeyser, "Swiss Recovery of Luxury Watch Market Provides Timely Lesson," *Dallas Times Herald* (November 12, 1989): D9.

5. Thomas Dudick, "Why SG&A Doesn't Always Work," *Harvard Business Review* (January–February 1987): 30–36.

6. B. Ames and J. Hlavacek, "Vital Truths about Managing Your Costs," *Harvard Business Review* (January–February 1990): 140–147. Dennis Weisman, "How Cost Allocation Systems Can Lead Managers Astray," *Journal of Cost Management* (Spring 1991): 4–10.

7. F. P. Strong, "Kodak: Beyond 1990," *Journal of Business & Industrial Marketing* (Fall 1987): 29–36.

8. Germain Boer, "In Defense of Contribution Margin Analysis," *Journal of Cost Management* (Summer (1989): 4–7.

TOSTITOS® Brand Tortilla Chips

In June 1988, Joshua Taylor, a senior product manager at Frito-Lay, Inc., scheduled a meeting with his brand group to review the performance of TOSTITOS® brand and SANTITAS® brand Tortilla Chips, two of the company's major tortilla chip brands. Both brands had come under competitive pressure in recent years because of the introduction of restaurant-style tortilla chips (RSTCs) by local producers in several regional markets. The purpose of the meeting was to assess the tortilla chip market and competitive activity and to develop the 1989 brand marketing plan. This plan would be presented to top management in late July.

FRITO-LAY, INCORPORATED

Frito-Lay, Inc., is a division of PepsiCo, Inc., a New York-based diversified consumer goods and services firm. Other PepsiCo, Inc., divisions include Pizza Hut, Inc., Taco Bell Corporation, Pepsi-Cola, Kentucky Fried Chicken, and PepsiCo Foods International. PepsiCo, Inc., recorded net income of $595 million on net sales of over $11 billion in 1987.

A nationally recognized leader in the manufacturing and marketing of salty snack foods, Frito-Lay makes LAY'S® brand, O'GRADY'S® brand, RUFFLES® brand, and DELTA GOLD® brand Potato Chips; FRITOS® brand Corn Chips; DORITOS® brand, TOSTITOS® brand, and SANTITAS® brand Tortilla Chips; CHEE·TOS® brand Cheese Flavored Snacks; and ROLD GOLD® brand pretzels. A sample of the company's major brands is shown in Exhibit 1. Other well-known Frito-Lay products include BAKEN-ETS® brand fried pork skins, MUNCHOS® brand potato crisps, and FUNYUNS® brand onion flavored snacks. In addition, the company markets a line of dips, nuts, peanut butter crackers, processed beef sticks, and GRANDMA'S® brand Cookies. Frito-Lay, Inc., recorded sales of $3.2 billion in 1987.

Regionality

Frito-Lay's market position varies by region within the United States, owing to consumer tastes and preferences and the presence of local or regional competitors. The popularity of tortilla chips is particularly affected by consumer tastes and preferences. For example, per capita consumption of tortilla chips in the northwestern United States is almost three times the consumption rate in the Northeast. Per capita

---

This case was prepared by graduate student Jane Lovett under the supervision of Professor Roger A. Kerin, of the Edwin L. Cox School of Business, Southern Methodist University, as a basis for class discussion and is not designed to illustrate effective or ineffective handling of an administrative situation. Certain names and data have been disguised. The cooperation of Frito-Lay, Inc., in the preparation of this case is gratefully acknowledged.

EXHIBIT 1

Frito-Lay's Major Brands

Source: Courtesy of Frito-Lay, Inc.

consumption growth rates also vary by region. During the period 1984 to 1987, per capita consumption in the Northeast increased 18 percent, whereas the growth rate in the Southwest was less than 1 percent (see Exhibit 2).

Although many firms market tortilla chips in the United States, only a small number of firms like Frito-Lay compete on a national scope. The remaining companies serve local or regional markets and provide products tailored to regional tastes. In addition, private-label or store brands are sold by chain supermarkets such as Kroger and Safeway. It is estimated that there are over 200 individual brands of tortilla chips.

EXHIBIT 2

Per Capita Consumption and Growth Rates for Tortilla Chips by Region

Region	*1987 Per Capita Consumption (Pounds)*	*Per Capital Consumption Growth Rate, 1984–1987 (Percentage)*
Midwest	2.02	16.1
Central	1.55	13.4
Southwest	2.28	0.9
Southeast	1.12	11.0
Northeast	0.90	18.0
East	1.11	8.3
West	2.31	10.4
Northwest	2.55	16.2
U.S. average	1.63	12.2

Frito-Lay Regional Marketing

The presence of regional variations in consumer taste, coupled with unique competitive conditions in different regional markets, prompted Frito-Lay to adopt a regional marketing orientation in 1984. The objective of this orientation was to combine the advantages of a large national firm, including scale economics and brand image, with a focus on the specific consumer and trade (retailer) needs of smaller, regional markets. Regional marketing groups, which manage 30 percent of the company's advertising and promotion budget, focus on region-specific programs, including pricing practices and sales promotion activities. This orientation gives Frito-Lay the flexibility to respond quickly to regional and local marketing opportunities and competitor actions.

TORTILLA CHIP MARKET

Tortilla chips are made from corn and are produced using a process that allows for different sizes and shapes. Tortilla chips are typically produced in strips, triangles, and circles. Tortilla chips come flavored and unflavored, with cheese and sour cream being the most popular flavors.

Tortilla chips have multiple uses. Consumers use tortilla chips for dipping, in cooking (in nachos and taco salads), and as a snack food. About 70 percent of tortilla chip volume is attributed to cooking and dipping. Unflavored chips are used mostly for cooking and dipping, whereas flavored chips are used primarily as a snack. Approximately 57 percent of annual tortilla chip sales are of the unflavored variety.

Frito-Lay created the tortilla chip product category in 1961 with the introduction of DORITOS® brand tortilla chips. The category has enjoyed consistent sales growth over the past 27 years. The average annual sales growth since 1981 has been 10.5 percent. With 1987 industry retail sales of $1.3 billion, the tortilla chip category ranked second among salty snack foods in sales volume, after potato chips.

Households purchasing tortilla chips were smaller than households purchasing other salty snack foods and tended to have no children. They had a higher income than the general population, were primarily in the 25–44 age bracket, tended to be white collar, and resided in large metropolitan areas with populations of over 1 million.

Tortilla Chip Competitors

Three types of competitors serve the tortilla chip market: (1) major branded tortilla chip producers with national or regional distribution, (2) two- or three-person operations producing local brands, and (3) private-label producers. National brand firms include Frito-Lay, Borden (La Famous brand tortilla chips), the Eagle Snacks Division of Anheuser-Busch (Cantina brand tortilla chips and El Charrito Nacho Cheese tortilla chips), and Keebler Company (Suncheros). Major branded regional tortilla chip firms include Laura Scudder in the western United States, Mission Foods Corporation in the western and southwestern United States, and Jimenez in the southwestern United States.

Large (national and regional) branded tortilla chip producers capture approximately 75 percent of tortilla chip dollar sales; small local producers capture 19 percent of industry dollar sales. Private-label tortilla chips, produced by local or regional firms on a contractual basis for supermarkets, account for 6 percent of industry dollar sales.

Major regional competitors are more concentrated and active in the western southwestern, and midwestern United States, whereas competition is fragmented and less aggressive in the eastern United States. Except in the East and the Northeast, tortilla chips are sold through supermarkets and grocery stores. In the East and the Northeast, tortilla chips are sold primarily through delicatessens, where they are viewed as a specialty product.

Emergence of Restaurant-Style Tortilla Chips

During the early 1980s, restaurant-style tortilla chips were introduced in several regional markets. Consumer taste tests indicate that these chips are considered to be of a lower quality. The name "restaurant-style tortilla chip" derived from their original use in Mexican restaurants, where they are used for nachos and for dipping with *pico de gallo*—a red hot sauce made with jalapeño peppers, onions, and spices. They are typically sold in supermarkets in one-pound bags and are used mostly for cooking (making nachos) and with dips. By 1987 RSTCs had achieved a substantial market share in several regional markets, despite little or no advertising. RSTCs accounted for 70 to 75 percent of tortilla chip pound sales on the West Coast (including the Northwest), 45 percent of pound sales in the Southwest, and 25 percent of pound sales in the Midwest. The 1987 RSTC unit volume market share in the United States was estimated to be 40 percent, according to industry sources.

RSTCs are unflavored, come in all shapes, and are typically priced below national and regional tortilla chip brands. Expressed as an index of prices, the average price differential between RSTCs and TOSTITOS® Tortilla Chips is 163. That is, if the price per pound for RSTCs were $1.00, the pound price for TOSTITOS® Tortilla Chips would be $1.63. The price differential between RSTCs and SANTITAS® Tortilla Chips is 106. This means that if RSTCs were priced at $1.00 per pound, SANTITAS® Tortilla Chips would sell for $1.06. The price differential varies by region of the country based on competitive activity (see Exhibit 3).

Few differences exist between consumers of RSTCs and consumers of national and regional tortilla chip brands. RSTC consumers generally tend to be slightly older and better educated and have slightly higher incomes.

EXHIBIT 3

Price Gap between Frito-Lay Tortilla Chips and Restaurant-Style Tortilla Chips by Region of the United States (RSTC = 100)

	Price Index	
Region	*TOSTITOS®* *Tortilla Chips*	*SANTITAS®* *Tortilla Chips*
Midwest	160	107
Central	147	111
Southwest	164	112
Southeast	157	102
Northeast	147	111
East	169	104
West	133	99
Northwest	149	107
National average	163	106

EXHIBIT 4

Example of Media Advertising for TOSTITOS® Brand Tortilla Chips, 1980

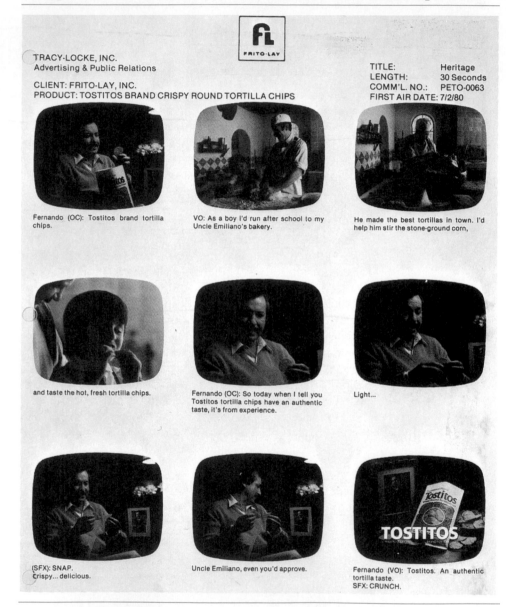

FRITO-LAY TORTILLA CHIP MARKETING

Frito-Lay produces and markets three branded tortilla chips: DORITOS®, TOSTITOS,® and SANTITAS® brand tortilla chips.

EXHIBIT 5

Example of Media Advertising for TOSTITOS® Brand Tortilla Chips, 1983

TRACY-LOCKE BBDO

TITLE: GROCER
LENGTH: 30 SECONDS
COMM'L NO.: PETO-3033
FIRST AIR DATE: 10/3/83

CLIENT: FRITO-LAY, INC.
PRODUCT: TOSTITOS® BRAND CRISPY ROUND TORTILLA CHIPS

GROCER: Two more.
CLERK: Don't all these tortilla chips make nachos?

GROCER: Yep.
FERNANDO: AHHHH...

FERNANDO: (Cont.) TOSTITOS Brand Tortilla Chips.

GROCER: But. . .Customers say one tastes best by themselves. TOSTITOS.

GROCER: Delicious, right out of the bag, they say.

FERNANDO: Incredibly thin, crisp and mild.

CLERK: Customer's always right!

FERNANDO: If you haven't tried TOSTITOS, you're missing an irresistibly delicious snack. TOSTITOS, America's best tasting tortilla chips.

CLERK: What about all these other chips?
GROCER: What other chips?

DORITOS® Brand Tortilla Chips

The DORITOS® brand tortilla chip, which pioneered the tortilla chip product category, was introduced as an unflavored, triangular tortilla chip in 1961. New flavored products were later introduced as line extensions of DORITOS® Tortilla Chips, including Nacho Cheese-flavor DORITOS® Tortilla Chips and Cool Ranch® brand fla-

EXHIBIT 6

Example of Media Advertising for TOSTITOS® Brand Tortilla Chips, 1986

TRACY-LOCKE

CLIENT: Frito-Lay, Inc.
PRODUCT: TOSTITOS® Brand Chilada
Flavor Tortilla Chips

TITLE: "Fernando Meets
The Adams Family"
LENGTH: 30 Seconds
COMM'L. NO.: PETO-6013
FIRST AIR DATE: 4/21/86

ANNCR (VO): Introducing 'Chilada.
SFX: ADAMS BELL RINGS.

LURCH: Yes.

FERNANDO: Tostitos Brand has a new
flavor.

MORTICIA: Isn't that sweet?

FERNANDO: No zesty. New 'Chilada. I
thought you'd like some.

GOMEZ: How did you know?

FERNANDO: I thought you'd like
exciting Mexican seasonings on a crispy
chip. (BREAK).

MORTICIA: We do think alike.

FERNANDO: Try 'em.

GOMEZ: If you insist.

ANNCR: New 'Chilada flavor. Peppers,
spices, and a touch of sour cream.

FERNANDO (VO): You like this new
flavor, Fester?
FESTER: Mmmm . . . that's very tasty.

EXHIBIT 7

Example of Media Advertising for TOSTITOS® Brand Tortilla Chips, Late 1987

TRACY-LOCKE, INC.
CLIENT: FRITO-LAY, INC.
PRODUCT: TOSTITOS® BRAND
TORTILLA CHIPS

TITLE: "FASHIONABLE REVISED"
LENGTH: 30 Seconds
COMM'L NO.: PETO-8073
DATE: 9/22/87

(Music under) FARNSWORTH: Things in our little part of the world are getting fashionable in the big city.

First this wearing apparel.

And now it's the food. Well, take some advice on the food, and go with the genuine article. It all seems to taste better.

Like these.

Made the old fashioned way. Stone-ground corn.

Stick with these. Don't embarrass me on this one.

(SFX: CRUNCH!)

AVO: Thin, crisp TOSTITOS® Brand Tortilla Chips.

The flavor's a legend.

EXHIBIT 8

Sales and Advertising and Promotion Spending Mix for TOSTITOS® Brand Tortilla Chips, 1985–1988

	1985	*1986*	*1987*	*1988*
Sales (millions of dollars, at manufacturer's prices)	$96	$88	$79	$72
Advertising and promotion mix (%):				
Media advertising[a]	71%	37%	27%	51%
Trade promotion[b]	21	47	44	38
Consumer promotion[c]	4	9	16	3
Other[d]	4	7	13	8
	100%	100%	100%	100%

[a]Media advertising includes electronic and print media directed at consumers.

[b]Trade promotion includes price reductions and print advertising directed at retail buyers and in-store displays.

[c]Consumer promotion includes coupons.

[d]Other includes special-events marketing.

vor DORITOS® Tortilla Chips. DORITOS® Tortilla Chips evolved into a flavored brand, with unflavored DORITOS® Tortilla Chips representing a declining percent of brand sales. DORITOS® Tortilla Chips are positioned primarily as a snack product.

TOSTITOS® Brand Tortilla Chips

A high-quality, premium-priced round tortilla chip, the TOSTITOS® brand tortilla chip was introduced nationally in 1981 as a complementary brand to DORITOS® Tortilla Chips. TOSTITOS® Tortilla Chips soon became a major brand in its own right, however. Although both flavored and unflavored products are sold, the unflavored TOSTITOS® Tortilla Chip has represented approximately 78 percent of total brand sales in recent years.

TOSTITOS® Tortilla Chips has been supported with major national media advertising, as well as trade and consumer promotion. According to industry sources, media advertising expenditures for TOSTITOS® Tortilla Chips were $9 million in 1985, $3.5 million in 1986, and $2.8 million in 1987. Although the TOSTITOS® Tortilla Chip was originally positioned as an authentic Mexican (stoneground corn) chip, it assumed a more competitive posture in 1982, with its positioning as the "best-tasting tortilla chip" (thin and crisp). In 1985 positioning shifted more toward product usage ("for sharing") and continued this way until a return to a more competitive posture occurred in 1987 ("best tasting"). Current advertising positions TOSTITOS® Tortilla Chips as the "ultimate tortilla chip." Exhibits 4, 5, 6, and 7 illustrate four of the positioning strategies for TOSTITOS® Tortilla Chips as reflected in television advertising. Dollar sales of unflavored TOSTITOS® Tortilla Chips have stayed relatively

EXHIBIT 9

Retail Market Share (Percentage) of TOSTITOS® Tortilla Chips

| Region | TOSTITOS® Tortilla Chips Share of Total Tortilla Chips | | | | Pound Market Share for Unflavored TOSTITOS® Tortilla Chips | | Dollar Market Share for Unflavored TOSTITOS® Tortilla Chips | |
| | Pound Market Share | | Dollar Market Share | | | | | |
	1987	1988	1987	1988	1987	1988	1987	1988
Midwest	15.6%	13.6%	18.0%	15.8%	24.6%	23.5%	32.5%	31.7%
Central	16.3	14.2	18.0	15.3	42.2	37.5	52.8	47.9
Southwest	24.4	23.6	25.7	25.1	35.8	34.2	41.8	40.6
Southeast	18.3	16.1	19.4	17.0	45.0	43.2	53.1	51.9
Northeast	6.8	4.7	7.7	5.4	23.7	19.0	31.5	26.6
East	12.9	9.4	14.6	10.7	37.8	30.0	47.1	39.3
West	6.5	6.2	8.5	7.7	6.5	6.6	10.3	10.0
Northwest	3.8	3.4	5.3	4.1	3.3	4.0	54.0	5.6

EXHIBIT 10

Sales and Advertising and Promotion Spending Mix for SANTITAS® Tortilla Chips, 1985–1988

	1985	*1986*	*1987*	*1988*
Sales (millions of dollars, at manufacturer's prices)	$3.4	$16.7	$21.0	$31.9
Advertising and promotion mix (%)				
Media advertising	0%	0%	0%	6%
Trade promotion	40	80	86	86
Consumer promotion	25	15	8	0
Other	35	5	6	8
	100%	100%	100%	100%

Note: See notes to Exhibit 8 for a description of the different types of advertising and promotion.

flat during the past few years, and sales volume of flavored TOSTITOS® Tortilla Chips has declined. Exhibit 8 gives an overview of sales and advertising and promotion effort for TOSTITOS® Tortilla Chips for the period 1985–1988. Exhibit 9 shows the TOSTITOS® Tortilla Chips market share data for 1987 and 1988.

SANTITAS® Brand Tortilla Chips

The SANTITAS® brand tortilla chip was introduced nationally in 1986 as Frito-Lay's competitive response to the growth in the RSTC segment. SANTITAS® Tortilla Chips are available in two shapes: triangular chips, designed primarily for cooking purposes, and strips, designed to accompany dips. Although no media advertising support was provided for SANTITAS® Tortilla Chips, sales in 1988 were $31.9 million, making it the nation's largest-selling RSTC brand. SANTITAS® Tortilla Chips sales and its advertising and promotion mix for the period 1985–1988 are shown in Exhibit 10. Exhibit 11 gives SANTITAS® Tortilla Chips market share data for 1987 and 1988. Frito-Lay executives believed that virtually all SANTITAS® Tortilla Chips sales were incremental to Frito-Lay, resulting in little cannibalization of either TOSTITOS® or DORITOS® Tortilla Chip sales.

Production Technology for TOSTITOS® and SANTITAS® Brand Tortilla Chips

TOSTITOS® and SANTITAS® Tortilla Chips are produced using a "wet corn" technology, in which stoneground corn is used to make a masa dough. Individual chips are formed from the masa and are then baked and fried. The wet corn technology used by Frito-Lay is considered to be the traditional approach for making tortilla chips. Identical production technologies coupled with equally high quality ingredients for TOSTITOS® and SANTITAS® Tortilla Chips result in identical production costs for both brands. The retail margin for both brands is about 36 percent.

EXHIBIT 11

Retail Market Share of SANTITAS® Tortilla Chips (Percentage)

| Region | SANTITAS® Tortilla Chips Share of Total Tortilla Chips | | | | Pound Market Share for SANTITAS® Unflavored Tortilla Chips | | Dollar Market Share for SANTITAS® Unflavored Tortilla Chips | |
| | Pound Market Share | | Dollar Market Share | | | | | |
	1987	1988	1987	1988	1987	1988	1987	1988
Midwest	2.8%	2.6%	2.2%	2.0%	7.4%	6.6%	6.6%	6.0%
Central	1.8	1.5	1.3	1.2	7.3	5.8	6.2	5.3
Southwest	4.0	5.4	2.8	3.7	7.2	9.9	5.7	7.8
Southeast	1.6	2.7	1.0	1.8	5.7	9.2	4.1	7.1
Northeast	1.7	2.2	1.1	1.5	9.3	11.6	7.5	9.9
East	1.4	2.2	0.9	1.5	6.0	9.0	4.4	7.2
West	4.4	5.4	3.7	4.2	7.5	9.8	7.9	9.7
Northwest	9.4	10.8	7.5	8.5	17.3	20.2	16.6	19.2

Marshall Museum of Art

In early 1992, Ashley Mercer, Director of Development and Community Affairs, and Donald Pate, Director of Finance and Administration, of the Jonathon A. Marshall Museum of Art and History, met to discuss what had transpired at a meeting the previous afternoon. The meeting, attended by the senior staff of the museum and several members of the museum's Board of Trustees, had focused on the financial status of the museum. The Marshall Museum recorded its third consecutive annual loss in 1991, and Mercer and Pate were assigned responsibility for making recommendations that would reverse the situation.

MARSHALL MUSEUM

The Marshall Museum of Art (MMA) is a not-for-profit corporation located in Universal City, a large metropolitan area in the western United States. Founded at the turn of the century, MMA was originally chartered as the Fannel County Museum of Fine Arts and funded by an annual appropriation from Fannel County. In the early 1960s, the name was changed to the Jonathon A. Marshall Museum of Art to recognize the museum's major benefactor, Jonathon A. Marshall. Marshall, a wealthy local landowner and philanthropist, had provided the museum with a sizable endowment. According to the terms of a $25 million gift given to the museum upon his death, the museum's charter was revised and its name changed. The charter of the museum stated that its purpose was

> To provide an inviting setting for the appreciation of art in its historical and cultural contexts for the benefit of this and successive generations of Fannel County citizens and visitors.

Randall Brent III, the Museum Director, noted that this charter differentiated the MMA from art museums and history museums. He said:

> Our charter gives us both an opportunity and a challenge. By spanning both art and history, the museum offers a unique perspective on both. On the other hand, a person can only truly appreciate what we have here if they are willing to become historically literate—that is our challenge.

In 1984, the MMA benefited from a $28 million county bond election, which led to the construction of a new and expanded facility in the central business district of Universal City, the county seat of Fannel County. The location, six blocks from the museum's previous site, had extensive parking availability and access through public transportation. The site was made available for $1.00 from Jonathon Marshall's real estate holdings. At the dedication of the new museum in January 1987, Brent said:

This case was prepared by Professor Roger A. Kerin, of the Edwin L. Cox School of Business, Southern Methodist University, as a basis for class discussion and is not designed to illustrate effective or ineffective handling of an administrative situation. The museum name and certain operating data are disguised and not useful for research purposes. Copyright © by Roger A. Kerin. No part of this case may be reproduced without the written permission of the copyright holder.

I will always believe that the greatest strength of our new museum is that it was publicly mandated. The citizens of Fannel County and the vision and generosity of Jonathon Marshall have provided the setting for the appreciation of art and its historical and cultural contexts. As stewards of this public trust, the Marshall Museum can now focus on collecting significant works of art, encouraging scholarship and education, and decoding the history and culture of art.

Museum Collection and Display

The MMA has over 15,000 works of art in its permanent collection. However, as with most museums, MMA does not display all of its collection at the same time because of space limitations. Artworks in the collection are rotated, with some periodically loaned to other museums.

The MMA collection includes pre-Columbian, African, and Depression-era art, as well as European and American decorative arts. The art is displayed in different portions of the museum, where the building architecture accents the display. For example, Depression-era art is displayed in an Art Deco setting of the 1920s and 1930s; decorative and architectural art of the late nineteenth century is displayed in the Art Nouveau wing. In addition, museum docents provide a historical context for the artworks during tours.

The museum collection is open for viewing Monday through Saturday from 10:00 A.M. to 6:00 P.M. and Thursday evenings until 8:00 P.M. Sunday hours are from 12:00 noon to 6:00 P.M. There is no charge for viewing the permanent collection; however, a modest fee of $3.00 to $5.00 is charged for special exhibitions. The museum is also available for private showings and is often used for corporate, foundation, and various fund-raising events during weekday and weekend evenings. Exhibit 1 shows museum attendance for the period 1983–1991.

EXHIBIT 1

Museum Attendance

Year	Total Museum Attendance	Special Exhibitions[a]	
		Attendance	Proportion of Total Attendance
1983	269,786	N/A	N/A
1984	247,799	N/A	N/A
1985	303,456	N/A	N/A
1986	247,379	N/A	N/A
1987	667,949	220,867	0.33
1988	486,009	140,425	0.29
1989	527,091	227,770	0.43
1990	468,100	203,800	0.44
1991	628,472	284,865	0.45

[a]Special exhibitions attendance includes attendance at private corporation, foundation, and fund-raising events held at the museum.

Museum Organization

The MMA is organized by function: (1) Collections and Exhibitions, (2) Development and Community Affairs, and (3) Finance and Administration. Each function is headed by a director who reports to the Museum Director, Randall Brent III. The museum has a staff of 185 employees. In addition, 475 volunteers work at the museum in a variety of capacities.

The Collections and Exhibitions staff, headed by Thomas Crane, oversees the museum's art collections, arranges special exhibits, is responsible for educational programming, and provides personnel and administrative support for museum operations that directly involve the artwork. The Finance and Administration staff, headed by Donald Pate, is responsible for the daily operation of the museum. The museum's profit centers (the Skyline Buffet restaurant, parking, museum gift shop, and special exhibitions events) are also managed by this function. The Development and Community Affairs staff, under the direction of Ashley Mercer, is responsible for marketing, public relations, membership, and grants. This function engages in fund raising for the museum, which provides supplemental funds for general operating support, endowment, and acquisitions. This function also handles all applications for foundation, federal, state, and local grants.

Museum Finances

Exhibit 2 shows the financial condition of the MMA for the period 1989–1991. Total museum revenues and expenses during this period are shown below:

	1991	1990	1989
Total revenue	$10,794,110	$7,783,712	$8,694,121
Total expenses	11,177,825	7,967,530	8,920,674
Net income (loss)	($ 383,715)	($ 183,818)	($ 226,533)

The three consecutive years of losses followed seven consecutive years of either break-even or profitable status. The cumulative loss of $794,066 had depleted the museum's financial reserves.

During a recent Board of Trustees meeting, several observations and projections were made that indicated that the museum's financial condition needed attention:

1. The appropriation from Fannel County would decline further as a result of the recessionary environment. Whereas the county appropriated about $2 million annually to the MMA in the early and mid-1980s, the museum could expect no more than $1.6 million in county appropriations in 1992 and for the foreseeable future.

2. Declining interest rates in 1991 and 1992 indicated that earnings from the museum endowment and investments would probably remain flat or decline.

3. Income from grants and other contributions in 1991 were extraordinary, and it was unlikely that the same amounts would be forthcoming in 1992.

4. Membership revenues were down for the fifth consecutive year. Membership represented the single largest source of revenue for the museum.

5. Income from auxiliary activities—those that were intended to produce a profit—continued to show a positive contribution to museum operations.

EXHIBIT 2

Summary of Income and Expenses, 1989–1991

	Year Ending December 31		
Operations	*1991*	*1990*	*1989*
Income			
Appropriations by Fannel County	$1,786,929	$1,699,882	$1,971,999
Memberships	2,917,325	2,956,746	3,134,082
Contributions	338,664	221,282	42,244
Grants	763,581	281,164	645,853
Investment income	27,878	28,537	32,205
Earnings from endowment	673,805	693,625	583,612
Other	149,462	128,628	196,195
Total revenue	$6,657,644	$6,009,864	$6,606,190
Expenses			
Personnel	$1,973,218	$1,086,177	$1,681,653
Memberships	854,461	869,043	906,314
Publications/public information	594,067	404,364	441,710
Education	616,828	519,805	542,076
Administration[a]	3,777,042	3,345,153	3,389,124
Total expenses	$7,815,616	$6,224,542	$6,960,877
Operating Income	($1,157,972)	($ 214,678)	($ 354,687)
Auxiliary Activities			
Revenue from auxiliary			
Special exhibitions	$1,655,200	$ 510,415	$ 451,347
Museum gift shop	1,596,775	606,503	810,123
Skyline Buffet	515,843	305,952	418,960
Museum parking	131,512	45,068	64,651
Museum Association	337,136	305,910	342,850
Revenue from auxiliary	4,236,466	1,773,848	2,087,931
Expenses from Auxiliary			
Special exhibitions	814,741	313,057	137,680
Museum gift shop	1,679,294	662,685	990,090
Skyline Buffet	592,051	457,841	462,475
Museum parking	31,168	16,528	16,536
Museum Association	344,955	292,877	353,016
Expenses from auxiliary	3,462,209	1,742,988	1,959,797
Profit from auxiliary activities	$ 774,257	$ 30,860	$ 128,134
Net income	($ 383,715)	($ 183,818)	($ 226,553)

[a]Administration expenses included mostly overhead costs, such as insurance, maintenance, utilities, equipment lease agreements, and so forth.

Special exhibitions and events were very profitable. Nevertheless, limited availability of special exhibitions in 1992, a declining number of scheduled events, and rising costs (for insurance as an example) indicated that the revenues from such activities would probably decline and costs increase in 1992. The Skyline Buffet restaurant, museum gift shop and parking, and the Museum Association were operating at about break-even.

MUSEUM MARKETING

As Director of Development and Community Affairs, Ashley Mercer was responsible for marketing at the MMA. Her specific responsibilities related to enhancing the image of the museum, increasing museum visitation, and building museum memberships. Reflecting on her responsibilities, she said:

> In reality, museum image, visitation, and membership are intermingled. Image influences visitation and membership. Visitation is driven somewhat by membership, but membership seems to also drive visitation and, in a subtle way, affects the image of the museum.

Museum Image

Interest in the public image of the MMA began soon after the new facility was dedicated in 1987. The new four-story building, situated downtown adjacent to skyscrapers, was occasionally referred to as the "marble box" by its critics, since the building facade contained Italian marble. When asked about the image of the MMA, Brent commented:

> It is basically correct to say that, in the mind of the public, the MMA has no image. There is nothing but this [building] that says,, "I'm a museum," or "Come in." There are a lot of people that are not interested in high culture and think this is a drive-in bank or an office building.
>
> Most museums in America have a problem with image. One of the things that makes me mad is that people think there is something wrong with the museum. The MMA is the most public museum in the country, and more heavily dependent on the membership contribution than any other [museum]. Like most, it is underendowed and underfunded from reliable public funds. This institution has chosen to be public, with free access, and this is very noble. It is wonderful that the museum has decided not to belong to an agglomeration of very rich people.
>
> This institution has more character than it thinks it has. It has the best balanced collection between Western and non-Western art of any museum in the country. We have not chosen to sell or promote the unique aspects of this collection or the museum's emphasis on historical context. What we have are the makings of an institution that is very different from other museums, and we ought to be able to make that into an advantage rather than apologize for it.

Other staff members believed either that an image existed but was different for the various publics the museum served or that the museum had not made a sufficient effort to create an image for itself. According to Ashley Mercer:

> Based on our marketing research, I think there are two distinctly different images. One is a non-image. People don't know what the museum is. They also don't know what we have to offer in the way of lunch, dinner, brunch, shopping, movies, etc.

They are not familiar with our collections. They are probably proud, however, that their community has a beautiful art and history museum.

The other image is that we are only for specific people. This image is probably based on our membership. About 85 percent of members are college-educated (compared to 70 percent of the county population of 2.5 million), 60 percent have household incomes in excess of $60,000 (compared to 25 percent of the county population), half are over 40 years old (compared to 25 percent of the county population), and 98 percent are white (compared to 75 percent of the county population).

Janet Blake, Staff Assistant in charge of membership, noted:

Among our membership, MMA is viewed as a community organization that has a cachet of class. It is exciting, educational, convenient, and inviting. It is a great place to bring visitors to our city for an afternoon of lunch and browsing.

A critic of the museum said:

The MMA has a definite image in my opinion. It's a great place to have lunch or brunch, buy an art or history book for the coffee table, and see a few things if time permits. Its parking facility is strategically located to allow its members to park conveniently for downtown shopping, particularly during the Christmas holidays.

Museum Visitation

Because there is a general belief that increased numbers of visitors lead to increased membership, Mercer's staff has historically focused its efforts on increasing the traffic through the museum. "Social, cultural, and educational activity in the museum is a major goal, and is not exclusive to the viewing of art," said Mercer. These efforts can be separated into general and outreach programs and programs involving special exhibition and events.

Press Relations The museum continually promotes its special exhibitions and activities by sending out press releases, and it maintains a close relationship with the local media. Stories about art and history, public programs, and human interest issues are often featured in the local media. A five-year anniversary party was held at the museum in early 1991, designed as a free special event aimed to involve the general public with the museum.

Education and Outreach The museum has many programs directed toward educating the public. Among these are public programs such as adult tours, school tours, lectures, art films, and feature films. The museum engages in programming to create community involvement and lends performing space to local performing arts organizations.

Special Exhibitions Public service announcements written by the museum are aired on local radio stations to promote special exhibitions. Advertisements are run in local newspapers in a five-county area for special exhibitions. For major special exhibitions, advertising is usually sponsored by a local corporation.

Ashley Mercer believed that these efforts increased museum attendance. For example, periodic visitor surveys indicate that on a typical day when only the permanent collection was available for viewing, 85 percent of visitors in the museum were non-MMA members. She added that even though less than 1 percent of nonmembers actually applied for membership during a visit, this exposure helped in the annual membership solicitation.

Museum Membership

According to Mercer:

> Museum membership and the revenue earned from membership play significant roles in the success and daily operations of the MMA. The museum and its members have a symbiotic relationship. Members provide the museum with a volunteer base, without which our cost of operation would be astronomical. Member volunteers provide museum tours, assist at the information desk, help in the gift shop and the Skyline Buffet, and are invaluable in recruiting new members and renewing existing members.
>
> The Museum Association was created to encourage membership involvement in the museum. The Association, with some 1,000 members, makes our volunteer effort possible—95 percent of our 475 volunteers are Museum Association members. The Association's assistance in fund raising is critical, and we appreciate what its members have done for the MMA. Last year alone, the Association was directly responsible for raising almost $350,000. In return, the museum sponsors social events for Association members, offers them lectures by authorities on art and history, and provides various other privileges not available to the general membership.

Member Categories, Benefits, and Costs The MMA has two distinct memberships: (1) personal and (2) corporate. These two memberships are further divided into categories based on dollar contributions and benefits received. There are six

EXHIBIT 3

Membership Benefits by Membership Categories

	Membership Category					
Benefits	*$50*	*$100*	*$250*	*$500*	*$1,500*	*$5,000*
Invitations to special previews/events	*	*	*	*	*	*
Free limited parking	*	*	*	*	*	*
Free admission to special exhibits	*	*	*	*	*	*
15% discount at Skyline Buffet and gift shop	*	*	*	*	*	*
Monthly calender	*	*	*	*	*	*
Discounts on films/lectures	*	*	*	*	*	*
Reciprocal membership in other museums		*	*	*	*	*
Invitations to distinguished lectures			*	*	*	*
Listing in Annual Report			*	*	*	*
Personal tours of exhibition areas				*	*	*
Invitations to exclusive previews/events					*	*
Free unlimited parking					*	*
Unique travel opportunities					*	*
Recognition on plaques in museum					*	*
First views of new acquisitions					*	*
Priority on all museum trips						*
Dinner with the Director						*

categories of personal membership ranging from $50 per year to $5,000 per year. Corporate memberships are divided into four categories ranging from $1,000 per year to $10,000 per year. These categories and participation levels were created in 1987 with the move to the new building. In 1991, there were 17,429 personal memberships and 205 corporate memberships.

Exhibit 3 shows the benefits received by each personal membership category. Exhibit 4 provides a breakdown of personal memberships by category and the revenue generated by each category over the past five years. In 1991, personal memberships accounted for almost 80 percent of membership revenue.

Corporate memberships provide many of the same benefits as the $500 or higher personal memberships. In addition, corporate members are given "Employee Memberships" depending on their category. For example, corporate members that fall into the $1,000 category are given 25 "Employee Memberships"; those in the $10,000 category are given 250 such memberships.

The direct cost of benefits provided by the museum to personal and corporate members was estimated by the museum's accounting firm in 1991. The museum was required to do this because of income tax laws that limited the deductibility of membership to the difference between the direct cost of membership and the value of the benefits received. The estimated total cost of member benefits provided exceeded $1 million.[1] An itemized summary of benefit costs by category is shown below.

Category	Benefit Cost
Regular ($50)	$ 631,016
Associate ($100)	81,903
Collector ($250)	64,135
Patron ($500)	39,628
Partner ($1,500)	99,567
Director's Club ($5,000)	15,975
Corporate (all categories)	125,576
Total cost	$1,057,800

The principal cost items in each category were (1) free admissions to exhibits, (2) parking, (3) the monthly calendar of museum activities, exhibits, and events, and (4) discounts at the Skyline Buffet restaurant and museum gift shop.

Member Recruiting and Renewals "Recruiting new members and renewing existing members is a major undertaking," said Mercer. While some recruiting and renewals occur at the museum during visitation, the recruitment effort mostly revolves around mail, telephone, and personal solicitations. Mail and telephone solicitations focus primarily on recruiting and renewing personal memberships in the $50 to $250 categories. Personal solicitations by the Museum Association and Friends of the MMA are used to recruit and renew personal memberships in the $500 to $5,000 categories and corporate memberships.

The MMA uses mailing and telephone lists obtained from other cultural organizations and list agencies. These lists are culled to target zip codes and telephone prefix numbers. Mail solicitations include a letter from the Museum Director, a

---

[1]The estimated cost of benefits exceeds the membership expense shown in Exhibit 2 because the cost of publications and other items is included in this estimate. These costs are allocated across several different items in Exhibit 2.

EXHIBIT 4

Personal Membership Categories and Revenues by Year, 1987–1991

Membership Category	Amount	Number of Members				
		1991	1990	1989	1988	1987
Regular	$50	13,672	12,248	13,483	16,353	17,758
Associate	$100	2,596	2,433	2,548	2,576	2,465
Collector	$250	364	325	397	461	454
Patron	$500	102	85	65	0	0
Partner	$1,500	604	638	679	741	882
Director's Club	$5,000	91	86	98	0	0
Total membership		17,429	15,815	17,370	20,131	21,559

		Membership Revenue[a]				
		1991	1990	1989	1988	1987
Regular	$50	$ 639,664	$ 556,120	$ 611,864	$ 600,188	$ 662,631
Associate	$100	234,871	232,398	249,317	244,961	242,981
Collector	$250	81,415	76,987	97,474	108,432	105,840
Patron	$500	48,100	44,293	35,500	0	0
Partner	$1,500	815,666	958,419	968,239	1,187,728	1,041,898
Director's Club	$5,000	406,673	405,016	458,938	282,219	0
Total membership revenue[b]		$2,298,449	$2,334,583	$2,485,352	$2,451,638	$2,079,330

[a]The number of memberships times the dollar value does not equal the amounts given as the membership revenue, since some memberships are given gratis.

[b]The inconsistency between these figures and the figures shown on the income and expense statement is due to memberships given gratis.

brochure describing the museum, and a membership application form. Telephone solicitations include a follow-up brochure and application form.

The economics of direct mail solicitation are illustrated below, based on an August 1991 mailing considered typical by Mercer.

Total mail solicitations	148,530
Total memberships obtained	1,532
Response rate	1.03%
Total membership revenue	$84,280.00
Total direct mail costs	$66,488.80

Two direct mail solicitations of this magnitude are conducted each year.

The solicitation process for personal memberships in larger dollar categories and corporate memberships relies on personal contact by museum volunteers and corporate member executives. Prospective members are identified on the basis of personal contacts and from the lapsed membership roster, the society page, other organizations' membership lists, and lower-membership-level lists. Once identified, these prospects are approached on a one-to-one basis. An initial letter is sent introducing the prospect to the museum. This first letter is followed by a personal telephone call or another letter inviting the prospect to an informal gathering at the museum. At the gathering, the prospect is introduced to other members and is asked directly to become a member.

Renewal efforts also include mail and telephone solicitation. In addition, membership parties, special previews, and special inserts in the monthly calendar of museum activities are used.

Museum records indicate that 70 percent of the $50 members do not renew their membership after the first year. Among those that do, 50 percent renew in each successive year. Members in the $100 to $500 categories have a renewal rate of 60 percent, and members in the $1,500 and $5,000 categories have a renewal rate of 85 percent. Mercer believed that less than 10 percent of personal members who do renew their membership increase the dollar value of their membership. Renewal rates among corporate members is about 75 percent, regardless of category.

CONSIDERATIONS FOR 1992

Ashley Mercer and Donald Pate met to discuss measures they might recommend to the Board of Trustees to reverse the deteriorating financial condition of the MMA. Pate noted that at an earlier meeting with his staff, personnel reductions were discussed. Specifically, he felt that a 10 percent reduction in personnel and administration costs was possible. Furthermore, his staff estimated that the appropriation from Fannel County, contributions, grants, investment income, endowment earnings, and other income would be 15 percent below 1991 levels. A "best guess" estimate from the Director of Collections and Exhibitions indicated that special exhibitions and events would generate revenues of $1.2 million and cost $675,000 in 1992. Parking revenues and expenses resulting from nonmember visitors would remain unchanged from 1991. Rough budgets for museum education programs indicated that an expenditure of $500,000 for 1992 was realistic, given planned efforts. Pate said that changes in other auxiliary activities for which he was responsible, namely, the Skyline Buffet restaurant and museum gift shop, were not planned.

Mercer was impressed with the attention Pate had already given to MMA's situation. She too had given consideration to matters of museum image, visitation, and membership prior to the meeting. Unfortunately, an earlier meeting with her staff had raised more issues than hard-and-fast recommendations. Staff suggestions ranged from implementing an admission fee of $1.00 per adult (with no charge for children under 12 years old) to instituting student (ages 13–22) and senior citizen (60 and older) memberships at $30. The need for institutional advertising was raised, since the MMA had only been promoting special exhibitions and events. Other staff members said that the benefits given to members needed to be enhanced. For example, raising discounts at the Skyline Buffet and gift shop to 20 percent was suggested. Another possibility raised was commissioning a "coffee table" book featuring major artwork at the museum to be given with personal memberships of $500 or more.

Mercer listened to these suggestions, knowing that some were unlikely to receive Board of Trustee approval. These included any proposal to increase expenses for Publications/Public Information (for example, new books and paid institutional advertising). She had already been informed that expenses for such activities could not exceed the 1991 expenditure. Improving the member benefit package seemed like a good idea. Increasing restaurant and gift shop discounts, even though 65 percent of the business for both was already on discount, seemed like a good idea at least at the margin. Pate said that he would give this suggestion consideration, but asked that Mercer think further about it in the context of the overall member-benefit package. Charging a nominal admission fee for nonmembers also seemed reasonable. Visitor surveys had shown that 50 percent of nonmember museum visitors said that they would be willing to pay a $1.00 admission fee for viewing the permanent collection (access to special exhibitions would continue to have admission fees). Furthermore, members could then be given an additional benefit, that is, free admission. However, Pate noted that the MMA had always prided itself on free access, and he wondered how the Board of Trustees would view this suggestion. Additional membership categories below $50 and for students and senior citizens also seemed to provide new opportunities to attract segments of the population that had not typically yielded members.

Mercer and Pate believed that their initial meeting had produced some good ideas, but both thought that they had to give these matters further thought. They agreed to meet again and begin to prepare an integrated plan of action.

Hanover-Bates Chemical Corporation

James Sprague, newly appointed northeast district sales manager for the Hanover-Bates Chemical Corporation, leaned back in his chair as the door to his office slammed shut. "Great beginning," he thought. "Three days in my new job and the district's most experienced sales representative is threatening to quit."

On the previous night, Sprague, Hank Carver (the district's most experienced sales representative), and John Follet, another senior member of the district sales staff, had met for dinner at Sprague's suggestion. During dinner he had mentioned that one of his top priorities would be to conduct a sales and profit analysis of the district's business in order to identify opportunities to improve the district's profit performance. He had stated that he was confident that the analysis would indicate opportunities to reallocate district sales efforts in a manner that would increase profits. As Sprague had indicated during the conversation, "My experience in analyzing district sales performance data for the national sales manager has convinced me that any district's allocation of sales effort to products and customer categories can be improved." Both Carver and Follet had nodded as Sprague discussed his plans.

Carver was waiting when Sprague arrived at the district sales office this morning. It soon became apparent that Carver was very upset by what he perceived as Sprague's criticism of how he and the other district sales representatives were doing their jobs—and, more particularly, of how they were allocating their time in terms of customers and products. As he concluded his heated comments, Carver said:

> This company has made it darned clear that 34 years of experience don't count for anything . . . and now someone with not much more than two years of selling experience and two years of pushing paper for the national sales manager at corporate headquarters tells me I'm not doing my job. . . . Maybe it's time for me to look for a new job . . . and since Trumbull Chemical [Hanover-Bates's major competitor] is hiring, maybe that's where I should start looking . . . and I'm not the only one who feels this way.

As Sprague reflected on the scene that had just occurred, he wondered what he should do. It had been made clear to him when he had been promoted to manager of the northeast sales district that one of his top priorities should be improvement of the district's profit performance. As the national sales manager had said, "The northeast sales district may rank third in dollar sales, but it's our worst district in terms of profit performance."

Prior to assuming his new position, Sprague had assembled the data presented in Exhibits 1 through 6 to assist him in analyzing the district sales and profits. The data had been compiled from records maintained in the national sales manager's of-

---

This case was prepared by Professor Robert E. Witt, of the University of Texas, Austin, as a basis for class discussion and is not designed to illustrate effective or ineffective handling of an administrative situation.

EXHIBIT 1

Hanover-Bates Chemical Corporation: Summary Income Statements, 1986–1990

	1986	1987	1988	1989	1990
Sales	$19,890,000	$21,710,000	$19,060,000	$21,980,000	$23,890,000
Production expenses	11,934,000	13,497,000	12,198,000	13,612,000	14,563,000
Gross profit	7,956,000	8,213,000	6,862,000	8,368,000	9,327,000
Administrative expenses	2,606,000	2,887,000	2,792,000	2,925,000	3,106,000
Selling expenses	2,024,000	2,241,000	2,134,000	2,274,000	2,399,000
Pretax profit	3,326,000	3,085,000	1,936,000	3,169,000	3,822,000
Taxes	1,512,000	1,388,000	790,000	1,426,000	1,718,000
Net profit	$ 1,814,000	$ 1,697,000	$ 1,146,000	$ 1,743,000	$ 2,104,000

fice. Although he believed the data would provide a sound basis for a preliminary analysis of district sales and profit performance, Sprague had recognized that additional data would probably have to be collected when he arrived in the northeast district (District 3).

In response to the national sales manager's comment about the northeast district's poor performance, Sprague had been particularly interested in how the district had performed on its gross profit quota. He knew that district gross profit quotas were assigned in a manner that took into account variation in price competition. Thus, he felt that poor performance in the gross profit quota area reflected misallocated sales efforts either in terms of customers or in terms of the mix of product line items sold. To provide himself with a frame of reference, he had also requested data on the north-central sales district (District 7). This district is generally considered to be one of the best, if not the best, in the company. Furthermore, the north-central district sales manager, who is only three years older than Sprague, is highly regarded by the national sales manager.

EXHIBIT 2

District Sales Quota and Gross Profit Quota Performance, 1990

District	Number of Sales Reps.	Sales Quota	Sales— Actual	Gross Profit Quota[a]	Gross Profit— Actual
1	7	$ 3,880,000	$ 3,906,000	$1,552,000	$1,589,000
2	6	3,750,000	3,740,000	1,500,000	1,529,000
3	6	3,650,000	3,406,000	1,460,000	1,239,000
4	6	3,370,000	3,318,000	1,348,000	1,295,000
5	5	3,300,000	3,210,000	1,320,000	1,186,000
6	5	3,130,000	3,205,000	1,252,000	1,179,000
7	5	2,720,000	3,105,000	1,088,000	1,310,000
		$23,800,000	$23,890,000	$9,520,000	$9,327,000

[a]District gross profit quotas were developed by the national sales manager in consultation with the district managers and took into account price competition in the respective districts.

EXHIBIT 3

District Selling Expenses, 1990

District	Sales Rep. Salaries[a]	Sales Commission	Sales Rep. Expenses	District Office	District Manager Salary	District Manager Expenses	Sales Support	Total Selling Expenses
1	$177,100	$19,426	$56,280	21,150	33,500	$11,460	$69,500	$ 388,416
2	143,220	18,700	50,760	21,312	34,000	12,034	71,320	351,346
3	157,380	17,030	54,436	22,123	35,000[b]	12,382	70,010	368,529
4	150,480	16,590	49,104	22,004	32,500	11,005	66,470	348,153
5	125,950	16,050	42,720	21,115	33,000	11,123	76,600	326,558
6	124,850	16,265	41,520	20,992	33,500	11,428	67,100	315,655
7	114,850	17,530	44,700	22,485	31,500	11,643	58,750	300,258
								$2,398,915

[a]Includes cost of fringe benefit program, which was 10 percent of base salary.

[b]Salary of James Sprague's predecessor.

EXHIBIT 4

District Contribution to Corporate Administrative Expense and Profit, 1990

District	Sales	Gross Profit	Selling Expenses	Contribution to Administrative Expense and Profit
1	$ 3,906,000	$1,589,000	$ 388,416	$1,200,544
2	3,740,000	1,529,000	351,346	1,177,654
3	3,406,000	1,239,000	368,529	870,471
4	3,318,000	1,295,000	348,153	946,847
5	3,210,000	1,186,000	326,558	859,442
6	3,205,000	1,179,000	315,376	863,624
7	3,105,000	1,310,000	300,258	1,009,742
	$23,890,000	$9,327,000	$2,398,636	$6,928,324

THE COMPANY AND THE INDUSTRY

The Hanover-Bates Chemical Corporation is a leading producer of processing chemicals for the chemical plating industry. The company's products are produced in four plants, located in Los Angeles, Houston, Chicago, and Newark, New Jersey. The company's production process is, in essence, a mixing operation. Chemicals purchased from a broad range of suppliers are mixed according to a variety of user-based formulas. Company sales in 1990 had reached a new high of $23.89 million, up from $21.98 million in 1989. Net pretax profit in 1990 had been $3.822 million, up from $3.169 million in 1989. Hanover-Bates has a strong balance sheet, and the company enjoys a favorable price-earnings ratio on its stock, which trades on the OTC (over-the-counter) market.

Although Hanover-Bates does not produce commodity-type chemicals (such as sulfuric acid), industry customers tend to perceive minimal quality differences among the products produced by Hanover-Bates and its competitors. Given the customers' perception of a lack of variation in product quality and the industrywide practice of limiting advertising expenditures, field sales efforts are of major importance in the marketing programs of all firms in the industry.

EXHIBIT 5

Northeast (#3) and North-Central (#7) District Sales and Gross Profit Performance by Account Category, 1990

District	(A)	(B)	(C)	Total
Sales by Account Category				
Northeast	$915,000	$1,681,000	$810,000	$3,406,000
North-central	751,000	1,702,000	652,000	3,105,000
Gross Profit by Account Category				
Northeast	$356,000	$623,000	$260,000	$1,239,000
North-central	330,000	725,000	255,000	1,310,000

EXHIBIT 6

Potential Accounts, Active Accounts, and Account Call Coverage: Northeast and North-Central Districts, 1990

District	Potential Accounts			Active Accounts			Account Coverage (Total Calls)		
	(A)	(B)	(C)	(A)	(B)	(C)	(A)	(B)	(C)
Northeast	90	381	635	53	210	313	1,297	3,051	2,118
North-central	60	286	499	42	182	218	1,030	2,618	1,299

Hanover-Bates's market consists of several thousand job-shop and captive (in-house) plating operations. Chemical platers process a wide variety of materials including industrial fasteners (for example, screws, rivets, bolts, and washers), industrial components (for example, clamps, casings, and couplings), and miscellaneous items (for example, umbrella frames, eyelets, and decorative items). The chemical plating process involves the electrolytic application of metallic coatings such as zinc, cadmium, nickel, and brass. The degree of plating precision required varies substantially, with some work being primarily decorative, some involving relatively loose standards (for example, 0.0002 zinc, which means that anything over two ten-thousandths of an inch of plate is acceptable), and some involving relatively precise standards (for example, 0.0003–0.0004 zinc).

Regardless of the degree of plating precision involved, quality control is of critical concern to all chemical platers. Extensive variation in the condition of materials received for plating requires a high level of service from the firms supplying chemicals to platers. This service is normally provided by the sales representatives of the firm(s) supplying the plater with processing chemicals.

Hanover-Bates and the majority of the firms in its industry produce the same line of basic processing chemicals for the chemical plating industry. The line consists of a trisodium phosphate cleaner (SPX); anesic aldahyde brightening agents for zinc plating (ZBX), cadmium plating (CBX), and nickel plating (NBX); a protective post-plating chromate dip (CHX); and a protective burnishing compound (BUX). The company's product line is detailed as follows:

Product	Container Size	List Price	Gross Margin
SPX	400-lb. drum	$ 80	`$28
ZBX	50-lb. drum	76	34
CBX	50-lb. drum	76	34
NBX	50-lb. drum	80	35
CHX	100-lb. drum	220	90
BUX	400-lb. drum	120	44

COMPANY SALES ORGANIZATION

Hanover-Bates's sales organization consists of 40 sales representatives operating in seven sales districts. Most sales representatives had formerly worked for a Hanover-Bates customer, and none were college-educated. Sales representatives' salaries range from $22,000 to $30,000, with fringe-benefit costs amounting to an additional 10 percent of salary. In addition to their salaries, Hanover-Bates's sales representatives receive commissions of 0.5 percent of their dollar sales volume on all sales up to their sales quotas. The commission on sales in excess of quota is 1 percent. District sales manager salaries range from $31,500 to $35,000. Sales managers are also eligible for a bonus based on district sales performance.

In 1988 the national sales manager of Hanover-Bates had developed a sales program based on selling the full line of Hanover-Bates products. He believed that if the sales representatives could successfully carry out his program, the following benefits would accrue to Hanover-Bates and its customers:

1. Sales volume per account would be greater, and selling costs as a percentage of sales would decrease.

2. A Hanover-Bates sales representative could justify spending more time with an account, thus becoming more knowledgeable about the account's business and becoming better able to provide technical assistance and identify selling opportunities.

3. Full-line sales would strengthen Hanover-Bates's competitive position by reducing the likelihood of account loss to other plating-chemical suppliers (a problem that existed in multiple-supplier situations).

The national sales manager's 1988 sales program had also included the following account call–frequency guidelines:

A accounts (major accounts generating $12,000 or more in yearly sales)—two calls per month

B accounts (medium-sized accounts generating $6,000–$11,999 in yearly sales)—one call per month

C accounts (small accounts generating less than $6,000 yearly in sales)—one call every two months

The account call–frequency guidelines were developed by the national sales manager after discussions with the district managers. The national sales manager had been concerned about the optimal allocation of sales effort to accounts and felt that the guidelines would increase the efficiency of the company's sales force, although not all of the district sales managers agreed with this conclusion.

It was common knowledge in Hanover-Bates's corporate sales office that Sprague's predecessor as northeast district sales manager had not been one of the company's better district sales managers. His attitude toward the sales plans and programs of the national sales manager had been one of reluctant compliance rather than acceptance and support. However, when the national sales manager succeeded in persuading Sprague's predecessor to take early retirement, no replacement was readily available.

Carver, who most of the sales representatives had assumed would get the district manager job, had been passed over in part because he would be 65 in three years. The national sales manager had not wanted to face the same replacement problem again in three years and also had wanted someone in the position who would be more likely to be responsive to the company's sales plans and policies. The appointment of Sprague as district manager had caused considerable talk, not only in the district but also at corporate headquarters. In fact, the national sales manager had warned Sprague that "a lot of people are expecting you to fall on your face . . . they don't think you have the experience to handle the job, in particular, and to manage and motivate a group of sales representatives, most of whom are considerably older and more experienced than you." The general sales manager had concluded by saying, "I think you can handle the job, Jim. . . . I think you can manage those sales reps and improve the district's profit performance . . . and I'm depending on you to do both."

Dell Computer Corporation
Reformulation Strategy

"Well, I'm certainly glad that's behind us," Michael Dell muttered to himself as he walked back to his office. "Now it's time to really concentrate on the future of the company and achieve our 50 percent sales growth goal this fiscal year."

Michael Dell, Chairman and Chief Executive Officer of Dell Computer Corporation, had just released his firm's second-quarter financial results. For the period May–July, 1993, Dell Computer had record revenues of $701 million, but the company experienced a first-ever quarterly loss of $75.7 million, and gross margins declined 16.2 percent (22.7 percent to 6.5 percent) compared to the second quarter of the previous fiscal year. Much of the loss was due to a one-time restructuring charge, but even without the restructuring charge the company would not have been profitable.

Dell Computer Corporation had closed out its 1993 fiscal year January 31, 1993, as the world's fifth-largest personal computer (PC) company, with sales in excess of $2 billion and profit of more than $100 million. Even so, the downturn in the world economy was beginning to take its toll, and the marketing activities of major competitors in late 1992, such as IBM and Compaq, began to undermine Dell's competitive position by early 1993. These uncontrollable events, when combined with certain product-line gaps, lack of inventory control, and a shortage of experienced upper-level managers, together with rapid international growth, culminated in the company's first-ever quarterly loss. As Joel Kocher, Dell President of Worldwide Sales and Marketing, so aptly noted, competition in the PC industry is no longer limited to technology. Instead, partly because of impending market saturation for desktop computers, the focus is on "inventory, execution, and supply." Indeed, due to the industry's adoption of open standards (essentially initial standard industry components popularized by IBM), few proprietary technologies exist anymore with respect to desktop personal computers.

THE COMPANY

The story of Dell Computer Corporation is the story of Michael Dell and his strategic vision. As a college freshman in 1983, Michael Dell began selling personal computer disk drive kits and related parts to enthusiasts at local meetings of PC users. Within a few months, he was selling "gray market" IBM PCs out of his dormitory room. By April 1984, Dell had dropped out of college and was devoting all of his energies to his burgeoning business. Operating out of a small storefront, he began

---

This case was prepared by Professor Robert A. Peterson, of the University of Texas at Austin, with the assistance of Marisa Manheimer, as a basis for class discussion and is not designed to illustrate effective or ineffective handling of an administrative situation.

to manufacture and market some of the first IBM "clones" under the brand name PC's Limited. By 1986, PC's Limited had grown to 400 employees and reached $69.5 million in annual revenues.

In 1988, at the age of 23, Dell took his company public. By the end of January 1990, annual sales had reached $388.6 million (see Exhibits 1 and 2 for pertinent sales and operating information), and Michael Dell was named *Inc. Magazine's* Entrepreneur of the Year. The following year *Fortune* listed Dell Computer Corporation as one of the 100 fastest-growing companies in the United States. During 1992 the company continued to expand both in the United States and internationally. By the end of 1992, Dell Computer employed approximately 4,700 people worldwide and had achieved sales as shown below. Also in 1992, Dell had its first "3 for 2" stock split and made the Fortune 500 list of top industrial corporations in the United States.

	Dell Computer Sales (in millions)	
Customer Group	*F1992*	*F1993*
Major corporate, government, and education accounts	$416	$953
VARs and systems integrators	137	274
Medium/small businesses and individuals	337	787
Total	$890	$2014

Source: Company records.

The Strategic Vision

According to analysts who follow the company, the success of Dell Computer Corporation can be traced to Michael Dell's strategic vision of a high-performance/low-price personal computer marketed directly to end users. Dell computers were not designed to be the most powerful or the most technically advanced. Instead, they were intentionally designed to be of higher-than-average quality and very reliable. Likewise, Dell computers were not designed to be the lowest-cost PCs available. The key strategic concepts of Michael Dell can be stated as "relatively high performance" and "relatively low price" combined in such a fashion as to produce exceptionally high value for buyers.

However, perhaps more important than the high-performance-to-price ratio was the manner in which Dell Computer marketed its products. Rather than marketing its computers through one of the currently existing (indirect) distribution channels—

EXHIBIT 1

Dell Computer Corporation's Net Sales, Fiscal Years 1985–1993[a] (Thousands of Dollars)

	1985[b]	*1986*	*1987*	*1988*	*1989*	*1990*	*1991*	*1992*	*1993*
Domestic	$6,195	$33,685	$69,450	$153,074	$218,204	$300,257	$358,877	$566,392	$1,283,899
International	—	—	—	5,963	39,606	88,301	187,358	323,547	730,025

[a]Fiscal years generally run February through January.
[b]May 1984–January 31, 1985.
Source: Annual reports of the company.

EXHIBIT   2

Dell Computer Corporation Operating Results, Fiscal Years 1987–1993[a]

	Percentage of Net Sales						
	1987	*1988*	*1989*	*1990*	*1991*	*1992*	*1993*
Net sales	100.0%	100.0%	100.0%	100.0%	100.0%	100.0%	100.0%
Cost of sales	76.9	68.5	68.5	71.8	66.7	68.3	77.7
Gross profit	23.1	31.5	31.5	28.2	33.3	31.7	22.3
Operating expenses							
Marketing and sales	10.2	13.0	15.0	16.0	16.2	16.1	11.0
General and administrative	4.6	4.2	4.8	4.5	4.8	4.4	2.3
Research, development, and engineering	2.3	3.5	2.8	4.4	4.1	3.7	2.1
Total operating expenses	17.1	20.7	22.6	24.9	25.1	24.2	15.4
Operating income	6.0	10.8	8.9	3.3	8.2	7.5	6.9
Other expenses	0.4	1.3	0.7	1.2	3.2	1.8	1.9
Income before taxes	5.6	9.5	8.2	2.1	5.0	5.7	5.0

[a]Fiscal years generally run February through January.

*Source:*Annual reports of the company.

traditional dealers, value-added resellers (VARs), and so forth—or by means of a sales force, Dell Computer initially marketed its computers directly to end users by means of direct-response advertising in selected computer magazines. Later it added telemarketing activities, an indirect sales force, and field sales representatives. Initially all products were distributed directly from the Dell factory to the end user by UPS or Airborne Express. This provided a single source for complete computing solutions, and total accountability to customers. No intermediaries, wholesalers, or retailers were utilized in the initial distribution channel. The industry recognized Dell as the pioneer of a unique form of direct-relationship marketing.

Interestingly enough, Michael Dell's direct marketing approach did not spring full-grown from his imagination. At age 13, he had already experimented with a mail-order stamp-collecting business.

As Dell Computer grew rapidly through its manufacturer-direct marketing strategy, its strategic vision evolved to include three key elements: maintaining a direct relationship with the end users of its products, developing high-quality products that are custom-configured and sold at reasonable prices, and providing industry-leading service and support.

The first key element, maintaining direct relationships with the end users of its products, is standard in all distribution channels used by Dell. For example, even the newer indirect channel (added in 1991), through which Dell sells PCs to end users by means of mass merchandisers, requires that all end-user buyers register their computers with Dell at the time of purchase. This process enables Dell to enter the new buyer into its catalog/mail-out database and immediately begin a direct relationship with the buyer.

The second key element of Dell Computer's success is its commitment to developing high-quality products that are custom-configured and sold at reasonable prices. The company prides itself on providing the highest-quality components and testing standards in the industry, and through innovative market segmentation, it offers a combination of competitively priced products and promotional bundles targeting specific market segments.

The final key aspect of Michael Dell's strategic vision that contributed to the success of Dell Computer Corporation is the unrelenting emphasis on the customer. Since customer satisfaction is dogma at Dell Computer, industry-leading warranty packages, installation, maintenance, repair services, and user support have always been first priority. Dell was the first company in the industry to offer manufacturer-direct toll-free, 24-hour technical support service and next-day, on-site, service programs that have become standard in the industry.

Distinctive Competency

The distinctive competency of Dell Computer in its early years resided in its innovative direct selling model more than anything else. Indeed, in several interviews in the 1980s, Michael Dell stressed his belief that the company's distribution channel was *the* most efficient way to market personal computers. Even the company's advertising reflected Dell's belief. For example, in the mid-1980s, company print advertisements contained a picture of a computer store with a red X drawn through it and featured the line "and you don't have to go there to buy it." (See Exhibit 3 for an example of a Dell Computer Corporation advertisement used in 1990.)

The success of the Dell selling model opened the door to literally hundreds of small PC manufacturers who found they only needed a telephone number and/or a post office box to enter the marketplace. Ultimately Dell Computer's success prompted even its largest competitors to expand into this direct channel. In 1992 both IBM and Compaq began offering new PC lines through direct distribution channels. IBM created a direct sales operation in late 1992 called Ambra, whereas Compaq created Compaq Direct in attempts to "Dell-ize" their selling methods.

What currently keeps Dell Computer competitive in the PC market is its ability to efficiently deliver new value-added services. Because it is becoming more difficult to distinguish among personal computers based on technology alone, and customers expect more value at lower prices, Dell approaches the PC desktop market, which has effectively become a commodity market due to the industry's adoption of open standards, with an array of custom-made products and services, which clearly sets the company apart from its competitors.

In mid-1993, Dell Computer launched a unique marketing campaign to further its market leadership in producing customized computing solutions for individual needs. This campaign was based on a new segmentation scheme wherein customers are profiled according to their "techno-type." Based on extensive research into customer computing needs and concerns, PC-use environment, and decision-making factors, Dell Computer structured the market for personal computers along two dimensions: extent to which advanced PC features are required and extent of connectivity (networking) requirements.

Company Sales Organization

As of mid-1993, Dell Computer Corporation had approximately 5,500 employees. The sales organization consists of Dell North America and Dell International. Although the majority of sales revenues are derived from the North American operation, sig-

EXHIBIT   3

Dell Computer Corporation Print Advertisement in 1990

HERE'S OUR NEW STORE, SO YOU'LL NEVER HAVE TO GO TO THEIR STORE AGAIN.

When you go out to buy computers, here's what you usually get:

A beefy mark-up.

Pressure to buy something you don't want.

That crummy feeling of not knowing what you're getting, because the salesman isn't sure what he's selling.

And, when there are problems, some stranger with a screwdriver taking your computer apart.

When you call Dell, on the other hand, here's what you get:

A frank talk with computer experts about what you need, and a recommendation about the best overall package for you.

TO ORDER, CALL
800-283-1490
IN CANADA, CALL 800-387-5752

FOR NETWORK/UNIX® INFO
800-678-UNIX

HOURS: 7 AM-7 PM CT M-F 9 AM-4 PM CT SAT

Customer configuration, with a long list of options including monitors, memory sizes, software, accessories and peripherals.

Service—often voted the best in the industry—by computer experts who know our computers inside and out.

A variety of financing and leasing◇ options.

A firm promise to build your computers, a configured systems test, and shipment by two-day air standard.

THE DELL SYSTEM 316SX 16 MHz 386™ SX.
The perfect low profile mainstream computer.

• Intel 80386SX microprocessor running at 16 MHz. • Standard 1 MB of RAM, optional 512 KB, 640 KB or 2 MB of RAM* expandable to 16 MB (8 MB on system board). • Page mode interleaved memory architecture. • LIM 4.0 support for memory over 640 KB. • Socket for Intel 80387™ SX math coprocessor. • 5.25" 1.2 MB or 3.5" 1.44 MB diskette drive. • Enhanced 101-key keyboard. • 1 parallel and 2 serial ports. • 3 full-sized 16-bit slots. • 12-month On-Site Service Contract provided by Xerox.◇
**Commercial Lease Plan. *Lease for as low as $82/month.* ◇*Xerox Extended Service Plan pricing starts at $220.* 40MB VGA Color Plus System $2,199
Price listed includes 1 MB of RAM. 20, 40, 80, 100 and 190 MB hard drive configurations available.

AD CODE 11X24

A 30-day, no questions asked, money back guarantee.

A one-year limited warranty.

And a great price, with no mark-up.

Call us now. Why waste a trip when everything you need is right in front of you?

Above and beyond the call.

Source: Company records.

nificant growth is also occurring internationally. In the first quarter of the 1994 fiscal year (February–April 1993), international sales represented 36 percent of total company revenues. This compared with 23 percent in the first quarter of fiscal year 1990. By the end of 1992 Dell was marketing personal computers in 95 different countries, either through selected distributors or wholly owned and operated subsidiaries. For example, international subsidiaries exist in Canada, France, Sweden, Germany, the United Kingdom, Australia, Japan, Asia, the Caribbean, and Central and South America. Through its manufacturing facility in Limerick, Ireland, Dell Computer supplies virtually all of its products sold in Africa, Europe, and the Middle East.

Over time the company has evolved from relying solely on direct marketing to employing account teams—groups of individuals that focus on potentially large orders. The purpose in doing so is to expand the initial customer base of small businesses and individuals (some of whom are called "hackers") to large corporations, government agencies (federal, state, and local), and medical and educational institutions. Whereas small businesses and individuals tended to purchase from Dell because of its low prices (and typically purchased only a small number of low-margin computers), large corporations, government agencies, and medical and educational institutions were believed to offer a much larger market for higher-priced (and high-margin) computers.

The Dell North American sales organization consists of four distinct entities: (1) commercial, (2) government, medical, and education, (3) direct sales, and (4) indirect sales. The commercial division focuses on Fortune 1000 firms and large privately held corporations, often employing account teams and field representatives. The government, medical, and education division markets Dell products to government entities and medical and educational institutions in much the same way as does the commercial division. The direct sales division specializes in small/medium businesses and the household/small or home office (SoHo) market through direct-response advertising, mailouts, and telemarketing. Although the direct sales division still accounts for approximately 40 percent of domestic revenues and represents the traditional Dell approach to distribution, its revenue growth has been relatively flat in recent quarters and is predicted to remain so.

It was the direct sales division's flat revenues that prompted Michael Dell to create the indirect sales division in 1991. Dell Computer entered the indirect market through the retailer CompUSA with a new brand name called Precision—a product line similar to that sold through the direct marketing channel. The Precision line is preloaded with the most current software on the market and is parity-priced with other value-line products offered in this channel. Since initiating the relationship with CompUSA, Dell has carefully formed alliances with distributors that have very low overheads and are extremely efficient. By 1992, Dell had expanded its presence in the indirect channel through retailers such as Sam's Club, Wal-Mart, Price Club, Costco, Staples, and Best Buy.

In addition to such mass retailers, the indirect sales division concentrates on marketing to value-added resellers, such as Falcon Micro Systems (a government reseller), original equipment manufacturers, and systems/network integrators, such as Andersen Consulting and EDS, often employing field sales representatives and account executives similar to the commercial division. While the creation of this division signaled a major change from Dell's traditional marketing strategy, the division has been relatively successful. Even so, nearly four-fifths of the company's revenues derive from its direct marketing efforts.

SELLING ENVIRONMENT

Oversimplifying somewhat, there are two major markets for personal computers, businesses and households. Each of these markets consists of numerous submarkets, segments, and niches. Business submarkets, for example, range from government entities to large publicly held firms (such as Fortune 500 companies) to small businesses with only a few employees. Overall, however, the business market is more heterogeneous than the household market. For instance, it consists of niches (for example, scientific laboratories) with very specialized performance needs with cost a secondary concern as well as government entities whose purchase decisions are based primarily on price. Even so, the household market is becoming less homogeneous as the growing SoHo market has very specialized needs.

Hence, as might be expected, the two major markets generally have different buying requirements. The household market consists of consumers using a computer for basic word processing and games as well as small/home office applications requiring complex financial and graphics software. The business market (medium to large-sized firms) requires sophisticated, powerful personal computers that are frequently networked (linked or connected together) to provide a variety of functions such as information sharing. The household market, on the other hand (except for "hackers" and the SoHo segment), is not as concerned with computing power or system capability. One of the primary concerns of the household market is cost. In general, personal computers sold to medium/large businesses tend to be on the high end of the price continuum and have higher margins. Exhibit 4 presents estimated domestic personal computer sales for selected application segments for the years 1993–1996.

Technology

Computer manufacturers such as Apple and Compaq respectively spend approximately 8 percent and 4 percent of their annual revenues on research and development. These funds are spent on new technology such as Pentium-based (586 mhz) systems, notebooks, subnotebooks, hand-held communications, and pen-based technologies. As the new Pentium technology increases the processing speed of PCs much like the 486 systems greatly improved upon 386 performance, computer companies are scrambling to master the technology and be the first to ship systems containing this high-speed microprocessor.

Notebook computers are portable (that is, battery-powered) PCs weighing from four to seven pounds that are capable of a wide variety of computing functions and frequently possess advanced communication capabilities. They took their name from the fact that their outside dimensions roughly correspond to those of a standard ring-binder notebook. Subnotebooks weigh a maximum of four pounds, about two to three pounds less than their counterpart full-sized notebooks, and often feature a pen-based technology. Typically they have a longer battery life but fewer capabilities than a full-sized notebook. Computer firms are scrambling to win over price-sensitive buyers who want the ability to take their office home with the new subnotebook products. Hewlett-Packard's Omnibook, Northgate's ZXP-XL2, Toshiba's Portege, and Compaq's Contura are all subnotebooks reaping profits from early entry into this market. Similarly, hand-held computing technology, which in-

EXHIBIT 4

Estimated U.S. Personal Computer Sales by Application Segment

						Sales						
	1993			1994			1995			1996	
Application Segment	Units (Thousands)	Dollars (Millions)		Units (Thousands)	Dollars (Millions)		Units (Thousands)	Dollars (Millions)		Units (Thousands)	Dollars (Millions)
Business/professional	9,507	$17,181		10,269	$18,295		10,754	$19,233		11,100	$20,574
Home/hobby	1,070	598		1,124	580		1,142	579		1,063	559
Scientific/technical	1,347	5,735		1,465	5,984		1,528	6,200		1,579	6,622
Education	1,294	1,446		1,380	1,503		1,424	1,571		1,443	1,707
Total	13,218	$24,960		14,238	$26,362		14,848	$27,583		15,185	$29,462

Source: Company records.

tegrates standard business tools such as a cellular phone, personal computer, fax machine, and personal organizer, is finding its own place in the market. AT&T's EO and Apple's Newton are in direct competition in this market. In general, a growth rate of nearly 90 percent per year is predicted for mobile computing technology.

Industry Sales Trends

By the end of 1992, more than 40 million personal computers had been sold in the United States. And, by the end of 1992, the total number of PCs sold to businesses and governmental and educational agencies cumulatively surpassed the number sold to households. Industry data show that small businesses and home offices (the SoHo segment) are the fastest-growing customer groups in the 1990s, even though sales to large businesses are still experiencing some growth. Sales to the former groups are expected to grow at an average annual rate of 25 percent through 1996, whereas sales to large businesses are expected to grow about 5 percent annually during the same time period.

The fastest-growing personal computer in the 1990s is expected to be the notebook. In 1990, fewer than 20,000 notebook computers were sold. By 1991, sales of portable/notebook computers in the United States were about $2 billion. By 1998 industry experts forecast annual notebook sales in the United States alone to be in excess of $25 billion, and worldwide sales to total $50 billion. At the present time, none of Dell Computer's major competitors are able to meet the demand for their notebook computers. Unlike desktops, most notebook technology is proprietary, and designing and building them require special skills beyond simply inserting chips and cards into motherboards.

Competition

Dell Computer Corporation's competitors vary from well-known firms such as IBM, Compaq, and Apple to nearly 200 "no-name" firms, many of which consist of only one or two entrepreneurs assembling personal computers in garages or storefront locations. It is common in the industry to refer to IBM, Apple, Compaq, and Dell as "tier 1" firms in terms of their sales. In 1992 IBM's personal computer sales totaled $7.7 billion; Apple's were $5.4 billion; Compaq's were $4.1 billion; and Dell's were $2.0 billion. "Tier 2" competitors consist of firms such as Gateway and ALR. There is a third tier of firms, such as Zeos and Austin Computer, each with sales of up to $100 million annually. In the past few years there has been considerable consolidation occurring in the industry through both bankruptcies and acquisitions. For example, in July 1993 AST purchased Tandy Corporation's PC business, overnight boosting its sales to more than $2 billion.

In 1992 the top ten PC manufacturers in the United States collectively held a 58 percent market share. This represented an increase of 6 percent from the comparable figure of 52 percent in 1990. Despite this consolidation, though, gross margins in the industry are relatively anemic and average slightly less than 30 percent.

Historically, firms such as IBM, Apple, and Compaq have possessed relatively high brand awareness. Even so, the brand awareness of non–tier 1 firms has steadily risen. Moreover, the price decline of PCs generally has not only squeezed the margins of all firms. It has greatly reduced the price advantages formerly held by second- and third-tier firms. Compaq and IBM in particular have become very aggressive in their marketing and created low-cost, low-price lines of PCs with brand names such as Compaq's Proline and IBM's ValuePoint to meet the demand of the fast-growing segment of price-conscious customers who are not concerned with advanced features. Partly as a consequence of industrywide price-cutting, once-successful PC manufacturers such as CompuAdd filed for bankruptcy.

A major trend began in the industry in 1991 and gained momentum in 1992 and early 1993. This was the tendency for firms that were fierce competitors to form strategic alliances and partnerships to both develop and market new products. For instance, Packard Bell and Zenith Data Systems agreed to jointly design and manufacture desktop and notebook computers, although each would be free to modify them for its particular markets. Likewise, IBM and Toshiba established an alliance to co-develop new portable computers. Motorola, IBM, and Apple partnered on the development of a new microprocessor called the Power PC, a direct competitor for the industry standard Intel microprocessor chip found in Dell and most other personal computers. Compaq, Intel, Microsoft, and VLSI Technology, Inc. formed an alliance for a mobile companion series that hooks into existing desktop networks. Apple and Siemens AG Private Communications Systems Group collaborated on the development of Notephone—a PC with fax and telephone capabilities.

DISTRIBUTION CHANNELS

Personal computer manufacturers use five primary channels to reach end users: (1) dealers/value-added resellers, (2) direct marketing, (3) mass merchandisers, (4) direct sales, and (5) systems/network integrators. Exhibit 5 contains estimated personal computer sales for several distribution channels through 1996.

Dealers/Value-added Resellers

The traditional channel used to reach personal computer buyers is the storefront dealer. Dealers are retailers that focus on selling personal computers and peripheral equipment to both the business and household markets. Some PC manufacturers sell exclusively through dealers. Generally, dealers operate out of facilities of 3,000 to 5,000 square feet and assume the marketing, servicing, and support functions for a manufacturer. Consequently, PCs sold through this channel tend to be on the high end of the price continuum. (Gross margins average 35–40 percent for dealers.) Major dealer chains include Computerland and Businessland. A subcategory of dealers consists of value-added resellers such as Microage. VARs are dealers that specialize in a particular market niche (often a vertical market such as educational institutions) and offer specialized services to that niche, such as complete hardware and software systems or special expertise in an application area.

Another type of dealer that merits special mention is the manufacturer-owned outlet. Although this dealer type is decreasing in popularity, some PC manufacturers market their computers through wholly owned company stores, usually in the range of 5,000 square feet or less. This permits considerable control over the distribution and selling process. The manufacturer-owned outlet can "showcase" the manufacturer's products because it does not have to share space with competing brands. Also, the manufacturer does not have to rely on intermediaries for sales, servicing, and support functions. As Exhibit 5 shows, in 1993 dealers accounted for the largest

EXHIBIT 5

Estimated U.S. Personal Computer Sales by Channel

					Sales				
	1993		**1994**		**1995**		**1996**		
Channel	Units (Thousands)	Dollars (Millions)	Units (Thousands)	Dollars (Millions)	Units (Thousands)	Dollars (Millions)	Units (Thousands)	Dollars (Millions)
Dealer								
Dealers	5,533	$10,955	5,859	$10,793	5,802	$10,669	5,521	$10,811
VARs	1,635	3,408	1,731	3,765	1,934	3,903	1,982	4,158
	7,168	$14,363	7,590	$14,558	7,736	$14,572	7,503	$14,969
Direct marketing								
Direct response	1,761	$3,165	1,731	$3,012	1,658	$2,862	1,699	$3,049
Direct outbound	503	974	400	1,004	414	1,041	425	1,109
Mail order	377	730	400	753	553	1,041	651	1,275
	2,641	$4,869	2,531	$4,769	2,625	$4,944	2,775	$5,433
Mass merchandise								
Mass merchants	1,006	$1,704	1,199	$2,008	1,243	$2,082	1,416	$2,495
Consumer electronics	604	1,169	692	1,305	760	1,431	807	1,580
Superstores	755	1,217	799	1,506	829	1,561	849	1,386
	2,365	$4,090	2,690	$4,819	2,832	$5,074	3,072	$5,461
Other	101	$195	266	$502	276	$520	425	$832
Total	12,275	$23,517	13,077	$24,648	13,469	$25,110	13,775	$26,695

Source. Company records.

proportion of personal computer sales. A major issue facing manufacturers using this channel is the amount of shelf space available for both new and existing brands.

Direct Marketing

Dell Computer Corporation pioneered the use of the direct-marketing channel. Personal computer manufacturers marketing through this channel typically use direct-response advertisements in computer magazines, direct mailings (catalogs, brochures, etc.), and both inbound and outbound telemarketing to reach potential customers and communicate with current customers. Firms marketing through this channel traditionally have competed on the basis of price and have offered "mainstream" personal computers, often known as "boxes" because of their simplicity and lack of features. Manufacturers using this channel have tended to spend little on research and development. Of the five primary distribution channels, this one has probably attracted the most competition because of the ease of entry and lack of capital requirements. According to industry forecasters, over the long term the market share of this channel will decrease somewhat. This likely decline is due to a variety of reasons, including both intense competition and shifting market conditions.

Mass Merchandisers

Until recently, relatively few personal computers were sold through mass merchandisers. However, as Exhibit 5 suggests, this distribution channel may become dominant in the near future, especially for the SoHo market segment. The term *mass merchandiser* is a bit misleading because it covers a variety of different types of retailers. For example, this distribution channel encompasses traditional retailers such as Sears and Dillards, which sell IBM personal computers among others, as well as specialized consumer electronics stores.

Perhaps the most important development among mass merchandisers is the "superstore" or "category killer." Based on the model of Toys R Us and Home Depot, several companies such as Computer City and CompUSA have opened large personal computer "supermarkets." These superstores typically range in size from 25,000 to 50,000 square feet and carry up to 5,000 different computer-related items. They operate on the principle of high volume, low prices, low margins (generally in the neighborhood of 10 percent or less), and minimal service and support. Most of the projected growth in sales among mass merchandisers can be attributed to an increase in the number of superstores, several of which offer their own brand of personal computers (for example, CompUSA's Compudyne brand).

Direct Sales (Field Sales)

The direct sales channel is typically used by manufacturers trying to reach businesses and government agencies. Since it is a relatively expensive channel because of the costs associated with supporting a field sales force, this channel type is typically not used for other than large corporate customers and/or major government agencies. Its advantages are flexibility, person-to-person contact, and the ability to work closely with a customer to solve unique computing problems and to target specific organizations and even individuals within an organization. Because of its size, IBM tends to dominate this distribution channel. Although exact sales figures are not available for this channel, it is believed that the channel has decreased in importance in recent years as PCs have become more user-friendly, prices have declined, and individuals at all levels of business and government have become more computer-literate.

Systems/Network Integrators

The fifth distribution channel is one of the fastest growing. This channel consists of what is termed "systems" or "network" integrators. Integrators are consulting firms that work with both personal computer manufacturers and end users to ensure that the end user purchases the right hardware (personal computers) and software for its specific needs. They may also help install a particular computer system or assist an end user in changing from one computer system to another. Systems/network integrators offer large corporate and government accounts a single hardware/software source and turnkey solutions to their computing problems. The largest integrators are Andersen Consulting and EDS. Since corporate and government end users frequently seek the advice of an integrator for personal computers, more and more computer manufacturer are trying to form alliances with them, especially because there is a trend toward systems/network integrators purchasing personal computers from a manufacturer and reselling them to an end user.

SEPTEMBER 1993

Following the release of his company's second-quarter financial results, Michael Dell began to draft an agenda for the upcoming strategy session of his senior management team. As he did so, his mind focused on the major issues that had to be addressed. Although he strongly believed that the company was well-positioned to meet the challenges facing it, he knew that to reestablish the momentum lost due to the second quarter's financial performance and regain the confidence of the marketplace, the company would have to act quickly and decisively. This meant squarely facing the two primary marketing issues that were appearing more and more to be firm albatrosses: notebooks and distribution. It also meant that the firm would have to decide if it wanted to position itself as a "manustributor," a company that simultaneously is a hybrid manufacturer and distributor.

The Notebook Decision

During the past eight years Dell Computer has met the challenge of developing products that kept up with the ever-changing computer industry. The current desktop product line that Dell offers takes advantage of industry-leading technology; however, its portable line has fallen short of industry standards.

In February 1992, Dell Computer entered the notebook market with a new color notebook based on the 25-megahertz Intel 386 SL microprocessor. This notebook was followed by the 320 SLi in June and the 325 SLc in December. Unfortunately, the notebook line was plagued with technical problems, one of which would result in a product recall. As a consequence of quality problems and the inability to design a notebook line that would be leading edge and incorporate the newest technologies, the company decided to phase out notebook computers in the first half of 1993. At the present time, less than 6 percent of Dell Computer revenues were derived from notebook sales, down from 17 percent in the summer of 1992 and considerably less than the 20–25 percent of revenues that other PC manufacturers were experiencing.

By the middle of 1993 notebook computers were the fastest-growing segment of the PC market. Hence, given customer demand and industry trends, it was clear that the company would have to replace its notebook line as quickly as possible. Unfortunately, determining the proper strategy to successfully bring a new notebook line to market was not so clear. The proper strategy would quickly close the existing product-offering gap due to the lack of a notebook and stem the direct loss of revenues (with customers possibly diverting to competitors) while simultaneously guarding against possible product quality and corporate image problems if the new notebook line was less than successful due to a forced and premature reentry. In brief, if Dell Computer is to maintain its growth momentum, it is necessary to introduce a new high-quality notebook line quickly. But a major question existed: How? As Michael Dell and his chief lieutenants discussed the notebook issue, it seemed as though at least seven different actions were possible.

The company could simply go back to the recently phased-out line and provide whatever enhancements would make it competitive. Or it could market other manufacturers' brands of notebooks simply to complement other Dell products. Either of these strategies would minimize the "down time" of not having a notebook line in the marketplace.

Some managers favored licensing the appropriate technology from other firms as another alternative to minimize the length of time it would require the company to produce a new Dell notebook. Others argued that Dell should develop a strategic alliance with a current notebook manufacturer or another "technology-wise" company and through some sort of partnership co-develop a new notebook line. Still other managers argued that Dell should simply find a contract manufacturer to produce notebooks under the Dell name so as not to lose its brand franchise. (Until June 1993, a sizable percentage of the Dell product line had been produced by SCI in Huntsville, Alabama.) One manager suggested that Dell simply purchase another company.

Finally, although there was wide agreement with respect to moving quickly, there was also considerable sentiment for Dell not to "rush into" a potentially bad situation by moving too rapidly. Rather, there was sentiment that Dell should assemble its own design team and design and manufacturer its own notebook line. The company had recently hired John Medica as Vice President for Portable Products. Medica, who had engineered the Apple Computer Powerbook, was very experienced in the notebook area (in its first year of existence, the Apple Powerbook achieved more than 400,000 unit sales) and it was his job to develop Dell's notebook strategy.

The Distribution Decision

There was virtual consensus among Dell's senior management team that to remain competitive the company must diversify its direct-centric distribution strategy. According to Dennis Jolly, Group Vice president of Indirect Sales, the company needed a balanced portfolio of channels, one that was not overly dependent on direct marketing. The question was how to achieve such an objective. (See Exhibit 6 for comparative PC shipment information for Dell and its major competitors.)

EXHIBIT 6

Estimated PC Shipment Percentages by Channel in 1992

	Percentage of Company Shipments			
Channel	*Dell*	*Apple*	*Compaq*	*IBM*
Dealers	0	63	68	65
Value-added resellers	15	5	15	8
Direct marketing	74	15	0	7
Systems integrators	3	5	6	5
Other (including mass merchandisers)	8	12	11	15

Source: Company records.

Although Dell Computer owed its early success to individual buyers, by 1993 the majority of its customer base (approximately 61 percent) consisted of large businesses. The remainder consisted of small/medium businesses and individuals. While large businesses account for the greatest proportion of company sales, and the computers they purchase have large gross margins, they must produce approximately 25 percent more revenue to generate the same profit margins as small/medium businesses and individuals. This is because of the higher marketing costs associated with selling to large businesses, such as the costs of maintaining account executives and field representatives, the need for evaluation units (try before you buy), and required volume discounts. These higher costs, when combined with projected segment growth rates, led Dell, as well as other PC manufacturers, to search for markets and distribution channels that would produce sustainable and profitable revenue growth. For example, in a significant strategy shift, Compaq Computer Corporation began offering its Presario line to consumers and home office users through mass retailers including Montgomery Ward, Service Merchandise, and Best Buy in August 1993.

Currently, Dell Computer markets its products through large retail chains such as Wal-Mart and Best Buy. However, several individuals in the company believe that Dell's position in the mass-merchandiser channel is still one of underdistribution as compared with IBM and Compaq, which are thought to be overdistributed. In 1992, for instance, IBM obtained 96 percent of its personal computer revenue through indirect distribution, whereas Compaq obtained 83 percent of its revenue through this channel. At the same time, the indirect channel accounted for only about 20 percent of Dell Computer's sales.

The vertical reseller segment consists of firms that target particular markets and develop software applications to meet the specific needs of these markets. For instance, many accounting firms that need industry-specific software often look to resellers to provide them with a "total solution" of both hardware and software. Recently Dell Computer has attempted to build partnerships with VARs and resellers through an aggressive advertising program (see Exhibit 7).

Systems and network integrators combine hardware, software, and peripherals—most often in a client/server environment—as a total package for a turnkey solution to customers. Because it is a relatively new channel to Dell, the company is not as well represented in it as are Compaq and IBM.

EXHIBIT 7

Dell Computer Corporation Reseller Advertisement

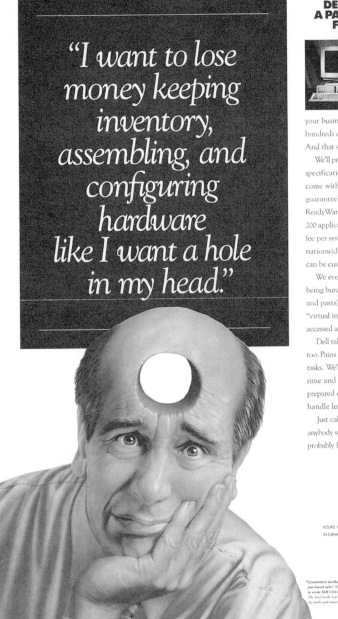

DELL INTRODUCES A PARTNERSHIP THAT FILLS THE VOID.

Finally, someone's come along with a partnership that can get rid of headaches and help you focus on the profitable parts of your business. Someone who's done it for hundreds of other VARS and Resellers already. And that someone is Dell.

We'll preconfigure systems to your customers' specifications at the factory. These systems come with Dell's exclusive compatibility guarantee. You'll get unique programs like ReadyWare,™ which let you choose from over 200 applications pre-installed for one low $15 fee per system. And we also have a flexible nationwide service and support program that can be custom-fit to your organization.

We even reduce your inventory costs (a.k.a. being burdened with warehouses of systems and parts) by maintaining a "virtual inventory" for you, easily accessed around the country.

Dell takes care of other pains, too. Pains like your administrative and support tasks. We'll direct ship to the user, saving you time and handling costs. Heck, we've even prepared competitive leasing options and will handle lease administration.

Just call Dell for an application kit. Because anybody who would ignore help like this should probably have their head examined.

DELL™

TO ORDER, CALL

800-247-2609

HOURS: MON-FRI 7AM-9PM CT SAT 10AM-6PM CT SUN 12PM-5PM CT
IN CANADA, CALL 800-668-3021. IN MEXICO CITY, 228-7811. #11004

Guarantees available in USA only for registered owners of Dell Performance Series systems purchased after 7/1/92. For a complete copy, please call our TechFax™ line at 1-800-950-1329 or write Dell USA L.P., 9505 Arboretum Blvd., Austin, TX 78759-7299. Attention Guarantees. The Intel inside logo is a registered trademark of Intel Corporation. Dell disclaims proprietary interest in the marks and names of others. ©1993 Dell Computer Corporation.

Source: Company records.

One channel where Dell Computer is conspicuously absent is the traditional dealer channel. Despite being the largest distribution channel, it is an enigma for Dell (partially because of its financial condition the company is not able to offer dealers the margins they traditionally require). In an interview published in the August 23, 1993, issue of *Computerworld*, the Chairman of Computerland stated that his company was not interested in marketing Dell computers because "we want to commit to someone who wants to be our partner. Dell doesn't really want to do that. They want to run the business and then try to find some cracks and crevices they can use us for, but whenever possible they want to go to the direct channel."

CHAPTER 11

Comprehensive Marketing Programs

An organization's comprehensive marketing program integrates the choice of which product or service markets to pursue with the choice of which marketing mix to use to reach target markets and, ultimately, create consumers. The process of formulating and implementing a comprehensive marketing program encompasses all the concepts, tools, and perspectives described in previous chapters.

The challenge facing the manager responsible for formulating and implementing a comprehensive marketing program divides into three related decisions and actions.[1] First, the manager must decide *where to compete*. Product-market choice determines the organization's customers and competitors. This decision is often based on the organization's business definition and opportunity and target market analysis. In this regard, the manager has multiple options ranging from concentrated marketing with a focus on a single product market to differentiated marketing whereby multiple product markets are pursued simultaneously. Second, the manager must decide *how to compete*. The means a manager has available reside in the marketing-mix elements or activities. Multiple options again exist. In a simple situation with two alternatives for each of the four marketing-mix elements, 16 different marketing-mix combinations are possible. Third, the manager must determine *when to compete*. This decision relates to timing. For example, some organizations adopt a "first-to-market" posture, while others take a "wait-and-see" stance concerning market-entry decisions.

Four issues are central to the design and execution of comprehensive marketing programs. First, a marketing manager must consider issues of *fit* with the market, the organization, and competition. Second, marketing-mix *sensitivities* and *interactions* must be considered as they relate to target markets. Third, issues of *implementation* must be addressed. Fourth, *organizational* issues must be taken into account. Each of these topics is discussed below.

PROGRAM FIT

A successful comprehensive marketing program must effectively stimulate target markets to buy, must be consistent with organizational capabilities, and must out maneuver competitors.[2] The fit of a program to a market is determined by the extent to which the marketing mix satisfies the unique needs and buyer requirements of a chosen target market. The fit of a program to an organization depends on the match between an organization's marketing skills and financial position, on the one hand, and the marketing mix being considered, on the other. Finally, the fit of a program to the competition relates to the strengths, weaknesses, and marketing mixes of competitors who are serving the target markets under consideration.

Establishing a program market fit can be a daunting task. For over 25 years, DuPont has explored applications for Kelvar, a synthesized material with five times the tensile strength of steel on an equal-weight basis. The chosen target market for Kelvar was tire makers that produced steel-belted radials. Despite the unique qualities of Kelvar, the marketing program did not persuade tire makers that Kelvar adequately satisfied their buying requirements.[3]

The importance of program-competition fit is illustrated by the evolution of the diet soft drink market. Sugar-free soft drinks, first introduced in 1947, were originally positioned as a product for diabetics and generated only modest sales. In 1962, Royal Crown introduced Diet Rite Cola. Diet Rite was heavily promoted, priced below regular soft drinks, and targeted at soft drink consumers. The company sold 50 million cases. In 1963, however, Coca-Cola (Tab) and Pepsi-Cola (Diet Pepsi) entered the market with massive advertising expenditures and quickly captured a dominant market share, eclipsing Royal Crown.[4]

MARKETING-MIX SENSITIVITIES AND INTERACTION

Many of the case analyses thus far have implicitly or explicitly focused on target-market sensitivity to one or more elements of the marketing mix. The Jones•Blair Company case in Chapter 4 is an example. When company management embarked on a planning effort, several views on how best to stimulate sales were voiced. One executive favored an increase of $150,000 in corporate brand advertising. Another argued for a 20 percent price reduction, and still another recommended hiring additional salespeople. Each of these executives implicitly suggested that the target market was most sensitive to the marketing-mix element he recommended.

In reality, however, the options are generally broader, and interaction effects between two or more marketing-mix elements must be considered. For instance, what would be the effect on sales of increasing corporate brand advertising *and* introducing a 20 percent price reduction? Would this action be more or less effective in stimulating sales than changing only one element of the marketing mix?

Although simultaneous consideration of marketing-mix sensitivities and interaction is a complex process, it is a necessity for the marketing manager. Consider the situation faced by John Murray, the marketing manager for DuPont's Sontara®, a polyester fabric used for disposable surgical gowns and drapes used in hospital operating rooms.[5] Murray's charge was to prepare a comprehensive marketing program that would meet two objectives for Sontara®: (1) maintain market share and

(2) persuade garment makers that DuPont could support them in promoting Sontara®
to end users and would remain a strong force in the disposable fabric business.

Murray thought that if sales-force/maintenance expenditures were raised from
the proposed level of $450,000 to a maximum reasonable level of $550,000 while
other spending was held to proposed levels, market share could reach 35 percent
of the total market. Similarly, if the other mix elements were increased to their maximum reasonable levels while the remaining expenditures were held at their proposed levels, market-share increases would be likely as well, although they would
not be as dramatic. Specifically, he thought:

- If instead of spending nothing on sales-force/missionary expenses, management spent $200,000, market share would increase to 33 percent.
- If trade support/maintenance expenses were increased to $100,000, a 33
  percent market share would result.
- If $100,000 were spent on trade support/missionary expenses, market share
  would be 33 percent.
- If advertising to intermediate users were increased to $50,000, the net effect
  would be a 1 percent increase in market share.
- An increase to $300,000 in advertising to end users would also result in a 1
  percent share gain.

Reductions in spending were thought to have the opposite effect. Reducing sales-
force/maintenance expenditures to zero while holding other spending at the proposed level was thought likely to reduce Sontara®'s share to 22 percent of the total
market during the next 12 months. Similarly, reductions to zero spending for sales-
force/missionary expenditures, trade support/maintenance, trade support/mission-
ary, advertising to intermediaries, or advertising to end users were thought likely to
reduce expected market share to 32,27,32,31, or 28 percent, respectively.

As a validity check on the above estimates, Murray described what he thought
would happen if all mix elements were raised simultaneously to their maximum reasonable expenditure levels or if all support was withdrawn from the product. He
thought that with maximum effort a 39 percent share could be realized, although he
was not sure how viable such an aggressive strategy would be for the long run. If
all support was withdrawn, he estimated that market share would drop to 22 percent in the next 12 months and then decline further.

This example demonstrates the complex relationships that exist among marketing-mix elements. It also illustrates the role of assumptions and judgment in considering marketing-mix sensitivities and interactions.

IMPLEMENTATION

Implementation is the third leg in developing a comprehensive marketing program.
Marketing managers have come to realize that poor implementation can hamper the
success of an otherwise brilliantly conceived program.

Among the wide variety of subtle factors that can make or break a marketing
program is timing. Failure to execute a marketing program when a window of opportunity opens can lead to failure or reduce the likelihood of success. For example, some industry observers believe that the success of Matilda Bay Wine Cooler,

introduced by the Miller Brewing Company, might have been hampered by poor timing on two counts. First, the popularity of wine coolers was declining. Second, the product was launched in the fall, typically a slow selling season.[6]

A second factor that can hamper implementation is not considering logistical aspects of a marketing program. When Holly Farms test-marketed a roasted chicken for distribution through supermarkets, consumer response was favorable. Holly Farms soon realized, however, that the roasted chicken was edible for only 18 days and it took 9 days to get the chicken from the production plant to supermarkets. As supermarkets could not be expected to sell the chicken within 9 days, Holly Farms had to halt its planned national introduction of roasted chicken.[7]

Effective execution of advertising and promotion, apart from expenditures, is a third factor in implementation. In short, the message conveyed to prospective buyers must be the right one. Revlon's Supernatural Hair Spray failed because the target market was unclear about what the product was supposed to do. Some people expected it to provide more holding power for their hair, and others expected less holding power.

Finally, implementation of a price-cost plan requires careful attention and monitoring. American Express Company's aggressive marketing program for its Optima credit card resulted in a $265 million charge against company earnings in late 1991. The charge was due to credit losses and costs related to the card's operations.[8]

Formulating a comprehensive marketing program is a formidable task that demands rigorous analysis and judgment, often without the benefit of complete information. At the same time, program planning and design cannot be separated from implementation issues. "What should we do?" cannot be separated from "How do we do it?" By assigning equal importance to program formulation and program implementation, marketing managers increase the likelihood that their comprehensive marketing programs will succeed.[9]

MARKETING ORGANIZATION

Emphasis on marketing implementation focuses attention on organizational structure. It is often said that strategy determines structure and that organizational structure, in turn, determines whether a marketing strategy is effective and efficiently designed and implemented.[10]

A central issue in creating an effective and efficient marketing organization is finding the proper balance between centralization and decentralization of marketing activities, including strategy formulation and implementation. The strategy of regional marketing, whereby firms attempt to satisfy unique customer needs and meet competitive demands in limited geographical areas, has prompted increased decentralization of strategic marketing decisions and practices. For example, regional marketing groups at Frito-Lay design and implement region-specific marketing programs, including pricing practices and sales promotion activities. They also manage 30 percent of the company's advertising and promotion budget. Efforts to "glocalize" marketing programs in the international arena have created elastic organizational structures that simultaneously strive for efficiencies, through scale economies in product development and manufacturing, and for effectiveness, through customization of advertising, promotion, pricing, and distribution in separate countries. As an example, Coca-Cola's concentrate formula and advertising theme are standardized worldwide, but the artificial sweetener and packaging differ across countries as do sales and distribution programs.[11] The relative emphasis on standardization versus customization in marketing strategy planning and execution ultimately manifests itself in organizational structure. For Frito-Lay and Coca-Cola, and an increasingly large number of other firms, the notion of "coordinated centralization" has produced domestic and global organizational structures that seek to foster adaptability to local conditions while preserving centralized direction in the pursuit of market opportunities and implementation of marketing programs.

NOTES

1. This discussion is based on Subhash C. Jain, *Marketing Planning and Strategy*, 4th ed. (Cincinnatti, OH: Southwestern Publishing Co., 1993): 23.

2. B. P. Shapiro, "Rejuvenating the Marketing Mix," *Harvard Business Review* (September–October 1985): 28–34.

3. DuPont's Difficulty in Selling Kelvar Shows Hurdles of Innovation," *Wall Street Journal* (September 27, 1987): 1, 23.

4. This example was extracted from S. Schnaars, "When Entering Growth Markets, Are Pioneers Better Than Poachers?" *Business Horizons* (March–April 1986): 27–36.

5. *E. I. DuPont de NeMours & Co.: Marketing Planning for Sontara and Tyvek*, University of Virginia, Colgate Darden School of Business Administration.

6. "Miller Jumps into a Cooler Cooler Market," *Business Week* (October 26, 1987): 36–38.

7. "Holly Farms' Marketing Error: The Chicken That Laid an Egg," *Wall Street Journal* (February 9, 1988): 36.

8. "Optima Backfires on American Express," *Wall Street Journal* (October 3, 1991): B1, B2.

9. See William G. Egelhoff, "Great Strategy or Great Strategy Implementation—Two Ways of Competing in Global Markets," *Sloan Management Review* (Winter 1993): 37–50.

10. Frank V. Cespedes, *Organizing and Implementing the Marketing Effort: Text and Cases* (Reading, MA: Addison-Wesley, 1991); "The Search for the Organization of Tomorrow," *Fortune* (May 18, 1992): 92–97.

11. John A. Quelch and Edward J. Hoff, "Customizing Global Marketing," *Harvard Business Review* (May–June 1986): 59–68; John Huey, "The World's Best Brand," *Fortune* (May 31, 1993): 44–54.

Tyler Pet Foods, Inc.

Executives of Tyler Pet Foods (TPF), Inc., looked forward to their meeting with representatives of Marketing Ventures Unlimited, a marketing and advertising consulting firm. The purpose of the meeting was to review the program for TPF's entry into the household dog food market in the Boston, Massachusetts, metropolitan area. TPF had sought out the consulting firm's services after discussions with food brokers who cited the tremendous potential for TPF in the household dog food market. These brokers had become aware that frozen dog food was being sold in small portable freezers in selected pet stores in a few cities in the southwestern United States. They believed these limited efforts represented a market opportunity for frozen dog food in supermarkets, where refrigerator space is more plentiful and where the majority of dog food is sold.

THE COMPANY AND THE PRODUCT

Tyler Pet Foods, Inc., is a major distributor of dog food for show-dog kennels in the United States. TPF has prospered as a supplier of a unique dog food for show dogs called Show Circuit Frozen Dog Dinner. Show Circuit was originally formulated by a mink rancher as a means of improving the coats of his minks. After several years of research, he perfected the formula for a specially prepared food and began feeding his preparation to his stock on a regular basis. After a short period of time, he noticed that their coats showed a marked improvement. Shortly thereafter, a nearby kennel owner noticed the improvement and asked to use some of the food to feed his dogs. The dogs' coats improved dramatically, and a business was born.

Show Circuit contains federally inspected beef by-products, beef, liver, and chicken. Fresh meat constitutes 85 percent of the product's volume, and the highest-quality cereal accounts for the remaining 15 percent. The ingredients are packaged frozen to prevent spoilage of the fresh uncooked meat.

PACKAGING AND DISTRIBUTION MODIFICATIONS

TPF executives recognized that modifications in the packaging of Show Circuit would be necessary to make the transition from the kennel market to the household dog food market. After some discussion, it was decided that Show Circuit would be packaged in a 15-ounce plastic tub, with 12 tubs per case. The cost of production, freight, and packaging of the meal was $6.37 per case, which represented total variable costs.

The cooperation of Tyler Pet Foods, Inc., in the preparation of this case is gratefully acknowledged. This case was prepared by Professor Roger A. Kerin, of the Edwin L. Cox School of Business, Southern Methodist University, as a basis for class discussion and is not designed to illustrate effective or ineffective handling of an administrative situation. Certain names have been disguised. Copyright © Roger A Kerin. No part of this case may be reproduced without written permission of the copyright holder.

The discussions with food brokers indicated that distribution through supermarkets would be best for Show Circuit because of the need for refrigeration. Food brokers would represent Show Circuit to supermarkets and would receive for their services a 7 percent commission based on the suggested price to retailers, which had yet to be determined.

THE MEETING

TPF executives listened attentively to the presentation made by representatives from Marketing Ventures Unlimited. Excerpts from their presentation follow.

During the course of the meeting, TPF executives raised a number of questions. The questions were primarily designed to clarify certain aspects of the program. One question that was never asked but that plagued TPF executives was "Will this program establish a place in the market for Show Circuit?" This direct question implied several subissues:

1. Was the market itself adequately defined?
2. What position would Show Circuit seek in the market? Should the program be targeted toward all dog food buyers or toward specific segments?
3. Could the food brokers get distribution in supermarkets given the sales program?
4. What should be TPF's recommended selling list price to the consumer for Show Circuit?
5. Could TPF at least break even in the introductory year and achieve a 15 percent return on sales in subsequent years?

TPF executives realized that they had to answer these questions and others before they accepted the proposal. The total cost of the marketing plan could be $300,000 to $500,000 which TPF executives considered reasonable, although it would stretch their promotional budget.

PROPOSAL OF MARKETING VENTURES UNLIMITED

The following is an excerpted version of the proposal presented to TPF.

The Situation

Our goal is to introduce and promote effectively the sale of Show Circuit dog food in the Boston market area. Show Circuit is the costliest dog food to prepare and will be available through supermarkets.

Show Circuit will be the first completely balanced frozen dog food available in a supermarket. It is of the finest quality and has been used and recommended by professional show-dog owners for years.

Yet, in spite of this history, Show Circuit is essentially a new product and is unknown to the general public. The fact that Show Circuit will be the only dog food located right next to "people food" in the frozen food section is an advantage that must be capitalized upon. Show Circuit's history of blue-ribbon winners is another plus. So, in essence, to market Show Circuit successfully, we must accomplish two objectives:

- Make the public aware of the brand name of Show Circuit, what the packaging looks like, and the fact that Show Circuit is a high-quality dog food.
- Direct the public to shop for dog food in the frozen food section.

The Environment

Sales of dog food will total almost $3.835 billion this year. Still, fewer than half of the dogs in the United States are regularly fed prepared dog food, which means the dog food industry has yet to tap its full potential.

This optimism is well founded. The dog food industry has been growing rapidly. The dog population, spurred on by the owners' desire for companionship or need for protection, is growing steadily and is expected to continue growing. Also, the trend toward using convenience foods in the household contributes to a lack of table scraps to be served to the dog, a fact that will only improve the prospects for selling prepared dog foods. One more important trend is that homemakers continue to invest their pets with human qualities and view them as members of the family. For years it's been a given that humans transfer their own wants and desires to their pets. Therefore, it comes as no surprise that dog owners spend more than $120 million annually for veterinarians' fees and medication for dogs and that about 30 percent of all dogs are fed exclusively from the table.

Supermarket chains, which dispense around $2.5 billion in dog food nationally, are amenable to opening up required shelf footage for these products, especially since the 25 percent gross profit margin they receive on pet foods is superior to the gross profit margins of 18 other departments located in most supermarkets. Approximately 65 percent of total dog food sales are made in supermarkets. Pet stores and veterinarians account for most of the remaining 35 percent. These percentages also apply to the Boston market.

Finally, the Boston market is growing rapidly in both population and median income. Furthermore, the dog and human populations are highly correlated. Our estimate that the Boston area has 1.5 percent of the U.S. population (and 1.5 percent of the dog population) makes this a great area for launching the product.

The Competition

There are about 1,000 dog food manufacturers in the United States. However, six firms—Ralston Purina, Carnation, Mars, Heinz, Quaker Oats, and Grand Met USA—capture 83 percent of dog food sales in supermarkets. The following ten brands of dog food command 43 percent of the $3.8 billion dog food industry:

Brand	Sales (Millions)
Alpo	$273.5
Dog Chow	260.8
Kal Kan Pedigree	260.0
Milk-Bone	167.7
Puppy Chow	150.0
Kibbles 'n Bits	140.0
Alpo Beef-Flavored Dinner	117.3
Gravy Train	91.2
Come 'n Get It	90.2
Mighty Dog	89.4

In addition to market share, the competition's advertising spending and forms of advertising used will be major considerations in planning Show Circuit's marketing strategy. Competitive data described in the presentation are shown in Exhibit 1.

EXHIBIT   1

Market Share and Sales for the Dog Food Industry at Manufacturers' Prices

Brand	Producer	Sales (Millions)	Market Share
Top Five Canned Dog Food Brands (Total Category Sales: $1.1 billion)			
Alpo	Alpo (Grand Met USA)	$273.5	25.8%
Kal Kan Pedigree	Kal Kan (Mars)	260.0	24.5
Mighty Dog	Carnation	89.4	8.4
Grand Gourmet	Carnation	68.8	6.5
Cycle	Quaker Oats	60.5	5.7
	Total	$752.2	70.9%
Top Five Dry Dog Food Brands (Total Category Sales: $1.9 billion)			
Dog Chow	Ralston Purina	$260.8	13.9%
Puppy Chow	Ralston Purina	150.0	8.0
Alpo Beef-Flavored Dinner	Alpo (Grand Met USA)	117.3	6.3
Gravy Train	Quaker Oats	91.2	4.9
Come 'n Get It	Carnation	90.2	4.8
	Total	$709.5	37.9%
Top Three Soft-Dry Dog Food Brands (Total Category Sales: $220 million)			
Kibbles 'n Bits	Quaker Oats	$140.0	63.6%
Tender Chops	Quaker Oats	50.5	23.0
Moist & Chunky	Ralston Purina	12.7	5.8
	Total	$203.2	92.4%
Top Five Moist Dog Food Brands (Total Category Sales: $165 million)			
Moist & Meaty	Ralston Purina	$ 37.0	22.4%
Gaines-Burgers	Quaker Oats	29.5	17.9
Ken-L Ration Special Cuts	Quaker Oats	14.5	8.8
Ken-L Ration Burgers	Quaker Oats	13.9	8.4
Smorgasburger	Quaker Oats	13.0	7.9
	Total	$107.9	65.4%
Top Four Snack-Type Dog Food Brands (Total Category Sales: $450 million)			
Milk-Bone	RJR Nabisco	$167.7	37.3%
Jerky Treats	Heinz	46.0	10.2
Chew-eez, etc.[a]	Superior	41.3	9.2
Meaty Bones	Heinz	37.0	8.2
	Total	$292.0	64.9%
Total Dog Food Sales (at manufacturers' prices): $3.835 billion			

[a]Superior products include Chew-eez, Wagtime Biscuits, Lickety Slicks, Glad-Wag, and other brands.

The Problems and Opportunities

Introducing a New Dog Food in a New Form This is an opportunity to educate the consumer. Until Show Circuit's program breaks, dog foods fall into five categories: canned, dry, soft-dry, moist, and snack-type (dog treats).

Canned dog foods average about 75 percent moisture and 25 percent solid materials. They are marketed either as complete foods or as supplementary foods.

Dry dog foods are usually produced as flakes, small pellets, or large chunks containing about 10 percent moisture and 90 percent solids. They are chewy, usually well rounded, and more economical than canned or moist foods.

Moist and soft-dry foods come in chunk or patty form and are about 25 percent moisture and 75 percent solids. They require no refrigeration and are made to look tempting to humans. These categories have shown the greatest percentage increase in recent years.

Dog food treats have a wide variety of ingredients and, while tasty, are not recommended as a complete food.

All these product forms are typically marketed in the same area of the store. The consumer must now be taught to shop for dog food in another part of the store—the frozen-food section. Fortunately, some of the pioneering work has been done already. A few Boston-area supermarkets carry a frozen dog treat called Frosty Paws, which sells for $1.89 for 14 fluid ounces. This product is often placed near ice cream.

Overcoming Objections to Frozen Dog Food   An objection must be anticipated regarding the requirement for thawing time and freezer space. Therefore, we should state on the container the thawing time, suggestions for quick thawing, how long the food will keep in the refrigerator, plus a gentle reminder to pull that container out of the freezer in the morning. Microwave instructions are a possibility.

Lack of Appeal of Frozen Dog Food   We can quickly turn this problem into an asset in our advertising ("the first dog food made to appeal only to dogs").

Pricing   We have considerable latitude in pricing as shown in Exhibit 2. Furthermore, while dog owners in general are price sensitive, they are also concerned about the health and welfare of their animal companion. Show Circuit's quality suggests a premium price.

Summary of Opportunities   We see Show Circuit seizing upon three opportunities:

EXHIBIT   2

Representative Prices of Dog Food Brands in Boston-Area Supermarkets by Product Form

Canned		*Dry*		*Soft-Dry*	
Mighty Dog:	$0.60/6 oz.	Dog Chow:	$3.49/5 lb.	Kibbles 'n Bits:	$3.89/4 lb.
Cycle:	$0.60/14 oz.	Gravy Train:	$3.39/5 lb.	Tender Chops:	$7.19/8 lb.
Alpo:	$0.60/14 oz.	Chuck Wagon:	$7.19/12 lb.		

Moist		*Treats*	
Moist & Meaty:	$3.49/4.5 lb.	Milk Bones:	$1.89/10 oz.
Gaines-Burgers:	$3.39/3.5 lb.	Jerky Treats:	$1.45/3 oz.
Ken-L Ration Special Cuts:	$3.49/3 lb.		

1. The opportunity to be first to tap the vast market potential of a complete frozen dog food in supermarkets
2. The opportunity to be among the first to claim to produce an organic dog food (Ralston Purina will soon launch Nature's Course, a dry dog food positioned as "organic")
3. The opportunity to lay the groundwork for entering the frozen cat food business (cat food sales total $2.4 billion)

Creative Strategies

Positioning Show Circuit will be positioned as the finest dog food available at any price and the only thing you will want to feed a dog that is truly a member of the family.

Concentration We believe our advertising should be directed to singles and young marrieds between the ages of 21 and 30 and people 50 years old and over. The reason is that single adults, young marrieds, and childless (older) couples regard their dogs as a part of the family. The dog sleeps on the bed and has free run of the house or apartment. When children enter the picture, the dog goes out to the back yard.

Concepts Because Show Circuit is such a unique product, there are a variety of concepts that can easily be applied, each with adequate justification:

1. The luxurious fur coat
2. The world's finest dog food
3. The guilt concept (shouldn't your dog eat as well as you do?)
4. Now your dog can eat what show champions have been eating for years.

All these will be touched on as the campaign progresses.

Creative Directions Initially, the campaign will focus attention on product identification and an introductory coupon offer.

Newspapers will supply a smaller, more retentive audience with facts to justify all claims. They will also supply the coupon, proven crucial to a successful introduction in the pet food market. The container and coupon will be prominently displayed, and the copy will emphasize Show Circuit's quality. Special-interest ads will appear in the society, sports, television, and dining-out sections. This unusual media placement is warranted by the product's unique qualities. Also, placement in these sections will pull a relatively low promotional budget out of the mass of food-section advertising.

Radio and television will provide access to a mass audience. Prime objectives are to register the brand name and the package design in the viewer or listener's memory. Because of the proven subliminal qualities of these media, an imaginative and all-important emotional approach will be taken.

Geographical Directions The entire campaign has been designed to accommodate product introduction outside the Boston market area. When the product goes national, the television spot will be ready, the introductory ads will be ready, the radio spots will be ready, and the immediate follow-up will be ready.

Sales Packet

The sales packet given to brokers should include, in the most persuasive form possible, the following categories of information:

1. Profits available in the dog food category
2. Chain store acceptance of dog food
3. Market potential
4. Suggested manufacturer's list price to consumers and quantity discount schedule
5. Information about Show Circuit
6. Information about the container
7. User endorsements
8. Promotional schedule
9. Order information
10. Reprint of ads and TV storyboard
11. Sample shelf strip

The packet should be designed to persuade the supermarket frozen-food buyer to provide freezer space to Show Circuit. Two major problems have to be overcome. Because of the organizational modes of supermarket buying departments, we will not be dealing with the regular pet food buyer. Instead, it will be necessary to persuade the frozen-food buyer to stock Show Circuit. The other major problem involves the usual higher margin for frozen foods. It will be necessary to persuade the buyer that greater product turnover will compensate for a potentially lower margin for Show Circuit.

Creative Strategy by Media

Creative strategies will differ by media. Print media will be utilized to position the product against its competition by comparing it to canned, dry, soft-dry, and moist categories. The print campaign will open with an attention-getting ad with a brief product history.

Television will carry the brunt of the attack. The most pressing problem is seen as the difficulty of finding the food in the supermarket, so the TV spot will emphasize location.

In order to give the campaign continuity, each ad will show the container. At the top of each of the ads designed to position the competition, the artwork reproduced on the container will be used.

No single breed of dog will be associated with the product. Both the container and the ads will show a variety of breeds from show dogs to mongrels.

The myth/fact format in newspapers will be utilized to take advantage of the current publicity dealing with the nutritional value of all-meat dog food and the continued trend toward more natural foods (see Exhibit 3).

The copy block dealing with Show Circuit will turn the problem of Show Circuit's being frozen into a product advantage.

Media Plan

Because dog food is heavily advertised, TPF must follow suit to compete.

General Media Strategy   Advertising objectives are as follows:

1. Create awareness of new brand
2. Obtain distribution through grocery outlets
3. Motivate trial through coupon redemption
4. Motivate trial through emotional impact of television

Collateral Advertising   Accomplishment of objective 2, getting distribution in grocery stores, is the main purpose of collateral advertising. The sales packet, containing fact sheets, shelf strips, the TV storyboard, and testimonial letters, gives the food broker an impressive story to tell to the supermarket buyer. This is recognized as the critical stage of the campaign, for without sufficient distribution, consumer advertising will be delayed.

Newspaper/Magazine   The primary purpose of newspaper advertising is distribution of coupons into the market. This will be accomplished by half-page ads in major Boston newspapers. As a secondary means of distribution, full-page ads will be placed in *Better Homes and Gardens* and *Dog Fancy* magazine for distribution throughout most of the Boston market area (see Exhibit 4). We expect that one out of ten sales will involve a coupon redemption.

EXHIBIT   3

Show Circuit Print Advertisement

Learn the facts about dog food.

Myth:

A diet of nothing but dry dog food is healthy for your dog

Fact:

Dogs are not born vegetarians. Dry dog food contains little if any meat. Dry dog food is inexpensive. Dry dog food is good to chew. And just by adding water, dry dog food melts into gravy. Dry dog food must be cooked which removes nutrition. It must be filled with additives and preservatives to keep it fresh. And because of the low meat content it must be fortified with various supplements.

Show Circuit

It's the perfect marriage of meat and cereal. 85% is federally inspected beef by-products, beef, liver and chicken. The other 15% is the finest cereal made. It promotes and insures digestion of the meat, plus supplies the vitamins and minerals meat cannot. Show Circuit is uncooked because cooking removes nutrition. And it's frozen for freshness — there's no need for additives or preservatives. Find Show Circuit in the frozen food section, right next to people food.

SHOW CIRCUIT.
Frozen Dog Dinner

**Now your dog can eat what
show dogs have eaten for years.**

EXHIBIT 4

Show Circuit Print Advertisement

The second phase of coupon distribution will be effected through 30-inch ads in the same newspapers. A final coupon distribution will be made through a 30-inch ad midway through the campaign. Newspaper insertion will be coordinated with TV flights.

Television The bulk of the budget will be placed in TV production and time. A sizable portion of the time budget will be spent on the "Late Night with David Letterman" show. Fixed space will be purchased within the first half-hour of the program. The remainder of the budget will reach daytime and nighttime audiences. Each flight will begin on a Monday, and newspaper advertising will be placed on Thursday of the following week.

Two basic approaches can be used for 30-second TV spots. The first approach capitalizes on the love of pet owners for their dogs. A somewhat frowzy, middle-aged, semi-greedy woman is shown enjoying a steak dinner—in contrast to an unappetizing cylinder of canned dog food. The spot ends on a close-up of the product. The storyboard for this spot is shown in Exhibit 5.

A second TV spot will emphasize location of the food in the supermarket. A description of the video and audio characteristics of this spot is as follows:

Video	*Audio*
Supermarket—long establishing shot of small boy with bulge under jacket	Announcer: There are many things to remember about new Show Circuit Frozen Dog Dinner.
Close-up of boy, as puppy pops out of top of jacket	Remember, although it's new to you, champion dogs have eaten it for years.
Manager walks by, boy hides dog, looks relieved	Remember, it contains all the vitamins your dog needs.
Close-up of sign indicating pet foods	Remember, Show Circuit is a perfectly balanced diet of meat and cereal. Remember, it doesn't come in a can.
Dolly shot of boy looking at competitive brands	
Close-up of boy and dog (sync)	Boy: I don't see it anywhere, Sparky.
Boy walks out of store past frozen-food compartment	Announcer: But most important, remember you find Show Circuit in the Frozen (bark) food section, where you shop for other members of your family.
People turn to stare	
Tilt down and zoom in on product	

EXHIBIT 5

Show Circuit Television Spot

SHOW CIRCUIT
Dog's Eye View
(A 30-second, full color, live-action commercial.)

HW: Ralphie, I don't understand you.

I buy you eighteen cent a can food.

I come straight home and feed you.

So why don't you eat, Ralphie?

What do you have against my cooking?

Long down-shot of dog food. Cylinder of dog food is covered in runny white gravy.

VO: It's a crying shame what some people feed their dogs.

VO: Now your dog can eat what show dogs have eaten for years. Show Circuit, a nutritious dog dinner so different it's found in the frozen food section—next to people food.

HW: Ralphie, think of all the hungry dogs in the world who would love to have your food.

EXHIBIT 6

Alternative Expenditure Levels for Introductory Program

| | Budget Levels | |
Item	$300,000	$500,000
Television[a]	$159,000	$329,000
Newspapers/magazines[b]	100,500	130,500
Collateral (sales pack)	9,750	9,750
Miscellaneous	5,250	5,250
Agency fees	25,500	25,500
Total	$300,000	$500,000

[a]The difference in television cost is due to the production of a second commercial and larger television schedule.

[b]The difference in newspaper/magazine cost is due to a larger number of insertions in *Better Homes and Gardens* and *Dog Fancy* magazines.

Program Budget The budget for the program described can be either $300,000 or $500,000 as shown in Exhibit 6. We see this cost as being the only incremental cost associated with the launch in the Boston market.

We believe that this expenditure is reasonable, since most major established brands are spending $7–8 million annually for ongoing nationwide media promotion. For a new product, a higher initial expense is necessary. For instance, Heinz Pet Products spent $30 million in 1991 to introduce Reward, a premium canned dog food. Ralston Purina spent $25 million to $30 million to introduce Nature's Course, a premium dry dog food. A line extension, Alpo Lite, with 25 fewer calories than regular Alpo, was launched recently with a $10 million advertising effort.

Chun King Corporation

Matthew Femrite and Robert Collins solemnly entered the conference room and looked over the piles of computer output and reports lying on the table. Collins glanced at Femrite and remarked, "Once again Chun King is at a crossroads. What we come up with in the next few days may well determine the future of Chun King. Before the week is over, we have to agree on a 1991 marketing strategy that the president can present to the board of directors in less than two months."

Femrite sat down at the table and muttered to no one in particular, "What should Chun King do? Should the company pursue an aggressive growth strategy and risk substantial losses, or should it follow a more conservative strategy designed to generate profits and throw off cash? What strategy will best meet the board's objectives?"

As Femrite started to silently mull over the options, Collins said, "Well . . . let's get started."

THE CORPORATION

For more than 45 years, Chun King has been a household word associated with Chinese food. Founded in Duluth, Minnesota, by Jeno Paulucci, the son of an Italian immigrant, Chun King nearly single-handedly introduced Americans to chow mein. Although Paulucci had been canning and selling bean sprouts and chop suey since the early 1940s on a limited basis, it was not until 1947, with $2,500 in his pocket, that he incorporated Chun King (named after the first Chinese city he could think of). The company grew rapidly and within three years sales reached $5 million. In the 1950s, bolstered by award-winning consumer advertising created by Stan Freeberg, sales increased every year. By 1965, they exceeded $50 million.

In 1966, Paulucci sold Chun King to R.J. Reynolds Industries for $63 million. He then went on to develop Jeno's Pizza, the first widely accepted frozen pizza. R.J. Reynolds directly managed Chun King until 1980, when it was placed under the control of Del Monte Foods, a division of R.J. Reynolds. After R.J. Reynolds and Nabisco merged in 1984, Chun King became a subsidiary of Hueblein. Nabisco managed its various business units by means of a portfolio approach—the business strategy and objectives of all units were designed to complement each other and provide an acceptable mix of profit and risk for the entire corporation. Under this approach, Chun King was managed for short-term profits; market share and sales were only secondary considerations.

A leveraged buy-out (LBO) took RJR-Nabisco private in 1988. One consequence of the LBO was that Nabisco was forced by the government to sell Chun King because of antitrust regulations. On October 1, 1989, two Singapore firms jointly pur-

The assistance of the Chun King corporation in the preparation of this case is gratefully acknowledged. This case was prepared by Robert A. Peterson, Professor of Marketing, the University of Texas, and Nick Mihnovets, Chun King Corporation, as a basis for class discussion and is not designed to illustrate effective or ineffective handling of an administrative situation. All names and sales and financial data have been disguised and are not useful for research purposes. Copyright © by Robert A. Peterson. No part of this case may be reproduced without the written permission of the copyright holder.

chased Chun King from RJR-Nabisco for approximately $52 million. At that time, its sales were in the neighborhood of $45 million, and its profit was $2 to $3 million. Since then Chun King has been a privately held company.

Management and Organization

As a stand-alone, independent company, Chun King has had to learn how to manage its own business functions. After being stripped of Nabisco corporate support, the firm had to establish its own accounting system, financial control system, and organizational structure. The new owners initially maintained a hands-off posture and allowed company management to do whatever it thought best for Chun King. Because production was in Cambridge, Maryland, but sales and management were headquartered in a Chicago suburb, Chun King developed an organizational structure that could most appropriately be termed "lean and mean."

At the head of the organization is Byron Jacobson (see Exhibit 1). Byron is a 32-year veteran with Chun King, having worked directly for Jeno Paulucci. Robert Collins, the vice president of sales and marketing, was promoted from a regional sales manager position. His background is in sales at a large packaged goods firm. Bradley Drier, the vice president of finance, was plant controller before Chun King was purchased from Nabisco. His experience is in the accounting and finance realm of plant management. The directors of personnel, quality control, and purchasing and the plant manager are all individuals who had previous experience in plant operations. All four were elevated under the new organization plan to administer their previous functions as well as take on added responsibilities. Only one new position was created; this is the director of distribution and customer service. A former Nabisco employee was brought in to head up this area.

Chun King has three regional sales divisions, with the head of each reporting to Robert Collins. Matthew Femrite is the midwest regional sales manager. In addition, though, he has the title of market manager. In that capacity he is responsible for

EXHIBIT 1

Chun King Corporation Organization Chart

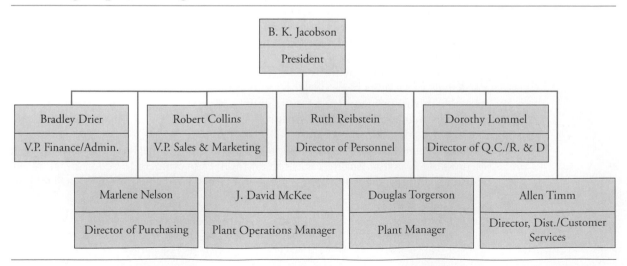

Source: Company records.

strategic marketing planning. All Chun King sales are made through food brokers, who receive commissions of approximately 3 percent of their sales in return for obtaining distribution in grocery stores and supermarkets. Presently Chun King has 60 brokers, a decrease of 5 from 1985, who collectively cover virtually the entire United States. However, without the prestige and backing of Nabisco, and with only three regional sales managers for the entire United States, Collins is concerned that the brokers are not being as aggressive in their distribution efforts as they should be.[1] Because of this, he has recommended to the president that, if Chun King wants to make progress in sales and marketing, it should hire at least two additional regional sales managers as well as a marketing associate to help Femrite with strategic planning. The projected annual cost (salary and expenses) of a regional sales manager is $78,000; the cost of a marketing associate is $55,000.

Product Line

The Chun King product line consists of offerings in five areas: sauces, noodles, main meals, packaged dinners (such as stir fry meals), and vegetables (see Exhibit 2). These products are off-the-shelf stable goods (canned goods). Because of the cost of ingredients, category gross margins range from 17 percent to 62 percent, as shown below.

Product Category	*Gross Margin Percentage*
Sauces	18–40%
Noodles	46–62
Main meals	25–45
Packaged dinners	17–31
Vegetables	17–39

Interestingly enough, although a line of frozen Chun King food exists, this is not part of Chun King. Not wanting to be in frozen foods, Nabisco had previously sold off the frozen food franchise to ConAgra. Several individuals in the company saw this as a potential problem, since consumers might be confused by seeing that the Chun King brand was being produced by two distinct companies. Yet others in the company saw this as a plus, since ConAgra would be likely to promote the Chun King name.

Promotion

For the most part, efforts to market Chinese food are directed at retailers rather than consumers. Accordingly, there is little money spent on consumer promotion and advertising using radio, newspapers, or television. With the exception of on-pack coupons, which are used throughout the year, most consumer promotions revolve about two Chinese holidays, Chinese New Year in January and Harvest Moon Festival in October. Chun King, for example, offers consumer coupons through free-standing inserts (FSIs) in Sunday newspapers to celebrate the Chinese New Year. An example of a Chun King FSI appears in Exhibit 3.

---

[1] *Case author's note*: Brokers are independent agents that do not take title to products they sell. Typically manufacturers allocate funds to brokers, in proportion to the brokers' sales, that the brokers can use for cooperative advertising, display space, or merchandising preference programs with the retail accounts they service.

EXHIBIT   2

Illustrative Chun King Products

Source: Picture courtesy of Chun King.

The majority of promotional activities are carried out for the trade. Chun King offers its retail accounts quarterly trade promotions ("off-invoice" price discounts) to encourage them to stock up on its products. In addition, it offers financial incentives that brokers can use in generating new business or defending current accounts against competitive incursions. The latter funds come from the "indirect trade" budget and are used to support cooperative retail advertising programs, merchandising performance incentives, display and stocking programs, and so forth.

THE MARKETPLACE

Since word of the LBO surfaced, Chun King has had to fend off attacks on its market share by La Choy, its major competitor. La Choy, previously a subsidiary of Beatrice Foods, was sold to ConAgra in mid-1990. As the market share leader, with about one-half of the retail market in shelf-stable Chinese foods, La Choy had slowly been eroding Chun King's distribution base with its marketing efforts. Because sales are in large part a function of shelf space—most retailers stock only one brand of shelf-stable Chinese food—both Chun King and La Choy use incentives and trade

EXHIBIT   3

Example of a Chun King FSI

programs to gain and defend shelf space. Perhaps sensing uncertainty at Chun King due to the LBO, La Choy intensified its attempts to gain distribution at Chun King's expense. Chun King management believes that the company lost about 230,000 cases in sales in the year prior to the finalization of the LBO because of La Choy's activities. This necessitated considerable spending on defense programs; in 1990 alone Chun King spent almost $464,000 to defend existing accounts by offering special price discounts and merchandising programs. This money came in large part from funds that would otherwise have been used to support trade programs.

At the time Femrite and Collins were meeting, there was considerably uncertainty as to what marketing strategies La Choy might follow under its new ownership. ConAgra was the second-largest marketer of prepared foods in the United States. It was known in the industry as a company with "deep pockets" and one that had a tendency to aggressively market its products. According to industry sources, La Choy would be dramatically changing its packaging in January 1991 to visually dominate shelf space in the oriental foods section of supermarkets and would unveil an extensive advertising campaign in February. In addition, industry sources thought that La Choy would be initiating a large consumer promotion in 1991 that would involve more than 400 million FSI coupons. At the same time, though, ConAgra required that its subsidiaries maintain relatively high (20 percent) rates of return. This financial requirement was thought to constrain La Choy's marketing spending, since it was assumed that La Choy had the same basic cost and margin structure as Chun King. Finally, ConAgra was basically a broker-focused organization, whereas the newly acquired Beatrice subsidiary had its own sales force. It was unclear whether the Chun King–La Choy battle would be waged as broker organization versus direct sales force or broker organization versus broker organization.

Chun King and La Choy are the only companies that compete in all five categories of off-the-shelf Chinese food. The third "major player" is Kikkoman. However, Kikkoman only competes in the sauces category, a category it tends to dominate and which appears to be one of the few growth areas in shelf-stable Chinese foods, primarily because of new products introduced by Kikkoman. Other competitors include China Boy, which competes in the noodles category; Geisha, which is the price leader in vegetables; and General Mills, which attempted to enter the packaged dinner category but is now thought to be exiting it. Although China Boy is not a large competitor, there is some concern among Chun King managers that it may be purchased and become a strong force in the marketplace. Chun King management currently believes that collectively Chun King, La Choy, and Kikkoman account for about 85 percent of all category volume (ACV). Exhibit 4 shows the case volume sold by the major competitors in each of the five product categories over a six-year period, as well as projected sales for 1991. In general, sales of shelf-stable Chinese food trended downward during the last half of the 1980s, whereas frozen, take-away, and away-from-home Chinese food sales were increasing. Some Chun King managers had gone so far as to speculate that the market for off-the-shelf Chinese food was effectively saturated.

STRATEGIC OPTIONS

Although it had been almost a year since Chun King had been acquired by the Singapore companies, the management at Chun King was not totally clear as to what the acquiring firms expected from it. As Femrite and Collins started reviewing the

EXHIBIT 4

Category Overview (Volume in Thousands of Cases)

Competitor/Category	Year						
	1985	1986	1987	1988	1989	1990	1991 (Projected)
Chun King							
Sauces	340	378	310	308	290	278	356
Noodles	267	273	232	236	215	185	211
Main meals	1,770	1,841	1,687	1,690	1,463	1,259	1,363
Packaged dinners (stir fry)	431	384	255	233	211	191	206
Vegetables	773	809	661	664	585	557	610
La Choy							
Sauces	1,048	1,085	1,115	1,146	1,183	1,242	1,254
Noodles	585	563	568	571	549	556	537
Main meals	4,096	3,820	4,046	3,797	3,666	3,641	3,342
Packaged dinners (stir fry)	421	398	332	346	394	374	331
Vegetables	2,187	2,132	2,114	1,994	1,935	1,858	1,745
Kikkoman							
Sauces	1,783	1,830	1,959	2,090	2,153	2,242	2,341
General Mills							
Packaged dinners (stir fry)	—	565	1,219	416	166	80	30
Other							
Sauces	310	398	453	498	512	586	591
Noodles	361	390	416	370	371	381	372
Vegetables	833	870	880	909	928	935	932

Source: Company records.

documents in front of them, they developed a list of objectives they believed the acquiring firms had for purchasing Chun King. They noted that the two firms may have different reasons for purchasing Chun King. In general, Collins and Femrite thought that Chun King may have been purchased because the companies wanted:

- A basis for further firm acquisitions in the United States
- Entry into the U.S. market and an existing distribution system for their own products
- Long-term sales and profit growth
- An opportunity to diversify their current operations

Even though Chun King management was uncertain as to the specific motives of the acquiring firms, it was required to develop a strategic business plan for the company for 1991. Within Chun King, opinions varied dramatically as to which marketing strategy would not only be most fruitful for the company but be most in line with the objectives of the Singapore firms. The president and vice president of finance believed that Chun King must deliver a profit in 1991. As they noted, the press had repeatedly reported that the Singapore firms "paid handsomely" for Chun King and that shelf-stable Chinese food was a "declining category" because of frozen food and take-out options. They believed, consequently, that the firms would want to prove the media wrong by showing a profit. In brief, they believed Chun King should follow a more-or-less status quo or conservative strategy in 1991.

Other Chun King managers, however, including Collins and Femrite, believed that Chun King should pursue an aggressive marketing strategy even though the company may not show a profit for several years. They argued that unless Chun King invests in new products and spends more on marketing activities, its market share will continue to erode and eventually it will lose its consumer franchise.

As Collins and Femrite sorted through the company's options and began developing a marketing plan, they started piecing together profit-and-loss statements. Because of changes in accounting systems and the fact that the fiscal year was not complete, certain sales and cost figures were only estimates, but, as Femrite pointed out, "We have to start someplace."

"Let's start with this," responded Collins, as he handed Femrite a sheet of paper containing summary income and expense items for Chun King (see Exhibit 5). "As you can see, Matt, we still have not received numbers for 1989 because Brad Drier has been unable to consolidate all the figures for that year. Anyway, I think the numbers we have in front of us are the most relevant. Remember that the 1990 numbers are still tentative because we have not yet received our year-end results."

"Furthermore," continued Collins, "remember that we have already projected a 12 percent growth in revenues for 1991 based on the distribution gains we are realizing at the end of 1990 as a result of our defensive spending this year, the fact that we will have a comprehensive marketing plan in place, and the introduction of our new lite soy and teriyaki sauces. Hence, no matter what option we decide to recommend to the board, I think we should use this growth rate as our starting point. Also, don't forget that we need to take into account continuing expenses from the spin-off—goodwill must be written off at 0.85 percent of net sales and we must pay the new owners a licensing fee equal to 2.4 percent of net sales. Interest expenses from the purchase and loans to finance operations will probably be the same in 1991 as in 1990."

"Fine," responded Femrite, "I agree completely. It's important, though, that we recognize that about three-quarters of the 12 percent anticipated sales growth will likely be due strictly to the $464,000 we spent to buy back distribution, and that we cannot continue to increase sales this way for a variety of reasons—both financial and competitive. In addition, I think we could project a further increase in revenues if we pursued an across-the-board, 5 percent price hike. A price increase seems reasonable in light of the extra activities and expenditures we would build into an aggressive strategy. Indeed, we may need a price hike to help profits in any case."

At that moment Tom Grant, one of the regional sales managers, entered the room. "Excuse me, guys, but I overheard you talking about a price hike. My gut feel is that a price hike may not be the way to go. While the 8 percent increase we took in 1988 turned out fine, I worry about the reaction of La Choy. I think we would all agree that La Choy is the price leader in every category but sauces, where Kikkoman has long led the way. If we need sales growth, why don't we simply buy back the frozen food business from ConAgra? I recently read that frozen oriental food sales are expected to increase 10 percent per year until the mid-1990s. That way we could consolidate the Chun King brand and gain an immediate sales increase. We could

EXHIBIT 5

Chun King Financial Summary (In Thousands of Dollars)

Category	Year					
	1985	1986	1987	1988	1989[a]	1990 (Projected)[b]
Net sales	54,363	52,098	48,088	51,291	44,748	39,164
Variable manufacturing costs	25,936	24,109	21,802	23,838		19,858
Fixed costs[c]	5,527	5,627	7,418	6,696		5,327
Marketing expenses						
Broker fees[d]	1,576	1,592	1,471	1,585		1,176
Off-invoice[e]	8,459	4,558	3,888	4,403		3,303
Indirect trade[f]	889	3,490	6,388	6,457		3,328
Consumer promotions[g]	2,964	3,037	2,143	2,896		2,136
Advertising[h]	693	133	0	0		0
Selling[i]	505	792	350	1,049		1,839
Marketing research	0	0	255	549		61
Administration	891	1,086	597	774		780
Goodwill	0	0	0	0		333
Licensing	0	0	0	0		940
Extraordinary[j]	0	0	0	0		824
Interest expense	0	0	0	0		513

[a]Final numbers unavailable, since Nabisco handled financial systems for first quarter. Consolidation of systems in process.

[b]Projected as of September 1990.

[c]Includes manufacturing overhead as well as all corporate overhead but not marketing administrative costs or interest expenses.

[d]Broker commissions are 3 percent of net sales.

[e]Direct price discounts given to retail accounts to get them to carry products represent a variable cost.

[f]Funds given to brokers that they can spend against a retail account for cooperative advertising, display space, or merchandising performance programs constitute a fixed cost.

[g]Coupons, free-standing inserts, etc.

[h]Advertising in mass media such as radio, television, or magazines.

[i]Includes costs of sales representatives.

[j]One-time restructuring expense not to be repeated.

Source: Company records.

also try selling through a new channel, such as fast-food restaurants, or, better yet, we could start distributing some of the authentic products our parent companies produce, such as oyster sauce, plum sauces, or soybean milk. Currently these products are being distributed by direct store delivery systems in the United States. By putting them in the Chun King distribution system, we could get a jump on competitors like La Choy that don't carry them. Besides, doing so would probably be looked at favorably by our parent companies."

"Your points are well taken, Tom," responded Femrite. "But La Choy followed our price increase almost immediately in 1988 and quickly followed Kikkoman's price increase in 1990, and I think it is likely to keep doing so. While I agree that we need to increase sales, we don't have any expertise in frozen foods, fast foods, or authentic foods. The first two require completely different manufacturing technologies and distribution channels. Our current brokers have no competency in these areas and probably would be upset if we moved into frozen foods or fast foods. Furthermore, I'm not sure that we have either the resources or the competency to move into authentic foods."

"Here," said Collins, "I have jotted down a few assumptions about activities and expenses for the two alternative strategies. Let's take these as a starting point when we develop marketing alternatives. [Exhibit 6 contains Collin's assumptions.] In addition, Brad Drier informed me yesterday afternoon that variable manufacturing costs will be approximately 48 percent of net sales in 1991 because he has been able to negotiate better supplier contracts. He also estimates fixed costs will increase by about $300,000 due to additional overhead from being a stand-alone corporation."

"As I see it then," stated Femrite, "the main differences between the two strategies are as follows. The conservative strategy is basically a status quo strategy wherein we increase marketing research and decrease consumer promotions but basically hold the line on all other expenditures and activities in order to show a profit. The aggressive strategy essentially means that we institute a 5 percent, across-the-board price hike, increase spending on consumer promotions and marketing research, establish one reserve for possible customer reactions to the price increase and one for possible competitive reactions, start developing new products, and add two regional sales managers and one marketing associate. In either strategy, though, we would be increasing our off-invoice activity to improve our position with retail accounts."

EXHIBIT 6

Strategic Plan Alternatives

Activity or Budget Item	Strategy	
	Conservative	*Aggressive*
Price protection reserve	None	Reserve 1 percent of sales
Consumer promotion	Decrease 1 percent from 1990	Increase 1 percent from 1990
Marketing research	Double 1990 budget	Quadruple 1990 budget
New product development	None	Budget $700,000
Defense contingency reserve	None	Budget $400,000
Off-invoice	Increase allocation 10 percent	Increase allocation 20 percent
Product line pricing	No change	Across-the-board 5 percent increase
Sales effort	No change	Add two regional sales managers at an annual cost of $78,000 each
Staff marketing support	No change	Add one marketing associate at an annual cost of $55,000
Indirect trade	No change	No change
Marketing administration	Increase 4 percent from 1990	Increase 4 percent from 1990

"My guess is that there is a .8 probability that there will be both customer and competitive reactions to the price hike. If there are reactions, and we aren't ready, I think we could suffer as much as a 3 percent revenue hit. If there are no reactions, the reserves will flow directly to the bottom line. Most important, I view the aggressive strategy as preparing for the future by investing $700,000 in new product development. The money would be spent on developing new sauces and noodle products and new packaging to compete with what La Choy is doing, new product marketing research, trade introductions, and consumer promotions. Although this investment will not generate any return for us in 1991, it should generate incremental sales of around $900,000 in 1992.

"I guess what we should do will hinge on our opinions as to where the market is going, the effectiveness of our marketing program, and what our competitors are likely to do. Indeed, even if we pursue a conservative strategy, I think it is likely that La Choy will be coming at us with both barrels: Perhaps we should think more seriously about Tom Grant's suggestions. Finally, although I think we need to look beyond 1991, we need to consider Byron's position also. How long can we stay in business if sales continue to decline?"

The Circle K Corporation

The Circle K Corporation is one of the leading specialty retailers in the United States and is the nation's second largest operator and franchiser of convenience stores. From fiscal 1984 (year-end April 30), when it embarked on a significant growth strategy, to fiscal 1990, the company acquired 3,326 stores and built another 983 stores while closing 899 units. During this period, sales increased from $1 billion in fiscal 1984 to almost $3.7 billion in fiscal 1990.

On May 15, 1990, the company and its principal subsidiaries filed for protection under Chapter 11 of the United States Bankruptcy Code. This action was taken because of the company's deteriorating financial condition, due in part to increased competition, a heavy debt burden from the expansion program, and the negative effect of merchandise and price policies instituted in 1989. Shortly after the bankruptcy filing, Circle K president Robert A. Dearth, Jr., announced that he was determined to reposition the company so that it could return to profitability and pay its debt in fiscal 1991.[1] Key elements of the plan to revitalize Circle K included a change in merchandising practices, increased promotional efforts, and an aggressive pricing program, all of which were designed to improve customer service and increase sales. In addition, opportunities to close or sell unprofitable stores would be pursued. Circle K's planned turnaround strategy was scheduled for implementation in the summer of 1990. Of critical concern to Circle K management was consumer and competitive response and the profitability of the announced strategy.

THE COMPANY

The Circle K Corporation, which is headquartered in Phoenix, Arizona, is the 30th largest retailer in the United States according to *Fortune* magazine. The company's convenience store business was begun by Circle K Convenience Stores, Inc., in 1951. In 1980, this company became a subsidiary of the Circle K Corporation. The Circle K Corporation is a holding company, which, through wholly owned subsidiaries, operates 4,631 convenience stores in the United States and related facilities. In addition, the Circle K Corporation has approximately 1,400 licensed or joint-venture stores in 13 foreign countries.

Circle K recorded an average annual increase in sales of 25 percent since fiscal 1984. The number of stores operated by Circle K increased by 14 percent per year during the period 1984 through fiscal 1990. Most of the increase in stores came from acquisitions. In the four years prior to fiscal 1989, when Circle K incurred an oper-

---

[1]"Circle K Squares Off with Its Creditors," *Wall Street Journal* (May 17, 1990): A4.

This case was prepared by Professor Roger A. Kerin, of the Edwin L. Cox School of Business, Southern Methodist University, as a basis for class discussion and is not designed to illustrate appropriate or inappropriate handling of administrative situations, or to be used for research purposes. The case is based on published sources, including the Circle K Corporation Annual Reports and Forms 10-K. The assistance of Angela Bullard and Deborah Ovitt, graduate students, in the preparation of this case is gratefully acknowledged. Copyright © by Roger A. Kerin. No part of this case may be reproduced without written permission of the copyright holder.

ating loss of $3.8 million, the company had recorded an average annual increase in operating profit of 25 percent. Exhibits 1 and 2 show the Circle K Corporation's consolidated financial statements for fiscal 1988 through fiscal 1990.

Stores and Unit Expansion

Circle K stores typically have 2,600 square feet of retail selling space. Most units are located on corner sites, have parking space on one or more sides, and are equipped

EXHIBIT 1

The Circle K Corporation's Consolidated Statement of Earnings (Thousands of Dollars)

	For the Year Ended April 30		
	1990	1989	1988
Revenues:			
Sales	$3,686,314	$3,441,384	$2,613,843
Other	50,238	53,507	42,879
Gross revenues	3,736,552	3,494,891	2,656,722
Cost of sales and expenses:			
Cost of sales	2,796,559	2,580,398	1,893,058
Operating and administrative	865,602	729,306	561,894
Reorganization and restructuring charge[a]	639,310	—	—
Depreciation and amortization	127,652	93,033	65,659
Interest and debt expense	126,799	95,912	56,608
Total cost of sales and expenses	4,555,922	3,498,649	2,577,219
Operating profit (Loss)	(819,370)	(3,758)	79,503
Gain on sale of assets[b]	—	32,323	8,198
Equity loss on foreign joint ventures	(15,064)	(1,784)	—
Earnings (loss) before federal and state income			
Taxes and cumulative effect of accounting change	(834,434)	26,781	87,701
Federal and state income tax (expense) benefit	61,565	(11,367)	(32,790)
Net earnings (loss) before cumulative effect of accounting change	(772,869)	15,414	54,911
Cumulative effect on prior years of change in accounting for income taxes	—	—	5,500
Net earnings (Loss)	($ 772,869)	$ 15,414	$ 60,411

[a]The company had been attempting a financial restructuring since October 1989. A review and assessment of operations by the Board of Directors resulted in a reorganization and restructuring charge of $639.3 million as of April 30, 1990. The charge includes (1) excess costs over acquired net assets and foreign investment; (2) abandonment, rejection, and reserves for fixed assets in nonperforming leased stores; (3) write-downs of real estate and other projects no longer under development, and (4) debt issuance and other costs.

[b]On October 31, 1988, the company sold all of its assets in connection with its manufacturing and distribution of fragmentary and block ice, sandwiches, and other fast foods. On October 27, 1987, the company sold a 50 percent interest in its wholly owned United Kingdom subsidiary.

Source: The Circle K Corporation, Form 10-K. Fiscal Year Ended April 30, 1990; The Circle K Corporation 1989 Annual Report. The statement of earnings information is accompanied by extensive explanations, which are an integral part of these consolidated financial statements.

EXHIBIT 2

The Circle K Corporation's Consolidated Balance Sheet, Abridged (Thousands of Dollars)

	April 30, 1990	April 30, 1989	April 30, 1988
Current assets:			
Cash and short-term investments	$ 50,205	$ 38,488	$ 44,216
Receivables	38,138	36,265	34,446
Inventories	175,308	239,916	191,000
Other current assets	39,865	94,341	109,851
Total current assets	303,516	409,010	379,513
Property, plant, and equipment (less accumulated depreciation and amortization)	836,123	1,068,489	708,314
Other assets	134,651	567,441	447,957
Total assets	$1,274,290	$2,044,940	$1,535,784
Current liabilites:			
Due to banks	$ —	$ 91,000	$ 60,000
Accounts payable	112,111	134,944	112,144
Other current liabilities	101,504	124,501	108,463
Total current liabilities	213,615	350,445	280,607
Liabilities subject to compromise	1,206,395	—	—
Long-term debt	54,651	1,158,563	844,065
Deferred income taxes	40,496	93,045	38,133
Other liabilities	130,915	45,359	17,191
Deferred revenue	32,285	19,632	24,767
Mandatory redeemable Preferred stock	42,500	47,500	47,500
Stockholders' equity	(451,567)	330,396	283,521
Total liabilities and stockholders' equity	$1,274,290	$2,044,940	$1,535,784

Source: The Circle K Corporation, Form 10-K, Fiscal Year Ended April 30, 1990; Circle K Corporation 1989 Annual Report. Balance sheet information is accompanied by extensive explanations, which are an integral part of these consolidated financial statements.

with modern equipment, fixtures, and refrigeration. Nearly all the stores are open seven days a week, 24 hours a day. The 4,631 stores operated by Circle K are located in 32 states. However, about 84 percent of the stores are situated in Sun Belt states ranging from California to Florida. The primary concentration of stores is in Florida (846 stores), Texas (735 stores), Arizona (679 stores), California (604 stores), and Louisiana (301 stores).

The present complement of stores was an outgrowth of an aggressive acquisition program begun in December 1983 with the purchase of the nearly 1,000-store UToteM chain. This acquisition was followed in October 1984 with the purchase of

Little General Stores, consisting of 435 units. In February 1985, Circle K bought 21 Day-n-Nite stores, and in September 1985, it acquired the 449-unit Stop & Go chain. The company purchased 189 units from National Convenience Stores in March 1987 and three months later bought 63 franchised 7-Eleven units from the Southland Corporation. In late 1987, Circle K's director of public relations announced that the company intended to have 5,000 stores by 1990.[2]

In April 1988, Circle K purchased the assets of 473 convenience stores, 90 closed stores, convenience store sites, stores under construction, and related facilities from the Southland Corporation. The company's last major acquisition occurred on September 30, 1988, with the purchase of the Charter Marketing Group. This transaction resulted in the addition of 538 gasoline and convenience stores. Circle K did not acquire any stores in fiscal 1990 because of its deteriorating financial condition, which led to the company's Chapter 11 bankruptcy filings. However, negotiations concerning the sale of 375 stores in Hawaii and the Pacific Northwest were initiated.

Product-Service Mix

Circle K stores sell over 3,800 different products and services. Food items include groceries, dairy products, candies, bakery items, produce, meat, eggs, ice cream, frozen foods, soft drinks, and alcoholic beverages (beer, wine, and liquor) where permitted. Fast food items, including fountain drinks, doughnuts, sandwiches, and coffee, are also sold. Non-food items sold by Circle K include tobacco products, health and beauty aids, magazines, books, newspapers, household goods, giftware, and toys. Food and non-food merchandise categories accounted for 50 percent of company revenue in fiscal 1990.

Circle K sells gasoline at 77.5 percent of its stores. Gasoline accounted for 48.6 percent of company revenue in fiscal 1990. In addition, the company provides a variety of consumer services. Consumer services include money orders, lottery tickets, game machines, and video cassette rentals. These services combined with interest income and royalty and licensing fees accounted for the remainder of company revenue.

Circle K had followed a program of continual testing and introduction of new products and services designed to appeal to a broader customer base and stimulate store traffic. According to the company's chairman of the board, Karl Eller, "We're a massive distribution system. Whatever we can push through that store, we will."[3] The addition of automatic teller machines (ATMs) or debit card programs at 1,146 stores and leased space at certain locations for Federal Express drop-off package service are recent innovations indicative of this strategy.

Efforts to sell and promote high-profit-margin products while cutting back on popular, though less profitable, merchandise proved costly for Circle K in the summer of 1989. While the gross profit margin for merchandise sales increased, dollar sales decreased (see Exhibit 3, which details sales and gross margins for merchandise and gasoline). Traditional customers did not want these products, according to Dearth, the company's president. An integral part of his merchandising plan for fiscal 1991 included tailoring product and service offerings to the particular ethnic or

---

[2]"Mergers of Convenience," *Progressive Grocer* (December 1987): 50–51; "Karl Eller's Big Thirst for Convenience Stores," *Business Week* (June 13, 1988): 86, 88; Circle K Corporation 1990 10-K Form.

[3]Lisa Gubernick, "Stores for Our Times," *Forbes* (November 3, 1986): 40–42.

EXHIBIT 3

The Circle K Corporation's Merchandise and Gasoline Sales and Gross Profit Percentage, Fiscal Years 1988–1990

Revenue Source	1990		1989		1988	
	Sales (Millions)	Gross Profit (Percentage)	Sales (Millions)	Gross Profit (Percentage)	Sales (Millions)	Gross Profit (Percentage)
Merchandise	$1,869.4	37.2%	$1,962.4	36.0%	$1,649.2	37.5%
Gasoline	1,817.0	10.8	1,479.0	10.5	964.6	10.6
Other[a]	50.2		53.5		42.9	
Total	$3,736.6		$3,494.9		$2,656.7	

[a]Other revenues consist of commissions on game machines and lottery tickets, money order fees, interest income, royalty and licensing fees, and other items.

Source: Circle K Corporation, 1990 10-K Form, pp. 30–31.

socioeconomic character of each store's clientele.[4] National Convenience Stores, Inc., with its Stop & Go stores, has adopted a similar program matching its merchandise with the demographics of surrounding neighborhoods. Early results from this merchandise program indicate that dollar sales will increase 4 to 5 percent.[5]

Advertising and Promotion Program

Circle K has historically used media advertising and special promotions to attract customers. In fiscal 1989, the company spent $4 million on advertising. This figure was down 41.2 percent from the fiscal 1988 advertising expenditures. For comparison, National Convenience Stores, Inc. (with 1,100 Stop & Go stores), spends about $12 million annually on advertising. Advertising as a percent-of-sales for the convenience store industry as a whole was 0.6 percent in 1989 and 0.3 percent in 1988 and 1987.

Circle K curtailed advertising in late fiscal 1990. "Circle K is not advertising and has not been," the company's national advertising manager said in April 1990. "We're going through bad times."[6] The company's most recent promotion was a "price-buster" campaign in Florida and Arizona. This campaign came to an end in the second quarter of fiscal 1990.

More aggressive advertising and promotion efforts were the second part of the turnaround strategy planned by Circle K. The company announced that a $100 million promotion would be launched in the summer of 1990.[7] The eight-week promotion would be centered on a "We're Driving Down Prices" game, which included some 180 million instant-winner, scratch-off tickets distributed to customers who made purchases at over 3,700 Circle K stores. Game tickets would feature instant-win merchandise discounts, theme park discounts, and grand prizes such as Jeep Wranglers, round-trip Continental Airline tickets, and Bayliner Capri 17-foot speedboats.

---

[4]"Circle K Squares Off with Its Creditors," p. A4.
[5]"Convenience Chains Pump for New Life," *Advertising Age* (April 23, 1990): 80.
[6]Ibid.
[7]"Circle K Unveils $100 Million Promotion," *Convenience Store News* (August 27–September 23, 1990): 12.

The game would be publicized by in-store window banners, ceiling danglers, and tent cards located near checkout counters. Outdoor signage near gasoline pumps was also planned. In addition, the promotion would be supported by radio and outdoor advertising. The objective of the promotion was to communicate a change in store prices by providing Circle K customers "more value for their dollar," according to a company press release.

This new promotional program planned for the summer of 1990 would compete directly against a similar initiative launched by 7-Eleven in April 1990.[8] 7-Eleven's program involved giving away six-ounce samples of coffee, fountain drinks, and Slurpees. The company was also giving away a coupon book, valued at $250, with discounts on 7-Eleven products as well as merchandise from Sears, Roebuck and Company, Radio Shack, and Children's Palace. 7-Eleven was promoting its program through television and radio advertising.

Pricing Policy

The third leg in the Circle K strategy involved an overall price cut of 10 percent to be implemented concurrently with the $100 million promotion and the change in merchandising practices. "Before, we had the attitude of gouging the customer for what we could get," said Dearth.[9] Historically, Circle K was able to charge premium prices for food and non-food items because of convenience of location, longer hours, accessibility, and fast service without long checkout lines. Promotional pricing of high-traffic items such as cigarettes, beer, bread, soft drinks, milk, and gasoline also was used periodically. These pricing practices had provided Circle K with the highest gross-profit-margin percentages in the convenience store industry. However, due to increased competitive pressures and rising costs during fiscal 1989, the company's gross-profit-margin percentage slipped to 25 percent for the first time since fiscal 1984. In addition, the Circle K Corporation incurred its first operating loss since its incorporation in 1980.

At the beginning of the 1990 fiscal year, Circle K boosted store merchandise prices by about 6 to 7 percent. According to industry analysts, store merchandise sales volume declined 8 to 10 percent. Gasoline sales volume dropped between 1 and 6 percent.[10] In February 1990, Circle K reversed the price increases. Merchandise dollar sales for Circle K in fiscal 1990 were 4.7 percent below fiscal 1989 levels, and company gross profit dropped 3.3 percent.

THE CONVENIENCE STORE INDUSTRY

The convenience store industry has been one of the fastest-growing sectors of retailing over the past 20 years. Since 1977, the number of convenience stores has grown at an average annual rate of 6.5 percent. Sales volume grew at an average annual rate of 17 percent. However, sales and store growth declined in the latter half of the 1980s. In 1989, the convenience store industry generated sales of $67.7 billion through an estimated 70,200 stores nationwide.

Convenience store industry profitability has fluctuated during the past five years.

[8] "Convenience Chains Pump for New Life," p. 80.
[9] "Circle K Squares Off with Its Creditors," p. A4.
[10] Ibid.

The industry gross profit margin fell to its lowest level in 1989 as a result of narrowing margins on store merchandise. The industry net profit margin before income taxes decreased in each of the past five years reaching a low of 0.4 percent in 1989. Rising costs of leasing, building, equipping, insuring, and operating stores coupled with financing costs attributed to store expansion contributed to this decline, according to industry analysts. A summary of industry sales, unit growth, and profitability is shown in Exhibit 4.

Competitors

The convenience store industry is highly fragmented. In 1989, 1,353 companies were listed as belonging to the National Association of Convenience Stores. According to Alex Brown and Sons, Inc., an investment banking firm, about 42 percent of total stores and 31 percent of industry sales were accounted for by convenience store chains with fewer than 50 stores.[11] The largest single convenience store chain is the Southland Corporation (7-Eleven). The largest U.S. convenience store operators in terms of sales and units are listed in Exhibit 5.

EXHIBIT   4

Convenience Store Industry Summary: 1980–1989

	Year									
	1980	*1981*	*1982*	*1983*	*1984*	*1985*	*1986*	*1987*	*1988*	*1989*
Sales, Including Gasoline										
Total sales (billions of dollars)	24.5	31.2	35.9	41.6	45.6	51.4	53.9	59.6	61.2	67.7
Year-to-year change (%)	31.0	27.3	15.1	15.9	9.6	12.7	4.9	10.5	2.7	10.6
Sales, Excluding Gasoline										
Sales (billions of dollars)	17.7	21.6	23.7	25.8	29.3	33.3	36.0	39.1	39.2	40.6
Year-to-year change (%)	22.9	22.0	15.7	8.9	13.6	13.3	8.4	8.6	—	3.6
Store Data										
Total number of stores (thousands)	44.1	47.9	51.2	54.4	58.0	61.0	64.0	67.5	69.2	70.2
Year-to-year change (%)	10.0	8.6	6.9	6.3	6.6	5.2	4.9	5.5	2.5	1.4
Sales per store (thousands of dollars) (excluding gas)	394.0	450.0	463.0	474.0	511.0	544.0	564.0	579.2	567.0	578.0
Year-to-year change (%)	11.0	14.2	2.9	2.4	7.8	6.5	3.7	2.7	2.1	1.9
Profitability Data										
Gross profit margin (%)										
Merchandise						32.5	35.5	35.9	36.4	32.1
Gasoline						7.3	11.2	10.6	11.5	11.7
Total						22.8	25.1	24.4	26.2	21.8
Net profit margin before income taxes (%)						2.7	2.6	2.2	1.9	.4

Source: Based on *The Convenience Store Industry* (Baltimore: Alex Brown & Sons, 1988): 3; *The State of the Convenience Store Industry 1990* (Alexandria, VA: National Association of Convenience Stores, 1990).

---

[11] *The Convenience Store Industry* (Baltimore: Alex Brown & Sons, 1988).

EXHIBIT 5

Largest U.S. Convenience Store Operators

Company	Key Chain(s)	Sales Volume (Millions of Dollars)	Number of Store Units (Approx.)
The Southland Corporation	7-Eleven, High's Dairy Stores, Quik Marts, Super 7	$7,950.3	7,200
Circle K Corporation	Circle K	3,441.4	4,631
Emro Marketing Co.	Speedway, Gastown, Starvin Marvin, Bonded	1,250.0	1,673
National Convenience Stores, Inc.	Stop N Go	1,072.5	1,147
Convenient Food Mart, Inc.	Convenient Food Mart	875.0	1,258
Cumberland Farms, Inc.	Cumberland Farms	800.0	1,150

Source: Company annual reports and 10-K forms; *Convenience Store News Industry Report 1989* (New York: BMT Publications, 1989).

Convenience store executives believe that their principal competitors are other convenience store chains, gas stations that sell food (g-stores), supermarkets, and fast food outlets. S. R. "Dick" Dole, an executive at the Southland Corporation, believed that competition for convenience stores depends on the product category:

> If you're talking about post-mix, coffee, and sandwiches, then our competition is the "fast feeders," like McDonald's and Burger King, and other convenience stores. If you're talking about beer and soft drinks, then our competition would be supermarkets, other convenience stores, and some g-stores, or a major oil company that operates a small convenience store with major emphasis on gasoline.[12]

Oil companies that operate g-stores engage in the most direct competition with convenience stores. Texaco, Chevron Corporation, Amoco Corporation, Atlantic Richfield Company, Coastal Corporation, Mobil Corporation, BP America, and Diamond Shamrock operate more than 600 g-stores each.[13] These well-capitalized companies, with the advantage of prime locations and newer stores, have become very aggressive in the creation of convenience-type stores. Although smaller than convenience stores in terms of retail selling space and number of items stocked (convenience stores stock 33 percent more items than g-stores), g-stores have focused on items traditionally viewed as convenience store staples—tobacco products, soft drinks, and beer.

Supermarkets have also been aggressive in trying to attract the convenience shopper. In particular, supermarkets have targeted the "fill-in" shoppers who typically populate the "eight items and under" express counters by offering extended store hours and prepackaged foods. This segment represents about $45 billion in annual sales. Supermarkets also cater to consumers who desire prepared foods for off-premises consumption. Prepared foods sold by supermarkets now account for

---

[12]"A Conversation with S. R. "Dick" Dole," *The Southland Family* (August 1986): 9.
[13]"Convenience Chains Pump for New Life," p. 80.

more than $2.4 billion in sales annually. Furthermore, industry research shows that supermarkets enjoy a better reputation among consumers for lower prices and higher-quality food than convenience stores.[14]

Convenience Store Customer and Purchase Behavior

About 90 percent of American adults (18 years or older) visit a convenience store at least once a year. Almost two-thirds of these shoppers visit a convenience store two to three times per month. The typical convenience store customer is a white male between the ages of 18 and 34 with a high school education who is employed in a blue-collar occupation. A profile of the convenience store customer is given in Exhibit 6.

Convenience store executives are sensitive to the fact that a stereotypic convenience store customer exists. They also recognize that opportunities for future sales growth exist in attracting women generally and particularly employed women, older consumers of both sexes, and professional and white-collar workers. According to a 7-Eleven executive:

EXHIBIT 6

Profile of Convenience Store Customers on a Given Day

	Convenience Store Customers (Percentage)	*United States Population (Percentage)*
Sex		
Male	57%	48%
Female	43	52
Age		
18 to 24	21	15
25 to 34	31	24
35 to 49	25	25
50 and over	23	35
Education		
Did not finish high school	19	18
Graduated from high school	62	60
Attended college	19	22
Annual Household Income		
Less than $10,000	14	13
$10,000 to $14,999	11	10
$15,000 to $19,999	12	10
$20,000 and over	48	48
Unknown	15	19
Race		
White	83	87
Nonwhite	17	13

Source: The Gallup Organization. Used with permission.

---

[14]"Convenience Store/Supermarket Market Segment Report," *Restaurant Business* (February 10, 1990): 125.

Two important demographic groups for 7-Eleven are the increased numbers of older people and working women. The elderly, the fastest-growing segment of the population, generally are not convenience store customers. Also, working women now represent 45 percent of the work force. By 1995, 80 percent of all women between the ages of 25 and 44 will be working. Right now, women represent less than one-third of our business. We must do a better job of attracting potential customers to our stores by developing programs that fit their needs.

The 24–45 age group is experiencing a tremendous growth in disposable income, which increases our need to upgrade our stores to meet their demands and tastes.[15]

Similarly, a Circle K executive said, "We feel we can appeal to other groups than the traditional blue-collar customer of the past. We'd like to skew more toward office workers and white-collar workers."[16]

Industry analysts also believe that a broadened customer base will be necessary if the convenience store industry is to prosper in the 1990s. They note that the U.S. population between the ages of 18 and 34 will actually shrink in the early 1990s. They also point out that the industry must expand its customer base to include more older, married, dual-income customers and women shoppers.

The principal purchases by the 643 customers who visit an average convenience store daily are gasoline, tobacco products, alcoholic beverages, prepared foods, and soft drinks. These five product categories account for almost 80 percent of convenience store sales. The average merchandise sale per customer visit was $2.29 in 1989.

Industry Trends and Concerns

Industry observers have identified several trends that are likely to affect convenience store industry growth and profitability prospects for the foreseeable future. These trends and their implications are outlined below.

The first trend relates to industry maturity and store saturation. Industry analysts cite several developments, some of which are documented in Exhibit 4.

1. Industry sales growth has slowed in recent years compared with growth rates in the 1970s and early 1980s. Similarly, the number of new stores being opened has leveled off, and consolidation is occurring as firms have elected to grow through acquisition.

2. Industry profitability has declined in recent years. The downward spiral in net profit margins has hampered the ability of firms to reinvest in their operations.

3. Store saturation is present in many geographic markets. Potentially overstored areas include the southwestern, southeastern, and western United States. Industry forecasters predict that the demand for convenience stores is such that the market can only support 400–500 new stores per year in the period 1990–1995.

A second concern is the lack of differentiation among convenience store competitors. According to a 7-Eleven executive, "The thing to overcome is the battle of sameness."[17] The lack of differentiation has often produced costly price competition

---

[15]"A Conversation with S. R. "Dick" Dole," pp. 9–10.

[16]"Convenience Store/Supermarket Market Segment Report," p. 134.

[17]"Convenience Chains Pump for New Life," p. 80.

in selected markets, most notably in Florida and Texas. Efforts at differentiation reflected in new products and services have often been met with an immediate response. "We are the worst thieves around," said a Circle K executive. "As soon as one of us finds something that works, the copycats go to work."[18]

A third trend is the changing sales mix between merchandise and gasoline. In the late 1970s, roughly 82 percent of convenience store sales were merchandise. By 1989, 60 percent of sales were merchandise. The increase in gasoline sales as a percentage of total revenue has affected industry profitability because of gasoline's lower gross profit margin and often higher equipment cost. Moreover, some industry watchers believe that oil company g-stores are better equipped to deal with the lower margins. These "low-price, high-volume" g-stores, with about 80 percent of their sales coming from gasoline, and supermarkets, with a growing commitment to serving the convenience-oriented consumer, have left convenience stores "stuck in the middle," say industry analysts.[19]

STRATEGY CONSIDERATIONS FOR FISCAL 1991

One week prior to the announced bankruptcy filing, Karl Eller resigned as chairman, chief executive officer, and board director of the Circle K Corporation. He did so to pursue personal business opportunities and to give the company's board of directors "the latitude to establish new objectives for the future."[20]

The principal elements of the announced strategy to revitalize the Circle K Corporation included (1) an overall price reduction of 10 percent, (2) a change in merchandise practices so that individual stores could stock items reflective of the socioeconomic characteristics of their trade areas, and (3) a $100 million advertising and promotion program. As the architect of the strategy, Dearth, Circle K's president, expressed no intention of downsizing the company or laying off any of the company's 27,000 employees when the bankruptcy filing was announced.

The initial reaction to the announced strategy was mixed. According to one of Circle K's bank creditors, "We would encourage any plan that generates income. We believe this [marketing] plan probably will."[21] However, industry analysts were skeptical. Some believed that the company's troubles would force it to sell about 10 percent of its stores. By August 1990, Circle K had terminated 400 leases on stores that had been shut down. These 400 leases were estimated to cost Circle K $1 million to $1.5 million per month. Furthermore, 201 unprofitable stores were scheduled to close in August 1990. In addition, the company had deals to sell 375 stores in Hawaii and the Pacific Northwest before its bankruptcy filing. These deals were delayed pending approval by the bankruptcy court. Savings from store closings, costs associated with terminating leases, and the potential gain on the sale of stores had yet to be determined.[22]

---

[18]"Stores for Our Times," p. 41.

[19]"Recent Events Show Plight of C-Store Chains," *National Petroleum News* (May 1990): 10.

[20]"Karl Eller Resigns as Circle K Chairman, CEO," *Wall Street Journal and Dow Jones News Wire* (May 7, 1990).

[21]"Circle K Squares Off with Its Creditors," p. A4.

[22]"Circle K Begins Closing 201 Unprofitable Stores," *Wall Street Journal and Dow Jones News Wire* (August 21, 1990).

Industry analysts also expressed doubts about the financial viability of specific elements of Circle K's turnaround strategy. Lower prices might attract customers and increase store traffic. However, gross profit margins would suffer. Furthermore, efforts to modify the merchandise mix would involve a substantial change in inventories, and the advertising and promotion program was expensive. According to a convenience store analyst, "I don't know where they will get the money."[23]

In affidavits filed with the Securities and Exchange Commission, Circle K management stated that it "believes, but has no assurances, that this plan will succeed in improving operating results." Moreover, the company "expects to continue to incur operating losses until the business plan is fully implemented and refined."[24] The question yet to be answered was "Could the announced strategy return Circle K to profitability as envisioned by its president?"

---

[23]"Circle K Squares Off with Its Creditors," p. A4.

[24]Circle K Corporation, Form 10-K, For the fiscal year ended April 1990, "Management's Discussion and Analysis of Financial Condition and Results of Operations," pp. 26, 30.

Volvo Trucks Europe

In early May 1989, Ulf Selvin, Vice President of Marketing, Sales, and Service for Volvo Truck Corporation, Europe Division (VTC Europe), was deep in thought. European Community (EC) directives aimed at creating a single internal EC market by the end of 1992 were reshaping the truck market in Europe. Truck buyers' sales support and service needs and demands were changing and becoming more pan-European. Competition was growing fiercer and increasingly pan-European as well.

VTC Europe had historically operated as a multi-domestic marketer, with each national importer management team responsible for the marketing, sales, and service of Volvo trucks within its country. Recently, however, programs had been initiated at both headquarters and importer level that were aimed at moving VTC Europe toward pan-European marketing. As Selvin reviewed the progress of these programs, he deliberated over whether or not VTC Europe should attempt to become a "Euro-marketer" and, if so, what the appropriate mix was between pan-European, regional, and national marketing of Volvo trucks in Europe. If he and his management team decided to move VTC Europe from multi-domestic to pan-European marketing, they would have to identify the critical steps that the company would need to take in order to make such a transition successful, including the implementation implications for VTC Europe's marketing strategy, marketing organization structure, marketing information systems, and human resource development policies.

BACKGROUND

Volvo Truck Corporation (VTC) is a wholly owned subsidiary of AB Volvo (Volvo). Headquartered in Göteborg, Sweden, Volvo is the largest industrial group in the Nordic region. Established in 1927 as an automobile manufacturer, the company gradually expanded its production to include trucks, buses, an extensive range of automotive components, and marine, aircraft, aerospace, and industrial engines. Beginning in the late 1970s, Volvo diversified into the food industry, finance, and the oil, fruit, and chemicals trade in order to increase the group's opportunities for growth and profitability and to counteract economic fluctuations. Volvo's structure and organization are characterized by decentralization and delegation of responsibility. Its myriad operations are united by the shared values of quality, service, ethical performance, and concern for people and the environment. The group's products are marketed around the world, with almost 90 percent of sales occurring outside Sweden in 1988. Volvo's sales and net income totaled Swedish kronor (SEK) 96,639 million and SEK 4,953 million, respectively, in 1988, up from 1987 levels of SEK 92,520 million and SEK 4,636 million, respectively.

The first Volvo truck was manufactured in 1928. It was an immediate success and was met with high demand. Volvo's truck production expanded rapidly in the

1930s and 1940s. The profits from truck building financed the company's total operations for most of its first 20 years. It was not until the late 1940s that Volvo's automobile production became more than marginally viable. By the late 1960s, however, this situation had reversed. Despite market leadership in Sweden and the rest of Scandinavia, Volvo's truck operations had become unprofitable because of heavy competition in new export markets, combined with problems with state-of-the-art truck models, which were placing severe stresses on Volvo's design and service departments. The truck business had become a drag on the company's automobile operations. Management contemplated divesting Volvo's truck operations but decided instead to form a separate truck division (VTC).

The creation of VTC marked the beginning of major investment in and continued expansion and profitability of Volvo's truck operations. During the 1970s and 1980s, VTC replaced its entire product line with new models and intensified its marketing efforts in international markets. Between 1979 and 1986, VTC became the first truck manufacturer to win the coveted "Truck of the Year" award three times. In 1981, VTC acquired the truck assets of the White Motor Company in the United States and formed the Volvo White Truck Corporation. In 1987, White Volvo joined with General Motors's heavy-truck division to form a joint venture, the Volvo GM Heavy Truck Corporation, with Volvo as the majority shareholder, with responsibility for management.

VTC's truck production grew dramatically between 1970 and 1980, from 16,300 to 30,200 trucks. By 1988, production had doubled to 60,500 units. During the 1980s, VTC's share of the world market for trucks in the heavy class—gross vehicle weight (GVW) of greater than 16 tons—doubled to 11 percent, and VTC became the world's second-largest producer of heavy trucks. In both 1987 and 1988, demand for Volvo trucks exceeded VTC's production capacity.

In 1988, VTC sold (delivered) 59,500 trucks worldwide. Exhibit 1 shows the breakout of VTC's 1987 and 1988 unit sales (deliveries) by market area. The two largest

EXHIBIT 1

Sales (Deliveries) of Volvo Trucks by Market Area and Size

Market Area	Number of Trucks Delivered	
	1987	1989
Europe	29,300	31,600
North America	13,200	21,500
White Autocar/WHITEGMC	11,100	9,800[a]
Volvo	2,100	1,700
Latin America	3,300	3,300
Middle East	500	700
Australia	400	800
Other Markets	1,000	1,600
Total	47,700	59,500
of which less than 16 tons GVW	6,500	6,500
of which greater than 16 tons GVW	41,200	53,000

[a]Includes GM's product line.

markets were Western Europe and North America, which accounted for 52 percent and 36 percent of sales, respectively. Almost 90 percent of unit sales were in the heavy class. VTC earned SEK 2,645 million on sales of SEK 22,762 million in 1988, which represented 34 percent of Volvo's 1988 operating income, up from 14 percent in 1986. Exhibit 2 contains graphs of VTC's sales, operating income, return on capital, and capital expenditure and development costs for the years 1984 through 1988.

VTC's organization chart is shown in Exhibit 3. Separate divisions are responsible for the manufacture and marketing of trucks in Europe, overseas, the United States, and Brazil. Trucks are produced in ten Volvo-owned assembly plants. Of the 60,500 trucks manufactured by VTC in 1988, 20,000 were produced in the United States, 17,200 in Belgium, 14,400 in Sweden, 3,700 in Scotland, 3,200 in Brazil, 1,500 in Australia, and 500 in Peru. VTC's trucks are sold through a network of 850 dealers operating with 1,200 service workshops in over 100 countries.

The product development division is responsible for the design and development of global truck concepts and components. It has development departments in Sweden, the United States, Belgium, the United Kingdom, Brazil, and Australia. About 6 percent of sales is invested in product development annually.

VTC EUROPE

VTC Europe is responsible for the production and marketing of Volvo trucks in Europe. The Western European market for heavy trucks grew 13 percent in 1988, to 175,000 vehicles, based on new truck registration statistics. Despite full capacity utilization of its plants, VTC Europe was unable to keep pace with the market growth. Its share of the Western European heavy truck market declined from 14.3 percent to 14 percent. The Western European medium-truck market (10–16 tons GVW) grew by 4.5 percent in 1988, to 42,000 vehicles. Volvo's share of this market declined from 10.6 percent to 9.0 percent. Exhibit 4 shows a comparison of new Volvo truck registrations and market shares by European country for 1987 and 1988.

Early 1989 registration figures indicated that Volvo was regaining lost share in Europe in both the heavy- and medium-truck markets, as shown in Exhibit 5. VTC Europe began 1989 with a large delivery backlog. The division dramatically improved its delivery precision between January and March 1989, moving from 56 percent to 80 percent of trucks being delivered within one week of scheduled delivery. However, delivery precision varied widely by country. As of March 1989, it ranged from 54 percent in Spain to 94 percent in Austria and Finland.

Distribution System

Two layers in the distribution system separate Volvo truck factories from Volvo truck customers. Each country's distribution network is headed by an importer that is responsible for marketing, sales, and service of Volvo trucks, parts distribution, and the creation and maintenance of a dealer network within its country. Of VTC Europe's 15 importer organizations, only 4—Austria, Spain, Portugal, and Greece—are independent importers. The other 11 are Volvo-owned. Importers purchase trucks from VTC Europe's corporate headquarters and sell them to the Volvo truck dealers within their countries, which in turn sell them to Volvo truck customers. VTC's European dealer network includes approximately 400 dealers and about 800 service points.

EXHIBIT 2

VTC Financial Trends, 1984–1988

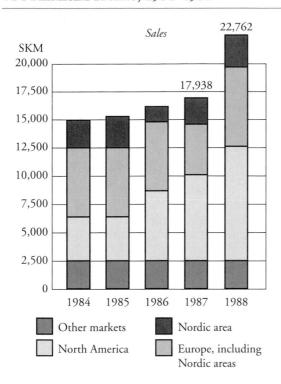

Sales

SKM

22,762

17,938

Other markets Nordic area

North America Europe, including
Nordic areas

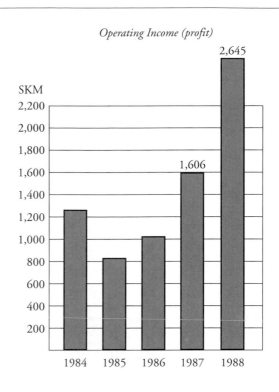

Operating Income (profit)

SKM

2,645

1,606

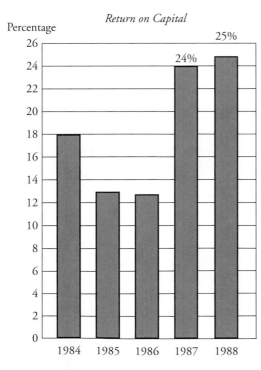

Return on Capital

Percentage

25%

24%

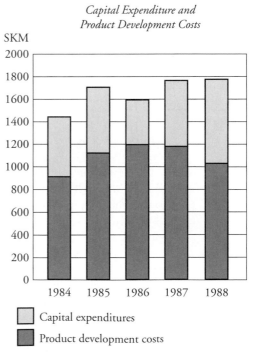

Capital Expenditure and
Product Development Costs

SKM

Capital expenditures

Product development costs

EXHIBIT 3

VTC Organization Chart

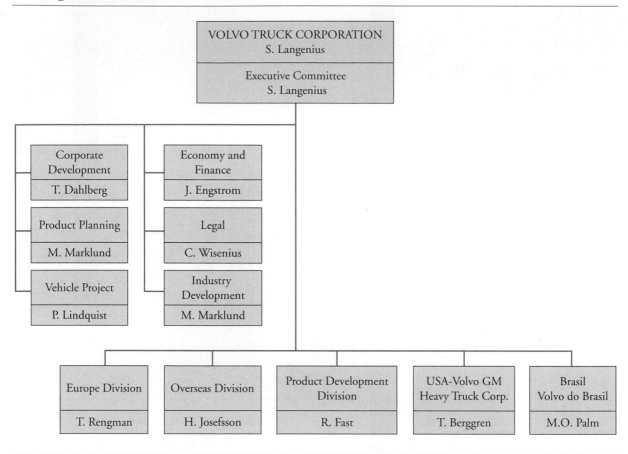

Almost all dealers are independent, although a few are Volvo-owned. All dealers are dedicated—that is, they sell only Volvo brand trucks.

The normal distribution network is rarely circumvented. Almost all sales are conducted through a dealer. VTC Europe headquarters sold directly to end customers only when selling to the governments of state-controlled countries like the former Soviet Union. Similarly, importers bypass their dealers infrequently. For example, the only customer to whom Belgium's importer makes direct sales is the Belgian army.

As a matter of course, importer organizations are headed and staffed by local nationals, although in a few cases a Swedish manager has headed an importer temporarily, during the transition from independent to Volvo-owned importership. Historically, importer managers are never transferred to work in the Swedish headquarters or in the importer organizations of other countries.

As one VTC Europe manager stated: "Importers are responsible for their country—period." Each importer's management is evaluated and rewarded on the sales volume, market share, and profit earned within its country. Importers negotiate transfer prices for the trucks they purchased from VTC Europe headquarters. These trans-

EXHIBIT 4

VTC Europe Sales (Registrations) and Market Share by Country, 1987 and 1988

Market	GVW Class[b]	Numbers of New Volvo Trucks Registered[a]		Market Share (Percentage)	
		1987	1988	1987	1988
Great Britain	> 10 tons	5,720	6,610	15.5	15.4
France	> 9 tons	4,340	4,580	10.9	10.3
Sweden	> 10 tons	2,970	3,030	50.9	53.7
Netherlands	> 10 tons	2,140	2,070	17.7	16.4
Italy[c]	> 9 tons	1,490	1,780	6.5	6.8
Spain	> 10 tons	1,010	1,700	6.5	8.4
Belgium	> 10 tons	1,600	1,600	21.6	20.1
Portugal	> 10 tons	1,020	1,280	29.9	27.1
Denmark	> 10 tons	1,310	1,130	29.8	33.0
Finland	> 10 tons	1,060	1,120	32.2	32.4
West Germany	> 10 tons	950	1,030	3.0	3.2
Norway	> 10 tons	1,280	800	40.6	37.5

[a]According to official registration statistics.

[b]Countries differ as to how they group their registration statistics by weight.

[c]Preliminary information.

fer prices vary from country to country. Importers have the responsibility to set the prices at which they sell trucks to their dealers. Prices to dealers and, consequently, prices to truck-buying customers, vary considerably by country, depending on local competitive pressures. For example, Belgium has no national truck producer. Consequently, the Belgian importer prices Volvo's trucks significantly higher than does the French importer, which faces fierce competition from a local manufacturer.

Marketing Communications

Prior to 1987, importers had complete control of the design and execution of marketing communications programs employed within their countries. In early 1987, Roger Johansson, marketing support manager for VTC Europe, developed a corporate communication platform. His objective was twofold. First, he hoped to encourage consistency in the visual presentation and underlying message of sales promotion and advertising materials across Europe, so as to enhance the total impact on customers of Volvo truck communications. Second, he aimed to improve the efficiency and cost effectiveness of the production of advertising and sales support materials. According to the communication platform, sales promotion and advertising activities were to be divided among all levels of the marketing organization—headquarters, importers, and dealers—based on which level was best suited for a given activity.

The platform was designed to remain in effect through 1989. Every three years a new communication platform was to be introduced. The platform did not dictate the actual content of messages that importers and dealers could use in their com-

EXHIBIT   5

Total Market New Truck Registrations and Volvo Share by Country

Market	For Year Ending[a]	Total Market Registration (>16 tons)	Volvo Market Share (>16 tons)	Total Market Registrations (10–16 tons)	Volvo Market Share (10–16 tons)
Sweden	3/89	5,541	51.5%	938	74.1%
Denmark	2/89	2,317	34.7	1,379	42.6
Finland	2/89	3,827	30.3	609	34.3
Norway	3/89	1,064	45.1	203	51.9
Great Britain	2/89	39,637	19.6	5,942	8.8
Ireland	1/89	1,782	14.2	672	1.4
Germany	2/89	28,157	4.2	5,593	2.4
Europe I	2/89[b]	83,962	18.1	14,851	14.8
France	3/89	35,921	11.3	8,371	7.3
Belgium	3/89	7,838	21.7	1,568	19.4
Luxembourg	12/88	385	31.9	86	19.8
Netherlands	1/89	9,419	16.0	1,489	22.0
Italy	2/89	27,198	7.5	13,328	2.0
Austria	2/89	3,751	14.5	1,072	7.8
Switzerland	12/88	3,349	15.4	476	19.7
Portugal	2/89	3,752	37.3	1,758	5.4
Spain	3/89	19,227	9.7	2,959	7.5
Greece	12/88	88	28.4	76	36.8
Israel	3/89	764	45.5	284	35.2
Europe II	2/89[b]	111,537	12.4	29,150	7.4
Europe Total (excl. Israel)	2/89[b]	195,263	14.4	44,288	9.6

[a]The most current registration information was used for each market.

[b]Markets with late information on registrations were estimated as of 2/89 for Europe I, Europe II, and Europe Total.

munications. Instead, it encouraged creativity in designing messages that took account of local circumstances, as long as the thinking behind the messages was consistent throughout Europe. Consistency was also encouraged by a visual identity program that strictly specified the logotypes, emblems, symbols, colors, typefaces, and layouts that were authorized for use throughout the marketing organization. Responsibility for complying with the precepts of the communications platform and visual identity program rested with the management of each importer organization.

Personal selling occurs almost solely at the dealer level. Each importer runs its own training programs for its dealer's salespeople. In addition, a state-of-the-art training facility in Göteborg is used to train both importer and dealer management whenever a new Volvo truck product is introduced. Importers and dealers are taught the features of the new truck, how those features translate into benefits for the potential buyers, and how to determine the bottom-line impact that the new truck will have on the potential buyer's profit-and-loss statement.

Service

In addition to selling trucks, Volvo dealers maintain and repair them. Each dealer is responsible for designing its local service system to suit its customers' needs. Each importer is responsible for coordinating service on a national level and ensuring consistency in dealer service offerings throughout its country. Volvo's service philosophy is based on the principle of preventive maintenance. Volvo dealers offer their customers service agreements with fixed prices for maintenance service and repair. Trucks that operate internationally can participate in Volvo Action Service Europe, which provides 24-hour assistance throughout Europe in the event of a breakdown. Volvo offers a DKV/Volvo credit card to its customers, which can be used at most Volvo workshops in Western Europe and at thousands of gas and service stations.

Volvo's service systems are not consistent across Europe. Service agreements made with a dealer in one country are not automatically valid at service centers in another country. Even when they are honored, prices for the same service or part often differ dramatically across countries, as does parts availability. Opening hours of service centers vary within and across countries, and the work habits and quality of mechanics differ significantly from country to country. According to importer management in Belgium, few Volvo truck owners use the DKV/Volvo credit card when traveling internationally. A customer explained why: "We do not use the DKV card anymore, except for fuel. Outside Belgium, we do not have the same discount; sometimes we find a difference of up to 22 percent in exchange rate and sometimes the card is simply not accepted." According to Jean de Ruyter, after-market manager of Volvo's Belgian importer, repairs made outside of a Volvo truck owner's home country typically result in a communication nightmare involving discussions among the customer, the repairing dealer, the importer, the customer's local dealer, and the importer in the customer's home country.

Market Segmentation

Historically, VTC Europe segmented its market solely on the basis of GVW. It divided the European truck market into three segments: heavy trucks (more than 16 tons GVW), medium trucks (7–16 tons GVW), and light trucks (less than 7 tons GVW). Volvo does not produce trucks for the light-truck market. Medium-duty trucks are further split into a 10–16 ton market, where Volvo has a truck range across Europe, and a 7–10 ton market, where Volvo sells a model on selected markets. Therefore, marketing management ignores this segment and concentrates on the other two, emphasizing the heavy-truck segment in which Volvo has achieved the bulk of its success concentrating on tractors for international transport.

Marketing Information Systems

VTC Europe does not have a standardized method of forecasting sales across Europe. Each importer develops its annual sales forecast using its own forecasting technique. The importers' forecasts are sent to VTC Europe's marketing planning and logistics department, which uses them as a starting point for making a total forecast. Forecasts are used to plan production and for long-term capacity planning. In both 1987 and 1988, several importers underestimated annual sales by as much as 25 percent, leading VTC Europe to underestimate its total sales substantially.

VTC Europe's marketing planning and logistics department conducts market research and market analysis. Market research includes both Europe-wide surveys and individual country surveys. Much of it is qualitative research intended to reveal how Volvo is performing relative to competitors. Results are shared with importer marketing managers. The department regularly tracks new truck registration statistics to try to discern market trends. It buys competitive production figures in order to learn the kinds of trucks that Volvo's competitors are building. The department also tracks Volvo's production, delivery precision, turnover rate, and market share by country.

In addition to research conducted by headquarters, importers commission marketing research in their own countries as needed. Most importer-initiated market research is conducted on a project-by-project basis, rather than on a recurrent basis. There is no standardized method of gathering data across countries.

THE EUROPEAN TRUCK MARKET

Between 1970 and 1988, truck sales made by Western European manufacturers grew at a compound annual rate of almost 1 percent. During that time, however, there were two exaggerated cycles. Sales boomed in the 1970s, peaking at 422,000 trucks (3.5 tons GVW and larger) in 1979. In the early 1980s, depression in Western Europe combined with collapse in demand from Middle East and African export markets. Sales bottomed out at 333,000 vehicles in 1984. Between 1984 and 1988, the Western European truck industry made a strong recovery. In 1988, sales reached 485,000 trucks. As Exhibit 6 shows, market growth was propelled by expansion in the heavy (greater than 16 tons GVW) and light (3.5–7.5 tons GVW) truck segments. Medium-truck sales (7.5–16 tons GVW) appeared to be in long-term decline. In 1988, approximately 310,000 new trucks (3.5 tons GVW and larger) were registered in Western Europe.

In 1950, there were 55 independent truck manufacturers in Western Europe. In 1989, there were 11. During the 1980s, several structural changes occurred in the European truck market. The most significant ones took place in the United Kingdom. Since the 1930s, both Ford and General Motors had based their European truck manufacturing in the United Kingdom. In 1986, Ford entered into a strategic alliance with Iveco, the truck subsidiary of Italy's Fiat, which led to the formation of Iveco-Ford. Ford ceded management control of both its U.K. operations and marketing to Iveco. A few months later, General Motors (Bedford-brand trucks) withdrew completely from truck manufacture in Europe after failed attempts to buy Enasa, MAN, and Leyland Trucks. The state-owned Leyland Trucks was losing more than $1 million per week when, in 1987, the U.K. government wrote off Leyland's substantial debts in order to facilitate its merger with the Dutch truck maker DAF. DAF received 60 percent of the equity of the merged company and effective control. The Rover Group received the remaining 40 percent equity stake.

In continental Europe, structural changes were less dramatic. West Germany's Daimler-Benz, the market leader in Western Europe truck sales, reduced production capacity in the early 1980s. The other West German truck manufacturer, MAN, had been heavily reliant on Middle East markets. The 1983 cancellation of a half-completed contract with Iraq left MAN financially crippled in the early 1980s. MAN's man-

EXHIBIT 6

Western European Truck Manufacturers' Sales by Truck Size

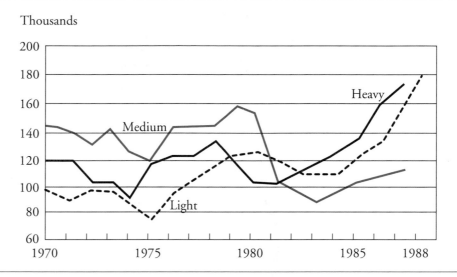

Thousands

Note: Heavy = more than 16 tons GVW; medium = 7.5–16 tons GVW; light = 3.5–7.5 tons GVW.
Source: *Financial Times*, May 3, 1989.

agement fought off a takeover attempt by General Motors, completely reorganized the company, concentrated on building up market presence in Western Europe, and regained profitability. In 1984, Iveco closed its unprofitable Unic truck plant in France, making RVI, the truck subsidiary of Renault, the sole truck producer in France. During the 1980s, RVI underwent a severe rationalization program. By 1987, it was profitable for the first time since its formation in the mid-1970s. Enasa, Spain's only independent truck producer, entered into a joint venture with DAF for the development of a modern truck cab range, which was introduced in 1987. Both of Sweden's truck manufacturers, Volvo and Saab-Scania, survived the recession in very good shape without restructuring in Europe.

There is no common classification of trucks throughout Western Europe. Although the definition of the truck market varies by country, each country maintains new truck registration statistics, which industry members use to calculate market shares. In 1988, the top five truck manufacturers accounted for almost 75 percent of total Western European truck sales (greater than 3.5 tons GVW). Daimler-Benz (23.7 percent) was the market leader, followed by Iveco (20.6 percent), RVI (11.4 percent), DAF (9.4 percent), and Volvo (9.0 percent). In the two segments in which Volvo competed, heavy trucks and medium trucks (10–16 tons GVW only), Volvo was number two and number four in the Western European market, respectively, as shown in Exhibit 7. In 1988, the market leaders by individual country were as follows: DAF (Leyland) in the United Kingdom, Daimler-Benz in West Germany, RVI in France, Iveco in Italy, Enasa in Spain, DAF in the Netherlands, Volvo and Daimler-Benz in Belgium, and Volvo in Sweden, Denmark, Finland, and Norway.

EXHIBIT 7

Western European Truck Market Shares by Manufacturer Based on New Truck Registrations

Manufacturer	Market Share (>16 tons GVW)		Market Share (10–16 tons GVW)	
	1987	1988	1987	1988
Volvo	14.3%	14.0%	10.6%	9.0%
Daimler-Benz	20.1	18.9	23.9	23.7
Iveco	12.8	13.6	24.9	27.6
RVI	11.9	12.3	14.3	16.3
DAF	10.8	11.6	8.0	8.7
Scania	12.4	11.0	1.3	.8
MAN	8.5	8.3	6.2	5.0
Pegaso	4.2	4.7	1.7	.6
ERF	1.6	2.1	0	0
WRIGT	1.7	2.0	1.0	1.0
EBRO	0	0	2.0	2.7
Other	1.7	1.5	6.1	4.6

Impact of 1992 on the European Truck Industry

The expression "1992" was shorthand for a campaign to turn the 12 EC member countries into one barrier-free internal market by the end of 1992. The community's goal was to create a market of 322 million people in which the free movement of goods, services, people, and capital was ensured. Among the 286 legislative reforms designed to fulfill this objective were ones aimed at liberalizing road haulage in the EC. Already, transport delays at customs posts had been shortened by the January 1, 1988, introduction of a "Single Administrative Document," which replaced the plethora of individual country documents previously required for inter-EC border crossings. Historically, inter-EC transport was strictly limited by a system of quotas that restricted the number of trips that haulers of one country could make into other EC countries in a given year. In June of 1987, the EC member nations agreed to increase these quotas by 40 percent per year in 1988 and 1989 and to abolish all road transport quotas to EC and non-EC destinations by January 1, 1993. As a result of these two measures, industry analysts expected a 30 to 50 percent increase in inter-EC trade by the year 2000.

The European Commission supported unrestricted cabotage—that is, freedom for a trucker registered in one EC country to collect and deliver loads between two points inside a second EC country. EC member states had not reached agreement on allowing unrestricted cabotage, but the Commission was pushing for agreement and implementation by the end of 1992. In 1989, restrictions on cabotage were partially responsible for 35 percent of all trucks on EC roads traveling empty. Unrestricted cabotage would give trucks more flexibility to contract short hauls on their return trips, which would enable them to avoid returning from a long trip with an empty truck.

Trucking companies had already begun to vie for position in the EC's post-1992 transport market. Industry analysts expected concentration in the road haulage industry via mergers, acquisitions, and strategic alliances, particularly among fleets specializing in international traffic. Many observers believed that medium-sized fleets would be squeezed out in favor of small specialized haulers and large efficient international haulers. Most believed that the scramble for business would result in a major shake-up of the EC transport industry, after which there would be likely to be fewer total competitors and, perhaps, a smaller total market for heavy trucks.

The implications for European truck manufacturers were several. Inter-European transporters had already begun to demand that truck producers supply consistent systems of service and sales support across Europe. As 1992 approached, pressures to harmonize both truck and parts prices throughout Europe would probably increase, as large fleet owners attempted to negotiate Europe-wide prices. In addition, "artificial" differences in truck product standards—that is, unique product standards that were designed solely to protect national markets—would likely disappear over time. Eventually, new trucks might be built to "Euro-specifications," in contrast with the existing situation in which "every European country had two unique possessions—a national anthem and a brake system standard." As large trucking companies became increasingly international, the loyalty of their truck buyers to locally produced vehicles would likely wane. Competition between truck producers was expected to intensify as was concentration within the industry.

VTC EUROPE'S MOVES TOWARD PAN-EUROPEAN MARKETING

Market Segmentation and Sales Forecasting

In 1984, VTC Europe took over its previously independent Belgian importer. Throughout the early 1980s, VTC had experienced heavy price competition and low profitability in Belgium. In order to develop a sound marketing strategy designed to increase the profitability of VTC's Belgian operation, while at the same time satisfying its customers, André Durieux, then marketing manager of VTC Belgium, commissioned an outside consultant, Professor Robert Peeters of the Université Catholique de Louvain, to perform a brand image study in the Belgian truck market. Peeters designed and executed a quantitative survey of a representative sample of truck owners in Belgium.

The first objective of the study was to conceive a truck market segmentation scheme that would help Belgian management decide the right customer groups to target in order to increase the profitability of its sales. The study also aimed to discover the criteria that were determinant to truck owners when choosing a make of truck and, for each criterion, the position that Volvo and each of its competitors held in owners' minds. A third goal of the study was to determine the marketing mix through which VTC Belgium could send the right message to its target segments in the ways which would best reach them and influence them to buy Volvo trucks.

One of the outcomes of this research was the development of a truck industry segmentation scheme that Belgian management used in reshaping its marketing strategy. In 1987, Pol Jacobs, VTC Belgium's marketing and business development manager, commissioned a follow-up study in order to assess the impact of Volvo's post-1984 marketing efforts on brand image in Belgium and to reveal any changes that had occurred in the makeup of the market by segment. Comparing the results of the second survey with those of the first showed that the pattern of Volvo's penetration of different market segments in Belgium had changed significantly between 1984 and 1987. Between 1984 and 1989, VTC Belgium improved its profitability almost tenfold. Jacobs was convinced that use of Peeter's segmentation scheme as a starting point from which to design Volvo's marketing strategy for Belgium had contributed to VTC Belgium's success. This segmentation scheme identified 60 unique segments based on four variables:

1. Fleet size
   a. Small (3 or fewer trucks)
   b. Medium (4–10 trucks)
   c. Large (10 or more trucks)
2. Gross vehicle weight (GVW)
   a. Less than or equal to 16 tons
   b. More than or equal to 16 tons
3. Transporter type
   a. Professional (firms whose primary business was transportation)
   b. Own account (firms that operated a truck fleet to conduct their primary business, for example, construction firms)
4. Principal truck usage
   a. Distribution (firms using trucks to transport goods)
   b. Construction (firms in the construction industry, where truck usage was primarily "off-the-road")
   c. National (firms that used trucks exclusively within a country's borders)
   d. International (firms that shipped across country borders)
   e. Others (firms not otherwise categorized)

Exhibit 8 shows the distribution of truck registration in Belgium, which was believed to be similar in other countries in the European Community. This analysis indicated that (1) truck registrations were almost equally split between professional and own-account transporters, (2) about 35 percent of trucks were operated within country borders, (3) 58.9 percent of trucks were under 16 tons GVW, and (4) about 43 percent of trucks were registered by large fleet (10 or more trucks) operators.

Peeters and Jacobs had also worked together to develop an econometric forecasting model, the intent of which was to improve the accuracy of Belgium's short-term (less than two years) sales forecasts. In 1989, the model was being tested in both Belgium and the United Kingdom. Ulf Norman, VTC Europe's manager of marketing planning and logistics, was supportive of expanding the model's use throughout Europe if it proved successful and reliable in the United Kingdom and Belgium.

Volvo Euro Truck Dealer and Eurofleet Task Forces

In late 1988, Selvin organized the "Volvo Euro Truck Dealer" (VETD) project. Its steering committee was made up of two VTC Europe headquarters service managers and five importer after-sales and service managers (from Belgium, France, Italy, the Netherlands, and the United Kingdom). Chaired by John de Ruyter, the steering committee was charged with establishing the project's objectives; coordinating the working process of the project among VTC, Volvo Parts Corporation (VPC), Volvo Dealer

EXHIBIT 8

Market Segmentation Grid (In Percentages of Total Truck Population)

	Fleet Size and Weight						
	Small (≤ 3)		Medium (4–10)		Large (≥ 10)		
Activity or Function	*≤ 16 t*	*≥ 16 t*	*≤ 16 t*	*≥ 16 t*	*≤ 16 t*	*≥ 16 t*	***Total***
Own-account transporters							
Distribution	7.3	4.5	1.1	1.8	0.4	2.1	17.2
Construction	0.1	1.1	0.9	1.4	1.7	1.6	6.8
National	4.7	1.6	1.4	3.8	1.7	3.6	16.8
International	1.3	0.9	0.2	1.3	—	1.4	5.1
Others	—	0.6	0.3	—	2.5	—	3.4
Professional transporters							
Distribution	1.1	0.8	0.9	1.6	—	1.6	6.0
Construction	0.2	1.6	—	0.4	—	1.2	3.4
National	1.4	1.5	1.4	3.0	2.5	8.5	18.3
International	0.2	0.7	0.5	6.1	0.4	14.7	22.6
Others	—	0.4	—	—	—	—	0.4
Total	16.3	13.7	6.7	19.4	9.2	34.7	100.0%

Note: First entry, for example, means that 7.3 percent of all truck registrations were less than or equal to 16 tons GVW, fleet owner-operators engaged in distribution.

Source: Dealer survey and truck registrations (disguised data).

Facilities (VDF), and the importers; organizing and providing education for the importers; advising VTC and VPC in policy matters relating to the project; allocating specific tasks to work groups; and motivating all parties involved to take an active part in the project.

By the end of March 1989, the VETD steering committee had established the project's objectives and the procedures that were to be followed at the importer level in order to realize those objectives. The fundamental objective of the VETD project was to create a common Volvo truck environment at all Volvo dealers in the EC (Switzerland and Austria were included in the project although they were not EC members). The desired Volvo environment was translated into specific "Euro Dealer Standards" that applied to the external, internal, and service environments of all Volvo dealers. The importers were charged with evaluating their existing dealerships, establishing an action plan for each dealer, and following up to ensure that the plans were correctly executed.

Both the objectives and the importer working procedures were presented to VTC Europe's importer truck division managers in April 1989. Each manager was directed to appoint within his organization a VETD staff that included one specialist who would be responsible for the project. The next step would be taken in June, when the importer's newly appointed VETD specialists were scheduled to be trained.

Around the time that the VETD project was initiated, Selvin created a "Eurofleet" task force composed of the truck division managers of each of VTC Europe's six largest importers and a headquarters liaison. The purpose of the task force was for the importers to work together to satisfy the needs of VTC's international fleet customers. Through May 1989, the Eurofleet task force had operated unsystematically, attending to each issue individually as it arose.

Pan-European Management Training

Selvin had identified 200 VTC importer and headquarter managers throughout Europe whom he targeted to attend a three-day training seminar at the Lovanium International Management Center in Belgium. The purpose of the seminar was for the managers to think through, and discuss together, the changes that were occurring in the European truck industry due to "1992" and the impact of those changes on VTC's business. Managers were to be trained in groups of approximately 35. The groups were to be cross-sectional, made up of managers from different countries and different functional areas, in order to foster the interchange of ideas and cooperation throughout the organization. The first seminar had been conducted in March 1989. The second one was scheduled for June 1989.

THE FUTURE OF PAN-EUROPEAN MARKETING IN VTC EUROPE

Selvin strongly believed that, in order to be successfully implemented, any attempts to move VTC Europe toward pan-European marketing would require the full support of both headquarters and importer management. Importer managers would not likely support a pan-European strategy that conflicted with their local interests or was perceived as being dictated from Sweden. Therefore, Selvin was convinced that it was crucial to involve managers from throughout the organization in the development and implementation of any future steps toward pan-European marketing.

Colgate-Palmolive Canada
Arctic Power Detergent

"We've got some important decisions to make on Arctic Power for 1988," said Linda Barton, Senior Product Manager for the brand. "As I see it, we can continue to develop our strong markets in Quebec, the Maritimes, and British Columbia or we can try to build market share in the rest of Canada." Ms. Barton was discussing the future of Arctic Power, one of Colgate-Palmolive Canada's leading laundry detergents, with Gary Parsons, the Assistant Product Manager on the brand.

"Not only do we have to consider our strategic direction," replied Mr. Parsons, "but we also have to think about our positioning strategy for Arctic Power. I'm for running the Quebec approach in all our markets." Mr. Parsons was referring to the Quebec advertising campaign, which positioned Arctic Power as the superior detergent for cold water cleaning.

"I'm not sure," said Ms. Barton. "We're making great progress with our current advertising in British Columbia. It might be more effective outside of Quebec. Remember, cold water washing is a newer concept for the western provinces. We have to overcome that obstacle before we can get people to buy Arctic Power. Let's go over the data again, then make our decisions."

THE COMPANY

Colgate-Palmolive Canada is a wholly owned subsidiary of Colgate-Palmolive, a large multinational with divisions in 58 countries. Worldwide company sales in 1986 were $4.9 billion with profits of $178 million. The Canadian subsidiary sales exceeded $250 million each year. Colgate-Palmolive Canada (CPC) manufactures a range of household, health, and personal care products. Among CPC's major brands are ABC, Arctic Power, and Fab (laundry detergents); Palmolive (dishwashing liquid); Ajax (cleanser); Irish Spring (bar soap); Ultra Brite and Colgate (toothpastes); Halo (shampoo); and Baggies (food wrap).

Under the product management system at CPC, product managers are assigned responsibility for specific brands, like Arctic Power. Their overall goals are to increase the sales and profitability of their brand. To meet these goals, the product manager supervises all marketing functions including planning, advertising, selling, promotion, and market research. In planning and executing programs for a brand

This case was prepared by Professor Gordon H. G. McDougall, of the Wilfrid Laurier University, and Professor Douglas Snetsinger, of the University of Toronto, as the basis for classroom discussion rather than to illustrate either effective or ineffective handling of an administrative situation. Names and proprietary data have been disguised, but all essential relationships have been preserved. Copyright © 1989. Used with permission.

the product manager usually is assigned an assistant product manager, and they work closely together to accomplish the brand goals.

Prior to the late 1970s CPC essentially followed the strategy of nationally supporting most of its brands. The result was the CPC was spread too thin with too many brands. There were insufficient resources to properly promote and develop all of the CPC line, and profits and market share were less than satisfactory. Beginning in the late 1970s and continuing to the early 1980s the Canadian division altered its strategy. An extensive review of the entire product line was conducted, and CPC moved to what was referred to as a regional brand strategy. Where a brand had regional strength, resources were focused on that area with the objective of building a strong and profitable brand in that region. For example Arctic Power had a relatively strong market share in Quebec and the Maritimes, where the proportion of consumers using cold water to wash clothes was considerably higher than the national average. Promotional support was withdrawn from the rest of Canada, and those resources were focused on Quebec and the Maritimes. Arctic Power was still distributed nationally but by the end of 1981, national market share was 4 percent consisting of an 11 percent share in Quebec, a 5 percent share in the Maritimes, and a 2 percent share in the rest of Canada. Over the next four years, marketing efforts were concentrated primarily on Quebec, and to a lesser extent the Maritimes. This approach worked well for Arctic Power. By the end of 1985, Arctic Power's national share had increased to 6.4 percent, share in Quebec had risen to 18 percent, share in the Maritimes was 6 percent, and less than 2 percent in the rest of Canada. With the increase in sales and profitability, the decision was made to target Alberta and British Columbia for 1986. The results of these efforts exceeded expectations in British Columbia but were less than satisfactory in Alberta.

THE LAUNDRY DETERGENT MARKET

The laundry detergent market was mature with unit sales increasing by approximately 1 percent annually and dollar sales increasing by about 5 percent each year (Exhibit 1). Three large consumer packaged goods companies, Procter and Gamble, Lever Detergents, and CPC, dominated the market. All three were subsidiaries of multinational firms and sold a wide range of household and personal care products in Canada. Procter and Gamble Canada had annual sales exceeding $1 billion, and its major brands included Crest (toothpaste), Ivory and Zest (bar soaps), Secret (deodorant), Pampers and Luvs (disposable diapers), and Head & Shoulders (shampoo). P&G held a 44 percent share of the laundry detergent market in 1986, due primarily to the large share (34 percent) held by Tide, the leading brand in Canada.

Lever Detergents with annual Canadian sales in excess of $400 million operated primarily in the detergent, soap and toiletries categories. Major brands included Sunlight (dishwasher detergent), Close-up (toothpaste), and Dove and Lux (bar soaps). Lever held a 24 percent share of the laundry detergent market, and its leading brand was Sunlight with a 13 percent share.

CPC was the only one of the three companies to gain market share in the laundry detergent market between 1983 and 1986. In 1986, CPC's total share was 23 percent, up from 16 percent in 1983. ABC, a value brand from CPC positioned to attract consumers interested in "value for less money," more than doubled its share between 1983 and 1986 and was the second leading brand with a 14 percent share.

EXHIBIT 1

Laundry Detergent Market—Market Shares (Percentages)

	1983	1984	1985	1986
Colgate				
ABC	6.0%	9.8%	11.8%	13.9%
Arctic Power	4.7	5.6	6.4	6.5
Fab	2.1	1.3	1.6	1.4
Punch	2.0	.7	.4	.3
Dynamo	1.0	.8	.6	.5
Total Colgate	15.8	18.2	20.8	22.6
Procter and Gamble				
Tide	34.1	35.1	32.6	34.1
Oxydol	4.9	4.2	4.0	3.3
Bold	4.8	4.2	3.2	2.3
Other P&G brands	4.7	4.8	4.4	4.3
Total P&G	48.5	48.3	44.2	44.0
Lever				
Sunlight	13.9	12.2	14.2	13.4
All	4.1	3.7	3.8	3.2
Surf	2.6	2.6	2.7	2.2
Wisk	3.8	4.1	4.1	4.4
Other Lever brands	.9	.8	.6	.4
Total Lever	25.3	23.4	25.4	23.6
All other brands	10.4	10.1	9.6	9.8
Grand Total	100.0	100.0	100.0	100.0
Total Market				
Tonnes (000s)	171.9	171.9	173.6	175.3
(% change)	2.0	0.0	1.0	1.0
Factory sales (000,000s)	$265.8	$279.1	$288.5	$304.7
(% change)	6.2	5.0	3.0	6.0

Source: Company records.

COMPETITIVE RIVALRY

Intense competitive activity was a way of life in the laundry detergent business. Not only did the three major firms have talented and experienced marketers, but they competed in a low-growth market where increased sales could be achieved only by taking share from competitive brands. A difficult task facing any product manager in this business was to identify the marketing mix that would maximize share while maintaining or increasing brand profitability—a task that had both long-term and short-term implications. In the long term, competitors strove for permanent share gains by building a solid franchise of loyal users based on a quality product and a strong brand image or position. These positioning strategies were primarily executed through product formulation and advertising campaigns. However, companies also competed through consumer and trade promotions (for example, coupons, feature specials in newspaper ads), tactics that were more short term in nature. Trade and consumer promotions were critical to maintain prominent shelf display and to attract competititors' customers. In virtually every week of the year, at least one brand of detergent would be "on special" in any given supermarket. The product manager's task was to find the best balance between these elements in making brand decisions.

Reformulating brands, the changing of the brand ingredients, was a frequent activity in the laundry detergent business. Reformulating a brand involved altering the amount and kinds of active chemical ingredients in the detergents. These active ingredients cleaned the clothes. Each of these cleaning ingredients was efficacious for particular cleaning tasks. Some of these ingredients were good for cleaning clay and mud from cotton and other natural fibers, while others would clean oily soils from polyesters, and yet others were good for other cleaning problems. Most detergents were formulated with a variety of active ingredients to clean in a wide range of conditions. As well, bleaches, fabric softeners, and fragrances could be included.

Thus laundry detergents contained different *levels* and *mixes* of active ingredients. The major decision was the *amounts* of active ingredients that would be used in a particular brand. In simple terms, the greater the proportion of active ingredients, the better the detergent was at cleaning clothes. However, all detergents would get clothes clean. For example, in a recent test of 42 laundry detergents, a consumer magazine concluded, "Yes, some detergents get clothes whiter and brighter than others—but the scale is clean to cleanest, not dirty to clean."

The Canadian brands of laundry detergent contained various amounts of active ingredients. As shown in the following table, Tide and Arctic Power had more active ingredients than any other brand.

Level of Active Ingredients of Laundry Detergents*

1	2	3	4	5
Some	Bold 3	ABC	—	Arctic Power
private	Oxydol	Fab		Tide
labels	Surf	Cheer 2		
	All	Sunlight		

*The scale of active ingredients increases from 1 to 5.

In fact, Tide and Arctic Power were equivalent brands in terms of the level of active ingredients. These two, referred to as the "Cadillacs" of detergents, had considerably higher levels of active ingredients than all other detergents. While the actual *mix* of active ingredients differed between the two brands (with Arctic Power having a greater mix of ingredients that were more suited to cold water washing), the cleaning power of Tide and Arctic Power was equal.

As the amount of active ingredients in a brand increased, so did the cost. Manufacturers were constantly facing the trade-off between cost and level of active ingredients. At times they had the opportunity to reduce unit costs by switching one type of active ingredient (a basic chemical) for another, depending on the relative costs of the ingredients. In this way, the level of ingredients remained the same; only the mixture changed. Manufacturers changed the physical ingredients of a brand in order to achieve an efficient per unit cost, to provide a basis for repositioning or restaging the brand, and to continue to deliver better consumer value.

Maintaining or increasing share through repositioning or other means was critical because of the profits involved. One share point was worth approximately $3 million in factory sales, and the cost and profit structures of the leading brands were similar. While some economies of scale accrued to the largest brands, the average cost of goods sold was estimated at 54 percent of sales, leaving a gross profit of 46 percent. Marketing expenditures included trade promotions (16 percent), consumer promotions (5 percent), and advertising expenditures (5 percent), leaving a contribution margin of 18 percent. Not included in these estimates were management overheads and expenses (for example, product management salaries, market research expenses, sales salaries, and factory overheads), which were primarily fixed. In some instances, lower share brands were likely to spend higher amounts on trade promotions to achieve their marketing objectives.

One indication of competitive activity was reflected in advertising expenditures between 1982 and 1986. Total category advertising increased by 12 percent to $14.4 million (Exhibit 2). As well, substantial increases in trade promotions had occurred during that period. While actual expenditure data were not available, some managers felt that twice as much was being spent on trade promotions as on advertising. For example, in Montreal over a nine-month period in 1986, Tide was featured in weekly supermarket advertisements 80 times and Arctic Power 60 times. Typically, the advertisement cost for the feature was shared by the manufacturer and the retailer. At times during 1986, consumers could have purchased Arctic Power or Tide for $3.49 (regular price $5.79). There was also a strong indication that the frequency and size of price specials on detergents were increasing. The average retail price of laundry detergents (based on the volume sold of all detergents at regular and special prices) had increased by only 4 percent in the past three years, whereas cost of goods sold had increased by 15 percent during the same period.

One final observation was warranted. Between 1983 and 1986, the four leading brands—Tide, ABC, Sunlight, and Arctic Power—had increased their share from 58.7 percent to 67.9 percent of the total market. The three manufacturers appeared to be

EXHIBIT 2

Share of National Media Expenditures, 1982–1986

	Percentages				
	1982	1983	1984	1985	1986
ABC	6.4	8.9	12.3	14.0	13.6
Arctic Power	6.1	6.1	6.7	7.2	9.3
Tide	21.0	17.8	19.1	16.4	29.7
Oxydol	5.1	4.5	5.9	6.6	6.4
Sunlight	14.1	10.8	10.5	9.1	11.3
All	10.3	5.5	6.9	7.7	4.0
Wisk	9.9	12.8	10.3	10.4	14.6
All other brands	27.1	33.6	28.3	28.6	12.1
Total	100.0	100.0	100.0	100.0	100.0
Total spending (000s)	$12,909	$13,338	$14,420	$13,718	$14,429
Percentage change	29.2	3.3	8.1	−4.9	5.2

Source: Company records.

focusing their efforts primarily on their leading brands and letting the lesser brands decline in share.

Positioning Strategies

While positioning strategies were executed through all aspects of the marketing mix, they were most clearly seen in the advertising execution.

Tide was the dominant brand in share of market and share of media expenditures. Tide's strategy was to sustain this dominance through positioning the brand as superior to any other brand on generic cleaning benefits. In 1986, four national and four regional commercials were aired to support this strategy. These commercials conveyed that Tide provided the benefits of being the most effective detergent for "tough" situations, such as for ground-in dirt, stains, and bad odors. Tide also aired copy in Quebec claiming effectiveness in all temperatures. Tide's copy was usually developed around a "slice of life" or testimonial format.

Other brands in the market faced the situation of going head-to-head with Tide's position or competing on a benefit Tide did not claim. Most had chosen the latter route. CPC's ABC brand had made strong gains in the past four years, moving from sixth to second place in market share based on its value position. ABC was positioned as the low-priced, good quality, cleaning detergent. Recent copy for ABC utilized a demonstration format where the shirts for twins were as clean when washed in ABC versus a leading higher priced detergent with the statement: "Why pay more? I can't see the difference." Sunlight, a Lever brand, had for several years attempted to compete directly with Tide and build its consumer franchise based on efficacy and lemon-scented freshness. Advertising execution had been of the upbeat, upscale lifestyle approach and less of the straightforward problem solution or straight-talking approaches seen in other detergent advertising. More recently, Sunlight had been moving toward ABC's value position while retaining the lemon freshness heritage. Sunlight was positioned in 1986 as the detergent which gave a very clean fresh wash at a sensible price. The final brand which attempted to compete for the value position was All. The advertising for All also claimed that the brand particularly whitens white clothes and gives them a pleasant fragrance.

Arctic Power had been positioned as the superior-cleaning laundry detergent, especially formulated for cold water washing. For the eastern market, Arctic Power advertising had utilized a humorous background to communicate brand superiority and its efficacy in cold water. For the western market a nontraditional, upbeat execution was used to develop the cold water market.

Wisk, which had received much attention for its "ring around the collar" advertising, competed directly with Tide on generic cleaning qualities and provided the additional benefit of a liquid formulation. Tide Liquid was introduced in 1985, but received little advertising support in 1986.

Fab and Bold 3 competed for the "softergents" market. Both products, which had fabric softeners in the formulation, were positioned to clean effectively while softening clothes and reducing static cling. Another detergent with laundry product additives was Oxydol, which was formulated with a mild bleach. Oxydol was positioned as the detergent that kept colors bright while whitening whites.

The other two nationally advertised brands were Cheer 2 and Ivory Snow. Cheer 2 was positioned as the detergent that got clothes clean and fresh. Ivory Snow, which was a soap and not a detergent, was positioned as the laundry cleaning product for infants' clothes which provided superior softness and comfort.

The Cold Water Market

Every February, CPC commissioned an extensive market research study to identify trends in the laundry detergent market. Referred to as the tracking study, its findings were based on approximately 1,800 personal interviews with female heads-of-households across Canada each year. Among the wealth of data provided by the tracking study was information on cold water usage in Canada. Regular cold water usage was growing in Canada and, by 1986, 29 percent of households were classified as regular cold water users (Exhibit 3). Due to cultural and marketing differences, Quebec (55 percent) and the Maritimes (33 percent) had more cold water users than the national average. A further 25 percent of all Canadian households occasionally (one to four times out of ten) used cold water for washing.

For households that washed occasionally or regularly with cold water, the most important benefits of using cold water fell into two broad categories (Exhibit 4). First, it was easier on or better for clothes in that cold water stopped shrinkage, prevented colors from running, let colors stay bright, and was easier on clothes. Second, it was more economical in that it saved energy, was cheaper, saved hot water, and saved electricity. Households in Quebec and the Maritimes mentioned the "economy" benefits more frequently, whereas households in the rest of Canada mentioned the "easier/better" benefit more often.

Arctic Power

Having achieved reasonable success in eastern Canada and having returned the brand to profitability, Linda Barton, Product Manager for Arctic Power, decided, for 1986, to increase the brand's share in Alberta and British Columbia. The brand plan is reported below.

E X H I B I T   3

Proportion of Households Washing with Cold Water, 1981–1986

| | *Percentages* | | | | | |
	1981	*1982*	*1983*	*1984*	*1985*	*1986*
National	20*	22	26	26	26	29
Maritimes	23	25	32	40	32	33
Quebec	35	41	49	48	53	55
Ontario	14	13	18	16	11	17
Prairies	12	12	13	11	10	17
British Columbia	13	19	20	17	22	21

*20 percent of respondents did five or more out of ten washloads in cool or cold waters.

N ≈ 1,800.

Source: Tracking study.

EXHIBIT 4

Most Important Benefit of Cold Water Washing, 1986

Reason	National	Maritimes	Quebec	Ontario	Man./Sask.	Alta.	B.C.
Stops shrinkage	22.7*%	19.4%	5.2%	32.7%	35.4%	35.4%	30.2%
Saves energy	16.5	12.5	32.1	8.2	2.1	9.9	12.9
Prevents colors from running	11.6	17.4	0.0	21.8	21.3	9.9	2.9
Cheaper	11.1	19.4	10.4	10.2	2.8	9.3	16.5
Saves hot water	9.7	9.7	15.5	6.8	11.3	3.1	3.6
Colors stay bright	8.8	4.2	7.8	11.6	9.2	6.8	7.9
Saves on electricity	8.7	19.4	0.5	8.2	5.7	16.1	25.9
Easier on clothes	8.5	11.1	6.7	8.8	10.6	13.7	5.0

*When asked what they felt was the most important benefit of cold water washing, 22.7 percent of all respondents said, "It stops shrinking." Sample included all households that washed one or more times out of last ten washes in cold water.

N = 956.

Only the eight most frequent responses are reported.

Source: Tracking study.

THE 1986 BRAND PLAN FOR ARCTIC POWER

Objectives

Arctic Power's overall objective is to continue profit development by maintaining modest unit-volume growth in Quebec and the Maritimes while developing the Alberta and British Columbia regions.

Long Term (by 1996) The long-term objective is to become the number three brand in the category with market share of 12 percent. Arctic Power will continue to deliver a minimum 18 percent contribution margin. This will require

1. maintenance of effective creative/media support,
2. superior display prominence particularly in the key Quebec market,
3. continued investigation of development opportunities, and
4. cost-of-goods savings programs where possible.

Short Term The short-term objective is to sustain unit growth while building cold water washing dominance. This will require current user reinforcement and continued conversion of warm water users. Specifically, in fiscal 1986, Arctic Power will achieve a market share of 6.5 percent on factory sales of $22 million and a contribution margin of 18 percent. Regional share objectives are Maritimes—6.3 percent, Quebec—17.2 percent, Alberta—5 percent, and British Columbia—5 percent.

Marketing Strategy

Arctic Power will be positioned as the most effective laundry detergent which especially formulated for cold water washing. The primary target for Arctic Power is women 18 to 49 and skewed toward the 25 to 34 segment. The secondary market is all adults.

Arctic Power will defend its franchise by allocating regional effort commensurate with brand development in order to maintain current users. In line with the western expansion strategy, support will be directed to Alberta and British Columbia in promoting the acceptance of cold water washing in those areas and thereby broadening the appeal among occasional and non-users of Arctic Power.

Media Strategy

The media strategy objective is to achieve high levels of message registration against the target group, through high message continuity and frequency/reach. Media spending allocation for regional television will be 75 percent on brand maintenance and 25 percent on investment for brand and cold water market development. Arctic Power will retain its number five share of media expenditure position nationally while being the number three detergent advertiser in Quebec.

		TV Spending	GRPs* per Week
1985	Plan	$1,010,000	92
	Actual	$ 990,000	88
1986	Plan	$1,350,000	95

*GRP (gross rating points) is a measurement of advertising impact derived by multiplying the number of persons exposed to an advertisement by the average number of exposures per person.

Arctic Power's 1986 media spending of $1.35 million is a 36 percent increase over 1985. This returns Arctic Power to its reach objective of 90 percent in Quebec, five points ahead of a year ago. In addition, two new television markets have been added with enhanced support in British Columbia and Alberta. Reach objectives will be achieved by skewing more of Arctic Power's spending into efficient daytime spots which cost less than night network and are more flexible in light of regional reach objectives.

Scheduling will maintain flighting[1] established in 1985 with concentrations at peak dealing time representing 40 weeks on-air in the east and 32 weeks in the west.

Copy Strategy: Quebec/Maritimes

The creative objective is to convince consumers that Arctic Power is the superior detergent for cold water washing. The consumer benefit is that when washing in cold water, Arctic Power will clean clothes and remove stains more effectively than other detergents. The support for this claim is based on the special formulation of Arctic Power. The executional tone will be humorous but with a clear, rational explanation (Exhibit 5).

---

[1]Periodic waves of advertising, separated by periods of low activity (as opposed to continuous advertising).

EXHIBIT 5

Quebec Campaign

Arctic Power . . . is made to
work in cold water . . . some
detergents are not . . .

Look . . . Arctic Power

. . . is formulated to release
more power and energy in cold
water

. . . some detergents are
formulated to

. . . work well in hot water

. . . but

. . . put them in

. . . cold and they start to
freeze up

In cold water . . . it makes a
difference which detergent you
use . . . you want clean like this

. . . and bright like this

Look for a pack like this

. . . and you'll get more power
in cold water.

Copy Strategy: British Columbia/Alberta

The creative objective is to convince consumers that cold water washing is better than hot and to use Arctic Power when washing in cold water. The consumer benefit is that cold water washing reduces shrinkage, color run and energy costs. The executional tone needs to be distinct from other detergent advertising in order to break through traditional washing attitudes and to do so will be young adult-oriented, light, "cool," and up-beat (Exhibit 6).

Consumer Promotions

The objective of consumer promotions in Quebec and the Maritimes is to increase the rate of use by building frequency of purchase among existing users. The objective in B.C. and Alberta is to increase the rate of trial of Arctic Power. In total $856,000 will be spent on consumer promotions.

Jan.	$0.50 In-pack Coupon—to support trade inventory increases and retain current customers in the face of strong competitive activity 400,000 coupons will be placed in all sizes in the Quebec and Maritimes distribution region. The coupon is for 6 L or 12 L sizes and expected redemption is 18 percent at a cost of $50,000.
April	To generate a 17 percent recent trial of regular-sized boxes of Arctic Power in B.C. and in Alberta a 500 mL salable sample prepriced at $0.49 will be distributed through food and drug stores. In addition, a $0.50 coupon for the 6 L or 12 L size will be placed on the pack of all samples. The offer will penetrate 44 percent of households in the region at a total cost of $382,000.
June	$0.40 Coupon through Free Standing Insert: to sustain interest and foster trial a $0.40 coupon will be delivered to 30 percent of homes in Alberta and B.C. The coupon is redeemable on the 3 L size and expected redemption is 4.5 percent at a cost of $28,000.
April/July	Game: Cool-by-the-Pool—Five in-ground pools with patio accessories will be given away through spelling POWER by letters dropped in boxes of Arctic Power. Two letters will be placed in each box through national distribution and will coincide with high trade activity and the period in which the desirability of the prizes is highest at a cost of $184,000.
Sept.	$0.75 Direct Mail National Coupon Pack (excluding Ontario)—To maximize swing buyer volume (from competition) in Quebec and encourage trial in the West a $0.75 coupon for the 6 L or 12 L size will be mailed to 70 percent of households in the primary market areas generating a 3 percent redemption rate at a cost of $212,000.

Trade Promotions

The objectives of the trade promotions are to maintain regular and feature pricing equal to Tide and encourage prominent shelf facing. An advertising feature is expected from each key account during every promotion event run in Quebec and the Maritimes. Distribution for any size is expected to increase to 95 percent. In the west, maximum effort will be directed at establishing display for the 6 L size, and four feature events will be expected from each key account. Distribution should be developed to 71 percent in B.C. and 56 percent in Alberta. Average deal size will be 14 percent off regular price or $5 per 6 L case. In addition, most trade events will in-

EXHIBIT 6

Western Campaign

CLIENT: COLGATE PALMOLIVE
PRODUCT: Arctic Power
TITLE: ''Cool It''
LENGTH: 30 Sec. TV

SINGERS: No!

Cool it.
Cool it.

Get some Arctic Power and
cool it.

Cold water washing that's the
way.

Up to date people save money
today . . .

they cool it.
Cool it.

Get some Arctic Power and
cool it.

You get less shrink.

You get less run.

And the laundry looks great
when you get it all done.

So cool it.
Cool it.

Get some Arctic Power and
cool it.

clude a $1 per case allowance for co-op advertising and merchandising support. The total trade budget is $3.46 million which includes $1 million investment spending in the west. The promotion schedule is shown below.

Arctic Power 1986 Promotional Schedule

Trade Promotions	Jan.	Feb.	Mar.	Apr.	May	Jun.	Jul.	Aug.	Sep.	Oct.	Nov.	Dec.
Maritimes	X			X		X			X		X	
Quebec	X	X		X		X	X		X		X	X
Alberta/B.C.	X			X		X		X	X			
East $0.50 coupon	X	X										
West sample/ coupon				X								
West $0.40 coupon						X						
National game					X	X	X	X				
National $0.75 coupon										X		

Results of the Western Campaign

In August of 1986, during the middle of the western campaign, a "mini-tracking" study was conducted in the two provinces to monitor the program. The results of the August study were compared with the February study. (Both studies are reported in Exhibit 7.) Market share for Arctic Power was also measured on a bi-monthly basis and the figures are shown below.

The campaign clearly had an impact—brand and advertising awareness had increased, particularly in Alberta (Exhibit 7). Brand trial within the six months had more than doubled in Alberta and was up over 25 percent in B.C. However, market share had peaked at 2.8 percent in Alberta and by the end of the year had declined to 1.9 percent. Market share in B.C. had reached a high of 7.3 percent and averaged 5.5 percent for the year.

Arctic Power Market Share

| | | | | 1986 | | | | | | Total |
	1983	1984	1985	D/J	F/M	A/M	J/J	A/S	O/N	1986
Alberta	0.7	2.3	1.7	1.4	1.1	2.8	2.8	2.4	1.9	2.1
B.C.	3.2	4.0	3.9	4.0	4.0	6.1	6.1	7.3	5.4	5.5

In attempting to explain the different results in the two provinces, Linda Barton and Gary Parsons isolated two factors. First, B.C. had always been a "good" market for Arctic Power with share figures around 4 percent, whereas Alberta was less than half that amount. Second, there had been a considerable amount of competitive activity in Alberta during the year. Each of the three major firms had increased trade and consumer promotions to maintain existing brand shares.

EXHIBIT 7

Results of Western Campaign

	Prelaunch (February 1986)		Postlaunch (August 1986)	
	Alberta	B.C.	Alberta	B.C.
Unaided Brand Awareness[a]				
Brand mentioned total (%)	13.3	20.3	18.1	24.2
Advertising Awareness				
Advertising mentioned (unaided)[b] (%)	1.9	7.9	20.3	11.5
Advertising mentioned (aided)[c] (%)	18.5	27.9	31.4	34.6
Brand Trial				
Ever tried[d] (%)	25.0	43.0	36.3	48.0
Used (last six months)[e] (%)	6.8	15.1	17.1	19.4
Image Measure[f]				
Cleaning and removing dirt	1.0	1.2	1.2	1.5
Removing tough stains	.7	.9	.9	1.4
Being good value for the price	.5	.9	1.0	1.4
Cleaning well in cold water	1.2	1.3	1.7	1.8
Conversion to Cold Water				
Average number of loads out of 10 washed in cold water	1.8	2.2	2.0	2.3

[a]*Question*: When you think of laundry detergents, what three brands first come to mind? Can you name three more for me? *Brand Mentioned Total* is if the brand was mentioned at all. On average, respondents mentioned 4.5 brands.

[b]*Question*: What brand or brands of laundry detergent have you seen or heard advertised? *Advertising Mentioned (Unaided)* is any mention of brand advertising mentioned.

[c]*Question*: Have you recently seen or heard any advertising for *Brand? Advertising Mentioned (Aided)* is if respondent said yes when asked.

[d]*Question*: Have you ever tried *Brand?*

[e]*Question*: Have you used *Brand* in the past six months?

[f]Respondents rated the brand on the four image measures. The rating scale ranged from –5 (doesn't perform well) to +5 (performs well).

Source: Tracking study.

ARCTIC POWER—1987

The 1987 brand plan for Arctic Power was similar in thrust and expenditure levels to the 1986 plan. Expenditure levels in Alberta were reduced until the full implications of the 1986 campaign could be examined. Market share in 1987 was expected to be 6.7 percent up marginally from the 6.5 percent share achieved in 1986 (Exhibit 8).

Each year, every product manager at CPC conducted an extensive brand review. The review for Arctic Power included a detailed competitive analysis of the four leading brands on a regional basis and was based primarily on the tracking study. In July 1987, Linda Barton and Gary Parsons were examining the tracking information which summarized regional information on four critical aspects of the market—brand image

EXHIBIT 8

Arctic Power Market Share and Total Volume by Region, 1983–1987E

Region	Market Share					1986 Total Volume* (000s litres)
	1983	1984	1985	1986	1987E	
National	4.7	5.6	6.4	6.5	6.7	406,512
Maritimes	5.3	5.7	6.3	6.3	6.3	32,616
Quebec	12.3	13.8	17.7	17.5	18.0	113,796
Ontario	.9	1.1	1.1	.8	1.0	158,508
Manitoba/Saskatchewan	.2	.2	.1	.1	.1	28,440
Alberta	.7	2.3	1.7	2.1	2.0	40,644
British Columbia	3.2	4.0	3.9	5.5	6.0	32,508

1987E = Estimated.

*All laundry detergents.

(Exhibit 9), brand and advertising awareness (Exhibit 10), brand trial and usage in past six months (Exhibit 11), and market share and share of media expenditures (Exhibit 12). Future decisions for Arctic Power would be based, in large part, on this information.

THE DECISION

Prior to deciding on the strategic direction for Arctic Power, Ms. Barton and Mr. Parsons met to discuss the situation. It was a hot Toronto day in early July 1987. Ms. Barton began the discussion. "I've got some estimates on what our shares are likely to be for 1987. It looks like we'll have a national share of 6.7 percent, broken down as follows: Maritimes (6.3 percent), Quebec (18 percent), Ontario (1 percent), Manitoba/Saskatchewan (0.1 percent), Alberta (2 percent), B.C. (6 percent)."

Mr. Parsons responded, "I think our problem in Alberta was all the competitive activity. Under normal conditions we'd have achieved 5 percent of that market. But the Alberta objective is small when you think about what we could do in our other undeveloped markets. I've been giving it a lot of thought, and we should go national with Arctic Power. We've got a brand that is equal to Tide and we've got to stop keeping it a secret from the rest of Canada. If we can duplicate our success in B.C., we'll turn this market on its ear."

"Wait a minute, Gary," said Ms. Barton. "In 1986 we spent almost $2 million on advertising, consumer and trade promotions in the west. Even though spending returned to normal levels this year, that was a big investment to get the business going, and it will be at least four years before we get that money back. If we go after the national market, you can well expect Tide to fight back with trade spending which will make our share or margin objectives even harder to achieve. On a per capita basis we'd have to spend at least as much in our underdeveloped markets as we spent in the west. We've got a real problem here. Our brand may be as good as Tide, but I don't think we can change a lot of consumers' minds, particularly the loyal Tide users. I hate to say it but for many Canadians, when they think about

EXHIBIT 9

Brand Images by Region, 1986

Image Measure	National	Maritimes	Quebec	Ontario	Man./Sask.	Alberta	B.C.
Arctic Power							
• Cleaning and removing dirt	1.4	2.0	2.5	0.8	0.4	1.0	1.2
• Removing tough stains	1.1	1.6	1.9	0.7	0.3	0.7	0.9
• Being good value for the price	1.1	1.4	2.6	0.3	0.2	0.5	0.9
• Cleaning well in cold water	1.6	2.1	2.8	1.0	0.4	1.2	1.3
ABC							
• Cleaning . . . dirt	1.0	1.9	0.5	0.9	1.1	1.2	1.6
• Removing . . . stains	0.5	1.1	0.0	0.6	0.8	0.7	0.9
• Being . . . price	1.5	2.4	0.8	1.5	1.3	1.7	2.1
• Cleaning . . . cold water	0.6	1.0	0.1	0.7	0.7	0.7	0.7
Sunlight							
• Cleaning . . . dirt	2.0	1.9	1.8	2.4	1.9	1.6	1.6
• Removing . . . stains	1.6	1.6	1.5	1.9	1.4	1.2	1.2
• Being . . . price	2.0	1.7	1.9	2.4	1.8	1.7	1.5
• Cleaning . . . cold water	1.4	1.1	1.5	1.7	1.2	1.1	0.7
Tide							
• Cleaning . . . dirt	3.4	3.7	3.2	3.6	3.5	3.3	3.2
• Removing . . . stains	3.0	3.1	2.8	3.3	3.0	2.7	2.7
• Being . . . price	3.1	3.1	3.3	3.1	2.8	3.0	2.4
• Cleaning . . . cold water	2.4	2.3	2.6	2.5	2.4	2.3	1.9

Respondents rated each brand on the four image measures. The rating scale ranged from −5 (doesn't perform well) to +5 (performs well).

N = 1816.

A difference of 0.2 is likely to be significant in statistical terms.

Source: Tracking study.

EXHIBIT 10

Brand and Advertising Awareness by Region, 1986

				Percentages			
	National	Maritimes	Quebec	Ontario	Man./Sask.	Alberta	B.C.
Unaided Brand Awareness[a]							
1. Brand Mentioned First							
Arctic Power	4.4	7.0	12.5	.0	.0	1.0	2.6
ABC	8.1	18.4	4.6	7.3	4.7	8.4	12.8
Sunlight	9.3	8.4	9.6	9.3	12.0	9.1	7.9
Tide	57.9	55.5	41.9	69.7	63.1	59.7	54.4
2. Brand Mentioned Total							
Arctic Power	23.0	43.5	49.8	5.0	3.0	13.3	20.3
ABC	61.3	82.6	47.9	64.0	56.1	67.5	64.9
Sunlight	58.1	60.2	50.8	65.0	58.5	62.0	46.6
Tide	94.8	95.7	88.8	98.0	97.3	97.4	94.4
Advertising Awareness							
1. Advertising Mentioned (Unaided)[b]							
Arctic Power	7.0	10.7	17.5	.7	.0	1.9	7.9
ABC	25.2	32.8	20.8	27.0	17.3	30.5	24.9
Sunlight	8.6	4.7	5.9	13.0	5.0	6.8	8.2
Tide	44.0	40.1	32.7	55.0	46.2	48.4	35.4
2. Advertising Mentioned (Aided)[c]							
Arctic Power	29.2	38.8	55.1	15.3	5.6	18.5	27.9
ABC	56.1	61.5	55.1	56.0	51.5	60.4	53.4
Sunlight	29.9	20.1	26.4	40.3	21.3	21.1	24.9
Tide	65.3	60.9	54.8	78.0	68.1	65.3	48.4

[a]*Question*: When you think of laundry detergents, what three brands first come to mind? *Brand Mentioned First* is the first brand mentioned. *Brand Mentioned Total* is if the brand was mentioned at all. On average, respondents mentioned 4.5 brands.

[b]*Question*: What brand or brands of laundry detergent have you seen or heard advertised? *Advertising Mentioned (Unaided)* is any mention of brand advertising mentioned.

[c]*Question*: Have you recently seen or heard any advertising for *Brand*? *Advertising Mentioned (Aided)* means respondent said yes when asked.

N = 1816.

Source: Tracking study.

EXHIBIT 11

Brand Trial and Used in Past Six Months by Region, 1986

Brand Trial	National	Maritimes	Quebec	Ontario	Man./Sask.	Alberta	B.C.
1. Ever tried[a]							
Arctic Power	42.4	67.9	75.6	19.7	20.3	25.0	43.0
ABC	60.4	83.9	50.8	60.0	53.5	62.7	67.9
Sunlight	66.3	65.6	59.4	75.0	67.1	58.1	58.7
Tide	93.6	91.0	90.1	97.3	95.0	91.9	92.1
2. Used (past six months)[b]							
Arctic Power	19.4	29.8	46.5	4.3	2.3	6.8	15.1
ABC	37.2	56.2	34.7	32.3	29.2	39.3	47.5
Sunlight	38.3	29.8	38.0	44.3	36.2	36.7	28.5
Tide	68.1	66.6	66.0	73.3	67.8	69.5	54.8

[a]*Question:* Have you ever tried *Brand?*

[b]*Question:* Have you used *Brand* in the past six months?

Note: On average, respondents had 1.3 brands of laundry detergents in the home.

N = 1816.

Source: Tracking study.

EXHIBIT 12

Market Share and Share of Media Expenditures by Region, 1986

				Percentages			
	National	*Maritimes*	*Quebec*	*Ontario*	*Man./Sask.*	*Alberta*	*B.C.*
Market Share							
Arctic Power	6.5	6.3	17.5	.8	.1	2.1	5.5
ABC	13.9	27.8	8.6	13.8	11.6	16.1	21.5
Sunlight	13.4	7.7	12.1	16.4	14.2	10.4	11.3
Tide	34.1	24.5	28.3	39.3	40.0	36.9	28.5
All other brands	32.1	33.7	33.5	29.7	34.1	34.5	33.2
Total	100.0	100.0	100.0	100.0	100.0	100.0	100.0
Share of Media Expenditures[a]							
Arctic Power	9.3	13.1	16.1	.5	1.4	16.0	13.1
ABC	13.6	14.7	9.1	18.4	17.3	12.1	12.1
Sunlight	11.3	11.1	11.1	12.6	10.2	10.1	9.8
Tide	29.7	27.8	25.1	33.1	38.1	30.2	28.7
All other brands	36.1	33.3	38.6	35.4	33.0	31.6	36.3
Total	100.0	100.0	100.0	100.0	100.0	100.0	100.0
Total $ ('000)	14,429	695	4,915	4,758	928	1,646	1,487

[a]The total amount of advertising spent by all brands was determined. The amount spent by each brand as a percentage of total spending was calculated.

Source: Company records.

washing clothes, Tide is the brand they think will clean their clothes better than any other brand. I agree that the size of the undeveloped market warrants another look. But remember, any decision will have to be backed up with a solid analysis and a plan that senior management will buy."

"I know that even if I am right it will be a tough sell," Mr. Parsons replied. "I haven't got it completed yet, but I'm working out the share level we will need to break even if we expanded nationally."

Ms. Barton responded, "Well, when you get that done, we will talk about national expansion again. For the moment we have to resolve this positioning dilemma. I don't like a two-country approach, but it does seem to make sense in this case. I think we might still want to focus on the brand in the east and continue to develop the cold water washing market in the west."

Mr. Parsons would have preferred to continue the discussion of national expansion but realized he would have to do some work and at least produce the share estimate before he raised the subject again and so replied, "I agree that Canada is not one homogeneous market, but that perspective can be taken to extremes. I worry that all of this data we get on the regional markets is getting in the way of good marketing judgment. I prefer a unified strategy and the Quebec campaign has a proven track record."

"Let's go over the data again, then start making our decisions," Ms. Barton concluded. "Remember, our goal is to develop a solid brand plan for 1988 for Arctic Power."

Swatch

In mid-1986 Chris Keigel returned from military service to become European marketing manager for Swatch, the new watch concept that had revolutionized the watch industry and brought Swiss watchmaking out of a 40-year slump. He knew that Swatch management in Biel, Switzerland, was concerned about maintaining sales growth and agreeing on long-term international strategy. Existing watch brands were renewing their strategies, and new competitors inspired by Swatch were mushrooming worldwide. Keigel had been requested to gather background information for an upcoming top management meeting called to arrive at a consensus on the very concept of Swatch, its international positioning, and viable product line extensions.

COMPANY BACKGROUND

Swatch watches are manufactured by ETA S.A., a century-old Swiss watch movement firm and a subsidiary of SMH (Société Micromécanique et Horlogère), the world's second-largest watchmaking concern after the Japanese firm Seiko. SMH was the result of a merger in 1983 between ASUAG (Allgemeine Schweizer Uhrenindustrie) and SSIH (Société Suisse pour l'Industrie Horlogère), Switzerland's two major watch manufacturers, rescued from bankruptcy by the major Swiss banks. In addition to Swatch, the SMH product line includes the well-known brands Omega, Longines, Tissot, and Rado. Swatch A.G. is a subsidiary set up in 1984 to handle the international marketing of Swatch watches. Its executive committee was composed of President E. T. Marquardt, Vice President American Operations Max Imgruth, Vice President Continental Operations Felice A. Schillaci, and Vice President Australasian Operations H. N. Tune.

WATCH TECHNOLOGY

Until the late 1950s, all watches were *mechanical*, that is, spring-powered, with movements comprising a hundred or more parts. In 1957, the first electric watch was marketed in the United States. A few years later, the American firm Bulova developed a *tuning fork* watch, battery-powered and accurate to within one minute per month. The *quartz*, that is, electronic, watch was invented in Switzerland in 1968 but first marketed in the United States by Hamilton. It improved accuracy to unheard-of levels. The quartz watch display was either the traditional "analog" type with hands moving around a face or "digital" with numbers appearing in a frame. Exhibit 1 gives a rough description of the components of four watch types.

This case was written by Helen C. Kimball, Research Assistant, under the supervision of Christian Pinson, Professor at INSEAD (European Institute of Business Administration). It is intended to be used as a basis for class discussion rather than to illustrate either effective or ineffective handling of an administrative situation. Reprinted with the permission of INSEAD. Copyright © 1987 INSEAD, Fontainebleau, France.

EXHIBIT 1

Major Components of Four Watch Types

	Mechanical	Tuning Fork	Quartz Digital	Quartz Analog
Energy source	Hair spring	Battery	Battery	Battery
Time base	Balance spring	Tuning fork	Quartz crystal	Quartz crystal
Electronic circuit	—	Simple	Integrated circuit	Integrated circuit
Transmission	Gears	Gears	Gears	Stepping motor/gears
Display	Hands	Hands	Numbers	Hands

The first digital watches used either light-emitting diodes (LEDs) or a liquid crystal display (LCD), which consumed less energy. By 1986 most quartz digital watches had LCDs. The switch to quartz was spectacular: whereas 98 percent of all watches and movements produced in 1974 were mechanical and only 2 percent were quartz, in 1984 the breakdown was 24 percent mechanical and 76 percent quartz.

THE WATCH INDUSTRY

Watchmaking was first developed in Switzerland by Swiss goldsmiths and French Huguenots. Swiss watchmakers were masters of precision workmanship and "Swiss made" became synonymous with quality. By 1970, however, the Swiss contribution to world watch production had dropped considerably (Exhibit 2). This trend continued into the 1980s, as less expensive and more accurate quartz watches and movements, mainly from Japan and Hong Kong, flooded the market. In 1984, 60 percent of quartz watches and movements produced were from Hong Kong, 30 percent from Japan, and only 7 percent from Switzerland.

Starting in the 1950s, the production of the major American firms (Timex, Bulova, Hamilton) gradually shifted overseas. By 1986, domestic production was considered virtually nil. While Switzerland's contribution to American import volume decreased from 99 percent in 1950 to 4 percent in 1984, the percentage of import volume from

EXHIBIT 2

Estimated Breakdown of World Watch Production, 1948–1985

	World Production[a]	Switzerland (%)	Japan (%)	Hong Kong (%)	United States (%)	Rest of World (%)
1948	31	80	—	—	—	20
1970	174	43	14	—	11	32
1975	218	34	14	2	12	38
1980	300	29	22	20	4	25
1985	440	13	39	22	0.4	25

[a]Millions of watches and movements.

Source: Federation of the Swiss Watch Industry.

Asia increased from 10 percent in 1970, primarily from Japan, to 92 percent in 1984, mostly from Hong Kong.

The Japanese industry was highly concentrated, with the two major firms, Hattori Seiko and Citizen, stressing the development of automated production lines and maximum vertical integration of operations. Compared with the multitude of Swiss watch brands, the combined product lines of these two plus Casio, the third major Japanese watchmaker, did not exceed a dozen brands. In contrast, the industry in Hong Kong was highly fragmented, with several manufacturers producing 10 to 20 million watches per year, and hundreds of small firms producing fewer than 1 million annually. These firms could not afford to invest in quartz analog technology, but with virtually no barriers to entry for watch assembly, they produced complete analog watches from imported movements and modules, often Swiss or Japanese products. The competitive advantages of the Hong Kong firms were low-cost labor, tiny margins, and the flexibility to adapt to changes in the market.

The spectacular rise of Japan and Hong Kong, particularly in the middle- and low-price categories, was primarily due to their rapid adoption of quartz technology, a drive to achieve a competitive cost position through accumulation of experience, and economies of scale. In 1972 the digital watch module cost around $200, and the same module cost only $0.50 in 1984. The Asian watchmaking industry's expansion had led to a chronic state of world oversupply, mainly in the inexpensive quartz digital range. This had been the cause of a number of bankruptcies and had incited watch manufacturers to turn to the quartz analog market, where added value was higher. In contrast to quartz digital technology, quartz analog technology was available only within the watch industry. Thus, the hundreds of watch assemblers scattered throughout the world were increasingly dependent on the three major movement manufacturers, Seiko, ETA, and Citizen.

THE WATCH MARKET

According to one industry analyst, the European OECD member countries represented around 30 percent of total world watch volume, the United States approximately 20–30 percent, and the Japanese market around 10 percent. Estimated annual market growth was approximately 4 percent.

Industry experts estimated 1984 wristwatch purchases in the United States to be 90–95 million units, a 400 percent increase over 10 years. By 1985 Americans were buying a new watch once every 2 years compared with once every 6–10 years a decade earlier. However, the U.S. market was considered to be near saturation with an average of 3.5 watches per owner. Buying habits had changed in Europe also, with the 8–20-year age group representing nearly half of all watch sales in 1985. When commenting on buying habits, industry experts pointed out that the industry was increasingly committed to the quartz analog, stressing the different meanings the digital and the analog had for the consumer (Exhibit 3). However, some of the more expensive Swiss watch manufacturers seemed to believe in a future trend back to mechanical.

The watch market was generally divided into five retail price segments (Exhibit 4). Swiss watches fell mostly in the mid- to expensive price ranges. To protect its mid-price niche, Seiko adopted a multibrand strategy, offering cheap watches under the Lorus, Pulsar, and Phasar brands with more expensive watches under the Credor, Seiko, and Lassale brand names.

EXHIBIT 3

A Comparison of Digital and Analog Watches

Digital	Analog
1. Time is represented by a sign	1. Time is represented by a symbol
2. The focus is on	2. The focus is on
The instant	Length of time
Numerical code	A pictorial code
Discontinuity	Continuity
Linearity and periodicity	Circularity and cyclical character
3. Signification	3. Signification
The time display is precise	Time display is imprecise
Time is imposed	Time can be negotiated
Monosemy: only one meaning	Polysemy: several meanings

Source: Adapted from Michel-Adrien Viorol "Un Problème d'Evolution du Produit Horloger," in "Les Apports de la Semiotique au Marketing et a la Publicité," IREP Seminar, 1976.

DEVELOPMENT OF SWATCH

Dr. Ernst Thomke joined ETA S.A. as president in 1978 after proving his success in the marketing department of Beecham Pharmaceuticals. He had been an apprentice in the production division of ETA before taking a Ph.D. in chemistry and a medical degree. In early 1980, after considering the sorry state of the Swiss watch industry, Thomke concluded that the future was in innovative finished products, aggressive marketing, volume sales, and vertical integration of the industry. Quartz analog technology was more complex than digital, but ETA was known for the technology it possessed for the production of high-priced, ultrathin "Delirium" movements.

EXHIBIT 4

Watch Industry Price Segments, 1984 (Swiss francs)[a]

Segment	Retail Price	Percent Units	Percent Value	Examples
A	8–30	60	10	Hong Kong LCDs, some cheap mechanicals
B	30–100	15	15	Swatch, Timex, Casio, Guess, Lip, Lorus, Dugena, Junghans, Yema, Jaz, Pulsar, Hamilton
C	80–250	20	45	Tissot, Seiko, Citizen, Casio, Lip, Yema, Jaz, Pulsar, Dugena, Junghans, Bulova, Hamilton, Herbelin
D	120–450	4	15	Omega, Longines, Eterna, Seiko, Citizen, Certina, Rado, Movado, Bulova
E	450+	1	15	Rolex, Piaget, Cartier, Audemars Piguet, Certine, Rado, Lassale, Ebel

[a]Dollar-to-franc exchange rates: 1983 = 2.10, 1984 = 2.20, 1985 = 2.30, 1986 = 1.84.

Source: Compiled from Federation of the Swiss Watch Industry records.

Thomke decided to develop a "low-price prestige" quartz analog wristwatch that could be mass produced in Switzerland at greatly reduced cost. Two ETA micro-mechanical engineers who specialized in plastic injection molding technology, Jacques Muller and Elmar Mock, were given the challenge of designing a product based on Thomke's concept. This required inventing entirely new production technology using robots and computers for manufacture and assembly. By 1981 a semi-automated process had been designed to meet Thomke's goal of a 15-SF factory price and seven patents were registered. The watch's movement, consisting of only 51 instead of the 90–150 parts in other watches, was injected directly into the one-piece plastic case. The casing was sealed by ultrasonic welding instead of screws, precluding servicing. The watch would be simply replaced and not repaired if it stopped. The finished product, guaranteed one year, was shock resistant, was water resistant to 100 feet (30 meters), and contained a three-year replaceable battery.

In April 1981 Thomke took his idea to Franz Sprecher, a marketing consultant who had worked at Nestlé before setting up his own consulting firm. As background for ETA's project, Sprecher studied prestige products like perfumes, successful mass-market brands like "Bic," and both designer and ready-to-wear fashion. He worked closely with advertising agencies in the United States on product positioning and advertising strategy. In addition to the name "Swatch," a snappy contraction of "Swiss" and "watch," this research generated the idea of downplaying the product's practical benefits and positioning it as a "fashion accessory that happens to tell time." Swatch would be a second or third watch, used to adapt to different situations without replacing the traditional "status symbol" watch.

Launch

Dr. Thomke arranged to have Swatch distributed in the United States by the Swiss Watch Distribution Center (SWDC) in San Antonio, Texas. SWDC was an American firm in which ETA held a minority interest and whose chairman, Ben Hammond, was instrumental in setting up and building Seiko distribution in the Southwestern states. Swatch was test marketed in December 1982 at 100 Sanger Harris department stores in Dallas, Salt Lake City, and San Diego, without any advertising, public relations, or publicity. The original test product line consisted of 12 rather conventional watches in red, brown, and tan. Opinions on test results were mixed, but the ETA team continued undaunted. Swatch was officially launched in Switzerland in March 1983 and then gradually worldwide. Exhibit 5 shows the fall 1983 collection as pictured in sales brochures.

Max Imgruth took over as president of SWDC in April 1983 and arranged a second test market in December 1983 through both the Zale Jewelry chain in Dallas and the New York department store Macy's, with television support created by Swatch's advertising agency, McCann-Erickson. Test market conclusions were that most of the watches in the 1983 fall/winter collection were not acceptable for the U.S. market. Imgruth recalled:

> Nothing happened. I tried to figure out what was wrong. The product was not very distinctive. It was not just the ad, it was the watches. It was close to the traditional watch. First of all, it was its positioning; second, the product; third, pricing; fourth, advertising. Basically, I ran down the marketing mix.

Imgruth became increasingly involved in product design and local adaptation of Swatch communication. He was appointed president of the newly created American

EXHIBIT 5

Swatch International Launch Collection

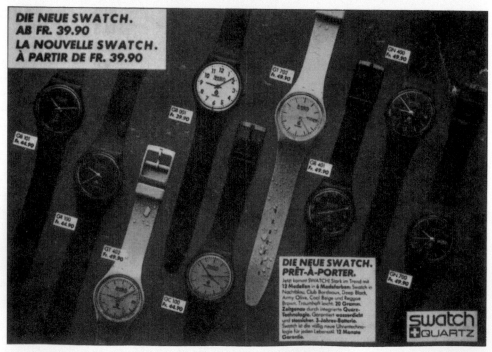

subsidiary Swatch Watch USA in early 1984. The American pricing strategy was modified and a direct sales force organized to replace SWDC that year. Managers hired to run Swatch Watch USA included Vice President of Operations Don Galliers, formerly in the watch strap business, and Marketing Manager/Creative Director Steve Rechtschaffner, age 27, a former member of the U.S. freestyle skiing team with experience in sales promotion. Exhibit 6 gives the perceived advantages and disadvantages of Swatch, in December 1984, in four countries.

Price

There were initially three prices for the Swiss launch: 39.90 SF for a model with only two hands, 44.90 SF for three hands, and 49.90 SF for three hands and a calendar display. In the United States, however, Swatch was first marketed at seven price points ranging from $19.95 to $37.50. Consumers did not seem to understand why certain watches cost more than others, so American prices were reduced to three in 1984: $25.00, $30.00, and $35.00. In 1986 one Swatch retail price was set throughout the world, based on the price in the United States of $30.00. Exhibit 7 presents the results of a survey on perceptions of Swatch retail prices in four countries.

EXHIBIT 6

Perceived Advantages and Disadvantages of Swatch

	Total (n = 800)	United States (n = 200)	France (n = 200)	Great Britain (n = 200)	West Germany (n = 200)
Positive Features					
Pretty shape	34.5[a]	34.0	33.5	20.0	50.5
Amusing, original	28.6	9.0	31.5	28.0	46.0
Waterproof	28.4	37.5	29.5	29.5	17.0
Fashionable, modern	24.5	7.5	30.5	24.0	36.0
Pretty, varied colors	22.6	31.0	13.5	18.5	27.5
Strong, resistant	22.1	24.5	27.5	24.5	12.0
Can be worn by anyone	16.0	30.5	9.0	12.5	12.0
Quality watches	14.8	28.0	8.0	4.0	19.0
Low price	14.5	3.5	32.0	5.0	17.5
Can be worn anywhere	12.6	13.5	13.5	11.0	12.5
Negative Features					
Uncomfortable plastic strap	16.0[b]	13.5	13.0	17.5	20.0
Too fashionable, too modern	10.3	2.0	6.5	9.5	23.0
Looks like a gadget, a toy	9.9	3.5	10.0	8.5	17.5
Does not match all styles of dress	8.4	1.0	4.0	14.0	14.5
Fragile	8.1	0.5	12.0	3.0	17.0
Too sophisticated face	7.4	6.0	3.0	8.5	12.0
Too much plastic	6.6	1.0	7.5	—	18.0
Too noisy	3.6	—	12.5	1.0	1.0

[a]Percentage of respondents indicating this feature in response to the question: "What, in your opinion, are the advantages of Swatch watches in comparison with other watches?"

[b]Percentage of respondents indicating this feature in response to the question: "And what are their disadvantages?"

Source: Delta International market study, December 1984.

EXHIBIT 7

Actual and Perceived 1986 Retail Prices of Swatch

United States (Actual Price = $30)

Perceived Price ($)	Total (n = 290)	Buyers (n = 99)	Potential Buyers (n = 140)	Nonbuyers (n = 51)
Less than 20	8[a]	3	9	16
21–30	57	62	56	49
31–40	26	25	26	25
41–50	6	7	6	2
51–60	2	3	2	2
More than 60	1	—	1	2

United Kingdom (Actual Price = £24)

Perceived Price (£)	Total (n = 202)	Buyers (n = 68)	Potential Buyers (n = 83)	Nonbuyers (n = 51)
Less than 10	4	—	4	12
11–15	10	3	14	14
16–20	39	44	36	35
21–25	22	38	16	12
26–30	8	4	10	12
31–35	1	1	1	2
36–40	2	—	4	2
More than 40	1	1	—	—

France (Actual Price = FF 250)

Perceived Price (FF)	Total (n = 200)	Buyers (n = 66)	Potential Buyers (n = 99)	Nonbuyers (n = 35)
Less than 100	10	2	11	20
100–150	9	2	12	14
151–200	17	8	23	17
201–250	41	74	32	3
251–300	7	9	5	9
301–400	4	3	4	3
More than 400	2	3	1	3

West Germany (Actual Price = 65 DM)

Perceived Price (DM)	Total (n = 200)	Buyers (n = 67)	Potential Buyers (n = 74)	Nonbuyers (n = 59)
Less than 20	3	3	—	7
21–40	11	6	12	14
41–60	38	27	42	44
61–80	39	58	34	22
81–100	7	4	8	8
101–200	3	2	3	3
More than 200	1	—	1	2

[a] Percentage of total responses to the question: "All the [Swatch] watches have the same price—could you estimate the price?"

Source: Qualitest A. G. market study, Zurich, August 1986, and company records.

From the start Thomke and Sprecher had decided that production contribution would have to be sufficient to finance massive communication. Manufacturing costs had been reduced substantially and wholesaler and agent margins could be decreased some. Retail margins would have to be kept high enough to motivate retailers. Exhibit 8 gives a comparison of costs and margins for traditional moderate-price Swiss and Japanese watches, low-price Hong Kong watches, and Swatch, in 1982–1983.

Product Line

Two Swatch collections of 12 different models each were marketed per year, in spring and fall. Styles were based on four major target groups geared to social behavior and trends: "classic," "hi-tech," "sports," and "fashion." Collections were designed by Kathi Durrer and Jean Robert in Zurich, with fashion consultants in New York, Milan, and Paris. At first there was only one large-size model, enabling mass production. In 1984, a smaller size was added. Limitation of sizes to these two enabled substantial reductions in production costs. Variations in the collections were made possible through face and watchband graphics and style. In the spring of 1984, Imgruth decided to name individual watches (for example, "Pin-stripe, " "Black Magic," "McSwatch," "Dotted Swiss") and tie each collection in with specific themes, starting with the "Skipper" line of sailing-inspired sport watches. Subsequent themes ranged from "Street Smart" paisleys and plaids to "Kiva" American Indian designs. Exhibit 9 illustrates selected watches from the 1984–1986 collections.

By fall 1984, Swatch management realized that a continuous system for pretesting the 80 to 100 models presented by the designers for each collection was essential for constant collection renewal. Franz Sprecher commented:

> The strategy should be to create bestsellers. This doesn't mean keeping the same collection for five years but improving the collection by identifying weak models and knowing whether to revamp them or create new models that will be leaders.

A collection of watches, including three scented "Granita di Frutta" models shown in Exhibit 9, were pretested in December 1984.[1] Test results, presented with the ac-

EXHIBIT 8

Breakdown of Costs and Margins for Low- to Moderate-Price Watches

	Swiss	*Japanese*	*Hong Kong*	*Swatch*
Retail price = 100%	100%	100%	100%	100%
(Retail margin)	(50%)	(55%)	(50%)	(45%)
Wholesale price	50%	45%	50%	55%
(Wholesale/agent margin)	(25%)	(16%)	(18%)	(11%)
Ex-factory price	25%	29%	33%	44%
(Contribution)	(4%)	(12%)	(3%)	(24%)
Manufacturing cost	21%	18%	29%	20%

Source: Company records.

---

[1]Granita di Frutta was a line of aromatic Swatches geared to the teenage consumer and consisting of pastel pink, blue, and yellow watches emitting strawberry, mint, and banana fragrances; it represented 80 percent of sales in the United States for the first two months in 1985.

EXHIBIT 9

Selected Watches from the 1984–1986 Collections

STREET SMART
(Fall–Winter 1985–86)

(Spring–Summer 1984)

COLOR TECH
(Fall–Winter 1985–86)

tual ex-factory sales figures for the collection, revealed no significant differences among the four countries involved (Exhibit 10).

Distribution

Until the mid-1970s most medium- and high-priced watches were sold through jewelry and specialist shops. Timex and other low-priced products sold through department and discount stores and some mail-order houses. The Swiss watchmakers, later followed by Seiko, had always placed emphasis on after-sales service and set up dealerships allowing jewelers to take up to 25 percent markups. As prices slipped, however, a gray market developed, fired by a drive for volume and a lack of control over distribution channels.[2]

---

[2]"Gray market" means parallel importing and distribution through unauthorized channels.

EXHIBIT 10

Preferences, Purchase Intentions, and Sales Data for 1985 Spring/Summer Swatch Collection in France, West Germany, Great Britain, and the United States

Swatch Code	Most Preferred Models[a]			Least Preferred Models[b]	Purchase Intentions[c] For Self				Ex-factory Sales Worldwide
	Total (n = 800)	Men (n = 400)	Women (n = 400)	(n = 800)	Total (n = 800)	Men (n = 400)	Women (n = 400)	Gift (n = 800)	(Thousands of Units)
GB 101	41.1%	63.3%	19.0%	2.0%	33.6%	57.0%	10.3%	27.0%	147
GA102	36.1	58.8	13.5	3.9	28.4	48.5	8.3	26.0	149
LB106	20.6	6.5	34.6	1.5	16.6	2.8	30.6	18.3	140
LM 104	20.4	3.3	37.6	2.3	18.1	1.0	35.3	21.0	70
GM 401	19.0	24.8	13.3	3.1	15.9	21.3	10.5	15.0	67
LW 104	18.3	3.8	32.8	3.5	15.1	1.3	29.1	16.6	246
LA 100	17.4	6.5	28.3	1.4	15.1	3.7	27.1	17.3	207
GN 401	17.3	31.8	2.8	4.3	15.1	28.3	2.0	11.8	63
GB 705	13.3	22.8	3.8	8.5	10.5	19.3	1.8	7.8	106
GW 104	12.9	11.8	14.0	7.9	8.0	5.8	10.3	9.9	221
GB 706	10.3	16.3	4.3	10.0	7.5	12.5	2.5	8.0	121
GK 100	9.9	11.5	8.3	48.9	6.3	7.3	5.3	8.0	286
GT 103	9.8	9.3	10.3	5.1	5.6	5.0	6.3	6.8	53
LT 101	9.5	1.8	17.3	3.1	7.1	0.3	14.0	10.3	53
LB 107	6.9	1.8	11.8	6.8	5.5	0.5	10.3	5.6	88
LW 107[d]	6.1	1.0	11.3	27.5	4.5	0.8	8.3	7.1	322
GJ 700	5.8	7.3	4.3	37.4	3.6	4.5	2.8	4.4	104
LN 103	4.1	0.8	7.3	2.6	3.3	—	6.5	5.6	64
LW 105[d]	3.9	0.8	7.0	17.3	3.0	0.3	5.8	4.6	213
GM 701	3.9	5.0	2.8	22.3	2.8	4.0	1.5	2.3	108
GB 403	3.5	4.5	2.5	13.9	2.5	1.5	1.5	2.9	78
LW 106[d]	2.4	0.8	4.0	27.1	1.5	—	3.0	3.1	152
LS 102	1.8	1.0	2.5	28.9	1.1	0.3	2.0	2.1	107
LB 105	1.5	0.8	2.3	5.0	1.3	0.8	1.8	1.6	118
LB 104	1.1	0.5	1.8	3.5	0.6	0.3	1.0	2.3	125

[a]Percentage of total responses to the question: "Here are a number of new Swatch watches. They come in two sizes, standard and small. Which are the three you like best?"

[b]Percentage of total responses to the question: "Which are the three watches you like least?" Responses were virtually the same regardless of sex.

[c]Percentage of total responses to the question: "Would you consider buying such a watch for yourself or as a gift?"

[d]"Granita di Frutta": 69 percent of those interested in these models as gifts claimed the recipient would be a girl under 15 years of age.

Source: Delta International market study, December 1984, and company records.

In the United States, Swatch watches were sold primarily in "shop-in-shops" at up-market department stores, some specialized watch retailers, sports shops, and boutiques. In Europe, Swatch was sold by the few existing up-market department stores but mostly by traditional jewelers and some specialized sports, gift, and fashion boutiques, mail-order houses, and duty-free shops. In France, as part of his launch strategy, the Swatch distributor Raymond Zeitoun, persuaded the prestigious jeweler Jean Dinh Van on the Rue de la Paix in Paris to sell Swatch for a few days. When the jeweler accepted "for the fun of it" and sales boomed, others followed suit. Zeitoun spoke of Swatch in France:

> Granted, it's an item without much of a margin but the profession has to change and widen its horizons. The advantage of Swatch is that it brings a lively atmosphere and a younger clientele to the store.

Discounting by distributors was not allowed, and the trade was warned to keep an eye out for counterfeits. Swatch Watch USA spent close to $1 million in 1984 to buy back Swatches displayed at less than the set price. Don Galliers recalled:

> We purchased 85–90 percent of gray market watches. Counterfeits appeared in 1985. We set up an international brand protection program with a very sophisticated information network. All new styles were copyrighted, counterfeiters caught at the source, and "confusingly similar" watch marketers taken to court. If we were spending $16–18 million a year on advertising, we could spend a couple of million to protect the brand.

Merchandising was considered fundamental and included sales promotional activities designed to catch the consumer's eye. Backed by 2.5-meter "maxi-Swatches," expensive and carefully designed display racks were "colorblocked," that is, arranged in rows of color. In-store videos played pop or rock music, and sales brochures were available in ample supply. In all countries, parties for the trade were organized for each collection launch to create a feeling of a "Swatch Club" encouraging retailers to give Swatch prime window space and exposure in spite of lower margins. One of Swatch's selling points with distributors was its very low return rate (0.3 percent in 1984 compared with the industry average of 5 percent), which virtually eliminated after-sales service problems and customer dissatisfaction.[3]

Exhibit 11 presents consumer preferences with respect to distribution of Swatch, and Exhibit 12 gives the breakdown of Swatch distribution channels in five countries. A breakdown of sales value and volume by distribution channel was not available.

In general, the attitude of the distributors toward Swatch watches was very positive, with the few negative comments limited to low profit margin, production-related delivery problems, skepticism about long-term success, and lack of distributor exclusivity. Galliers commented on Swatch's distribution strategy in the United States:

> Swatch's success was built on limited distribution. We should not sell more than 5 million Swatches in the United States in any single year, to keep it rare, in demand. You can't always get what you want so when you see it you'd better buy it. For a trendy article like this, if you accelerate too much into the market, you risk making it become a fad.

Product Line Extensions

While its major competitors, Seiko, Citizen, and others were diversifying into other applications of electronics and "superwatches" complete with televisions, computers, or health monitoring systems, Swatch, mainly through the initiative of Swatch Watch USA, had moved into a range of accessories and ready-to-wear apparel designed to express a "Swatch" life-style (Exhibits 13 and 14).

---

[3]The return rate is percentage of watches returned on warranty.

EXHIBIT 11

Consumers' Store Preferences for Buying Swatch, 1986

Store	Switzerland (n = 212)	United Kingdom (n = 202)	France (n = 200)	West Germany (n = 200)	United States (n = 290)
"Fine fashion" department stores	68[a]	28	56	57	53
Regular department stores	29	35	16	13	70
Sport shops	14	25	22	22	37
Jewelers	50	73	44	61	35
Boutiques	12	10	28	11	32
Clothing shops	17	12	4	11	31
Discount stores	—	7	—	—	19
Drugstores	—	—	—	—	10
Mail order	5	14	3	2	9
Supermarkets	8	4	6	3	2
Others	6	3	2	2	—

[a]Percentage of total responses to the question: "Listed on this card are different shops where you could buy a Swatch. From which of these shops would you prefer to buy a Swatch?" (Several answers are possible.)

Source: Qualitest A.G. market study, Zurich, August 1986.

One of the reasons given for expanding into accessories and apparel was the need to fill out the available space in the shop-in-shops. "Funwear" and "Fungear," manufactured in Hong Kong and the United States, were designed by Renee Rechtschaffner, Steve's wife and the winner of a Swatch-organized contest at the Fashion Institute of Technology. By the last quarter of 1985, nonwatch items accounted for one-third of Swatch sales in the United States. Aided awareness scores for Swatch accessories available only in the United States are presented in Exhibit 15.

EXHIBIT 12

Swatch Distribution Channels, 1985–1986

Channel	Switzerland		United Kingdom		France		West Germany		United States	
	1985	1986	1985	1986	1985	1986	1985	1986	1985	1986
Department stores	10[a]	10	6	9	3	11	19	22	82	71
Jewelers	85	78	87	78	95	79	73	59	3	2
Sport shops	—	—	0.1	0.1	—	—	6	16	1	2
Fashion shops	5	12	6	12	—	—	2	4	6	12
Others[b]	—	0.2	0.4	0.5	2	10	—	—	8	14
Total number of stores (including branches)	590	511	1708	1273	2634	2266	1030	511	6437	4634

[a]Percentage of total number of outlets.

[b]Gift and card shops, drugstores, college bookstores, military exchanges, catalogs, etc.

Source: Company records.

EXHIBIT 13

Swatch Accessories and Apparel

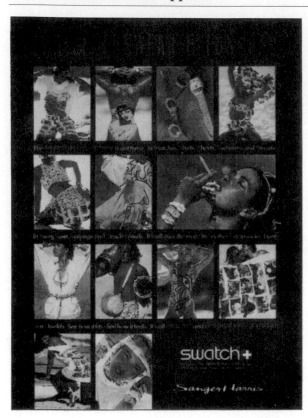
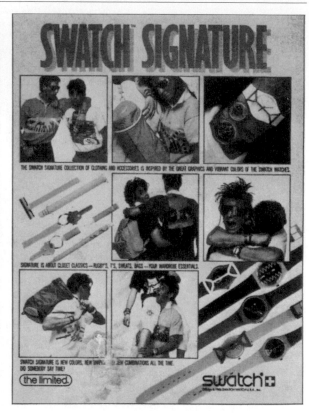

Fashion retailing in the United States was stimulated by six "market weeks" per year to launch each new season (spring, spring-summer, summer, back-to-school, fall-winter, holiday) and introduce products to retailers nationwide. At Swatch Watch USA, preparation of each market week began almost a full year in advance with market and sales analyses, fashion forecasts, and theme development (watches and accessories) covering approximately two months for each season followed by gradual decisions and presentations throughout the rest of the year on design, color, prints, prices, quantities, range, advertising, public relations, and promotion. Coordination of production and delivery with "fickle fashion" was a tricky business that relied on very short lead times. Perpetual innovation was also difficult to maintain. Galliers commented:

> We don't have the flexibility of the traditional watch industry, where if you miss it this year you can launch it next year. We also don't have the normal 18-month development time to field the watch after a one-year design time. Our whole cycle is built on the concept that every six weeks there is something new at the Swatch counter.

In the spring of 1986, under license from the Coca-Cola company, the American subsidiary also started marketing a line of Coca-Cola watches. They contained traditional ETA and not Swatch technology quartz movements and did not bear the name Swatch.

EXHIBIT 14

Swatch Clothing and Accessories, 1984–1985

Date	Product	Description	Retail Price
Fall 1984	Swatch Guard	Protective, decorative device for watches	$3
Fall 1984	Maxi-Swatch	2.5-meter Swatch wall clock	$150
Spring 1985	Shields	Sunglasses	$35
Spring 1985	Chums	Eyeglass holders	$5
Spring 1985	Signature line	Umbrellas, T-shirts, sweatshirts with watch graphics	$12–38
Spring 1985	Gift set	Keyholder and Swiss pen-knife	$45
Spring 1985	Parafernalia	Italian pens, stationery items, key rings, safety razors	$7–15
Fall 1985	Fungear line	Knapsacks, belts, bags	$10–65
Fall 1985	Funwear line	Unisex casual wear (pants, tops, sweats, shirts, shorts, skirts) linked to watch themes	$12–65

Communication

Thomke and Sprecher had adopted a global communication strategy for Swatch to establish a distinctive brand personality. The company issued strict directives on use of the Swatch logo, baselines, layout, and the Swiss cross. The Swatch communication budget was split more or less evenly between advertising/store promotion (50 percent) and public relations/special events (50 percent). Local agencies were in

EXHIBIT 15

Aided Awareness of Swatch Accessories in the United States, 1985

	Total Sample (n = 895)	Age 12–18 (n = 219)	19–24 (n = 234)	25–34 (n = 442)
Shields	17[a]	43	13	8
Bags	16	37	12	8
T-shirts	15	36	13	6
Guards	11	27	10	4
Gift sets	9	20	10	3
Chums	8	20	6	3
Beach boxes	8	18	4	5
Maxi-Swatch	8	17	7	3
Pocket knives	6	15	5	2
Pens and pencils	6	13	3	3
Razors	3	5	3	1

[a]Percentage of respondents indicating this accessory in response to the question: "Please tell me which of the following Swatch accessories you are aware of."

Source: "Attitude and Awareness of Swatch in Various Markets" study, McCann-Erickson, July 1985.

charge of public relations, promotion, publicity, and special events, including contests, concert tours, and sports events. McCann-Erickson in Zurich was in charge of all advertising and designed ads for local adaptation in different countries through the use of voice-overs for commercials and strips of copy in the respective languages for print ads. Roger Guyard, Regional Manager for France, explained:

> We want to have a global image with the same image in England as in Australia. Where we are different from the others is in our launch events and promotions, adapted to each country and each population.

The Swatch communication target audience was described by McCann-Zurich as "all men and women between 15 and 39 years of age, particularly between 20 and 29, opinion leaders/trend-setters, extroverts who are nonetheless group-dependent, young fashion wearers, and both active and passive sports fans." For Felice Schillaci, vice president of continental operations, Swatch was "a brand for the young at heart, no age group, no 18 to 29, it's a state of mind, an attitude."

Public Relations

Heavy emphasis was placed on testimonials and endorsements by opinion leaders as well as special events including sponsoring of musicians and artists, exhibitions, and competitions at which gadgets, leaflets, and "Swatch magazines" were distributed (Exhibit 16). Swatch promotion was often unsolicited, such as when Princess Diana wore not only her husband Prince Charles's watch at a polo match but also two Swatches, just when Swatch was introducing the ideas of man-size watches for women and "multiple Swatch accessorizing." Swatch also benefited from massive publicity through the press. According to Elmar Mock:

> Management's stroke of genius was not to hide its engineers. We were on great terms with the newspapers who created an advertising effect, quite naturally, without the slightest solicitation.

Limited edition watches were launched with elaborate parties. The first was designed by Kiki Picasso and distributed to 100 celebrities at a cocktail party in Paris. There was the diamond-studded "Limelight" ($100) available in both Europe and the United States. Then there were the "Breakdance" watch ($30) and four watches designed by New York artist Keith Haring ($50) marketed in the United States only. Swatch's French public relations agency claimed that the strategy behind these serial watches was to manage the production-related scarcity by "creating a frenzy through rarity." Organization of advertising and events revolved around the development of a "Swatch cult" and using connections. In 1984, for instance, Max Imgruth organized a celebrity advertising campaign through a photographer in California who persuaded a number of stars to be in Swatch ads in exchange for a Rolex or Piaget gold watch. These included Lauren Hutton, Donna Mills, Lee Majors, and Ivan Lendl.

Advertising

Swatch advertising and promotion budgets are given in Exhibit 17, with industry media expenditures in the United States in Exhibit 18. Don Galliers explained that Switzerland had a strict policy whereby roughly 30 percent of the product's retail price would go to advertising. Swatch advertising relied primarily on films for tele-

EXHIBIT 16

Major Special Events Organized or Sponsored by Swatch

Date	Country	Event
March 1984	Germany	13-ton giant Swatch on Commerzbank building, Frankfurt
April 1984	France	Urban Sax saxophonist group at the Eldorado theater in Paris to collaborate launch; first Swatch magazine
August 1984	United States	Ivan Lendl, U.S. Tennis Open
September 1984	United States	World Breakdancing Championship at the Roxy, New York
September 1984	France	First street art painting show with the French artists Les Frères Ripoulin, Espece Cardin theater, Paris
November 1984	United States	The Fat Boy's music sponsorship at Private Eye's, New York, to introduce "Granita di Frutta" to the trade
October 1984–January 1985	United States	New York City Fresh Festival: breakdancing, rapping, graffiti artists
January 1985	United States	World Freestyle Invitational/Celebrity Classic, Breckenridge, Colorado
March 1985	France	IRCAM "copy art" show, Paris; limited edition (119) Kiki Picasso design watches; second Swatch magazine
Spring 1985	United States	Hi-fly freestyle windsurfing team sponsorship
May 1985	England	Second street art painting show, Covent Garden, London, with Les Fröres Ripoulin and English street artists
June 1985	Switzerland	Art fair in Basel; third street art painting show with 50 European artists
Summer 1985	Sweden	Oestersjo Rallyt (Segel-Rallye)
September 1985	France	Cinema festival, Pompidou Center, Paris, with Kurosawa's film Ran; Mini City magazine
September 1985	France	"Le Defile": Jean-Paul Gaultier and Regine Chopinot fashion/dance show, Pavilion Baltard, Paris
September 1985	England	Andrew Logan's Alternative Miss World, London
October 1985	Belgium	"Mode et Anti-Mode" fashion show, Brussels
Fall 1985	United States	Thompson Twins' concert tour sponsorship
November 1985	Spain	Swatch launch party, the Cirque, Barcelona
November 1985	United States	"Limelight" launch party, Los Angeles (for trade)
November 1985	International	Freestyle World Cup sponsorship
November 1985	Japan	Giant Swatch in Tokyo for launch of Swatch
January 1986	United States	Fashion show (for trade) at Private Eye's, New York

E X H I B I T   16   (*continued*)

January 1986	United States	Pierre Boulez orchestra concert tour
January–November 1986	England	"Time & Motion Competition," Royal College of Art, London
February 1986	England	Feargal Sharkey tour
February–March 1986	Germany	Swatch Freestyle World Cup, Oberjoch
March 1986	Switzerland	"Arosa" freestyle skiing weekend with retailers
March 1986	Austria	"Exposa" jewelry fair with Swatch balloons
March 1986	France	"Waterproof Paris": Daniel Larrieux's subaquatic ballet performance
April–October 1986	Canada	Giant Swatch, Swiss Pavillion, Expo 86, Vancouver
May–September 1986	Sweden	Swatch Funboard Cup sponsorship
June 1986	France	Fourth street art painting show, fourth Swatch magazine
June 1986	Italy	"Sasswatchgala Mailand." launch event
July 1986–February 1987	Switzerland	First International Swatch Freestyle Youth Camp, Zermatt
July 1986	International	Second Himalaya Super Marathon sponsorship
July 1986	Netherlands	Srachenflug Festival sponsored by Swatch

vision and cinema. Print ads, accounting for approximately one-third of total advertising expenditure, were used worldwide to reinforce awareness of each collection and current trend themes. They ran from April to June and from September to December every year. Swatch print media plans included sport, fashion, and avant-garde magazines (for example, *Vogue, Elle, Cosmopolitan, Sports Illustrated, L'Equipe, Rolling Stone, The Face, City*), as well as magazines geared to the young (for example, *Just 17, Jacinte, Madchen, Seventeen*) and occasionally general news publications (for example, *Stern, Der Spiegel, Figaro, Tiempo*).

Swatch Watch USA has an in-house department that adapted the McCann-Erickson ads and created its own ads. Samples of print ads used in the United States are shown in Exhibit 19. Imgruth commented on global advertising:

> We adapted the spots in a way that made sense, different wording, cut them a little bit with McCann here, knowing full well that what the Swiss wanted to achieve, a brand created and sent in directly from Switzerland, was impossible. A watch is not consumed like Coca-Cola. It is not a daily need. This is emotional and you have to play local emotions.

Felice Schillaci explained that the loyal Swatch customer in the United States fell in the 10- to 16-year-old age bracket. Reliable data on the Swatch buyer profile in Europe were not available but buyer age group brackets in the United Kingdom were estimated to be 20 percent under 18, 40 percent between 18 and 24, 30 percent between 25 and 34, and 10 percent over 34. Management in the United States felt that catching consumers at an early age would get them to stick with Swatch as they grew up and the enthusiasm they generated would rub off on those older. By 1986 in New York City and Los Angeles, where Swatch awareness was at a maximum, Swatch Watch USA had limited television commercials to MTV to avoid over-

EXHIBIT 17

Swatch Budgets, 1983–1986

Swatch Advertising Budget[a] (Thousands of Swiss Francs)

Country	Launch	1983	1984	1985	1986
Switzerland	March 1983	459	620	964	1,107
United Kingdom	March 1983	922	2,398	2,398	2,767
West Germany	September 1983	2,275	4,182	2,706	2,706
United States	September 1983		9,480	32,838	33,404
Austria	January 1984		244	429	472
France	April 1984		2,610	2,423	2,583
Belgium	April 1984		199	295	307
Netherlands	May 1984		148	430	369
South Africa	September 1984		301	133	92
Australia	September 1984		562	883	984
Norway	October 1984			243	246
Sweden	October 1984			571	615
Denmark	March 1985			151	184
Finland	May 1985			236	246
Japan	October 1985			NA	NA
Spain	October 1985			1,230	2,460
Italy	June 1986				3,524

Swatch Public Relations and Special Events Budget[b]
(Thousands of Swiss Francs)

		1983	1984	1985	1986
Central promotion budget			3,690	4,920	6,150
Switzerland	March 1983			258	184
United Kingdom	March 1983			369	633
West Germany	September 1983			300	209
United States	September 1983			3,978	886
Austria	January 1984		29	29	37
France	April 1984		898	1,204	1,291
Belgium	April 1984		139	253	246
Netherlands	May 1984		118	209	260
South Africa	September 1984		18	31	49
Australia	September 1984			86	123
Norway	October 1984			47	80
Sweden	October 1984			77	209
Denmark	March 1985			c	61
Finland	May 1985			c	37
Japan	October 1985			NA	NA
Spain	October 1985			492	1,599
Italy	June 1986				1,458

NA = Not available.

[a]"Advertising" includes production of ads, media spending, in-store programs, etc.

[b]This budget includes music and sports promotions, special events, etc.

[c]Paid for by distributor.

Source: Company records (disguised data).

EXHIBIT   18

1985 Watch Brand Media Spending in the United States

Brand	Share of Voice[a]	Brand	Share of Voice[a]
A-Watch	1.15%	Omega	1.02
Bulova	0.60	Piaget	1.56
Cartier	0.83	Pulsar	9.74
Casio	3.35	Rado	1.87
Certina	0.13	Rolex	5.05
Citizen	10.33	Seiko	11.17
Ebel	0.97	Swatch	7.05
Gucci	2.16	Timex	15.22
Guess	0.03	Tissot	0.32
Hamilton	0.32	Z-Watch	0.01
J. Lassale	7.32	Total	86.32%
Longines	1.77	Others	13.68
Lorus	4.36	Total advertisers	100.00%

[a]Share of voice = percentage of total industry media spending.

Source: Compiled from 1985 Broadcast Advertisers Reports, Inc. and Publishers Information Bureau, Inc., figures.

saturation.[4] A firm specializing in TV and radio youth audience surveys conducted an analysis for Swatch of American consumers, based on interviews in 15 cities and including reactions to a random sample of eight Swatch ads (Exhibit 20). Scores for recall of Swatch advertising in five countries are presented in Exhibit 21. Watch brand awareness scores in the same countries are presented in Exhibits 22 and 23.

Competition

When asked to define the competition, Swatch management's responses varied. Swatch was generally credited with having opened up a new market niche (Exhibit 24). By 1986, however, the market was flooded with Swatch imitations, some bearing similar brand names, for example, Watch, Watcha, Swiss Watch, Smash, Swatcher, A-Watch, La-Watch, P-Watch, Q-Watch, Zee-Watch, as well as counterfeits using the brand name Swatch. Many Swatch imitations were produced in Hong Kong or Taiwan for distribution in the United States, Europe, or other major markets. These could look strikingly similar to Swatch, some were even similar in quality and very price competitive, and the company was involved in a long series of legal proceedings to fight off the competition.

Timex, one of the companies worst hit by the LCD watch glut, had launched a line of colored fashion watches called "Watercolors," priced slightly below Swatch. Timex was also rumored to be preparing a new advertising campaign for its "Big-Bold-Beautiful" fashion watch line for women, introduced in the summer of 1986 and targeted to an older age group than Swatch. According to one industry expert,

---

[4]MTV is a music video cable TV station watched primarily by 12- to 24-year-olds.

EXHIBIT 19

Selected Swatch Print Ads in the United States

EXHIBIT 20

A Psychographic Segmentation of Consumers in the United States

	Age			
	Children (6–10)	*Teeny Boppers (11–15)*	*Young Teen Rockers(11–15)*	*Students (11–15)*
Profile/Interests	TV: Jem rock cartoon, *Nikelodeon*. Males: He-man, Transformers, G.I. Joe. Females: Care Bears.	Almost 100% female. Middle/middle-upper-class suburban, clique oriented, very fashion conscious: trendy, outrageous style, favor Sourthern California over Europe/NYC look. Like partying, dancing, hanging out at malls. Music: Breezy pop love songs, New Wave. Main hero: Madonna.	80% male, 20% female. Middle/upper-middle-class suburban, mall creatures, macho, heavy-metal look. Hard rock concerts, partying (but isolated, not in cliques). Main heroes: Stallone, Schwarzenegger, Iron Maiden ("Madonna is useless").	50% male, 50% female. Middle/lower-middle class, very conservative, like professional and participation sports. Music: no allegiance to type of music or artist.
Media	Network TV, MTV.[a]	MTV-crazy, fashion magazines, Top-40 radio.	AOR[b] radio, critical MTV watchers.	Network TV, AM radio.
Shopping Habits	Dependent on parents. Stores: department stores,malls, etc.	Heavy consumers. Stores: department stores, record stores, malls.	*Not* shopping oriented. Stores: record stores, department stores, malls.	Consider shopping not an event. Stores: Sears, K-Mart, chain drugstores.
Reaction to Swatch	42% awareness (of which 4% ownership, 76% interest in teeny bop models). Consider it "cool," something the big kids wear. Parents' interests: durability, price, large face numbers, traditional styles, models that won't become unfashionable.	*Very* positive— provides a sense of identity—is a life-style magnifier but becoming too commonplace, boring. Line extensions: negative. Too expensive, not cool, "Swatch is not a clothing line, but a rock 'n roll time piece."	High awareness due to visibility in schools but strong negative bias: Swatch represents teeny bopper life-style, "price too high for a piece of plastic." Only 16% wear watches, but 72% desire to purchase Swatch if positioned correctly (NB: are currently "undersymboled").	Price and function outweigh fashionability Swatch too wild for their life-style yet potential interest to "fit in" (80% unawareness of traditional styles).

[a]MTV is a leading national "basic cable" TV music station.

[b]AOR = Album-oriented rock.

[c]CHR = Contemporary hits radio.

Source: Compiled from a Burkhard, Abrams, Douglas, Eliot market study, 1986.

EXHIBIT 20 (*continued*)

	Age		
	Rockers *(16–22)*	*Preppies* *(16–22)*	*Trendies* *(16–22)*
Profile/Interests	60% male, 40% female. Long hair, clique oriented, committed to rock groups, very frequent concertgoers (for music, not as a social event). Like fast cars, comedy and horror movies, 100% American rock 'n roll. Dislike short hair, New Wave, disco. Music: *pure* rock 'n roll (no synthesizers, drum machines). Hero: ZZ Top.	Career-oriented, traditional views, "controlled" hippies wildness in style (designs more than colors), concerts (more as social even than for music), participation sports. Like dating, movies. Music: "Yuppie" rock/folk/pop. Like songs more than artists.	Movement similar to but smaller scale. Exist only in U.S. art and culture capitals. Avant-garde tastes; outspoken on issues they consider important. Left socially and politically. Go to clubs, not concerts. Music: anti–rock 'n roll, anti–popular groups.
Media	AOR radio, MTV (77% regular viewers).	Cable TV, some MTV, some fashion magazines, radio (AOR, CHR,[c] light rock mix) but low station loyalty.	Trendy, artsy magazines and newspapers, anti-MTV, anti–commercial radio.
Shopping Habits	Like all things "American."	Stores: mainstream department stores.	Consider fashion a vehicle of expression, rejection of anything too popular.
Reactions to Swatch	Aware of wild Swatch styles *only*. Like its disposability, price. Dislike what it stand for: glitzy, hi-tech graphics, New Wave, dancing, slick ads, male model geeks. "A girl's/bopper's watch." Consider multiple Swatch ownership too trendy.	92% awareness. Prefer traditional designs, price, fashionability, reliability, practicality. Dislike its young teen image. 73% prefer dressier watches (silver/gold Rolex look) for "special events"; strongly "antidigital." Line extensions: too expensive, unnecessary.	73% wear no watch. Very negative image of Swatch: "a rip-off," "a toy," "the corporate world," "fast-food of time pieces."

EXHIBIT 20 *(continued)*

	Age		
	Transitionaries *(22–32)*	*Older Casuals* *(22–43)*	*Weekend Hippies* *(33–43)*
Profile/Interests	Conservative, social climbers, wildness (as observers, not participants), competitive sports. Music: "intelligent" rock 'n roll.	The hidden mainstream, ultraconservative, *very* family-oriented, fast-food patrons, socially inactive, disinterested in fashion. Music: traditional.	Mellowed former hippies. Look like but hate being called Yuppies; still subscribe to basic 1960s principles. Music: mood music, "New Age" movement.
Media	Females: fashion magazines. Males: *Time, Newsweek, Sports Illustrated.* Not MTV (only 16% regular viewers).	Network TV. Local newspapers (even *National Enquirer*–type tabloids).	Cable TV (critical viewers) but not MTV, radio (as background music). Weekend newspaper supplements, traditional magazines (*Time, Newsweek,* etc.).
Shopping Habits	Pro-American but respectful of foreign-made goods; appreciate quality/ value; balance between fashion and conservatism. Stores: major mainstream department stores (91% source of potential Swatch purchase for 76% aware).	Traditional brands (e.g., Timex, Bulova, Casio for watches).	Heavy shoppers, appreciate quality products. Stores: upscale department stores (I. Magnin, Saks) for females, mainstream department stores for men.
Reactions to Swatch	Positive: consider it a great leisure tool, like its durability, disposability, price, reliability. Line extensions: high awareness but overpriced for females, not really credible for males.	Watches are functional. Awareness: 12% aided, 4% unaided.	High awareness, but 43% of those have never seen one. Cheap, teen-item image; but functionality, light weight durability. Line extensions: overpriced, not functional, too gaudy. High awareness of competing brands.

EXHIBIT 21

Aided Recall of Watch Advertisements

Brand	United States				Switzerland			
	Total (n = 99)	Buyers (n = 99)	Potential Buyers (n = 140)	Nonbuyers (n = 51)	Total (n = 212)	Buyers (n = 90)	Potential Buyers (n = 87)	Nonbuyers (n = 35)
Swatch	67[a]	79	66	47	78	88	70	74
Omega	6	9	6	—	19	22	17	14
Rolex	31	32	25	45	20	29	10	23
Seiko	35	35	36	29	16	22	6	23
Cartier	14	7	16	25	16	22	10	11
Timex	41	37	46	35	4	3	2	11
Gucci	16	17	15	16	—	—	—	—
Citizen	18	17	21	12	5	3	3	11
Pulsar	11	12	14	—	—	—	—	—
Bulova	10	6	12	14	—	—	—	—
Casio	10	14	11	—	6	7	5	6
Longines	11	12	11	12	15	18	9	20
Guess	14	18	12	14	—	—	—	—
Tissot	8	12	7	—	50	50	45	60
A-Watch	10	10	13	—	—	—	—	—
K-Watch	—	—	—	—	—	—	—	—
M-Watch	—	—	—	—	13	18	6	20
Club Med	—	—	—	—	—	—	—	—
Dugena	—	—	—	—	—	—	—	—
Kiple	—	—	—	—	—	—	—	—
Lorus	4	—	4	—	—	—	—	—
Yema	—	—	—	—	—	—	—	—

(continued)

661

EXHIBIT 21 (continued)

Brand	United Kingdom				France				West Germany			
	Total (n = 202)	Buyers (n = 68)	Potential Buyers (n = 83)	Nonbuyers (n = 51)	Total (n = 200)	Buyers (n = 66)	Potential Buyers (n = 99)	Nonbuyers (n = 35)	Total (n = 200)	Buyers (n = 67)	Potential Buyers (n = 74)	Nonbuyers (n = 59)
Swatch	50	56	53	39	50	62	46	34	67	70	69	61
Omega	5	10	—	8	—	—	—	—	19	18	24	14
Rolex	17	16	22	12	15	17	12	17	34	31	39	31
Seiko	30	35	28	27	30	32	30	26	31	30	36	25
Cartier	11	12	13	6	—	—	—	—	—	—	—	—
Timex	23	26	19	24	21	23	23	9	22	24	26	15
Gucci	—	—	—	—	—	—	—	—	—	—	—	—
Citizen	15	18	18	6	58	64	56	49	—	—	—	—
Pulsar	—	—	—	—	4	3	5	—	6	16	—	—
Bulova	—	—	—	—	—	—	—	—	—	—	—	—
Casio	11	15	11	6	11	11	10	14	—	—	—	—
Longines	3	6	4	—	—	—	—	—	13	13	11	14
Guess	9	13	10	4	—	—	—	—	—	—	—	—
Tissot	4	4	6	—	—	—	—	—	12	14	11	10
A-Watch	—	—	—	—	—	—	—	—	—	—	—	—
K-Watch	—	—	—	—	4	6	3	—	—	—	—	—
M-Watch	—	—	—	—	—	—	—	—	—	—	—	—
Club Med	—	—	—	—	5	6	2	9	—	—	—	—
Dugena	—	—	—	—	—	—	—	—	15	15	15	15
Kiple	—	—	—	—	11	12	10	9	—	—	—	—
Lorus	—	—	—	—	—	—	—	—	—	—	—	—
Yema	—	—	—	—	14	17	12	14	—	—	—	—

aPercentage of total responses to the question: "Which of the watches on this list have you recently seen or heard advertised recently?" No figure indicates that the brand was not listed on the card.

Source: Compiled from a Qualitest A.G. study, Zurich, August 1986.

EXHIBIT 22

Unaided Awareness of Watch Brands in Europe and United States

Brand	Switzerland (n = 212)	Great Britain (n = 202)	France (n = 200)	West Germany (n = 200)	United States (n = 290)
Swatch	66[a]	49	47	66	62
Timex	—	74	24	17	57
Seiko	15	45	37	26	50
Rolex	26	34	17	58	40
Gucci	—	—	—	—	15
Cartier	8	8	21	20	14
Citizen	—	6	11	19	12
Pulsar	—	2	—	—	11
Bulova	—	—	—	—	11
Casio	—	20	4	3	9
Longines	9	—	—	—	9
Guess	—	—	—	—	6
Tissot	58	—	3	10	6
A-Watch	—	—	—	—	2
M-Watch	5	—	—	—	—
Coca-Cola	—	—	—	—	2
Dugena	—	—	—	26	—
Lorus	—	2	—	—	—
Yema	—	—	8	—	—
Lip	—	—	23	—	—
Kelton	—	—	36	—	—

[a]Percentage of respondents mentioning this brand in response to the questions: "What brands of watches can you spontaneously think of?" then "And which else?"

Source: Compiled from a Qualitest A.G. market study, Zurich 1986.

the Timex range did not seem to have any "winners," at least not in Europe. Seiko's Lorus line was expanded in 1984 to include "Swatch-like" fashion models, priced lower than Swatch and doing well when they had special design features. The first solar-powered wristwatch was also launched under the Lorus brand name in 1986. Competitors wondered, however, if Seiko was really committed to competing with Swatch since nonwatch products, for example, personal computers, printers, and audio and video equipment, were to be increased to 30 percent of worldwide sales by 1989. Don Galliers summarized the challenge in the United States:

> If you want to take significant market share away from the existing well-established brand, you have to spend three times the amount of advertising that brand spends. To kick us where we hurt worse, in delivery and depth, they'll have to build up $75 million worth of initial inventory, in addition to the $100 million investment in production facilities. That's one hell of an investment!

EXHIBIT 23

Unaided Awareness of Watch Brands in the United States

Brand	1983 (n = 1641)	1984 (n = 1669)	1986 (n = 1783)
Timex	84[a]	84	82
Seiko	36	41	39
Bulova	52	44	38
Elgin	20	21	18
Rolex	8	12	18
Hamilton	14	12	13
Longines	12	10	10
Waltham	12	9	8
Casio	4	4	8
Swatch	NA	NA	7
Pulsar	2	4	7
Omega	7	4	5
Citizen	3	4	5
Caravelle	4	4	2
Piaget	1	1	2
Lorus	—	1	2
Cartier	1	2	1
Tissot	—	1	1
Gucci	NA	NA	1
Guess	NA	NA	1
A-Watch	NA	NA	1

[a]Percentage of respondents mentioning this brand in response to the question: "Will you please tell me all the brands of watches you can think of?"

Source: Compiled from the Gallup Organization, Inc., figures.

Citizen apparently did not feel it necessary to launch a Swatch-like product, preferring to focus on its specialization, digitals, and technically sophisticated watches. At first Casio, specialized more specifically in calculators and extremely price-competitive multifunction digital watches, did not jump on the Swatch bandwagon either. In 1986, when the shift from digital to analog watches became apparent, however, Casio launched "Color Burst," a line of quartz analog fashion watches, waterproof to 50 meters, retailing at less than the price of Swatch. Sales were reported to be rather disappointing.

Swatch management claimed that only the very large firms could compete with ETA on price and that smaller firms undercutting Swatch on price were left with virtually no margin to compete with Swatch's intensive communication. Swatch refused to enter into a price war with its competitors. According to Jacques Irniger, ETA marketing manager, Swatch spent more than double the watch industry's average ad expenditure for a *single* brand: "Competitors can copy our watch but not our media spend. They will also have trouble duplicating some of Swatch's promotional stunts." Examples of "Swatch-like" fashion watches with limited market response were the

EXHIBIT 24

A Perceptual Map for Swatch and Other Leading Brands in West Germany

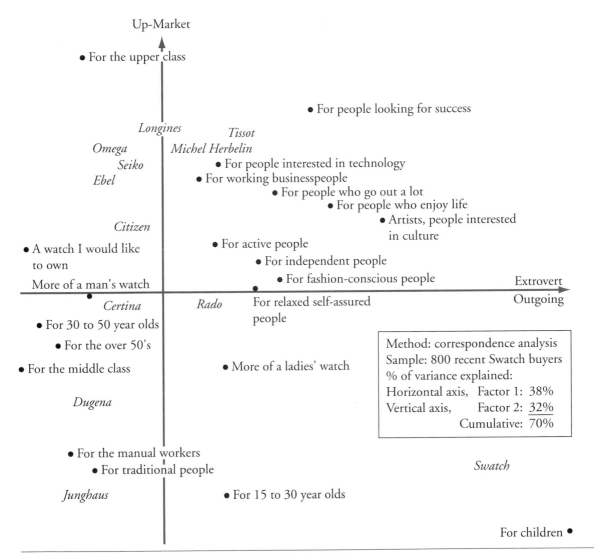

Up-Market

• For the upper class

• For people looking for success

Longines

Tissot

Omega   Michel Herbelin

Seiko   • For people interested in technology

Ebel   • For working businesspeople

• For people who go out a lot

• For people who enjoy life

• Artists, people interested
 in culture

Citizen

• A watch I would like   • For active people
to own
 • For independent people

More of a man's watch   • For fashion-conscious people   Extrovert

Outgoing

Certina   Rado   For relaxed self-assured
people

• For 30 to 50 year olds

• For the over 50's

Method: correspondence analysis
Sample: 800 recent Swatch buyers
% of variance explained:
Horizontal axis, Factor 1: 38%
Vertical axis,   Factor 2: 32%
                   Cumulative: 70%

• For the middle class   • More of a ladies' watch

Dugena

• For the manual workers

• For traditional people   Swatch

Junghaus   • For 15 to 30 year olds

For children •

Source: ECS Conseil S.S., August 1986.

"Twist" by Accurist and the "American Graffiti" watch by Gillex in the United Kingdom. According to Ernst Thomke, "In an era when superbly accurate quartz watches sell for $10, the key is not technology but image." Exhibit 25 presents Swatch's image in five countries.

Brands explicitly positioned as fashion accessories varied from one country to another and it was difficult to obtain a global view of the situation as well as market share data to determine the relative threat presented by such brands. Designer watches (for example, Gucci, Dior, Givenchy, Nina Ricci, Yves Saint Laurent, Ralph

EXHIBIT 25

Swatch Image in Five Countries

Swatch	Switzerland				United Kingdom			
	Total (n = 212)	Buyers (n = 90)	Potential Buyers (n = 87)	Nonbuyers (n = 35)	Total (n = 202)	Buyers (n = 68)	Potential Buyers (n = 68)	Nonbuyers (n = 83)
is Swiss made	39[a]	43	37	31	15	13	17	14
is reasonably priced	36	44	34	20	32	32	34	27
is a sports watch	33	31	39	23	24	28	23	22
is continuously introducing new models (colors, dials)	32	30	37	26	14	10	23	6
is a watch for all occasions (business, sports)	30	37	32	9	31	35	25	33
is a highly fashionable watch	25	27	31	9	37	25	41	31
is mainly for young people	17	17	18	11	27	25	22	37
is waterproof	15	16	16	9	10	10	8	14
is the ideal present	14	17	16	—	11	15	8	10
has good ads	10	13	7	11	8	6	8	12
is a trendy watch	8	4	8	17	22	16	30	18
is a high-quality watch	7	9	6	3	29	32	23	33
is a quartz watch	6	4	7	9	3	1	6	3
is shockproof	5	4	7	—	10	9	5	20
attracts attention	3	2	3	3	24	25	25	20
I would like to own more than one	1	1	1	—	1	1	—	—

Swatch	France				West Germany				United States			
	Total (n = 200)	Buyers (n = 66)	Potential Buyers (n = 99)	Nonbuyers (n = 35)	Total (n = 200)	Buyers (n = 67)	Potential Buyers (n = 74)	Nonbuyers (n = 59)	Total (n = 290)	Buyers (n = 99)	Potential Buyers (n = 140)	Nonbuyers (n = 51)
is Swiss made	13	12	14	11	21	25	11	29	16	16	16	14
is reasonably priced	24	30	19	26	16	15	16	15	26	31	24	18
is a sports watch	43	52	37	43	44	51	47	31	28	30	26	27
is continuously introducing new models (colors, dials)	30	29	31	29	50	61	53	32	19	20	20	12
is a watch for all occasions (business, sports)	23	18	25	23	18	21	23	8	14	16	16	8
is a highly fashionable watch	18	15	21	14	33	19	39	41	25	27	24	25
is mainly for young people	38	23	44	49	40	30	30	63	16	12	13	33
is waterproof	8	15	5	3	8	9	14	—	17	22	16	10
is the ideal present	23	26	26	9	12	18	14	2	12	12	14	6
has good ads	5	8	4	3	16	9	20	19	16	8	21	20
is a trendy watch	29	21	28	43	10	3	4	24	25	16	27	35
is a high-quality watch	6	9	4	6	6	6	4	8	20	28	16	12
is a quartz watch	8	5	9	9	8	13	4	7	6	6	7	4
is shockproof	9	12	5	14	5	6	8	—	8	10	7	6
attracts attention	14	11	14	17	15	12	12	22	32	35	35	31
I would like to own more than one	11	15	10	3	1	2	1	—	6	9	5	—

[a] Percentage of total responses to the question: "Which *three* statements on this card do you think of as the most important ones in describing Swatch?"

Source: Qualitest A.G. study, Zurich, August 1986.

Lauren, Calvin Klein, Guy Laroche, Lanvin, Hermes, Benetton), although often in a different price range from Swatch, that is, segments C and D (see Exhibit 4), were a growing trend and the actual concept of "fashion watch" did not appear clear in consumers' minds. Responses to the question "Please tell me all the brands of fashion watches you can think of" included such diverse brands as Timex, Swatch, Bulova, Citizen, and Rolex. Franz Sprecher's definition of a fashion watch was "a watch not only colorful but with accessorizing potential and meaning, a statement of the fashion trends at a specific period of time."

In Europe, moderately priced fashion watches included Kelton, an inexpensive French watch brand launched by Timex in the early 1960s. After initial rejection by the traditional jewelers' network, Kelton had been very successfully distributed through mass distribution channels. The breakdown of Kelton sales in France was estimated to be 45 percent from "tabacs" (registered tobacconists), 30 percent from supermarkets, and 25 percent from department and variety stores. Kelton was also distributed in the United Kingdom, Portugal, and Italy. Prices ranged from 99 to 320 French francs. K'Watch, Kelton's response to Swatch launched in June 1984, was priced at 249–270 FF. Kelton brand awareness was very high in France, and it had a young, inexpensive, active, and fashionable image. Philippe d'Herbomez, Kelton marketing manager, commented:

> When you think about the Swatch strategy you realize that the product was launched on the Kelton concept: "Vous vous changez, changez de Kelton" (Time to change, change your Kelton!), but the consumer more readily changes his Swatch than his Kelton since with every new Swatch collection the previous ones become virtually obsolete. When Swatch was launched, Kelton was no longer very fashionable and had become expensive in comparison with Asian watches. The 1987 Kelton collection is a series of new lower-priced products. Our distribution is wearing thin also so we plan to open up new outlets and invest in communication with emphasis on our well-known, successful slogan.

Other fashion watches had mushroomed in the wake of the Swatch success. The M-Watch, an inexpensive (38 SF) traditional quartz watch containing ETA movements, was launched by Mondaine in Zurich at the same time as Swatch and distributed by the Swiss supermarket chain Migros. In May 1984 the French firm Kiple launched "Kip'Marine" priced at 210–440 FF and distributed through supermarkets, stationers, "tabacs," and variety stores.

In October 1984, Dr. Konstantin Theile, ETA marketing manager during the development of Swatch, left ETA to launch the new brand TIQ (Time Inter Corporation A.G.). This new nonplastic, leather-strapped, silent, and reparable waterproof quartz watch priced at 70–150 SF targeted an "optimistic, individualistic, fashion-conscious consumer" aged 25–35 but slightly more conservative than the Swatch consumer. Production costs were three times those of Swatch, and TIQ granted the usual margin to the trade. Distribution was through up-market department stores, established jewelers, and fashion boutiques. To quote Theile:

> Not everybody wants to wear a noisy irreparable plastic watch. It is frustrating to become attached to your watch only to find out that your model cannot be repaired and is no longer available.

By early 1985 the French firm Beuchat had introduced a series of metal and plastic strap watches with original and fun faces: a sports line illustrating 27 different sports, a "crazy" line including a face with hands turning counterclockwise, and a "corporations" line illustrating different professions. Distribution was the same as Swatch and prices were slightly higher. Beuchat's plans were to expand into promotional watches, starting with BMW, the German auto company. Under license from Club Méditerranée, the French firm Marckley CDH had launched waterproof metal and plastic quartz watches distributed worldwide through selective channels. Prices were also slightly higher than Swatch. Marckley did not invest in advertising for the "Club Med" watch but point-of-sales promotion included an aquarium display containing a submerged watch.

The American firm Le Jour started testing a $49 kaleidoscope color fashion watch called "Sixty" in 1986. Sales, mainly through department stores, were reportedly encouraging. In the spring of 1986 a Swiss entrepreneur launched "The Clip," a clip-on waterproof, shock-resistant, silent, and reparable quartz watch designed to be worn "anywhere except on the wrist" and sold through the same distribution channels as Swatch. Launched in Switzerland at 40 SF and 50 SF, The Clip was introduced in France, Spain, West Germany, and England in the summer and rolled out to the United States in the fall. E. A. Day, managing director of Louis Newmark, the Swatch distributor in the United Kingdom, commented:

> It is too early to discuss the future of The Clip. It does appear to sell well when promoted, but once the promotion ends, sales drop back dramatically.

In the summer of 1986, the Swiss firm SAMEL S.A. had introduced "Sweetzerland," a water-resistant quartz watch with a two-year battery that snapped in and out of interchangeable elastic terrycloth wristbands in different colors, priced at $40. Distribution was through jewelry stores, fashion boutiques, accessory and sports shops, perfumeries, and up-market department stores in France, West Germany, Austria, Benelux, Italy, Spain, and Portugal, as well as the United States through a California subsidiary.

Sekonda, an English firm importing watches from the USSR and Hong Kong, launched a new line of fashion watches in 1985, under the brand names "Spangles," "Phantom," and "Nostalgia." Prices ranged from L15 to L20. A mechanical watch named "Hotline," with style variations on the dial and strap, appeared in West Germany and Switzerland in 1986. It was explicitly aimed at preteenage groups and retailed mainly in department stores for 30 DM. Other European fashion watches in roughly the same price category as Swatch included Avia, Alfex, Orion, Zion, Video Clip, and Hip-Hop.

The Meeting

Chris Keigel checked the fashionable collection of Swatches on his wrist. It was time to make major decisions for the future of Swatch, and the meeting with Thomke, Marquardt, Imgruth, and Sprecher was approaching fast. He perused the sales figures in Exhibit 26. Keigel knew that Swatch guards and shields, the Parafernalia line, and the Coca-Cola watches yielded profit margins exceeding that of Swatch watches, whereas other items in the United States extended product line did not. Apparel profit margins had dropped and sales were lagging behind forecasts. Swatch management knew that the transport and other costs involved in importing this line to Europe might put prices out of line, especially since the clothing was designed specifically for the American market. He also knew that Max Imgruth was pushing for six

EXHIBIT 26

Swatch Sales, 1983–1986

	Swatch Watches (Thousands of Units or Swiss Francs)						January–August 1986	
	1983		1984		1985			
Country	Units	Francs	Units	Francs	Units	Francs	Units	Francs
World	1,319	27,901	4,496	114,057	10,168	284,832	8,321	209,954
United States	135	NA	1,242	42,475	4,659	167,562	3,817	102,824
Switzerland	NA	NA	1,032	23,451	924	21,707	595	14,585
France			399	8,910	756	17,710	667	14,824
England	NA	NA	455	7,140	762	14,288	24	9,694
West Germany	NA	NA	202	4,514	712	17,152	587	16,837
Japan					141	3,374	18	646

	Extended Product Line (Thousands of Units or Swiss Francs)					
	1984		1985		January–August 1986	
Item	Units	Francs	Units	Francs	Units	Francs
Swatch guards	7	10	3,617	4,280	2,637	3,721
Chums	18	26	104	226	24	6
Bags			224	2,497	134	1,042
Shields			141	2,418	87	1,381
Knives			263	1,236	4	20
Clocks			4	248	1	77
Umbrellas			181	1,606	109	359
Apparel			620	6,279	1,898	18,877
Parafernalia			387	1,175	440	464
Coca-Cola watches					194	3,392

Source: Company records (disguised data).

collection changes per year but remembered hearing Franz Sprecher advocate a more conservative approach:

> We can't just announce "Here comes our collection" to the trade. We are an accessory, we are not making fashion. What is most important is what the consumer will think. Are we really enough of a fashion product in the eyes of the consumer to make a planned line extension into fashion wear? If Calvin Klein, Ralph Lauren, or Benetton make a watch, that works because they are established fashion firms, but I have never seen it work the other way around. There is a lot of competition in the department stores, whole floors of T-shirts, and where is our expertise?

Zantac (A)

It was July 1989. Dr. Martin Preuveneers, International Marketing Director for Zantac,[1] Glaxo's £1.3 billion[2] antiulcer drug, the world's best-selling pharmaceutical product, was preparing recommendations in order to ensure that Zantac would reach the £2 billion sales goal that Glaxo's directors had set for June 1993. Zantac had achieved its leadership after an intense, five-year global battle against Tagamet, another antiulcer drug made by SmithKline Beecham and the industry's previous best-seller. The challenge now was to sustain Zantac's leadership. Losec, a new antiulcer product from the Swedish company Astra, first introduced in Sweden during 1988, looked like the most serious competitor. Dr. Preuveneers wanted to make sure that Losec would not be able to do to Zantac what Zantac had done to Tagamet.

COMPANY BACKGROUND

Zantac is a product of Glaxo Holdings plc, a U.K.-based company with headquarters in London. In 1989, Glaxo was the world's third-largest pharmaceutical company (Exhibit 1), and one of the most profitable (Exhibit 2). Zantac accounted for 50 percent of its sales.

Dr. Preuveneers was responsible for the analysis of all Zantac-relevant market and product information worldwide, and for the formulation of Glaxo marketing strategies for Zantac. Although he had no responsibility for results and no formal authority over any other department or country, his position at the interface between Glaxo's senior management, Glaxo's R&D company, and the operating companies allowed him to influence all decisions regarding Zantac.

Glaxo's operating companies decided how to position Zantac, when to introduce which line extensions, how much marketing resource to devote to Zantac versus other products, and the promotional mix. Marketing costs amounted on average to 25 percent of operating company sales. Of these, about 60 percent went on the sales force (medical representatives), 5 percent on sales force promotional material (for example, visual aids), 5 percent on advertising (medical journals, direct mail,

---

[1]Zantac's generic name was ranitidine hydrochloride ("ranitidine"). Although Glaxo's policy was to use the same brand name worldwide, due to conflicts with locally registered brand names and comarketing arrangements, ranitidine was also marketed under the following brand names: Antak (Brazil); Azantac and Raniplex (France); Zantic and Sostril (Germany); Ranidil, Trigger, and Ulcex (Italy); Zinetac (India); Azantac (Mexico); and Coralen, Quantor, Ranidin, and Ranix (Spain).

[2]During 1989, the average US $ / £ sterling exchange rate was $1.64 to £1.

This case was written by Reinhard Angelmar and Christian Pinson, Professors at INSEAD, with the assistance of Hugh Dixson, MD, MBA, and the cooperation of Glaxo Holdings plc. It is intended to be used as a basis for class discussion rather than to illustrate either effective or ineffective handling of an administrative situation. Although the case is based on a real situation, some names and figures have been disguised. The information in this case has been obtained from Glaxo, public sources, and industry interviews. Zantac is a registered trademark of Glaxo; Tagamet is a registered trademark of SmithKline Beecham; Losec is a registered trademark of Astra. Copyright © 1992 INSEAD, Fountainebleau, France.

EXHIBIT 1

1989 World Rankings

Ethical Pharmaceutical Products

1989 Rank	Product	Company	Indication	Share of All Eth. Pharmaceuticals %	Sales Growth[a] 1986–87 %	Sales Growth[a] 1987–88 %	Sales Growth[a] 1988–89 %
1	Zantac	Glaxo	Ulcer	1.8	35	27	21
2	Tagamet	SmithKline Beecham	Ulcer	0.9	5	2	−1
3	Renitec/Vasotec	Merck	Hypertension	0.9	210	78	31
4	Adalat	Bayer	Hypertension	0.8	31	20	11
5	Capoten	Bristol-Myers/Squibb	Hypertension	0.8	48	34	15
6	Voltaren	Ciba-Geigy	Inflammation	0.7	17	11	44
7	Tenormin	ICI	Hypertension	0.7	16	15	9
8	Naprosyn	Syntex	Inflammation	0.6	15	25	8
9	Cardizem	Marion Merrell Dow	Angina	0.5	66	53	30
10	Feldene	Pfizer	Inflammation	0.5	−2	13	3
			Industry Growth:		11	14	11

[a]Based on constant exchange rates.

Ethical Pharmaceutical Products

1989 Rank	Company	Home Country	Share of All Eth. Pharmaceuticals %	Sales Growth[a] 1986–87 %	Sales Growth[a] 1987–88 %	Sales Growth[a] 1988–89 %
1	Merck & Co.	U.S.	3.8	20	22	16
2	Bristol-Myers/Squibb	U.S.	3.5	18	21	14
3	Glaxo	U.K.	3.3	29	28	22
4	SmithKline Beecham	U.S./U.K.	3	11	8	4
5	Ciba-Geigy	Switzerland	2.9	11	9	13
6	Hoechst	Germany	2.7	3	11	8
7	American Home	U.S.	2.6	7	7	6
8	Bayer	Germany	2.3	13	18	23
9	Eli Lilly	U.S.	2.2	12	5	18
10	Sandoz	Switzerland	2.1	19	14	14
	Industry Growth:			11	14	11

[a]Based on constant exchange rates

Source: Glaxo.

EXHIBIT 2

Glaxo Holdings plc
Key Financial Figures (in £ millions) (The financial year ends on June 30)

	1989	1988	1987	1986	1985	1984	1983	1982	1981
Total group sales	2,570	2,059	1,741	1,429	1,186	915	779	663	537
Pharmaceuticals sales	2,557	2,027	1,698	1,361	1,060	779	615	504	414
Ranitidine sales[a]	1,291	989	829	606	432	248	97	37	—
Ranitidine's sales growth	31%	19%	37%	40%	74%	156%	162%	—	—
Ranitidine's share of group sales	50%	48%	48%	42%	36%	27%	12%	6%	—
After-tax profit	688	571	496	400	277	169	109	80	61
R&D Expenditure	323	230	149	113	93	77	60	50	40
Net assets	2,318	1,809	1,471	1,108	846	697	565	481	442
Shareholders' equity	2,291	1,784	1,450	1,090	827	675	542	428	382
Return on net assets[b]	44%	47%	52%	56%	49%	39%	35%	31%	22%
Return on shareholders' equity[c]	30%	32%	34%	37%	33%	25%	20%	19%	16%
Number of group employees	28,710	26,423	24,954	24,728	25,634	25,053	27,768	28,106	28,218

[a]This includes the sales of ranitidine to licensees and associates.
[b]Based on profit before taxes and interest (EBIT).
[c]Based on after-tax profit.

etc.), 5 percent on scientific congresses and educational events, 5 percent on clinical studies with local opinion leaders, 10 percent on product sampling, and the remaining 10 percent on the cost of the operating company marketing department.

INDUSTRY BACKGROUND

All new pharmaceutical products have to obtain approval from each country's health or regulatory authorities before market introduction. Manufacturers have to provide data from tests on animal and human subjects (clinical trials) that demonstrate the efficacy and safety of the product. The approval decision can take two to three years for products based on new chemical entities. The terms of approval are highly specific, and defined: (1) the indication(s) for which the drug is approved; (2) the presentation (for example, a 300-mg tablet); (3) the dosage (for example, once a day); and (4) the length of treatment (for example, four weeks). Any change in these specifications requires new data, and a new application and approval. Approval of changes generally takes less than one year.

Zantac was approved for distribution only in pharmacies and hospitals, and patients needed a doctor's prescription to obtain it. This differentiates so-called "ethical" products like Zantac from "over-the-counter" (OTC) or "self-medication" products like aspirin and antacids.

General practitioners (GPs) account for about 85 percent of all antiulcerant prescriptions. Specialists, especially those practicing in research hospitals, play an important role by carrying out clinical trials, and as opinion leaders. Manufacturers' medical representatives are the main source of information about drugs for many GPs:

> The representative helps me memorize the indications, the treatment regimen, and the interactions; that's what I need for prescribing. I am not competent enough to match the subtle differences between patients with the subtle differences between different products; I want the rep to explain this.
>
> (from a market research study)

Contact time per visit varies between 5 and 15 minutes, during which up to four products are promoted. Visits are carefully scripted, and presentations supported by visual aids, PC-presentations and the like. The danger is to appear somewhat mechanical and depersonalized:

> You always know what's in the visual aids: "our curve is higher than . . ."; it's written in large letters—you feel like they are teaching us to read. They are like trained monkeys: they recite their lesson, without comprehending it; when you ask a question about another indication for their product, they are lost.
>
> (from a market research study)

What the representatives say to doctors, as well as other aspects of drug promotion, are highly regulated. For example, representatives are obliged to provide doctors with a health-authority approved data sheet comprising the following information: (1) indication(s); (2) dosage and treatment length; (3) drug interactions, when present; (4) side effects, when present; and (5) warnings, when appropriate. If a company detects a violation by a competitor it can obtain a discontinuation of the promotion in question. Brand advertising of ethical drugs to the general public, for example via network TV, is generally forbidden.

In countries that operate a reimbursement system for prescription payments, Zantac is rated for at least 60 percent reimbursement. The U.S. market constitutes an exception, with more than 50 percent of the prescriptions being paid for directly by the patients. Few doctors have an accurate perception of drug costs, and high prices tend to be seen as indicating high quality. Due to spiraling health-care costs, price sensitivity is increasing, especially in the hospital market.

ULCER DISEASE

Ulcers are erosions in the mucous membrane, which lines the muscular walls of the gastrointestinal tract. Ulcers that appear in the upper and lower part of the stomach are called peptic ulcers. Reflux, another form of ulcer, occurs at the lower end of the esophagus as a result of backward flow, or reflux, of acid gastric juice from the stomach. Ulcers cause stomach pain attacks that last for a few hours and tend to occur daily for some days or weeks. They then disappear only to recur a few weeks or months later. Ulcer complications, like bleeding and stomach perforation, can be lethal. In the United Kingdom, as many people die from peptic ulcers every year as are killed on the roads.

Approximately 1–2 percent of the adult population in Western society has an ulcer in any one year, and about 10–15 percent of the population has an ulcer at some time during their lives. Factors thought to be important for developing an ulcer include smoking, and frequent use of aspirin and nonsteroidal anti-inflammatory drugs (NSAIDs), which are prescribed to relieve the symptoms of arthritic conditions. While ulcers occurs in men and women of all ages, its incidence is significantly higher in people over 60 years old.

Patients usually come to GPs when self-treatment of stomach pain fails. Because symptoms are not always clearcut, it is often difficult to distinguish ulcers from nonulcer stomach problems like dyspepsia and gastritis.[3] Accurate diagnosis requires referring the patient to a gastroenterologist for a test. Initial prescriptions of antiulcerants are usually made without testing. Fast pain relief is the most important treatment objective for doctors and patients, followed by rapid healing and product safety. The disappearance of pain does not guarantee that the ulcer is actually healed. This poses "compliance" problems, since some patients stop treatment as soon as the pain disappears. Most doctors are now requesting tests after treatment.

THE H2-BLOCKER (H2-ANTAGONIST) REVOLUTION IN ULCER TREATMENT

Each day, the body produces one to two liters of gastric juice, with acid peaks occurring around meal times and in the early morning hours. Gastric juice plays a part in the digestive process, kills microorganisms and helps solubilize certain minerals, especially iron and calcium. But excessive gastric acidity has traditionally been seen as the major direct cause of ulcers.

Prior to the introduction of Tagamet, antacids such as Tums and Maalox were the main nonsurgical ulcer treatment. Antacids neutralize acid already in the stomach and provide short-term pain relief but do not accelerate healing, unless very large and frequent doses are used. The only really effective treatment for serious ulcer disease at the time was surgery. While offering a significant reduction in ulcer recurrence (only 10–20 percent over a five-year period), surgery was unpleasant, costly, and always involved some risk.

Tagamet, the generic name of which was cimetidine, was the first of a new class of antiulcerants called H2-blockers or H2-antagonists. Instead of merely neutralizing already existing acids, H2-blockers reduce the level of acid production (see Exhibit 3). They do this by blocking the histamine (H2) receptor, which is an important controller of gastric acid production. Tagamet was the brainchild of Dr. James Black, working in the British laboratories of the U.S.-based pharmaceutical company Smith, Kline and French (SmithKline). Dr. Black was subsequently awarded the Nobel Prize in Medicine for his discovery of Tagamet and another breakthrough drug.

In November 1976, Tagamet was launched first in the United Kingdom, followed rapidly by launches in other countries, including the United States, where the regulatory authority rated it a "major therapeutic gain," an accolade given to a mere 3 percent of new drugs. Tagamet was priced far above any other frequently prescribed drug. Its 1982 introduction in Japan completed Tagamet's worldwide launch.

TAGAMET AND SMITHKLINE IN 1981

Tagamet's success exceeded SmithKline's wildest dreams. By 1981, Tagamet had not only become the favored medical ulcer treatment, but had also put the stomach surgeons out of business. The total market for antiulcerants exploded from £100 million in 1976 to £600 million in 1981, thereby making Tagamet the world's best-selling

---

[3]Dyspepsia refers to a diverse group of symptoms, for example, abdominal pain, heartburn, flatulence, which patients may have whether or not an ulcer is present; gastritis refers to an acute or chronic inflammation of the stomach.

EXHIBIT 3

How Antiulcerant Products Work

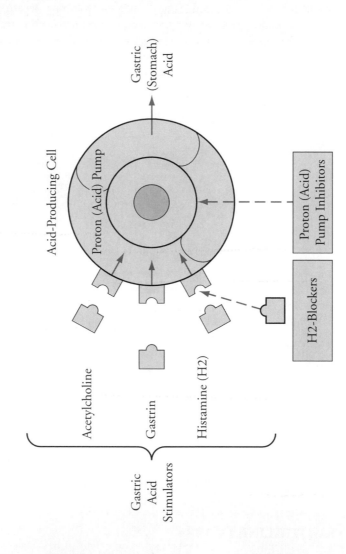

Gastric
(Stomach)
Acid

Acid-Producing Cell

Proton (Acid) Pump

Proton (Acid)
Pump Inhibitors

H2-Blockers

Acetylcholine

Gastrin

Histamine (H2)

Gastric
Acid
Stimulators

ethical pharmaceutical product, sold exclusively by SmithKline's own, fast-growing country organizations. Thanks to Tagamet, SmithKline had become a darling of Wall Street, which had coined a new word: "Tagamania."

To ensure the company's future beyond Tagamet, SmithKline targeted other indication areas for similar breakthroughs, and acquired companies outside pharmaceuticals. But Tagamet still accounted for about 65 percent of SmithKline's 1981 $1.2 billion ethical pharmaceutical sales, 39 percent of the corporation's $2 billion sales, and an estimated 60 percent of its $370 million corporate net profits.[4]

Tagamet came mainly in the form of pale green tablets, which patients were to take four times per day: three times a day with meals, and again at bedtime. Although SmithKline had obtained U.K. approval for a simpler twice-daily regimen, it did not actively promote it.

Tagamet produced pain relief after several days of treatment. Its healing rate was 80 percent (that is, 80 percent of the patients entering treatment were healed) after six weeks of treatment. Ulcers recurred in two-thirds of the healed patients within a year. SmithKline had obtained approval for long-term maintenance treatment, but did not strongly promote this concept.

The data sheets mentioned the possibility of side effects like gynaecomastia (tenderness and swelling of the breasts in males), reversible liver damage, and mental confusion in the elderly and very ill, as well as possible interactions with other drugs such as the tranquilizer Valium. Researchers had discovered these side effects and drug interactions, the incidence of which was estimated at 1 percent of the treated persons, only after several years of widespread use of Tagamet—by 1981, over 11 million patients around the world had been treated with Tagamet. But most practitioners had never encountered these side effects, and those who had, often attributed them to other factors. Tagamet's safety was generally seen as very high, as evidenced by the lack of serious consequences in cases of extreme overdose, and by several ongoing long-term studies in Europe and the United States. Whether Tagamet produced male sexual dysfunctions like impotence and reduced sperm production was the subject of as yet inconclusive debate among researchers.

Physicians prescribed Tagamet for a myriad of digestive disorders, turning it into "the ultimate cure for belly-ache." Nonapproved uses added up to an estimated 30 percent of Tagamet's sales. Patients were so convinced of its superiority that doctors felt they had little choice but to prescribe Tagamet.

DEVELOPMENT OF ZANTAC

When Glaxo's researchers learned of Dr. Black's breakthrough in 1972, they quickly redirected their own antiulcer project. The new objective was to improve on Tagamet. They discovered that a part of the molecule, previously regarded as vital to Tagamet's effectiveness, could be replaced with different chemical structures. Exploration of an alternative structure, thought to be more selective in its action, hence producing fewer side effects, resulted in the chemical synthesis of ranitidine in August 1976. In October 1981, Zantac was ready for launch.

---

[4]During 1981, the average US $ / £ sterling exchange rate was $ 2 to £ 1.

To achieve this unusual speed, Glaxo had to abandon its traditional sequential development approach in favor of a parallel, simultaneous process:

- A multi-million-pound investment in production facilities was made before the animal trials were finished, that is, before Zantac's safety was established.

- Clinical trials were started in November 1978 in over 20 countries. Previously, trials had commenced in the United Kingdom first, and then started gradually in other countries.

- Time-saving considerations entered all decisions, including the choice of tablet color: "We wanted to avoid any registration problems as a result of the color we chose. After all, different colors have different significance in different markets. We went for white to play it safe," explained one member of the development team.

- In March 1981, the approval package was put together, with 26 countries serviced within two months.

The U.K. and Italian health authorities happened to be the first ones to approve Zantac for acute and maintenance treatment of peptic ulcers and reflux. No clinically significant side effects and drug interactions were noted (see Exhibit 4).

SmithKline was not alarmed by Zantac ("How can you improve on Tagamet?" was its official position), nor was it impressed by Glaxo. Industry analysts shared this attitude, citing the following arguments:

"The first major drugs in new therapeutic classes normally do far better than newer products unless the therapeutic benefits of the follower are very noteworthy."

"Tagamet's known side effects are not major deterrents to prescribing so that, even if Zantac's side effect profile proves to be lower, doctors may well prefer to prescribe a product perceived as having a longer track record of large-scale usage."

"Tagamet's economies of scale will be so enormous by the time Zantac is launched that Zantac may not be able to be marketed at a more competitive price."

"About 40% of Tagamet's current sales arise in the USA, where Glaxo representation is considerably lower than that of SmithKline."

"On the most optimistic realistic assumption . . . we would be most surprised if Zantac's eventual sales ever exceeded £100m worldwide."

(from an industry analysis; 1980)

KEY DECISIONS FOR ZANTAC

Glaxo UK, the U.K. operating company, recommended that Zantac be priced 10 percent below Tagamet's daily treatment cost, to allow Zantac to capture 10 percent of the U.K. antiulcerant market. The recommendation was based on a considerable amount of market research that showed that doctors saw Zantac basically as a "me-too" product with no significant medical benefits compared to Tagamet.

EXHIBIT   4

Main Characteristics of Tagamet and Zantac, 1981

	Tagamet (cimetidine)	Zantac (ranitidine hydrochloride)
Product and Indications		
Presentations	Pale green tablets: 200mg, 300mg, 400mg Ampoule for injection	White tablet: 150mg Ampoule for injection
Relative potency, active substance	1	5
Approved main indications	Acute and maintenance treatment of peptic ulcers; acute treatment of reflux	Acute and maintenance treatment of peptic ulcers; acute treatment of reflux
Acute Treatment (Peptic ulcer)		
Total daily dosage	1000mg 1200mg (North America)	300mg
Number of administrations per day	4 (3 × 200mg with meals plus 400mg at night) (in North America: 4 × 300mg) 2 (2 × 400mg)	2 (2 × 150mg)
Approved treatment length	4 to 6 weeks	4 weeks
Maintenance Treatment (Peptic Ulcer)		
Number of tablets per day	1 or 2 × 400mg	1 × 150mg at night
Other Aspects		
Efficacy	80% of patients healed after 6 weeks	80% of patients healed after 4 weeks
Side effects	Breast swelling in males (gynaecomastia) Reversible liver damage Mental confusion in the elderly and very ill	No serious side effects have been reported
Drug interactions (products the effect of which is influenced by the antiulcerant):	Anti-coagulants of valium	No clinically significant interactions have been reported
Cautions:	Reduced dosage in patients with impaired kidney function	Examine patients with severe kidney problems

Source: Medical literature and industry sources.

Although in theory Glaxo UK was just one of many subsidiaries, the tradition of U.K.-led product development and launch had always given the U.K. operating company a strong influence on global marketing policy. With a 27 percent share of Glaxo's total sales, the United Kingdom was also by far the most important market for Glaxo. Glaxo's international coverage reflected Britain's colonial heritage. For example, Glaxo's sales were larger in Nigeria than in the United States.

For Glaxo's senior management, the Zantac situation evoked memories of Ventolin, an asthma drug launched by Glaxo some years earlier. Although Ventolin became a rather successful product, one senior executive expressed Glaxo's hindsight regret:

> With proper commercial exploitation Ventolin could have become one of the world's largest pharmaceutical products. First, Ventolin was underpriced. We simply never appreciated how different it was from existing products. We just priced it at their levels. Second, we didn't have sufficient geographical presence.

Glaxo's track record of outstanding research but poor marketing had earned it a reputation as "the only university quoted on the Stock Exchange." But Sir Paul Girolami, Glaxo's chief executive, was determined that Glaxo would never again fail on product exploitation. Born in Venice, Italy, educated in Britain, and qualified as a chartered accountant, Sir Paul had entered Glaxo in 1965 as a financial controller before becoming its financial director in 1976 and chief executive in 1980.

In a fiery meeting of senior executives, Sir Paul ignored the carefully compiled market research on Zantac and, despite the perception that Tagamet was already priced as high as the market would bear, ordered that Zantac be launched at a significant premium over Tagamet. Sir Paul reasoned that if Glaxo's own marketing organization did not recognize the superiority of its new drug by charging a substantial premium, then no one else would. To ensure that Zantac would not suffer from Glaxo's weak position in the major countries, Sir Paul decided to enter marketing alliances with other pharmaceutical companies wherever necessary.

While these decisions delighted Glaxo's researchers, they provoked little enthusiasm among the operating companies. Many were skeptical and waited to see the results from the first countries where Zantac was about to be launched, namely the United Kingdom and Italy.

THE U.K. LAUNCH OF ZANTAC

Tagamet's position in the United Kingdom, where it commanded a 90 percent market share, was extremely strong. The discovery and development of this breakthrough drug in Britain were the pride of the British medical community, and its extensive patient base had generated a flood of publications testifying to the drug's effectiveness and safety. These were also the dominant themes in SmithKline's advertising (Exhibit 5).

Several months prior to Zantac's launch, SmithKline's 75-member sales force, about the same size as Glaxo UK's, began to warn doctors about the arrival of this new drug, which they claimed had no advantages over Tagamet and a much shorter safety record. This created significant awareness (31 percent unaided awareness among GPs) and interest in Zantac prior to its launch. SmithKline also started to promote its twice-daily regimen in order to preempt Zantac. The difference between the newly promoted twice-daily dosage (800 mg) and the habitual four-times-a-day dosage (1,000 mg), plus the yet different U.S. dosage (1,200 mg), created uncertainty and doubts in doctors' minds.

Glaxo UK enjoyed an above-average reputation for research, effective products, and the quality of its medical information. They were able to obtain health authority agreement for a price of £0.91 for a day's treatment, compared to £0.52 for Tagamet. This resulted in a 17 percent price premium for the approved four-week treatment cycle over Tagamet's habitual six-week treatment cycle. In fact, most doctors ended up prescribing Zantac for the habitual six weeks.

For Zantac's launch in October 1981, Glaxo hosted a conference of gastroenterologists from around the world. Senior Glaxo R&D managers were very active, giving interviews to the business press and other media. A sample of press echoes follows: "Super-pill from Glaxo" (*Newcastle Evening Chronicle*, October 15); "Drug cuts out sex problems" (*Darlington Evening Despatch*, October 15); "A new anti-ulcer drug which does not affect people's sex lives, was launched in Britain today by Glaxo" (*Oxford Mail*, October 14).

EXHIBIT 5

Tagamet: Selected U.K. Campaigns Prior to Zantac's Launch, 1977–1981

Tagamet

(cimetidine, SK&F)

The H₂ receptor antagonist
A British Discovery

A real breakthrough

Due to its dramatic reduction of gastric acid secretion Tagamet has achieved quite remarkable results in peptic ulcers and reflux oesophagitis.

Complete healing of duodenal and gastric ulcers (proven endoscopically) is seen in most patients after 4 weeks' treatment.

Complete healing or marked improvement of reflux oesophagitis has frequently been obtained within 6 weeks.

Early symptomatic relief is normally achieved in patients receiving Tagamet treatment.

Furthermore, Tagamet is well tolerated with minimal side effects which, together with its convenient dosage, makes Tagamet well suited to everyday treatment.

Tagamet—for patients with suspected or confirmed benign gastric or duodenal ulcer or reflux oesophagitis, and for patients in whom the reduction of acid secretion is likely to be beneficial.

The discovery

Until recently, one aspect of gastric physiology remained paradoxical—histamine was known to be a potent stimulant of gastric acid, yet conventional antihistamines were totally inactive in this area. Confronted by this apparent anomaly investigators began to suspect that there might in fact be two types of receptor site for histamine—one mainly

for allergic reactions (H₁) and the second for gastric acid secretion (H₂).

In 1964, the SK&F research team set out to find a new class of therapeutic agent by chemical modification of the histamine molecule. They were seeking an agent capable of blocking the action of histamine at the H₂ receptor site, just as conventional antihistamines do at the H₁ site. After 12 years of extensive research, this search has resulted in the development of Tagamet the H₂ receptor antagonist, with the fundamental property of controlling gastric acid secretion.

A real breakthrough in the medical treatment of peptic ulcers and reflux oesophagitis

Update (UK), March 1977

'Tagamet'
The long and the short of it

Tagamet
cimetidine

Unique control of gastric acid secretion

World Medicine (UK), May 5, 1979

A Mark of Recognition

1978

Two years ago, Smith Kline and French Research Institute received the Queen's Award for Technological Achievement resulting from H₂ receptor antagonist research and the development of cimetidine.

Since it became generally available over three years ago, 'Tagamet', by its unique action in reducing gastric acid, has revolutionised the treatment of disorders such as duodenal ulcer, benign

gastric ulcer and reflux oesophagitis, where acid plays a part.

For many patients it has brought a new standard of pain relief and healing. In the United Kingdom alone 'Tagamet' has been prescribed for an estimated one million patients.

Tagamet
cimetidine

SK&F

Doctor (UK), February 21, 1980

Vital statistics

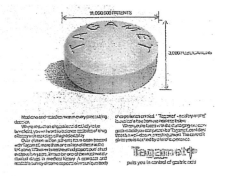

Tagamet
puts you in control of gastric acid

SK&F

GP (General Practitioner), UK, May 15, 1981

The launch campaign positioned Zantac as a new, advanced H2-blocker that was "fast, simple and specific" (Exhibit 6), which doctors interpreted to mean "faster, simpler, and safer" than Tagamet. Smith Kline responded by emphasizing its "tried and trusted" reputation and extensive safety record (Exhibit 7).

ZANTAC'S LAUNCH IN ITALY

Tagamet, which was promoted by SmithKline's 95 medical representatives, had a 39 percent share of the Italian antiulcerant market. Because of the lack of effective patent protection in Italy, ten copies of Tagamet had another 16 percent of the market.

To preempt copiers and increase promotional presence, it was decided to enter a comarketing agreement with the Italian company Menarini. Glaxo sold ranitidine to Menarini, whose 220 representatives promoted it under the brand name Ranidil. In parallel, Glaxo Italy's 250 representatives promoted ranitidine under the brand name Zantac. Both brands were priced identically, at more than twice Tagamet's daily treatment cost.

Zantac was launched in October 1981, at about the same time as in the United Kingdom. Each doctor was exposed every two to three weeks to Glaxo's ranitidine, compared to every three months for SmithKline's Tagamet. Glaxo Italy managed to involve Italian opinion leaders, and carried out extensive sampling and advertising (see Exhibit 8).

Zantac and Ranidil took off at an incredible speed, capturing 80 percent of the Italian H2-blocker market one year after the launch, with Zantac's share slightly exceeding that of Ranidil. Meanwhile, Glaxo UK obtained a 23 percent share for Zantac (see Exhibit 9). The speed with which Tagamet was blown out of the market in Italy silenced the skeptics inside Glaxo.

ZANTAC'S WORLDWIDE LAUNCH

In Germany, ranitidine was launched in October 1982 by Glaxo GmbH in parallel with a company set up jointly with the German company E. Merck, by a total sales force of 160, as against 100 for SmithKline. The two ranitidine brands, Zantic and Sostril, were priced at a 60 percent price premium (daily treatment cost) over Tagamet, and made good inroads against Tagamet (Exhibit 9).

News from Europe slowly made its way to the SmithKline organization in the United States, where Tagamet held a 90 percent share. The news tended to emphasize Tagamet's continued sales progression in Europe, and its good showing in the United Kingdom. While SmithKline increased its U.S. sales force from 725 to 850, Glaxo concluded a copromotion agreement with Roche Inc., under which the latter's 700 representatives and Glaxo Inc.'s 450 representatives were to launch the same brand, namely, Zantac.[5] A growing number of articles talked about this forthcoming new antiulcerant product.[6]

---

[5]According to industry sources, the arrangement was as follows: (1) Each year all sales up to an agreed level went to Glaxo, irrespective of which company made the sales; (2) sales above this level were split between Glaxo and Roche, with Roche having the larger share; (3) the agreed level for Glaxo's "front sales cut" increased each year.

[6]Broad coverage was given to a study in which impotence and breast swelling in 9 out of 19 men treated with Tagamet disappeared when these patients were subsequently given Zantac. Experts were quick to point out that all of the patients in the study were suffering from a rare gastric disease and given nearly four times the recommended dose of Tagamet. Nevertheless, a warning that high Tagamet doses could cause reversible impotence in men was added to Tagamet's data sheet.

EXHIBIT 6

Zantac: U.K. Launch Campaign, 1982

Zantac is target specific

No interference with major body systems

CNS function[1,2]

Zantac does not cross the blood-brain barrier in significant amounts, thus it is most unlikely to cause or exacerbate confusion or dizziness in elderly patients.

NEW

Endocrine function[3,4]

No anti-androgenic effects have been detected: hence gynaecomastia and loss of libido cannot be anticipated.

Liver enzyme function[5]

Zantac has not been shown to provoke interactions with other drugs, including those metabolised by the P450 mixed function oxygenase enzyme system in the liver. There are no known contra-indications to the use of Zantac.

The fast, simple and specific way to promote peptic ulcer healing

The benefits of highly specific H₂ blockade

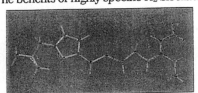

80% ulcers healed in one month[1] Rapid pain relief, rapid healing of the ulcer.

No dosage simpler in peptic ulcer treatment
One tablet b.d. in the healing phase.
One tablet daily in maintenance.
No need to link medication with mealtimes.

The fast, simple and specific way to promote peptic ulcer healing

Glaxo

NEW Zantac

A British advance from Glaxo

The benefits of highly specific H₂ blockade

EXHIBIT 7

Tagamet: Selected Campaigns Following Zantac's Launch, United Kingdom, 1981–1983

GP(UK), October 30, 1981   GP (UK), December 11, 1981

GP (UK), November 4, 1983

EXHIBIT 8

Zantac: Selected Launch Campaigns Outside the United Kingdom, 1981–1983

il nuovo trattamento dell'ulcera peptica

dalle ricerche Glaxo

Italy (1981-82)

Italy (1981-82)

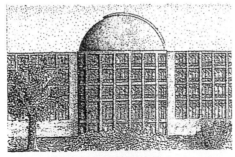

"Universität mit Börsennotierung"

So wird Glaxo wegen seines hohen Forschungspotentials in Finanzkreisen bezeichnet.

Zu Recht, denn therapiebestimmende Substanzen aus der Glaxo-Forschung haben weltweit neue Maßstäbe gesetzt. Engagement und Erfolg in Forschung und Entwicklung medizinischer Innovationen kennzeichnen die Bedeutung von Glaxo als pharmazeutisches Unternehmen.

Glaxo
Glaxo Pharmazeutika GmbH · 2060 Bad Oldesloe

Germany (1982)

Germany (1982)

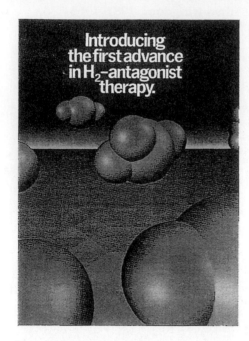

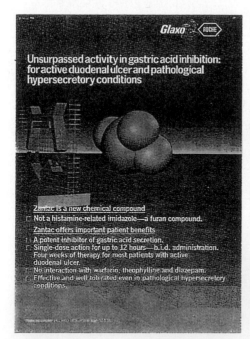

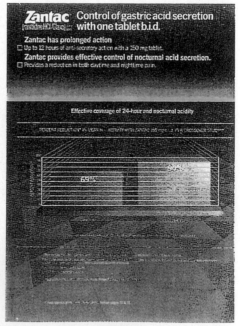

* 2 pages with medical prescribing information not shown here

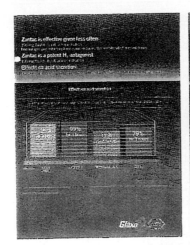

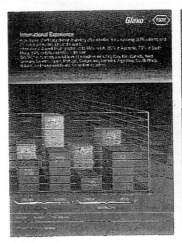

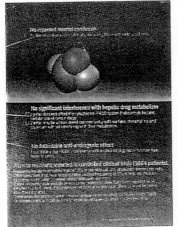

EXHIBIT 9

Zantac Penetration of H2-Blocker Market in Five Major Countries

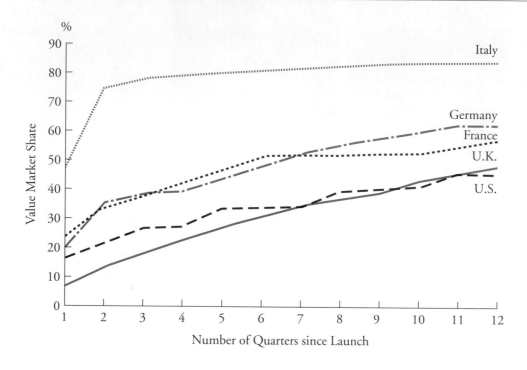

Source: Glaxo.

When the U.S. regulatory authority finally approved Zantac, it gave it a "C" rating, indicating that it made "little or no" contribution to existing drug therapies. Zantac was launched in the United States in June 1983, at a 20 percent price premium (daily treatment cost) over Tagamet. It was positioned as a more potent, more convenient, and safer product (see Exhibit 8). SmithKline responded by emphasizing Tagamet's safety: "Tagamet's side effects are generally low in incidence, well defined, mild in nature, and reversible. Zantac is a new drug in the U.S. and it hasn't been on the market that long. Its clinical profile is still evolving," argued Tagamet's product director at the time of Zantac's U.S. launch. Medical experts generally agreed with SmithKline. To counter Zantac's twice-a-day convenience argument, SmithKline presented a study showing no difference in compliance among patients taking tablets twice or four times a day. Even so, SmithKline applied to the FDA for approval of a twice-a-day dosage for Tagamet. In mid-1984, one year after its introduction, Zantac obtained 28 percent of the US H2-blocker market.

In order to increase barriers for Zantac's anticipated launch in France, SmithKline signed a comarketing agreement with the French company Pharmuka, which resulted in the launch of a second cimetidine brand (Edalène), shortly before Zantac's entry in November 1984. Glaxo concluded a comarketing agreement with the French company Fournier. They launched Zantac and Raniplex at a 50 percent price premium (daily treatment cost) over cimetidine. Their combined sales forces outnumbered the cimetidine sales forces by 70 percent, partly because Glaxo France doubled its own sales force by hiring a "mercenary" freelance sales force. French doctors were generally aware that the four H2-blocker brands in reality represented only two different products. They accepted the two ranitidine brands, choosing between them on the basis of chance ("Representative X was the first to visit me"), nationality ("I prefer to prescribe the French ranitidine"), merit ("Glaxo invented it; I favor the firm which has done the research"), or like/dislike for a specific representative. But the new cimetidine brand Edalène was seen as a mere commercial manipulation and never took off:

> I would be deceiving patients if I told them that Edalène is a new product. It isn't. I've been prescribing Tagamet for years. One needs a reason for switching, and I don't see any.
>
> (from a market research study)

With Zantac's launch in Japan in November 1984, in cooperation with the Japanese company Sankyo, Glaxo virtually completed Zantac's worldwide launch in a record three years.

ZANTAC'S POSTLAUNCH MOVES

Postlaunch clinical comparisons showed that the ulcer healing rate of Zantac (twice daily) was 6 percent higher than that of Tagamet (four times daily). Comparison of the twice-daily regimens resulted in a still greater 12 percent superiority for Zantac. Two studies published in leading U.S. and U.K. medical journals in 1984 and 1985 showed that the annual relapse rate during maintenance treatment, that is, the percentage of healed patients who experienced an ulcer recurrence during the following year despite continuous treatment, was about twice as high for Tagamet (30 percent) as with Zantac (12–15 percent). Glaxo used these two studies throughout the world as proof of Zantac's superior effectiveness, particularly in maintenance,[7] and set out to persuade doctors that ulcers needed long term maintenance treatment (see Exhibit 10). They wanted to change the way doctors thought about and treated ulcers: from an acute, curable disease to a chronic, lifelong illness requiring treatment forever.

Glaxo also pioneered a further simplification of the dosage regimen, from twice daily to once-a-day at bedtime. This was based on the discovery that nighttime reduction of acidity mattered most. The once-a-day regimen, which initially required patients to take two 150-mg tablets at the same time, became even simpler when Glaxo launched a once-a-day 300-mg tablet.

SmithKline followed with its own once-a-day 800-mg tablet. They reduced Tagamet's price and advertised its price advantage, a move unheard of for a branded ethical pharmaceutical manufacturer. SmithKline also obtained official approval to promote Tagamet for nonulcer dyspepsia (see Exhibit 11).

---

[7]It was later realized that the differences in effectiveness resulted probably from the differences in potency between the recommended dosage regimens. Because Zantac was five times more potent than Tagamet, the equivalent Tagamet dosage for acute treatment should have been 1,500 mg (vs. 800 mg for the actually recommended twice-daily regimen), and for maintenance treatment it should have been 750 mg (vs. the approved 400 mg).

EXHIBIT 10

Zantac: Example of Maintenance Campaign (Visual Aid), United Kingdom, 1984

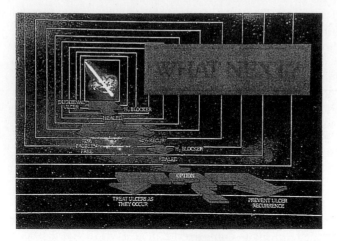

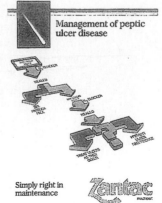

Management of peptic
ulcer disease

Simply right in
maintenance

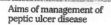

Aims of management of
peptic ulcer disease

⊚ Maintain patient symptom free

⊚ Maintain patient ulcer free

⊚ Incur no new problems

⊚ Maintain acceptable lifestyle

Simply right in
maintenance

Zantac. Simple dosage
in maintenance

150mg at night

TO HELP PREVENT RELAPSE

and in treatment.

150mg b.d.

ON TWO TABLETS AT BEDTIME
FOR DUODENAL ULCER

FOR FOUR WEEKS

Maintenance with confidence.
Treatment with simplicity.

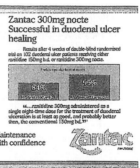

Zantac 300mg nocte
Successful in duodenal ulcer
healing

Results after 4 weeks of double-blind randomised
trial on 102 duodenal ulcer patients receiving either
ranitidine 150mg b.d. or ranitidine 300mg nocte.

84% 95%

"...ranitidine 300mg administered as a
single night-time dose for the treatment of duodenal
ulceration is at least as good, and probably better
than, the conventional 150mg b.d."

Maintenance
with confidence

Zantac. Proven superiority
in the prevention of
duodenal ulcer relapse

Two clinical trials using identical randomised, double-blind
protocols were carried out, using endoscopic examinations every
4 months to determine relapse status in the U.K. and U.S.

	Ranitidine 150mg at night	Cimetidine 400mg at night
U.S. trial	15%	29% (p <0.05)
U.K. trial	12%	30% (p <0.05)

2 major multicentre trials
involving 579 patients with
recently healed duodenal
ulcers

"...the use of ranitidine
[Zantac] 150mg at night
represents a true
therapeutic gain in the area
of duodenal ulcer
prophylaxis."

Significantly fewer relapses on Zantac
than with cimetidine.

Maintenance
with confidence

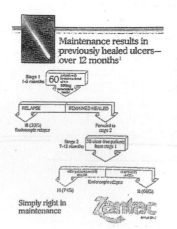

Maintenance results in
previously healed ulcers—
over 12 months[1]

Stage 1
1–6 months 60

RELAPSE   REMAINED HEALED

18 (30%)
Endoscopic relapse

Forward to
stage 2

Stage 2
7–12 months 36 ulcer-free patients
from stage 1

Endoscopic relapse

14 (7.1%)   14 (66%)

Simply right in
maintenance

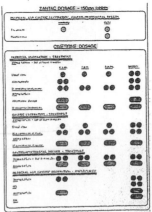

ZANTAC DOSAGE – 150mg tablets

EXHIBIT 11

Tagamet: Selected Promotional Material, United Kingdom, 1985

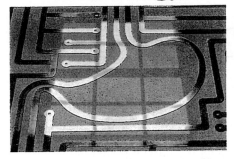

Gastro-technology

Tagamet
cimetidine

the leading H₂ antagonist*

96% of duodenal ulcers healed...

In a large multicentre study[1] involving
547 patients, 'Tagamet' 800 mg given at
bedtime completely healed 79% of
duodenal ulcers in 4 weeks,
and 96% in 8 weeks.

Tagamet
cimetidine

£10 less expensive than ranitidine...

for the recommended duodenal ulcer healing course.

A 28-day calendar pack of 'Tagamet'
800 mg tablets is £10.82 less expensive
than a 30-day treatment pack of
ranitidine. This represents a 65%
difference based upon original pack
prices taken from 'Mims', April 1985.

The price of the 'Tagamet' 800 mg tablet
calendar pack has since been reduced.

Tagamet
cimetidine

The only H₂ antagonist recommended for persistent acid-related dyspepsia...

'Tagamet' is recommended for
persistent acid-related dyspepsia with
or without peptic ulceration.

For full information see 'Tagamet'
data sheet.

GP (UK), May 24, 1985

Zantac, however, was first to obtain U.S. approval for reflux during 1986, a memorable year for Glaxo. Zantac overtook Tagamet in terms of global sales, thus becoming the biggest pharmaceutical product worldwide and the first to ever hit the $1 billion sales landmark. This earned Zantac an entry to the *Guiness Book of World Records*. But competition was heating up.

CHALLENGES FROM OTHER H2-BLOCKERS

July 1986 saw the launch of a third H2-blocker, whose generic name was famotidine. Famotidine was developed and first launched in Japan by the Japanese company Yamanouchi. In most other countries it was marketed by the U.S.-based Merck and Co, the world's largest pharmaceutical company, under the brand name Pepcid[8] at a price about 10 percent below Zantac. Merck's promotional support appeared to be limited, due to internal competition with other higher-margin and more exciting products. Famotidine was seven to eight times more potent than Zantac but appeared to have no other significant differentiating feature vis-à-vis Zantac. Its worldwide launch was virtually completed in early 1989, and its global market share was 12 percent.

The U.S.-based company Eli Lilly launched another H2-blocker under the brand name Axid,[9] first in the United Kingdom in mid-1987, and subsequently in other major markets. Axid was similar to Zantac and priced about 10 percent below. Like Zantac and Famotidine, it was rated as making "little or no" contribution to existing drug therapies by the U.S. regulatory authority. Axid's 1989 global market share was 2 percent.

SmithKline maintained its price aggressiveness, and the expiration of Tagamet's patents during 1992 was expected to focus attention even more on price.[10] They further extended Tagamet's indications and stepped up line extensions, offering the greatest variety of presentations among all H2-blockers. Most of these achieved only minute market shares, while some succeeded but might have hurt Tagamet's image:

> The launch of Tagamet's 200 mg effervescent tablet put Tagamet in the same category as antacids. In some countries, Tagamet has become the Alka-Seltzer of the rich.

> (a Glaxo manager)

A 1988 U.S. copromotion agreement with DuPont led to a 10 percent increase in Tagamet's U.S. sales force effort. SmithKline's mid-1989 merger with the U.K.-based pharmaceuticals company Beecham, resulting in a new company called SmithKline Beecham, was also expected to strengthen Tagamet.

The four main H2-blockers (Zantac, Tagamet, Pepcid, and Axid) accounted for 75 percent of global 1989 antiulcerant sales (Exhibit 12). The remaining 25 percent were shared by various products such as sucralfate (strong in the United States under the name of "Carafate" and in France as "Ulcar"), seaweed extracts (Japan), and by niche products like the recently launched Cytotec from the U.S. company Searle, which was targeted mainly at NSAID-induced ulcers.

---

[8]Other major brand names for famotidine were Pepdine (France), Ganor and Pepdul (Germany), and Gaster (Japan).

[9]Other major brand names for this product were Nizax (Italy, Denmark), Cronizat and Zanizal (Italy), Nizaxid (France), Calmaxid (Switzerland), and Naxidine (Netherlands).

[10]Zantac's patents would be challenged in 1995, but Glaxo was confident of being able to maintain patent protection for Zantac until 2002.

EXHIBIT 12

Worldwide Antiulcerant Market Size and Shares, 1981–1989

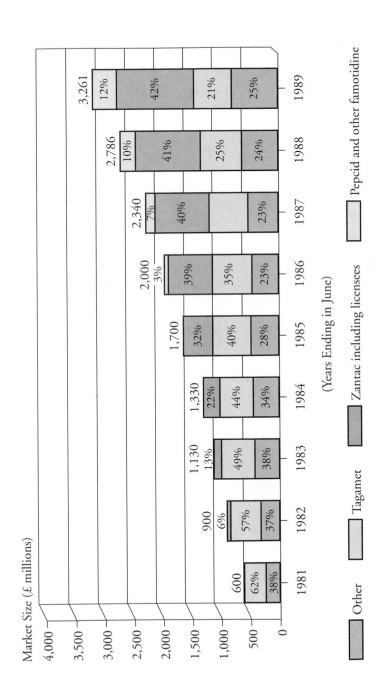

Market Size (£ millions)

(Years Ending in June)

Other   Tagamet   Zantac including licensees   Pepcid and other famotidine

Source. Glaxo.

ZANTAC IN 1989

Zantac's global share was 42 percent, with country shares varying significantly (Exhibit 13). Glaxo maintained a strong sales force presence (Exhibit 14). One-third of all Glaxo visits were exclusively devoted to Zantac. During multiproduct visits, Zantac was usually promoted in first position. Glaxo rarely promoted more than two products during a visit and preferred to multiply its sales forces. In some countries, each GP was visited by three different Glaxo representatives, each belonging to one of three separate Glaxo GP sales forces with their own management. Each sales force emphasized a different aspect of Zantac: One focused on Zantac's use in acute peptic ulcer, the second on maintenance treatment, while the third talked about reflux. Hospitals were visited by dedicated hospital sales forces.

Different visual aids were developed for each sales force. As other companies emulated Glaxo's sales force and brand multiplication strategies, some doctors developed strong negative reactions. Signs saying "Co-marketers keep out" appeared on some doctors' doors!

To monitor sales force call frequency, behavior during the visit, and sales force communication effectiveness, a representative sample of doctors was surveyed every one to two weeks and asked to recall visits, brand names, key messages, and other aspects of the visits (for example, samples and promotional material left behind). To monitor the impact on sales, Glaxo tracked the relation between sales force share and market share (Exhibit 15).

Glaxo also carefully evaluated the effectiveness of its advertising (see Exhibits 16 to 18 for examples of advertising research in Germany, the United Kingdom, and the United States, respectively).

ASTRA'S LOSEC: A NEW TYPE OF ANTIULCERANT

In March 1988, the Swedish company Astra launched Losec,[11] the generic name of which was omeprazole, in Sweden. Losec presented itself in pink/brown gelatine capsules containing coated 20-mg granules to be taken once a day before breakfast. Astra was the largest northern European pharmaceutical company with 1988 sales of 6.3 billion krona (U.S. $1 billion) and net profits of 682 million krona. Northern Europe accounted for 27 percent of Astra's sales, the United States and Japan each for 10 percent, and Italy for 1 percent. Prior to Losec, Astra's small gastrointestinal business (1.4 percent of 1987 sales) consisted mainly of antacids.

Losec represented a new class of drugs called proton (acid) pump inhibitors. Proton pump inhibitors follow the same general treatment strategy as H2-blockers, namely, to heal ulcers by reducing gastric acidity. The major difference is that they act directly on the final site of gastric acid production, the so-called proton or acid pump (Exhibit 3). Their impact on gastric acid reduction is more powerful and of longer duration than that of H2-blockers. Several other companies were known to be developing proton pump ionhibitors, whose launch was expected from 1993 on. Lansoprazole, by the Japanese company Takeda, seemed the most interesting and advanced proton pump inhibitor under development.

---

[11]Other major brand names of this product were: Antra (Germany), Mopral (France), and Prilosec (United States).

Antiulcerant Market Shares (in Value) in Six Major Countries, 1986–1989

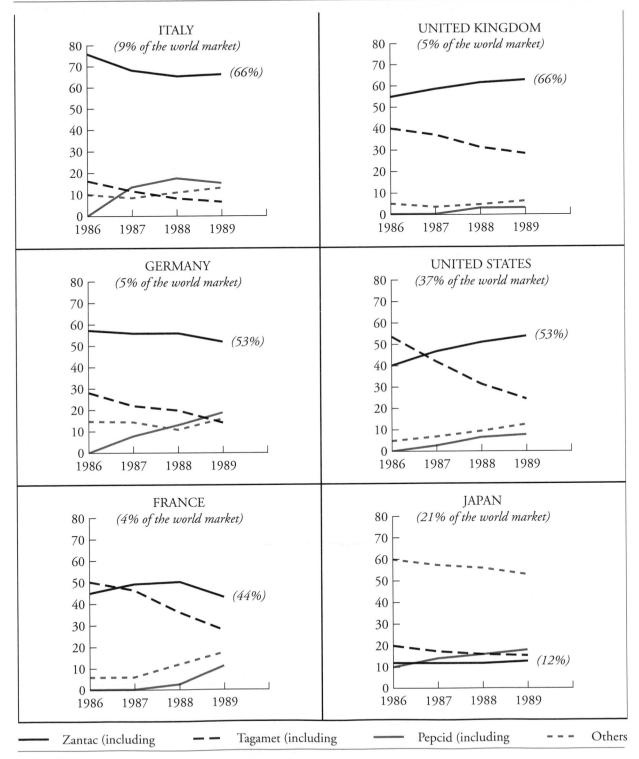

ITALY
(9% of the world market)
(66%)

UNITED KINGDOM
(5% of the world market)
(66%)

GERMANY
(5% of the world market)
(53%)

UNITED STATES
(37% of the world market)
(53%)

FRANCE
(4% of the world market)
(44%)

JAPAN
(21% of the world market)
(12%)

Zantac (including   Tagamet (including   Pepcid (including   Others

Source: Glaxo.

EXHIBIT 14

Size of Antiulcerant Sales Forces in Five Major Countries, 1989

	Germany		France		Italy		United Kingdom		United States	
	Number of reps.	Share of reps.	Number of reps.	Share of reps.	Number of reps.	Share of reps.	Number of reps.	Share of reps.	Number of reps.	Share of reps.
Zantac	240	16%	285	21%	432	14%	191	24%	2 600	31%
Other ranitidine	220	14%	200	15%	741	23%	-	-	—	
Total ranitidine	460	30%	485	36%	1,173	37%	191	24%	2 600	31%
Tagamet (b)	100	7%	200	15%	173	5%	120	15%	1 330	16%
Pepcid	350	23%	240	18%	681	21%	218	28%	1,500(a)	18%
Losec	160	10%	130(c)	10%	478	15%	65	8%	1,500(a)	18%
Other	462	30%	300	22%	691	22%	199	25%	2 850	35%
Total	1,532	100%	1,355	100%	3,196	100%	793	100%	8 280	100%

aLosec was to be marketed in the United States by Merck, whose sales force was currently promoting Pepcid.
bThe figures for Tagamet do not include Beecham's sales force.
cThis figure does not include potential comarketers or copromoters.
Source: Glaxo and industry interviews.

Clinical comparisons between Losec and Zantac showed the following picture (Exhibit 19):

- Several studies claimed faster pain relief for Losec.

- For peptic ulcers, Losec produced significantly higher healing rates after two and four weeks of treatment, but after eight weeks of treatment there was no significant difference.

- In reflux, Losec had superior healing rates at all points in time.

- Losec was able to heal ulcers which could not be healed by H2-blockers, so-called refractory ulcers.

- Patients relapsed at the same rate as after treatment with Zantac.

- As with Zantac, no clinically significant side effects had been reported.

- Losec had similar potential drug interactions as Tagamet, but so far, actual clinical evidence was limited.

In mid-1989, Losec was already approved for sale in 15 countries and launched in 10, accounting for approximately 5 percent of global antiulcerant sales. Of the major countries, only France and the United Kingdom had approved Losec until now. Approvals generally were for acute treatment of peptic ulcers and reflux. The United Kingdom provided the exception, allowing Losec only for acute treatment of refractory peptic ulcers ("second line treatment"). Maintenance treatment was not approved anywhere.

Astra's short-term intention was to obtain approval for acute ulcer and reflux treatment in all countries; longer-term, it intended to obtain approval for maintenance treatment as well. Because of the need for extensive, long-term studies, maintenance approvals were unlikely before 1992 at the earliest.

EXHIBIT 15

Zantac: Sales Force Visit Share (SFS) and Unit Market Share (UMS) in a Major Country, 1988

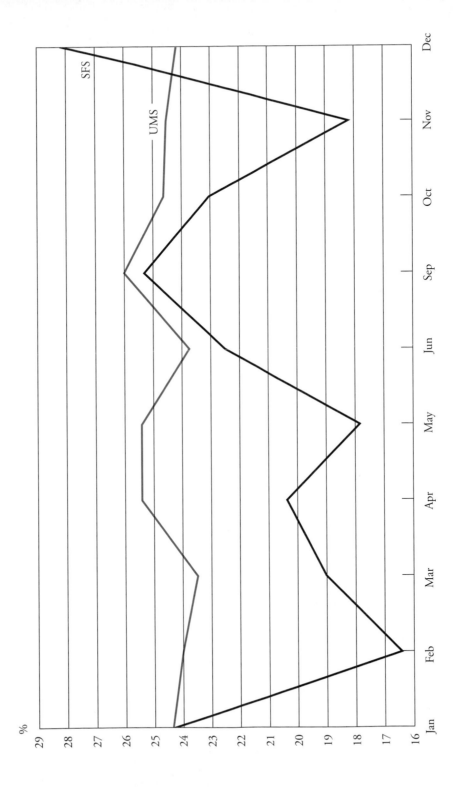

EXHIBIT   16

Zantac: Attention and Eye Movement Ad Tests (Germany), 1985–1987

Test ads

WAS HAT
DER HAMBURGER
MIT ZANTIC
ZU TUN?

Translation and test results

Date: 16/10/85

What has a hamburger got to do with Zantac?

Be at the office on time in the morning. No time for breakfast. A quick cup of coffee standing up, then off.

By lunchtime, the stomach is making itself heard. Thank goodness for the hamburger. It fills you up and doesn't take much time. The next appointment is pressing.

Day in, day out, rushing around, no time to eat. The toughest stomach could not hold out.

Explain to your patients the connection between nutrition, stress and stomach pain. Tell them to take time for their meals. And prescribe against acid and pain in an H2-blocker that works quickly and safely.

<u>Studies:</u>   *(30 doctors, 20 advertisements studied)*

	Recall	Recognition
Zantic	10/30	28/30
Best ad	10/30	28/30
Worst ad	0/30	3/30

Was hat der
Arbeitsplatz
mit Zantic
zu tun?

Date: 3/6/87

What has the workplace got to do with Zantac?

In Germany each year more than 750,000 people suffer from duodenal and stomach ulcers.

For these patients in the past this has meant a long sick-leave, possibly an even longer hospital stay and even the risk and expense of a surgical operation.

Now with Zantic 300 they are soon free of pain and quickly cured. The number of hospital stays and operations can be drastically reduced. From the patient's point of view the cost of ulcer treatment can be greatly diminished.

<u>Studies:</u>   *(30 doctors, 16 advertisements studied)*

	Recall	Recognition
Zantic	13/30	16/30
Best ad	13/30	19/30
Worst ad	4/30	6/30

Source: Glaxo GmbH and Institut für Kommunikations-forschung von Keitz GmbH

EXHIBIT 16 (continued)

Figures in red show % of doctors who looked at this element at all, figures in blue show average time they spent looking at each element (in seconds)

Figures show % of doctors who looked at this element first

Note: Subjects were asked to go through an issue of the Arzte Zeitung (a medical periodical). Their eye movements were recorded by a special camera.

Source: Glaxo GmbH and Institut für Kommunikations-forschung von Keitz GmbH.

EXHIBIT 17

Zantac: Tests of the "Volcano" and "Ball of String" Ads, United Kingdom, Spring and Autumn, 1989 (N = 200 GPs)

Exhibit 17
Zantac: Tests of the "Volcano"
and "Ball of String" Ads,
UK, Spring and Autumn 1989

(N=200 GPs)

	Spring 89	Fall 89	Spring 89	Fall 89	Spring 89	Fall 89	All ads on the data base [b] Spr'g 89	Fall 89	All ads on data base running 1-3mths	10-12mths	All ads on data base in same therapy class Spr'g 89	Fall 89
Recall from visual (brand blanked out) [a]	54%	67%	60%	75%	59%	68%	50%	51%	51%	67%	61%	62%
Recall from complete ad	60%	68%	60%	75%	55%	56%	50%	50%	51%	63%	59%	61%
Product associated with "blanked out" visual [c]												
Zantac	28%	38%	36%	52%	30%	41%	25% [d]		25% [d]		N.A.	
other	7%	10%	4%	7%	4%	5%						
don't know/N.A.	17%	7%	19%	11%	21%	20%						
not seen ad	46%	40%	40%	25%	41%	32%						
Main messages conveyed by complete ad (unprompted)												
ulcers can reoccur	21%	26%	32%	33%	18%	10%						
ulcer treatment	34%	30%	24%	25%	9%	14%						
long term treatment		9%	7%	14%	20%	20%						
healing		9%	14%	13%								
for burning pain	24%	16%	9%	12%								
ulcers last forever					17%	19%						
ulcer craters	14%		10%		14%	12%						
painful	10%		4%									
effective					15%	9%						
no message	2%	2%	10%	3%								
Interest [e]	0.91	0.7	0.8	0.71	-0.44	-0.14	-0.07	-0.06	-0.1	0.16	-0.01	0.06
Impact	1.2	1.03	1.03	1.12	-0.62	-0.24	-0.05	-0.04	-0.07	0.23	0.02	0.12
Attractiveness	0.77	0.56	0.75	0.68	-0.7	-0.59	0	0.01	-0.0	0.29	-0.12	-0.06
Informativeness	0.6	0.6	0.58	0.67	-0.28	-0.14	0.06	0.07	0.0	0.22	0.27	0.28
Credibility	0.83	0.83	0.83	1.07	0.44	0.51	0.27	0.28	0.28	0.4	0.45	0.51
Relevance	1.09	1.19	1.15	1.11	0.67	0.63	0.52	0.53	0.5	0.5	0.63	0.7
Ulcer disease is a chronic condition [f]	1.08	1.34	1.39	1.59	N.A.	0.66						
Zantac should be used long term to reduce risk of relapse	0.48	0.74	0.69	1.00	N.A.	0.71						

a With all means of brand/manufacturer recognition removed from the advertisement, subjects were asked whether ad has been seen prior to interview.
b MARS (volcano) and MRO (ball of string) data bases.
c When presented with the blanked out ad., the GPs were asked to state which product they associated with the visual.
d Average product identification values for all ads in the MARS/MRO data bases.
e Interest and 6 other dimensions below were rated on a scale of 2 to -2.
f Agreement with statement was rated on a scale of 3 to -3.

Source: Glaxo Pharmaceuticals Ltd., 1989.

aWith all means of brand/manufacturer recognition removed from the advertisement, subjects were asked whether ad has been seen prior to interview.
bMARS (volcano) and MRO (ball of string) data bases.
cWhen presented with the blanked out ad., the GPs were asked to state which product they associated with the visual.
dAverage product identification values for all ads in the MARS/MRO data bases.
eInterest and six other dimensions below were rated on a scale of 2 to minus 2.
fAgreement with statement was rated on a scale of 3 to minus 3.
Source: Glaxo Pharmaceuticals Ltd., 1989.

EXHIBIT 18

Zantac: Ad Tests among Doctors, in United States, 1989

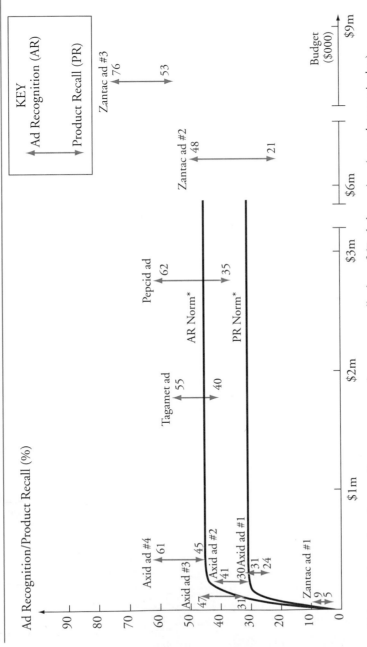

Ad Recognition/Product Recall (%)

KEY
Ad Recognition (AR)
Product Recall (PR)

Zantac ad #3 76 53

Zantac ad #2 48 21

Pepcid ad 62 35

Tagamet ad 55 40

AR Norm*

PR Norm*

Axid ad #4 61
Axid ad #3 45 47
Axid ad #2 41 31
Axid ad #1 31 24
30
Zantac ad #1 9 5

Budget
($000)

$1m $2m $3m $6m $9m

*Ad recognition and product recall norms correspond to average recall values of 67 ad observations (same therapeutic class).

*Ad recognition and product recall norms correspond to average recall values of 67 ad observations (same therapeutic class).
Source: Glaxo.

EXHIBIT   19

Main Characteristics of Zantac and Losec, 1989

	Zantac (ranitidine hydrochloride)	Losec (omeprazole)
Pain relief		Claimed to be faster.
Acute ulcer healing rates:		
Peptic ulcer (average)		
- after 2 weeks	52%	67%
- after 4 weeks	80%	92%
- after 8 weeks	92%	92%
- typical approved treatment length	4 weeks	2 to 4 weeks
Reflux oesophagitis (range)		
- after 4 weeks	27–67%	67–85%
- after 8 weeks	38–65%	85–96%
- typical approved treatment length	6 weeks	4 to 8 weeks
Relapse rates	Both products have similar relapse rates.	
Side effects	No significant side effects have been reported for either product.	
Drug interactions	None of clinical significance. Potentially the same as for Tagamet.	

Source: medical literature and industry sources

The important and highly visible United States was one of the many countries in which the approval decision was still pending. On March 15, 1989, the Advisory Committee to the U.S. registration authority recommended that Losec be approved only for refractory reflux. This highly restrictive recommendation was motivated by concerns about a potential cancer risk.

Data sheets for some countries indeed mentioned the possibility of carcinoid risk and explicitly cautioned against maintenance usage. Trials of Losec had been suspended in 1984 for about a year when carcinoids (that is, benign tumours) were observed in the acid-producing cells in the stomach of rats after prolonged administration of Losec. It appeared that these carcinoids were the ransom for Losec's superior potency: when acid completely disappeared from the stomach, other substances increased which eventually produced the stomach carcinoids in rats but, so far, not in other animals or humans.

Astra's entry strategy was similar across countries. Losec was priced between 50 percent and 100 percent above Zantac for daily treatment cost. Positioning emphasized the following themes: (1) Losec is a breakthrough product; (2) Losec has a "precise mechanism of action"; and (3) Losec provides fast pain relief and healing (see Exhibit 20). Involvement of opinion leaders in clinical trials and conferences created an awareness and image for Losec prior to the actual launch. Its image was that of an innovative product with side effects (among GPs), or that relieves pain and heals (among gastroenterologists). Lansoprazole was perceived to be very similar to Losec (see Exhibit 21). During launch, Astra typically targeted hospitals first, followed by GPs.

EXHIBIT 20

Losec: Selected Launch Campaigns, 1988–1989

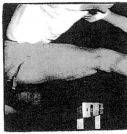

weden (1988)

Snabbhet!

Föjsamhet!

Precision!

Speed	Compliance	Precision
Losec gives a fast result	Losec is easy for the patient to remember	Losec works directly on the final steps of acid production

Sweden (1989)

EXHIBIT 20 (*continued*)

Losec: Selected Promotional Material, 1989

HOE TERUGHOUDEND BEN JE BIJ DE ONTDEKKING VAN EEN NIEUWE THERAPEUTISCHE KLASSE?

De ontdekking of creatie van een geheel nieuwe therapeutische klasse: elke farmaceutische wetenschapper droomt ervan. Want dan ben je écht grenzen aan het verleggen. Het is Astra gelukt. Met de ontwikkeling van Losec® [omeprazol]. Een geneesmiddel dat een regelrechte doorbraak in de behandeling van maagzuur-gerelateerde aandoeningen betekent. Losec werkt sneller. En beter. Bij méér patiënten. Omdat het volgens een geheel nieuw principe werkt. Als eerste geneesmiddel remt Losec het zuurproducerende enzym H⁺/K⁺·ATP-ase (de zuurpomp). En beheerst daarmee direct de bron. In ruim 20 jaar onderzoek zijn de effecten van Losec nauwkeurig en uitgebreid gedocumenteerd. De klinische voordelen spreken voor zich. Bij ulcus duodeni. Bij ulcus ventriculi. Bij reflux oesophagitis. Daarom hebben wij onze laatste terughoudendheid laten varen.

LOSEC

EEN DOORBRAAK IN DE BEHANDELING VAN MAAGZUUR-GERELATEERDE AANDOENINGEN

"HOW RESERVED ARE YOU ABOUT THE DISCOVERY OF A NEW THERAPEUTIC CLASS?" The Netherlands (1989)

Above is the title of the Dutch launch ad for Losec. The ad continues: "The discovery or creation of a completely new therapeutic class: every pharmaceutical scientist dreams about it".

The ad goes on to say that Astra have succeeded with the discovery of omeprazole and describes it as a breakthrough in the treatment of acid-related diseases.

"Losec workes faster. And more rapidly. In more patients." And concludes: "Therefore we have let our last reservations go". The illustration was commissioned by Astra from a Dutch artist.

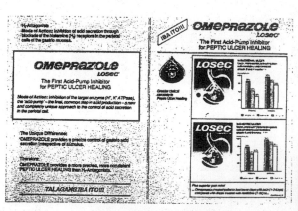

The Philippines (1989)

UK (1989)

EXHIBIT 21

Perceptual Maps of Leading Antiulcerant Brands in France, 1989

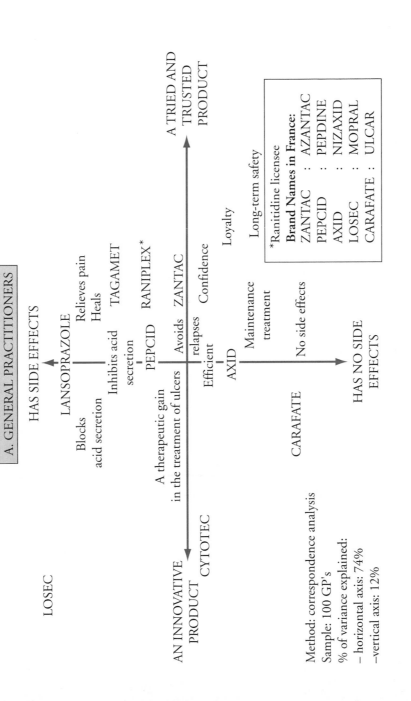

A. GENERAL PRACTITIONERS

HAS SIDE EFFECTS

LANSOPRAZOLE
Relieves pain
Heals   TAGAMET
Blocks
acid secretion
Inhibits acid
secretion
PEPCID   RANIPLEX*
Avoids   ZANTAC
relapses   Confidence
A therapeutic gain   Efficient   Loyalty
in the treatment of ulcers   AXID   Long-term safety
Maintenance
treatment
No side effects

CYTOTEC
CARAFATE

LOSEC

A TRIED AND
TRUSTED
PRODUCT

AN INNOVATIVE
PRODUCT

HAS NO SIDE
EFFECTS

*Ranitidine licensee
Brand Names in France:
ZANTAC : AZANTAC
PEPCID : PEPDINE
AXID : NIZAXID
LOSEC : MOPRAL
CARAFATE : ULCAR

Method: correspondence analysis
Sample: 100 GP's
% of variance explained:
– horizontal axis: 74%
– vertical axis: 12%

Source: Glaxo France

EXHIBIT 21 (*continued*)

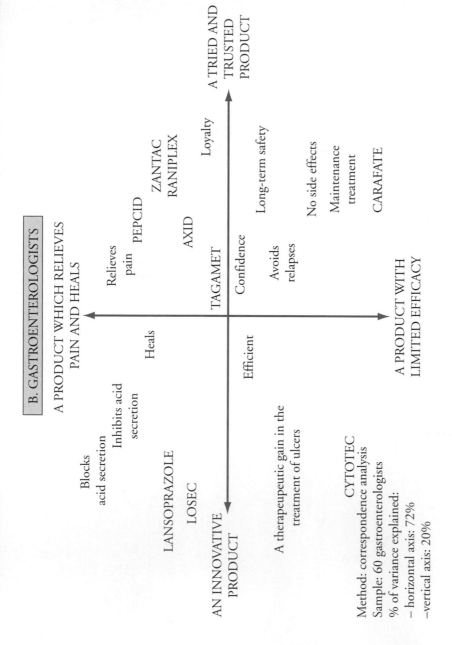

B. GASTROENTEROLOGISTS

A PRODUCT WHICH RELIEVES
PAIN AND HEALS

Blocks
acid secretion

Inhibits acid
secretion

Relieves
pain   PEPCID

ZANTAC
RANIPLEX

AXID

Loyalty

A TRIED AND
TRUSTED
PRODUCT

Long-term safety

Heals

TAGAMET

Confidence

No side effects

Maintenance
treatment

CARAFATE

LANSOPRAZOLE

LOSEC

Efficient

Avoids
relapses

AN INNOVATIVE
PRODUCT

A therapeupeutic gain in the
treatment of ulcers

A PRODUCT WITH
LIMITED EFFICACY

CYTOTEC

Method: correspondence analysis
Sample: 60 gastroenterologists
% of variance explained:
– horizontal axis: 72%
–vertical axis: 20%

Source: Glaxo France

Data from the European launch countries showed that Losec achieved a 12 percent value share of the antiulcerant market six months after launch, of which about six share points came from Zantac. Three-fourths of the Losec prescriptions were for reflux.

Astra already had, or was expected to conclude, marketing partnerships in the United States, Japan, Italy, France, and some other countries. In the United States, Losec registration and marketing was handled by Merck and Co., which already marketed Pepcid. Exhibit 14 includes estimates of the size of the sales forces expected to promote Losec in five major countries.

ISSUES FOR ZANTAC

Reviewing events since 1981, Dr. Preuveneers sought the real reason behind Zantac's rise to become the world's number one pharmaceutical product. Was Zantac simply a clearly superior product? Had SmithKline made so many blunders that victory had been easy? Was it merely luck on Glaxo's part? Or was there another explanation?

Over the last eight years, Glaxo had been transformed from a U.K.-centered company to one with a truly international outlook. This was reflected in Glaxo's international board of directors, and in the operating companies throughout the world, where local managers had replaced the British expatriates. The influence of the United States, which accounted for 41 percent of Glaxo's total 1989 sales, was on the rise, as indicated by the recent appointment of Dr. Ernest Mario, an American and previously head of Glaxo Inc., to the position of Glaxo Chief Executive.

EXHIBIT 22

Glaxo's New Product Pipeline, 1989

Brand Name Indication Areas	Estimated Number of Worldwide Patients (millions of patients)	Estimated Launch Date	Estimated Annual Sales Three Years after Worldwide Launch (£ million)
Zofran for severe nausea and vomiting associated with cancer therapy such as chemotherapy and radiation	1	End of 1989	£ 75
Flixonase nasal spray for hayfever *Cutivate* cream ointment for skin rashes	35	End of 1989 (both products)	£ 175
Imigran for migraine and cluster headache	35	First half of 1991	£ 450
Severent a long acting treatment for asthma	25	First half of 1992	£ 250

Source: Industry analyses.

EXHIBIT   23

Antiulcerant Indication and Geographic Segments: 1989 Segment Size and Average Future Growth Rates

	Peptic Ulcer	*Reflux*	*Nonulcer*	*Total*	*Total*	*Average Future Growth*
United States	13%	7%	17%	37%	£1207	16%
Europe	18%	7%	8%	33%	£1076	17%
Japan	14%	0%	5%	19%	£620	11%
Rest of world	9%	2%	0%	11%	£358	15%
Total	54%	16%	30%	100%		
Total size	£1761	£522	£978		£3261	
Average Future Growth (p.a.)	13%	23%	15%			15%

Source: Glaxo.

Looking to the future, Dr. Preuveneers was concerned about possible declining commitment to Zantac within Glaxo. Some argued that Glaxo's resources should be concentrated on the promising new products nearing market introduction (see Exhibit 22). Dr. Preuveneers wondered how he could demonstrate the importance of Zantac for Glaxo's future growth.

A second issue was what segments he should emphasize. While total antiulcerant sales were predicted to grow at an average 15 percent during the coming four years, growth prospects of different geographic and indication areas varied (Exhibit 23). In the peptic ulcer area, 65 percent of sales were for acute, and 30 percent for maintenance treatment. The remainder went for preventive treatment of NSAID-induced peptic ulcers via coprescriptions of antiulcerants, a recent indication area that might grow anywhere between 13 percent and 40 percent p.a. Zantac's share was similar across all indication segments.

The challenge for Zantac as industry leader was to continue to develop the market and, at the same time, to defend its share against new entrants. Not everybody within Glaxo was taking Astra seriously. How likely was it really that Astra would be able to repeat the success with Losec that Glaxo had achieved with Zantac, and what could Glaxo do to prevent this from happening?

Dr. Preuveneers's task was now to formulate recommendations enabling Zantac to maintain its leadership and achieve the objectives set by Glaxo's directors.

Preparing a Written Case Analysis

 Chapter 3 outlined an approach to marketing decision making and case analysis. The purpose of this appendix is to provide a more detailed description of what is involved in a thorough written case analysis through the use of an example. The following case—Republic National Bank of Dallas: NOW Accounts—describes an actual problem encountered by bank executives. The case is accompanied by a student analysis in the format described in Chapter 3. The student analysis shows how to organize a written case and the nature and scope of the analysis, which includes both qualitative and quantitative analyses. You should read and analyze the case before examining the student analysis.

Republic National Bank of Dallas
Now Accounts

INTRODUCTION

In early 1977, Ruth Krusen, marketing officer for Republic National Bank of Dallas (RNB), was asked to assess the impact on Republic Bank of offering NOW (negotiable order of withdrawal) accounts if they became legal nationwide. Specifically, she was asked to:

The cooperation of Republic National Bank of Dallas in the preparation of this case is gratefully acknowledged. This case was prepared by Professor Roger A. Kerin, of the Edwin L. Cox School of Business, Southern Methodist University, as a basis for class discussion and is not designed to illustrate effective or ineffective handling of an administrative situation. Certain data have been disguised.

1. Determine the impact on profits that Republic National Bank could anticipate from NOW accounts

2. Recommend a NOW account marketing strategy

NOW accounts, which are effectively interest-bearing checking accounts, have
been in use since 1972 in New England. In early 1977, however, a bill was introduced into Congress that would allow commercial banks and thrift institutions in all
50 states to provide this service.[1] Despite some opposition in Congress, observers
were of the opinion that legislation enabling NOW accounts would be passed by
the first quarter of 1978 and would become effective January 1979.

BANKING IN TEXAS

Texas is a "unit banking" state. This means that individual banks cannot operate
branch banks. The regulation that limits a bank to a single location was specified in
the state constitution of 1876. In 1971, however, amendments to the Bank Holding
Act allowed individual banks to acquire smaller institutions if the identity of the acquired bank was maintained. Since 1971, large banks in Texas have formed holding
companies to improve their lending capability in order to better serve large commercial accounts. By 1977, 33 bank holding companies were operating in Texas.
Holding companies owned 250 of the state's 1,360 banks and held about 55 percent
of the state's total bank deposits in 1977.

Three of the largest bank holding companies in Texas are based in Dallas. Each
operates its largest bank in downtown Dallas. First International Bancshares, which
operates First National Bank, is the largest bank holding company in Texas. Republic
of Texas Corporation operates the Republic National Bank of Dallas and is the second-largest holding company. Mercantile Texas Corporation operates Mercantile
National Bank and is the fifth-largest bank holding company in terms of total assets.

Banking activity in Texas generally corresponds to pockets of urban and commercial growth. Accordingly, banking activity is concentrated in the Dallas–Fort Worth
and Houston metropolitan areas. The San Antonio metropolitan area has shown a
dramatic increase in banking activity due in part to population growth and increased
economic growth.

COMPETITIVE SITUATION IN DALLAS

The Dallas banking market consists of 57 banks in the city of Dallas and an additional 43 banks in Dallas County. At the end of 1976, the 57 banks in the city of
Dallas recorded total deposits of $13.27 billion. The 43 banks in Dallas County
recorded deposits of about $1.25 billion.

Three large downtown banks dominate the Dallas banking market. At the end
of 1976, Republic National Bank, First National Bank, and the Mercantile National
Bank accounted for approximately 78 percent of total bank deposits in the city of
Dallas and 71 percent of Dallas County bank deposits. Republic National Bank was
the leader with approximately $4.6 billion in deposits, followed closely by First

---

[1]Thrift institutions include mutual savings banks, cooperative banks, credit unions, and savings and
loan associations. Thrift institutions differ from commercial banks in that only banks have the authority
to accept demand deposits or checking accounts or offer commercial loans.

National Bank with $4.4 billion. Mercantile National Bank recorded total deposits of about $1.3 billion at the end of 1976. These three banks are located within walking distance of one another, as well as of some 12 other banks.

Competitive activities of Dallas banks have historically focused on retail (consumer) or wholesale (business) bank account development. Banks located in suburban areas typically emphasized the retail business, whereas downtown banks emphasized the wholesale business. Nevertheless, the Dallas competitive environment in recent years has been characterized by aggressive bank marketing efforts on both fronts. According to one observer of the Dallas banking scene:

> The competitive marketing furor is fierce, and it's not just the catchy advertising themes. . . . There's a scramble going on to repackage consumer services, put forth new services, cross-sell services, and woo corporate customers. There's Saturday banking, extended hours banking, 24-hour tellers, foreign currency sales, cash machines, no-charge checking package deals, automatic payroll deposits, pension fund management services, computer billing services, specially arranged travel tours, traveler's checks to spend on travel tours, equipment leasing, credit card loans, loan syndications, lock boxes, and on and on. First National Bank in Dallas alone lists more than 400 different bank "products" in its inventory of services.[2]

Krusen confirmed the observation that the Dallas banking market was competitive. She noted that RNB continues to be competitive in banking services, but "the question of how aggressive we should be has not been resolved at least as regards retail account marketing." RNB has at least as many bank services for customers as competitors do, if not more services than are offered by the vast majority of commercial banks in Dallas.

In addition to commercial banks, savings and loan associations (S&Ls) also compete for passbook savings accounts among Dallas County residents. At the end of 1976, deposits of the 22 Dallas County–based savings and loan associations were $2.85 billion. Dallas Federal Savings was the largest savings and loan association with about $909.6 million in deposits, or about 32 percent of total deposits. Texas Federal Savings and First Texas Savings combined accounted for approximately $992 million in deposits, or 35 percent of total deposits. Dallas-based savings and loan associations operated approximately 150 offices in Dallas County. Savings and loan associations based outside Dallas County also operated about 50 offices in the county.

Savings and loan associations have aggressively sought deposits in recent years. Dallas-based associations have historically outpaced the national average for savings and loan deposit volume growth. Savings associations have emphasized two competitive advantages in their passbook savings marketing programs. First, they could pay $5\frac{1}{4}$ percent on passbook savings, whereas commercial banks were limited by law to 5 percent on passbook savings. Second, they could develop branch operations with a common name, whereas commercial banks were limited to a single location in Texas.

Savings and loan associations have placed greater emphasis on consumer, or installment, loans in recent years. Texas is unique among states in that it allows savings associations to provide installment loans, and some associations have used this opportunity to attract deposit volume. According to an industry observer, "S&Ls have historically attracted older customers. Installment loans are a useful service to bring

---

[2]Dave Clark, "A Big Pitch for Bucks," *Dallas–Fort Worth Business Quarterly* 1, no. 2.

in younger customers, introduce them to S&Ls, and get them to open a passbook savings account."

Credit unions also represent a competitive force in the Dallas market. By the end of 1976, 218 credit unions were located in the city of Dallas and its immediate environs. These credit unions operated 232 offices. Combined, credit unions held over $666 million in assets and served almost one-half million members.

Credit unions compete effectively in the Dallas market in three ways. First, they offer consumer, or installment, loans to their members at competitive interest rates. They hold a significant share of the automobile loans in the Dallas market. Second, credit unions hold substantial funds in member savings accounts. Third, credit unions provide share drafts to their members. A *share draft* is a withdrawal document that permits credit union members to make payments from interest-bearing savings accounts. These drafts resemble checks but are actually drafts drawn on a credit union and payable through a bank.

REPUBLIC NATIONAL BANK

Republic National Bank was founded in 1920. At that time, the bank was called Guaranty Bank and Trust, and it held a state banking charter. After several name changes, the present name was adopted in 1937, and RNB obtained a national bank charter. Today, RNB is the largest member of the Republic of Texas Corporation bank holding-company system. By the end of 1977, RNB would be ranked twenty-first in the United States in total assets and deposits and would be the largest bank in Texas and the South in terms of total assets, deposits, loans, and equity capital. Also by the end of 1977, RNB would be ranked 150th among the 500 largest banks in the non Communist world, according to *American Banker* magazine. RNB had total assets exceeding $6 billion and a net income of approximately $36.3 million by that time.

Retail Account Marketing

Although figures are not available for competing banks, RNB is considered to have one of the largest, if not the largest, retail account bases in the Dallas area. According to Krusen, this occurred as a result of RNB's historic position of "taking chances on the little guy and community service." It was estimated that about 55 percent of RNB's retail checking accounts in 1977 were under $500. Exhibit 1 shows the distribution of accounts by account size.

This philosophy is communicated in RNB advertising. Beginning in the late 1960s with its "Silver Star Service" campaign and continuing with the "Star Treatment" advertising campaign, RNB communicated to present and potential customers that they were special and that RNB had a number of special services to provide them. In early 1977 the "Republic National Bank *Is* Dallas" campaign was launched, with Orson Welles narrating television and radio advertising spots and the Dallas Symphony playing the theme music. This campaign was designed to reflect the mutual traditions of RNB and Dallas residents as progressive and growth-oriented, as well as emphasize the interdependence of banking leadership and service with the prosperity and quality of Dallas life. Marketing research has shown that RNB has had the highest "top-of-mind awareness" of any bank in the Dallas area since 1975.

E X H I B I T   1

Estimated Distribution of Personal Checking Account Balances in Early 1977

Account Size	Percentage of Accounts	Percentage of Total Checking Account Deposits
Under $200	32%	3%
$200–$499	23	3
$500–$999	14	4
$1,000–$4,999	18	13
$5,000–$9,999	7	11
$10,000–$24,999	3	13
$25,000–$100,000	2	20
Over $100,000	1	33
	100%	100%

Number of personal checking accounts: 45,000

Personal checking account deposits: $150 million

Note: Figures reported in this exhibit reflect approximations drawn from *1977 District Bank Averages: Functional Cost Analysis* (Dallas: Federal Reserve Bank of Dallas, 1977).

Retail Account Services

RNB retail account marketing efforts have resulted in a variety of traditional as well as innovative bank services for its customers. For example, RNB provides its Teller 24® Service, which is an automatic bank teller/cash machine. This service operates 24 hours a day at 26 locations around the city of Dallas and in six other Texas cities. Another innovation, the *Starpak* Account, is a complete package of banking services provided to customers for a fixed monthly fee of $3. Exhibit 2 gives a description of this service. RNB personal checking is highly competitive in the Dallas market, with no service charge for accounts that maintain a minimum monthly balance of $400. A $1 charge accrues to accounts with a minimum monthly balance of $300, a $2 charge with a minimum monthly balance of $200, and a $3 charge with no minimum balance requirement.

Retail Checking Account Revenue and Cost Estimates

In the course of preparing her report, Krusen contacted the RNB Controllers Division to obtain revenue and cost data on retail checking accounts. The Controllers Division report, based largely on Federal Reserve statistics, indicated that approximately 85 percent of retail checking account deposits were investable. In other words, about 15 percent of checking account deposits must be held in reserve. Ninety-six percent of savings account balances were investable.

The Controllers Division also indicated that RNB would realize an average yield on loans and securities of about 7.5 percent in 1977. Krusen noted that this figure

EXHIBIT 2

Components of Republic National Bank's Starpak Account

1. *Unlimited Checking*—There's no minimum balance requirement, no per check charge, and no limit on the number of checks you write when you have a Starpak personal checking account.

2. *Free Personal Checks*—They're prenumbered and personalized with your name, address, and phone number, and you can order as many as you need any time you need them.

3. *Reduced Loan Rates*—With this feature alone, many people make Starpak pay for itself. At the end of the loan period, we'll refund 10 percent of the total interest you paid on installment loans of $1,000 or more, when the loan has been repaid as agreed. Of course, your loan is subject to normal credit approval.

4. *No Bank Charge for Traveler's Checks*—Or for Money Orders or Cashier's Checks when you show us your Starpak Account Card.

5. *Free Safe Deposit Box*—We'll give you the $5 size free. Or take $5 off the rent for a larger size.

6. *Combined Monthly Statement*—Your monthly statement can include status reports on any or all of the accounts you and your spouse have at Republic. You select the accounts you want the Combined Statement to cover. We can include your checking, savings, personal certificates of deposit, and even personal loans. Yes, you'll also receive separate regular statements on each of your Republic accounts you include in the Combined Statement.

7. *Numerical Check Listing*—Your monthly statement will report each check in the order written. That makes it much easier to reconcile your statement each month.

8. *Automatic Overdraft Protection*—This optional service gives you additional peace of mind and the opportunity to take advantage of an exceptional bargain. It works this way. If the checks you write exceed your balance, we'll cover the overdrafts up to the limit of your Republic Master Charge or VISA Credit. Finance charges for deferred payment will apply at the normal rate. Repayment will be through your monthly Master Charge or VISA account payment.

9. *Teller 24® Service*—You can get cash from your Starpak Checking Account, or your Republic Master Charge or VISA Card, at any of 26 Teller 24 machines located in Dallas and six other Texas cities, and at 12,000 banks nationwide. With Teller 24 your money is available 24 hours a day, 7 days a week.

10. *Automatic Loan Repayment*—If you have an installment loan at Republic, we will, at your request, withdraw your monthly loan payment from your Starpak Checking Account. It's a good way to make sure you can take advantage of the 10 percent interest refund.

11. *Automatic Savings Account Deposits*—If you've never been able to save before, this plan solves the problem. Just tell us how much and on what day of the month. On the date you specify, we'll automatically transfer the amount you select from your checking to your savings account. Then, to help your savings grow even faster, we'll pay the highest interest rates allowable.

12. *Starpak Account Card*—It identifies you as a preferred customer of Republic National Bank, entitled to the privileges and special savings available with your Starpak Account.

13. *No Separate Charges*—All these Starpak services are available for the flat monthly fee of $3. There's no separate charge.

Plus these other services available to all Republic National Bank customers—We pay postage both ways when you bank by mail. We'll validate your in-bank parking stub when you bank. And you'll have a personal banker assigned to your accounts so that you can call for advice or assistance with any banking need.

Source: Bank brochure.

was the lowest experienced by RNB in recent years. In 1974 RNB had realized an average yield of 10.59 percent. Other figures obtained directly from Federal Reserve statistical averages for commercial banks with total deposits of over $200 million were as follows:

Service and handling charge revenue per account per month:	$1.56
Account cost per month (including checks, deposits, and other assignable overhead):	$5.24

NOW ACCOUNTS

NOW accounts came into being as the result of the attempt of a Massachusetts mutual savings bank to circumvent the prohibition against thrift institutions' offering checking accounts. After a two-year regulatory and legal battle, Consumer Savings Bank of Worcester, Massachusetts, won its case and in June 1972 began to offer a savings account on which checklike instruments called negotiable orders of withdrawal could be written. Other mutuals in Massachusetts and New Hampshire soon followed suit.

Although regulatory authorities persist in regarding the NOW account as a savings account on which checks can be written, from a consumer point of view (and from an operational point of view) it is a checking account that pays interest. As consumers gradually became educated about NOWs, commercial banks began to lose customers to this attractive type of account, with which they were unable to compete. In response, federal and state laws were passed permitting commercial banks as well as mutuals and S&Ls in Massachusetts and New Hampshire to offer NOW accounts starting in January 1974. As of March 1976, financial institutions in the other New England states were granted the same powers. In two of the states (Connecticut and Maine), state-chartered thrifts had been empowered to offer checking accounts a few months earlier.

In New England, NOW accounts may be offered to individuals and to nonprofit organizations (except that in Connecticut, thrifts can offer NOWs only to individuals).[3] A uniform rate ceiling of 5 percent applies to all institutions. Excerpts from a report prepared by the RNB Marketing Division on the development of NOW accounts in New England are presented in the appendix at the end of this case.

NOW ACCOUNT MARKETING STRATEGY

The task facing Krusen was difficult for a number of reasons. First, the only NOW account information available pertained to the New England experience. Although this information would be useful in gauging the rate of adoption of NOW accounts, it was not entirely clear how the Dallas-area banks and thrift institutions would react. Second, several contingency plans would have to be charted. If NOW accounts were not deemed appropriate for RNB by top management, then Krusen would have to recommend a strategy to maintain the RNB customer base. This strategy would depend on whether a "free" NOW account program became popular in the Dallas area

---

[3]At the time of this case and for analysis purposes, only retail (personal and nonprofit) checking accounts were affected by NOW accounts in the Dallas area.

or a more conservative approach was adopted by competitors. If the NOW account was adopted by RNB, she realized, the NOW account package (separate account or part of an existing bank service) and the price (service charges, if any) would have to be defined. The package and price would be, in part, determined by the competitive environment that developed and the cost of NOW accounts.

Timing was a third consideration. Should RNB be a leader and set the competitive tenor in the market or take a "wait and see" stance? Finally, if RNB decided to adopt the NOW account, then a question of communications would arise. For example, should RNB quietly inform present customers of NOW account availability or actively communicate availability to the Dallas market as a whole via an advertising program?

APPENDIX: NOW ACCOUNTS IN NEW ENGLAND, A REPORT PREPARED BY THE MARKETING DIVISION OF REPUBLIC NATIONAL BANK OF DALLAS

The objectives of this investigation of NOW accounts in New England were

1. To learn the speed and magnitude of NOW account impact as a basis for estimating the impact on RNB
2. To identify and evaluate various marketing strategies and their possible relevance to our own market

Penetration of NOWs

Reaction of New England financial institutions given the power to offer NOWs is shown in Exhibit A.1. It indicates the percentages of thrifts and commercial banks that were offering NOWs by August 1976 and the market shares of commercial banks. By August 1976 mutual savings banks in Massachusetts and New Hampshire had been able to offer NOWs for 50 months, commercial banks for 30 months. In the other states, all institutions had been able to offer them for only 6 months.

EXHIBIT   A.1

NOW Account Adoption in New England as of August 1976

	Percentage of Institutions Offering		Commercial Banks' Share of NOW Market	
	Thrifts	Commercial Banks	Percentage of Accounts	Percentage of Balances
Massachusetts	94[a]	72	32	52
New Hampshire	81[a]	64	43	62
Connecticut	69	53	35	74
Maine	32	40	68	81
Vermont	23	29	89	93
Rhode Island[b]	25	75	83	85

[a]Mutual savings banks only; in each state two-thirds of the savings and loans also offer NOWs.

[b]Rhode Island has a unique situation of affiliated mutual savings banks and commercial banks. Figures in exhibit refer only to unaffiliated thrifts and commercial banks. NOWs are offered by 66 percent of the affiliated group.

Despite the resistance of commercial banks in Massachusetts and New Hampshire to offering NOWs. Exhibit A.1 shows that a substantial majority are now providing them. In the other New England states, commercial banks have moved more quickly to adopt NOW accounts. This is one of the reasons that they have a larger share of NOW accounts and balances than do commercial banks in Massachusetts and New Hampshire. Nevertheless, even in the latter states, commercial banks have captured more of the total NOW balances than have thrifts.

One conclusion supported by the data is that the competitiveness of financial institutions is directly related to the degree to which the state's population is concentrated in large urban markets.

The additional data on Massachusetts and New Hampshire shown in Exhibit A.2 indicate the substantial impact of NOWs in the personal payment account market. Exhibit A.2 shows that after four years, 72 percent of checking account balances in New Hampshire have been converted to NOWs and 44 percent have been converted in Massachusetts. Thrifts have captured 27 percent of this market in New Hampshire and 21 percent in Massachusetts.

Marketing Strategies

Massachusetts and New Hampshire As simple as the concept of an interest-bearing checking account appears to be. NOW account introduction in New England produced an initial confusion of positioning, pricing, and marketing strategies.

Positioning For a variety of reasons, thrifts initially positioned NOWs as savings accounts with a special convenience feature in getting access to funds. Consumers who opened them did not regard them as checking accounts and there was relatively low account activity. Adding to the confusion, when banks began to offer NOWs, some of them were very negative in their presentations. They told customers, in effect, "We have NOW accounts, but you don't really want to spend your savings, do you?"

In time, thrifts and then banks became more daring in presenting NOWs as accounts that were identical in function to checking accounts but paid interest. NOWs are by now recognized as a substitute for checking accounts, are opened instead of checking accounts (or an existing checking account is closed when it is realized that it is no longer needed), and have virtually the same level of activity as checking accounts.

EXHIBIT A.2

Personal Payment Accounts, August 1976

	Personal Payment Balances	
	Percentage in NOWs	*Percentage in Thrifts*
New Hampshire	72%	27%
Massachusetts	44	21

Note: Personal payment accounts consist of all checking balances plus 80 percent of NOW balances. The 20 percent of NOW balances estimated to have come from savings accounts have been deducted.

Pricing   Pricing was initially fairly conservative. In New Hampshire NOWs were usually offered at a lower rate of interest than a savings account, while in Massachusetts per-item charges were prevalent. Then a price war began and increasing numbers of institutions offered free NOWs—that is, maximum rate of interest, no service or item charges, and no minimum balance requirements.

The proportion of institutions offering free NOWs increased until mid-1975, but since then the trend has been reversed, largely because late entrants into the field have offered less generous terms. It has also been true that some institutions that previously offered free NOWs have imposed charges or minimum balance requirements.

The free NOW resulted from a variety of causes and motives:

1. At the time of introduction, money market rates were so high that the cost of NOW funds might still allow a margin of profit.
2. Thrifts were inexperienced in the costs involved in servicing checking accounts.
3. Some thrifts were determined to establish a good market share early, regardless of short-run lack of profitability.
4. In the major market areas, there was a free checking environment.

Price and service package   Pricing structures on NOWs in New England are as varied as checking account charges have historically been. The possibility of competing through the interest rate paid is the only new element. When NOW accounts are not free, some variant of the following occurs:

1. *Interest rates.* Initially, some institutions paid less than the maximum rate on savings accounts. However, under competitive pressure, rates rose to the 5 percent ceiling in all major markets. However, some institutions do not pay on a day-of-deposit to day-of-withdrawal basis. While very few now pay only on collected balances, several large banks are contemplating going in that direction. A few banks pay only on minimum balances.
2. *Balance requirements.* Balances above which the NOW account is "free" range from $200 to $1,000. In most cases, this is the minimum balance, although one large bank, Shawmut, has an average balance requirement.

   What happens when the balance goes below the minimum varies. In some cases, no interest is paid; in others, a transaction or service fee is imposed; and in some cases, both. In some isolated markets, fees are imposed on all accounts, but in competitive major markets, NOWs become free at some balance level.
3. *Transaction charges.* Charges per check range from 10 to 25 cents. Usually, the charge is levied on all checks if the balance is below the required level. In some cases, a certain number of checks are free (5 to 15 per month), and in some other cases the number of free checks is related to balances (for example, 5 checks per $100 of average balance).
4. *Service charge.* Some banks charge flat fees rather than per-transaction charges. Fees generally are $1 or $2.

Other New England States   By the time NOW accounts were authorized in the other New England states, both thrifts and commercials had had the opportunity to assess the cost and competitive impact of NOWs in the two original states, and money market conditions had changed. These facts are reflected in the response of financial institutions in offering NOWs. Commercial banks have moved more rapidly than they did in Massachusetts and New Hampshire. At the same time, both thrifts and commercial banks have been more conservative in pricing.

Connecticut Thrifts have moved aggressively to offer both checking accounts and NOWs. Although free checking prevails in major Connecticut markets and although about one-third of the thrifts offer free NOWs, large Connecticut banks have offered NOWs on conservative terms (high minimum balances with transaction charges for lower-balance accounts). The effect of this strategy is reflected in the high average balances of commercial bank NOWs—over $4,000.

Rhode Island The financial market is highly concentrated in a very few institutions. Six months after NOWs became legal, six of the nine commercial banks affiliated with thrift institutions, six of the eight unaffiliated banks, and one of the four unaffiliated thrifts were offering NOWs. None of them offered free NOWs. As in the checking account market in this state, relatively high minimum balances are required. It should be noted that because of the thrift commercial bank affiliations, a majority of thrifts have in effect been able to offer checking accounts to their customers.

Maine Thrifts have concentrated harder on selling checking accounts than on offering NOWs. Neither thrifts nor commercial banks have moved very fast to offer NOWs. Few offer them free.

Vermont This state shows the slowest gain in institutions offering NOWs. None offers them free.

STUDENT ANALYSIS

Republic National Bank of Dallas
Now Accounts

STRATEGIC ISSUES AND PROBLEMS

Ruth Krusen, marketing officer for RNB, has been given responsibility for (1) determining the profit impact RNB could anticipate from NOW accounts and (2) recommending a contingency plan for a NOW account marketing strategy. Her task involves a number of important factors. She must assess the likelihood that the Dallas competitive environment will be liberal or conservative in its marketing of NOW accounts. An important consideration is RNB's role in affecting this environment, given its dominant position in the Dallas market and its posture regarding aggressiveness in retail account marketing. Ultimately, she must make a "go–no go" decision. A "go" decision requires a recommendation on the form of the service, its target market, its price reflected in service charges, and promotion. A "no go" decision must take into consideration RNB's competitive position without NOW accounts and measures to minimize their impact. The problem facing RNB is how to retain its dominant competitive position given an environmental threat (NOW accounts) while at the same time preserving profitability and its customer base.

DALLAS RETAIL BANK MARKETING

Financial institutions compete with each other—or avoid direct competition—in terms of primary markets served and the character of the marketing mixes employed. Banks emphasize either the wholesale (business) market or the retail (individual) market. Savings and loan institutions (S&Ls) and credit unions focus on the retail market.

The *product-service* element of a bank's marketing mix consists of (1) the variety of accounts provided (checking, savings, savings certificates); (2) the sources of funds for customers (installment loans, commercial loans); (3) frills (package accounts such as RNB's Starpak, safety deposit boxes); and (4) service delivery systems (nature of statements, speed of banking service, accuracy in recording transactions, friendliness of personnel, and the like). S&Ls and credit unions use the same product-service elements, although the nature of the mix varies. S&Ls do not offer checking accounts; credit unions provide share drafts, which have similarities with checking accounts. Both offer savings accounts and S&Ls offer savings certificates. S&Ls and credit unions provide funds for installment loans; S&Ls are also major sources of mortgage loans. Frills are less apparent in S&Ls and credit unions than in banks.

The *distribution* element is reflected in the number of locations at which financial institutions can operate. Banks in Texas are limited to a single location by the unit banking regulation. However, S&Ls and credit unions have multiple locations. The case notes that about 200 S&L offices existed in Dallas County and 232 credit union offices operated in Dallas County. *Convenience* in personal finance is influenced by the distribution factor. The *price* element is evident in interest rates and service charges on personal accounts. Regulations limit banks to 5 percent interest on savings; S&Ls can offer $5^1/_4$ percent. Service charges vary between banks. The *communication* element includes advertising, sales efforts of bank officers and tellers, gifts, and promotion gimmicks.

In short, banks, S&Ls, and credit unions compete through their primary market focus and marketing mix. NOW accounts will change the way financial institutions compete, however. To a large extent, NOW accounts will transform S&Ls and credit unions into banks!

INSIGHTS FROM THE NEW ENGLAND EXPERIENCE

The NOW account experience, based on the data in the report of the marketing division, reveals the following:

1. The faster commercial banks move to adopt NOW accounts, the larger their share of NOW accounts and NOW account balances.

2. Cannibalization of checking accounts occurs when NOW accounts are available; 72 percent of checking account balances in New Hampshire have been converted to NOW accounts, and 44 percent of checking accounts in Massachusetts have been converted to NOWs. These figures developed over 50 months (four years) after the NOW introduction (see Exhibit A.2).

3. Exhibit 1 in the case provides some evidence that NOW account balances are high. This could mean that those individuals with high checking account balances are more likely to switch to NOWs. Alternatively, the Connecticut experience would indicate that minimum balance requirements increase NOW account balances. Data for Massachusetts and New Hampshire—both of which experienced "free NOWs"—would tend to support the point that individuals with high account balances convert to NOWs.

4. NOW account usage activity approaches checking account activity; hence checking account costs are merely transferred to managing NOW accounts.

5. Competitive activity, reflected in the NOW package provided, reveals that "free NOWs" were initially provided. Financial institutions subsequently offered less generous terms, however.

6. NOW account packages differ greatly with respect to minimum balances, service charges, and positioning against checking and savings accounts.

Results from the New England experience suggest that three scenarios are possible in the Dallas market.

Environment	*Environment Description*
No NOW adoption:	Financial institutions refrain from adoption.
Liberal NOW adoption:	NOWs are adopted with no minimum balance, service charges, 5 percent interest, an active promotion/communication program.
Conservative NOW adoption:	NOWs are adopted with some form of minimum balance, service charges, less than 5 percent interest, little promotion or communication.

Numerous factors will affect the likelihood of each environment's developing in the Dallas market.

Factors in favor of a no-NOW environment:

1. The New England experience suggests that a no-win possibility exists for all financial institutions. For example, banks will have to pay interest on previously interest-free funds, and S&Ls and credit unions will incur costs not previously encountered.

2. Money market rates are quite low at present, suggesting little spread to make an adequate profit margin.

Factors in favor of a NOW environment:

1. The New England experience suggests that where NOWs are legalized, they are adopted in some form, by someone.

2. If the Dallas market is competitive *and* various financial institutions are vying for deposits, then NOWs offer a means to attract deposits. Moreover, the New England experience suggests that "getting in first" is crucial. "Followership" is not rewarded.

3. S&Ls are poised to take some advantage of NOWs in that their interest rate paid on deposits will fall from $5\frac{1}{4}$ percent to 5 percent, assuming a 5 percent ceiling level.

Factors in favor of a liberal NOW environment:

1. Thrifts might view NOWs as a way of gaining deposits quickly.
2. S&Ls will benefit from NOWs even if 5 percent interest is offered on NOW accounts, since they are currently paying $5\frac{1}{4}$ percent on savings.
3. Share drafts provided by credit unions have characteristics similar to those of NOWs; NOW accounts would seem like a logical extension.

Factors in favor of a conservative NOW environment:

1. This appears to be the trend in New England states.
2. Dallas banks do not generally offer free checking.
3. Money market rates are low.

It would seem that a potential determinant of how the NOW environment evolves will be the decision of RNB, given its dominance in the Dallas banking market. RNB's dominant position would seem to affect the environment *only* if RNB acts immediately with a well thought out NOW account program. NOWs are probably inevitable— that is, the no-NOW environment seems unlikely. The question, then, is whether a liberal or a conservative NOW environment will develop. The environment could be influenced by RNB.

REPUBLIC NATIONAL BANK

RNB dominates the Dallas financial market. Its assets alone ($6 billion) are almost ten times *total* assets of all credit unions ($666 million). RNB's deposits ($4.6 billion) exceed the total for *all* S&Ls ($2.85 billion). RNB has the largest deposit base of all Dallas banks *and* the largest retail account deposit base in Dallas.

Nevertheless, RNB management apparently has not resolved how aggressive the bank should be in retail account marketing efforts. The aggressiveness issue would seem to be related to the bank's emphasis on the wholesale rather than the retail business.

Exhibit 1 in the case indicates that about 55 percent of RNB's checking accounts are under $500. However, 96 percent of total checking account balances are accounted for by accounts of $500 and up, and 53 percent of total deposits are accounted for by accounts of over $25,000. The average account size is $3,333 ($150 million in deposits divided by 45,000 accounts). A profitability analysis of checking account sizes reveals that RNB loses money on accounts that are less than $500 on an annual basis (see Exhibit 1 in this analysis). This profitability analysis indicates that accounts below $500 produce *a loss* of $519,210 annually:

Accounts under $200:   14,400 accounts × ($24.24) = ($349.056)

Accounts $200-$499:   10,350 accounts × ($16.44) = ($170.154)

Loss   = ($519.210)

More important, this analysis provides important data on the pricing of NOW accounts and the form of the service, as I will discuss later.

EXHIBIT 1

RNB Retail Account Profit Analysis (Based on Exhibit 1 in the Case)

Account Size	Average Interest Revenue per Account[a]	+	Average Service/ Handling Revenue per Account[b]	=	Average Revenue per Account	−	Account Cost[b]	=	Profit/ (Loss)
Less than $200	$19.92		$18.72		$38.64		$62.88		$(24.24)
$200–$499	27.72		18.72		46.44		62.88		(16.44)
$500–$999	60.71		18.72		79.43		62.88		16.55
$1,000–$4,999	153.47		18.72		172.19		62.88		109.31
$5,000–$9,999	333.93		18.72		352.65		62.88		289.77
$10,000–$24,999	920.83		18.72		939.55		62.88		876.67
$25,000–$100,000	2,125.00		18.72		2,143.72		62.88		2,080.84
Greater than $100,000	7,083.00		18.72		7,101.72		62.88		7,038.84

[a]Computed as follows: $\dfrac{\text{Account size deposit volume}}{\text{Number of accounts in category}} \times 85\% \times 0.075.$

For an account size of $200, using Exhibit 1 data: $\dfrac{\$4.5 \text{ million}}{14,400} \times 0.85 \times 0.075 = \$19.92$

[b]Annualized average account revenue and cost given in the case where Service/handling charge revenue per account per month = $1.56; Account cost per month = $5.24

PLAN OF ACTION

There are two primary alternatives open to RNB: to offer NOWs or not to offer NOWs. If NOWs are considered, then the form, price and promotion must be determined. The alternatives are:

1. Do not offer NOW accounts.
2. Offer NOW accounts with no conditions and promote them heavily or modestly.
3. Offer NOW accounts with conditions and promote them heavily or modestly.

The advantages and disadvantages of the options available to RNB can be outlined as follows.

1. Not offering NOW accounts:

   Advantages

   - RNB is dominant and has the resources to wait and see what will happen.
   - The impact on revenue of offering NOWs would be too severe. Assuming that *all accounts* are cannibalized by NOWs and the interest yield drops from $7\frac{1}{2}$ percent to $2\frac{1}{2}$ percent because of 5 percent interest on NOWs, the interest revenue lost will be about $6.0 million.

Checking Deposits		Percent Investable		Investable Deposits
$150 million	×	85%	=	$127.5 million

				Interest Revenue
$127.5 million	×	0.075	=	9,562,500
$144 million	×	0.025	=	−3,600,000
Interest revenue lost				$5,962,500

Note that NOW accounts are viewed as savings accounts, and 96 percent of deposits are investable.

Disadvantages

- RNB will lose an opportunity to be an innovator or the "first to market," which has been shown in New England to be advantageous.

- Erosion of accounts may occur, as individuals switch to institutions offering NOW accounts. This factor is particularly important if *large* accounts switch, and they are most likely to do so, since they stand to benefit most from NOW accounts.

2. Offering NOW accounts with no conditions:

Advantages

- Nonconditional NOWs will have a dramatic impact on the Dallas banking market. Banks offering them will most likely attract deposits and accounts in great numbers, particularly since they are a better deal than checking accounts with minimum balances or service charges, *plus* they give interest!

- Nonconditional NOW accounts will set the competitive tenor of the market; retail banks not offering them may be unable to compete.

- By offering nonconditional NOWs, RNB will keep current accounts from being attracted to competitors (preemptive cannibalism).

Disadvantages

- This strategy could be very expensive. As noted earlier, in addition to the account costs, a loss of interest of $6 million is possible.

- This strategy will cannibalize checking accounts almost totally.

3. Offering NOW accounts with conditions:

Advantages

- A minimum-balance condition would allow RNB to accept only those accounts on which it can make money.

- A service/handling charge condition would also result in greater account selectivity.

- A break-even analysis shows how RNB can determine a minimum balance given current service charge and account costs per year. The break-even point is the point at which total revenues (interest plus handling/service charges) minus total costs (account cost per month) equals zero. Since RNB will net 2.5 percent in account interest revenue, has an $18.72 handling and service revenue per account per year ($1.56

× 12 months), and has an annual account cost of $62.88 ($5.24 × 12 months), I solved for the minimum account balance as follows:

$$\text{Profit} = \frac{\text{acct. interest}}{\text{revenue}} + \frac{\text{handling/}}{\text{service charge}} - \frac{\text{acct.}}{\text{cost}}$$

$$0 = 0.025X + \$18.72 - \$62.88$$

$$\$44.16 = 0.025X$$

$$\$1{,}766.40 = X$$

Thus RNB breaks even at an account size of $1,766.40, given existing handling/service revenue per account and account maintenance costs. This minimum balance level would be a condition that from 80 percent to 90 percent of RNB's accounts could meet (see Exhibit 1 in the case).

Disadvantages

- This strategy leaves RNB open to being undercut by competitors if conditions are too stringent.
- Overly complex conditions and the likelihood of customers' being unexpectedly hit with service charges could hurt goodwill, particularly among larger-balance account holders.

NOW ACCOUNT MARKETING STRATEGY

The previous analysis indicates to me that RNB should offer NOW accounts immediately to set a competitive tone in the market and create a "rational" NOW environment. By doing so, RNB will assume a leadership position.

The principal *target market* should be current customers with large account balances. The emphasis should be on preemptive cannibalism. There is probably little to be gained from new customers. The RNB NOW *account should be offered with conditions*. It is recommended that RNB set a minimum balance of about $1,500. Moreover, RNB should incorporate NOWs into one of its package accounts, such as the Starpak Account. The promotional effort should be modest and directed. Specifically, direct mail to current customers is recommended.

Advertising opportunity. Conditions suggesting that a product or service would benefit from advertising: (1) there is favorable primary demand for the product or service category, (2) the product or service to be advertised can be significantly differentiated from its competitors, (3) the product or service has hidden qualities or benefits that can be portrayed effectively through advertising, and (4) there are strong emotional buying motives for the product or service.

Brand equity. The added value a brand name bestows on a product or service beyond the functional benefits provided.

Brand leveraging. The practice of applying an existing brand name to new entries in different product-service categories.

Break-even analysis. The unit or dollar sales volume at which an organization neither makes a profit nor incurs a loss. The formula for determining the number of units required to break even is:

$$\text{Unit Break-even} = \frac{\text{total dollar fixed cost}}{(\text{unit selling price} - \text{unit variable cost})}.$$

Bundling. The practice of marketing two or more product or service items in a single "package" with one price.

Business definition. The characterization of an organization's customers, customer needs, and means or technology used to satisfy the needs of customers.

Cannibalism. The process whereby the sales of a new product or service come at the expense of existing products (services) already marketed by the firm.

Channel captain. A member of a marketing channel with the power to influence the behavior of other channel members.

Channel conflict. A situation that arises when one channel member believes another channel member is engaged in behavior that is preventing it from achieving its goals.

Contribution. The difference between total sales revenue and total variable costs or, on a per-unit basis, the difference between unit selling price and unit variable cost. Contribution can be expressed in percentage terms (contribution margin) or dollar terms (contribution per unit).

Cost of goods sold. Material, labor, and factory overhead applied directly to production.

Cross-elasticity of demand. The responsiveness of the quantity demanded of one product or service to a price change in another product or service.

Distinctive competency. An organization's principal strengths or qualities that are imperfectly imitable by competitors and provide superior value to customers.

Diversification. A product-market strategy that involves the development or acquisition of offerings new to the organization and the introduction of those offerings to publics (markets) not previously served by the organization.

Dual distribution. The practice of distributing products or services through two or more different marketing channels that may or may not compete for similar buyers.

Effective demand. The situation when prospective buyers have both the willingness and ability to purchase an organization's offerings.

Exclusive distribution. A distribution strategy whereby a producer sells its products or services in only one retail outlet in a specific geographical area.

Fixed cost. Expenses that do not fluctuate with output volume within a relevant time period (usually defined as a budget year), but become progressively smaller per unit of output as volume increases. Fixed costs divide into programmed costs, which result from attempts to generate sales volume and committed costs, which are those required to maintain the organization.

Full-cost price strategies. Those that consider both variable and fixed costs (total cost) in the pricing of a product or service.

Gross margin (or gross profit). The difference between total sales revenue and total cost of goods sold or, on a per-unit basis, the difference between unit selling price and unit cost of goods sold. Gross margin can be expressed in dollar or percentage terms.

Harvesting. The practice of reducing the investment in a business entity (division, product) to cut costs or improve cash flow.

Intensive distribution. A distribution strategy whereby a producer sells its products or services in as many retail outlets as possible in a geographical area.

Life cycle. The plot of sales of a single product or brand or service or a class of products or services over time.

Market. Prospective buyers (individuals or organizations) who are willing and able to purchase the existing or potential offering (product or service) of an organization.

Market-development strategy. A product-market strategy whereby an organization introduces its offerings to markets other than those it is currently serving. In global marketing, this strategy can be implemented through exportation, licensing, joint ventures, or direct investment.

Market evolution. Changes in primary demand for a product class and changes in technology.

Market-penetration strategy. A product-market strategy whereby an organization seeks to gain greater dominance in a market in which it already has an offering. This strategy often means capturing a larger share of an existing market.

Market redefinition. Changes in the offering demanded by buyers or promoted by competitors.

Market segmentation. The breaking down or building up of potential buyers into groups on the basis of some sort of homogeneous characteristic(s) (for example, age, income, geography) relating to purchase or consumption behavior.

Market share. Sales of a firm, product, or brand divided by the sales to the served "market."

Market targeting (or target marketing). The specification of the specific market segment(s) the organization wishes to pursue. Differentiated marketing means that an organization simultaneously pursues several different market segments, usually with a different strategy for each. Concentrated marketing means that only a single market segment is pursued.

Marketing audit. A comprehensive, systematic, independent, and periodic examination of a company's—or business unit's—marketing environment, objectives, strategies, and activities with a view of determining problem areas and opportunities and recommending a plan of action to improve the company's marketing performance.

Marketing-cost analysis. The practice of assigning or allocating costs to a specified marketing activity or entity in a manner that accurately displays the financial contribution of activities or entities to the organization.

Marketing mix. Those activities controllable by the organization that include the product, service, or idea offered, the manner in which the offering will be communicated to customers, the method for distributing or delivering the offering, and the price to be charged for the offering.

Net profit margin (before taxes). The remainder after cost of goods sold, other variable costs, and fixed costs have been subtracted from sales revenue or, simply, total revenue minus total cost. Net profit margin can be expressed in dollar or percentage terms.

Offering. The sum total of benefits or satisfaction provided to target markets by an organization. An offering consists of a tangible product or service plus related services, warranties or guarantees, packaging, etc.

Offering mix or portfolio. The totality of an organization's offerings (products and services).

Operating leverage. The extent to which fixed costs and variable costs are used in the production and marketing of products and services.

Operations control. The practice of assessing how well an organization performs marketing activities as it seeks to achieve planned outcomes.

Opportunity analysis. The process of identifying opportunities, matching the opportunity to the organization, and evaluating the opportunity.

Opportunity cost. Alternative uses of resources that are given up when pursuing one alternative rather than another. Sometimes referred to as the benefits not obtained from not choosing an alternative.

Payback period. The number of years required for an organization to recapture its initial investment in an offering.

Penetration pricing strategy. Setting a relatively low initial price for a new product or service.

Positioning. The creation of impressions about a product, service, or organization. A product or service can be positioned by (1) attribute or benefit, (2) use or application, (3) product or service class, (4) product or service user, and (5) competitors.

Price elasticity of demand. The percentage change in quantity demanded relative to a percentage change in price for a product or service.

Product-development strategy. A product-market strategy whereby an organization creates new offerings for existing markets through product innovation, product augmentation, or product-line extensions.

Pro forma income statement. An income statement containing projected revenues, budgeted (variable and fixed) expenses, and estimated net profit for an organization, product, or service during a specific planning period, usually a year.

Pull communication strategy. The practice of creating initial interest for an offering among potential buyers, who in turn demand the offering from intermediaries, ultimately "pulling" the offering through the channel. The principal emphasis is on consumer advertising and consumer promotions.

Push communication strategy. The practice of "pushing" an offering through a marketing channel in a sequential fashion, with each channel representing a distinct target market. The principal emphasis is on personal selling and trade promotions directed toward wholesalers and retailers.

Regional marketing. The practice of using different marketing mixes to accommodate unique consumer preferences and competitive conditions in different geographical areas.

Relevant cost. Expenditures that (1) are expected to occur in the future as a result of some marketing action and (2) differ among marketing alternatives being considered.

Scrambled merchandising. The practice of wholesalers and retailers to carry a wider assortment of merchandise than they did in the past.

Selective distribution. A distribution strategy whereby a producer sells its products or services in a few retail outlets in a specific geographical area.

Situation analysis. The appraisal of operations to determine the reasons for the gap between what was or is expected and what has happened or will happen.

Skimming pricing strategy. Setting a relatively high initial price for a new product or service.

Strategic change. Environmental change that will affect the long-run well-being of the organization.

Strategic control. The practice of assessing the direction of the organization as evidenced by its implicit or explicit goals, objectives, strategies, and capacity to perform in the context of changing environments and competitive actions.

Strategic marketing management. The analytical process of defining the organization's business; specifying the purpose of the organization; identifying organizational opportunities; formulating product-market strategies; budgeting financial, production, and human resources; and developing reformulation and recovery strategies.

Success requirements. The basic tasks that must be performed by an organization in a market or industry to compete successfully. These are sometimes "key success factors," or simply KSFs.

Sunk cost. Past expenditures for a given activity that are typically irrelevant in whole or in part to future decisions. The "sunk cost fallacy" is an attempt to recoup spent dollars by spending still more dollars in the future.

Trade margin. The difference between unit sales price and unit cost at each level of marketing channel. Trade margin is usually expressed in percentage terms.

Trading down. The process of reducing the number of features or quality of an offering and lowering the purchase price.

Trading up. The practice of improving an offering by adding new features and higher-quality materials or augmenting products with services and raising the purchase price.

Value. The ratio of perceived benefits to price for a product or service.

Variable cost. Expenses that are uniform per unit of output within a relevant time period (usually defined as a budget year); total variable costs fluctuate in direct proportion to the output volume of units produced. Variable costs includes cost of goods sold and other variable costs such as sales commissions.

Variable-cost price strategies. Those that consider only direct (variable) cost associated with the offering in pricing a product or service.

Working capital. The dollar value of an organization's current assets (such as cash, accounts receivable, prepaid expenses, inventory) minus the dollar value of current liabilities (such as short-term accounts payable for goods and services, income taxes).

Subject Index

Accuracy of information, 113
Acquired immune deficiency
    syndrome (AIDS), 430, 431–34
    incidence and cost of, 432–33
Addiction, smoking as, 478–80
Advertising
    collateral, 575
    cooperative advertising
        allowances, 284
    make-or-buy decision relating to,
        276
    of orange carbonated soft drinks,
        304–5
Advertising budget allocation,
        278–79
    in Morgantown Furniture case,
        287
Advertising opportunity, 277
Advertising strategies
    of Circle K Corporation, 594–95
    of Godiva Europe, 325–29
    of Goodyear Tire and Rubber
        Company, 401
    in household furniture industry,
        287
    for Niconil, 488
    for Sun Chips™ Multigrain
        Snacks, 177, 181
    for Swatch, 652–64
    for Tyler Pet Foods, Inc., 574–78
AIDS-related complex (ARC), 430
Airline Deregulation Act of 1978,
    226
Alopecia, 86
Alternative courses of action, 32–33
Alternatives
    analysis of, at Upjohn Company,
        86–88
    identifying best, 33–35
    plan for implementing chosen,
        35–36
Ambulatory health-care services and
    facilities, 200–201
American Dental Association (ADA),
    250
Androgenetic alopecia, 86
Ansoff, H. Igor, 5
Application, positioning by, 163
Assets, current, 25
Asynchronous transfer mode (ATM),
    492, 499–501
Attractiveness of opportunity, 42,
    43
Audit, marketing, 13
    of Marshall Museum of Art,
        532–37
Availability of information, 114
Aversion therapy for smoking, 478

Bain, Alexander, 454
Balding, treatments for, 86–88
Banking industry, 710–12, 720
    investment, 193–94
Behavioral self-monitoring for
    smokers, 478–80
Better Business Bureau, 246
Bidding, competitive, 428–29
Big Six, 187, 188, 193
Blitz, George, 345
Blitz strategy, 279
Brand equity, 164
Branding offerings, 164–65
    private branding (private label),
        165, 222–23, 397
Brand leveraging, 164
Break-even analysis, 20–21, 159, 426
    impact of price changes on profit
        and, 424–25
Break-even point, 21
Break-even pricing, 426

Brokers, 581
Budget, master, 12
Budgeting, 1, 12
    for communication strategy,
        277–80
    at Tyler Pet Foods, Inc., 578
Bundling, 157
Business analysis, 159
    in American Airlines case, 227–32
Business definition, 1, 2–3
Buyer behavior
    in carbonated soft drink industry,
        301–2
    in chocolate market, 316–17
    convenience store customer,
        598–99
    furniture, 284–86
    in home entertainment industry,
        384–85
    in mouse marketplace, 264–66
Buyers
    defining market by, 42–43
    information requirements of,
        272–73, 274, 362, 365

Cadbury, John, 297
Canadian Dental Association, 250
Cannibalism, 8
    assessment of, 23–25
    at Goodyear Tire and Rubber
        Company, 402
    offering mix and, 158
    by P&G Downy Enviro-Pak,
        471–72
    by private-label product, 223
    by Sun Chips™ Multigrain Snacks,
        180–83
Capital, working, 25
Carpal tunnel syndrome, 262, 263,
    269
Carpet and rug industry, 416–18
Case analysis, 33, 37–40
    approaching case, 37
    communicating, 39–40
    example of, 719–25
    formulating, 37–39
Category killer, 557
Cells in matrix, 46
Centralization
    coordinated, 567
    decentralization and, balance
        between, 566
Certified public accountants (CPAs),
    187
Change, strategic, 507–8
Channel captain, power of, 368–69
Channel conflict, sources of, 368
Channels.
See Marketing channels
Channel strategy, 11
Chinese food market, 582–84
Chocolate market, 314–17
    consumption, 314–16
    purchase behavior in, 316–17
Class discussion of case studies, 39
Clinics, 200
Coffee, market structure for, 44
Coffee consumption, 97–98
Coffee industry, 98–104
Collateral advertising, 575
Comarketing agreements, 682,
    688–89
Committed costs, 17
Communication budget, 277–80
    at Club Med España, 345, 353,
        355, 357
    at Honeywell, Inc., Spectronics
        Division, 343, 344
    at Morgantown Furniture, Inc.,
        287–89

Communication strategy, 271–361
    for American Airlines, 239–41
    analytical framework for, 272
    for Cadbury Beverages, Inc.,
        296–311
    for Club Med España, 345–61
    communication mix, 271–72,
        274–77
    evaluation and control of
        communication process, 280
    for Godiva Europe, 312–30
    for Honeywell, Inc., Spectronics
        Division, 331–44
    information requirements in
        purchase decisions, 272–73,
        274, 362, 365
    for Logitech, 268–69
    for Morgantown Furniture, Inc.,
        282–95
    objectives of, 273–74
    organizational capacity and,
        275–76
    purpose of, 271
    push versus pull, 276–77
    for Swatch, 651–52
    target-market characteristics and,
        275
    for Volvo Trucks Corporation,
        Europe Division, 607–9
    for Warner-Lambert Ireland,
        487–90
Company sales force, 275–76
    of Honeywell, Inc.'s Spectronic
        Division, 334
    independent sales reps vs.,
        275–76, 293–95
    at Morgantown Furniture, Inc.,
        283, 293–95
Competency, distinctive, 4
    of Dell Computer Corporation,
        549
Competition, fit of program to, 564
Competitive analysis, 154–55
Competitive bidding, 428–29
Competitive-parity approach, 278
Comprehensive marketing
    programs, 563–708
    at Chun King Corporation,
        579–89
    at Circle K Corporation, 590–601
    at Colgate-Palmolive Canada,
        617–36
    implementation of, 565–66
    marketing-mix sensitivities and
        interaction, 564–65
    marketing organization and,
        566–67
    program fit, 564
    for Swatch, 637–70
    at Tyler Pet Foods, Inc., 568–78
    at Volvo Trucks Europe, 602–16
    for Zantac, 671–708
Computers
    notebook, 552–54, 558–59
    personal computer industry,
        261–62, 555
Concentrated marketing, 47
Conceptual pricing strategies, 427
Constraints in problem definition,
    32
Consumer research. See Buyer
    behavior; Marketing research
Contingency plans, 13
Continuousness, concept of, 280
Contribution analysis, 20–25
Contribution margin, 21
Contribution-margin approach, 510
Contribution per unit, 21
Contribution pricing strategy, 425,
    426–27

Control process, 506–62
    considerations in, 514
    for Dell Computer Corporation,
        546–62
    for Hanover-Bates Chemical
        Corporation, 539–45
    marketing channel control,
        512–14
    marketing-cost analysis, 508–9
    for Marshall Museum of Art,
        528–38
    operations control, 506, 508–14
    product-service mix control,
        509–10
    sales control, 510–12
    strategic change and, 507–8
    strategic control, 506
    for TOSTITOS® brand Tortilla
        Chips, 516–27
Convenience store industry,
    595–600
    competitors, 596–98
    customers and purchase behavior,
        598–99
    industry trends and concerns,
        599–600
Conversion, costs of, 6
Cooperative advertising allowances,
    284
Coordinated centralization, 567
Coors, Adolph, 119
Corporate finance services, 186,
    190–93
Cost(s)
    committed, 17
    of conversion, 6
    of defining market segments, 45
    experience (learning) effect and,
        465–67
    fixed (indirect), 17, 425
    of information, 116
    of marketing channels, 513–14
    marketing-cost analysis, 508–9
    opportunity, 9
    order-getting, 513
    order-servicing expenditures, 513
    pricing strategies and, 425–29
    programmed, 17
    relevant, 17
    sunk, 17–18
    variable (direct), 16, 422, 425
Cost allocation, 508–9
Cost of goods sold, 16, 26
Cost per thousand (CPM), 278
Credit unions, 712
Cross-elasticity coefficient, 424
Cross-elasticity of demand, 424
Culture, organizational, 258
Currency of information, 113–14
Current assets, 25
Current liabilities, 25

Data versus information, difference
    between, 514
Dealers, 555–57, 562
Decentralization and centralization,
    balance between, 566
DECIDE (decision-making process),
    31–37
Decision analysis, 33–35
    value of information and, 112–13
Decision factors, enumerating,
    32–33
Decision making
    evaluating decision, 36–37
    steps in, 31–37
Decisions, make-or-buy, 275–76
Decision tree, 10, 34
Dell, Michael, 546–47, 549, 551,
    558, 559

Demand
  cross-elasticity of, 424
  effective, 42–43
  price ceiling set by, 422
  price elasticity of, 423–24
  primary, 273–74
  selective, 273–74
  variable-cost pricing and, 427
Demand-impact analysis, 239, 240
Density of distribution, 365–66, 367
Depth of repeat, 180, 185
Dewey, John, 32
Differential channel pricing by
  Logitech, 268
Differentiated marketing, 47
Direct distribution for Carrington
  Carpet Mills, Inc., 419–20
Direct investment, 7
Direct mail campaign
  for Marshall Museum of Art,
    536–37
  for Niconil, 490
Direct-marketing channel, 548, 549,
  557
Direct sales (field sales) channel,
  557–58
Direct (variable) costs, 16, 422, 425
Direct vs. indirect distribution,
  363–64
Distinctive competency, 4
  of Dell Computer Corporation,
    549
Distribution, effective, 366. See also
  Marketing channels
Diversification, 8–9, 10
Dog food industry, 570–71
  market share and sales for, 571
Downsizing, 162
Drucker, Peter, 31
Dual distribution, 367
Due diligence, 186

Effective demand, 42–43
Effective distribution, 366
Effectiveness versus efficiency, 506,
  514
"80–20 rule," 509
Einstein, Albert, 27
Elasticity of demand, price, 423–24
Elimination of offering, 162
Enis, Ben, 45
Environmental changes, 9
Environmental issues, 469–70
Environmental opportunity, 4
Ethical pharmaceutical products,
  rankings of, 672
Ethics, 13–14
European Community (EC), 602
  Curtis Automotive Hoist and,
    implications for, 80–83
  history of, 80–81
  impact of 1992 on European
    truck industry, 612–13
  MacTec's strategy in, 141–42
European truck market, 610–13
Exclusive-distribution strategy, 365,
  366
  of Hendison Electronics
    Corporation, 388–89
Expected monetary value of
  "perfect" information (EMVPI),
  112, 113
Expenses. See Marketing expenses
Experience (learning) curve, 461,
  462, 463, 464–67
Exporting, 7

Facsimile machine industry, 454–59
  commercial development of, 456
  competitive and marketing
    environment, 456–57

industry suppliers in, 458–59
  market segmentation of, 457–58
  origins of technology, 454–56
Fiber optics, 332, 496
Fiber-optics industry, 331–33
Field sales (direct sales) channel,
  557–58
Finance, 16–30
  contribution analysis, 20–25
  liquidity, 25
  margins, 18–20, 21
  operating leverage, 25–26
  relevant and sunk costs, 17–18
  variable and fixed costs, 16–17,
    425
Financial contribution of market
  offerings, appraising, 509–10
Fit, program, 564
Fixed costs, 17, 425
Florida Orange Growers Association,
  6
Focus group studies, 134, 153–54
Ford, Henry, 45
Formula-based approach to
  communication budgeting,
  277–78
Frame-relay transmission service,
  497–98
Frequency, 278
Full-cost pricing, 425–26
Furniture industry. See Household
  furniture industry

General and administrative
  expenses, 26
Glass-Steagall Act of 1933, 195
Glocalization, 11, 566
Goals, specifying, 3
Gross margin, 18, 26
Group presentation of case, 39
G-stores, 597

Harvesting, 162
Health-care business, 89–90
  hospital industry, 199–201
  in Ireland, 481
Health maintenance organizations
  (HMOs), 200
Health Protection Branch (HPB) in
  Canada, 249
Hill-Burton Act, 199
HIV (human immunodeficiency
  virus), 430
  anti-HIV drug treatment, 433–34
  incidence and cost of, 432–33
Home entertainment industry,
  384–85
Horizontal media, 278–79
Hospital industry, 199–201
Household furniture industry,
  284–87
  advertising practices in, 287
  buyer behavior in, 284–86
  consumer expenditures in, 284
  distribution in, 286–87
H2-blocker (H2-antagonist) for ulcer
  treatment, 675–77
Human immunodeficiency virus
  (HIV), 430, 432–34
Hypothermia, treatment of post-
  operative, 443–48
  competing technologies, 445–46
  competitive products for, 446–48
  hospital market for, 448–52

Idea generation/idea screening, 159
Implementation
  of comprehensive marketing
    program, 565–66
  plan for, 35–36

Income statement, pro forma,
  26–27
Independent sales representatives,
  275–76, 293–95
Indirect (fixed) costs, 17, 425
Indirect vs. direct distribution,
  363–64
Information. See also Marketing
  research
  appraising value of, 112–14
  best means for obtaining, 115–16
  determining cost of, 116
  relevant, 33, 114
  requirements in purchase
    decisions, 272–73, 274, 362,
    365
  specification requirements for,
    115
  strategies for analysis and
    interpretation of, 116–17
Information-acquisition process,
  managing, 114–17
Information versus data, difference
  between, 514
Innovation
  product, 8
  production process, 464
Insect control, 374–76
Insect growth regulator (IGRs) case,
  372–82
  effectiveness of IGRs, 374–76
  product development and
    marketing, 377–81
Insecticide market, premise, 376–77
Intensive-distribution strategy, 365,
  366
Intermediaries, density of, 365–66.
  See also Marketing channels
Intermediary requirements,
  satisfying, 368–69
Intermediate pricing strategy, 428
Internal-warming technologies, 446
Investment, direct, 7
Investment banking industry,
  193–94
Ireland, Republic of
  health care in, 481
  smoking in Republic of, 477–78

Joint venture (strategic alliance), 7,
  82, 555, 559

Korn, Arthur, 454

Labor efficiency, 464
Labor learning curve, 462, 463
Launch campaigns for Zantac,
  680–89
Laundry detergent market, 618–19
  intense competitive activity in,
    619–24
Learning (experience) curve
  phenomenon, 461, 464–67
  example of, 465–67
  labor learning curve, 462, 463
  sources of, 464–65
  strategic implications of, 467
Leather Industries of America, 8
Leverage, operating, 25–26
Leveraging, brand, 164
Liabilities, current, 25
Licensing, 7
Life cycle
  communication objectives and,
    273–74
  concept of, 160–61
  importance of positioning in, 162
  learning curve and, 467
  pricing and, 422
  product, 160–61, 262
  service, 161

Line extension, 169
  by Procter and Gamble, 250, 251
Liquidity, 25
Logistical aspects of marketing
  program, 566

Make-or-buy decisions, 275–76
Management training at Volvo
  Trucks Corporation, Europe
  Division, 616
Manufacturer-owned outlet, 555
Margins, 18–20, 21, 26
Market
  defining, 42–45
  fit of program to, 564
Market-development strategy, 6–7,
  10, 273
Market evolution, 507
Marketing audit, 13
  of Marshall Museum of Art,
    532–37
Marketing channel control, 512–14
Marketing channels, 362–420
  for Bateson battery chargers,
    148–49
  for Carrington Carpet Mills, Inc.,
    416–20
  channel-modification decisions,
    369–70
  channel-selection decision,
    363–67
  for Club Med España, 354–55, 361
  for Dell Computer Corporation,
    548, 549, 555–62
  direct vs. indirect distribution,
    363–64
  dual distribution, 367
  for Godiva Europe, 322–24
  for Goodyear Tire and Rubber
    Company, 390–402
  for Hendison Electronics
    Corporation, 383–89
  for household furniture industry,
    286–87
  intermediary requirements,
    satisfying, 368–69
  for Konark Television India,
    403–15
  for Logitech, 268
  profitability analysis for, 512–13
  push versus pull communication
    strategy and, 276–77
  strategic change and, 507
  for Sun Chips™ Multigrain
    Snacks, 177, 182
  for Swatch, 646–48, 649
  for Swisher Mower and Machine
    Company, 215–17
  trade relations, 368–69
  for Volvo Trucks Corporation,
    Europe Division, 604–7
  for Zoëcon Corporation, 372–82
Marketing communication mix,
  271–72, 274–77
Marketing communication strategy.
  See Communication strategy
Marketing control. See Control
  process
Marketing-cost analysis, 508–9
Marketing expenses
  of Club Med España, 356–60
  of Colgate-Palmolive Canada, 621,
    625, 631
  of Frito-Lay's® Dips, 68, 72
  of Honeywell, Inc., Spectronics
    Division, 339, 340, 343, 344
  of Jones•Blair Company, 56
  of Morgantown Furniture, Inc.,
    283–84
  of Nestlé Italy, 103, 104
  for orange soft drink brands,
    305–7

of Procter and Gamble, Inc.,
  Scope, 249
in *pro forma* income statement,
  26
for Strike ROACH ENDER test
  market, 380, 382
for Sun Chips™ Multigrain
  Snacks, 180
of Swatch, 655, 656
of Tyler Pet Foods, Inc., 578
of Upjohn Company, 94, 95
Marketing information systems at
  Volvo Trucks Corporation,
  Europe Division,
  613–16
Marketing mix, 5, 10–12
  sensitivities and interaction,
    564–65
Marketing program fit, 564
Marketing research, 111–55
  for Bateson Corporation, 149–52,
    154
  choosing types of analysis and
    interpretation, 116–17
  for Club Med España, 353, 354
  defined, 111
  for Godiva Europe, 329–30
  on home entertainment buyers,
    384–85
  on hospital market for
    hypothermia treatments,
    448–52
  information-acquisition process,
    managing, 114–17
  for MacTec Control AB, 142–44
  for Morgantown Furniture, Inc.,
    289–92
  for Ms-Tique Corporation, 131–36
  for Procter and Gamble, Inc.,
    Scope, 246–49, 252
  for South Delaware Coors, Inc.,
    120–28
  value of information, appraising,
    112–14
  for Volvo Trucks Europe, 610
Marketing strategies
  for Bateson battery chargers,
    145–46
  for Chun King Corporation,
    584–89
  for Circle K Corporation, 590,
    600–601
  for Club Med España, 352–55, 360
  for Colgate-Palmolive Canada, 625
  for Curtis Automotive Hoist,
    79–80
  development of actionable, 117
  for Frito-Lay, Inc. Sun Chips
    Multigrain Snacks, 185
  for Frito-Lay's® Dips, 67–68, 69,
    70, 71
  for Godiva Europe, 320–27
  for Hendison Electronic
    Corporation, 385–88
  for MacTec Control AB, 141–42
  for Nestlé Italy, 106–9
  reformulation. *See* Control
    process
  for TOSTITOS® brand Tortilla
    Chips, 520, 522, 523, 524–26
  for Tyler Pet Foods, Inc., 573–78
  for Upjohn Company, 92–95
Market-penetration strategy, 6, 10,
  12, 273
  for Logitech, 262–63
Market-potential analysis, 47–48
  for Augustine Medical, Inc.,
    448–52
  for Curtis Automotive Hoist,
    76–78, 81
  for Frito-Lay's® Dips, 63–65

for Jones*Blair Company, 52–54
for MacTec Control AB, 144
for Nestlé Italy, 98–104
for Swatch, 638–39
for Tyler Pet Foods, Inc., 570–71
for Upjohn Company, 85–86
Market redefinition, 507
Market segmentation, 45–46
  for Dell Computer Corporation,
    552
  of facsimile machine industry,
    457–58
  of mouse marketplace, 264–66
  positioning for different market
    segments, 163
  for Strike ROACH ENDER, 378–79
  for Volvo Trucks Corporation,
    Europe Division, 609, 613–14,
    615
Market share
  of Colgate-Palmolive Canada, 618,
    619, 629, 631, 635
  defined, 44
  of facsimile machine
    manufacturers, 457
  as indicator of performance, 509
  of P&G Downy Enviro-Pak,
    471–72
  of TOSTITOS® brand Tortilla
    Chips, 525
  of Volvo Trucks Corporation,
    Europe Division, 604, 607, 608
  of Zantac, 694, 695
Market size
  contribution analysis and, 23
Market targeting, 47
  for Bateson battery chargers,
    147–51
  for Frito-Lay's® Dips, 62–63
  for Nestlé Italy, 109–10
  for Upjohn Company, 85–86, 95
Markup or mark-on, 18–19
Markup pricing, 425–26
Marts, 287
Mass merchandisers, 557
Master budget, 12
Media, vertical and horizontal,
  278–79
Media selection, 278
  at Honeywell, Inc., Spectronics
    Division, 337–39
Media strategy of Colgate-Palmolive
  Canada, 625–36
Medicaid, 199
Medicare, 199
Merchandising, scrambled, 507
Mergers and acquisitions, 187,
  192–93, 194
Minor emergency centers, 200
Mouse marketplace, computer,
  262–66
  buyer behavior in, 264–66
  competition in, 266
  market development, 262–64
Mouthwash market, Canadian,
  244–49

National Home Furnishings
  Foundation, 282
National Pork Producers Council,
  164
Net income before (income) taxes,
  27
Net profit margin (before taxes), 20
Neuhaus, Jean, 317
New-offering development
  at American Airlines, 232–42
  at Bateson, 147
  Frito-Lay, Inc., Sun Chips
    Multigrain Snacks, 171–76
  Frito-Lay's® Dips, 65–67

at Honeywell, Inc., Spectronics
  Division, 334–35
at Logitech, 269–70
P&G Downy Enviro-Pak, 470–75
at Price Waterhouse, 186, 193,
  195–98
process of, 159–60
at Zoëcon, 377–81
New-offering pricing, 427–28
Notebook computers, 552–54,
  558–59
NOW Accounts, case on, 709–10,
  715–25

Objectives, 3, 32
  pricing, 421
Offering(s), 43
  appraising financial contribution
    of market, 509–10
  assessing performance of, 509
  branding, 164–65
  concept of, 156–57
  decisions related to, 156
  elimination of, 162
  harvesting, 162
  life cycle concept and, 160–61
  modifying, 161–62
  nature of, communication mix
    and, 274–75
  new-offering development
    process, 159–60
  positioning, 162–64
Offering development. *See* New-
  offering development
Offering-market matrix, 46–47
Offering mix (portfolio), 157–62
  additions to, 158–59
  defined, 157
Operating leverage, 25–26
Operations control, 506, 508–14
  considerations in, 514
  in Hanover-Bates Chemical
    Corporation, 539–45
  marketing channel control,
    512–14
  marketing-cost analysis, 508–9
  product-service mix control,
    509–10
  sales control, 510–12
Opportunity(ies)
  advertising, 277
  identifying, 1, 4–5, 41–42
Opportunity analysis, 41–42
  at Curtis Automotive Hoist, 80–83
  for Frito-Lay's® Dips, 68–73
  at Jones*Blair Company, 59–61
  at Nestlé Italy, 97–98
  at Tyler Pet Foods, Inc., 571–73
Opportunity costs, 9
Opportunity evaluation, 42, 43
Opportunity-organization matching,
  42
Optoelectronics, 333–34
Order-getting costs, 513
Order-servicing expenditures, 513
Organization
  capacity of, communication
    strategy and, 275–76
  culture of, 258
  definition of business of, 1, 2–3
  fit of program to, 564
  identifying opportunities of, 1,
    4–5, 41–42
  purpose of, specifying, 1, 3
Organizational structure of
  marketing, 566–67
Orphan Drug Act of 1983, 439
Outdoor Power Equipment Institute
  (OPEI), 218
Outdoor power equipment (OPE),
  retail distribution of, 221

Packaging
  for Godiva Europe, 321–22
  of Strike ROACH ENDER, 380
Paint industry, analysis of, 52–54
Paulucci, Jeno, 579
Payback period, 159–60
Payoff table, 34–35
Penetration pricing strategy, 428
Performance measurement,
  contribution analysis and, 23
Performance of offerings, assessing,
  509
Performance review of sales
  personnel, 511–12
Personal computer industry, 261–62
  strategic alliances in, 555
Pharmaceutical industry, 673–74
Plan for implementation, 35–36
Plaque, 255
Positioning strategies, 162–64
  of Colgate-Palmolive Canada,
    619–20, 622
  for CRUSH soft drink, 309–11
  for orange carbonated soft drinks,
    304–5
  of Procter and Gamble, Inc.'s,
    Scope, 244–45
  of Strike ROACH ENDER, 378–79
  for Zantac, 682
Preferred provider organizations
  (PPOs), 200
Premarket test (PMT) of Sun
  Chips™ Multigrain Snacks,
  172–76
Premise insecticide market, 376–77
Prescription products, marketing,
  486–87
Price, Samuel Lowell, 188
Price elasticity of demand, 423–24
Price strategy. *See* Pricing strategy
Pricing
  conceptual orientation to, 422
  markup, 425–26
  objectives, 421
  price as indicator of value,
    422–23
  profits and, 421, 424–25
Pricing policy
  of Circle K Corporation, 595
  of Godiva Europe, 322
Pricing strategy, 11, 421–505
  for American Airlines, 239
  for Augustine Medical, Inc.,
    443–53
  break-even pricing, 426
  for Burroughs Wellcome
    Company, 430–42
  for Chun King Corporation, 586
  for Club Med España, 361
  competitive bidding, 428–29
  conceptual, 427
  full-cost, 425–26
  for Goodyear Tire and Rubber
    Company, 398–401
  learning (experience) effect and,
    467
  for Logitech, 263–64, 268
  new-offering, 427–28
  for P&G Downy Enviro-Pak, 469,
    474
  for Procter & Gamble, Inc.,
    468–75
  for Strike ROACH ENDER, 380
  for Sun Chips™ Multigrain
    Snacks, 177, 180
  for Swatch, 643–45
  technical, 427
  for Tyler Pet Foods, Inc., 574
  for U.S. SemiCon Corporation,
    454–67
  variable-cost, 425, 426–27

Pricing strategy *(cont)*
   for Warner-Lambert Ireland, 476–91
   for WilTel, Inc., 492–505
   for Zantac, 678–80
Primary care, 200*n*
Primary demand, 273–74
Private brand (private label), 165
   for Swisher Mower and Machine Company, 222–23
   in tire industry, 397
Private placements, 194
Problem definition, 32
Problems versus symptoms, recognizing, 514
Product. *See* Offering(s)
Product augmentation, 8
Product-comparison technique, 336
Product development. *See* New-offering development
Product-development strategy, 8, 10
Product innovation, 8
Production process innovations, 464
Product life cycle, 160–61, 262
Product line
   of Chun King Corporation, 581
   of Goodyear Tire and Rubber Company, 398–401
   of Swatch, 645–46
Product line extensions, 8
   of Swatch, 648–51
Product-market strategies, formulating, 1, 5–12
Product redesign, 465
Product-service mix control, 509–10
Product-service mix of Circle K Corporation, 593–94
Product standardization, 465
Product strategy, 10
   for Bateson battery chargers, 146
   for Logitech, 267–68
   for Sun Chips™ Multigrain Snacks, 176–77
Profit
   contribution analysis of, 22
   effect of operating leverage on, 25–26
   price and, 421, 424–25
Profitability analysis, 48, 159
   for marketing channels, 512–13
   of Republic National Bank of Dallas, 722–23
Profitability of retail outlet, 365
   of tire retailers, 397
Pro forma income statements, 12, 26–27
Program fit, 564
Programmed costs, 17
Promotion strategies, 10
   of Chun King Corporation, 581–82, 583
   of Circle K Corporation, 594–95
   of Colgate-Palmolive Canada, 627–29
   of Honeywell, Inc.'s Spectronic Division, 335–44
   of Strike ROACH ENDER, 380, 381
   of Swatch, 652–64
Proton (acid) pump inhibitors, 694
Psychographic segmentation, 658–60
Public accounting industry, 186–88
Public relations
   for Niconil, 490
   for Swatch, 652, 653–54
Public security issues, 194
Pull communication strategy, 276–77
Pulse strategy, 279
Purchase decisions, information

requirements in, 272–73, 274, 362, 365
Purpose of organization, specifying, 1, 3
Push communication strategy, 276–77

Qualitative appraisal of value of information, 113–14
Qualitatively based approaches to communication budgeting, 278
Quantitative appraisal of value of information, 112–13

Rack jobbers, 130
Rate-of-return pricing strategy, 426
Reach, 278
Redesign, product, 465
Reference value, 423
Reformulation and recovery strategies, 13. *See also* Control process
   for laundry detergents, 620
Regional bell operating companies (RBOC), 501
Regional marketing, 11, 566
   Frito-Lay, 518
Regulatory environment for Canadian mouthwash market, 249–50
Relevant costs, 17
Relevant information, 33, 114
Repeat, depth of, 180, 185
Repeat rates for Sun Chips™ Multigrain Snacks, 180, 183, 184
Repetitive strain injuries, 263
Resale, manufacturer's control over, 366
Research. *See* Marketing research
Resellers, value-added, 555
Reseller segment, vertical, 560
Resource mix, changes in, 464
Resources, addition of new offerings and, 158
Retail level, channel selection at, 365–66
Return on investment (ROI), 160
Revson, Charles, 43
Riding lawn mower industry, 218–21

Saccharin/cyclamate sweeteners, 250
Sales
   industrial, 52
   in *pro forma* income statement, 26
   trade, 52
Sales analysis, 159
   in Hanover-Bates Chemical Corporation, 539–45
Sales control, 510–12
Sales force
   company vs. independent, 275–76, 293–95
   cost of representatives, 420
   of Hanover-Bates Chemical Corporation, 543–45
   of Honeywell, Inc., Spectronic Division, 334
   of Lea-Meadows, Inc., 293–95
   of Morgantown Furniture, Inc., 283, 293–95
   of Warner-Lambert Ireland, 490–91
   of Zantac, 694, 696, 697
Sales-force budget allocation, 279–80
   for Morgantown Furniture, 287–89
Sales forecasting
   at Volvo Trucks Corporation, Europe Division, 609–10, 613–14

   at Warner-Lambert Ireland, 485
Sales organization for Dell Computer Corporation, 549–51
Sales potential. *See* Market-potential analysis
Sales strategy
   of Logitech, 268
   for Sun Chips™ Multigrain Snacks, 177
   of Warner-Lambert Ireland, 490–91
Sales volume as index of performance, 509
Savings and loan associations, 711–12
Schweppe, Jacob, 297
Scrambled merchandising, 507
Segmentation
   market. *See* Market segmentation
   psychographic, 658–60
Selective demand, 273–74
Selective-distribution strategy, 365–66
   of Hendison Electronics Corporation, 389
Sensitivity analysis, 21–22
Service. *See* Offering(s)
Service life cycle, 161
Share draft, 712
Shaving cream, marketing analysis case on, 130–36
Shelf goods, 52
Simon, Herbert, 31
Situation analysis, 3, 33
   Honeywell corporate campaign and, 336
Skimming pricing strategies, 427–28
   of Logitech, 263–64
Smoking
   as addiction, 478–80
   in Republic of Ireland, 477–78
Snack-food industry, 170–71
Social responsibility, 13–14
Soft drink industry, carbonated, 299–302
   marketing in, 301–2
   orange category, 302–7
   purchase and consumption behavior in, 301–2
   structure of, 299–300
"Speaking for the Industry" approach, 336
Specialization, work, 464
Standardization, product, 465
Strategic alliance (joint venture), 7, 82, 559
   in personal computer industry, 555
Strategic change, 507–8
Strategic control, 506
Strategic marketing management, analytical processes of, 1–13
Strategy selection, 9–10
Subnotebooks, 552
Substitutes, 423, 424
Success measures, 32
Success requirements, 4
Sufficiency of information, 114
Sunk costs, 17–18
Supermarkets, 597–98
Superstore, 557
Surface-warming technologies, 445–46
Surveys, 154
Symptoms versus problems, recognizing, 514
Systems/network integrators, 558

Target markets. *See also* Market targeting

   for Club Med España, 352
   communication strategy and characteristics of, 275
   for Honeywell, Inc., Spectronics Division, 336–37
   for Warner-Lambert Ireland, 486–87
Task approach, 278
Technical pricing strategies, 427
Telecommunications industry, 501–2, 504
Television industry in India, 403–4
   television manufacturers, 405–6
Test market, 154, 160
   for Frito-Lay, Inc., Sun Chips Multigrain Snacks, 176–85
   for Swatch, 641–43
   for Zoëcon Corporation, 378–81, 382
Timing of marketing program, 565–66
Tire industry, 391–97
   original equipment tire market, 391–92
   replacement tire market, 392–97
   retail distribution and marketing in, 394–97
Tortilla chip market, 518–19
Tourist industry, Spanish, 348–52
Trade margin, 18–19
Trade relations, 368–69
Trading up and trading down, 161–62
Trial rates for Sun Chips™ Multigrain Snacks, 180, 183, 184
Truck market, European, 610–13
Turnaround strategy of Circle K Corporation, 590, 600–601
Twain, Mark, 117

Ulcer disease, 674–75
   treatment of, 675–77
Uncertainties, 32–33
U.S. Federal Drug Administration (FDA), 84
Use, positioning by, 163
User, positioning by, 164
Use tests, 154

Value
   defined, 422
   price as indicator of, 422–23
Value-added resellers, 555
Variable-cost pricing, 425, 426–27
Variable costs, 16, 422, 425
Vertical media, 278–79
Vertical reseller segment, 560

Watch industry, 638–39
   competition in, 656–69
   strategic change and transformation of, 507–8
Watch market, 639–40
Watch technology, 637–38
Waterhouse, Edwin, 188
"We're Number One" technique, 336
Wholesalers
   quantitative assessment of eliminating, 370
   selection of, 366–67
Working capital, 25
Work specialization, 464
Written case analysis, 39–40, 709–25
   example case, 709–19
   student analysis, example of, 719–25

Company Index

Abbott Labs, 436
Accurist, 665
Adolph Coors and Company, 6
AHV Lifts, 78
Alex Brown and Sons, Inc., 195, 596
Alladdin Mills, 417
Alps, 257, 266
ALR, 554
American Airlines, Inc. case, 224-42
American Express Company, 566
American Hamilton, 447
American Home Products, 672
American Hospital Supply, 369
American Monarch, 152
American Yard Products, 220, 221
Ameritech, 501
AMEX Electronics, 461
Amoco Corporation, 394, 417, 597
AMP, 333
Amphenol North America, 333
AMR Corporation, 224
Andersen Consulting, 551, 558
Anheuser-Busch Companies, Inc., 6,
    14, 128, 170, 518
A&P, 12
Apollo, 257
Apple Computer, Inc., 7, 257, 261,
    276, 365, 552, 554, 555, 559
Ariens, 220
Arm and Hammer, 163
Arthur Andersen and Company, 187,
    188
AST, 554
Astra, 671, 694-707, 708
ASUAG (Allgemeine Schweizer
    Uhrenindustrie), 637
Atlantic Richfield Company, 597
AT&T, 157, 257, 261, 333, 497, 501,
    502, 504, 554
Augustine Medical, Inc. case, 443-53
Austin Computer, 554
AutoZone, 146, 148
Avis, 164

Bar Maisse, 82
Bassett, 284
Bateson Corporation, battery
    chargers case, 145-55
Bayer, 672
Beatrice Foods, 582
Beaulieu Group of America, 417
Beecham, 692
Bell Atlantic, 501
Bell South, 501
Benjamin Moore, 53
Berne Manufacturing, 78
Best Buy, 551, 560
Beuchat, 668-69
Bloomingdale's, 369
BMW, 151, 669
Bobst Graphics, 256
Booz, Allen, and Hamilton, Inc., 159
Borden, 9, 62, 65, 165, 170, 188, 518
Boyle-Midway Division of American
    Homes Products, 372, 373, 376
BP America, 597
Bridgestone Corporation, 391, 394,
    396
Bristol-Myers, 188, 433
Bristol-Myers/Squibb, 672
Brown-Forman Distillers Corporation,
    117
Browning Group, 142-44
Bulova, 637, 638
Burlington Industries, 417
Burroughs Wellcome Company,
    Retrovir case, 430-42, 456, 457
Bush, 405
Businessland, 368, 555

Cable & Wireless, 502
Cadbury Beverages, Inc., CRUSH
    brand case, 296-311

Cadbury Schweppes PLC, 7, 296,
    297, 299
Café do Brasil, 101, 104
Campbell Soup Company, 116, 164,
    313, 314, 322, 325
Canadian Tire, 76, 77, 79
Canon, 457
Carnation, 570, 571
Carrington Carpet Mills, Inc. case,
    416-20
Casio, 639, 664
CC Corporation, 257
Centel Communications Systems, 494
Charles Chips, 170
Charles of the Ritz, 164
Charles Riley Consultants
    International, 352
Charter Marketing Group, 593
Chevron Corporation, 394, 597
Chief, 149
Children's Palace, 595
China Boy, 584
Chrysler, 79, 392
Chun King Corporation case, 579-89
Ciba-Geigy, 672
Cincinnati Sub-Zero, 447
Circle K Corporation, 590-601
Citizen, 507, 639, 648, 664
Clorox Company, 160
Club Med España case, 345-61
Club Mediterranée, 345-47, 669
Cluett Peabody and Company, 32
Coastal Corporation, 597
Coca-Cola, 9, 47, 114, 276, 299, 301,
    302, 303, 564, 566-67, 650
Colgate-Palmolive, 245, 469, 473
Colgate-Palmolive Canada, Arctic
    Power detergent case, 617-36
Collins & Aikman, 417
Compaq Computer Corporation, 261,
    368, 546, 549, 552, 554, 555,
    560
CompuAdd, 555
CompUSA, 551, 557
Computer City, 557
Computerland, 555, 562
ConAgra, 581, 582, 584, 586
Consorzio Sao Caffé, 103
Consumer Savings Bank of
    Worcester, Massachusetts, 715
Continental A.G., 396
Continental Bank, 494
Convenient Food Mart, Inc., 597
Coopers and Lybrand, 187, 188
Cooper Tire and Rubber, 396
Coors, Inc., 119-20
Corné Port Royal, 325
Corning Glass Works, 333
Corte Inglese, 319
Costco, 248, 551
Cottern and Company, 221
Crippa and Berger, 103
Crown, 405
Cumberland Farms, Inc., 597
Curtis Automotive Hoist case, 74-83

Daewoo, 456
DAF, 610, 611, 612
Daimler-Benz, 610, 611, 612
Dallas Federal Savings, 711
Day-N-Nite stores, 593
D-Con Company, 372, 376
Dean Witter Reynolds, 195
DEC, 333
Dell Computer Corporation,
    reformulation strategy case,
    546-62
Del Monte Foods, 579
Deloitte Touche, 187, 188
Delta Tire, 397
Depraz, 257

Diamond Rug & Carpet, 417
Diamond Shamrock, 597
Diamond Star, 392
Dillards, 557
Domino's Pizza, 4
Dr. Pepper/7Up, 299, 301
Drexel Heritage, 284, 286
DuPont, 8, 188, 334, 417, 564-65,
    692
Dyanora, 405
Dym S.A., 353, 354

Eagle Snacks Division of Anheuser-
    Busch, 170, 518
Eastman Kodak, 158
Ebauches S.A., 508
EBRO, 612
ECI Corporation, 460, 461
EDS, 551, 558
Elan Corporation, 480, 490
Eli Lilly, 436, 672, 692
El Nacho Foods, 32, 33-35, 112-13
Emro Marketing Co., 597
Enasa, 610, 611
ERF, 612
Ernst and Young, 187, 188
ETA S.A., 637
Ethan Allen, 284
Exxon Corporation, 4-5, 188, 394,
    457
Exxon Information Systems, 456

Fabergé, 164
Falcon Micro Systems, 551
Federal Express, 2, 164
Fiat, 610
Fieldcrest/Cannon, 417
Filenes, 319
Firestone Auto Master Care Centers,
    394
Firestone Tire and Rubber, 76, 77,
    79, 280
First Boston, 195
First International Bancshares, 710
First National Bank, 710-11
First Texas Savings, 711
Folger's, 6, 44
Ford Motor Company, 35, 79, 151,
    392, 610
Fournier, 689
Frito-Lay, Inc., 8, 11, 167-70
Frito-Lay, Inc., Sun Chips™
    Multigrain Snacks case, 167-85
Frito-Lay, Inc., TOSTITOS® brand
    Tortilla Chips case, 516-27
Fujitsa, 457

Gateway, 554
Gaymar Industries, 447
GE Aerospace, 494
Geisha, 584
General Electric, 157, 164, 333, 367
General Foods, 9
General Mills, 158, 584, 585
General Motors, 79, 151, 164, 276,
    369, 392, 426, 603, 610, 611
Gerber Products Company, 9, 47, 115
Gillette Company, 8, 42, 158, 367
Gillex, 518
Glaxo Holdings plc, 434
Glaxo UK, 678-79
Glidden, 53
Gnostic Concepts, Inc., 333
Godiva Europe case, 312-30
Godiva International, 313, 324, 328
Godiva Japan, 313
Godiva USA, 313, 327
Goldman Sachs, 195
Goodyear Auto Service Centers, 401,
    402
Goodyear Tire and Rubber Company,
    76, 77, 79, 390-402, 509

Goodyear Tire Dealers, 401, 402
Goodyear Tire Stores, 394
Grand Met USA, 570, 571
Groupe Michelin, 97, 391, 394, 396,
    398
Grundig, Gmbh., 411
GTE, 501

Hamilton, 637,638
Hanes Corporation, 5
Hanover-Bates Chemical Corporation
    case, 539-45
Harris/3M (now Lanier Worldwide),
    456
Hattori Seiko, 639
Heinz Company, H.J., 165, 368, 570,
    571
Heinz Pet Products, 578
Hendison Electronics Corporation
    case, 383-89
Henredon, 284
Hercules, 417
Hertz, 164
Heublein, 579
Hewlett-Packard, 2, 188, 257, 552
Hoechst-Roussel Pharmaceuticals
    Inc., 90, 672
Hoffman-LaRoche, 434
Holly Farms, 566
Home Depot, 47, 53, 54, 220, 557
Honda, 220, 369
Honda of U.S., 392
Honeywell, Inc., Spectronics Division
    case, 331-44
Horizon Industries, 417
Hosworth Air Engineering Ltd., 447
Hyundai, 392

IBM, 188, 257, 261, 333, 365, 369,
    428, 507, 546, 549, 554, 555,
    557, 560
ICI, 672
Illy Caffé, 103
I Magnin, 320
Imperial Chemicals Industries, 53
Importadores Quetzal (Quetzal
    Importers) case, 49-51
Ingersoll-Rand, 364
Intel, 555
Interface, Inc., 417
Isuzu, 392
ITT, 333
ITT Cannon, 334
Iveco, 611, 612
Iveco-Ford, 610, 611

JCPenney, 146, 149, 220, 221, 286
Jeno's Pizza, 579
Jimenez, 518
John Deere, 220
Johnson and Johnson, 164
Johnson and Son, Inc., S. C., 132,
    372, 376, 378
Jones, Caesar and Company See Price
    Waterhouse case
Jones•Blair Company case, 52-61
JPS Textile Group, Inc., 417

Kearney, A. T., 9-10
Keebler Company, 170, 518
Kelly-Springfield Tire Company, 397,
    401
Kelton, 668
Kentucky Fried Chicken, 65, 167,
    516
Kikkoman, 584, 585, 586, 587
Kimberly-Clark Corporation, 273
Kiple, 668
Kmart, 53, 54, 149, 220, 221
Kodak, 509
Konark Television India case, 403-15
KPMG Peat Marwick, 187, 188
Kraft, 62, 63, 65, 70

Kroger, 170
Kubota, 220
Kussmaul Electronics Company, 152
KYE (Genius), 256, 264, 266
KYE/Mouse Systems, 266

La Choy, 582–84, 585, 586, 587, 589
Lanier Worldwide, 456
Laura Scudder, 518
Lavazza S.p.A., 99–101
Lawn Boy, 220
Lawn Chief Manufacturing, 220, 221
LDDS, 502
Lea-Meadows, Inc., 293–95
Lee Tire and Rubber Company, 397, 401
Lehman Brothers, 195
Le Jour, 669
Léonidas, 318, 324–25
Lever Detergents, 618, 619, 622
Leyland Trucks, 610
Little General Stores, 593
Loblaws, 469, 475
Logitech, Inc. case, 256–70
Lord & Taylor, 320
Lotus Development Corporation, 157
Louis Newmark, 669
Lowes, 221
Lucky-Goldstar, 456
Lundbeck, 484

McCann-Erickson, 641, 654
McDonald's, 161, 300, 510
MCI, 497, 501, 502, 504
MacTec Control AB case, 137–44
Macy's, 641
Magnavox Corporation, 365
MAN, 610–11, 612
Manor Memorial Hospital case, 199–210
Manson and Associates, 120–28, 129
Marckley CDH, 669
Marion Merrell Dow, 672
Mark and Spencer, 319
Mars, 570, 571
Marshall Museum of Art case, 528–38
Matsushita, 384, 457, 459
Maxwell House, 6, 44
Mazda, 392
Menarini, 682
Mercantile National Bank, 710, 711
Mercantile Texas Corporation, 710
Merck, E., 682
Merck & Co., 436, 672, 692, 707
Merrell Dow, 245, 246
Merrill Lynch, Pierce, Fenner and Smith, 8, 195
Mete Lift, 78
Metra-Seis, 349
Metropolitan Life Insurance Company, 158
Mexus, Inc., 461–63
MGM Grand Air, 224, 229, 230, 231, 233
Microage, 555
Microsoft, 256, 257, 261, 263–69, 555
Midstates, 215
Migros, 668
Mike Sells, 170
Miller Brewing Company, 128, 566
Milliken & Company, 417
Minnetonka, Inc., 158
Mission Foods Corporation, 518
Mitsumi, 266
Mobil Corporation, 597
Mohawk Carpet, 417
Mondaine, 668
Mondose, 325
Montgomery Ward, 53, 394, 560
Morgan Stanley, 195
Morgantown Furniture, Inc. case, 282–95
Motorola, 333, 456, 459, 464, 555

Mouse Systems Corporation, 262, 264, 265, 266
Ms-Tique Corporation case, 130–36
MTD, Inc. (formerly Modern Tool and Die), 220
Murata, 457, 462
Murray of Ohio, 220

Nabisco, 579, 580, 581
National Convenience Stores, Inc., 593, 594, 597
National Semiconductor, 459, 464
NCR, 507
Neiman Marcus, 320, 369
Nestlé Italy case, 96–110
Neuhaus, 319, 325
NeXT, 261
Nissan, 151, 369, 392
Noma, 220
North American Philips, 384
Northern Automotive, 146, 148
Northgate, 552
Nummi (GM-Toyota), 392
NYNEX, 501

O.R. Concepts, 448
Ocean Spray Cranberries, Inc., 117
Olivetti, 257
Onida, 405
Open Systems Foundation, 261
Orgill Brothers, 215
Orkin, 376, 377

Pacific Telesis, 501
Packard Bell, 266, 555
Pan Am, 224, 231, 239
Panasonic, 457
Payless Cashways, 47
Peerless/Galaxy Carpet, 417
Pegaso, 612
Pennzoil Motor Oil, 276
Pep Boys, Inc., 148
PepsiCo, Inc., 7, 65, 167, 299, 301, 302, 303, 516
PepsiCo Foods International, 65, 167, 516
Pepsi Cola Bottling Group, 65
Pepsi-Cola Company, 167, 300, 516, 564
Perstorp Corporation, 137
Petro-Canada, 79
Pfizer, Inc., 246, 251, 436, 438, 672
Pharmaseal, 447
Pharmuka, 688
Philadelphia Electric Company, 494
Pillsbury, 35
Pirelli Group, 396
Pitney Bowes, 457
Pizza Hut, Inc., 65, 167, 516
Power King, 220
PPG Industries, 53
Price Club, 248, 551
Price Waterhouse case, 186–98
Primax, 266
Procter and Gamble, Inc., 6, 7, 9, 45, 89, 91, 158, 163, 164, 170, 280, 296, 307, 364, 618, 619
Procter and Gamble, Inc., Scope case, 243–55
Procter and Gamble Italia, 103
Proctor and Gamble, Inc., Downy Enviro-Pak case, 468–75
Prudential Securities, 195
Purolator, 2

Quaker Oats, 8, 570, 571
Queen Carpet, 417

R.J. Reynolds Industries, 579
Radio Shack, 595
Ralph Lauren, 369
Ralston Purina, 165, 570, 571, 573, 578
Rand Corporation, 432
Rauscher Pierce Refsnes, Inc., 195
Reebok International, Ltd., 41–42

Renault, 611
Republic National Bank of Dallas, NOW accounts case, 709–19
Republic of Texas Corporation, 710, 712
Revlon Cosmetics, 43, 566
Ricoh Company Ltd., 256, 363, 457
RJR Nabisco, 170, 580
Robinson Humphrey, 195
Roche Inc., 682
Rockwell International Corporation, 459
Rohr Industries, 9
Rolls Battery Engineering, 152
Rover Group, 610
Royal Crown, 564
RSCG, 353, 355, 358
RVI, 611, 612

Saab-Scania, 611
Safeway, 170
Saks Fifth Avenue, 320
Salomon Brothers, 195
Salora, 405
SAMEL S.A., 669
Sam's Club, 551
Samsung, 456
Sandoz, Ltd., 373, 672
Sanger Harris, 641
Sanyo Electric, Inc., 369
Sao Café, 101
Saturn, 392
Scania, 612
Schauer Manufacturing Company, 152
Schering-Plough, 436
SCM Corporation, 53
Scott and Sons Company, O. M., 6
Searle, 692
Sears, Roebuck and Company, 2–3, 53, 54, 146, 149, 164, 220, 221, 286, 390, 394, 401, 402, 557, 595
Segafredo-Zanetti, S.p.A., 101
Seiko, 507, 646, 648, 663
Sekonda, 669
Service Merchandise, 560
7-Eleven, 507, 593, 595, 596
Sharp, 457
Shaw Industries, 417
Shell Oil, 188
Sherwin-Williams, 53, 54
Siemens AG, 555
Silitec, 266
Singer, 9
SMH (Société Micromécanique et Horlogère), 637
Smith Barney, Harris Upham and Company, 195
SmithKline Beecham, 671, 672, 675–77, 678, 680, 682, 688, 689, 692
Snapper, 220
Snyder's, 170
Sony, 384
South Delaware Coors, Inc. case, 119–29
Southland Corporation, 364, 593, 596, 597
Southwestern Bell, 501
Sperry-Univac, 333
Sprint, 497, 501, 502, 504
SSIH (Société Suisse pour l'Industrie Horlogère), 637
Staples, 551
Stop & Go, 593, 594
Strategic Brands, 246
Subaru, 392
Sumitomo, 396
Swatch A.G., 637
Swatch Watch USA, 54, 648, 650
Swisher Mower and Machine Company case, 211–23
Swiss Timing, 257

Swiss Watch Distribution Center (SWDC), 641
Syntex, 672

Taco Bell Corporation, 65, 167, 510, 516
Takeda, 694
Tandy Corporation, 554
Teledyne Battery Products, 152
Terminix, 376, 377
Texaco, 597
Texas Federal Savings, 711
Texas Instruments, 2, 459, 464
Thomasville, 284
Thomson, 384
3M, 457
Time Inter Corporation A.G., 668
Timex, 507, 638, 646, 656, 663, 668
Toro, 220
Toshiba, 459, 552, 555
Toyota, 151, 369, 392
Toys R Us, 369, 557
Triton Biosciences, Inc., 434
Troy-Bilt, 220
Truedox, 266
True Value Hardware, 221
Trumbull Chemical, 539
TSC (Tractor Supply Company), 221
TWA, 224, 231, 239
Tyler Pet Foods, Inc. case, 568–78

Uniroyal Goodrich Tire Company, 97
United Airlines, 230, 231, 232
U.S. SemiCon Corporation case, 454–67
Upjohn Company, 84–95, 436
US West, 501
USX, 188
UToteM, 592

Van Heusen, 279
Vanner, 152
Viajes Melia, 350
Videocon, 405, 406
VLSI Technology, Inc., 555
Volvo, 392
Volvo GM Heavy Truck Corporation, 603
Volvo Truck Corporation (VTC), 602–4
Volvo Trucks Corporation, Europe Division case, 602–16
Volvo White Truck Corporation, 603

W.R. Grace, 188
Wagons-Lits, 350
Wal-Mart, 47, 53, 149, 368, 401, 551, 560
Walt Disney, 188
Warner-Lambert Company, 244, 245, 367, 476
Warner-Lambert Ireland, Niconil case, 476–91
Wellcome PLC, 431, 434, 435
Western Auto, 146, 149, 221
Wheat Belt, 215
Wheelhorse, 220
White, 220
White Laboratories, 132
White Motor Company, 603
William Blair, 195
Williams Companies, Inc., The, 492–93
WilTel, Inc. case, 492–505
World Carpets, Inc., 417
WRIGT, 612

Xerox, 456, 457

Yamanouchi, 692

Zale Jewelry, 641
Zenith, 384
Zenith Data Systems, 555
Zeos, 554
Z-nix, 266
Zoëcon Corporation, insect growth regulators case, 372–83

Brand Index

ABC laundry detergent, 617, 619, 621, 622, 632-35
Accudrop, 484
Accupro, 477
Acura, 369
Adalat, 672
Ajax (cleanser), 617
Alfex watches, 669
All detergent, 619, 621
Allen's (beverage), 297
Alpo, 570, 571, 572
Alpo Beef-Flavored Dinner, 570, 571
Alpo Lite, 578
ALTOSID®, 373
Always, 243
Aqualex System, 137-44
Aquamatic, 447
Aquatred tires, 398, 399, 400
Arctic Power detergent, case on, 617-36
Armstrong tires, 396
Arriva tires, 398, 400
Arrow shirts, 32
Atlas brand tires, 394
Atoll (beverage), 297
Attends, 243
Avia watches, 669
A-Watch, 656, 661-64
Axid (H2-blocker), 692
AZT. See Retrovir

Baggies (food wrap), 617
Bair Hugger® Patient Warming System, 443-45, 452-53
Baken-Ets®, 65, 168, 516
Bali (beverage), 297
BF Goodrich tires, 391, 392, 394, 396
Big Mow mowers, 215
Big O mower, 215
Black Flag, 372
Blanketrol 200, 447
Bob's Big Boy, 65
Bold 3 (detergent), 622
Bold (detergent), 244, 619
Bounce, 244
Bourbon coffee, 99
Bridgestone tires, 392, 396
Brut, 164
Bugles, 158
Bulova watches, 656, 661, 662, 663, 664, 668
Busch, 14
BUX (processing chemical), 543

Café Kimbo, 104
Caffeine-free Diet Coke, 302
Caffeine-free Diet Pepsi, 302
Canada Dry, 297, 298, 299
Cantina brand Tortilla Chips, 518
Capoten (drug), 672
Carafate (H2-blocker), 692
Caravelle watches, 664
Cardizem (drug), 672
Cartier watches, 656, 661-64
Cascade, 244
Casio watches, 656, 661, 662, 663, 664
CBX (processing chemical), 543

Cepacol, 245-50
Certina watch, 656
Charbonel, 323
Check-Up toothpaste, 158
Cheddar and Bacon dip, 66
Cheddar and Herb dip, 66
Cheddar and Jalapeno dip, 66
Cheer 2 detergent, 622
Cheer detergent, 164, 244
CHEETOS® brand Cheese Flavored Snacks, 65, 168, 169, 516
Chew-eez, 571
Chuck Wagon, 572
CHX (processing chemical), 543
Citizen watches, 656, 661, 662, 663, 664, 668
Citrus Hill orange juice, 507
Clamato, 297
Clarion, 244
Clearasil, 244
Cleocin Phosphate Sterile Solution, 89
Climator, 447, 448
The Clip, 669
Close-up toothpaste, 618
Club Med watches, 661, 662
Coca-Cola, 114
Coca-Cola Classic, 47, 302
Coca-Cola watches, 663
Colgate Fluoride Rinse, 245, 247
Colgate oral rinse, 247-50
Colgate toothpaste, 617
Come 'n Get It, 570, 571
Comet, 244
Compudyne, 557
Condensed Milk, 96
Contura (subnotebook), 552
Cool Ranch Doritos®, 172
Cooper tires, 396
Coors beer, 120
Corné, 318
Corné Port Royal, 314, 323, 329, 330
Corné Toison d'Or, 313, 314, 323, 324, 329, 330
Corsa tires, 398, 400
Cortaid, 89
Cover Girl, 244
'C'Plus, 297
Craftsman, 164, 220, 221
Credor watches, 639
Crest toothpaste, 45, 244, 468, 618
Crisco oil, 243, 468
CRUSH soft drink case, 296-311
Cub Cadet brand mower, 220
Curtis Lift, 74-76, 79-80, 82-83
Cutivate, 707
Cycle dog food, 571, 572
Cytotec (H2-blocker), 692

Daisies, 158
Daskalides, 318, 329, 330
DDC (drug), 434
DDI (antiviral drug), 433-34
Decathlon tires, 398, 400
Delta Gold®, 65
DELTA GOLD® brand Potato Chips, 516
Dentyne chewing gum, 476
Dexxa brand mouse, 264, 267
DIANEX®, 373
Diet Coke, 47, 302

Diet Pepsi, 302, 564
Diet Rite Cola, 564
Dilzem (drug), 476, 480
Dog Chow, 570, 571, 572
Doritos®, 65, 68, 168, 169, 175, 177, 183
DORITOS® brand Tortilla Chips, 516, 518, 521-24
DOS, 261
Douglas-brand tires, 391, 401
Dove (bar soap), 618
Downy Environ-Pak case, 468-75
Downy fabric softener, 468, 469
Doxidan (drug), 90
Dr. Pepper, 302
Dramamine, 89
Duncan Hines baking mixes, 243, 468
Dunlop tires, 392, 396
Dynamark (mower), 221
Dynamo detergent, 619

E.D. Smith, 297
Eagle brand snacks, 170
Eagle tires, 398, 400
Ebel watches, 656
Edalène (drug), 688, 689
El Charrito Nacho Cheese tortilla chips, 518
Elgin watches, 664
Enchilada Bean Dip, 65, 66
EO (hand-held computer), 554
Equal (sugar substitute), 423

Fab laundry detergent, 617, 619, 622
Faemino (coffee), 103
Fauchon (chocolate), 323
Feldene (drug), 672
Firestone tires, 392, 396
Fleecy, 469
Flixonase, 707
FLYTEK®, 373
Fontaine ch., 323
Frigor (chocolate), 96
Frito-Lay's® Dips case, 62-73
Fritos®, 65, 167
FRITOS® brand Corn Chips, 516
FUNYUNS brand onion flavored snacks, 65, 168, 516

Gah (coffee), 103
Gaines-Burgers, 571, 572
Gala (chocolate), 96
Gatorade, 8
GE brand, 384
GENCOR®, 373, 378, 382
General Tire, 392, 396
Genesis carpet, 417
Gérard Ronay, 323
GINI brand, 297, 299
Glynase PresTab, 89
Goodyear, 391, 392
Goodyear Eagle brand, 390
Grand Gourmet, 571
Grandma's® brand Cookies, 65, 168, 516
GrassHandler, 220
Gravy Train, 570, 571, 572

Green Products, 469
Gucci watches, 656, 661-64
Guess watches, 656, 661-64
Guys brand snacks, 170

Hag (coffee), 103
Hall's cough drops, 476
Halo shampoo, 617
Hamilton watches, 656, 664
HDC Interface, 334-35
Head & Shoulders, 244, 618
Hédiard (chocolate), 323
Hip-Hop watches, 669
HIRES soft drink, 296, 297, 298
Holland House, 297, 298
Huggies diapers, 273
Huskee, 221

Imigran, 707
Infiniti, 369
Interferon, 439
Invicta tires, 398, 400
Irish Spring (bar soap), 617
Ivory Snow, 622
Ivory soap, 468, 618

Jalapeno Bean Dip, 65, 66
Jean Naté, 164
Jeff de Bruges, 323, 324
Jell-O, 164
Jerky Treats, 571, 572
Joy (dishwashing liquid), 244

KABAT®, 373
Kal Kan Pedigree, 570, 571
Kaopectate, 89
Kelly-Springfield, 391, 396
Kelton watches, 663
Kelvar, 564
Ken-L Ration Burger, 571
Ken-L Ration Special Cuts, 571, 572
Kenmore, 164
Kibbles 'n Bits, 570, 571, 572
Kiple, 661, 662
Kip 'Marine, 668
Kraft Cheese Whiz, 63
Kraft Hot Nacho Dip, 63
Kraft Nacho Cheese Dip, 63
Kraft Nacho Dip, 63
Kraft Premium Jalapeno Cheese Dip, 63
K-Watch, 661, 662, 668

La Famous brand tortilla chips, 518
Lansoprazole, 694
Lassale watches, 639, 656
LAY'S® brand, 8, 65, 167, 183, 516
Lee tires, 391
Le Notre, 323, 324
Léonidas, 323, 324, 329, 330
Lexus, 369
Lip watches, 663
Listerine mouth wash, 244, 245, 247, 248, 249, 250, 476
Listermint, 245, 247-50
Logitech, 264, 267, 268, 269
Longines watches, 656, 661-64

L'Oreal, 96
Lorus watches, 639, 656, 661-64
Losec (antiulcerant), 671, 694-707, 708
Luvs diapers, 243, 618
Lux (bar soap), 618

Maalox, 675
Macintosh computer, 257, 261
Maggi, 96
Magnavox, 384
Maison ch., 323
Malvern, 297
Mandarin Orange Slice, 300, 302, 303, 304, 305, 310
Marie's, 65, 72
Marzetti's, 65
Matilda Bay Wine Cooler, 565-66
Max Factor, 244
Meaty Bones, 571
Metamucil, 244
Mete Lift, 79
Michelin tires, 391, 392, 394, 395, 396, 398
Michelob, 14
Microsoft Office, 157
Mighty Dog, 570, 571, 572
Mild Cheddar dip, 66
Milk Bones, 570, 571, 572
Minute Maid Orange, 302, 303, 304, 305, 310
Minute Maid orange juice, 507
Mitchell's (beverage), 297
Mite coffees, 103
Moist & Chunky, 571
Moist & Meaty, 572
Mon chéri, 315, 329, 330
Mondose, 324
Motrin IB Tablets and Caplets, 89, 90
Mott's, 297, 298
Mountain Dew, 302
Mr. Clean, 244
Mr & Mrs "T," 297, 298
MTA 4700, 447
MTD mower, 220
Multi-Mile tires, 396
Munchos®, 65, 168, 516
M-Watch, 661, 662, 663, 668
Mycitracin, 89

Naprosyn, 672
Natural Light (beer), 14
Nature's Course, 573, 578
NBX (processing chemical), 543
Nescafé, 96, 97, 105, 106-10
Nesquick, 96
Nestlé Powdered Milk, 96
Neuhaus chocolate, 318, 323, 324, 329, 330
Newton (hand-held computer), 554
NeXtStep, 261
Nicobrevin, 484
Niconil case, 476-91
Nicorette, 484, 485, 487
Notephone, 555
Noxzema, 244
Nutrasweet, 423

Oasis, 297
O'Boisies, 170
O'GRADY'S® brand, 65, 172, 183, 184, 516
Oil of Olay, 244
Old Colony, 297
Omega watches, 656, 661, 662, 664
Omnibook, 552
Optima credit card, 566
Orion watches, 669
Orzoro (beverage), 96, 110
OS/2, 261
Oxydol detergemt, 164, 244, 619, 621, 622

Palmolive (dishwashing liquid), 617
Pampers diapers, 243, 468, 618
Panasonic brand, 384
Pantene, 244
Pepcid, 692, 696, 707
Pepsi-Cola, 7, 302
Pepto Bismol, 244
Pert, 244
PHARORID®, 373
Phasar watches, 639
Philco, 384
Piaget watches, 656, 664
Picante Sauce Dip, 65, 66
Pilot (Series 15) mouse, 267, 268
Pirelli, 396, 398
Planter's, 170
Plax, 243, 246-50
Portege (subnotebook), 552
Powerbook, 559
Power PC, 555
Precision computer, 551
PRECOR®, 373, 377-78, 382
Presario, 560
Presentation Manager, 261
Pringles®, 170, 243
Progaine Shampoo, 95
Proline, 555
Prontos®, 171
Proselect carpet, 417
Pulsar watches, 639, 656, 661-64
Punch detergent, 619
Puppy Chow, 570, 571
Pure Spring, 297

Quasar brand, 384

Rado watches, 656
Raid, 372
Raniplex (drug), 689
RCA brand, 384
Red Cheek, 297, 298
Regatta tires, 398, 400
Rejuvenator, 145, 148, 154
Renitec/Vasotec, 672
Retrovir, 430-42
Reward, 578
Ride King mowers, 211, 212-18, 223
Roach and Flea Killer, 376
Roach Traps, 376
Rogaine Topical Solution, 84-95
Rold Gold®, 65, 168, 516

Rolex watches, 656, 661, 662, 663, 664, 668
Rose's, 297, 298
Royal Crown (RC) Cola, 300
Royale, 243
Ruffles®, 65, 167, 169, 183, 516
Rumbles®, 176

SAFROTIN®, 373
SANTITAS® Tortilla Chips, 168, 516, 519, 526, 527
Saturn, 369
ScanMan, 267, 270
Schick razors and blades, 367
Schweppes, 297, 298
Scope, 243-55
Sears tires, 396
Secret (deodorant), 244, 618
Seiko watches, 639, 656, 661-64
Sensor razor, 8, 158
7Up, 302
Severent, 707
S4S tires, 398, 400
Show Circuit Frozen Dog Dinner, 568-69, 570, 572-78
Smartfood®, 168, 170
Smorgasburger, 571
Soft and Silky, 130-36
Soft Sense, 132
Soft Shave, 132
Softsoap, 158
Sontara® (fabric), 564-65
Sostril (drug), 682
Splendid Decaffeinato, 103
Splendid Oro and Classic, 103
Sprite, 47, 302
SPX (processing chemical), 543
STARBAR®, 373
Strike FLEA ENDER®, 373, 378, 381
Strike ROACH ENDER®, 372, 373, 378-82
Stuffers®, 176
Suncheros, 518
Sun Chips™ Multigrain Snacks, 167-85
SUN-DROP soft drink, 296, 297, 298
SUNKIST, 297, 298, 299, 303, 304, 305, 309, 310
Sunlight (dishwasher detergent), 618, 619, 621, 622, 632-35
Sunny Delight, 243
Supernatural Hair Spray, 566
Surfak, 90
Surf detergent, 619
Sussex, 297
Swatch watches, 11, 637-70
Sweetland Bed Warmer and Cast Dryer, 448
Sylvania, 384

Tab, 564
Tagamet (H-2 blocker), 671, 672, 675-77, 680, 682, 684, 688, 689, 691, 692, 696
Taster's Choice, 96
TEKNAR®, 373
Tender Chops, 571, 572

Tenormin (drug), 672
T-40 (mower), 215, 216
Theolan (drug), 480
Thermadrape, 448
Thornton's (chocolate), 323, 324
Tide laundry detergent, 164, 244, 468, 618-22, 631-36
Tiempo tires, 398, 400
Timex watches, 656, 661, 662, 663, 664, 668
Tissot watches, 656, 661-64
T-Metric tires, 398, 400
Toppels®, 176
Tostitos® brand Tortilla Chips, 11, 65, 168, 169, 516-27
Total cereal, 507
Toyo tires, 396
Trackman, 267
Trina, 297, 299
Trina Colada, 297, 299
TriNaranjus, 297, 299
Tums antacid, 507, 675
Turfmaster, 221
Tylenol Cold & Flu, 164
Tylenol P.M., 164

Ultra Brite toothpaste, 617
Unicap vitamins, 89
Uniroyal, 391, 392, 394, 396
Uniroyal-Goodrich tires, 398
Unix, 261
Unix System 5, 261

Valium, 677
Valrhona (chocolate), 323
ValuePoint, 555
VAPORETTE® flea collars, 373
Velveeta Mexican, 63
Ventolin (drug), 679
VET-KEM®, 373
Vicks cold care products, 244, 468
Vida (beverage), 297, 299
Vidal Sassoon, 244
Video Clip watches, 669
Voltaren (drug), 672

Walden Farms, 65
Waltham watches, 664
Whistles, 158
Windows, 257, 261, 267
Wise, 170
Wisk detergent, 619, 621, 622
Wrangler tires, 398

Yard Pro, 221
Yema watches, 661, 662, 663
Yokohama tires, 396

Zantac case, 671-708
Zantic, 682
ZBX (processing chemical), 543
Zest, 618
Zion watches, 669
ZODIAC®, 373
Zofran, 707
Zovirax, 434
Z-Watch, 656
ZXP-XL2 (subnotebook), 552